Untrammeled Approaches

THE COLLECTED WORKS OF JACQUES MARITAIN
Volume 20

Honorary Editor-in-Chief
Theodore M. Hesburgh, C.S.C.

Editors
Ralph McInerny
Frederick Crosson   Bernard Doering

Acknowledgments

A grant from the Homeland Foundation enabled this series to get under way.

Untrammeled Approaches

JACQUES MARITAIN

Translated by
Bernard Doering

Preface by
Ernst R. Korn (Heinz R. Schmitz)

University of Notre Dame Press
Notre Dame, Indiana
1997

Copyright © 1997
University of Notre Dame Press
Notre Dame, IN 46556

Originally published as *Approaches san Entraves*
Librairie Arthèm Fayard, 1973

Manufactured in the United States of America

Library of Congress Cataloging-in-Publication Data

Maritain, Jacques, 1882-1973.
  [Approaches sans entraves. English]
  Untrammeled approaches / Jacques Maritain; edited by Bernard Doer-
ing.
     p. cm. — (The collected works of Jacques Maritain; v. 20)
  Includes bibliographical references.
  ISBN 0-268-04300-0 (alk. paper)
  1. Philosophy. 2. Theology. I. Doering, Bernard E. II. Title. III. Series:
Maritain, Jacques, 1882-1973. Works. English. 1996; v. 2011.
B2430.M33A6713 1996
194—dc20   96-26434
                                                                        CIP

∞The paper used in this publication meets the minimum requirements of the
American National Standard for Information Sciences—Permanence of Paper for
Printed Materials, ANSI Z39.48-1984.

CONTENTS

PREFACE

IN SPEAKING OF THE PERIOD just before their conversion and entry into the Church, Raïssa Maritain wrote in *We Have Been Friends Together* (*Les Grandes Amitiés*): "We still thought that to become Christian meant to abandon philosophy forever. Well, we were ready—but it was not easy—to abandon philosophy for the truth. Jacques accepted this sacrifice. The truth we had so greatly desired had caught us in a trap."[1] This Truth which had drawn them to itself and which had made itself known to them,—what was it going to ask of them? For Jacques Maritain, it was to serve this same Truth by devoting all his energies to the work of philosophy, which, among all our ways of knowing, can most rightfully claim the title, *the knowledge of the truth, "ipsa est maxime scientia veritatis."*[2] With an untiring energy, his thought never ceased from that moment on to lead philosophical research to ever higher levels of which the present book marks one of the high points. Whether it is bent on elucidating some philosophical question posed by the real, or whether its purpose is to reflect on philosophy itself—Maritain's work bears witness to the grandeur and the dignity of that philosophical knowledge which St. Thomas Aquinas loved so deeply and whose noble nature (in the tradition of Aristotle, but better than his master) he made known to us.

It is not without some merit here to remind ourselves of this noble conception of the work of philosophy. Indeed, in order to follow the avenues opened up by these *Approaches*, it is very important, to have an accurate view of the *opus philosophicum* and of the requirements that are proper to it. Moreover, this book happens to pose a doctrinal problem of major importance which requires considerable work of innovation, and must be settled once and for all. It is not surprising then that certain metaphysical considerations, because they govern the entire discussion, are proposed here from the very outset.

Metaphysical knowledge is the highest wisdom of the natural order which is accessible to man by the powers of his nature alone. However, if Aristotle is right to see in it a more than human science and St. Thomas a divine science, *"non humana sed divina,"*[3] it is because in order to arrive at such lofty knowledge, our natural way of operating must go beyond itself. Metaphysics con-

---

1   Raïssa Maritain, *We Have Been Friends Together,* translated by Julie Kernan (Garden City, N.Y.: Image Books, Doubleday, 1961), p. 138.

2   St. Thomas Aquinas, *In Metaphysicam Aristotelis,* lib. II, lect. 2, ed. Cathala, § 297.

3   *Ibid.,* § 68.

stitutes, in reality, the most difficult and the most arduous form of knowledge for the rational animals that we are because it bears on that which is furthest removed from the perception of our senses: the highest causes of being and its most universal principles and, for this very reason, the most immaterial. Because it is concerned with what is fundamental and absolutely primary to all reality, namely, being, such a science is not ordered to any other: "*sola ista maxime propter se est.*"[4] And this is the reason why it is sovereignly free "*maxime libera.*"[5] If this is so, can it then be the property of a nature, which, like ours, in so many ways is held in bondage? Aristotle had thought it impossible. But St. Thomas, who affirms that metaphysics is divine knowledge because it has God as its object,[6] adds that it is divine by yet another claim: God possesses it eminently, "*ipse tamen maxime habet*"; better yet, He is in truth the only one to possess it, being the only one to have a perfect understanding of it.[7] Man will never use it as its master, he will never dispose of it as of a possession, but only as of a thing which is loaned to him.[8] Now although we can attain such wisdom only very imperfectly and, as a result, to a very modest degree, yet what we can attain of this wisdom, is incomparably more valuable than what we can arrive at by the other forms of knowledge.[9] If such knowledge is the first in dignity and the queen of the noblest faculty of our nature, it should be treated with the greatest respect.

Precisely as a divine form of knowledge, "*scientia maxime divina,*" it deserves the greatest honors—and it is not St. Thomas, for whom it is "*maxime honorabilis,*" the most honorable of the sciences,[10] who would refuse it these honors. At the very moment when he shows that there are wisdoms much higher than the great wisdom of metaphysics and at the very point where he establishes that theology is superior to philosophy, he does not cease to affirm philosophy's divine character.[11] For all that, he has no intention of absorbing philosophy into theology (as is the case today with a theologian like Karl Rahner for whom philosophical knowledge is a kind of "anonymous theology").[12] And he does not intend either to dissolve it in some mystical movement (according to a process inaugurated by the first *philosophus teutonicus*, Jacob Boehme, and

---

4   *Ibid.*, § 59.

5   *Ibid.*, § 60. For St. Thomas, "ipsa sola est libera inter scientias," § 58.

6   *Ibid.*, § 64.

7   *Ibid.*

8   *Ibid.*

9   *Ibid.*, § 60.

10   St. Thomas Aquinas, *In Metaphysicam Aristotelis*, lib. I, lect. 3, ed. Cathala, § 64.

11   *In Boetii de Trinitate*, prooemium, q. 2, a. 2: "*Haec scientia* [i.e., the science of theology] *est altior illa divina quam Philosophi tradiderunt.*"

12   "Inevitably in any philosophy, theology, in a thematic way, is already put into practice . . ." Karl Rahner, *Ecrits théologiques*, volume VII (Paris: Desclée de Brouwer, 1967), p. 49.

taken up again by a whole school of German philosophers). For whatever may
be the role that the higher forms of wisdom (the theology and the wisdom of
the saints) are called to play with regard to philosophy, St. Thomas never
forgets that they have natural reason as a foundation and that they are, as a
consequence, strictly rational forms of knowledge: *"perfectum opus rationis."*[13]
As Jacques Maritain pointed out, "Thomistic philosophy . . . is wholly rational:
no reason issuing from faith finds its way into its inner fabric; it derives intrinsically from reason and rational criticism alone; and its soundness as a philosophy
is based entirely on experimental or intellectual evidence and on logical
proof."[14] How can one do greater honor to the human spirit (which, at the
highest point of spiritual tension that is natural to us, is a created participation
in the divine intellectual power itself) than to make manifest the supra-human
dignity of philosophy, and to affirm at the same time that it is the *perfect work
of reason* (however small a part of it we are able to attain). To celebrate the
excellence of that metaphysical knowledge toward which man tends in his
most highly spiritual elan is to recognize the excellence of human reason made,
as it is, for the most sublime things and capable (be it only with owl's eyes) of
contemplating the source of being and the ultimate center of all intelligibility.

If others than St. Thomas form for themselves an entirely inadequate and
unworthy idea of philosophy and delight in miserably disfiguring it (let us
think once more of Karl Rahner for whom philosophy is nothing more than a
certain "precomprehension of man by himself"),[15] it is because they have been
instructed by masters who hate reason and combat in it "the most implacable
enemy of thought."[16] Not recognizing that philosophy in its pure essence is a
rational knowledge, they will go so far as to ask theology to establish philosophical knowledge "in its proper autonomy."[17] But this is the very negation
of philosophy which, free by birth, can possess its autonomy only from itself.
Bearing within itself its own justification, it is born when our mind—in and
by the judicative act of a purely intellectual intuition[18]—seizes upon that which

---

13   Cf. St. Thomas Aquinas, *Sum. Theol.*, IIa-IIae, q. 45, a. 2.

14   Jacques Maritain, *An Essay on Christian Philosophy* (New York, Philosophical
      Library, 1955), p. 15. An English translation of *De la Philosophie chrétienne* (Paris:
      Desclée de Brouwer, 1933).

15   K. Rahner, *Ecrits théologiques*, p. 42: "Even philosophy in the strict sense of the
      term can be nothing else than the exact presentation and methodical explication,
      reflected upon and carefully controlled, of this comprehension of the self."

16   Martin Heidegger, *Chemins qui mènent nulle part* (Paris: Gallimard, 1962), p. 219.

17   K. Rahner, *Ecrits théologiques*, pp. 43–44: "It is essential to understand both the
      fact that and the way in which theology at one and the same time detaches from
      itself as other that intrinsic element of its own reality, which it establishes in its
      own autonomy and cannot in any other way establish the real condition of its
      own being."

18   Cf. *infra*, ch. XI, *Reflections on Wounded Nature*.

constitutes the first actuality of a thing and at that moment when the vast field of being in its infinite extension and its analogical richness unfolds before its eyes. It does not depend on some other knowledge but on being which is its proper object and from which it holds its nature. Dependence on being, yes. But this very dependence is its life and its glory.

Founded on being and its mysterious richness, metaphysical wisdom cannot attain its plenitude directly. It will remain, in fact, indefinitely perfectible and will never be completely attained. This is to say that it will always have to *progress* and to *learn*. In order to advance in the knowledge of its object—not by way of authority but by way of intellectual evidence and by rational demonstration—and in order to converse *tête-à-tête* with being, it has its own methods and its own means of investigation. Is this to say that other forms of knowledge do not interest it and that, in order to know better the ontological mystery of things, it finds nothing in the sciences of nature or in the "human sciences" by which it can gain knowledge to help it advance in its own work? Would there be nothing to draw from the great religious cultures of humanity, from its admirable myths and from the work of its great poets? And when there is question of theology and of the revelation of Him Who called Himself the Way, the *Truth*, and the Life and Who came into the world only in order to bear testimony to the truth, does the *maxime scientia veritatis* have nothing to learn there either? If today many reject the very idea of learning, metaphysics which, precisely as wisdom, is a free knowledge, is too jealous of its freedom to let anything whatever prevent it from seeking out truth wherever it may be found and learning from what it finds. It is because philosophy suffers no constraint that nothing can prohibit it from acquiring knowledge from other human sciences and also from divine revelation which *teaches* it certain truths, even philosophical ones. "God alone is not subject to being taught, the angels themselves learn from one another; being taught does not stifle the freedom of the mind, but merely attests that it is a created freedom. And for every created spirit truth holds primacy even over the quest for knowledge, however noble this quest may be."[19] To say that philosophy has much to learn from faith and from theology is to raise a very complex and difficult problem to which Jacques Maritain, I believe, has offered a decisive response in his works: *An Essay on Christian Philosophy* and *Science and Wisdom*. If I insist here on returning to the principles which govern the discussion and determine its solution, it is because they are of capital importance not only for the philosopher but for philosophy itself. In fact, "speculative issues of the highest importance as to the nature of philosophy and the intellectual value of faith, are involved in these questions, and the answers we shall give them should have a decisive practical bearing on certain basic spiritual attitudes. For the philosopher will shape his life and thinking in a particular way if he has to keep his philosophic

---

19   Jacques Maritain, *An Essay on Christian Philosophy*, p. 35.

labors apart from his life of prayer (supposing he has one). And he will shape them in an entirely different way to the extent that he believes, contrariwise, that he ought to join them in an organic and living unity and strive in his personal activities to have the *opus rationis* quickened and activated by his life of prayer and by contemplative wisdom—while fully safeguarding its absolute rigor and special purity."[20]

For the philosopher who has received the grace of Christian faith must avoid a twofold danger: on the one hand, of *confusing* faith and reason (in which case, there is no longer a distinction between them but absorption of the one into the other or substitution of the one for the other) and, on the other hand, of *separating* them, by yielding to the temptation "to cut off reason in its own proper activities from higher sources of light, and, on pretext that his object is purely natural, to look upon the philosopher himself as dwelling in a condition of pure nature."[21] Let us note parenthetically that in pointing out this twofold danger against which philosophical reason in its relation to faith must be on guard, I am certainly not forgetting that it is good form today not only to *separate* faith and philosophy but to *oppose* them, Philosophy which is *scientia maxime divina* is then regarded as the spokesman of unbelief and of atheism. And—an absurd enterprise (but whose contradiction remains hidden for those who have eyes only for the fashion of the day)—it is this pseudo-philosophy which is busy denying the revealed mysteries. And at the present time certain theologians, in order to acquire some understanding of divine revelation, run to these same pseudo-philosophers to ask their help!

When St. Thomas comes across statements contrary to faith in the sayings of philosophers, he never attributes them to philosophy itself, for he never denies the nobility of philosophy which is the science of the truth. He knows that we have received from God, along with our nature, the light of reason and, along with grace that light of faith, which does not destroy our natural knowledge but rather perfects it. To say that these two forms of knowledge which we receive from God contradict each other (which implies that at least one of them is erroneous) is to maintain that for our mind God is a source of falsity and error. But this is impossible and such an affirmation is blasphemous. Because philosophy is the science of truth, it cannot contradict a revelation which bears the very seal of ultimate Truth. And this is why, when St. Thomas finds in the books of philosophers an affirmation opposed to faith, he has this admirable response (which shows the high esteem he has for philosophy): this does not come from philosophy but rather from its misuse due to the deficiency of reason,—"*hoc non est philosophiae, sed magis philosophiae abusus ex defectu rationis.*"[22]

---

20   Jacques Maritain, *An Essay on Christian Philosophy*, p. ix.

21   *Ibid.* p. 8.

22   St. Thomas Aquinas, *In Boet.*, prooemium, q. 2, a. 3. St. Thomas says the same thing apropos of things contrary to the faith, "*non sunt philosophiae, sed potius error*

In order to avoid the twofold peril we have just mentioned and to which the Christian philosopher exposes himself if on the one hand he neglects to *distinguish* between faith and reason and if on the other hand he omits to *unite* in an organic and vital manner that which he began by distinguishing, it must be recognized that between faith and reason, between philosophical knowledge and those forms of knowing rooted in faith that are theology and mystical wisdom, there is neither separation nor confusion but synergy and life-giving solidarity.

Let us begin by pointing out that this vital synergy between the light of theological faith on the one hand (that faith by which God enables our mind to share—even though it be, it is true, through inevidence—in that knowledge by which He knows Himself from all eternity) and the natural light of reason on the other hand, operates differently according to whether there is a question of theology or a question of philosophy. In the first case, faith *elevates* reason in its proper activity in order to help it attain a *supernatural object*, whereas in the second case, reason illumined by faith has to do with a formal object which is of the *natural* order. If, in the two cases, the role that faith plays is different, it is because the object of theology and that of philosophy are essentially different.

Theology is a certain impression in us of the very knowledge of God Himself and of those who see Him face to face. Its proper object is the mystery of God supernaturally revealed for the scrutiny of reason. And therefore theology cannot be a kind of "metaphysics of the revealed" (in which philosophy would apply itself to studying, by its sole light, the truths which God proposes to the assent of our faith) because the statements of faith, inasmuch as they are an expression of the mystery of God, have a supernatural meaning which escapes every purely natural gaze. In order to acquire some understanding of divine revelation, in order to penetrate and scrutinize with reason's halting steps, its richness and its intelligible power and in order to make it shine bright in our mind—this is the work of theology, our reason must receive a supplementary light: it must be perfected and enlightened by the light of infused faith. Neither reason left to its natural powers, nor the light of faith by itself alone (insofar as it is immediate adherence to ultimate Truth) can ensure the result of the human effort of penetrating the truths that revelation proposes (for theology is in itself a rational science acquired by human effort). In other words, the light of theology is neither the simple light of faith (which transcends that of theology) nor the light of our natural reason (which is inferior to theological light). In order to be made capable of exploring, in its rational and discursive way, the truths we hold by faith, our reason must be elevated above itself by this same faith as an instrumental cause.

Here all the initiative comes from faith, which, as principal agent, takes

vel abusus ejus" (*ibidem*).

possession of the powers that are proper to reason for its own ends. Because of the indispensable role of reason and of the discourse proper to its nature, the quality communicated to our cognitive power, that is to say the *habitus* by which the latter is proportioned to the theological object, is in itself rational and naturally acquired,[23] but because this role of reason is a ministerial role, this *habitus* is *supernatural in its root* or in its origin.

If we turn now to philosophy, what is the role of faith, of theology, and of the wisdom of the saints in its regard?

Philosophy, we have said, is founded on the natural light of reason. And so when we consider it in its pure essence, precisely as philosophy, "it is independent on the Christian faith as to its object, its principles, and its methods."[24] However, this is a consideration relating only to the *nature* of philosophy, to philosophy considered in its *abstract essence* without taking account of the concrete or *existential state* in which philosophy, in actual fact, finds itself situated. This state depends on the conditions of existence and of the exercise of reason which is the work of philosophy; in other words, this state depends on the existential situation of man himself. If humanity has never failed to question itself about its origin, about its destiny, about what makes of the existence of each one of us a matchless adventure which sometimes disheartens us, at other times exalts us, it has learned to know the meaning of its march through history and the full truth about itself only through the revelation of Him Who created man in His image, Who called all of humanity to share His life and His eternal beatitude, Who has not abandoned man to his strayings and his faults, but Who sent His only Son in order to save him. God Himself became man in order to divinize us. This is astonishing good news. Faith, not reason, is its bearer.

However this revelation of faith concerns reason itself, not only from the fact that its field of investigation is considerably enlarged by this, but more radically still from the fact that the light of faith touches it in its very depths. If the first thing, and the most manifest, to be considered is the objective contribution which philosophical reason receives from revelation, this contribution is not what is most vital to it. What pierces to the very heart of its life is the gift of faith itself whose light brings down to us that knowledge which God has of Himself and of all things. The nature of our reason will certainly not be changed, but through participation in the divine knowledge which is supernaturally communicated to us, reason finds itself situated in a better and more perfect state even in what concerns its natural activity. For the grace of faith not only raises our minds to a new level; it also binds up those wounds whose traces are found in each of our natures. Better still, the light of faith strengthens and stimulates reason in its natural vitality itself. If, in the case of

---

23 John of St. Thomas points out that the object of theology "*pertinet ad habitum naturalem et naturaliter acquisitum.*" *Curs. theol.*, vol. I, disp. 2. a. 12.

24 Jacques Maritain, *An Essay on Christian Phliosophy*, p. 8.

theology, reason receives from faith the communication of an instrumental power by which the power proper to reason exercises itself at a new and higher level, in the case of philosophy, that is to say when reason sets itself to scrutinize being by its own proper light, the illumination which it receives from faith does not raise it to a new level, but strengthens it in its activity as principal cause. The truth is that in this last case where reason acts on its own behalf, philosophy is *princeps* and *domina*, whereas in working on behalf of theology it is *ancilla* (but not *serva*). The fact that philosophical reason receives from the grace of faith a medicinal aid (which does not mean that *gratia sanans* makes deviations impossible, even very serious ones), the fact that philosophical reason is sustained and strengthened in its own life by the power of faith, this constitutes a subjective contribution of capital importance for philosophical activity. Let us add that philosophy, insofar as it is a certain perfection of the intelligence, is also made firmer and more sure of itself by theology and mystical wisdom (thanks to the vital solidarity and dynamic continuity of those *habitus* of which the higher strengthen the lower in their order). The *habitus* of mystical contemplation "clarifies and soothes, spiritualizes the philosophic *habitus* within its own order. And in the light of theology, metaphysical truths take on a radiance so immediate and convincing that in consequence the philosopher's labors are blest with a new facility and fruitfulness, Henceforth, in fact, metaphysics cannot assume its fullest proportions in the human mind without experiencing the attraction of theology."[25]

If it is true that the attraction exercised on philosophy by these higher lights enables it "to achieve some degree of self-detachment and be relieved of some of its ponderousness,"[26] it is nevertheless necessary to note that, whatever the conditions of its formation and of its exercise in the soul may be, philosophy remains a work of reason. This unifying and multiform participation, this dynamic continuity within this threefold Christian wisdom do not come about at the expense of the formal distinction of objects, and the fact that philosophy is attracted by higher wisdoms does not give it another formal object; otherwise this would do violence to the very nature of philosophy. In undergoing the attraction of the other wisdoms and in receiving their vivifying influx, philosophy does not submit to a movement imposed from the outside; rather it obeys its own nature and *its natural aspirations to know, as best as possible, everything that comes within its domain.* In its communion with theological and mystical wisdom, it loses not one single element of its own identity. On the contrary, in this communion it will be more fully itself and more strictly faithful to its nature as philosophy because then the *scientia veritatis* will itself be even truer, since it will then have a better knowledge of the vastness of being.

In speaking of philosophy considered in its existential state which is that of reason in a Christian order, Jacques Maritain often used the term "Christian

---

25   Jacques Maritain, *An Essay on Christian Philosophy*, pp. 26–27.
26   *Ibid.*, p. 28.

philosophy." If today he proposes to designate it by another word, it is first of all because the name Christian philosophy is too suggestive of a philosophy that is not free but bound by some restriction or other of a confessional nature. There is however a more profound reason for changing the vocabulary on this point. The truth is that the term "Christian philosophy" runs the risk of hiding from our mind's eye that we are no longer concerned here with philosophy considered simply as such, but with philosophy that has come to its full maturity, with *philosophy considered fully as such.*[27] What is fundamentally at stake here is much more than a change of vocabulary. It is a question of indicating that the state in which philosophy finds itself in a Christian order is not only a better state for reason, but a state in which philsoophy as such attains its proper plenitude and attains it only there.

The growth in awareness of this fact marks a historical turning point of capital importance for philosophical reason itself to the degree that it implies the growth in awareness by philosophy of the breadth of its own domain.

This domain is above all that of the formal object of the philosopher: *being* as it is accessible to natural reason. But being has an infinite amplitude; and it includes higher degrees, which are offered to our mind by faith and the supernatural order and which, without being the formal object of philosophy, are objects which concern it eminently and which it receives from a higher wisdom. As soon as it makes contact with being, the intelligence thirsts for being in its totality. Far from compartmentalizing the mind and enclosing it within the limits of its formal object—as is the case for the specialized sciences (chemistry, biology, etc.; a physicist devoted to a specialized sector of physics does not understand what a physicist devoted to another sector is saying!)— philosophy, which is already a form of wisdom, refuses to compartmentalize the intellect and to imprison it in its formal object (according to an only too prevalent narrow-minded conception, which misconstrues both being and the mind). It is the formal object itself of the philosopher who is fully a philosopher which asks him to consider objects of a higher order, which are objects of a science superior to his own, that is, the science of theology. It asks this of him certainly not in order to acquire *full knowledge (savoir)* of them (a knowledge which depends on a higher order than his and is the affair of the theologian), but in order to complete as much as possible, *in his own perspective,* his quest for *being to which his intelligence is assigned.*

In theology there are certainly *objects beyond* the formal object of philosophy, but to which the latter requires the philosopher to apply himself by way of personal research which has no pretension whatever of leading to a demonstrated certitude. The views and opinions resulting from this personal research, which are naturally subject to the control of the theologian, may eventually be of use to him.

And understood thus as objects of thought proposed by the philosopher,

---

27   Cf. *infra*, ch. XVII, "Along Unbeaten Pathways," p. 421.

indeed affirmed by him at his own risk and peril, such points of research belong to the *domain of philosophy*, when it is that of a Christian. They are its most noble and most precious objects. And they are part and parcel of a philosophy set free by the full sense of being, a philosophy which will have nothing to do with compartmentalizing the mind or keeping it shut up within the limits or the barriers of its own formal object. Philosophical reason is required by its formal object to go *beyond itself* from the moment that there is question of objects which in their own particular manner bear on *being*. The objects in question are *necessary* and *indispensable* to such a philosophy which owes it to itself, from the moment that it reflects at the very beginning on what it is, to consider them as included in the extension of its own domain as *essential elements* (although dependent on a knowledge higher than its own).

The idea that I am maintaining is that the domain of philosophy, because it is a form of wisdom, extends far beyond its own formal object and embraces, for conjectural research, all that is accessible to our mind in the treasures of being, thanks to other modes of knowing.

By virtue of its formal object, philosophy is a science and a wisdom of the purely natural order, a work of reason alone. But from the very fact that it bears on being, it overflows the limits of its formal object, in order to reach other zones of being, even the highest; but in this case it is no longer science or wisdom but has become simply an instrument of research. For the mind will never renounce aspiring to adequation with being.

Let us think of a man who owns a magnificent garden and who gives his most attentive care to the beautiful flowers which he grows there. Will this gardener-philosopher, and should he, spend his whole life behind his garden walls? He knows that beyond those walls is all of Nature, with its forests, its mountains, its snows, its oceans, and that the care of this immensity has been entrusted to other specialists, specialists of the second great wisdom, let us call them angel-theologians. Are they going to keep him from opening his gates and, while continuing to tend his own garden, from visiting the vast expanse of Nature, and looking at it with his own eyes, with no pretension of acquiring that *knowledge* of nature which belongs to the angel-theologians, even at the risk of stumbles, sprains, and falls resulting from his temerity? It is certainly better for him and for his mind to risk such things, for which he alone would be responsible, and better too perhaps for the angel-theologians with whom he is in dialogue, than never to go beyond the walls of his garden; for if he takes his walks outside at his own risk and peril, it may very well be that they would suggest to him some very good ideas that the angel-theologians who are in charge of Nature never thought of themselves.

What is it that gives philosophy, when understood in its full sense, the right to cast its gaze on objects which formally depend on a science superior to its own? Are we not involved here in an impossible quarrel about competence between philosophy and the science of theology? No, this is not the case at all, and to pose the problem in these terms is to misconstrue completely the views proposed here. For it is quite evident that theology alone has the *competence* to pronounce with scientific certitude on questions that fall within its proper domain. Here theology alone is *qualified* to do the work of *theological science*. If the philosopher submits to the theologian his own views on a particular theological question, it is as an *hypothesis of research*. However—and this is the point which matters—such a research is not only legitimate, it is necessary for the philosophical enterprise itself. The philosopher has no mission to elaborate a theological treatise. If he considers that theological questions are research goals for his own particular science, he does no more than draw the consequences for his own science from what St. Thomas teaches about the vital connection and solidarity between metaphysical wisdom and wisdoms rooted in faith, theological wisdom above all. For the metaphysical *habitus* touches the theological *habitus* directly, according to the law that the lower touches at its summit the lower limit of what is immediately above it. But how is the communion between the two *habitus* established? If the light of theology strengthens metaphysical reason, it is by proposing theological objects to reason, for it is the object which governs here. The theological *habitus* itself is born in the mind only when the latter has taken possession of truths which constitute the object of theology. From the point of view of receiving its perfection from the *habitus*, the mind is dependent on the object which is revealed to it. All the light is communicated through the object.

In setting his sights on being, the philosopher, from the very outset of his work, encounters matters which at one and the same time and in one way or another are both philosophical and theological. And this does not occur only when he reflects on his own work as a philosopher,[28] or when he considers human things in a more general way or the conduct of human life,[29] but even when he is concerned with the infra-human world,[30] subject as it is like everything else to divine government. Does he not know by faith that what is accomplished for the salvation of man concerns *all of creation*?[31] But not only does being which it encounters require philosophy to turn its gaze above its formal object; it is again theology itself, by the very fact that it proposes to our mind objects more elevated than those of philosophy, which invites the latter to enlarge the dimensions of its domain. To say, as St. Thomas does, that philosophy cannot take on its full development in our minds without the support of the theological *habitus*, is to affirm at the same time that philosophy cannot be fully itself without being concerned in its own way with theological

---

28   Cf. *infra*, ch. XI, *Reflections on Wounded Nature*.

29   Cf. *infra*, ch. IX, *Love and Friendship*.

30   Cf. *infra*, ch. VI, *Toward a Thomist Idea of Evolution*, and ch. VII, *Concerning Animal Instinct*.

31   Cf. St. Paul, Rom., VIII, 19–23. See also St. Thomas, *Summa contra Gentiles*, lib. IV, c. 55.

questions, in other words, without the philosopher applying himself to the consideration of theological questions from his own particular perspective—which requires that he himself participate, in however modest a manner, in the theological *habitus*.

St. Thomas refused to compartmentalize the mind because he knew that this would be to sin against it. When he tells us that philosophy, if it is put in the service of theology, must be brought into conformity with the dimensions of faith, *"philosophia est ad metas fidei redigenda,"*[32] he certainly does not ask philosophy to do what is impossible for it, nor to do violence to its very nature. This extension of philosophy to the dimensions of faith is valid also when philosophy works to advance its own work. It must be noted however that such an enlargement of philosophy is carried out in an essentially different manner depending on whether philosophy is fulfilling its office of *ancilla* in the service of theology or whether it is working in its own behalf. In the first case it is integrated, as an *instrument* of theology, in a procedure and in the service of an enterprise which at each stage of its elaboration is *formally* theological. In the work which it then carries out, philosophy is entirely dependent on the theological habitus. In the other case, however, where philosophy is working in its own behalf, conforming itself to the dimensions of faith requires that philosophy seek help in the theological habitus itself (which the philosopher must possess at least in elementary form) in order to be able to turn its gaze toward objects theological in themselves, but which it is necessary and indispensable for philosophy to consider if it is to push to the very limit of its own domain.

Is this to practice theological science? Not at all.

The remarks of a theologian like Father Congar concerning the person of the Church are rather complex but very significant.[33] The reflection of the Christian philosopher, when he scrutinizes (as a philosopher) some point relating to theology, is certainly a *reflection of theological nature*, but his manner of approaching the theological object, his free demeanor in conversing *tête-à-tête* with it, in short his *procedure* is altogether different from the procedure which the *theologian must* follow when he wishes to practice theological *science*.

If philosophy, taken in the strictest and fullest sense of the term, recognizes fully and affirms clearly its relation to theology, would it not be more fitting to call it by a new name: *theo-philosophy*? This designation seems quite accurate and guarantees liberty of research and of vocabulary, freeing us (because the

---

32   *In Boet.* prooemium, q. 2, a. 3.

33   "Jacques Maritain often insists on his professional title of Christian *philosopher*. He refuses to be classified as a 'theologian,' but he still does theology since he insists on thinking out his faith. And perhaps from this very point of view, he remains a philosopher. He speaks of grace and of the Church almost like a naturalist of the supernatural, as of physical types of realities: after all, these are *concrete* realities, which in fact have a certain nature, a certain ontology." (*Revue Thomiste*, 1971, no. 4, p. 633.

relation to theology is frankly indicated) from the ambiguous vocabulary of those philosophers who present themselves as pure philosophers while harboring hidden theological agenda.

The whole of German philosophy in which Nietzsche saw "an insidious theology" or "a masked theology" is the most typical example. Indeed, this system of thought, from Boehme to Heidegger (and the philosophy of Nietzsche himself, however atheistic it claims to be, is no exception), proceeds in disguise, concealing under a philosophical vocabulary a claim of an entirely different order. Is it not the duty of philosophy, freed by faith and come to its full maturity, to indicate openly and frankly its relation to the theology inscribed in its natural aspirations? It is not because of its connection with theology (and also with a certain mysticism) that German philosophy must be called to account. What must be held against it is that it began by *separating* and *opposing* philosophy, theology, and mysticism to one another, and ended up by absorbing theology and mysticism into philosophy itself.

What has taken place now that, with the Lutheran revolution, the unity of this threefold Christian wisdom has been broken and its dynamic continuity destroyed? Each of the three continues to aspire toward that whole from which it was separated. And each one now strives separately to realize alone the work which needs the cooperation of all. That is to say that each part takes upon itself the work of the whole and ends up turning itself into the whole. And this is the source of the worst confusions and of the worst forms of totalitarianism. In observing the spectacle which is offered by the history of German philosophy, one notices various totalitarian systems of knowledge which differ among themselves only in the fact that it is one part or another which has substituted itself for the whole. Thus Boehmian mysticism takes upon itself that very work which on the one hand is the province of theology and on the other of philosophical knowledge. And this "mystical theosophy" has been so successful in substituting itself for philosophy that Jacob Boehme can appear in the eyes of a Hegel to be the "first German philosopher." In the case of Hegel himself, philosophy turns itself into theology (and mysticism too) and proposes to lead humanity toward its salvation (for must not the theologian teach in such a way as to contribute to the salvation of souls?). And, returning once again to Father Rahner, it is theology (according as it bears the mark of a Heidegger whose thought is more mystical than philosophical) which takes upon itself the work of philosophy.

However it may be with these strayings and with these serious deviations, this "masked theology," in spite of everything, remains tributary to the vital unity of Christian wisdom as well as to the loftiest aspirations of philosophy. In actual fact, where the work of philosophy is concerned with the priceless jewels of being which it examines freely as best it can by advancing personal opinions, it is here that philosophical work, while attaining its highest level, is also more humble than ever since it knows full well that the scientific verification of such jewels depends on mental equipment very superior to its own.

If the present book marks a historical turning-point whose importance must be recognized, it is first and foremost because here philosophy becomes conscious of what is demanded of it when it is fully itself, that is, when it is no longer in its beginning stages, as in the case of Aristotle, or especially when it is no longer mandated, as in the case of St. Thomas, to be the *ancilla* of theology. Such a growth in awareness by which philosophy reaches its complete freedom is in itself an outcome of considerable importance and implies for philosophy itself a change of perspective which, if it has nothing spectacular about it, is really the equivalent of a revolution. But the word *revolution* is very inadequate when there is question of signifying the progress which has been realized here. For in the realm of the mind there is neither the din nor the clamor of proud violence which ordinarily accompany what history calls revolutions. In the kingdom of the mind, changes take place in silence and humility. (And this is why they often remain so long unrecognized.) On the other hand, in the spiritual order progress is made neither by destruction nor by substitution. If philosophical thought has arrived here at its loftiest state, it has not been by uprooting and pushing over the tree of metaphysics. Rather, by drawing on all the sap within its system, this tree has grown to the size its nature destined for it so that it might produce its noblest fruits. It is by fidelity to its very being and to the demands inscribed in it as the *scientia maxime divina* that metaphysics rises up to cast its gaze beyond the frontiers of its own formal object.

With regard to the historical importance of this change of perspective for philosophical activity, it should be noted also that in becoming more deeply conscious of its vast domain and of the work required for any kind of progress (and which needs workers ready to sacrifice everything for the truth), philosophy is in a position to put back on a sure footing a modern intelligence which is staggering under the weight of four centuries of history. In order to carry out such a task, philosophy must be able to discern—and for this it must more than ever be instructed in theology—philosophical wisdom's authentic cry for help in the very failures of modern philosophy.

If the name *theo-philosophy* then belongs to a philosophy that has attained its full maturity (more than ever conscious of its strictly philosophical nature, even as it receives and makes use of higher lights), if this name belongs to it because it emphasizes admirably the nobility of philosophical science,[34] from another point of view, the name of *Seinsphilosophie* suits it even better. In reality,

---

34   Let us not forget that for Aristotle and St. Thomas, metaphysics, because it is a science of divine things, is called *theology.* Cf. *In Metaph.*, lib. VI, lect. I, ed. Cathala, § 1168. (Dans la *Sum. theol.* Ia, q. 1, a. 1, ad 2um, St. Thomas distinguishes between theology founded on divine revelation and theology which is part of philosophy.)

metaphysics is a limited knowledge, *modica cognitio*, not only because we never succeed here on earth in possessing it perfectly, but above all because in its beginning stages it is not ensconced, as is theological science, at the very heart of the knowledge of God, in whose light theology shares by theological faith. Philosophy rises to the knowledge of God beginning with the knowledge of the things we find all around us. It is here first that metaphysics encounters its proper object: being as attained by natural reason. If by its most sublime name, philosophy is called *theo-philosophy*, it prefers the name of *Seinsphilosophie* because this name reminds it of its humble origins at the same time as of its highest object: the deity which is subsistent being itself.

Up till now I have been concerned with philosophy itself. I have certainly spoken of it at too great a length, and also too imperfectly (my excuse being that it was important to show the progress which these *Approches sans entraves* have brought about in philosophy by helping it to become more fully itself).

I would like to end this preface with a few brief remarks about some more particular aspects of the present book.

From the day when Raïssa passed to the other side of the veil and was no longer, except invisibly, at his side, Jacques Maritain, despite the fatigue of age and problems of health, published a considerable number of books.[35] But, using the few moments and the little strength that this work left him, he also wrote a considerable number of articles, especially in *Revue Thomiste* and in *Nova et Vetera*, on the most varied of subjects. It is these essays, along with a few unpublished or privately published texts, that the present volume brings together. Like no other contemporary thought, Jacques Maritain's thought is turned toward the conquest of new territories and new regions for philosophy. It is characterized by an extraordinary curiosity and by a force and a freshness that indefatigably moves it to push its investigations further and further into the field of reality.

Because, in *Approches sans Entraves*, philosophy is completely set free by faith and because his advance follows its course in as untrammeled a manner as possible, the present book is the work of an intrepid explorer who ventures, alone, into the *Neuland*. This explains the very free pace and style of the discussion as well as the variety of the questions he grappled with, questions which bear on theology as well as on metaphysics, the philosophy of nature, moral philosophy, and epistemology. With indefatigable attention and an admirable openness to everything present to it, Philosophy here ranges freely over the vast reaches of the degrees of being. This is why the profound unity

---

35   Let us mention first of all texts by Raïssa that he published: *Notes sur le pater* (1962), *Journal de Raïssa* (1963), et *Poèmes et Essais* (1968); and then his own books: *Dieu et la Permission du Mal* (1963), *Carnet de Notes* (1965), *Le Mystère d'Israël* (1965), *Le Paysan de la Garonne* (1966), *De la Grâce et de l'Humanité de Jésus*, (1967), *Pour une Philosophie de l'Education* (1969), *De l'Eglise du Christ* (1970).

of this book comes above all from Maritain's constant concern as a thinker, endowed with an exceptional boldness of vision, to open doors and cut new paths in all the regions of philosophy. From this point of view alone, his present work constitutes a contribution of the greatest importance to philosophical thought. In addition it gives us an indication of the admirable fecundity of *Seinsphilosophie* as well as its power of self-renewal characteristic of every living organism.

Needless to say, these *Approches* do not send us on *Holzwege* or along some indistinct woodcutters' trail where the mind loses its way in the depth of some trackless forest? Nor are these *Approches* in any way like the position of Schopenhauer who took himself for a *Wegweiser*, a "signpost which indicates the way" but does not itself budge to follow the path. The *Seinsphilosophie* does not send the mind off into obscure wooded thickets, nor does it open up paths without entering upon itself. In trying "to open doors and to clear the way a little,"[36] this author has pushed on, more than once, to the very end of the road he opened up. It is not surprising then that in this book are found some of the most important and most luminous pages in all his writings.

If at times they are also difficult pages, it is because such a thought can do no other, under pain of denying the nobility of metaphysics and the aspirations of our nature, than draw us always deeper into the mystery of being and toward its highest light. "If we consider human nature as such, and by itself alone, we must say that it includes within itself, essentially, a *natural* aspiration toward something infinitely above it and which it knows nothing about (we know what that is only through faith)."[37] Metaphysics, which is the loftiest knowledge accessible to our natural powers alone, includes, we have seen, inscribed in its nature, such an aspiration toward something which far surpasses it. And this is why a humanity which does not recognize the nobility of metaphysics has already lost the sense of its own grandeur and prepares itself to be devoured by its animality. If these *Approches* are so priceless, it is because they teach metaphysics that no one can tear away this aspiration without leading it miserably astray; in the same way they teach us that if we try "to tear from ourselves this aspiration toward the *naturally impossible*, which is as essential to us as our skin, to that same extent we bring about the debasement our very nature."[38]

Heinz R. Schmitz (under the pseudonym of Ernst R. Korn)

After receiving the proofs of this volume, the author died suddenly. They were corrected by some of his friends, under the responsibility of the Cercle d'Etudes Jacques et Raïssa Maritain.

---

36   Cf. *infra*, ch. XI, "Reflections on Wounded Nature," p. 237.

37   Jacques Maritain, *infra*, ch. XVII, "Along Unbeaten Pathways."

38   *Ibidem.*

MARITAIN CHRONOLOGY

1882
November 18, Birth in Paris, son of Paul Maritain and Genevieve Favre.

1883
September 12, Birth of Raïssa Oumansov in Rostov-on-the-Don.

1893
The Oumansov family arrives in Paris.

1898–1899
Jacques studies rhetoric at Lycée Henri IV and meets Ernest Psichari.

1900
Jacques meets fellow student Raïssa Oumansov at Sorbonne

1901
Jacques meets Charles Peguy
Peguy, in the winter of 1901–1902, prompts Raïssa and Jacques to take Henri Bergson's course at the Collège de France

1902
Jacques and Raïssa engage to marry.

1904
November 26, Jacques and Raïssa marry.
They come upon the writings of Leon Bloy.

1905
June 25, first visit to Bloy.
Jacques passes *agrégation* in philosophy.

1906
June 11, Jacques and Raïssa (and Vera Oumansov) baptized in the church of St. John the Evangelist in Paris.
August 25, Jacques and Raïssa leave for Heidelberg, where they will spend two years studying biology. Raïssa's sister Vera comes to live with them and remains for the rest of her life.

1907

September 8, Encyclical *Pascendi* deals with Modernism.

1908

June, returns to France.
September, Peguy regains his faith.
The Maritains acquire P. Clerissac as their spiritual director.
Jacques's employment consists in work on Orthographic Dictionary.

1909

October, Maritains take up residence in Versailles, where they will remain until 1923.

1910

June, "Reason and Modern Science," Jacques' first published article
appears in the *Revue de Philosophie*.
September 15, Jacques begins to read the *Summa theologiae* and is en-
thralled.

1912

Jacques becomes professor of philosophy at the Lycée Stanislas.

1913

February 13, conversion of Ernest Psichari.
October, Jacques's first book *Bergsonian Philosophy* is published.

1914

June, Jacques named adjunct professor of the History of Modern Philoso-
phy at the Institut Catholique.
August 2, outbreak of World War I.
August 22, death of Ernest Psichari.
September 5, death of Charles Peguy.
November 15, death of Pere Clerissac.

1917

Jacques called up, spends brief time at Camp Satory, is not kept.
November 3, death of Leon Bloy.
March 26–April 8, first visit to Rome; audiences with Benedict XV and
with Cardinal Billot on the subject of the apparitions at La Salette.

1918

Becomes joint heir, with Charles Maurras, of Pierre Villard. Takes 1918–
1919 year off to work on first volumes of a projected Manual of Philosophy.

1919

Associated with new *Revue Universelle*, in charge of philosophy; contributes many articles at first, tapers off and stops in July 1926.
The Thomist Circle meetings begin.

1920

Art and Scholasticism published.

1921

Theonas published.

1922

Jacques and Raïssa privately print *Prayer and Intelligence* (*La vie d'oraison*).
July 20, first meeting with Charles Journet in Switzerland.
October 4, Reginald Garrigou-Lagrange preaches the first retreat of the Thomist Circle at Versailles.
Antimodern published.

1923

June 5, Jacques and Raïssa installed at 10 rue de Parc, Meudon, where they will live until the outbreak of World War II.
September 26–30, second retreat of Thomist Circle, at Meudon. These will be held every year except 1936 that the Maritains are in residence in Meudon.
December 14, Jacques tries to persuade André Gide not to publish Gide's homosexual work *Corydon*.

1924

Réflexions sur l'intelligence et sur sa vie propre published.

1926

Published exchange of letters with Jean Cocteau, who had regained his faith at Meudon.
Meets Olivier Lacombe and Julien Green.
December 20, Action Française condemned by Pius XI after several months of discussion with Charles Maurras in which Maritain and Garrigou-Lagrange took part.

1927

Primauté de spirituel published.
Charles de Bos converted. (Eventually would teach for a few years at Notre Dame.)
Jacques Maritain called to Rome by Pius XI.

1927 (cont'd)

Pourquoi Rome a parlé published with essays by Maritain and others on the condemnation of Action Française.

1928

Peter Wust, German Catholic philosopher, visits Meudon.
Emmanuel Mounier becomes regular participant at Meudon.
Jacques's chair changed from History of Modern Philosophy to that of Logic and Cosmology.

1929–1930

Maritain on leave while he writes *Distinguer pour unir, ou Les degrés du savoir*.
The Angelic Doctor and *Religion and Culture* published.

1931

March 21, meeting of the Société française de Philosophie on the topic of Christian Philosophy. Brehier, Gilson,and Maritain among participants.

1932

Le songe de Descartes published.
Distinguer pour unir published.
De la philosophie chrétienne published.

1933

First visit to Toronto and Chicago.
Du régime temporel et de la liberté published.
Sept leçons sur l'être published.

1934

Pour le bien commun manifesto.

1935

Frontières de la poésie published.
Science et Sagesse published.
La philosophie de la nature published.
Maritain writes "Pour la justice et pour la paix," prompted by Mussolini's invasion of Ethiopia.
Lettre sur l'indépendance published.

1936

Humanisme Intégral published.
Jacques and Raïssa visit Argentina (July 26–November 7).

1938

October 1, departs for United States, returns at Christmas.
Questions de conscience published.
Situation de la poésie, written in collaboration with Raïssa, published.

1939

La Crépuscule de la civilisation published.
Quatre essais sur l'esprit dans sa condition charnelle published.
August 5, death of Charles de Bos.
September 3, declaration of war.

1940

With Raïssa and Vera, leaves for America. Spends January and February in Toronto, in March move to New York. After the fall of France and the formation of the Vichy government, decides to remain in U.S. In September, Maritains installed at 30 Fifth Avenue.

1941

January 4, death of Bergson.
A travers le désastre published.
Confession de foi published.
La pensée de saint Paul published.
First volume of Raïssa's *Grandes Amitiés* published.

1942

Les Droits de l'Homme et la loi naturelle published.

1943

The Thomist devotes a jumbo issue to Maritain.
Christianisme et Démocratie published.
Education at the Crossroads published.

1944

Principes d'une politique humaniste published.
De Bergson à Thomas d'Aquin published.
June 6, Normandy beachhead established.
September, *A travers la victoire.*
November 10, return to France, appointed French ambassador to the Vatican.

1945

Second volume of *Grandes Amitiés* published.
April 1, departure for Rome.

1947

Court Traité de l'existence et de l'existant, La personne et le bien commun published.

November 6, Maritain president of French delegation to UNESCO conference in Mexico.

Resigns as ambassador to accept appointment at Princeton.

1948

Raison et raisons published.

June 27, arrives in New York.

August 19, arrives in Princeton.

1949

La signification de l'athéisme contemporain published.

Revue thomiste devotes a number to the work of Maritain.

June 4, death of Maurice Blondel.

Buys 26 Linden Lane, Princeton, where he will live until 1960 and bequeath to the University of Notre Dame.

1951

Man and the State published.

Neuf leçons sur les notions premières de la philosophie morale published.

1952

June, retires from Princeton University.

1953

Creative Intuition in Art and Poetry published.

Approches de Dieu published.

1954

Suffers coronary thrombosis in March. Begins *Carnet de notes*.

February, death of Paul Claudel.

1957

Reflections on America published.

Founding of the Jacques Maritain Center at the University of Notre Dame.

1959

Liturgie et contemplation, written in collaboration with Raïssa, published.

December 31, death of Vera.

1960

Le Philosophe dans la Cité published.
The Maritains return to France, where the ailing Raïssa dies July 7 in Paris. She is buried at Kolbsheim.
La Philosophie morale published.

1961

Visits U.S. in January, in March installs himself at Toulouse near the Little Brothers of Jesus. In autumn, again visits U.S.

1962

October 11, opening of first session of Vatican II.

1963

June, death of Pope John XXIII and election of Paul VI.

1965

February, *Carnet de notes* published.
September, visits Paul VI at Castel Gandolfo.
December 8, close of Vatican II. The Pope presents Maritain with a message addressed to intellectuals.

1966

Autumn, last trip to the U.S.
November 3, *Le Paysan de la Garonne* published.

1967

De la grâce et l'humanité de Jesus published.

1970

De l'Eglise du Christ published.
October 15, Maritain dons the habit of the Little Brothers of Jesus at Toulouse and in 1971 takes his vows.

1973

April 28, death of Jacques Maritain at Toulouse. On May 2, he is buried at Kolbsheim with Raïssa.

I

IN THE SECRET OF FAITH

CHAPTER I

BEGINNING WITH A REVERIE

ESCHATOLOGICAL IDEAS[1]

FOREWORD

THE KIND OF ESSAY, OR RATHER POEM, which this Foreword precedes is not even an hypothesis which one would wish might someday become an accepted theory. It is a conjectural essay destined to remain conjectural. And it is also a question addressed to theology—the question of knowing whether without any guarantee that such is really the case—it is permitted to a Christian to form for himself, as purely imaginary possibilities, certain ideas and certain hopes concerning mysteries about which the scriptural texts and revelation give us only a few indications, and apropos of which, consequently, it seems that within well-defined limits reverie may give itself a certain scope.

The author confesses that he attaches some importance to his reveries; they have been a help to him. He believes that they might be of some help to others as well. Julian Green remarks in his *Journal* that hardly anyone preaches today on the Last Ends of man. The most likely reason is that in order to provide a setting for the eternal diamonds of faith, we continue to make use of an imagery and a conceptualization which have changed very little from the time of the cathedrals and of Dante, and which should have been renewed and carefully worked out in our own times. For want of something better, why not have recourse to some unfettered daydreams, which are attentive to the data of faith, but which remain day-dreams all the same?

Because reflections carried out in this way have nothing to do with theologically demonstrable or theologically probable conclusions, but rather with a kind of free play of the mind, within the solid walls of those certitudes established by faith, it seems quite natural that a share of initiative be left to these day-dreams, as well as to the imagination, and to simple Christian common sense. Because we know how dangerous it is for a philosopher to trespass on the terrain of theology, we have taken care not to do so. Our purpose is not at all theological; nor is it philosophical. It is one of simple common sense when it is Christian and when, after taking account of what the

---

1   *Editor's footnote*: Privately circulated. Thirty mimeographed copies were made in April 1939, and again in October 1961.

theologians teach, it feels its way along the paths opened up by day-dreams in a zone which the lights of revelation leave in the dark, except on the outer edges.

This is also why our essay is not an essay in the ordinary sense of the word, but rather a kind of poem: the poetic form of expression naturally suited to those things which cannot be attained by ordinary ways of knowing, even though in their own way they bring nourishment to our minds. In addition we thought it necessary to bring out in the highest possible relief and color all the implications of our thought. At the same time we should remind ourselves that we must never confuse poetic assertions with doctrinal affirmations. Let us say that in the final analysis the pages which follow, far from being simple folklore, belong to the same literary genre as that little monastic poem, undoubtedly translated from the Greek: *The Virgin's Journey through Hell*, mentioned by Dostoïevski in *The Brothers Karamazov* and very popular in Russia before Peter the Great.[2]

In looking over these pages once again after an interval of more than twenty years, I have thought it best to make only a few corrections of detail and to add a few notes.[3] I have had thirty copies made, and I intend to distribute a number of them among a small group of friends in whose advice I have the greatest confidence. Need I add that my reveries, as is the case with everything I write, were conceived and brought to light in a spirit of faithful submission to the judgment of the Church, a judgment to which I adhere in advance, if it should ever happen that the Church should consider worthy of its attention so modest and completely conjectural an imaginative essay.

J. M.
The North Atlantic, on board the *Flandre*, October 3, 1961

ESCHATOLOGICAL IDEAS

*A conjectural essay destined for
those who are not unaware of the
the distinction between nature and
grace and the value of analogy.*

IMAGERY

For the purposes of symbolic imagery, I will picture the world of the Last

---

2   Cf. Book V, chap. v.

3   In 1972 and for the present [1973] edition, I also corrected quite a few passages in the first four paragraphs of this work.

Ends as a star in a dream, gravitating around the sun which one side faces at all times while the other side remains in continual darkness.

* * * * * * * * * *

The sun never sets, and an unending day shines on that hemisphere where the predestined live.

In a high country of supernatural mountains, there is an abundance, a superabundance of snow, more beautiful and softer than ours, not cold but cool and invigorating, an image of grace, under the delicious warmth of a loving and life-giving sun, which is the Lamb. It is there, in the realm of glory and of vision, that the Blessed dwell, and where the heavenly Jerusalem rises in incorruptible splendor. As far as the snows extend, there extend as well the streets, the squares, and the dwellings of the City, whose ramparts will reach their full dimensions when the snows have covered all the valleys and plains of the hemisphere of the predestined.

* * * * * * * * * *

The land drops off into wide valleys. Here there is still snow, but also sorrow and its shimmering waters. Here smoke and flames leap up, which afflict the heart and darken the sky, but rays of the sun and of hope pierce through. These are the valleys of Purgatory.

As the souls are gradually set free, the depths of the waters of affliction, and the flames too, subside in the valley. On the day of resurrection, the entire land will be covered with the sacred snows of the mountains. Purgatory will be no more. But everywhere there will be a holy light. And these valleys and mountains too will become the valleys and mountains of the paradise of glory, of sacred Beatitude.

* * * * * * * * * *

At the farthest shores, where the valleys end, the hemisphere of night begins; that night without end. Steep, unscalable banks, beyond which is found, not the sea, but chaos, *magnum chaos firmatum est*. A desert of despair and desolation, where no order reigns, but only eternal horror. Tempest driven waves of mud and slime in their violent current wash down the rocks of hell.

Mutinous matter, gold, oil, iron, and coal, and all the ores of our pride and greed, transfigured in their fury, are locked in hideous combat. Fire rages everywhere. It burns in a ferocious night where not a single star, not the slightest glimmer of light runs across the sky. This is the empire of disordered nature, set loose against guilty souls. In this immense magma the damned move about.

However far it may be from the hemisphere of the Blessed, there is a high country that rises above the plains of horror. It also has valleys and mountains, with plants and flowers. The fire cannot touch it. No, there is no snow, but delicate moss and prairies. There is no desolation there, but well-ordered nature. And above this continent the nocturnal sky is resplendent with the most varied and ravishing constellations. A moon, more beautiful than our own, but which like ours does no more than reflect, dispenses its light. This is the land of Limbo, the land of natural happiness, where the soul does not see God face to face, and which, because of that, is still a kind of hell compared to Glory.

REFLECTIONS AND CONJECTURES
I

The blessed see God through His essence; they love Him with all the force of nature and of grace, according to a sovereign necessity which is at the same time a sovereign spontaneity. They now possess what they have always wanted.

With regard to all those goods which are not Goodness Itself, they are free, with a freedom of choice that is supernaturally impeccable. The Lamb enlightens them; and they exult to see in Mary the flawless and almost divine holiness of a little daughter of Israel who is no more than a simple creature; they exult to see the royal generosity of the Mother of the Savior and of all who have been saved. They communicate with the angels in endless revelations; they and the angels tell one another the history of this poor world and of all the fragile deeds immortalized in their holy memories. Of all that has been done, nothing is lost; all is poetry and song.

And their bodies, when they rise again by the power of the resurrection of Christ, and of His glory—miraculously drawn again from the potency of matter and finding themselves once again, though transfigured, in their exact singularity, since the entelechy of each one restores to every single body all its distinguishing features—their glorified bodies will enjoy the privileges of impassibility, subtlety, agility, brightness, which theology enumerates, and which will render space and time completely subject to them. Among themselves and with all nature that has been set free, risen souls will enjoy inexhaustibly marvelous forms of communication.

The resurrection of their bodies will be an event of joyous celebration for the separated souls.

And when the souls detained in the valleys of Purgatory are set free one by one, do you not think that each new deliverance will be another cause of joyous celebration? And so—throughout the course of discontinuous time—there will still be a kind of history in the world of eternity.

II

What are we to think of the sufferings of Purgatory? God takes no delight in the suffering of creatures, and suffering as such is not a good, like pleasure, it is only a surplus which "is added" to an ontological process. It is through the love of charity with which these sufferings are endured and which renders them in a certain sense voluntary[4] that the punishments of Purgatory cleans and purify souls.[5]

In an effort get an inkling of how this is so, it might be useful to recall first a few preliminary data.

How could there be the slightest *macula* in the souls of Purgatory? The stain (*macula*) or darkness of sin, which is the absence of grace, was removed from the soul during earthly life at the same time that mortal sin was forgiven (supposing that this soul was guilty of mortal sin), if it did penance and was restored to the state of grace; and as far as venial sin[6] is concerned, it left no *macula* in the soul here below.[7] Likewise, venial sin itself and any trace of guilt have completely ceased to exist for the souls in Purgatory. From the very moment when death separated them from their bodies, they began immediately to rejoice in a fervent charity that wipes out any venial guilt; they are absolutely guiltless, they are holy. But if *guilt* has disappeared, *punishment*— the privation of the vision of God—still remains due for the duration of this exile because after this present life there is no longer any possibility of merit and because those disorders of which the soul was guilty on earth require, for their reparation, the severities of the order of justice.[8] This is what is called *reatus poenae*, or the debt of punishment. This debt, contracted by some fault, relates to the demands for "compensation" or for a kind of "reverse shock" by virtue of which the order of things (either among themselves or in relation to God), when it is disturbed somewhere, recoils in repercussive punishment on

---

4   Cf. *Sent.* IV, d. 21, q. 1, a. 1, q^{la} 4.—*Sum. theol.*, Suppl., Appendix, q. 1 (*de Purgatorio*), a. 4.

5   "*Habent autem istae poenae quod sint purgatoriae ex conditione eorum qui eas patiuntur, in quibus est caritas per quam voluntatem suam divinae voluntati conformant, ex cujus caritatis virtute poenae quas patiuntur eis ad purgationem prosunt.*" St. Thomas, *Comp. theol.*, c. 182.

6   The souls in Purgatory are there because of their *venial sins* and in order to suffer the pains these sins deserve. Mortal sin is related to the final end, and in this case the soul chooses something else than God for its final end. Venial sin relates to the means used, and in this case the soul uses means incorrectly, all the while going toward its Final End. In both cases the created order is disturbed, but in the first case far more seriously. "*Peccata mortalia sunt per aversionem a fine ultimo,*" says St. Thomas (*Comp. theol.*, c. 175). *Peccata venialia non respiciunt ultimum Finem, sed viam ad Finem ultimum.*"

7   *Sum. theol.*, Ia-IIae, q. 89, a. 1.

8   Cf. *de Malo*, q. 7, a. 11: corp. et ad 17m.

the author of the fault, according to the laws of the good which, automatically, "do evil" and turn toward deterioration when an act has been posited in violation of these laws and of the limits of that act. And in the end, on whom should this deterioration fall if not on the agent of the fault when through his liberty as the intelligent and voluntary cause (and as *first* cause—though deficient—with regard to the evil as such) he has by his own initiative (the *first* initiative with regard to the evil as such) taken upon himself the complete responsibility for that fault? In this way the truth of God as head of the universe of liberty—that is to say of His justice—is made manifest to all. This manifestation, required by the harmony of things themselves, of the divine perfection of justice and of the truth in all things, wounded as they are, compensates exactly for the privation of love, and of good diffused in the creature, for which the fault is responsible. For this universal harmony, creative wisdom has established from all eternity a quantum of love and of created lovableness. Both God and created things are deprived of this by the fault. Punishment, not as suffering, but as a manifestation of that sacred truth which measures all things by their exact weight, is the compensation for this privation. Payment will have to be made down to the last penny—if in the blood of Christ love has not already remitted the debt (*sicut et nos . . .*).

So what has to be paid in Purgatory is the price which compensates for the privation introduced into the universal harmony by a disordered change of direction toward perishable goods—in other words the debt which still remains for a more or less extended time as the effect of venial sin committed here on earth. (For while eternal punishment is due to turning away from Being itself, temporal punishment is due to the disordered turning toward beings).

Now separated souls can no longer merit.[9] But the punishment they suffer is accepted with love. And this love of charity which no longer merits, and which can no longer grow, produces, in the soul which suffers and wants to

---

9   In the *Commentary on the Sentences* St. Thomas admitted that with respect to the remission of venial sins there could still be meritorious acts in Purgatory: "*Post hanc vitam non potest esse meritum respectu praemii essentialis. Sed respectu alicujus accidentalis potest esse, quamdiu manet homo in statu viae aliquomodo. Et ideo in purgatorio potest esse actus meritorius quantum ad remissionem culpae venialis*" (*Sent.* IV, d. 21, q. 1, a. 3, q^{la} 1. Cf. *Sum. theol.*, Suppl., Appendix, q. 1, a. 6: corp. et ad 4m). In this case the difficulty to which we are trying to respond here no longer exists. It is still rather unsettling to admit that the state *in viam* persists even if it is *respectu alicujus accidentalis* for a soul who has done with the time of trial and upon whom sentence has been passed—and who besides, being separated, is not a "person." And so St. Thomas later abandoned this opinion ("*post hanc vitam non est status merendi*," he declared purely and simply in *de Malo*, q. 7, a. 11, for indeed every venial sin was effaced from the soul by the sovereign act of charity toward God that the soul produced at the instant when it was separated from its body by death and made its entry into Purgatory).

suffer, a welling up of goodness in act capable of raising the level of the harmony in creation and of its intrinsic quantum of goodness, and thus of compensating, by dint of pouring forth goods from the treasury of patience, for the privations which the evil of the free creature had caused God and all created things to undergo.

Therefore in Purgatory not only is there compensation for evil by the justice and the manifestation of holy truth, but this manifestation and this compensation repair things themselves, and in them compensate for evil (the venial sin formerly committed) by the intrinsic goodness accumulated in them by their acceptance of punishment. And so—henceforth without merit, and without the overabundance and overcompensation due to the payments of Christ and of the saints (if not through the prayers of the Church Militant)—the goodness of the punishment borne in love repairs little by little the damage done to the created order, through an almost physical process of quantitative accumulation of justice that has been loved, accepted, assimilated, and cherished in love.

In the end, when Mercy and Justice have completed their work, all debt of punishment has been paid; the spotless soul, which had been washed clean from the moment it was separated from its body and entered into Purgatory by the holy violence of an act of love of God's wildly ardent love, is now set free and passes through the eternal gates.

There is a Purgatorial fire.[10] Is it the same as the fire of of Hell? Certainly not.[11] For, as a wholly spiritual fire, it causes us to feel in all their depth the

---

10   "*Igne crucientur ad tempus*," wrote Clement VI in 1351 (*ep. ad Consolatorem*, Denzinger-Schömetzer, 1067). St. Thomas uses the same expression *ignis purgatorius* (cf. *Sum. theol.*, Suppl., Appendix, q. 1, a. 6 and 7).

11   There was a time when, dazzled by the word *ignis*, I admitted they were the same, something I regret very much. I forgot that in sacred language the same word does not always have the same meaning. St. Thomas knew this very well, and indeed concerning this very word he wrote: "*In eisdem verbis Sacrae Scripturae latet multiplex intellectus*," cf. *Sum. theol.*, Suppl., q, 7, a. 7, ad 3m. (Nevertheless in his young years—*Sent.* IV, d. 21, q. 1, a. 1, q[1a] 2; Suppl., Appendix, q. 1, a. 2—he too advanced the opinion that it is the same fire which torments the damned in Hell and purifies the just in Purgatory: an opinion still shared by many in the West at the time of the Council of Florence, which refused, and rightly so, to give it any official status. If St. Thomas, instead of proposing this only as an offhand remark or as a conjecture without any proof to support it, had taught this formally, I would not hesitate to take my distance from him on this point.) From the abyss of Hell, the infernal fire of the damned does not reach the upper region, the highest level of the Underworld, which is Limbo, where nothing comes to trouble the natural happiness of those who reside there, whether for all time, as is the case with children who died without baptism, or for a certain time, as with the just who died before the resurrection of Christ. How could this fire rise as far as that place which is in no way a part of the Underworld, as far as the holy place that Purgatory is? The *ignis purgatorius* is, as I have indicated in the text, absolutely different from the fire of Hell.

ugliness and the stupidity of the failings committed here on earth, and which now hold up our entry into beatitude, and it makes our regret all the more intense as it causes our hope and love to burn brighter. Such a fire is the instrument not only of God's merciful justice, but also of His divine love, and it reaches the soul at the very center of love. This is why, in my imagery, I said that the rays of the sun and of hope break through. It acts as a sign or as a kind of sacrament,[12] it is like a witness through whom God makes clear to the soul

---

After this, if there is still question of the eternal fire into which the damned have been plunged, I would like to recall here a few points concerning it.

As a classic manual of theology points out (H. Hurter, s.j., *Theologiae dogmaticae Compendium*, III, Innsbrück, 1908, no. 651, pp. 620–621), it must be held that the fire of hell is real, not just metaphoric, something really physical or corporal, not purely moral or spiritual. But that does not in any way imply that it is the same fire that we experience, nor is it that "fire" which the Ancients regarded as one of the four elements. "*Vere enim scribit Augustinus*, De Civit. Dei, XX, 16: '*Qui ignis cujusmodi sit, hominem scire arbitror neminem, nisi forte cui Spiritus divinus ostendit.' Id tamen videtur defendendum eum esse aliquid externum, physicum, corporale, verum producens dolorem non mere internum, morale, spirituale.*" The fire of the damned in Hell, according to an opinion held by theologians of recognized authority, would be the fury with which the order of the universe takes its revenge on the author of the disorder which sin introduces into the cosmos—the world of bodies in this way inflicting, under the action of the First Cause, a torment experienced spiritually by the fallen spirits, angels and separated souls, and a physical torment felt in the bodies of the damned once they have risen. Cf. Charles Journet, "Les Anges et le cosmos," *Nova et Vetera*, 1953, no. 2, pp. 138–153.

We might add here that the eternal Fire mentioned in the Gospel (Matt. xxv, 41) includes corporal and physical fire, the instrument *par excellence* for the pain of the senses, which is what we are talking about, but also and of primary importance the deprivation of the beatific vision and beatific love. "In the wish to include in 'the eternal fire prepared for the devil and his angels' the pain of the senses, which is secondary, it would be vain to wish to exclude the pain of eternal privation, which is primary." Charles Journet, *loc. cit.*, p. 144.

As regards the pain of the senses, it is commonly taught that if the fire of Hell, even though corporal, causes the souls of the damned to suffer, it is because it holds them prisoner, invincibly bound to it, fixed in the corporal world to something they wants to get free from and which is repugnant to their nature. This is what constitutes the nature of the suffering produced by the corporal fire of Hell as an instrument of divine justice, in the souls of the damned and in the fallen angels.

But what is more important is that this same fire is a sign of their total abandonment, permitted by divine justice, to their own perverse wills and to the endless torments that their pride inflicts on them.

And what is still more important, as Father Journet points out, it is the pain of damnation, the eternal privation of that blessed vision of God, which at one and the same time they both desire and detest.

12   I say a *kind* of sacrament, because properly speaking a sacrament is something sensible received through the senses. But God can make use of a purely spiritual fire, exalting and enkindling, I suppose in this case, the Gift of Knowledge, as a

not only the stupidity of the faults, however venial they may be, which soiled it on earth (and which it has already recalled, without ever having seen them in such a vivid flash of light), but also the nobility and the beauty to which it was called and of which it has deprived itself, as well as the grandeur, which it did not recognize, of God's designs for it. And so a suffering and a sadness which reach the very roots of its being but which leave it hope, and the certitude of being saved—and which come from pure love—are continually roused in the soul. It asks to suffer, it thirsts for purification, out of love of justice and out of love for Love Itself. It is not in this place by constraint; it has thrown itself of its own accord, far from the snows which it longs for, into the valleys of the cleansing fire. It has what it wants now (while waiting to have what it has always wanted).

III

In the midst of the hemisphere of night, in the continent of Limbo crowned with stars, there is also a history, and events of far-reaching consequence. It is there that the soul of Christ came one day, swift and victorious, when it descended into Hell. It went only to Limbo,[13] but the rest of Hell knew of the

---

sign of His merciful justice, by means of which He causes certain cruel truths to be seen in their fullness.

13   *Sum. theol.*, IIIa, q. 52, a. 2.

But can we not ask if, in accepting, during His agony on the Mount of Olives, that frightful chalice, the very thought of which made Him sweat blood: taking on Himself *all the sins of the world*, Christ did not force Himself to empty to the very last drop that cup of abomination; and if then, during His descent into Hell (which lasted one day and two nights), His holy soul, after having visited Limbo, did not next descend into the Hell of the damned, to make them look upon the Savior they wanted nothing to do with, and for a moment to feel on His soul the weight of the malediction which the Father so infinitely dear to Him reserved for those who, making perverse use of the inviolable gift of human freedom, refused to the very end to be healed of the sins of the world and chose evil above everything else. For God and His Christ want all men to be saved, and this divine will was checkmated by these men for all time. And can we not think that such a rejection was one of the reasons why Jesus said on the cross: "My God, my God, why hast thou forsaken me?"

Concerning the visit to Limbo, St. Thomas tells us (IIIa, q. 52, a. 5) that there Christ immediately, and in the same place (*ibid.*, ad 3m), freed the holy Fathers by delivering them from original sin, but further on (IIIa, q. 56, a. 2; qu. 57, a. 6: corp. and ad 2m) he also says that it is His Resurrection which raised up these souls, and His Ascension which made them ascend to heaven along with Him. In my opinion it would have been better to express this a little differently, for example by saying: in his visit to Limbo Christ filled with joy the hearts of the Just of the Old Law, by announcing to them that the moment had come for their liberation and the end of their exile; but it was when they left Limbo, on the

event and bent its knee; the soul of Jesus could not enter into the world where there is no redemption: a reservation which seems stamped with a certain sadness (what surprise is He perhaps preparing?)

In Limbo there were not only the souls of the little children who had died without having received the sacraments of the law of Nature or of the Old Law, because of which in former times, *in fide ecclesiae*, God remitted original sin, as He does now—but this time because they enter immediately into beatitude— through the efficacy of baptism. There—in the bosom of Abraham—was that throng of the souls of the *parvuli* who had died with these sacraments, and who, with a radical longing, awaited the coming of their Redeemer so they could enter into heaven; there was that immense multitude of all the souls of those men and women who had died in the state of grace, and who with an actual expectation awaited the coming of their Redeemer in order to enter heaven and who had been waiting there in pressing throngs for centuries. And not only four thousand years, but hundreds of thousands of years, as many as paleontology requires. The beliefs of Antiquity had scarcely deceived these holy souls at all concerning their ultimate fate, for it was in those kinds of Elysian Fields that, without any suffering or distress—but with what nostalgia to see God!—they became bored with the pale asphodels and with the imperfect natural felicity of separated souls. Without bodies or any life of the senses from which to draw ideas, their intelligence informed by their spiritual substance knew quite intuitively of His coming. But their intelligence did not have a force intensive enough (this is why man needs multiple ideas to articulate) to achieve anything but a too general, imprecise, and hazy knowledge of the world and of God. From time to time angels came to comfort them with their natural light, to accustom them to concepts of sublime intellectuality, and without doubt also to illumine and console them with their light of grace. Their hearts kept watch in charity; hope and supernatural faith were alive in them like their love.

But one day eternity was shaken, the soul of their Savior comes like a May breeze to set them free; He speaks to them, He instructs them, He gathers them together for their departure. Behind Him, as one, as a single swarm of bees filled with joy, they leap across the abyss on Easter Day, and rushing into the blessed vision, they leave behind in the land of Limbo the souls of those little children who died without the sacraments. They have also left behind their faith and hope but not their charity. They see, they possess, they love. They have what they have always longed for.

morning of their Savior's Resurrection, that the liberation which had been announced was fully accomplished. At that moment they entered into glory. As for our Lord's Ascension, was this not a sign of what concerned Him alone, namely the fact that during the forty days during which He showed Himself to the witnesses of His Resurrection, He now resides forevermore, in glory and majesty, in the kingdom of the Blessed, where He sits at the right hand of the Father.

As for the souls of the little children, they were sleeping in Limbo. On earth they had never made a human act of deliberate will; they had not chosen their last end, they were therefore not fixed in a last act of their mortal life. This is why they were sleeping. What is in store for them now? Acts of childish animality? As separated souls, they are no longer children. Acts of freedom? They left their bodies before the age of reason. To take the initiative in the act of deliberating about oneself and of determining one's last end, which is eminently an act of the person as such—does not belong to the separated soul. And without this act, the source of all others, no other free act can come into existence.

In short the separated soul is not in the state which is suited to that divine impulse which might awaken in it, according to the order of nature, the first act of intelligence and the first act of will. For that it will have to wait for the resurrection of the body. The separated souls of the little children—of those who had been washed clean of original sin and of those who had not—were asleep in Limbo before the coming of the Lord.

Those who had received the sacraments before Christ were set free at His coming, like the souls of the others who were saved. They are awakened, and what an awakening! Their first human act—as the first human act now of the souls of the Little baptized children who have died—is to see God.

The souls of the little children who died without the sacraments before Christ continue to sleep in Limbo. The actualization of their intelligence by their substance remains virtual and does not pass to second act. They enjoy perfect repose, perfect sleep, sweet nirvana. They sleep in peace, waiting for their bodies to be restored to them.[14] At that time they will awaken, not to the Beatific Vision, but to the life of nature and natural happiness. As soon as they are again united with their now incorruptible flesh—risen, not in the virtue of the resurrection of the Savior, but through a kind of over-splash or repercussion from it, setting in motion the miracle of the natural order (supernatural *quoad modum*) called for by the natural incompleteness of the separated soul— then, these human persons now and forever fixed in the right direction will produce, in the discontinuous time proper to spirits, their first deliberate act; and this act will bear on their last end, it will—in the natural order—constitute

---

14   This idea of sleep in Limbo for the souls of little children who died long ago without the sacraments of the ancient Economy of Salvation, now without the sacrament of baptism, in my opinion is founded on reason. Do certain people find this idea contestable, seeing that it departs a bit from the general perspective that St. Thomas held to on this point? Though they may try to present this to us as a case of poetic license, such is certainly not the case for us, for from our point of view this is an idea that is very simply true. We might add that to sleep does not mean to sink into a state of pure inertia; it is the humblest of our vital operations, as worthy of appreciation as it is indispensable. And then there is no sleep without dreams (whether we remember those dreams or not). What keeps us from thinking that in their sleep the *parvuli* enjoy the sweetest of dreams?

God as the end of all their action; they will love God more than themselves, with a natural love that is perfect in its kind, incapable of attaining to community of life with God, but which will nevertheless cherish more than all else the All Itself.

What can be said of the condition in which they will live? They still carry the blemish of Adam's sin, with which they came into the world here on earth, and which has not been effaced in them. The temporal sanctions entailed in this they have fulfilled on our earth, by the death which they underwent, and by all the sufferings to which they were exposed, and by the wounds of nature which had remained in them. All this now is finished for them. The sole sanction to which they remain subject—and which is in itself the greatest—is to be eternally enclosed in the order of nature alone—but of a nature henceforth preserved from all fault. In short they find themselves in an absolutely new condition, which exists only there, the state of *pure nature raised to its highest degree.*[15] For these creatures there will be realized what is very improp-

---

15   I know that, after man fell by his own fault from the state of grace in which he had been created, the state of pure nature has never existed in this world and remains only a mere abstract possibility with regard to our life on earth, a concept which corresponds to nothing real. On the other hand, if it had ever existed in this world, it would have included death—just as it would have included the possibility of falling into error and evil—which is normally implied in the nature of the rational animal if it has not been raised to a higher level. But what I am thinking of here is the state of nature *raised to its highest degree, or to the highest point of its proper order after the general resurrection* and under the conditions implied in the resurrection which exclude death—as well as the possibility of falling into error and evil—for all those who, in Limbo too, will live under new heavens and on a new earth.

I know too that human nature will not reach the fullness of its perfection except in those who have been raised up and will see God, with the result that in Limbo, to however high a degree human nature will have been raised, it will be capable of no more than a relative perfection, due to the inviolate rectitude of the natural order, and of no more than an imperfect happiness, consisting in the absence of all pain and an exultation in every kind of joy: all of this is sufficient for the subject at hand.

Finally I know that it is our nature to aspire toward what is naturally impossible (cf. below the chapter "Along Unbeaten Pathways,") and that this will be the case as well for the inhabitants of Limbo after the resurrection of the body. This is why I said a few lines later in those pages, that a *kind of melancholy* will be mixed with their happiness, without however changing it: for the joys included in this happiness will be so numerous, so noble, and so beautiful that in regard to the acuity of their consciousness they *will completely eclipse* this melancholy. (And certainly they will have no need, as do people in this world who have not received the Christian revelation, to construct mythologies to satisfy their desire to go beyond nature. Such a desire will remain latent and ineffective for them, covered over by the brilliance of their perpetual joys.)

Is this all? Alas! No. There remains a question which as far as I know theologians have not touched upon, which concerns the resurrection of babies who

erly called philosophic or natural "beatitude," that beatitude which Leibniz called a path through pleasures—but which is not beatitude, for this word designates *absolute* (therefore supernatural) happiness; rather let us call it natural felicity, happiness in movement, natural knowledge of God, philosophical contemplation which will increase without end but will never attain the divine essence in itself. The natural love which accompanies it will also increase without end, in its own order.

But however great this natural love of God may be, it will never attain to the smallest grain of charity. Is not a single good of grace worth more than all the goods of nature combined? The souls of whom we are speaking, those of the risen in the land of Limbo, will remain eternally deprived of these goods of grace, of eternal life. Their felicity is not beatitude, it remains infinitely far from it, they will never know absolute happiness. This is why, while being filled to overflowing with all the goods to which nature is entitled when it is righteous, while enjoying felicity according to nature, they are "damned," "lost" (and here the analogical polyvalence of these words becomes clear to us), they inhabit the hemisphere of night, Hades—the higher regions of Hell.

---

died without baptism. The way I see it they will remain in Limbo till the day of the resurrection of the body. Theoretically their souls, until that day, will remain the souls of children. Then suddenly they will be roused from sleep (or from some state of infantile happiness) to inform once again and forever a body. What body? The bodies of the risen, St. Thomas tells us, will be the same—*idem numero*—as they had here below, but their age will the perfect age of the human being, namely the age at which fullness of growth is attained and still remains far from the portals of decrepitude, in short the lovely age of youth at the peak of its capacities. Is it then for risen bodies twenty or thirty years old that the souls of unbaptized babies will become the substantial forms after the general resurrection? Why certainly. Whatever chutzpah it takes to believe this, that I have. And I believe just as brashly that the souls of these beautiful young people, taken aback by their ignorance, will have to acquire quickly the same maturity with regard to the things of the spirit as their bodies have with regard to their organs and limbs. And how will this happen? Why evidently because the holy angels will rush to teach them. They will be the teachers and professors, acquitting themselves of their task with much greater expertise than ours did for us here below. What a beautiful opportunity for the angels to carry out their mission as attentive administrators of the entire material universe which theology recognizes for them? Without embarrassment I hold all this to be entirely believable, and just as admirable as it is believable. And if an old philosopher has the effrontery to tackle questions which in the eyes of human prudence it would be wiser to leave in the night of the unknowable, then in his poor way he does nothing more than imitate his master Thomas Aquinas, who never stepped back from any question proposed to him, however incongruous it might have been.

If the reader, in the flower of his youth, should prefer to think that I am nothing more than a poor old fool, I would certainly take not the slightest umbrage, for at ninety years of age this is the very name that one becomes accustomed to apply to oneself every day in many little circumstances of daily life.

(This footnote was added in November 1972)

What is more exciting for a philosopher, and more instructive, than this fact that the state of pure nature at the best of its own order is the same as that in which, when the flesh has risen (and, in my opinion, only then), the souls of the children who have died without baptism will be found! It is doubtless for this reason and because in this way all the degrees of being will find their fulfillment, that I feel so attached to the notion of Limbo.

Neither fire nor punishment of the senses. The punishment of damnation, of which they will suffer only a kind of melancholy, will in no way alter their purely natural happiness. And even before the resurrection, the souls of these children do not suffer at all from this melancholy, whether they are asleep in Limbo as I imagine they are; or whether, on the contrary, one accepts that there they already exercise acts of knowledge; in either case they experience no affliction whatsoever, because (1) at the summits of the state of pure nature where they find themselves, they possess such a happiness that it eclipses for them the desire, natural in us, to surpass nature, and in them, as in the souls of Purgatory, there are not found the unconditioned aspirations of grace; (2) it is not through their fault that they are deprived of the vision of God, and they have God in a certain way, in the way of pure nature, in the mirror of creation; (3) they are not envious, and having themselves everything to which their nature as such can lay claim, they rejoice rather in the happiness of the elect, supposing that they are aware of the existence of these elect.[16] But although they do not feel its effects, it is a punishment nevertheless with regard to the destination of the human race, and the fall of Adam. *Felix culpa* nevertheless: for if not they, at least their happier, blessed, sisters have profited from the redemption which this fall brought about. And they are happy that their sisters are blessed, and they admire and love Jesus, with a natural love—just as they

---

16   St. Thomas, in *de Malo*, says that children who died without baptism have not the slightest idea of the glory possessed by the elect or of the fact that the sovereign good consists in the vision of God: with the result that not even a shadow of regret will pass over them. Let us have confidence in this great Doctor's charity and perspicacity, both of which, in his mature years, were no longer satisfied by what he had written, with the same intention, in the *Commentary on the Sentences* many years before: "*Pueri nunquam fuerunt proportionati ad hoc quod vitam aeternam haberent: quia nec eis debebatur ex principiis naturae, cum omnem facultatem naturae excedat, nec actus proprios habere potuerunt, quibus tantum bonum consequerentur: et ideo nihil omnino dolebunt de carentia visionis divinae; imo magis gaudebunt de hoc quod particibabunt multum de divina bonitate, et perfectionibus naturalibus. . . . Defectus talis gratiae non magis tristitiam causat in pueris decedentibus non bapitzatis quam in sapientibus hoc quod eis multae gratiae non fiunt quae similibus factae sunt.*
       "*Ad quintum dicendum, quod quamvis pueri non baptizati sint separati a Deo quantum ad illam conjunctionem quae est per gloriam, non tamen ab eo penitus sunt separati; imo sibi conjunguntur per participationem naturalium bonorum: et ita etiam de ipso gaudere poterunt naturali cognitione, et dilectione.*" Sent. II, d. 33, q. 2, a. 2: corp. and ad 5m.

love Beauty and Goodness. And the holy angels—who can cross the chaos, and who like stars illumine the night of Limbo—tell them the stories of Paradise.

After the end of time, this will be the condition of the highest part of the world of those who will never see God; such will be the state of the summits of Hell, in other words of the summits of the state of pure nature raised to its highest degree.

Oh, little children who have died without baptism, rejected though you have never done evil, you are not an accident in the divine economy, a peculiar case from which the theologians, pressed on all sides, extricate themselves as they can, an insignificant parenthesis. Your role is great, and your destiny well determined and very significant. You are the first fruits of natural felicity, of nature divinely restored.

IV

Of the other inhabitants of Hades, of the damned, we know that they are fixed in the final act by which, at the moment when their soul separated itself from their body, they did not want God. Not only can they not change, but they do not wish to either, they will never want to change. Since they desire happiness like every creature, this place of misery is intolerable, they would like to leave it. But they prefer to suffer everything rather than to renounce themselves as their final end, their pride suffers in this way with a kind of enthusiasm, and in this sense they do not want to leave Hell (they want to change constantly in Hell, from evil desire to evil desire; they choose not to leave Hell, or to change their evil desire into a good desire). They are gorged with regrets, with remorse; they do not aspire to Heaven, with constancy they *prefer* Hell. Their choice is made; they have put their beatitude in their pride. They do not ask God to leave Hell; they will never ask this; they wish to remain in Hell. They do not wish to see God, although formerly, on earth, many of them may have had in them grace and the aspirations of grace. But they hate God and the beatitude of the saints; they make fun of it; and they envy the saints; they hate them for having a good which they do not have and which they hate. The punishment of damnation, the privation of seeing God tortures them, not because they aspire to the vision without being able to attain it but because they know that this vision is the supreme good, which they envy because it deifies, which they detest because it is holy, and which they do not want at any price. It grieves them to have missed it through their own fault; yet they never cease to refuse it in their hatred. And so they are in a consubstantial contradiction, a heart-rending conflict; they love God the source of being and they hate God the author of glory; in spite of themselves they love God whom they detest with all their heart (their free will). They are disunited, dissociated to their very core, convulsed on themselves. It is the same with the demons. And in the same way, although all the gifts and the dignity of their spiritual nature remain intact in them, a languor, a nauseating asthenia wounds their terrible strength from within.

Their blasphemies, their cries of anger, which they emit endlessly, are an expression of this internal conflict. Their despair is not that they are no longer able to hope; it is that they never want to hope; they hate hope. They know very well that there is no remedy; they know all that refusing God entails. They prefer this. Because what they love above all else is to be great by themselves. They have what they wanted before; they have what they want now.[17]

They stand against God forever. For all eternity they refuse Him. For all eternity their created liberty chooses evil; first cause of Nothingness, the god from below.

As to damnation, the punishment of the damned is their fault itself, closed back upon themselves. The justice of God is His patience.

Unimaginable patience! He allows creatures made in His image to refuse Him as last end, scorn Him, treat Him as a piece of dirt, and for all eternity. They are deprived of their end, a just punishment, and the principal punishment of Hell. But an irremediable fault because they themselves absolutely refuse this end.

In mortal fault there is not only an aversion from God; but at the same time the conversion toward a created good taken as final end. The creature remains attached to all these perverse ends which it has chosen as its god (for there is no incompatibility among them, as between the uncreated end and the created ends, for they are but the multiple faces of a single idol). And all the deformations of its being and of its action consequent to these false standards, and the sufferings they entail, are a natural effect inevitably produced by the choices which it has made. Here again it has what it wanted, and the divine patience does not intervene in the irony of things.

Here again the punishment of Hell, according as it implies the pain of sense, is not a just punishment arbitrarily established (as such or such fine for such or such misdemeanor), but a just punishment naturally determined; naturally engendered by the fault.

This pain of sense is not only the internal punishment of which I have just spoken. There is also the fire of Hell, of which it is actually one of the effects. Attracted at once by sin and the blemish of sin and by the call for an exact compensation which emanates from the fault of the free creature, this fault

---

17   Cf. St. Thomas, *Comp. theol.*, c. 175: "Si voluntas malorum post mortem obstinate firmatur in malo, semper appetent ut optimum, quod prius appetierunt: non ergo dolebunt se peccasse. Nullus enim dolet se prosecutum esse quod aestimat esse optimum. . . . Etiam tunc mallent peccata illa (quae commiserunt) committere, si facultas daretur, quam Deum habere."

itself, and the whole string of evils which it drags in its train, deprives the order of creatures among themselves and with God of a certain quantum of good and of love.

But here it is not as it is in Purgatory, which, as we have seen above, has its own fire, entirely different from that of Hell; here the punishment is not received in Love, it cannot accumulate in good and in love qualifying the harmony of creation and raising the level of the created. It is not endured through love; it is wasted for the creature; all the good that it would have brought to this lost world is itself lost at each instant. The manifestation of eternal truth, or of eternal justice, is the only compensation for the fault here, without any reparation in the universe of the creature itself being joined to it.

The fire of Hell does not afflict the soul only because it is riveted to it through constraint; it acts also, and principally, as an instrument by which divine justice communicates to the created intelligence *truth* which is the nourishment of spiritual beings, and which in this case tortures it; this *truth* portrays to it the stupidity and the ugliness and the horror of what it has committed, and the happiness and the beauty which it has mistaken and defiled. And neither sin nor the stain of sin is wiped out, nor is the goodness immanent in the created order increased by so much as the thickness of a hair. Everything is engulfed in hatred and negation.

Because the soul remains turned against God and fixed in hatred, the fire is of no use to it, and burns it eternally. To have made a child weep—out of real malice, that is to say as a turning away from God—the tears of this little one will not last forever. But the punishment will last forever because the guilty soul, which would very much like it end in order to suffer less does not wish that it stop in reality; because it refuses to *accept* it at any moment and will never permit that this suffering repair anything whatsoever in being. In this way the damned soul itself attests that its fault of a moment by its very nature struck at what is eternal in man.

After the resurrection of body, the damned will suffer in their bodies as well. Fire, as the vengeance of the wounded cosmos, according to the laws of an absolutely unimaginable physics, will attain the flesh that is again one in substance with the soul—a soul fixed in its love of self above all else.

Chosen as instrument by the First Cause, it inflicts pain on pure spirits and on souls. In its own order it afflicts bodies, even those that are incorruptible. And it burns without end, for where there is no charity, the universe wounded by sin, and revolting against a disorder that charity alone could have repaired, can never be appeased.

Are we to believe that the damned remain there in immobility, with nothing else to do but endure their sufferings, like turnips in a stew pot? I think not. The state of the damned is a state of life—in a second death. A state of existence, and therefore a state of activity. And these are famous men and famous angels, to whom a certain grandeur must not be refused, however false that grandeur may be; for it is precisely grandeur as such that they have preferred to love. And, as I have said before, it is first and foremost his *patience* that God shows in their regard.

The damned are active, they work all the time, they have the religion of work. They build, they organize, and what they build crumbles because of their division and their hatred. But they continue to build and to work without ceasing. They engage incessantly in politics. Their life should not be imagined as very different from our own (if it is true that the more human history advances, the more it reflects its terminal conditions; and supposing that this wretched life should endure forever, would this not be a kind of "Hell"?) Think of our big cities today, of their prisons, their factories, their drugs, their parliaments, their dictators, their destitution, their despair, their forced slavery, the corruption of their varied crimes. The damned will build cities in Hell, towers and bridges. They will wage battles there. They will undertake to organize the abyss, to imipose order on chaos. The more they lay out roads and install their marvelous technologies, so much the more will chaos prove cruel and hostile to them. But in evil itself and in all their activity as damned souls, they still show those ontological gifts and energies of which as creatures they could not be deprived unless they ceased to exist.

And there it is. This will continue forever, and each will have his due. Not only his due but exactly what he wanted. And eternal justice will shine bright in the Hell's dark night (without uncreated love being absent from it, since they are beings, and since they are not punished, says St. Thomas, as much as they deserve); and eternal love will shine bright in the light of the holy city (without uncreated justice being absent from it, for on the contrary it will be raised there to its fullness). All truth is fulfilled. *Tell the just man that all is well.*

V

"'All is well,' cry the just. But everything could be better. It is well that God be patient to the end, but it is His love which cries out in our mouths, He has given us His love, not His patience. How could our love, this love which He has given us, be content to see God hated endlessly, and endlessly blasphemed by beings who have issued from His hands, to see crime endlessly added to crime? And among these damned there are some whom we have loved, there are some whom we still love, as much as St. Paul loved his race, for which he wished to be anathema. No, we shall not cease, we shall continue to pray and to cry out through the Blood of the Savior, ah! without having, we know it very well, the slightest right to have our request granted, yet giving vent freely, *gratuitously*, what else can we do, to the folly of our love."

This cry of love beyond love, this ultimate overflowing of the ground-swell of boundless charity, and this excess that will still well up, even after all perfection has been accomplished, all measure adjusted—is this not the *supercompensation* by virtue of which love alone will finally have its victory, and the blood of Jesus triumph over the defeats suffered by the Redemption?

And so, according to the words of Ernest Hello which Bloy took up again and orchestrated, the saints will cry out their appeal *from Thy Justice to Thy Glory.*

And why could their prayer not be granted? Why could not the answer to the excess of their love be the excess of a miracle—a miracle of goodness in justice itself? God can make a man out of a stone; He can change bread into the Body of Jesus Christ. It is no more difficult *by a miracle* to change the will of a man or an angel, to raise up and rectify in its inmost being a will that is dead and confirmed in evil. It is by virtue of the order of nature that the will of the damned is fixed in evil in an absolute and immutable manner. A miracle, and a miracle alone, can change this. I mean leaving them in Hades, and simply transferring them from the abyss to the summits of an eternal Hell.

Precisely because it is a miracle, it leaves intact, while transcending it, the order of things established according to the eternal laws of natures and the eternal justice of God. To anyone who agrees to go beyond an imagery which has nothing theologically necessary about it, and to understand all the analogical diversities that reality acknowledges, in the very bosom of Hell and its punishments, it seems that the possibility of such a miracle is conceivable in accord with the revealed formulas and sacred writ concerning the state of the damned.

Pierced to its very center, the will, confirmed till then in evil, *is turned about* miraculously, as toward the true end of all nature, toward God the author of nature, toward the God it loved and detested at one and the same time. Now it loves Him above all else, with that same natural love which, at the time of the resurrection of the bodies, wells up naturally in the souls of the children who died without baptism and which, in the case we are speaking of, the will now receives through a pure miracle. This "pardoned" damned soul (still damned but pardoned) leaves the lower regions, leaves the fire, and is transported to Limbo. There it will enjoy, although it remains wounded, that natural felicity mentioned above, and which is still a kind of Hell compared to glory. Through pure mercy, it is introduced to that condition whose first fruits were brought to our attention by the souls of the little children who died without baptism—but under a different form in their case because they are innocent.

No one leaves Hell; no one passes out of its gates; we are concerned here with no more than a transfer *within* the infernal regions, a passage from the lower places to the higher places of Hades, from the abyss to Limbo. And I do not say that this transfer *must take place*—who can know this? It depends on the pure divine will. I ask simply: Is it not *possible* that it take place—*if God wills it* (and who would dare to impose limits on Him)? And are we not permitted to hope for this?

Supposing that the outcome be such, the principal punishment of Hell remains in any case eternal, that pain of loss, which these adults, unlike the children, know they have incurred through their personal fault.

And the fire of Hell itself remains eternal, *secundum substantiam;*[18] it continues to burn without end in all the infernal regions distinct from Limbo. But those who were plunged into that fire have been drawn out—miraculously.

And it remains ever true to say that *in itself* the pain of sense is eternal because it presupposes that the soul is established in evil, in conformity with the nature of the immutable options of pure spirits. But if by a miracle the soul is drawn from evil, it is also freed from the pain of sense, insofar as it is caused by the Fire of Hell—there is nothing left now to catch fire.

Though in another sense, as we shall see further on, it can be said that in actual fact the pain of sense as well continues forever.

And it will remains always true that these pardoned souls are lost souls. They are not saved, not redeemed (and through their fault). Lost for grace and for glory, for that end which is such that if God had not ordained them to it, He would have created neither the world nor these beings. *Sine decore gratiae,* without grace, which is preeminently the light and the splendor of the soul, they remain nocturnal. Beautiful creatures of the night.

But they are saved from the fire, drawn from the waterless abyss, from their own abyss. And this not through the proper effect of the Blood of Christ which would have redeemed them, but through the cries of the saved and of those redeemed *in sanguine Christi,* and therefore through an indirect effect of the Blood of Christ, bringing life not to them but to the saved, that is, through a repercussion of the Redemption passing beyond its proper effect. "Ero mors tua o mors, morsus tuus ero inferne" (Hosea xiii, 14). "As for you, for the blood of your covenant with me, I will bring forth your captives from the waterless pit" (Zach. ix, 11).

And so, through the prayers of the saints (and not only of the saints, but of their head, Jesus in His glory, and of His Mother) a damned soul is drawn from the fire, but not from Hell. It is restored to the norm of nature, not of grace or of glory.

Those who remain in the fire only rage and blaspheme and despair all the more at the departure of their companion. For they do not believe in divine mercy, which for them is nothing but hypocrisy. And they do not want to be made good by a miracle, such an idea exasperates them.

And now, let this miracle be renewed at intervals of time as great as one

---

18   As I noted above (p. 9, n. 11) this is a physical and corporal fire, and as such will
      burn without end.

would wish; since eternity exhausts all time, it will inevitably come about that at a certain moment the lower regions of Hades will be completely emptied.

If such is the case, Lucifer doubtless will be the last one changed. For a time he will be alone in the abyss and will think himself the only one condemned to endless torments, and his pride will know no bounds.

But for him also there will be prayers, there will be cries. And in the end he too will be restored to good, in the order of pure nature, brought back in spite of himself to the natural love of God, borne miraculously into that Limbo whose night glitters with stars. There he will once more assume his office of prince—still damned, in regard to glory; loved once again, in regard to nature.

He remains fallen forever, forever humiliated, for he had been created in the state of grace and is now reduced solely to the goodness of his nature. He contemplates the infinite abyss which separates these two states. He bears for all eternity the scars of his wounds; for he remembers what he has lost, and what he now loves. Humiliated for all time, he is humble now.

There will be Milky Ways of regret and of sadness in the natural felicity of the pardoned. True beatitude, beside which everything else is as nothing, they must never look to have, they will never see the divine essence; and this is an eternal privation—a painfully felt privation because, unlike the children who died without baptism, they were called personally to the glory in which the three Divine Persons give themselves to the blessed and make of them "gods by participation" and because they refused this glory. They know that they were made for this joy, and that they missed it through their own fault. They missed the end for which Love destined them. To have been miraculously restored, and put in possession of the simple end of their nature, gives them a truer feeling, though without torment or revolt, of what they have lost.

And for similar reasons it can be said that, spiritually, the pain of sense also continues for them (in an analogical sense, but all the more real because, even though they suffered by means of fire, it was above all spiritually that their soul suffered). The evil which they remember having done will no longer gnaw at them through fire but will continue to afflict them by the thought that they have not made up for that evil and that they have cut themselves off by their own accord from the order of the goods of grace, from the perfect accomplishment of the designs of the Father; never will they live by the life of the Lamb, never will they know "the delicious taste of the Holy Spirit," never will they be filled with charity—and all this through their own fault. Nevertheless to this very sorrow which crowns, without diminishing it, their happiness at seeing the order of nature fully accomplished in them, they give their full consent; they know it is just, it dignifies them, and they thank God for it.

Natural felicity, or the final state of the children who died without baptism, will be the same, once the flesh has risen, as if they had been created in pure nature raised to its highest level; and no sadness, no sorrow will be joined to it; however, even in this final state, their nature, as I have noted above, will be subject to a certain melancholy, the shadow caused by the privation (even if they are unconscious of it, as St. Thomas would like) of all they would have a right to by the general call of the human species to the life of grace, if Adam had not sinned. Ontologically speaking, and in an analogical sense, it is a kind of punishment, a kind of condemnation, but unlike that of the pardoned because the little children experience no pain or sorrow.

Natural felicity, or the final state of the pardoned is substantially the same, a state in which pure nature brought to its highest level will receive forever all kinds of those joys to which the desires of the intelligent and free creature tend directly, according to the order of nature. But in them nature, even in its final state, remains wounded, as I have just explained. The risen Redeemer keeps His wounds for divine glory; the pardoned of Hades keep the scars of their wounds for divine justice. But now they love this justice, according to the wisdom of right reason. Exulting in their pardon and giving thanks for this supreme miracle of love, they know themselves unworthy of beatitude. Too happy, if I may put it this way, at having been restored to natural felicity, by their own initiative they exclude themselves voluntarily—this time not because they are confirmed in evil but because they are confirmed in natural justice—from that divine vision to which they aspire with an inefficacious natural desire but of which their rational will wants them to remain deprived.

There will always be an unbridgeable chasm between Paradise and Hell, between eternal day and eternal night.

On the one side are glory and formal participation in the life of the Trinity, in the very joy of the divine essence; the creature is deified.

On the other side the creature is left in his natural condition as a creature, *issued* from God and not *brought back* into Him by participation in the uncreated; the creature without grace or glory, nature restored to itself and to its own good, after what an adventure!; restored to itself and to the good proper to its nature in its final state and its eschatological moment—after having, while *in via*, been botched by evil (for a greater good, for that good of the elect for which Hell is the ransom)—and while still keeping in its final state (I am speaking of the pardoned) those wounds which it had inflicted on itself along the way. And it is still "lost," if it is true that God would not have made nature if He had not ordained it to grace. And the fire which like an ocean surrounds the continent of Limbo, and the memory of the lower regions of Hell, of the tortures suffered there, and of the obstinacy in evil, and of the rage and the blasphemy in which the damned were immersed before their pardon, all these things bear witness for all time to the catastrophe from which the Blood of the Redeemer has drawn *all men*: the elect for the beatitude of glory, the damned who have been pardoned for the "blemished" felicity of nature, which they owe to the prayer of Christ and His blessed members.

When all the inhabitants of Hades have been reunited in Limbo, when all the damned have been pardoned (still damned, but pardoned) a hymn of gratitude will rise toward the Church Triumphant, toward God and toward Jesus and toward all the elect for their great cry of love. It will be the song of nature; of poor beautiful nature, remaining only nature but restored; the hosanna of vanquished Hell.

And from the Jerusalem of glory, what a hymn, what a cry of eternal joy, what an amen of jubilation, as unrestrained as—more unrestrained, more overflowing than—had been the cry of supplicating love! Then Christ and the Church will be definitively and superdefinitively triumphant. Then love will have definitively and superdefinitively conquered all.

> *Quia fortis ut mors est dilectio;*
> *dura sicut infernus aemulatio.*

And when God looks down at Hades, He will rejoice in Limbo, and in the eternal manifestation of His justice, and in the felicity of those creatures both damned and pardoned at one and the same time, who had wanted nothing to do with Him and for whom the cry of His elect had wrested from Him a last, an *after-last* miracle, a miracle *after* everything had come to an end; a miracle of goodness in justice itself, one which does not abolish but confirms and consummates the order of justice.

And He rejoices in the lower regions of Hell and in the fire burning there eternally because they have been emptied of every rational creature.

And He smiles in seeing how the work of the damned had organized this chaos, and what beautiful techniques they had made use of in their constructions of hatred—attesting thereby that even in the wicked creature confirmed in evil there was still present, inasmuch as there was being, a vestige of Himself and something to render homage to His goodness.

Nantes-Meudon
April 24–28, 1939

POSTSCRIPT

Something that could easily lead the human mind astray and tempt it with metempsychosis, it seems to me, is the idea that the eternal fate of men could be sealed up at the end of lives that have been in so many cases complete failures, so full of accidents, of absurd misfortunes, of impediments of misery, so over-burdened with animal darkness, scarcely human in the true sense or worthy of the spirit. After this brief boot camp for born losers, suddenly an eternity of happiness or of misery! Can this be serious? Would there not be necessary at least a few good chances before this final sentence to lead an existence less dangerous spiritually, to bring to a somewhat successful conclusion a life of a creature endowed with reason? The trouble is that if one begins with metempsychosis, there is no way out of it; the horror of the wheel of reincarnations is another scandal.

There is no solution to the problem if one pictures the just Judge infinitely magnifying (univocally) our bookkeeper type of justice; if one does not imagine that God has disposed things precisely in such a way that in this pell-mell jumble lie hidden the secrets and the incomprehensible marvels of His *supero-verflowing* mercy.

And from this very moment. For through the Blood of Christ the most wasted life, the most loused-up of all, can take on some value, in some way become productive, be fruitful as is possible for neither angels nor separated souls. And for all eternity.

CHAPTER II

IN HOMAGE TO OUR DEAR GODFATHER LEON BLOY[1]

I

BEFORE HE BECAME BISHOP OF DAX, Monseigneur Bezac exercised his priestly ministry at Perigueux, Léon Bloy's native city, and there he organized, some years ago now, an astounding public homage in Bloy's honor. I want to thank the Bishop for having invited me to speak today about a man whom Raïssa, Véra, and I loved so tenderly (without him we would not have become Christians), and who hated the abjection of our times as much as our times hated his thirst for the absolute. The literary world has now finally made up its mind to recognize and to admire this extraordinary witness of the Holy Spirit. But during the whole of his life, he was a Poor Man consigned to constant distress, a Solitary Man crying out in the desert, one Misunderstood and victim of the conspiracy of silence that surrounded him and who, only at the very end of his terrible journey through life, had the comfort of a few cherished friendships from men who had read his works and became passionately interested in them, friends like Pierre Termier and Georges Rouault.

I would like first of all therefore to speak, briefly but still at sufficient length, of the life of Léon Bloy.

He was born on the 11th of July, 1846, the same year in which the Apparition of La Salette took place. His father was a engineer in the Department of Bridges and Highways, an austere and petty-bourgeois anticlerical, who rejected, as Stanislas Fumet tells us, "the authoritarian ascendency of the parish priests and the 'mummeries' of religion as unworthy of a definitively free man who agrees to subject himself, for the good of humanity, solely to the notion of inevitable progress."[2] It was because of his father that Bloy associated the idea of an "engineer" with such a state of mind; and this is why he might very well be expected to feel such apprehension the day on which he received the first letter from Pierre Termier, engineer in the Department of Mines and member of the Institut, who asked to see him, and who became for him such an admirable friend. He had discovered Bloy's books through his eldest daughter Jeanne, whose poetic soul felt a fraternal affinity with the soul of this Pilgrim of the Absolute. Would you like to hear his testimony concerning Leon Bloy? "He is

---

1   *Editor's footnote*: A lecture delivered at Dax on the 11th of March, 1968. Cf. *Nova et Vetera*, 1968, no. 2, pp. 81–103.

2   Stanislas Fumet, *Léon Bloy captif de l'absolu* (Paris: Plon, 1967).

at one and the same time," he wrote,[3] "judge in the service of divine justice, promulgator of the Absolute, a beggar praying on the church steps; and yet he is an artist, because he cannot imagine that God is not beauty itself, and because he wants to put into his work as brilliant a reflection as possible of the glorious vision which is in Him. Nothing is beautiful enough for the monument he is erecting; nothing is beautiful enough for Truth and for Love. 'I wanted,' he says somewhere, 'to be the sculptor of the Word': a sculptor never satisfied, who dreamed perpetually of undiscoverable marbles and of a bronze whose secret is lost. Neither the frightful harshness of his life, nor the constant injustice of men, nor the all too prolonged silence of God are capable of curbing his ardor."

As for the mother of Léon Bloy, in whose veins flowed a little Spanish blood, her role with regard to her son was entirely different from that of her husband, and her influence on him incomparably more profound. Humble and gentle, she was a prayerful soul, and "a Christian from the old days." Thanks to her, Léon Bloy wrote, "Christian teaching descended in me to immense depths where one day I would find it again, after horrible periods of complete, integral darkness, which dominated my thought and was miraculously increased by all my experiences of sin and of suffering."[4] "Why," she wrote to him in 1866, at the time when this boy of twenty years was rebelling against God, "have you rejected without profound examination the faith of your childhood? . . . But your heart needs a center which it will never find on earth. It is God, it is the infinite that you need, and towards which all your aspirations push you. You are one of those chosen few to whom God communicates Himself and on whom he lavishes His love, once such men have agreed to make an act of humility by submitting themselves to the darkness of faith."[5] And it is important above all else to notice that, through a thirst for abnegation which is found again in her son, she had, wrote Léon Bloy, "abdicated her maternal rights into the hands of Mary, making the Blessed Virgin *responsible* for my entire destiny." She never ceased, he added, to tell him that Mary was his "true mother, in a very special and very absolute manner." As he would write to Paul Bourget at a time when he was not yet horrified by this novelist, "She offered to suffer for her children and to do their penance. In a council of a mysterious and ineffable sublimity, it was agreed between her and God that she would make the absolute sacrifice of her health and the complete abandonment of every joy and of every human consolation, and that in return she would be granted the entire and perfect conversion of that child of hers who needed it most."[6] In fact

---

3   *Ibid.*, p. 263.

4   Cf. Jacques Petit, *Léon Bloy* (Paris: Desclée de Brouwer, 1966), p. 17.

5   *Ibid.*, p. 18.

6   Cf. Stanislas Fumet, *Léon Bloy captif de l'absolu*, p. 33.

she at once lost her health completely and irretrievably, and remained immobilized by paralysis until her death (in 1877).

The childhood of Bloy was spent in dreaming and in weeping. What he did learn came much later—and was self-taught. At eighteen, he left for Paris where he became an architect's assistant and where for several years he almost died of hunger. At this time he went through a period of violent revolt against God. Disgusted by the mediocrity of the Christian world, he had begun to hate the Church; he would describe himself later as "a Communard converted to Catholicism."[7] At twenty-two he began to find his faith once again; at twenty-three he returned to it "definitively, irrevocably and sacramentally,"[8] with such profundity, and in a way that was absolutely irrevocable. The instrument of this return to the faith was Barbey d'Aurevilly, who for his part joined an unshakable faith to a dazzling literary talent and to a most irregular moral life. It was thanks to Bloy that he died with the sacraments.

The other friends of Bloy who played a truly important role in his life, though not as central as that of Barbey, were, first of all, Ernest Hello, and then Villiers de L'Isle-Adam, whom, I believe, he came to know somewhat later. Here, let me point out how essential it is to recall that in France, at the time in question, Renan and Positivism reigned supreme. In the eyes of the entire lay intelligentsia religion seemed to have fled to the sacristies for refuge. So that we have to do here with the very first pioneers of the Catholic Renaissance in France, and they were, these three men, Barbey, Villiers, Hello, solitaries, dare-devils, spiritual soldiers of fortune.

It was the same with Bloy. I would add that he was a sort of bedazzled prophet, of extraordinary intuitive genius, in a kind of wild primitive state, possessed by the Holy Spirit. He was filled with supernatural gifts of extraordinary power joined to the sensitivity of a pure poet in which the ways and tools of reason played almost no role at all—"I understand only what I divine," he liked to say so that it is not very surprising to find in him sometimes, along with the prodigiously penetrating intuitions of a visionary which enabled him to touch the ineffable and to reveal the most profound truths, an enormous naïvete as well concerning matters of secondary importance. We must note also, and he did so himself, that he experienced immense impulses of a love obsessed by the desire for God which overflowed its banks and because of which, due to his affectionate loving nature, his life was filled with lapses, with remorse, with confessions, and with relapses, that left him tortured by moral anguish in the midst of material destitution.

As for Barbey d'Aurevilly, he was, at that time, the High Constable of Letters. He was a dandy full of pride and of scorn, but of grandeur also, with lacy ruffles on his shirt-front and cuffs; he steadfastly played out his role until his very death, and kept himself in character with as much courage as childishness.

---

7   Jacques Petit, *Léon Bloy*, p. 15.

8   *Ibid.*, p. 19.

For his part Villiers led a *vie de bohème* in the midst of dire poverty all the while vindicating his rights on the Island of Malta, on the pretext that one of his ancestors had been Grand Master of the Knights of Malta. If this did little to help him in his days of distress, at least this haughty poet had an authentic nobility of soul and of spirit. Nor did he lack a certain sublime impertinence. Bloy liked to recall, with appropriate gestures, his reply to some imbecile who, sitting down beside him at a table in a cafe, said to him in the most jovial tone of voice, while with his hand he made circles in the air toward the clouds: "Well, Villiers, still like that, like that, like that?" Villiers answered him in funereal tones, while making the same gesture in the opposite direction, toward a point on the floor (and toward the cellar): "And you, still like that, like that, like that?" Or again, when another imbecile, a more or less celebrated confrere, spoke to him, Villiers approached him, considered him more and more closely with extreme concentration, and concluded, greatly discouraged: "I am looking at you, but it does no good, *I cannot see you . . .*"

In Ernest Hello also, Bloy admired certain dazzling sayings, in particular this one: "Talent does whatever it wants, genius does what it can." "Filled with flashes of genius," as Léon Bloy said of him, Hello was nevertheless completely ignored by his times. His puny body concealed a very lofty soul and an ardent spirituality. It was he whom we must thank for the first translations of Ruysbroeck and of Angela of Foligno. In short, he was the precursor of that discovery of the great spiritual writers and of the great mystics in whom interest later became so widespread. But he complained miserably of being unable to transmit his message and of having not a single reader.

Parenthetically, we would do well to remark that without Barbey there would have been no Bloy, and without Hello there would have been no Garrigou-Lagrange. It was the reading of a book by Hello, *L'Homme*, that converted the young Garrigou, then a student of medicine, and made a Dominican of him. Without Bloy, many men would never have given themselves as best they could to the task of arousing our contemporaries. "I owe him everything," Bernanos said. Let me say a word, in passing, on what today is called the advancement of the laity. I do not wish in any way to denigrate organizations in which laymen band together and stand shoulder to shoulder under the aegis of the clergy, and which certainly have their usefulness. But I do not think that it is through *organization* that the essence of their mission is transmitted to laymen as members of the Church of Christ . . .

I have just spoken of three friends who had a certain influence on Léon Bloy, during what may be called his formative years. It must be mentioned too that he was an assiduous reader of the philosopher Blanc de Saint-Bonnet, and took delight in repeating his maxim: "A holy clergy makes for a virtuous people, a virtuous clergy makes for a worldly people, a worldly clergy makes for an impious people." and above all, that Bloy never ceased to declare his gratitude to a priest "of rare distinction and of exquisite sweetness,"[9] the Abbé Tardif de

Moidrey, to whom he was introduced by Hello and who taught him to decipher the Holy Scriptures, guiding him on the path of a sacred interpretation in which the pupil would surpass his master. It was also Abbé Tardif who initiated Bloy in the devotion to the Apparition of La Salette, in which the Blessed Virgin appeared all in tears to two little shepherds, to whom she said in her message to "her people": "From the time that I have been suffering for you. . . ." "She weeps as she alone can weep," Bloy wrote in *Vie de Mélanie.* . . . "Reason loses its way here. A beatitude which 'suffers' and weeps! Is it possible to conceive of such a thing?"[10] This Abbé Tardif de Moidrey published a precious commentary on *The Book of Ruth* for which Claudel had a profound admiration. "It was Léon Bloy who led me to Abbé Tardif," one reads at the beginning of Vol. III of his *Commentaires et Exégèses* which appeared in 1963. And Claudel adds: "It is no small honor for Léon Bloy that such a man could judge him worthy, in the shadow of *Celle qui pleure*, to be his associate for a number of months and the depository of his knowledge, of his inspirations and of his thought."

In a letter of 1897 to Octave Mirbeau,[11] Bloy wrote: "I entered the life of Letters at the age of thirty-eight, after a frightful childhood and in the wake of an unspeakable catastrophe which had cast me down from a purely contemplative existence. . . ." These lines allude to the extraordinary and tragic adventure—of capital importance in his life—through which he passed with the woman whom in *Le Désespéré* he would call Véronique, but whose real name was Anne-Marie Roulé,[12] He had met her in 1877: a poor prostitute who had been fascinated from their very first encounter by Bloy's look and who had fallen in love with him. He led her to change her life, then to devote herself to prayer—all this not without painful lapses and terrible heartbreaks, during the first year of their love. A two months' retreat which he made at the Trappist monastery of Soligny resolved nothing. But one day in September, 1878, in the chapel of Sacré-Coeur de Montmartre, Anne-Marie found her "road to Damascus"—"the love of God," wrote Léon Bloy, "struck her like a thunderbolt." And from that moment they lived together chastely in that purely contemplative life which he mentioned in his letter to Mirabeau. He became her spiritual guide, with the help of Abbé Tardif, who, alas, for them died at La Salette the 28th of September, 1879; and he was also her lover, dazzled by the illuminations he received from her.

Bloy was persuaded that Anne-Marie was led by the Spirit of God along exceptionally elevated paths; and I have no doubt that this great soul was favored with authentic contemplative graces and probably very high ones—I have every confidence in Bloy on this point. In any case these graces unfortu-

9   Stanislas Fumet, *Léon Bloy captif de l'absolu*, p. 59.

10   *Vie de Mélani.*

11   June 13, 1897.

12   Cf. Jacques Petit, *Léon Bloy*, p. 24.

nately became more and more mingled with a dangerous exaltation of human origin due to the difficult and morally exhausting life in which they were both involved—and due also, I believe, at least in part, to what was less good in the influence of Ernest Hello with whom they had a rather close association at that time, and one of whose foibles was seeking out the extraordinary. (It is said of Hello, I do not know if this is authentic—that he had gone to see the Curé of Ars, and when asked about him, is supposed to have replied: "Oh! he does not do anything particularly extraordinary.")

For three years Bloy and Anne-Marie together lived this life of contemplation; they went to Mass and received Holy Communion every morning, and they did nothing but think of God or read books on spirituality. But in Anne-Marie the exaltation I just mentioned only increased, at the expense of her mental equilibrium. Finally, the *unspeakable catastrophe*: poor Anne-Marie went mad in June 1882. She had to be confined in a mental asylum; she never recovered her reason, and Bloy never saw her again.

It was after this that Bloy plunged into literature like a gladiator into the midst of beasts, as God's witness in a world of careerists and of renegades. He collaborated in *Chat noir*, frequented some men of letters, published two books and the four issues of a review he founded and called *Le Pal*. This was still a preliminary period which did not last long. But everything was really under way now—his magnificent and imperishable work, the frightful struggle in solitude and neglect, the light he brought to souls, and the admirable and mysterious deepening of his intimacy with God—that all began with and continued after his first great book, *Le Désespéré*, published in 1887. This was, as you well know, a kind of *roman à clef*, in which under fictitious names he described in a very recognizable manner many of the more or less famous writers of his time, painting for them a "true" portrait of themselves—that is to say, not at all a portrayal of poor wretches whom he saw passing by amid the deceptive semblances of this world, but a portrayal of those detestable realities which they had come to symbolize for him (I shall return to this point presently). This was all documented rather exactly, although, no doubt, with a certain exaggeration, by Huysmans: as a result everyone in the book recognized himself, and so Bloy was immediately accused of calumny animated by a furious hatred. The only reaction of the literary world was silence—total, implacable silence. It was forbidden to speak of Léon Bloy. A few people interested in beauty and in poetry read and admired him, but the number of copies of his books printed during his lifetime never went beyond two thousand, with royalties of fifty centimes per volume sold. His poverty continued, worse than ever.

It continued after his marriage, in 1890, to Jeanne Molbech, a great-hearted Danish woman whom he had converted. He had met her the year before,[13] in

---

13   Cf. Stanislas Fumet, *Léon Bloy captif de l'absolu*, p. 85; and the preface of Jeanne Léon-Bloy to *Lettres à sa fiancée*. It was at the home of François Coppée that she

the drawing-room of Mlle. Read, after returning from the wake of Villiers de L'Isle-Adam (Villiers and Barbey died in 1889). "Who is that man?," Jeanne Molbech asked (she knew only that he had published *Le Désespéré*). "A beggar," replied the woman friend to whom she had put the question. Jeanne's immediate reaction was: "I shall marry him." She had "felt then that it was destiny" as she herself once said. Six months later they were married. The carnal lapses which had long tortured Bloy were now at an end. The love of Jeanne gave him self-mastery and a blessed support in all his sufferings. She was a marvelous companion for him and thanks to her he won forever complete freedom for his soul and for his inspiration. She lived in perfect communion with him, and no one understood him better than she. Somewhat austere in outward appearance, she showed by her actions the depths of her goodness and generosity.

In marrying Bloy, she had also married suffering and poverty. They lost two small boys, André and Pierre, who died very young (for at that time destitute poverty reigned in their home). Their daughters Véronique and Madeleine, whom they cherished, were their joy on this earth. But for them too, especially during the years of their childhood, life showed no tenderness.

Pitiless poverty still reigned there when we met Léon and Jeanne Bloy, in 1905. I remember that at the time of our first visit, Léon Bloy wore a jacket closed at the top because he did not have money enough to buy a shirt. I remember also a certain excursion with him through Paris to some frightful pawn shop; it was in the early period of our friendship; in order to renew the temporary lease for the grave of his little André, he had to find the money he needed to avoid the pauper's grave for his son. How can one forget the immense sadness which overwhelmed him then, and which darkened his great sorrowful eyes?

And I remember the gentleness and the tenderness of this extraordinary man, the wonderful hospitality of these poor people, in whose house the wings of miracle seemed to beat noiselessly. In these lodgings on the street of the Chevalier de la Barre of Montmartre, which sheltered so much human suffering—there reigned a supernatural peace.

It was later, after Termier entered their life, then after they moved to Bourg-la-Reine, in 1911, in the house where Péguy had lived, that black poverty's vice loosened its grip a little. And then also, to warm their hearts a bit, there were at least their friends Pierre Termier and his daughter Jeanne, Georges Rouault, Felix Rauguel, Ricardo Vinès, Georges Auric, Jean de la Laurencie, Léopold Levaux, Jean and André Baron, Henry de Groux, whose friendship returned to Bloy in 1916, that "humble Brother Dacien who, too poor to buy Bloy's books which he wanted to study in depth, copied them out by hand."[14]—and his godchildren (Raïssa, Véra, and I, baptized on June 11,

---

next saw him.

14   Raïssa Maritain, *Les Grandes Amitiés*, "Livre de Vie" 18–19, p. 405 (ch ix, § [6]).

1906; Pierre van der Meer and his son Pierre-Léon, baptized on February 24, 1910; Christine van der Meer, who was born a Catholic and returned to God at the same time as her husband) . . .

What else is there to say? With the eyes of my soul I see Bloy once again in the evening, surrounded by his loved ones, kneeling on the floor, reciting the rosary. I see him too at the first light of dawn—at that time when, as he put it, the heart, "not yet sullied by the base glamor of light unburdens itself before peaceful tabernacles," making his way with heavy and weary steps toward the first mass of the morning, as he did each and every day. He drew his life from the Holy Scriptures. Each night he recited the office of the dead. "We have to pray," he wrote. "We must endure the horror of this world, we must pray to remain pure, we must pray for the strength to *wait*. There is no despair, there is no bitter sadness for the man who is constant in prayer. Let me tell you. If you only knew what right and what authority I have to say this."

And once again in my mind's eye I see his final communion, received with very humble love, on All Saint's Day, in his poor sickroom, while in the distance the church bells pealed for high mass and throughout the whole world the Church chanted the gospel of the beatitudes.

He died on Saturday the 3rd of November, 1917, "towards evening at the hour of the Angelus, without a death-rattle and without agony."[15] "On October 31st," Raïssa writes in *Les Grandes Amitiés*, "While I was at his bedside he confessed to me that he was in great suffering. 'You are suffering for your godchildren,' I said in my great desire to help him in some way, But he went on: 'The baseness of my nature is expiated by. . . .' His voice was scarcely audible and I did not hear the last words. 'I wish I could do something for you,' he said a moment later with great tenderness. And I replied, my heart breaking with pity: 'You have done everything for me, since you brought me to know God.' I added: 'I wish I could take your suffering upon me.' 'Don't say that!' he said with a certain vivacity, and then looking at me solemnly, 'You don't know what you are asking.'"

If he spoke this way to his godchild, it was because he remembered the day when, impelled by his living faith in the mystery of the Communion of Saints, he had asked to suffer "all that a man can suffer, in order that his friends, his brothers and souls unknown to him who were living in darkness might receive help,"[16] and it was also because he remembered the terrible manner in which his prayer had been heard.

I continue Raïssa's account: "During those days of cruel suffering," she writes, "whenever he spoke, he still took extreme care in regard to exactness of language and purity of expression. But he spoke very little, his rare words emerged from a deep silence, not inert but intensely vigilant, an august silence

---

Cf. p. 431 (ch ix, § [18], pp. 434–435, ([§ 20]).

15   Jeanne Bloy, *Conclusion to La Porte des Humbles*.

16   *Lettres à sa Fiancée*.

which filled us with respect and fear, in which we felt that alone, truly alone, as he had written, he was facing his God and looking upon his life, passing over in his heart for the last time the mysterious promises he had been given, accepting in the night of faith these final purifications. . . .

"He seemed to be suffering acutely—but remained in great peace. A few days before his death, at the end of a painful night, he had said to his wife: 'I alone know the strength that God has given me for the combat.' It was with this strength that he faced his death agony.

"There was not the slightest shadow of fear in him; only deep wonder in the face of death which came without the bloody martyrdom he had expected and had prayed for with all his heart for so many years.

"We saw this peace and this wonder on his face in the very last hours of his life. A martyrdom of blood would have been in his soul the illuminated picture of the constant martyrdom he had suffered during those long and hard years in which his life and labors had no other aim than to give witness to Truth and Faith and God's demands."

II

It is this poor man entirely alone in the combat, treated by our intelligentsia during the whole of his life as unworthy of existence, who enriched the treasury of French letters with incomparable masterpieces: *Le Désespéré, La Femme Pauvre, Le Salut par les Juifs, Celle qui pleure,* the two volumes of *Exégèse des lieux communs, Méditations d'un Solitaire, Le Sang du Pauvre, Le Symbolisme de l'Apparition, Dans les Ténèbres, Le Mendiant ingrat* and the seven other volumes of the *Journal* of Léon Bloy, to name only his greatest books.

It seems to me that in the second part of this talk it would be fitting to read to you some selected texts. This is not an easy thing, for the citations which I would have to make would last hours—the *Pages de Léon Bloy,* chosen by Raïssa and published by Mercure de France, make up a volume of 400 pages. A quarter of an hour will be sufficient to read the texts which I have chosen somewhat at random.

First of all, on Bloy himself:

"Pity cannot extinguish anger in me, because *my* anger is the daughter of an infinite foreboding. . . . My anger is the effervescence of my pity."

"However insane this may appear to you, I am, in reality, an obedient and tender-hearted person. This is why I write implacably, having to defend Truth and to bear testimony to the God of the poor. My most vehement pages were written *out of love* and often with tears of love in hours of unspeakable peace."

On Poverty:

"Poverty is nothing less than the Bride of the Son of God, and when their golden anniversary is celebrated, barefoot and starving beggars will run together from the very ends of the earth in order to be witnesses of it."

"Man is situated so close to God that the word *poor* is an expression of tenderness. When the heart bursts with compassion or with love, when one can almost no longer hold back one's tears, it is this word which comes to one's lips . . ."

And now for the Bourgeois. These texts are taken from *Exégèse des lieux communs*. Bloy was the exact opposite of an anarchist who hates "the bourgeois"; he was a Christian who hated *the Bourgeois*, with a capital 'B', a name symbolic of detestation of all grandeur, and of the unique preoccupation to save one's skin and one's little business in the lower places of this world. Commonplaces are the natural linguistic provender and the security blanket of this Bourgeois mentality. And Bloy undertook the exegesis of these commonplaces in order to show that the Bourgeois, without knowing what he is saying, utters in each of them stupefying mysteries and things that turn everything upside down.

First example: "I do not wish to die like a dog," says the Bourgeois. Bloy comments: "Why should he not wish to die like a dog when he has lived his whole life like a pig?"

Second example: "All truths are best not spoken." There are others, Bloy adds, "There are others, in greater number, which are better not heard. Therefore, one must make a choice in both cases, which supposes the discernment of angels, and of what angels!

"A truth which would expose its divulger or its witness to some disgrace clearly would not be good to utter. One's skin must be saved above all, everyone to his own trade, the Bourgeois is not a martyr. But neither is he a confessor, or a penitent hungry for humiliations, and those truths which he finds offensive, he prefers to ignore.

"This is all very well, but then here's something strange. If one suppresses at the same time those truths that are dangerous to proclaim and those that are offensive to hear, what is left? I have been looking in vain, for in the end I cannot see a third category.

"Let us say it then without beating around the bush, *No truth is good to utter*, for such is the true meaning of this text. Perhaps even, there is no Truth at all. Pilate, who saw It face to face, was none too sure."

Another example: "To have a heart of gold."

"What a privilege! No more palpitations, no more emotions, no more foolish love, no more ill-considered enthusiasm. He is as quiet as a mouse and happy as a pig. Cessation of all absurd phenomena. He no longer gnaws his heart, his heart no longer bleeds. He does not have a heart of bronze, nor a heart of stone, still less the heart of a lion, but a handsome shining organ, shaped like a mollusk and hollow, all gold, and perfectly insensitive. This is the inestimable privilege of the true Bourgeois."

Last example: "He who gives to the poor, lends to God."

"If you think about it, this is a most dangerous situation. Whoever says lender says creditor. The mortal enemy of the creditor is the debtor, The consequence is frightful. In giving to the poor, one exposes oneself to the enmity of God, since one lends to Him. Therefore, one must never give to the poor, if one wishes to keep God's friendship . . ."

But let us leave the *Exégèse des lieux communs* and pass on to more serious texts. Here are a few on Suffering:

"The nature of things cannot be changed and man will always be the impassioned slave of Suffering. . . . This is something so very precious that it is impossible to do without it and so common that one must be a genius to perceive its value." "Man has places of his heart which do not yet exist and into which Suffering enters so that they may come to be. . . . I would never finish if I wanted to describe the marvelous effects of Suffering on man's faculties and on his heart. *It is the auxiliary of creation.*"

"For more than thirty years I have desired the only real happiness, Sanctity. The result makes me ashamed and frightened. 'All that remains for me is to have wept,' said Musset. I have no other treasure. But I have wept so much that in this regard I am rich. When we die this is what we can take with us: the tears we have shed and the tears which we made others shed; this will be our capital of beatitude or of terror. It is on tears that we will be judged, for always the Spirit of God 'hovers over the waters.'"

Now, on the mystery of souls:

"It is the most banal of illusions to think that one is really what one appears to be, and this universal illusion is corroborated, all through life, by the tenacious imposture of all our senses. Nothing less than death is required to make us realize that we have always been mistaken. At the same time that our identity, so completely misunderstood by us, is revealed to us, inconceivable abysses will unveil themselves to our *true* eyes—abysses within us and outside of us. Men, things, events will finally be divulged to us, and each will be able to verify the affirmation of that mystic who said that after the Fall, the whole human race fell into a profound sleep."

And on the mystery of Him Who, as St. Thomas Aquinas says, *took on Himself all human suffering*:

"Jesus is at the center of everything, He assumes everything, He bears everything, He suffers everything. It is impossible to strike a creature without striking Him, to humiliate anyone without humiliating Him, to curse or to kill anyone without cursing or killing Christ himself. The basest churl whether he wants to or not must borrow the Face of Christ to receive a slap, from no matter what hand. Otherwise, the slap would never reach him and would remain suspended, amid the planets, forever and ever, until it met the Face which pardons . . ."

And on the mystery of the Holy Books:

"The sacred text is not obscure, but mysterious. Mystery is luminous and impenetrable. Obscurity is essentially penetrable because man can be swallowed up in it."

Next, a text on the Blessed Virgin:

"It is clear that Mary is not God, although she is the Mother of God. However, nothing can express her dignity. Theologically it is as impossible to adore her as it is to exaggerate the cult of honor which belongs to her. The glory of Mary and her ecumenical excellence defy hyperbole. She is that fire of Solomon which never says: 'Enough!' She is the earthly Paradise and the heavenly Jerusalem, She is the one to whom God gave everything."

And then, on anti-Semitism: "Suppose that people around you should speak continually of your *father* and your *mother* with the greatest scorn and treat them with nothing but insults or outrageous sarcasm, how would you feel? Well, this is exactly what happens to Our Lord Jesus Christ. We forget, or rather we do not wish to know, that our God-made-man is a Jew, by His nature the Jew *par excellence*, the Lion of Judah; that His Mother is a Jewess, the flower of the Jewish race; that all his ancestors were Jews; that the Apostles were Jews, as well as all the Prophets; and finally that our entire sacred liturgy is drawn from Jewish books. How, then, can we express the enormity of the outrage and blasphemy which consist in vilifying the Jewish race?"

And on the Jewish people:

"The Jews are the eldest of all, and when everything is in its proper place, their proudest masters will consider themselves lucky to lick their wandering feet. For everything has been promised to them, and in the meantime they do penance for the earth. The birthright of the firstborn cannot be annulled by some punishment, however rigorous it may be, and God's word of honor is unchangeable because 'His gifts and His vocation are without repentance.' It was the greatest of converted Jews who said that, and the implacable Christians who claim to eternalize the reprisals of the *'Crucifigatur'* had better remember it."

And three more texts, upon which it would certainly not be inopportune to meditate today.

The first was written in 1897; although the verbs are in the past tense, it has a prophetic meaning regarding the moral ideal which seems to prevail in our day. Bloy wrote in *La Femme Pauvre*: "The command given . . . by the Almighty One of Hell was *to wipe out the memory of the Fall*. Then, under the pretext of restoring man, the ancient Meat was born again with all its consequences. All rhythms belonged to Lust."

The second is made up of a single line and shows all the misery of our sexualist psychology and of our aphrodisiac civilization: *"What troubles love,"* wrote Bloy, *"is the senses."*

The third—and I hope without expecting too much that the translators charged with putting the liturgy into French will one day appreciate its importance—is the following: "The words of Holy Scripture," wrote Léon Bloy, "nourish the soul and even the intelligence in the way the Eucharist does, without it being necessary to understand them."

Let me add that what I fear with most translators (not with the great ones like Claudel) is that they believe it their duty to make everything comprehensible. God is not comprehensible, and His word is essentially mysterious. Words must be permitted to render testimony to the divine transcendence by going beyond the measure of our human clarities. But in order for us to speak to the Most Holy God it is His most holy word which liturgical prayer puts on our lips. And after all, it is to God, is it not, that we speak in prayer even when we pray in common.

Finally, to conclude this second part of our talk here are some isolated thoughts of Léon Bloy.

I make my way, ahead of my thoughts in exile in a great column of Silence.

Lord, I weep very often. Is it from sadness at thinking of what I suffer? Is it from joy at remembering You?

Here is my secret for writing books to please you: It is to cherish with all my soul—even to the point of sacrificing my life—such souls as you, known or unknown, who are called to read me some day.

We ask God for what we want and He gives us what we need. All that happens is adorable.

When one speaks lovingly of God, all human words are like blind lions seeking a spring in the desert.

The visible is the footprint of the Invisible.

Suffering passes away—to have suffered does not.

A heart without affliction is like a world without revelation. It sees God only by the feeble glimmer of twilight.

Our hearts are filled with angels when they are filled with affliction.
Providence is a Pactolus of Tears.
There is but one sadness—Not To Be SAINTS.

III

In the third and last part of this too long conference, I would like to propose to you a few remarks on the vocation of Bloy as poet and as Christian.

As I have noted before, there is a mystical impatience at the very source of his art. Inconsolable over not being already in possession of the vision of divine glory, he did not use human language, as metaphysicians and theologians do in their formulas, in their effort to express, according to the imperfect mode of our concepts, what we can come to know of transcendent reality. On the contrary, he used human language in an attempt to evoke those very things which in this reality surpass the mode of our concepts, and remain unknown to us. In short, he used the signs of language and of the understanding only in order to indemnify himself for being deprived here on earth of the beatific vision—which no sign will ever be able to express precisely—and his words tended less to express truths directly than to procure, as he said, the sensation of mystery and of its effective presence.

For him, therefore, it was above all a question, of "giving the idea and the impression of mystery," that is to say of our inability to see when face to face with that light which illumines our minds, and of giving at the same time, through the most sumptuous flowering of images, a sensible likeness of that truth of which we do not yet have the intuition and which we know only "through a glass, darkly." "It is indispensable," he said, "that Truth exist in Glory. Splendor of style is not a luxury—it is a necessity."

If he seemed dazzled at times by this necessity, to the point of pushing the splendor of style and of images too far, I think that the profound reason for this is the heart-rending experience he had of the abyss which exists between the realities of which we catch a fleeting glimpse in the mystery of Faith and that coldness, that kind of tranquil indifference of the words through which our language expresses them. When we say, "the Son of God died for us on the Cross," "Christ rose from the dead,"—these are, in the common realm of our speech (and also, very often, of our wandering thought), *statements*, assertions *like all the others*; as when we say: "Napoleon died at Saint-Hélène" or "the airplane for Paris leaves at 10 o'clock." However, as soon as there is question of the divine mystery, the *thing* designated is Fire, a fire more devouring than all the fires of earth together. Should not the words we use then set our entrails on fire, and make a Pentacostal fire flame from our mouths? It is the office of all great poets to surmount in some way or other, and at whatever price, this inadequation of the sign with respect to the mystery of life immanent in the reality signified. But in the case of Léon Bloy—and it is, I believe, a unique case—since the reality signified is the infinite fire of the unfathomable Truth of God, it was necessary to do violence to art and to the works which the poet fashions from words, in order to bring them to a superhuman excess, which is still unworthy of the reality which they evoke—in other words, in order to rouse us for a moment from the sleep into which, as is said in one of the texts I cited, the human race has been plunged since the Fall.

Such is the task that Bloy had assigned himself as artist, and in which he consumed himself: a supreme effort of poetry which overflowed from his contemplative prayer and which, in comparison to the treasures glimpsed in that prayer, was like a resplendent rag. For Bloy knew very well that the silence

of adoration will always praise God better than any word. *Silentium tibi laus.*
This is why he said: "I am simply a poor man looking for his God, calling to
Him with sobs along all the pathways." Yes, but this poor man had received
the gift of art as the elephant receives his trunk. And in a page which I shall
cite at greater length in my final considerations, he wrote something which in
a way, it seems to me, goes back to the things which I was trying to suggest a
moment ago: "Our inexpressible misery is to mistake the incessantly clearest
and the most living statements of Scripture for inanimate figures or symbols.
We believe, but not *substantially*. Ah! The words of the Holy Spirit should enter
and flow into our souls like molten lead into the mouth of a parricide or a
blasphemer. We do not understand that we are the members of the Man of
Sorrows . . ."

*   *   *   *   *   *   *   *   *   *

The same kind remarks must be made concerning Léon Bloy's outbursts of
violence and his apparent ferocity. In them must be seen first of all the effect
of a very special kind of *abstraction*, not philosophical, certainly, but artistic or,
if you wish, an abstraction of typification, to which I have already alluded:
Every event, every gesture, every individual given *hic et nunc*, under the gaze
of this terrible visionary, was instantaneously transposed, torn from its con-
tingencies, from the concrete conditions of the human ambiance which explain
it and make it plausible, and transformed into a pure symbol of some devouring spiritual reality.

We must see in them also an effect of his strange absorption in his own
interior world. He was one of "those whom the clamors of Disobedience
importune, and who live withdrawn in their own souls." A boundless melancholy, natural and supernatural, weighed down on him; a certain number of
apperceptions of a deadly acuity, such as mystical gifts can awaken in a soul
of this kind, filled his heart; a crucifying vision of man's forgetfulness of God
and of His Love, of the hatred of the Poor, of the abjection and of the cruelty
characteristic of a world which has rejected the Gospel, made the Passion of
our Lord perpetually present to him. This is what existed for him: this spiritual
universe—and his faithful suffering. The rest was phantoms, useless and
uncertain show. And with these apperceptions existing in him from the first,
in their keen certitude, and already exerting pressure from all sides on his
mind, it was enough for some external object, passing into the shadow of his
suffering, to present some appearance of the vices or of the lukewarmness
which he hated, for him to seize upon it as a detestable symbol and subject it
to his indignation as an "obedient judge." Sometimes his blows could go
astray; the chosen victim might merit neither the stake nor scalping, might be
worthy on the contrary of all kinds of laurels: but through the perishable form
of this victim he struck at the invisible monster, the monument of spiritual
iniquity which oppressed his heart and the hearts of a great number of his
brothers.

*   *   *   *   *   *   *   *   *   *

It was convenient for people to reproach him for his injustices. I have just indicated why they were in reality, however disagreeable they might have been for some of his contemporaries, only injustices of appearance or of show. They were the inevitable *metaphors* of his avenging poetry, which aimed at *something else*, in that invisible world of which the visible is only an ephemeral footprint and which alone mattered for him.

For if in the reality of his heart there was in Léon Bloy a constant passion that obsessed and devoured him, it was indeed his zeal for Justice, even if the ardor of this zeal seemed at times to be somewhat careless of the moral virtue of the same name. "I die for need of Justice," he said. And again: "I am eaten up by the need for Justice, as by a dragon which has been starving since the time of the Flood." In the first letter he wrote to his fiancée he confided to her that he "loved Justice more than anything else in the world."

As I once wrote, what makes his character special in the spiritual order is this insatiable passion for Justice. His heart was continually oppressed by the weight of the incalculable injustice which is the princess of this world. Using the famous words of St. Gregory VII, while modifying them a bit, he might have said: Because I have loved justice and hated iniquity, for this reason I live in a perpetual exile. This is why this obedient Christian felt himself in a communion of impatience with all the rebels of the earth, but his was an impatience turned toward Heaven and toward the coming of the Kingdom of God. This is why he entered so deeply into the mysteries of Suffering and of Abandonment, of all sufferings and of all abandonments: the suffering and abandonment of the Poor, the image of God; the suffering and abandonment of Israel, the people of God; the suffering and abandonment of Mary, the Mother of God.

His special mission was to echo the terrible threats of the Gospel against all those who already have their consolation.

*   *   *   *   *   *   *   *   *   *

Finally let us ask ourselves: What was at the source, at the deepest center of his very life and of his relations with God, of his *existence* as a Christian? As Bishop André Baron pointed out recently in an admirable homily[17] given on the 50th anniversary of the death of Léon Bloy, it was the adherence of his whole soul to that truth in which, in the Apostles' Creed, immediately after our profession of faith *in sanctam Ecclesiam catholicam*, the very life of the unity and holiness of the Church is revealed to us and in the dogma of the Communion of Saints. "From this treasure, scarcely inventoried through the centuries, Léon Bloy," said Bishop Baron, "drew so many marvels that to evoke them today seems to me the most perfect way for us, in crossing the fragile wall

---

17   Delivered in Saint-Germain-l'Auxerrois, November 3, 1967.

which separates us from him, to gain some part of that indescribable knowledge which he now enjoys in eternity."

"Bloy's entire existence—and to my mind his whole work," continues Bishop Baron, "is substantially linked with the Communion of Saints. It does not even seem that one can truly approach his soul, if one does not seek to discover how this mystery invaded the mind and the heart of Léon Bloy from the moment he regained his Faith. There are four stages that mark the path of his discovery, The Communion of Saints first of all awakened in him the grandiose vision of faith which illuminates the action of men, intervening at every period in God's Plan for the world; next it revealed to him the properly divine power which the quality of Christian confers for acting within this plan; then it led him to contemplate the origins of this power, wholly rooted in the conformation of the Christian to the God-Man on the Cross; and finally this mystery allowed him to see something of the prodigious effects which the Communion of Saints puts within reach of the poor sinners that we are."

"The Communion of Saints!" wrote Bloy, "What do these two words mean for the majority of Christians who repeat them every day as an article of their faith? The less ignorant are obliged to accept that such is the theological designation of the Church, the Mystical Body of Christ, of which all the faithful are the visible members. This is rudimentary.

"But how many are there who, going beyond this postulate, are capable of thinking—along with the Apostles—that only the demons are outside the Church [let us understand clearly, as Bloy indicates, five lines further on, outside *potential* membership in the Church], that no human being is excluded from the Redemption and that even the darkest pagans are virtually Catholic, heirs of God and co-heirs of Christ!

"If all men without exception were not potentially saints, the ninth article of the Creed would make no sense; there would be no Communion of Saints. It is the harmonious grouping of all souls since the creation of the world, and this concert is so marvelously exact that it is impossible to escape it. . . . The word 'reversibility' had to be invented, for whatever it's worth, in order to give some inkling of this mystery."

"It was his incessant contemplation of the Communion of Saints which aroused in Bloy a hunger and thirst that were never satiated to 'drag,' as he put it, multitudes to God"[18]—and also a desire to "suffer beyond measure" for souls. If he did not fear to write such words as these: "I say that someone loves me when that someone accepts to suffer by me or for me. Otherwise this someone who claims to love me is only a sentimental usurer who wants to install his vile business in my heart," it was because he knew that every true love has its proper place in the Communion of Saints or at least tends toward it obscurely, and that, as Bishop Baron says, "the threads which bind souls

---

18   André Baron, citation from the homily.

together in the Communion of Saints are knotted in the warp and woof of suffering."[19] And Bishop Baron continues by citing the page from which I read a few lines at the beginning of this third part, and which is one of Bloy's most precious pages, from his last book, *Dans les Ténèbres*: "Well, what are we, Lord God, but the members of Jesus Christ, his very members. Our unspeakable misery is to mistake unceasingly for inanimate figures or symbols the clearest and the most living statements of the Scriptures, We believe, but not *substantially*. . . . We do not understand that we are the members of the Man of Sorrow, of the Man who is supreme Joy, supreme Love, supreme Truth, supreme Beauty, supreme Light and supreme Life, only because he is madly in love with supreme suffering, the pilgrim of the last agony, who has come running to endure it, across the Infinite, from the depths of eternity, and on whose head are heaped in a dreadfully tragic unity of time and place and person, all the elements of torture amassed in each human act, accomplished in the duration of each second, over the whole surface of the earth," since the Fall.

"So we can start from there," Léon Bloy continues, "to measure all things. In declaring us members of Jesus Christ the Holy Spirit has invested us with the dignity of redeemers and when we refuse to suffer, we are precisely simoniacs and prevaricators. We are made for this, and for this alone. When we shed our blood, it flows on Calvary and from there over the whole earth. Woe to us, therefore, if that blood is poisoned! When we shed our tears which are 'the blood of our souls,' they fall on the heart of the Virgin and from there on all living hearts. Our status as members of Jesus Christ and sons of Mary has made us so great that we can drown the world in our tears, Woe therefore—triple woe—if they are poisoned tears!"

And here is the end of the chapter: "From the top of the Mountain symbolized, as it would seem, by the mountain of temptation, all empires can be seen, that is to say all the moral virtues, invisible from any other point, and love alone, great, passionate, ravishing love, can provide the strength to reach this summit. The Saints sought out the society of the Passion of Jesus. They believed the word of the Master when He said that he possesses the greatest love who gives his life for his friends. In every age, ardent and magnificent souls have believed that in order to do enough, it was necessary to do too much, and that it was in this way that the kingdom of Heaven is won . . ."

In the Preface of this same book, which was published after the death of the author, Jeanne Léon-Bloy tells us that one night during his last illness, Bloy heard these words from Our Lady: "You and I, dear child, are the People of God."

What a marvelous response, at the moment when the life of the Pilgrim of the Absolute was about to end, to the total gift which his mother had made of him, when he was still only a child, to the compassionate Virgin. And what a

---

19   *Ibid.*

sublime summation, in a few words of infinite significance, of the truths taught us by that Communion of Saints which embraces the whole People of God, the sons of Eve redeemed and sanctified by the Blood of Christ and now become sons of Mary and, along with them, the immaculate Queen of Heaven, their Mother. As Bishop Baron says: "She who, on Calvary, was consecrated Mother of the Church in the adoption, declared by Jesus from the height of the Cross, of the beloved disciple, because she had accepted that the blood of her son be shed drop by drop for mankind—she now makes up along with us the People of God because we in our turn have accepted to take our humble and painful part in the salvation of the world in the Communion of Saints."

When Léon Bloy was given the grace of hearing Mary's words, his sickness still left him enough strength to write; and during that same night he wrote the short chapter in which, in order to make of it a hymn in honor of the Virgin, he discreetly alludes to the words of final blessing which rewarded him for all his sufferings. Here are those lines: "You and I, dear child, are the People of God. We are in the Promised Land and I myself am this blessed land, even as I was once the Red Sea which had to be crossed. Remember! My Son has said that those who weep are blessed and it is because I have wept all the tears and suffered all the agonies of generations, that all generations will call me blessed. The marvels of Egypt are nothing, neither are the marvels of the Desert, in comparison with the dazzling light which I bring you for all Eternity."

II

A LOOK AT SOME QUESTIONS OF A
PRIMARILY PHILOSOPHICAL ORDER

CHAPTER III
ON METAPHYSICS (I)

CONCERNING TRUTH[1]

IT IS IMPORTANT MORE THAN EVER for Christians to reflect on truth. For it is the very meaning of truth which today is obliterated and threatened for many people. It seems to crumble away under our very eyes, along with the sense of divine transcendence and the sense of mystery.

In our reflections on truth I think it is fitting to begin from the top, with supernaturally revealed Truth. This is normal from the point of view of Christian thought. It is normal, for anyone who has received the gift of faith, to begin these kinds of reflections with faith, with what is highest and most precious in our intellectual equipment. The Christian has the privilege of finding himself face to face with *absolute Truth*, of that Truth which is God Himself, and of God Himself revealing Himself. In adhering to this absolute truth the Christian will bring into play, spontaneously and in lived actuality, *in actu exercito*, those great things about truth which philosophy discovers on its own, when it understands for example that truth is the adequation of the intellect and the real, or that being is the proper object of the intelligence, which finds its life and its freedom in adhering to it.

Philosophy knows these things *in actu signato*, in signified act or by way of conceptualization. But there is an enormous advantage in having *lived*, in having experienced in exercised act these great themes concerning truth before conceptualizing them philosophically.

And it is in faith in God Who is subsistent Truth, in faith in uncreated Truth and in incarnate Truth, that we live them to a sovereignly eminent degree.

I. SUPERNATURALLY REVEALED TRUTH

1. The first point concerns the sacred importance, absolutely essential and absolutely preponderant, of *Truth* in the Gospel and for Christian faith.

I am the Way, and the TRUTH, *and the Life* (John xiv, 6)—*He* [the Word] *was the* TRUE LIGHT *that enlightens every man coming into the world* (John i, 9)—*and the*

---

1   *Editor's footnote*: A Seminar given to the Little Brothers of Jesus, in Toulouse on March 31, 1965.

Word became flesh . . . full of grace and TRUTH (John i, 14). Jesus, subsisting Truth, Incarnate, came *to bear witness to the* TRUTH (John xviii, 37)—*The Spirit is* TRUTH (I John v, 6)—The Holy Spirit is *the Spirit of* TRUTH (John xiv, 17; xv, 26; xvi, 13)—*Father, sanctify them* IN THE TRUTH (John xvii, 17)—We are OF THE TRUTH (I John iii, 19)—*He brought us forth by the word of* TRUTH (James i, 18)—*The* TRUTH *will make you free* (John viii, 32)—*. . . those who worship must worship in spirit and* TRUTH (John iv, 24)—*Let us profess the* TRUTH *in love* (Ephes. iv, 15)—*Those who are to perish because they did not receive* THE LOVE OF THE TRUTH *which would have saved them* (II Thessal. ii, 10)—*All shall be condemned who did not* BELIEVE IN THE TRUTH (II Thessal., ii, 12).

The absolute certitude of faith is founded on divine *Truth*. "I believe firmly everything that Your Holy Church believes and teaches because You, Who are Truth Itself, revealed it to Her."

This truth of faith is the infinitely transcendent truth of the mystery of God. And nevertheless, God has willed that this infinitely transcendent truth be expressed (the prophets of Israel, the teaching of Christ, and the definitions of the Church) in human concepts and words. This is characteristic of the Judeo-Christian revelation. Revelation is not unformulable; it is *formed*. This is so because the Second Person of the Trinity is the Word and because the Word became flesh. The concepts and words that transmit revelation to us are at once *true* (they make what is hidden in God actually *known* to us) and essentially *mysterious* ("*in aenigmate*": they remain disproportionate to the Reality which they attain without either circumscribing or comprehending it). In the obscurity of faith we enter into possession already here below of absolute Truth, which we shall see clearly only in the light of glory. This is why we can *worship in spirit and* IN TRUTH.

2. CHARITY AND TRUTH.[2]—*In veritate et charitate* (II John iii).

Charity has to do with persons; truth, with ideas and the reality attained through them. Perfect charity toward our neighbor and complete fidelity to the truth are not only compatible; each calls for the other.

In fraternal dialogue, the deeper love is, the more each one must declare without any attenuation what he holds to be true (otherwise he would do wrong, not only to truth as he sees it, but also to the spiritual dignity of his neighbor).

And the more freely I affirm what I hold as true, the more I should love whoever denies it (I do not show my neighbor the tolerance demanded by brotherly love unless his right to *exist*, to *seek the truth and to express it* according to his lights, and *never to act or speak against his conscience* is recognized and

---

2   Cf. my study "Qui est mon prochain?" in *Principes d'une politique humaniste* [OE C VIII, p. 279 f.; please note that hereafter all citation cross-referencing the *Oeuvres Complètes* will appear in brackets], and our study "Tolérance et Vérité," in *Le Philosophe dans la cité* [OE C XI, p. 73 f.].

respected by me at the very instant when this neighbor takes sides against those truths which are dearest to me).

And if I truly love him whom I regard as being in error, I must *suffer* to see him deprived of the truth which it is given me to know. This does not seem to be the case today for certain pseudo-ecumenists[3] who quiver with joy in sniffing out the slightest odor of heresy in their dear separated brethren. They love the latter more than truth. If they loved truth above everything else, they would suffer—both for the truth and for their brothers—that their brothers are in error and that the truth is not recognized. This element of suffering and of heartbreak is the indispensable mark of the Cross of Jesus and is an integral part of fraternal dialogue. Such dialogue, on the other hand, would degenerate completely if the fear of displeasing my brother entered into balance with my duty to declare the truth. It would be very dangerous to confuse "loving" with "seeking to please." *Saltavit et placuit.* This dancer pleased Herod's guests; it is difficult to say whether her heart was burning with love for them.

3. EFFICACY AND TRUTH.—*"Non in fortitudine equi"* (Ps. cxlvi, 10).

The Church is open to the world, she is attentive to the effort of men and to the movement of history, she does not wish to neglect anything that is good in this effort and this movement. She wishes us to do justice to nature. If there are in the world many things we are asked to renounce, either in order to avoid evil or in order to cooperate in the redemptive work of Christ, our sacrifice is all the more meritorious as the goods in question are more valuable. If the saints despise the world, it is certainly not that the world is in itself worthy of scorn; it is because in comparison with Him to Whom they have given their heart, even what is resplendent with the greatest of beauties is, according to the saying of St. Paul, "like dung." The Christian soul has always known these things and today is becoming more deeply aware of them. But it knows also that to the extent that it refuses the Blood of Christ, the world surrenders itself to a "Prince" of perdition and is, according to the word of St. John, "situated in evil."[4] Loving the world with a redemptive love, as Christ loved it, the Church suffers and prays, and proclaims the word of God in order that the world may know divine truth better and better, and in order that it may conform itself to the will of the Father; she is wary of conforming to the lusts, the prejudices, or the passing fancies of the world. In this sense, Chesterton was right in saying: "The Catholic Church is the only thing which saves a man from the degrading slavery of being a child of his age."[5] And with incomparably greater authority, it has been said also: *"Do not be conformed to this world"* (Rom. xii, 2). And the Lord himself told us: "Do not be afraid, I have

---

3   True ecumenism means love; it does not mean stupidity.

4   "Mundus totus in maligno positus est" (I John v, 19).

5   *L'Eglise catholique et la Conversion* (Bonne Presse, 1952).

overcome the world" (John xiii, 33).[6] The technocratic civilization into which the world is entering today seems to have chosen efficiency for its supreme law. This is why men will desperately need the witness which the Church renders to the absolute primacy of truth.

To neglect efficiency would be culpable childishness. This is why the Church renews her means at each great new period of history. But it is not enough to say that the efficacy of means is ordered to Truth, when Truth has been served first; it is necessary to understand also that in the domain of the kingdom of God, it is truth which is *the source and the measure of efficacy itself.* He Who is the Truth is also the Way—and the Life.

Nowadays, there is a tendency in many people (and even, without their clearly realizing it perhaps, in many Christians) to give *efficacy* primacy over *truth.* What does it matter if the means used are sullied or not with error as long as they are effective in gathering men together in the Good Shepherd's flock?

That is a flagrant absurdity since the Good Shepherd is precisely Truth itself. Even if one does not realize it, this is actually a way of denying Christ (for every truth, even the humblest, bears witness to the Light which enlightens every man coming into the world). And it exposes Christian souls to a deadly disintegration, by ruining their internal unity and their spiritual equilibrium.

If things were carried to the extreme, these poor souls would be asked to adhere by faith to supernatural truth without believing in any truth of the natural order (except the more and more ephemeral truths of positive science), in other words on an ocean of complete skepticism or philosophical and (by repercussion) theological indifferentism. The result would finally be the defection of a great multitude, The day when efficiency prevails over truth will never come for the Church, for then the gates of Hell would have prevailed against her.

II. TRUTH OF THE RATIONAL ORDER
"Rationabile obsequium vestrum" (Rom. xii, 1)

4. One is thus normally led to descend from considerations concerning supernaturally revealed truth to considerations concerning truth of the rational order.

How indeed could we know with full certitude supernaturally revealed truth, to which our mind is not naturally proportioned, if we could not know

---

6   The world and its ambivalence are a great mystery. I spoke of this a bit, if I recall correctly, in *Humanisme intégral* [OE C VI, p. 291 f.]. But see especially *Pour une philosophie de l'histoire,* chap. iv, §§ 4 and 5 [OE C X, pp. 722–730]. See also Raïssa's *Le Prince de ce monde* (and in the *Journal,* p. 221, fragment 39, of the "Feuilles détachées").

with full certitude the truths of the rational order which, precisely insofar as they are rational, are naturally proportioned to our mind? Grace perfects nature and does not destroy it. It is essential to man to aspire to truth, and he has the capacity to attain truth by his own powers—little by little and however imperfectly—in those things which depend on the experience of the senses or to which this experience gives us access indirectly.

Moreover there are truths of the rational order which revelation itself says are accessible to us. Thus it is our faith which asks us to believe that the existence of God can be attained with full certitude by the paths of reason.

And many other similar truths have a necessary connection with the data of faith and are presupposed by them. For example, the axiom that man is made for truth, and again, the existence of the sensible world, the existence of free will, the spirituality and the immortality of the human soul. . . . Such a list can be extended, to the point that certain philosophers have been able to think that a whole metaphysics is implied in the revealed datum.

5. But then another question arises, and one of extreme importance: Since there are truths of the rational order of which the human mind can acquire full certitude, does it not follow from this that an organic network of fundamental truths, in other words a *doctrine* which is essentially *grounded in truth*, is possible (in the philosophical order and also—when there is a question of acquiring by rational mode some understanding of the revealed mystery—in the theological order)?

We answer: Yes, it is indeed necessary, since man is made for truth, that a doctrine essentially grounded in truth be possible for the human mind—on condition that it not be the work of one single person (clearly too weak for such a work) but on the contrary that it rely, in its respect for common sense and common intelligence, on the efforts of the human mind since prehistoric times, and embrace the work of generations of the thinkers with contrasting views—all of this being one day brought together and unified by one or several persons of genius.

In giving such an answer, I do not intend to discuss the positions of those who in great numbers today regard the pluralism of philosophical doctrines as something normal *de jure*. My intention is rather to dispel a misunderstanding and to show that, contrary to what is often believed, one can understand clearly the idea that a *doctrine essentially grounded in truth is possible* only if one recognizes at the same time the pluralism of philosophic doctrines, which I do not say are normal *de jure*, but which I say, because they must *inevitably occur, are normal de facto*, in Christian lands as well as in non-Christian lands—and this by reason of the conditions of the exercise of human subjectivity in philosophers.

On the one hand it would be a great illusion indeed and a great absurdity to imagine that a philosophical doctrine grounded in truth is by that very fact complete or perfect, nay more, that it contains ready-made, beforehand, the answers to all the questions which will arise in the course of time. Doubtless one can say that a doctrine essentially grounded in truth is a *true* doctrine; but it is necessary to eliminate immediately any possibility of ambiguity. What do the words "a *true* philosophy" or "a *true* theology" mean? They mean that, its principles being true, and organized among themselves in a manner which conforms to the real, such a philosophy or such a theology is therefore equipped to advance from century to century toward more truth. But there is an infinite number of truths which it has not yet attained. And such as it presents itself at a given time, it can itself include a number of accidental errors.

Not only is it never finished and must always progress, but it implies necessarily, in order to free itself from those limiting conditions due to the mentality of a given period of culture, a perpetual process of *self-recasting*, as is the case with all living organisms. And it has the duty to understand intelligently the diverse doctrines which develop from age to age in opposition to it, to disengage their generative intuition, and to save those truths which they hold captive. But, being given the conditions of the exercise of human subjectivity, it is certainly to be feared that those who adhere to this doctrine grounded in truth will more or less neglect the duty of which I have just spoken, as well as the process of self-recasting which I have also mentioned.

On the other hand, being given the conditions of the exercise of human subjectivity, it is inevitable that in every epoch a certain number of minds, and great minds, devoted above all to research and fascinated by some particular truth or other which they have discovered (ordinarily, through the stimulant of some error), will give rise to other doctrines, succeeding one another from century to century, which contrast more or less violently with the doctrine grounded in truth envisaged here as possible. The minds of which I am speaking will burn themselves up like mayflies in the truth they have discovered. And it will be the office of the doctrine essentially grounded in truth to save and to liberate this truth in a coherent universe of intelligibility. But they will have contributed effectively to the progress of philosophy.

And so, as I noted above, we can see that to recognize the possibility of a lasting doctrine essentially grounded in truth, but which, in actual fact, being a common work, advances more slowly, is at the same time to recognize as inevitably *normal de facto* (or by reason of the subject) the existence of other doctrines which, each an individual work, and for this reason ephemeral, indicate a more rapid advance on some particular point, but an advance paid for with a tribute of error.

And we can understand likewise how those who see in the development of philosophy no more than a succession of individual works will be inclined to hold as necessary *de jure* (as if it were required by the object itself) a doctrinal pluralism which in reality is undoubtedly normal (on the part of the philosophizing subject with the human condition being what it is), but only as necessary *in actual fact*.

III. THE ROLE OF THE COMMON DOCTOR
"Da nobis, quaesumus, et quae docuit intellectu conspicere . . ."
(Prayer of the Feast of St. Thomas Aquinas)

6. At this point we must turn to questions concerning the doctrine of St. Thomas Aquinas. As a matter of fact that doctrine "essentially grounded in truth," of which I have just spoken in order to affirm that such a doctrine is certainly *possible*, evidently might have remained in the state of mere possibility. I mean that this doctrine might never have been *formed*, and could have remained no more than that virtual term, not really attained, to which the contrasts and conflicts between the many doctrines which succeed one another in course of history seem to tend. It happens however that the testimonies of the Supreme Pontiffs (which have been promoted with particular urgency since Leo XIII but had begun as early as the canonization of St. Thomas) show that the Church (on the basis of her own human experience, and certainly not on the basis of the deposit of revelation) thinks that *in actual fact*, and through a succession of providential encounters, that doctrine essentially grounded in truth to which the human intellect aspires has not remained a mere possibility. Its realization is found in a philosophy and theology that is destined to ceaseless progression, that of St. Thomas Aquinas.

It is important however, not to forget what authentic Thomism is (I do not like this word *Thomism*, but in default of another word I am obliged to use it). Authentic Thomism is not an end point. Nor is it the doctrine of any *single man*. Certainly all those elements that St. Thomas took up and brought to unity were due more than anything else to the labor of the Fathers of the Church and of the Doctors who preceded him, of the great seekers of Greece and of the great inspired minds of Israel. But what all this represents precisely is the mass of treasures (accumulated with the natural and supernatural help of Providence)—treasures of the slow acquisitions of reason, those of the wisdom disseminated by Christ and the apostles, and those of the wisdom of the Old Testament. These are centuries-old treasures—which rise, some from the depths of the ages, others from more recent epochs of human history, and which at a certain period were knit together into an intelligible organism purposely *formed* and destined to grow forever, and through the centuries to extend its immense supple arms ever preoccupied with taking new truths into its embrace. For such an adventure privileged preparations were certainly needed, the most important and the holiest of which depended on the Judeo-Christian revelation, and of which the most weakly human (but endowed with a catalytic power as far as the technique of knowledge is concerned) depended on what is called the "miracle of Greece" and on the exceptional genius of Aristotle; and later there was need for another privileged moment in history, as well as the privileged instrument of the exceptional genius of Thomas Aquinas, along with the grace of his holiness. And afterwards, all through the ages, other particularly favorable moments and other specially aided workers will be needed as well. But are not exceptional strokes of luck and privileged events characteristic of the adventures of the kingdom of the spirit?

We can certainly note in passing that Holy Mother Church is *Mulier unius libri*—and this single book is *The Bible*. But in the case of St. Thomas Aquinas, when she asks us to pay special heed to him among all the Doctors of the Church, it is so that we might pay heed also—and not only through him, but, as much as we can, through the original work of all great thinkers—to the innumerable human voices which have contributed something to the truth and which the Angelic Doctor was able to change from discord into harmony. It is so that we might also listen to all those voices which after him have already contributed and will continue to contribute something to the truth, and which his principles, his doctrine, and his spirit will ennable us to change from discord into harmony.

7. Is it necessary to add that authentic Thomism is not, according to the caricature which its enemies and, alas, some of its defenders have drawn of it, a kind of intellectual police force or ecclesiastical constabulary, mounting guard to defend the past and whatever is considered rightly or wrongly to be the acquired truth, preoccupied with nothing but the refutation of error, and suspecting every new intellectual germination of malice or heresy.

Authentic Thomism will always be suffering the birth pangs of new truths that have to be discovered, recognized and integrated. The keys which it is busy making are for the purpose of opening doors, not closing them. Authentic Thomism is not a closed system; it is a wisdom that is essentially *open* and without frontiers by the very fact that it is a doctrine in movement and vital development.

It is *open* to the new questions and to the new truths which the evolution of culture and science enable it to propose. It is *open* to the contributions of the new philosophies which appear with each epoch and to the new truths brought by these philosophies, even though they may be sullied with error. Such an openness, I might note in passing,[7] supposes an effort of mind to transcend for a moment one's own conceptual language in order to enter into the conceptual language of others, and to return from this intellectual journey having grasped the particular intuition which is the life of the new philosophy in question.

Authentic Thomism is *open* to the diverse *problematics* (that is, to the diverse organizations of problems) which it may very well be proper for it to put to use, whether such a Thomism sets them up itself with the progress of time or whether it goes forth to seek them in other universes of thought (Oriental thought, Islam, Hinduism, Taoism)—renewing them all in the light of the great

---

7   Cf. our study "Coopération philosophique et justice intellectuelle," in *Raison et raisons* [OE C IX, p. 271 f.].

fundamental intuitions of the philosophy of being. I am thinking, for example, of what might be brought to us by a Christian and Thomist Hindu, who would have a thorough knowledge, along with a kind of filial piety and connaturality, of the Vedantic schools of thought and their proper modes of intellectual approach.

Thus we can have some idea of what it is possible to derive from the same primary intuitions and from the same philosophical wisdom—and within that same wisdom and doctrine—along with the *problematics* and forms of *expression* that differ according to times and places and according to the individual genius of this or that participant in this vast continuous concert.

This is what Thomism is by nature, and the form it is called to take among men in the course of time to come, because above all it is an insatiable hunger and thirst for truths to be seized upon and assimilated.

8. One more remark. Pascal made a distinction between the geometrical mind and the shrewd or subtle mind. Bergson, likewise distinguished between minds which see things principally through spatial perspectives and minds which see them through the perspectives of living durations and of qualitative differentiations. It is clear that minds with predominantly spatial or spatializing perspectives will have an instinctive loathing for those privileged moments or privileged events which I just mentioned, and will tend to see in time a homogeneous unfolding, in which what took place once can be repeated indefinitely at other equally favorable moments. Why then would it not be possible to do again at other moments in time what St. Thomas did in baptizing Aristotle by adapting other great philosophers to the service of theology? Thus in the eighteenth century we saw a kind of Cartesian theology. Today certain people would like to see appear a kind of Hegelian theology, which they imagine would have a better chance of success.

It is undoubtedly easy to picture things this way. But facility is not truth. And for those who look closely at reality, the mirage offered to the mind by such a way of looking at things quickly vanishes. In fact, as I have already noted, every great modern philosophy is essentially an individual work, the discovery of one single man. And at the same time, unlike the work of St. Thomas Aquinas, it lays resolute claim to being a completed synthesis; and this is why it can exercise an enormous, diffuse influence after this one man. But it will have a very short life expectancy as a formed and articulated body of doctrine. It will inevitably give way to other individual doctrines. In other words it is a closed system, not an open wisdom. Hegel might very well have considered his philosophy the supreme summit of the entire effort of human thought (in reality it was only the summit of the thought of one particular epoch). By the very fact that in his eyes it was the supreme revelation of wisdom, he could not regard it as an instrument for future discoveries in a search that will never come to an end. No great modern philosophy lays claim or can lay claim to be made for the assimilation of all the truths that have been discovered, even with the help of error, by all the other doctrines in their endless diversity. Each is enclosed within itself.

It is therefore impossible to do with these philosophies what St. Thomas did with Greek thought and with Aristotle as a catalyst. The only thing that would be accomplished in using them to construct a theology is a succession of theological systems fundamentally foreign to one another, offered individually as valid for each successive epoch. All of which would result in a definitive theological relativism and the ruin of all *truth* in that domain where our reason tries, in a faltering and stammering way, to express things divine.

Finally the absurdity of the point of view I am criticizing here, which would like to *repeat* with any great philosopher what St. Thomas did with Aristotle, is even more evident if we remember that the great modern philosophies, far from being pure philosophies, drew their life from the debris of the theology to which they considered themselves heirs and burdened themselves with the many problems attributable to that theology which philosophy had supposedly dispossessed. Is it possible to find in disaffected theologies and in antitheologies, the philosophic *ancilla* that theology needs?

For symmetrically opposite reasons, but which lead to identical conclusions, the same must be said about the great philosophies of the Orient. Whether they were born of a great religious tradition as in India, or have their origin from another as in China, they are in fact theologies as well as philosophies, or substitutes for theology. I noted a moment ago that Thomism could draw help from Hinduism in renewing its problematic. I did not say, an idea that would be an absurdity, that Catholicism could use Hinduism to replace the theology of St. Thomas by a theology founded on Shankara or on Ramanuja.

IV. THE POPES AND ST. THOMAS AQUINAS

9. Earlier I recalled above the importance of the constant testimony of the Sovereign Pontiffs in favor of the philosophy and the theology of St. Thomas. I must now add that with regard to the translation into *practical* formulation of these testimonies, a great change seems desirable today which would indicate a *re-establishment*, a putting back into place, of at least as great a significance as the "restoration" proclaimed by Leo XIII.

What I mean is that, instead of seeking somehow within the Church to impose by way of authority the teaching of the principles and the doctrine of St. Thomas Aquinas, it is by turning toward the ways of *liberty* that the Church, in order to attract attention to the intrinsic truth of these principles and this doctrine, would seem able to recommend them most effectively today. In speaking this way, I realize I am entering into a domain that is in no way my own, but that of the teaching Church. However, each of us is certainly free, after all, to humbly express his desires and hopes, even if they concern areas that are beyond him and even if he has some reason to doubt that he will ever see them realized.

Every philosophical or theological doctrine is a human doctrine, and therefore, however true it may be, it cannot be imposed in the dogmatic order and in the name of the *truth of the faith* (even though a certain number of philosophical or theological truths may be imposed as necessarily attached to the deposit of revelation). If the Church still wants somehow to impose by way of authority the teaching of some philosophical or theological doctrine, it can only be by recommending it in the order of discipline and in the name of *prudence*, according as this doctrine appears to be safer and posing less of a risk. There is no doubt that such a procedure is legitimate in itself; but in actual fact it runs the risk by its very nature of inevitably provoking the result directly opposite to what it had intended, for it is truth, not safety, which matters in every struggle for knowledge (with all the "beautiful dangers," as Plato put it, which must be encountered). And to recommend a doctrine, solely on the basis of discipline and prudence, as being "safer," is the best and most effective way to turn away from it many minds which cannot necessarily be called reckless or proud because they have turned elsewhere.

On the contrary, by having recourse to the *reversal* of method I alluded to, and by insisting solely on the truth of Thomism on a plane that is neither dogmatic nor simply prudential, but *free*—I mean on the plane of that freedom which the Mystical Body itself has in order to discern for its own intellectual life here below its best instruments of truth, and to seek the assurance of their help, just as on the plane of the freedom which each person has in his search for decisive intuitions and primary certitudes—then the philosophy of St. Thomas would have some chance of being recognized as having a really vivifying and ordering influence on the research in which Christian thought is engaged.

10. While putting human reason to work in the service of the faith and of revealed truth, the Church, the Mystical Body of Christ, has a particularly clear consciousness of the demands of its own intellectual life here below because it is particularly assisted by the Holy Spirit in the person of that leader who here on earth has charge of her universality. In the lofty consciousness which she has of herself in the person of the Vicar of Christ, the Church is certainly free, *for the progress of its own thought, to adopt by preference* a particular philosophy and theology (which are human sciences); and she is certainly free to *declare* her preference through the voice of the Vicar of Christ, with just as much freedom as a particular human person is entitled to in adopting by preference the doctrine which he or she holds to be true and in making public declaration of that preference.

But how does it best suit the Church to declare her preference for the philosophical and theological doctrine of Thomas Aquinas and to lead her faithful to share that preference, in particular those who have some mandate to teach? If the remarks I have proposed above are correct, in its hands nothing less exalted than the very demands of the truth of the faith, and of the preservation of the deposit of revelation, has the *decisive power* to *oblige* minds—but these demands cannot be invoked in the present case. It consequently remains that the best means at the disposal of the Church is to appeal, not to obedience and docility, but to the freedom of the human mind, and its devotion to the truth. *Let her address an urgent appeal to all those who have ears to hear, let her declare loudly her need that the living tradition of the doctrine of St. Thomas Aquinas continue to develop and progress from age to age!* It is not important that this appeal be heard by all, nor even that it be heard by the majority. What is essentially important is that it be heard by a few, and it will certainly be heard by a few, enough that the torch continue to pass from hand to hand. These few, having turned toward the Angelic Doctor, will perceive the light of truth in his eyes.

As far as the others are concerned—all those who could not or would not see for themselves the truth of the principles and the doctrine of St. Thomas— let them know that they are free to follow other masters and to join other schools or to create some new school, from the moment that in good conscience—and this is everyone's absolute duty—they try sincerely to seek out the truth alone, and on condition also that whatever doctrine they subscribe to teaches nothing, on the theological level, that is opposed to the revealed deposit or is incompatible with it, and that it preserve, on the philosophical level, those truths of the natural order which have a necessary connection with that deposit.

Such are the things which I would be extremely happy to hear the teaching Church tell us someday . . .

11. The reversal of method or of practical approach which seems to me desirable with regard to the testimony rendered by the Church to the doctrine of St. Thomas—a testimony which henceforth would be rendered, no longer in the name of the disciplinary authority[8] of the Church, but in the name of the

---

8   I have not forgotten that canon 1366-2 of the *Code of Canon Law* (of 1917) requires those professors to whom the Church has confided the teaching of rational philosophy to treat these matters *ad Angelici Doctoris rationem, doctrinam et principia*. And it would certainly be deplorable to abolish this canon, for such a change would inevitably be misunderstood and regarded as a kind of renouncement. But the canon in question could be interpreted, in saying that it has the force of an imperative prescription concerning the great truths relating to the deposit of Revelation. These great truths find solid grounding in a most eminent way in the Thomist synthesis (They can of course be recognized by other doctrines also). But as far as thomism itself is concerned, taken in the specificity

freedom of the Church herself and of the freedom of each person to use human reason in the service of truth—I am persuaded that only such a reversal would be capable, not only of disconcerting the contemners of St. Thomas, but also of knocking down the prejudices of many of those who in great numbers today have taken sides against him more or less irresponsibly (in most cases without even realizing the gravity of the stakes involved). Many sincere minds would thus be led to give serious consideration to the problem, even in this strange world of professors who often—either out of laziness and routine, or on the contrary out of a desire of originality, or again because they have an itch to be in line with the fashion of the day, or simply because a certain mental mediocrity gives them the illusion of scientific "objectivity"—seem to consider it a duty of state to betray the very illuminating mission which the Church of Christ has entrusted to them.

Finally it is clear that the Supreme Pontiff alone has the language necessary to make clear the reasons for this great movement of confidence in the dynamism of *freedom in the service of truth,* which I am speaking about very awkwardly and clumsily, just as he alone can make it come to pass. This is why for a moment I have let myself dream of the declaration which he could formulate in this respect. I think that with regard to the role of St, Thomas in the intellectual life of the Church, and with regard to the future of Christian philosophy, of theology and of its related sciences, such a declaration would have a remarkable power of renewal if, while appealing, in the name of the sacred mission of the Church to those who are disposed to devote themselves completely to the diffusion and to the progress of the thought of St. Thomas, it took care forthrightly to put at ease those who, in the service the Catholic faith, have chosen other philosophical and theological paths, and if it expounded in the most explicit manner how and why the necessary continuity and the necessary development through the centuries of the doctrine providentialy *formed* by Thomas Aquinas do not prevent but rather suppose, as I have indicated, the pluralism of philosophical systems which develop on their own and which succeed each other in the world and under the overarching canopy of the Church.

Let me repeat once again, what is essentially important is that from the living waters of common human thought, which from the far distant past have made their way underground, once they have been gathered together by the angels of God to well up like a spring to the surface of the earth, there gush forth a life-giving stream which will never stop, even though sometimes—indeed, many times—it may appear weak and thin in volume (but never in intensity). What is absolutely necessary is that it exist and act and that it continue to act and to exist.

---

and the integrity of its organization as a body of doctrine, canon 1366 has no more than the force of a counsel through which is passed along "the urgent call to all those who have ears to hear," about which we spoke earlier.

V. CONCERNING CHRISTIAN PHILOSOPHY

12. Let me add to these already far too extended reflections two additional remarks concerning Christian philosophy.

In the first place, it seems to me that in our time, and through the ecumenical perspectives opened up by the Council, the role of Christian philosophy, if finally it develops normally, appears to be of singular importance. By the fact that of its very nature it has its origin in reason, not in revelation, it does not, like theology, have to engage in a fraternal dialogue with the theological systems of the great non-Catholic Christian families, or of the great non-Christian religions, a dialogue which inevitably runs into painful and more or less irreconcilable oppositions. The object of its research are the supreme truths of the natural order, of which reason is capable of grasping by its own power, while being aided and raised up in its own order (since this philosophy is Christian) by the strengthening support of faith. It follows from this, not only that its dialogue with non-Christians is much easier, and that each of the interlocutors can receive from the other precious contributions for his own thought, but also that in this area the possibilities of intellectual *agreement* are much vaster. The spontaneous interest which Moslem or Hindu thinkers take nowadays in certain aspects of Thomist philosophical research is an indication of what I am proposing here.

In the second place, it may be said that when the classical role of *ancilla theologiae* was attributed to philosophy, Christian antiquity actually had in mind philosophies born in pagan lands and more or less successfully baptized and which theology made use of as instruments while at the same time correcting them. If there is question of a philosophy that is already Christian, it may be asked if things do not change a bit, and if the servant, while retaining her instrumental role, does not also become an auxiliary associated in research. Theology is essentially *of the Church* and *in the Church*. But Christian philosophy, even though, inasmuch as it is Christian, it is not *of the world*, nevertheless, inasmuch as it is a philosophy, it is essentially *in the world*. In its own light, therefore, it touches upon many problems whose reality demands to be recognized by all Christian wisdom, but in which, because they are not found directly in a perspective of Church, theology on its own would perhaps not think of taking an interest. It is as "associated in theological research" that Christian philosophy, after having studied as best it can the problems in question, brings them under the purview of the theologian, to whom it belongs in the last resort to pass judgment on them.

CHAPTER IV
ON METAPHYSICS (II)

LETTER ON PHILOSOPHY AT THE TIME OF THE COUNCIL[1]

YOUR BOOK IS SUCH A COURAGEOUS, timely, ample, and luminous testimony to truth, and of such high intellectual quality, that with all my heart I thank both of you for having written it and God for having inspired it.

What a stroke of good fortune that it has appeared just before the last session of the Council. And the fact that it is a dialogue, a dialogue between two eminent lay philosophers, and that these two philosophers are sons of dear Poland, cannot fail to make more evident its universal value and add to its authority.

It will help, I am confident, to weaken the disastrous prejudice which links "Thomism" and "conservatism" in certain minds (both adversaries and self-styled defenders of St. Thomas). It will also help to force those among the Council Fathers who dream of getting rid of St. Thomas to reflect a bit and to avoid the worst.

However, unless an extraordinary breath of the Holy Spirit passes over the Council (which is always possible), I have very serious doubts that any positive declaration of the Council will accomplish in fact the wish that you formulate in admirable terms in the conclusion when you say (p. 171) that the Church should remind, not only Christians, but the entire world, that the salvation of human culture in its totality depends on its never losing sight of the importance of metaphysical wisdom, of the philosophy of being, and hence of the work of St. Thomas, "that last great metaphysician of humanity who left us such an admirable example of the contemplation of being."

But as you indicate in your very accurate analyses in the third part of the book, even a "failure of Thomism," if God should permit it, "would only be one more avatar in its seven-century-old history" (and finally would perhaps be no more than a momentary regrouping as a prelude to a new and more vigorous advance).

This letter would become an entire volume—a repetition of yours!—if I

---

1   *Editor's Footnote*: A letter addressed to Jerzy Kalinowsky and Stefan Swiezawski, August 20, 1965, on the occasion of the appearance of their book *La Philosophie à l'heure du concile* (Paris: Sociéte d' Editions Internationales, 1965). Cf. *Nova et Vetera*, 1965, no. 4, pp. 242–249.

tried to express in explicit detail how much I agree with you on all the great themes which you treat and on all the great perspectives in which you have taken your positions. I must limit myself therefore to a few remarks or commentaries in the margins of your text, about certain points which struck me with particular force.

I like very much what you say about the historical plurality of *philosophies* and the essential unity of *philosophy*,—this seems to me to be fundamental. The error of many today (of my friend Etienne Borne, for example) is to believe that there is question of a pluralism that is necessary *de jure*, as if no doctrine were capable of being "true," that is to say sufficiently well grounded in order to grow ever in truth (not only on its own, but also by profiting from other doctrines). It is a question of a *de facto* pluralism, but one that is *inevitable*, given human nature. That "Thomism" may not be synonymous with "philosophia perennis" is true in the sense in which you speak. But can it not be said also that Thomism is the "philosophia perennis" *as it is doctrinally organized*, so as to assimilate endlessly the truths present in other philosophies that are less complete and more eager to discover something new than to carry out the work of integration in the truth?

"Every Christian is a theologian just as every man is a philosopher" (p. 70). How true this is! And it illuminates with an indispensable light that "advancement of the laity" which we hear so much about today, and rightly so without any doubt, but on condition that it mean above all the call of the laity to the fullness of Christian life, and first and foremost in the order of *intelligence* and in the order of *contemplation*. While for many it seems to mean a simple call to Christian *temporal action*, something that would end up in a new kind of clericalism, in which, not the Prince or the State, but the laity in its ensemble, would become the temporal instrument of a clergy convinced (at least subconsciously) of what Conrad of Megenburg expressed in such savory fashion.[2]

It seems to me that what you say of the primacy of the intuition or contemplation of existential being characterizes exactly what Thomism is *in its essence*. But does this not entail a distinctive *property* (and one more visible to men) which I would like to call the *openness* of Thomism to every reality, wherever it may be found, and to every truth, whatever its source. In this sense, Thomism is the only doctrine which is not the work of *one man*, but that of all human generations, a work gradually taking organized shape, thanks to geniuses like Aristotle and St. Thomas, and destined to grow forever. Whereas each "modern" doctrine appears as the doctrine of *one man*, closed in on itself and excluding (instead of assimilating progressively) the true elements present in other doctrines.

Another remark relates to what you say so rightly (p. 139) of the philosophical intuitions of St. Thomas. The misfortune of ordinary Scholastic teaching,

---

2   "Genus laicorum est populus ignarus. . . . Debet regi a clero, quoniam sapientis est regere . . ." (p. 115)

and above all of the manuals, has been to neglect in actual practice this essential intuitive element, and to replace it from the start by a pseudo-dialectics of concepts and formulas. Nothing can be done as long as the intellect has not *seen*, as long as the philosopher, or the apprentice-philosopher has not had the intellectual intuition of being. From this point of view I might point out the pedagogical value of a year of initiation into philosophy centered entirely on the necessity of leading the mind to the intuition of being and of those other fundamental intuitions which are the life of Thomist philosophy.

Finally there is a particularly delicate question which underlies the preoccupations of many of the Fathers of the Council. It comes from the fact that philosophy is essentially a work of freedom, and that no *human* doctrine (and this is the case for theology itself, even though it is rooted in the faith) can be *imposed* on minds by the Magisterium of the Church. [At this point Maritain repeats almost verbatim what he said in Part IV (The Popes and St. Thomas Aquinas) about freedom of research in philosophy and theology and the imposition of Thomism by way of authority with all the harmful effects of such an imposition. He then concludes.] I have no particular sympathy for Canon 1366-2, requiring that professors treat philosophical and theological matters *ad Angelici Doctoris rationem, doctrinam et principia.* However, since this canon exists, it would clearly be deplorable to seek its abrogation, for this would give rise to the worst misunderstandings and would seem to deny the very preference of the Church. But one could interpret this canon as expressing a wish (*I am, like St. Thomas, the contemplative of being!* 3).[3]

I am thinking here of much more of *research* than of teaching. Would it not be best to explain to professors that they must not confuse their research with their teaching and that, in theology especially, if they have not *seen* the truth of Thomism, they should be faithful at least to those principles and those great truths formulated by St. Thomas, but which are "supra-Thomist," and which the magisterium has made its own. And if they feel themselves incapable of this, they should seek employment in some other profession than teaching.

So let us not forget that, as Plato said, "Beautiful things are difficult." Given human nature and the sin of Adam, it cannot be imagined that all professors of philosophy and theology will experience the intuition of being and, turning toward St. Thomas, perceive in his eyes the light of truth. Undoubtedly those who receive this gift will always remain relatively small in number. The main thing is that they be there and that they bear testimony.

Then another problem arises immediately. All you have written, with such great competence and from such an illuminating experience about the necessity of a thorough reorganization of the teaching of philosophy (and theology) in Catholic universities (the importance of *seminars*, etc.) is right on the mark. But if what I have just pointed out is correct it must be added that, with regard

---

3   "To the question: *Sector Thomas, who are you?* today he ends up replying: *Like St. Thomas, I am a contemplative of being.*" (p. 109)

to St. Thomas in particular, the perspective of the official *organization* of studies, however indispensable it may be, remains insufficient. A crucial role must also be accorded to free initiatives, which therefore do not enter into a curriculum that is fit for everyone, but which, because they answer profound needs of the human soul, can be undertaken by certain individuals (both priests and laymen) and by certain groups.

Let me give you an example. Quite recently a small group of students at the Sorbonne asked our friend Olivier Lacombe to introduce them, in some informal private lectures, to the thought of St. Thomas. These *causeries* went very well and should certainly be encouraged and developed. This is the kind of free initiatives I spoke of. And it is important to point out here that it is at the request of students that the whole thing got under way—the Christian soul has such a thirst for philosophical and theological truth that it will one day or another make itself known.

If we want to push these considerations further, it seems to me that we would have to add that the work accomplished by St. Thomas, and the gifts he received, are the greatest charismatic gift that God has bestowed on His Church. And speaking more generally, the fact that human intelligence produces either works of truth in philosophy and theology or works of beauty in art and poetry, so elevated by gifts from on high that they can help souls enter into the depths of the supernatural life, supposes charismatic gifts of far greater importance than the gift of tongues or even healing the sick (and these are gifts, which like all charismatic gifts, come without having asked permission and which procure for those who receive some participation in them a privileged chance to feel their own immeasurable misery, to accept blows and be obliged to embrace the Cross. This question of charisma which we have brought up is a very real one but one that goes counter to the organizational mania of our technocratic age.

Evidently these charisma should be subject to some control by the Teaching Church. In particular those free initiatives among the Thomists that the Church needs so much ought to sustain certain organic relations with that official teaching which is the general responsibility of the hierarchy. It is still a fact though that in themselves they are of another order than the teaching. Particular areas of freedom must be permitted where the initiative does not come from the hierarchy. I have no doubt that in heaven St. Thomas takes personal care of his doctrine on earth (amid all the avatars you spoke about).

P.S.—There are still a few small points of detail I hope you will permit me to mention quickly.

1. You have correctly pointed out that the insistence of Gilson on the existential perspective of Thomist came chronologically *before* the invasion of contemporary existentialism. The same can be said of myself. It was in studying St. Thomas in depth that these things became apparent to me, and this has

nothing to do with some kind of adaptation or other to the existentialist fashion.

2. Your severity with regard to Cajetan is expressed with a nuance and moderation that make me grateful to you. You know that my position with regard to the great commentators is not the same as Gilson's. They are far from being infallible and have often hardened our differences. I gladly recognize the serious deficiencies of Cajetan. But it remains my position that these great minds (and especially John of St. Thomas—from whom on occasion though I do not hesitate to separate myself) are like very precious optical instruments which enable us to *see much more clearly* certain depths of St. Thomas' thought (even though other depths are given short shrift by them).

3. Natural Law. It seems to me that it might be advisable to make a bit more precise what you say on p. 64. "Metaphysics is the foundation of natural law, starting with moral law and the moral conscience . . ." I believe that metaphysics and moral philosophy afford us—and this is of capital importance—the *reflexive justification* of natural law. But it seems important to me to note explicitly that natural law is not a conclusion deduced from philosophy. It is also natural in the sense that it is *naturally known,* as it were by an instinct of the intelligence, in other words by connaturality (hence the imperfections of its formulations among primitive men and the constant progress of these formulations in the course of human history). Let me point out that this is a point I tried to examine thoroughly in my (as yet unpublished) lectures at Princeton.

4. You seem to be saying (perhaps I have misunderstood you) that, since philosophy as such is by its very nature a work of freedom, no philosophical thesis can incur the condemnation of the Church. I agree completely that there are perhaps much better means (will they ever be found?) than "condemnation" and anathema to put minds en guard against error. This function of calling attention to a danger nevertheless remains a necessary one. And if a theological thesis can be the occasion of calling attention to a danger, why not a philosophical thesis as well, if either of them is incompatible with revealed dogma? There is question here of two human sciences but sciences which touch on certain truths in a deposit for which the Church is responsible.

Let me make use here of a kind of Chestertonian paradox. If I had to choose between a period when one of my sentences (either because it was in error or because it was misunderstood) ran the risk of having me burned at the stake or a period when I could say absolutely anything at all without incurring absolutely any risk whatsoever, I would think that the first period, as barbarous as it might be, would show more honor to the intellect than the second and to the importance of what the intellect offers to the world.

Please do not take me for an enemy of freedom because of this little tirade. The fact remains that "religious freedom" is absolute only with regard to the State. . . . (Yet the State still has the right to dissolve sects practicing murder, collective suicide or collective debauchery.) With regard to the Church, from the moment that I have freely opted for its creed, I am bound by that creed, unless I decide to abandon the Catholic Faith and leave the Church . . .

CHAPTER V
ON METAPHYSICS (III)

DIVINE ASEITY[1]

IF WE CONSIDER THE DEVELOPMENT of Cartesian thought, can it not be said in the final analysis that in the tradition of a great metaphysical idealism like Fichte's, the God of Descartes appears logically after two centuries as an existence without an essence, as a pure faceless "I" who posits himself by his own will, in positing becoming.

According to one of its aspects, one of the "cuttings" of Descartes' thought, the peremptory reason the divine essence is properly inaccessible to reason, would then be that, according to the secret virtualities of Cartesian thought, God has no essence or nature. God is nothing more than Existence and Efficiency. That the Cartesian God is an existence without essence is so true that the ideal essences themselves are an expression of His creative freedom. Not finding in Himself the reason for things, if I may put it this way, God creates this reason for things arbitrarily. He is the efficient cause, the creative cause of intelligible necessities, just as He is the creative cause of the world, just as He is finally the cause of his own being, of His own existence. God could have made mountains without valleys and square circles. The intelligible necessities implied in the essence of the circle and of the mountain were for Descartes the work of God's creative freedom and not a created participation in the necessary essence of God as He sees it from all eternity.

I just now referred to Fichte. With Hegel we have an idea which posits itself and develops dialectically. In this case we cannot say that we are in the presence of an existence without an essence nor of a freedom without a nature; on the contrary there is question of an idea—an "essence"—which will provide everything through its self-development; but the existential thrust, if I may use this term, is transmitted in this case *inside* the essence. Now this is intrinsically contradictory, antinomic, since absolutely undetermined being is identical to non-being, and so Hegel's famous dialectical development comes into play. And it is thanks to this development that existence under the various types of becoming—existence which henceforth is a becoming—is reintroduced into essence itself and into logic (shattering both of them).

On the other hand, if we consider now forms of idealism that are not as

---

1   Editor's footnote: *Nova et Vetera*, 1967, No. 3 (pp. 189–206). This study first appeared in Toronto, in *Medieval Studies* 5, 1943, pp. 39–50.

grandiosely metaphysical as that of Hegel and Fichte, but rather anti-ontologi-cal, we can say, along with Mr. Brunschvicg, for example, that these forms of idealism are characterized as refusing any nature and any structure or any essence to thought, knowing thought being conceived on the model of moral freedom and as advancing from discovery to discovery, from invention to invention, but itself being without form, without structure. We could say that this is an existence without essence, a god without a face.

Finally, if we consider certain anti-idealist reactions with ontological ten-dencies, as that of Mr. Louis Lavelle, we see in his book on "Act" that, without giving a systematic value, I believe, to the expression, calls God in passing "a freedom without a nature." In his case I believe it is no more than a word uttered in passing; I do not think it has here any systematic doctrinal meaning. I imagine that his way of speaking depends rather on the acceptance of the idea of nature understood univocally, in the sense of those natures we know here below. This would be quite an affair to work out; many philosophers today do not grasp the analogical scope of the word *nature* and reduce nature to material nature and in this case it is logical to refuse it to God.

But enough of this parenthesis. I was saying that there is a philosophical line which begins with Descartes, and which goes in the direction of a certain *libertisme*, represented by Secrétan, Lequier (and perhaps, according to an entirely different spirit, Fichte also depends on Descartes from this point of view). At the end of this *libertistic* line we find the idea that God exists *because He wills it*. This is the extreme limit of the notion of *causa sui* when it is carried over to pure Act, and in this acceptation the line of the freedom of spontaneity is abandoned in order to pass over to that of the freedom of choice. This is an extremist way of understanding the pure actuality of God while refusing Him an essence or a nature properly so called. God exists through His freedom, or He exists as an absolute fullness of freedom, the word *freedom* being taken in the sense of freedom of choice, of absence of necessity; that is to say, that God, if it can be expressed in this way, is at the summit, at the highest point of the absence of necessity, *he exists without any necessity whatsoever*, by a pure act of free will; consequently He could annihilate Himself—we must surely go that far!—just as He could make mountains without valleys and square circles. This is one of the extremes to which we are led by this notion of existence without essence considered as characterizing pure Act.

For Thomists the problems which I have just indicated never existed; this tendency is completely absent among them. Their entire metaphysics was so steeped in the analogicity of being that they could not even imagine as possible the thought that the notion of essence, an essentially analogical notion, could be refused to God.

Yet, at certain moments we find in them something which *resembles* this idea, but which in reality has a very different meaning. What we do find among them is an affirmation of a general significance, of universal extension, which does not apply exclusively to the notion of essence, but to all the notions that can be predicated of God. It is the theme of general and universal extension which maintains that what is called apophatic or negative theology is superior to what is called cataphatic or affirmative theology. All of which in the final analysis means that, in the thought of Scholastic writers, mystical theology, by way of unitive contemplation, is superior to concepts and superior to theology *per modum cognitionis*, by way of knowledge.

This position signifies in general that even the perfections which exist in God in a formal-eminent way, that is to say while retaining in Him their typical and proper intelligibility, such as goodness, intelligence, wisdom, etc., do not exist in Him according to the mode in which we know them and in which they exist in things. And so it is equally true, or even truer in this sense, to deny them to God as to affirm them of Him. This is a thesis which Denis the Areopagite had made classical in the Middle Ages.

One could look for example at that text of the *Summa Theologiae* in which one of the objections recalls the doctrine of Denis according to which it is truer to refuse all these names like goodness, wisdom, etc., to God than to attribute them to Him. And St. Thomas replies[2] that "Denis said that these names must be denied to God because what is signified by each name does not fit God according to the mode of signification of that name, but according to a better mode."

According to this understanding of the *mode of signification*, it is proper to refuse even these perfections to the divine being, that is to say, to know God by way of an "ignorance" which introduces the intelligence itself into the transcendence of that mode according to which these perfections exist in God—a knowledge by way of ignorance which by this very fact can no longer proceed through concepts, that is to say, by attributing to God this or that perfection—and which is better than notional and rational knowledge, better than abstract theological constructs or better than knowledge by way of knowing.

This doctrine is true, according to the Ancients, even with regard to *existence*. And yet St. Thomas declares at each instant that God is *ipsum esse subsistens*. If we consider the *mode* according to which the word and the concept "to exist" signifies its object, then that *mode* which itself corresponds to the mode, to the way by which the things we know exist, a knowledge of such a kind that it surpasses the attribution of existence to God, is the supreme knowledge we can acquire of Him, or rather receive from Him by virtue of our union with Him.

Here is a text from Book I of the *Commentary on the Sentences*:[3] "When we proceed toward God by way of remotion [the two other ways are those of causality and eminence], we deny Him in the first place corporeal things, and

---

2   Ia, q. 13, a. 3, ad 2.

3   *Sent.* Lib. I, dist. viii, q. 1, a. 1, ad 4.

in the second place intellectual things as well, according as these attributes are found in creatures, like goodness and wisdom. . . ." He is good, but not in the way things are good; He is wise, but not in the way creatures are wise." So divine existence alone remains in our intellect, and nothing else, *quia est*, that He exists. This is all that is left notionally in our intelligence. "This is why He is there as if in a kind of confusion. But at the ultimate level, we deny to God existence itself according as it exists in creatures; it is then that He dwells in a kind of darkness of ignorance, according to which, as much as it is proper to our condition *in via*, we are most perfectly united with God, as Denis says, and this is the darkness in which God is said to dwell." It is evident then that this doctrine applies just as much to *esse* as to the other perfections.

However, St. Thomas always considered *esse*—the act of existence considered this time in its analogical transcendence and no longer according to the mode of signification of the word *to exist*—as the formal constitutive (according to our manner of conceiving) of the divine nature.

Among others there is the following text taken from the *Commentaries on the Book of Causes*:[4] "According to the Platonists the first cause is above being, *supra ens*, insofar as the essence of goodness and of unity, which according to them is the first cause, surpasses separated being itself, *ipsum ens separatum*." Even in the case of being itself, it was not from the perspective of the act of being, of *esse*, that the Platonists conceived it; it was from the perspective (a perspective in truth limited to what is created) of *ens*, of something "be-ing," of something "having existence." And it is logical that they should put the good and the one above something that is "be-ing"; for the idea of *ens* is no longer that of the *good* and the *one*. And in separating it we leave it as it is. The separated *ens* is not *goodness*, and goodness will always be above it. Because the separated *ens* (like the *separated* good or the *separated* one!) is the created that has been sublimated; it is not the uncreated; it is not God. God is subsistent *esse*, which implies all other perfections in pure act. According to the Platonists God is *supra ens* because the separated Good is above the separated Existent. "But according to the truth of things, the first cause is *supra ens*, above the existent, inasmuch as it is infinite existence itself, *ipsum esse infinitum*."

In another text of St. Thomas there is a very beautiful expression of this general doctrine:[5] "What I call the 'act of existing' is the actuality of all acts, and for this reason it is the perfection of all perfections—*hoc quod dico esse est actualitas omnium actuum et propter hoc est perfectio omnium perfectionum*." We could examine other texts and always find the same teaching: "The highest degree of human knowledge of God is to know that one does not know God, *quod sciat se Deum nescire*, inasmuch as one knows that what God is exceeds the totality of even those things we attain of Him by our intelligence."[6]

---

4   *Expositio super Librum de Causis*, lect. VI.

5   *De Potentia*, q. VII, a. 2, ad 9.

6   *De Potentia*, q. VII, a. 5, ad 14.

Likewise in the *Commentary on the Divine Names*: "This is what it means to know God: to realize that concerning God we do not know what His essence is. . . . And so, he who knows God in such a state of knowledge is illumined by the very depths of divine wisdom which we have no way to fathom."[7] Knowledge, not by concepts, but by illumination; here St. Thomas is certainly thinking of mystical knowledge, and not of theology by mode of rational knowledge. "Indeed our perception that God is above all things, not only those things which exist, but even those things we can arrive at by our intelligence, comes for us from the incomprehensible depths of divine wisdom.[8] And so, "at the very highest point of our knowledge we know God as unknown." These are the words of Denys in his *Mystical Theology* which are echoed by St. Thomas: "*In finem nostrae cognitionis Deum tanquam ignotum cognoscimus.*" The same teaching is found in the *Summa contra Gentiles*:[9] "And this is the peak and highest perfection of our knowledge in this life, as Denys says in his *Mystical Theology*, that we are united to God as the unknown."

This does not mean of course that in the order of cataphatic theology, of theology as doctrine where we proceed by concepts and by notions, we must deny God existence, goodness, intelligence, etc. This doctrine in no sense has the slightest claim whatever to any validity as some form of agnosticism. It affirms only that whatever we know validly and certainly of God still remains infinitely below Him.

And so, whatever we have just said about all the divine perfections, goodness, intelligence, justice, wisdom, mercy, and even the divine *esse*, we must evidently say of his essence as well. There is no cause for surprise that the scholastics have said of His *essentia* what they said of His *esse*, and this is why Albert the Great could say: "I maintain: God is an essence; but immediately and more strongly I deny it, saying: God is not an essence since He is not among those things which are defined for us by genus, difference and number."[10] That is to say, we must refuse God the notion of essence, and we must exclude it from God insofar as there is question of the way in which the word *essence* receives its signification and of the way in which it is properly applied to created things from which we get our notion of essence. This is why Albert the Great continues: "And after that, from this opposition I infer: God is an essence above every essence, and, proceeding in this way, my intelligence is established in the infinite and drowns itself there."[11]

There is no question whatever of conceiving God as an existence without an essence, even though he may seem to say this, if one does not pay close

---

7   Cap. VII, lect. 4.

8   *Ibid.*

9   *Contra Gentiles*, Lib. III, cap. 49.

10   Ia, tract. iii, q. 13, membrum 1.

11   *Ibid.*

attention, if one takes note only of the expression he used: "And I deny it more strongly, saying: God is not an essence." He does not say this in the sense in which modern philosophers have thought it. There is question here of a teaching which has an absolutely general application, which concerns all divine perfections, all notions that we can express about God, and which refers back to the superiority of apophatic or negative theology over cataphatic or affirmative theology.

We find similar texts among the Fathers of the Church. St. John Damascene, for example: "Concerning God, it is impossible for us to say what He is in Himself; it is more exact to speak of Him by the exclusion of everything else. He is in fact nothing of what exists. Not that He does not exist in any way, but because He is above everything that is, above being itself."[12] St. Basil says: "The works of God are diverse, but His essence is simple. It is by His works that we say we know God, but we cannot pretend to rise to His essence." If we took this sentence out of context, we could claim that for St. Basil too God is an existence without essence. But he continues: "If the operations of God do actually come down to us, His essence remains beyond our reach; to know that we cannot grasp it, this is the knowledge that we have of it."[13] From the instant they say that God's essence is above our thoughts and beyond our reach, they attribute to Him a clearly determined essence.

Throughout the whole tradition of Christian philosophy, the notion of essence in theodicy and in theology has such importance that beatitude itself consists in seeing the divine essence, in knowing God in His essence.

II

What we have just discussed is the question of knowing whether God's privilege of existing without any kind of potentiality must be translated by the characteristically Thomist formula: "In God existence and essence are identical," the essence of God is to exist, or on the contrary, by another formula which at first glance might seem to be saying the same thing, but which in reality is fundamentally different: "God has no essence," God is an existence without an essence, an act of existing, an *esse*, without *essentia*.

I would like to point out here that the formula in question: "God has no essence," since the time of Descartes, has assumed great importance in modern thought, even though Descartes himself did not specifically propose it. This formula is already found among the Ancients, and St. Thomas knew it. Here is what he said in his opusculum *De Ente et Essentia*: "After the considerations expounded in the preceding chapters, we see how essence is found in different beings (or at the different degrees of being). Indeed, in substances we find a

---

12   *De Fide Orthodoxa*, I, 4 (PG 94, 800).

13   *Letter I to Amphilocus* (PG 32, 869).

three-fold way of having an essence. The first mode is that of God whose essence is His very act of existing, and this is why there are certain philosophers who said that God has no quiddity or essence," and St. Thomas adds immediately: "because His essence is nothing else than His existence."[14] Who are these *aliqui philosophi*, these certain philosophers who said that God has no quiddity or essence? In his commentary on *De Ente et Essentia*, Cajetan writes: "There is question here of certain Platonists," he does not become more specific. "They say that God has no essence and that He is a pure existence, *quasi pura existentia sit*."[15] Rather than of Platonists, there is question of Arab philosophers and in particular of Avicenna, as Father Roland-Gosselin points out in his edition of *De Ente et Essentia*.[16] In the metaphysics of Avicenna we find the following very characteristic formulas: "Every being which has a quiddity (every being which has an essence) is caused . . . and the first being has no quiddity (has no essence)."[17] A little further on: "It is manifest that the First Being has no genus nor any quiddity." And again: "The universe has a principle which is necessarily *esse*, pure existence not contained under any genus or under any definition . . . free from quality, from quantity and *from quiddity*."[18] For Avicenna it is the same thing to say that God is without essence and to say that He is not definable, not contained under any definition, or again that He is not contained in a genus. The consequence of this is that for Avicenna the word essence or quiddity designates an element of resemblance or if you prefer an intelligible stuff which is found univocally in a number of realities, such as the generic nature and the specific nature, and hence an intelligible stuff distinct from *esse*, distinct from the act of existing.

On this last point St. Thomas agrees with Avicenna; it is the doctrine which he has made classic; there is a real distinction between *essentia* and *esse*, between essence and the act of existing; wherever *essentia* is enclosed within a genus, there is a single nature univocally common to several.

These remarks explain for us the formulas that Avicenna used a moment ago. For him the word *essentia* connotes a nature *enclosed within a genus*; and if the word *essentia* has this meaning, then it must be said that God has no essence; it is like saying that God is not enclosed within a genus, God has no generic essence, no specific essence.

These considerations help us to understand as well why St. Thomas, in the text of *De Ente* which I cited, while alluding to "certain philosophers" who say that "God has no quiddity or essence," seems immediately to excuse that

---

14   *De Ente et Essentia*, at the beginning of Chapter 6; this sixth chapter of the old editions has become Chapter 5 in the edition established by Father M.-D. Roland-Gosselin (Kain, Belgium: Le Saulchoir, 1926).

15   Ed. M.-M. Laurent (Turin, 1934), p. 170.

16   *Loc. cit.*

17   Lib. VIII, cap. 4.

18   Lib. IX, cap. 1.

formula, which he appears to consider as a simple hyperbole of language, which signifies nothing else than *ejus essentia est suum esse*. And further on in the same chapter St. Thomas tells us that "God is only existence, *Deus est esse tantum* . . . and it is by the very purity of this existence that He is distinct from every other existence," which is the act of an essence distinct from its existence. And this is why, "although being only existence," He possesses all the other perfections and all the other "nobilities" which are in things, but under a more excellent mode. When he tells us: "God is *tantum esse*, only existence," he means: God has no other essence than His existence, or again, as he says in the *Commentaries on the Sentences*, his existence is his quiddity, "*esse suum est quidditas sua.*"[19]

I come now to the discussion to which these pages are consecrated. If we give to the expression *"Deus est esse tantum"* (God is only an existent, God is only the act of existing) a sense of *exclusion* in relation to the notion of essence, if the expression no longer signifies: God has no other essence than to exist, but signifies rather in the full force of the term: God has no essence, God is an existence without an essence, then we have a formula which links up with many more or less secret, more or less hidden tendencies of modern metaphysics; but then it is also a formula which deserves a special criticism because it is completely erroneous.

What kinds of valid criticisms can we offer to contradict the assertion: God is an existence without an essence? The first criticism is that such a proposition is due to a univocal conception of *nature* or of *essence*. This is so true that in the created order itself certain philosophers, as we noted at the beginning of this study, already deny a nature to anything spiritual. They form for themselves an idea of nature or essence so univocal that their notion has application only to natures composed of matter and form, to natures which contain materiality. If this is so, if materiality is necessarily and intrinsically implied by the notion of essence or nature, we would have to say that spirits do not have natures, or that spirit does not have any nature. And it is quite clear that if we refuse an essence to created spirits or to the created spirit, with all the more reason we would have to refuse it to God.

What does this notion of nature or essence mean? Let us go back to *De Ente et Essentia*; there we find some very interesting explanations by St. Thomas himself. He tells us[20] that "the Philosopher, in the fifth book of the *Metaphysics*, teaches that being (*ens*) expresses itself in two ways. In the first way when it is divided according to the ten categories; in the second way when it signifies the truth of a proposition. And in this second sense, we can give the name being (*ens*) to anything about which we can form an affirmative proposition, even if the object of thought in question posits nothing in things. In this way we can give the name beings (*entia*) even to privations and negations." In fact

19   *Sent.* Lib. I, dist. viii, q. 4, a. 2.

20   *De Ente et Essentia*, cap. 1.

we can form true propositions about beings of reason such as privations and negations. We can say that the affirmation is opposed to the negation, and that blindness is in the eye. "But on the other hand, in the first sense, only that which posits something in extra-mental existence can be called being (*ens*). In this first sense, blindness and beings of reason are not beings (*non sunt entia*)." After positing this, St. Thomas continues: "The name essence is not taken from being understood in the second sense; as a matter of fact privations are called beings in the second sense (they are called beings of reason) and they have no essence. But the notion of essence is taken from being understood in the first sense, and this is why the Commentator says in the same place: Being understood in the first sense is that which signifies the essence of the thing. And because being understood in this sense is divided into the ten categories, the word essence must signify something common to all those natures by which diverse beings find their place in diverse genera and species. Thus it is that humanity is the essence of man."

And so we see St. Thomas immediately affirm the analogicity of the notion of essence, since the notion of essence is found throughout the ten categories of Aristotle; if it were enclosed in a genus, it would be enclosed in one of these ten categories, which is proof that it is not a predicamental, but an analogical notion.

"And," he continues,[21] "because that by which a thing is constituted in its proper genus or in its proper species, is that which is signified by the definition indicating what the thing is, it follows that the name essence has been changed by the philosophers into quiddity. This is what Aristotle frequently calls the *quod quid erat esse*, which we can translate as the intelligible constitutive, *hoc per quod aliquid habet esse quid*. It can also be called form insofar as the certitude and the intelligible value of each thing is signified by the word form," because form is the reason for the knowability and the certitude of things. "And in the third place it is also called nature," inasmuch as the essence is ordered "to the proper operation of the thing."

And so *nature* signifies essence insofar as it is ordered toward operation; *quiddity* signifies essence insofar as it is the intelligible constitutive capable of being defined, and finally the word *essence* itself is used insofar as through it and in it the being has existence, "*Essentia dicitur secundum quod per eam et in ea ens habet esse.*"

So from the outset St. Thomas, following Aristotle, shows us that the notion of essence is an analogical notion, common to the ten predicaments; and it can therefore emigrate (if I can use this term) all the way to the very cause of being, it remains valid not only when applied to created being, but to uncreated being as well which is beyond any human definition, but which is capable of uttering itself to itself. Hence, if someone says that God has no essence, it is because he

---

21   *Ibid.*

has adopted a univocal conception of essence, whereas this is an essentially analogical notion.

Let us note here in passing that another word, the word *substance*, creates even more difficulties for St. Thomas. The word *substance* cannot be as immediately, or as easily freed from its original reference to created being. Why? Because the word *substance* properly designates one of the predicaments, the very first, one of the ultimate genera. To the question,[22] "Is God in the predicament of the substance?" St. Thomas answers that He is not. God is above any predicament. God is outside every predicament or every genus, and a little further on he explains[23] that though God is absolutely not an accident, yet He cannot be properly called a substance for two reasons: because the word substance comes from *substare*—to stand under accidents—and thus is correlative of accident; and in the second place because substance signifies a quiddity, an essence which is other than its existence.

If we take the word *substance* in its strictest and most proper sense, it signifies an essence which is other than its existence, it is enclosed in the first predicament, it cannot be applied to God, it is a division of created being. "If, however, we do not insist on this most proper sense of the word substance, we can say in a broad sense that God is substance, which then means above every created substance, considering only what perfection there is in the substance, such as not existing in another, etc." ". . . And so, because of the fundamentally different way in which substance is attributed to God and to creatures, this word is used not univocally, but analogically of God and of creatures."[24] The same teaching is found in the *Summa Theologiae*:[25] "The word substance does not mean only that which exists of itself; because existence cannot determine a genus [whereas substance is a category]; the word substance signifies an essence which properly exists *per se, non in aliud*; this existence, however, is not the very essence of the substance. [The word *substance*, taken in its most proper sense, refers to an essence distinct from its existence.] So it is evident that God is not in the genus of substance." But further on, in treating the Trinity, when there is question of showing that the word person can be affirmed of God, St. Thomas resorts to the notion of substance, this time in a wider sense, since person is defined: "*rationalis naturae individua substantia*"—an individual substance of a rational nature. In this case: "The word substance is properly used of God inasmuch as signifies something that exists of itself, *existere per se*,"[26] inasmuch as it has been stripped of its strictest meaning, according to which it designates an essence distinct from its existence.

---

22   *Sent.* Lib. I, dist. viii, q. 4, a. 2.

23   *Ibid.* ad 1.

24   *Ibid.*

25   Ia, q. 3, a. 5, ad 1.

26   Ia, q. 29, a. 3. ad 4.

We see then that the word *substance* is transferable to God; the notion of substance is transferable to God by a special operation of purification and of extension, if I may put it this way, which "transcendentalizes" and makes analogous a notion that was originally univocal, since originally, in the most proper sense, this word designates a category, a supreme genus. Parenthetically, the same can be said of the notion of relation which originally and properly designates one of the categories and which however can be transcendentalized in order to be transferred to God Himself, in whom it applies to the Divine Persons.

The notion of essence, to the contrary, is from the very first like being itself, analogous and transcendental, and if this analogous and transcendental character of the notion of essence is well understood, we see immediately that the notion of essence or nature—what a thing is, or the intelligible constitutive of a being—does not include *necessarily* either matter or potentiality. If it did of necessity include matter, the notion of essence would refer to natures that are determined *ad unum*, in the sense that they would all be determined to *a particular effect*, as is the case with material natures; and this would be so according to the *conditions of construction* of these natures. In this particular sense the first analogate of the word *essence*, as far as our way of knowing is concerned, would refer to material things which, as a matter of fact, are determined to a particular effect by reason of their conditions of construction. But if we move over to spirits, to spiritual natures, the notion of nature no longer signifies a being determined to a particular effect, but a being determined to a certain infinite, since the intellectual nature is determined to being itself, and this is an infinite ocean, not a particular effect. In the same way the will is determined to the good. Here the notion of determination *ad unum* is again present but in a completely analogical way. There is a transfiguration when we pass from the determination *ad unum* of a material nature to the determination *ad unum* of the intelligence or of the will. And this is so, not according to the conditions of their constructions, but according to their relation to the object, that the intelligence and the will are determined.

The notion of essence or of nature does not necessarily include matter, nor does it necessarily include potentiality. It is only insofar as it is created that it signifies potency. This is an absolutely necessary condition of every *created* essence, to be potency with regard to existence.

This fundamental thesis of St. Thomas, that essence in all created things is their potency with regard to existence, must not prevent us from seeing another aspect of things, namely that essence is fundamentally act and perfection; it is an act, it is a perfection, it is the intelligible constitutive of things; it is an act, it is a perfection which is still a potency in relation to another act, in relation to the act of existing.

Let us recall here the words of St. Thomas in *De Potentia* which we have already cited: "What I call being or existence, *hoc quod dico esse*, is the actuality of all acts, *actualitas omnium actuum* [he does not say *omnium potentiarum*], and for this reason it is the perfection of *all perfections*."[27] And let us note that it is the same for other perfections, such as intelligence and will, which in creatures imply potentiality; these are "operative potencies,"—this very expression, even though in this case it refers to energies and activities, helps us understand that something potential is still present in them, that they are not their very act itself of intellection or volition. There is a very real distinction between *intellectus* and *intellectio*, between *voluntas* and *volitio*. So the relation of essence to existence in creatures is precisely the same as the relation of *intellectus* to *intelligere* or of *voluntas* to *velle*. The relation of the intellectual faculty to this kind of existence or superexistence in act which intellection is, is a relation of potency to act in creatures.

However we say that in God there is *intellectus* in the same way as there is *intelligere*, there is intelligence in the same way as there is intellection, there is will in the same way as there is volition. In God there is no distinction, not even a virtual one, between *intellectus* and *intellectio*; in God there is no distinction, not even a virtual one, between *voluntas* and *velle*, precisely because in creatures these same things are distinct according to potency and act. Therefore in God there is nothing on which to base even a minor virtual distinction between *voluntas* and *velle* or between *intellectus* and *intelligere*. In God there is not even a minor virtual distinction between these particular things; rather *intellectus*, or the perfection designated by the word *intellectus*, and the perfection designated by the word *voluntas* are properly attributed to God in a formal and eminent way. And it is in exactly the same way that in God there is not even a minor virtual distinction between essence and existence; rather the notion of essence applies to God in a formal and eminent way. It cannot be said that God has no essence or that He is an existence without an essence. What must be said is that God has an essence which is the very infinity of existence *a se*.

Our first argument consists in pointing out that to refuse God an essence is to fabricate a univocal idea of *essence* or *quiddity*. The second argument consists in pointing out that this implies a univocal conception of *existence* itself, of the very act of existing, a univocity which is unthinkable and which goes against the intelligibility of that first intelligible which is being.

Let us note that every *esse* implies an *essentia*, every act of existence implies an essence, a *quod quid est*, an intelligible constitutive (since this is what an essence is. An *esse*, an act of existence without an essence, would be an *esse* without intelligibility). Let us go back here to all those discussions which concern the abstraction of being; it is not possible to make a perfect abstraction of *esse*, of existence, by putting aside every nature, every intelligible determination. One can think of animal without thinking confusedly of all the different species of animals; animality, realized *in the same manner* in all its different

---

27   *De Potentia*, q. VII, a. 2, ad. 9.

species, can be abstracted perfectly from the specific differences which are extrinsic to it: *perfecte praescindit a differentiis specificis;* univocal differences can be abstracted perfectly from their specific differences. But being itself, *ens* (described as "that whose very act is to exist"), cannot be abstracted perfectly from diverse beings, for in an implicit or confused way it envelops all those beings. Likewise, *esse*, the act of existing cannot be perfectly abstracted from the essences which exercise it, from the essences in which it is received, as a surface or a mathematical line can be abstracted from the extended material subject.

Here I believe there exists among certain philosophers what might be called a pseudo-mathematization of metaphysical concepts. hey conceive metaphysical concepts, for example the concept of *esse*, the notion of *esse*, as if this notion could be abstracted from its subjects in the same way and just as completely as a mathematical notion is abstracted from the material subject in which it is realized. This is to confuse the metaphysical order with the mathematical order and is to form a conception of *esse*, of existence itself, that is completely erroneous. More often than one would think, the proper intelligibility and the essential analogicity of the notion of existence can, in fact, be lost sight of, only to be replaced by a notion in which the imagination plays as much a role as the intelligence, by a notion of existence which, like mathematical notions, seeks its resolution in the imaginable; it is here then, in the imagination, that *esse* can be completely abstracted from its "inferiors," as we say in logic, and this is absolutely false.

III

To define existence, or *esse*, is evidently impossible, but when we attempt to describe it, we often say that it is *positio extra nihil*, outside of nothingness. By considering this expression we best realize the ambiguity, of the pseudo-mathematization I mentioned just a moment ago. This metaphysical position *extra nihil*, outside of nothingness, is altogether different from the position of a point in space—a mathematical position in which the point in question does not terminate or complete anything else and in which any point at all posited in this way is exactly the same as any other, except as regards its situation. *On the contrary*, in the case of existence, there is question of an effectuation which varies with the existing nature itself and which it receives from the first Being. Let us remember the words of St. Thomas:[28] *"Deus, simul dans esse, producit id quod esse recipit"*; at the same time that God gives existence, He produces that which receives existence. Let us say that the influx of God passing through the causes which produce a being causes that being *to exist*.

In other words, in an attempt to make this metaphysical idea more tangible,

---

28   *De Pot.*, q. III, a. 1, ad 17.

we could say that the nature of this being is run through completely by something transcendent which vivifies it, which "existentifies" it intrinsically, in such a way that the nature in question carries out of itself, and from the very depths of its self, the act of *esse*, the act of existing, as the proper perfection of its nature or essence. The act of existing is a certain energy, indeed the energy *par excellence*, and this is in no way evident when we picture existence to ourselves as the mathematical position of a point in space.

So therefore existence is received, but it is received as an *exercised activity*, as an act exercised by the essence, and that act is different according to the natures which exercise it. It is not a simple position in space, a pure repetition of the same thing in the eyes of the imagination which pictures one point and then another point, designated in space. An atom exists in a way that is not that of a living being. We could say that in the atom, as in every other being, existence is exercised, but not for itself. It is exercised by the individual substance and, so to speak, *of that substance* (in the sense that the existence of one atom is not that of another atom), but of that substance as part of the universe. It is not precisely "its own" (in the sense that it "belongs to" that substance or that it exists "for" that substance). The atom, a non-living body, participates in the *esse* of the universe, which, certainly, is not a single and unique *esse*, which is diversified in each corporal substance, but which in each case depends on all the others as causes of that existence (*concausae*) and is turned toward the whole. The very existence of the non-living is oriented toward the whole, destined for the whole, for the entire universe. Its action is oriented toward the outside, and the same can be said of its *esse*, to which the action is consecutive. The living being on the other hand exercises existence in a different way. The existence of the living being is not only of that living substance; it belongs to it and exists for it. Its *esse* without a doubt depends on the universe, but more and more, as one moves up the ladder of living beings and draws closer to the spirit, more and more it depends on the universe as *condition* (the universe furnishes the conditions of existence of the living being, especially of the corporeal-spiritual living being), less and less is the universe its *cause* properly speaking. The existence of the living being is oriented toward itself, to overflow afterwards toward the outside.

Spiritual writers like to use the comparison of a canal with the basin of a fountain. One should not be a canal pouring out the gifts of God which pass through it. Rather one should be a basin receiving His grace so that afterwards, when it has attained a certain fullness, it can pour that grace forth on others. This comparison has a value which is not solely spiritual; it also has a metaphysical value, and we can say that existence in non-living beings is symbolized by a canal; in living beings, the more they advance in the imma-nence of life and its activity, the more their existence takes on the form of a basin. The more existence is enriched within, the more internal intensity this existence then has to pour itself out, in such a way that the living being in question becomes capable of *giving itself.* It must be in possession of itself in order to be able to give itself.

These remarks were made to underline the fact that intelligible "existence," which is signified by a single word, in reality varies through all the stages of the ontological ladder. Things do not exist in the same way because each essence exercises existence in its own way and as the expression and the fundamental actuality of the ontological reserves that are typical of it. In other words, existence is not a univocal notion, but an analogical notion.

Pursuing this train of thought, we understand that if we imagined the pure Act as pure existence without a nature, without an essence, we would be led to all the impossibilities implied in the idea of the univocity of being, in the univocal conception of being; for then the infinite transcendence of God would be sought by hypothetically *dissociating esse* and *essentia* (since this view considers that of itself *essentia* necessarily implies potentiality, then in order to have a pure act it is necessary to have a pure existence, without essence). *Esse* is disjoined from *essentia*, existence from nature, any essence or nature is rejected, *but in order to preserve 'esse,'* in order to preserve the act of existing, I am speaking of the couple essence-existence, from which the first term has been dropped. So that in this view, *esse* is really thought of as infinitely enlarged, but which in the end is the same as the *esse* offered to our intelligence by things, which is still the *esse* with the mode of signifying that the concept of being has in our mind, but all the while supposing that the being so signified is infinitely extended, if I might put it this way, in a quantitative fashion. This is a false conception of analogy. Passage is made from one degree to another and to the highest degree along the same line. This is not analogy; this is univocity. M. Penido showed this very clearly in his book *Le Rôle de l'analogie en théologie dogmatique.*[29] He warned against this false conception of analogy.

An exact notion of analogy would escape anyone who saw things in the way I just described. And so, thinking he was ensuring the transcendence of God, he would in reality be attributing to Him the same *esse*, the same existence as that of things, but "infinitized." By virtue of its internal logic such a conception would imply a kind of emanationist position (the ultimate term of the secret tendency, stronger than the philosopher himself, of every univocist philosophy toward monism). The source of all things would be pictured as a pure *esse* without essence, which would multiply itself, pulverize itself by becoming the *esse* of numberless essences sprung from it.

The exact notion of analogy entails, and this is what is forgotten in the view I have described, an intrinsic, qualitative, not quantitative, transfiguration of the object of intellection; so that the signified of our concepts, the *significatum*, remains, but in God the mode of their signifying fails, without our knowing how. The *mode of signifying* of our concepts—a mode which we must of necessity continue to use because it is our mode of conceiving—remains

29   M. T. L. Penido, *Le Rôle de l'analogie en théologie dogmatique* (Paris, 1931).

essentially imperfect and deficient with regard to the signified object, when that signified object is God, the First Cause.

And this deficiency, this radical imperfection of the mode of signifying of our concepts, holds just as well for *esse*, for existence, as it does for *essentia*, for nature. Both objects of notion, while being realized formally in God (formally-eminently), are transfigured in God. They are formally in God, but transfigured in a way that we are absolutely incapable of representing to ourselves. It is in this sense that negative or apophatic theology is superior to affirmative or cataphatic theology because God is not like any of those things that exist, and once again, this holds true for *esse* itself as for goodness, justice, etc.

This transfiguration of the notion when it is applied to God holds just as well for the act of existing as for His nature. The notion of essence is just as formally-eminently proper to God as is that of existence. And we know God's existence like His essence, not as they are in themselves, but imperfectly and by analogy. In short, with regard to God, the infirmity as well as the solidity of the concept of *esse*, of existence, are the same as those of the concept of essence.

CHAPTER VI
ON THE PHILOSOPHY OF NATURE (I)

TOWARD A THOMIST IDEA OF EVOLUTION[1]

1. I HAVE GIVEN IN TODAY TO THE DESIRE we often experience to tell what we are thinking to those we love very much, even though our thoughts are in a very imperfect state. I would like to share with you (in four stages) a certain philosophical approach, which has occurred to me and which I think is correct and full of possibilities but of which I can offer no more than an elementary elaboration (years would be required to do this completely), by confronting it according to the means at my disposal with the most recent data of either paleontology or animal psychology. In any case, it seems clear to me that it is a philosophical basis and elucidation that are lacking in the present studies and discussions of the origin of man. I am persuaded that if we took hold of this affair *by the philosophical end of the stick*, we would see a whole pile of things cleared up, and we would see that a just and reasonable solution is not really so difficult to find.

To tell the truth, it is not one single conference, but four, that I intend to inflict on you.[2] Today's conference will be devoted to some lengthy preambles which I consider necessary. (A bit of the philosophy of nature will not do us any harm.) The more carefully worked-out views which I would like to propose to you on the origin of man will come in the second and third conferences. The fourth will be dedicated to points of view where there will be no lack of hypothetical and arbitrary elements—but the hypothetical and the arbitrary elements will be *honest* ones, I mean conscious of being so and proposed as such—on Evolution in general and on the state of man before and after the fall: views that are dependant on what I would like to call "le petit véhicule," or little wisdom, because there is no wisdom on the level of old peasants like me without a bit of laughter and humor.

BY WAY OF PREFACE

2. But first of all, by way of preface, in order to place ourselves in the perspective of *great* wisdom, this time, of that great and exalted theological

---

1   *Editor's footnote*: Conference given to the Little Brothers of Jesus in Toulouse on the 12th and 13th of January, 1967. Cf. *Nova et Vetera*, 1967, no. 2, pp. 87–136.

2   As a matter of fact, I have had neither the time nor the strength to prepare more than this one.

wisdom ("le grand véhicule"), I would like us to read together a few passages from the beginning of an admirable chapter of *Contra Gentiles*, lib. IV, chap. 11, where St. Thomas treats of the degrees in the hierarchy of different natures, the lowest degree being that of inanimate bodies, which produce something only by acting on each other (transitive action).

Immediately above inanimate bodies come plants, whose seed is produced from within, *ex interiori*. "This is the first degree of life, for living beings are those that move themselves to act" or that are endowed with an immanent activity.[3] And yet in the plant kingdom, where what proceeds from the interior emanates little by little toward the exterior, this life is imperfect: "In the end it is the flower which emanates from the tree, then the fruit, distinct from the tree, but still attached to it, but which once ripe separates itself completely from the tree, and falls to earth, where through its seed it produces another living plant. And the very principle of such an emanative process comes from without, for it is from the earth that the sap of the tree is nourished."

The level of life above that of plants is that level which belongs to the sensitive soul; what it causes to emanate doubtless comes from without, moving further and further into vital intimacy; the process moves from the external senses, which receive from without the form of the sensible thing, to the imagination, then to the treasury of the memory. If the beginning and the

---

3   A living being is one that is endowed with *immanent activity* or that is self-per-
     fecting. It is worthy of note that there is a correspondence between this philo-
     sophical definition (whose implications are infinitely vast but which apply first
     and foremost to living organisms) and the definition of organic life given by the
     eminent scholar Oparine—as if it were a reflection or translation of the other on
     the level of empiriological knowledge: "The particularity which qualitatively
     differentiates the life of all the other forms of movement in matter (and in
     particular of open non-organic systems) is the following: in living bodies,
     individual chemical reactions by the tens, indeed by the hundreds and thou-
     sands, whose ensemble makes up the metabolism, are, on the one hand, strictly
     coordinated in time and space and are combined in a continuous order of
     self-renewal, and, on the other hand, this order is unfailingly directed toward
     the self-preservation and self-reproduction of the entire living system in its
     ensemble; it is adapted in a very particular fashion to the mission of assuring the
     existence of the organism in the given conditions of its exterior milieu." (A.
     Oparine, *L'Origine et l'évolution de la vie* (Moscow: Ed. de la Paix, s. d.), pp. 12–13).
         Mister Oparine must certainly realize that such a pronouncement puts him
     very close to Aristotle. Is this perhaps why he has a rather ambiguous position
     with regard to Aristotelian entelechy? Sometimes he reproaches it with being
     "idealist" (*Ibid.*, p. 6), at other times (p. 13) he recognizes that Aristotle pointed
     out the "rationality of structure existing in all organisms without exception and
     that his entelechy, "a principle which has its end in itself," "designates that
     specific property of living beings"; it is only "later" that "this doctrine of Aristotle
     on entelechy took on a clearly idealist character."
         How desirable it would be that the doctrine of hylomorphism, its true meaning
     and implications, be better understood by eminent scholars!

term of such a process derives in this way from two different areas (the outside and the inside), it is because no sensitive power can turn back on itself or reflect upon itself, *"non enim aliqua potentia sensitiva in seipsam reflectitur."*

Finally there is a supreme and perfect degree of life, *"qui est secundum intellectum,"* which belongs to the intellect: "For the intellect reflects upon itself and can know itself, *seipsum intelligere potest."*

But intellectual life itself comprises a hierarchy of different degrees, for the human intellect, even though it can know itself, nevertheless takes the very beginnings of its knowledge *from without*; as a matter of fact in man there is no intellectual knowledge without images, *"non est intelligere sine phantasmata."*

Among the angels intellectual life is on an even higher level of perfection, in which knowledge of self does not come from something external; it is by itself that the angel knows itself. *"Per se cognoscit seipsum."* Nevertheless, although the *intentio intellecta* (Be careful here! *Intentio intellecta*, intellected intention, means intention *conceived* by the intellect or engendered by it from itself; it is the idea by which something is known, an idea known by reflection. In short it is that intentional determinant interior to the mind which would prove so dear to Husserl). Even though the *intentio intellecta* in the angels does not have its origin in images, and even though in them it is intrinsic in every respect, *omnino intrinseca*, it does not constitute their substance because in the case of the angels their intellection is not identical to their existence, *non est idem in eis intelligere et esse.* (The angel has an idea of itself, but that idea is not its being.)

It is to God that the ultimate perfection of life belongs, for in Him intellection is not something other than existence, *"non est aliud intelligere et aliud esse."* (God has the idea of Himself, and this idea is His being.)

St. Thomas continues, I call *intentio intellecta* that which the intellect conceives within itself of the thing that is known. *"Dico autem intentionem intellectam id quod intellectus in seipso concipit de re intellecta."* In our case, it is neither the thing itself which is known or perceived by the intellect, *"neque ipsa res quae intelligitur,"* nor the substance itself of the intellect, *"neque ipsa substantia intellectus,"* but a certain similitude of the thing known conceived by the intellect, *"quaedam similitudo concepta intellectu de re intellecta, quam voces exteriores significent"*: a similitude which words of our language signify on the outside. This is why the conceived intention is itself called the interior word which is signified by the exterior word. And the fact that the conceived intention in question is not the thing known within us, *res intellecta*, is the reason why it is one thing to *know the thing* and an entirely different thing to *know the conceived intention* itself, something that the intellect does when it reflects on its own work; *"aliud est intelligere rem et aliud est intelligere ipsam intentionem intellectam, quod intellectus facit dum super opus suum reflectitur."* It follows from this that the sciences of things and the sciences of intellective intentions (logic and dialectics) are distinct from one another.

Here we see clearly the fundamental realism of St. Thomas and how, long before their time, he burst the great bubbles of Hegelian dialectics and Husserlian phenomenology. It does no harm to point this out parenthetically.

And now let us leave the human intellect to return to the divine intellect. *"Creator coeli et terrae, visibilium omnium et invisibilium,"* let us not say in the equivocal phrase, as does the French translation of the *Credo* presently in use: *of the visible and invisible universe*; let us say rather: *of all things visible and all things invisible*, the world, men, and angels.

At the peak of all creation and of the pyramid of the degrees of life, or of increasing interiorization, there are the pure spirits. And infinitely above this summit, there is God in His absolute transcendence. God is Life in its infinite sovereign and entirely inexpressible perfection: inexpressible except in the uncreated Word. God is Life as pure Act of intellection and of love subsisting by Itself. It is in the line of intellectuality that St. Thomas considered Him in the text we are reading. And what is his conclusion?

"Therefore, since in God *esse est intelligere*, to exist and 'to intellect,' are the same thing, in Him the *intentio intellecta*, the *conceived intention* or the interior word, is His intellect itself; and because in Him the intellect is also the *res intellecta*, the thing known or perceived by the intellect—for He knows Himself, and in knowing Himself He knows all things—, it must be concluded that in God knowing Himself, *the intellect*, and *the thing known by Him*, and the *conceived intention*, are one single, identical reality, *relinquitur quod in Deo intelligente seipsum sit idem intellectus et res quae intelligitur et intentio intellecta.*"

I. ON A MAJOR TEXT OF ST. THOMAS

3. The preface is over, and I now come to my presentation. For the sake of clarity I have divided it into a certain number of points.

My first point bears on *another major text of St. Thomas*.

Again this text is taken from the *Contra Gentes*, from book III, chap. 22. And here too there is question of a hierarchy of degrees, no longer in the order of ascending perfection of activity proper to natures, as was the case in the text I just cited, but this time in the order of the ascending perfection of *forms* and the movement of *generation*, or of *substantial transformation*, which at different levels characterizes all beings of the material universe.

"Prime matter," writes saint Thomas, "is first of all in potency to the form of the *element*.

"But existing under the form of the element, it is in potency to the form of the *mixed body* (or of the compound), elements being the matter of the mixed body.

"And considered under the form of the mixed body, it is in potency to the *vegetative soul*: for it is a soul that is the act (or the substantial form) of the plant (since a plant is a living being, or a being endowed with immanent activity).

"And likewise the vegetative soul is in potency to the *sensitive* soul, as the sensitive soul is to the *intellective* soul: as it appears in human generation, in which the fetus lives first by plant life, then by animal life, and finally by human life.

"But after this form—the intellective soul—we do not find, in those things subject to generation and to corruption (or to substantial transformation), any subsequent or worthier form.

"And so the highest degree of the whole order of the movement of generation is the human soul, and it is toward this that matter tends as toward its ultimate form.

"The elements then exist for mixed bodies, which exist for living beings, among which the plants in turn exist for the animals and the animals for man. Indeed man is the end of the whole movement of generation."

4. This is a very important text on which we would do well to reflect. You will notice that here there is question of a hierarchy or of *the order of the ascending perfection of forms* in those beings subject to the movement of substantial transformation.

But there is still more in what St. Thomas tells us. For the order of ascending perfection under consideration here implies a *tendency* in the beings in question, an aspiration toward the form of a higher metaphysical level, and in the final analysis toward the ultimate form, which is absolutely superior in the order of those things where substantial transformation reigns, namely towards the human soul. The existence of this *tendency* is indicated in the lines I just read (matter "*tends* toward the human soul as toward the ultimate form"). It is indicated even more forcefully in the texts of the same chapter which precede the text I read and where St. Thomas tells us that "prime matter *tends* toward its perfection, which consists in acquiring in act the form to which it was at first in potency, even though it then ceases to have the other form that it had in act previously; and so in reality, it receives *successively* all the forms to which it is in potency, in such a way that all its potency is eventually reduced to act, something that could not take place all at once."

Let us note then that according as it exists at a given level in the transcategorical[4] hierarchy under consideration, matter *tends* toward a higher level,

---

4   By this word I mean that the hierarchy in question concerns absolutely fundamental general characteristics which designate the ("metaphysical") thresholds of perfection in being, thresholds which matter necessarily tends to pass over. The levels of such a hierarchy are steps, more or less high, in the crossing of an absolute threshold. (The step is less high when matter becomes informed by the form of the compound. It is much higher when it becomes informed by the form of a living being, and highest when it receives the form of the human being—the intellective soul.)

On the other hand, if there is question of the immense multiplicity of more or less perfect forms and of those species totally immersed in matter—non-living

where it will be informed by a form of a higher order. And if it tends in this way toward a higher level, it is because it tends toward *the divine similitude, "in divinam similitudinem,"* with a view to deeper and deeper participation. And as we read again in the same chapter, to the degree that an act tends toward what is more distant and more perfect, *"quanto aliquis actus est posterior et magis perfectus,"* all the more fundamentally, *tanto principalius, the basic inclination of matter moves in the direction of that act,* in other words, and these words are those of St. Thomas, toward the ultimate form which is the human soul.

So here we find clearly indicated the immanent *tendentiality* of the hierarchy of levels in the entire order of substantial transformation or of "generation" in the very broad sense which the Scholastics give to this word. If bodies deprived of knowledge tend toward an end, says St. Thomas in chapter 24, it is because they are directed toward that end by their Creator, as the arrow is shot toward its target by the archer. But to tend toward a good is to tend toward the divine similitude. And it is *because* each being in nature tends toward the divine similitude that it tends toward its own good—as we have also just seen, toward a higher level of perfection, which is *transnatural* with regard to its own nature.[5] And when we come to natures endowed with intelligence, even the human intellect, however inferior it may be in comparison to the pure spirit, has for its ultimate end to see God, *"finis cujuslibet substantiae intellectualis, etiam infimae, est intelligere Deum,"* the end of every intellectual substance whatever it may be. even the lowest, is to see God, *intelligere Deum,* says St. Thomas in chapter 25; in such a way that man has a natural desire or appetite for the vision of God,[6] which is not only something preternatural with regard to a given nature, but something supernatural, that is, superior *to the entire order of nature.*

---

or living—which the spectacle of nature presents to us, there is in their regard no predetermination in the aspirations by which *materia prima* tends toward its perfection through all those actuations to which it is in potency.

5   A bit of commentary might be useful here: Matter under the form of an element tends toward the form of a compound (a higher transcategorical level); under the form of a compound it tends toward a vegetative soul; under the form of the latter toward the sensitive soul, and under this form toward the intellective soul. Hence, a tendency toward a determined transnatural form.

But when there is question of living beings it must be added, and this is something quite different, that (in the evolutionist perspective, and this is our perspective) each living being (at least inasmuch as it was part of the evolutive stem), while tending toward the good of its specific nature, tended likewise, during the prehistorical ages, to pass over, at least in its line of descent, to *some* specific (ontological) form, higher up on the evolutive scale, and hence transnatural with respect to its own specific nature.

6   This, I should note in passing, is a desire of *nature* which is but one with the very being of the intellect, even in a man who would fall far short of knowing *by his reason,* as he can and ought, God as the *Cause of being.* And this desire of nature is accompanied by an elicit desire for *grace* in one who, *by faith,* knows God *as his*

5. Let us return to the world of nature and to our consideration of the degrees of perfection in the order of the "movement of generation and corruption," or of substantial transformation. Here we find, at one and the same time, *a hierarchy of (transcategorical) degrees and a general tendency toward higher degrees, and toward the ultimate degree which is that of the intellective soul or of the human being.* What does this mean, if not that St. Thomas, who had no idea of what we call Evolution, has given us in advance, in chapter 22 of book III of *Contra Gentes* that we have read, the true basis of a philosophy of Evolution and the metaphysical principles of a truly evolutionist thought. All we have to do is add the *historical dimension* and to extend so to speak *through the course of Time* the hierarchy of degrees of perfection which we have been considering: at one stroke we have the Evolution of the material cosmos and of living beings, in a philosophical view that is in accord with that image of Evolution which science, on its own epistemological level, tries somehow or other to give each of us.

It would be utterly foolish to seek in St. Thomas a Teilhardian philosophy of Evolution. Perhaps I will consider this matter in detail in another seminar. Let it suffice for me to note in passing that for St. Thomas there were *substantial transmutations* causing a true passage from one nature to another, whereas in the case of Teilhard (the thought of this great poet of Evolution lacked the evolutionary concept *par excellence*, the concept of the *change of being*), for him everything was in everything, and what he called evolution (as was the case with many evolutionists who were not sufficiently metaphysicians) was no more than a kind of unwrapping. On the other hand, for a St. Thomas who would have had the idea of Evolution, it is not a generalized Incarnation, an *encosmized Christ* who is the mover in this process; it is God, the creating and sovereignly transcendent Intellect, directing all things toward their end and elevating life toward its higher forms. What St. Thomas gives us in the text we have read is a rough sketch of a *Thomist philosophy of Evolution*, not an Evolution served up with a Theilhardian sauce, but the kind of Evolution whose problem scientific data has been laying ineluctably for a century now at the feet of the philosophers.

II. ON HUMAN GENERATION ACCORDING TO ST. THOMAS

6. My second point concerns human generation according to St. Thomas, I mean according to his philosophical ideas—for their part, scientific ideas have undergone enormous change since his day. It is the philosophical ideas that I am interested in. (Parenthetically, let me note immediately that in St. Thomas' day, the commonly held scientific or pseudo-scientific idea of human *seed* was completely erroneous. On the one hand, completely lacking the microscopic

---

Savior and his Friend, who will grant an immediate vision of Himself, in his essence, to the glorified intellect.

analysis that we have today, this seed was considered no more than "spumous matter" which was not yet organized or living; this was a case of simple scientific ignorance. On the other hand, and here I would see a *faux pas* of human reason based on totally exterior observation of animal copulation, reinforced perhaps by a vague ethico-social prejudice concerning the superiority of the "stronger sex," it was imagined in those days that the active or actuating role in fecundation was strictly limited to the male gamete, the female gamete playing no more than a role of passive potency. But these erroneous pseudo-scientific notions have absolutely nothing to do with the idea, taken in itself and in its philosophical significance, that St. Thomas proposes concerning embryological development. End of parenthesis.)

You will recall that in that chapter of *Contra Gentes* which gives us beforehand a rough outline of a philosophy of Evolution, St. Thomas teaches that "the vegetative soul is in potency to the sensitive soul. And the sensitive soul to the intellective soul: *as appears in human generation, where the fetus lives first by plant life, then by animal life, and finally by human life.*" This theory is constantly taught by St. Thomas, and this is why he says also that when the human embryo passes in its development from vegetative life to animal life and from animal life to human life, it passes each time through a substantial transformation of generation and corruption, the word *corruption* here meaning in this case not destruction of a substance giving birth to another substance, but only the fact that in its development the same substance (i.e., the same suppositum *virtually* human from the outset, and which will become *formally* human when it receives an intellective soul) at a given moment loses the form that animated it, and which gives place to a superior form.

This philosophical view of St. Thomas has been abandoned, I believe, by most modern theologians, who admit in general that the intellective soul, the spiritual soul, is infused into the embryo *at the very instant of its conception.* If we were forced to abandon the views of St. Thomas concerning human generation, this would simply prove that the comparison he used to illustrate his rough outline of an anticipated philosophy of Evolution was worthless. And the text we read would be even more astonishing and would offer us no more that a rough outline of an anticipated philosophy of Evolution, without any application to human generation which was mentioned there as an example and comparison.

But I have no intention of abandoning St. Thomas' views on human generation; I consider them true and singularly enlightening.

For it is indeed true that the intellective soul, a substantial form that is purely spiritual but which informs a body, causes man to live not only with intellective life, but also with sensitive and vegetative life. It has also, according to St. Thomas—as an informing form—what a simply vegetative or sensitive soul would have.[7]

---

7   Cf. *Sum. Contra Gent.*, II, cap. 89: The intellective soul is "*anima perfectior quae est*

But it has this power on a higher level: the vegetative life of a human being, endowed with its spiritual soul, is, I do not say more vigorous, but I do say *more complex, more refined, and at the same time, more delicate* than the vegetative life of a plant or an animal. The same can be said of its sensitive life. And this necessarily supposes a *disposition of the body*—the ultimate disposition on which the great Commentators insisted— adapted to and demanding such a life. (In fact, the soul, "being united to the body as its form, is united to it only as to that body *of which it is properly the act*,"[8] in other words, whose organization is duly proportioned to it and is disposed uniquely to this particular body.) And the ultimate disposition which the intellective soul requires supposes a brain, a nervous system, and an already highly developed motor-sensitive psychism (and which are, indeed, in the process of rising even higher than in the rest of the animal kingdom.) To admit that the human fetus, from the instant of its conception, receives the intellective soul, while the matter is still in no way disposed with respect to it, is in my view a philosophical absurdity. It is just as absurd to call a fertilized ovum a *baby*. This is a complete *misunderstanding* of the *evolutive movement*, which in truth would be mistaken for a simple movement of augmentation or of growth, as if by dint of growing bigger a circle would turn into a square, or the *Petit Larousse* would become *The Divine Comedy*.

7. Why have theologians accepted such an opinion? As far as I know, for two reasons: (1) because abortion is a crime in the very first stages of gestation as well as in the last; (2) because the Virgin was immaculate from the very moment of her conception.

But these two reasons in no way prove that the fetus receives an intellective soul at the very moment of its conception.

With regard to the first reason, concerning the crime of abortion: St. Thomas says clearly that the embryo lives first of all by vegetative life, then by sensitive life; but he also says that from the instant of its conception, and even beforehand in the human seed, *human nature* is *virtually* present, and is thus *transmitted to the embryo*, really transmitted to the embryo. For "virtually" means *really*, even though it may not mean "formally."

To kill a being which possesses human nature virtually (really-virtually), and which is made to be a man, is evidently the same as killing a man.

As far as the second reason is concerned, that is, the Immaculate Conception of Mary: it is precisely because from the very instant of its conception the human embryo is in virtual possession of its *human nature*, but a human nature deprived of grace and disordered by the sin of the first man, the father of the human race, that from the very instant of its conception the human embryo also has within it virtually, but really (really-virtually), *original sin*. The entire doctrine of St. Thomas on the transmission of the first sin is based on this point.

---

nutritiva et sensitiva simul."

8   *Ibid.*

So, to say that the Virgin, redeemed and pardoned ahead of time by the foreseen merits of her Son, was immaculate from the very moment of conception, in other words that she was miraculously preserved from the transmission of original sin, or from a *fallen* human nature, means that she was free from original sin as it exists virtually (really-virtually) from the very first stages of the embryonic development of all other men, and *formally* from the very last stage of that embryonic development at which they receive a rational soul. This is what is meant by the Immaculate Conception, and whatever may have been the views of St. Thomas on what at his time had not yet been proclaimed a dogma of faith, the teaching of St. Thomas on human generation is in perfect accord with this dogma, *just as perfectly* as with the dogma of the transmission of original sin to all other men.

Thus the two reasons proposed by modern theologians to insist that the rational soul is infused from the very first instant of conception are invalid. And, by virtue of the considerations which I have just indicated, the theory that the rational soul is infused from the very first moment of conception is philosophically untenable.

8. But, in conclusion, let us go back to what St. Thomas thought about human generation. Notice that St. Thomas does not say that the embryo *is a mere vegetable* during the first phase, and then *a mere animal*, before becoming a human being. Such an interpretation would be grossly inaccurate. St. Thomas says something entirely different: that possessing a human nature *virtually* from the very beginning—the human embryo during the first stage *lives by vegetative life* and in the following stage *by sensitive life*. It is a being which from the very first instant is *made to be a man*, and which becomes *formally* what from the very beginning it has already been *virtually* and by that fundamental life force on which it depends. This being becomes a man formally, a body informed by a rational soul, after having passed through a stage in which its body is informed *for a time and in the process of becoming* (in via), by a vegetative soul, and during another stage in which its body is informed *for a time and in the process of becoming* (in via) by a sensitive soul. This is the *evolutive movement* proper to human generation.

What St. Thomas saw by a stroke of genius is the absolutely typical reality, unique in its kind, of the *evolutive movement* or *evolutive development* of the human embryo: a corporeal substance *numerically one* (one and the same suppositum) which is transformed from one stage to another (as a mere seed at first, developing and then *evolving* according to the vegetative life characteristic of the vegetable kingdom, then as a more perfect organism, developing and then *evolving* according to the sensitive life characteristic of the animal kingdom). In order that at the end of this process it may become formally what it was virtually from the very beginning, at each stage it becomes *formally something else*, substantially something else, that is, informed by a different soul—we would say today that it recapitulates in itself, in the intra-uterine development of that being which is the head of material creation, *the evolution of life* which after centuries has attained its final end in man.

Those theologians who brush aside with an offhand gesture, indeed, with a smile of condescension, what St. Thomas thought of human generation, have not understood this at all.[9]

This old peasant would like to point out, if he might, that the two reasons whose invalidity he demonstrated a moment ago and which claim to establish the thesis of the immediate infusion of the rational soul, even though accepted by a number of modern theologians, are, in the first case concerned with the

---

9   I have not forgotten that, as Father Karl Rahner notes in his book *Science, Evolution et Pensée chrétienne* (Paris: Desclée de Brouwer, 1967), p. 113, "the medieval doctrine according to which the spiritual soul comes into existence only at a rather late stage of embryonic development, and not from the moment of conception," "has regained a bit of ground in our day." Certainly this is all to the good. However, is it always for solid *ontological* reasons, or again for *moral* reasons, but whose particular objective this time is somewhat suspect? This is another question entirely. As far as Father Rahner himself is concerned, it is for very solid ontological reasons (the same as ours—this says it all, does it not, about our well-known arrogance) that he looks with favor on the Thomist theory of the development of the human embryo; and he notes very pointedly: "Having accepted this, it can very well be said that the ontogenesis thus understood corresponds to human phylogenesis . . ." (*Ibid.*, p. 114).

If this peasant is happy to have had occasion to cite a text of Father Rahner about which he finds himself in substantial agreement, he must nevertheless add that the case is not the same with the ensemble of the work from which this text is taken. I have great esteem and great respect for this author and for the doctrinal intentions which inspire him, but I am afraid that these intentions are betrayed only too often by the artificial difficulties and the ambiguities that become inevitable the moment that, in treating of the "*dialogue between theology and science*" little or no consideration is given to the indispensable role that *philosophy* (and not the philosophy of Heidegger) and a firmly grounded philosophical epistemology ought to play in such a dialogue (as holding their rightful place *between* science and theology). On the other hand the same difficulties and ambiguities arise the moment that an effort is made to restore in their integrity those theological truths neglected by Teilhardian evolutionism, all the while holding firmly to the vision of the world presupposed by it, and the idea of the relationship between divine action and the world inherent in that vision (for which it is an axiom—accepted by Rahner—that "God operates in each thing by means of secondary causes," *ibid.*, p. 115). Hence the importance attached to a notion, in my opinion very ambiguous, like that of "auto-transcendence" (*ibid.*, pp. 107 ff.). Secondary causes played an essential role in the appearance of man at the end of evolution (as they do in the generation of each human being), but the human soul is created by God, and this is an operation that does not take place by means of secondary causes. The same is the case for the infusion of grace (when it does not take place by means of those "secondary causes" which the sacraments are, even though in this case secondary causes certainly play an important *preparatory* role).

moral order (confronted with a truth of the moral order—that abortion is a crime at whatever stage of gestation it takes place—they had recourse to the most immediately plausible notion, the notion which seemed to be the most readily *applicable*, to take account of this truth); and in the second case with the *dogmatic* order (confronted with the dogma of the Immaculate Conception, that again turned immediately to the notion which seemed to *fit in* most easily with this dogma). They did not seem to take pains, as St. Thomas, who did not work solely to reconcile one notion with another, always did, to assure the ontological bases for a theological thesis. Here, apropos of a particular problem which may appear minimal in itself, we can see a small indication (and there are more serious ones) of the lack of metaphysical interest among many theologians, who do not take the trouble to instruct the *ancilla* in that truth which is within its domain, and who make use of any philosophy or ideosophy which happens to be in style at the moment.

One more point to end this section. I detest concordism, but I would like to point out to you, as a curiosity, a rather unexpected analogy. From the philosophical perspective of St. Thomas there are three stages in the evolutive development of the human embryo: (1) a stage when it has a vegetative soul as its substantial form; (2) a stage when it has a sensitive or animal soul for its substantial form; (3) a stage when it finally has that rational soul which is the human soul for its substantial form.

So then, from the purely scientific point of view of the embryologists, who are indeed strangers to such philosophical points of view and whose criteria are purely morphological and physiological, what are we told? Embryology tells us[10] that there are three distinct stages in the development of the human embryo: (1) a stage when, at a very delimited time after the first differentiations which have gotten it under way (about the 18th day), it is called an *embryo*, and which continues from the end of the first month to the end of the second; (2) a stage when it is called a *foetus*, which goes from the 3rd month to the end of the 6th, and during which the functions of "motricity" awaken; (3) a stage when it is called a *viable foetus*, which goes from the 7th month to the end of the 9th, during which it ends up taking on a decidedly human appearance.

Once again three stages! This of course proves nothing, but it's still nice to notice.

III. CONTINUATION OF OUR CONSIDERATIONS ON HUMAN GENERATION

9. In my third point, which I come to now, I would like to follow up on our considerations of human generation.

---

10   Cf. A. Giroud and A. Lelièvre, *Elements d'embryologie* (Paris: Libr. Le François, 1965), pp. 65–81.

Taking account of the data obtained by science, what *philosophical* description, what *philosophical* analysis can we try to propose of the evolutive movement or the evolutive development of the embryo when we are considering it in the case of the human being?

At the very beginning there is first of all the seed: the male gamete, which is the spermatozoon, and the female gamete, which is the ovule.

Since both are detached or separated from the organism of the genitor, it is quite clear that they do not live by the life of that organism or by the life of a body informed by a rational soul. They are like two complementary halves of a living being, made to produce by their union a single new living being, the egg, or the fecundated ovule. They are both living, but by an imperfect (vegetative) life, incapable of living very long separated from one another or of growing and engendering another being like itself. The form, let us call it "ontic," which informs them is not properly a vegetative soul but rather a transient (vegetative) form, drawn from matter at the moment of their separation from the generating organism. At the very instant that the two gametes come together, the form in question of each one returns into the potency of matter, while a vegetative soul is educed from it, informing the new living being at the point of its entry into existence.

But we must be careful here. They are not only what they are. There is something which *passes* in them and through them, and which is of immensely greater worth than they are in themselves. *Human nature* passes in them and through them—virtually as I said above. By *virtue* of the human generative act, human nature, which is that of the two genitors, passes virtually in and through the seed.

10. Now here we are face to face with that devilish word *virtue*, which is so troublesome because the routines of thought and especially of language traitorously push us to reify it and to misunderstand it completely. It is not a thing, *res*; and yet it is real. Let us have the courage to look at it directly, to discuss and demythologize it.

"Virtue" refers essentially to the *instrumental* order. All the art of Michelangelo passed in and through his chisel; it did not pass as a thing (a certain *habitus* in the soul of Michelangelo), but as the *virtue* of that art or his power, in the fire of artistic creation to control, in the fire of artistic creation, the slightest movements of his hand and chisel. From the intelligence and the sensitivity of the sculptor the controlling power and the controlling virtue of his art pass into his hand and his chisel. If Michelangelo had been paralyzed, his art would have remained intact in his soul, but the virtue or the controlling power of his art would not have passed into his hand and his chisel.

Another example: the words of human language which are at the same time signs and instruments. I can pronounce words like a parrot, without *thinking* them, putting into them absolutely nothing of my intelligence or my heart; in which case absolutely nothing passes through them. Whoever hears them receives them like a stone. But if I think with all my heart some truth while pronouncing these words and want to communicate it to another, then something passes through them in the manner in which I pronounce them. My thought itself, my very intelligence, my very heart? Surely not; they are formally mine and remain formally within me. What then? A little demon-messenger emanating from them and passing at a gallop through my thoughts? This is a myth. What does pass along is my thought, my intelligence, my heart, but is by the *virtue* of their action tending toward an end, which continues to operate in an instrument,—virtue animating my voice, *controlling every movement of my voice*, in such a way that it truly carries the *sense* of what I am thinking and saying. Then words attain their end, moving the hearer in his intelligence and his heart.

There is a still better comparison I would like to use in this particular case. I am thinking of a symphony composed by a musician and played by an orchestra.

First of all there is the intellect of the musician who creates the symphony. To do so he makes use of instrumental signs—musical notes and other instrumental signs which he inscribes on the pages of the score as he invents the symphony. Next it is all the energies of the members of the orchestra, blowing into their trumpets and sawing away on their violins, which bring the symphony to our ears as a musical work in act. If it is well played, then all the art, intelligence, and heart of the composer pass *virtually* and instrumentally through the orchestra to attain their end, and illuminate our hearts. They pass into the orchestra by *virtue* of the intellectual act of the composer, which is communicated to the orchestra and controls its every movement.

I would say that this *virtue* is a certain transmitted or communicated *form*, but, and this is a capital point, it is not an entitative form informing a *thing*, a *res* to which it would give its constitution in being. It is a *transitive* form, it is the FORM OF A MOVEMENT, not of a *being*, it is the *form of a movement* by which that movement is regulated in the very impermanence of its passage in time. Hence this form itself is essentially passing, transient, like the impulse imparted to the arrow by an archer; and it lasts, that is continues to exercise its controlling causality in the thing in movement, only as long as the movement itself lasts. When the movement ceases, having attained its term or its end, when the arrow reaches its target, when the symphony has been performed, at that very moment the virtue communicated to the arrow or to the orchestra, ceases to exist. That *form of the movement* which directed and controlled the energy which, from the physical energy *in actu* of the archer or the spiritual energy *in actu* of the composer, passed instrumentally into the arrow or into the orchestra, no longer has any existence.

All of this means that *virtue*, in the strict sense in which I use the word, depends on *formal* causality, and in no way on *efficient* causality. When we imagine that *virtue* exercises an *efficient* causality, it becomes a myth, justly made laughable by that *virtue dormitive* which Molière held up to ridicule. It exercises no efficient causality whatever, only a formal causality.

In a formula which is a bit long, but which I hope is complete, I would say that virtue is *the form of a caused movement by which the action of the efficient cause, when it is not instantaneous, controls the whole instrumentality which leads to the final effect, as long as the process of causation lasts.*

Now it seems to me that the comparison of the symphony can be applied in a certain way to the evolutive movement of human generation. Let us just imagine that in producing sounds the symphony produces a being, a sonorous tree which from one mutation to another becomes a sonorous eagle whose wings spread over the whole concert hall. Then the virtue which caused the control of the intellectual act of the composer to pass into and through the orchestra has attained its end; by it the intellectual act of the composer has produced a work.

In the ovule fecundated by the spermatozoon and which lives a completely vegetative life, and has no more than a vegetative soul, human nature is present *virtually* because the virtue of the generative act, which proceeds from the spiritual souls of the genitors insofar as their souls inform their bodies (to put it more succinctly, the *virtue of the human generative act*, i.e., the fecundation of a human ovule by a human spermatozoon) passes into and through this fecundated ovule and its vegetative life. This is the *form of a movement*, the form of an evolutive movement. And it will pass through the embryo all during its evolutive development, until it attains it goal: a formally human being, a body informed by a rational soul.

The ovule, then the embryo, is the orchestra playing the score, thanks to the energy of the musicians. The orchestra conductor is the virtue—passing into the fecundated ovule, then into the embryo up to the last stage of its development[11]—from the human generative act, that is, the controlling and directive form of the evolutive movement caused by this act. The musicians are the physico-chemical and biological energies of the ovule and the embryo, in particular the genes which are contained in the chromosomes and which might be compared (limpingly, I'm afraid) to the different groups of musicians playing a particular category of instruments.

11. And now I've done with *virtue* (if I might put it this way). To finish what I have to say about human generation I would like to make a few more remarks (oh, no more than five) which I will try to make as brief as possible (though I really do not have much success in this regard).

First remark. Hereditary continuity is guaranteed by reproductive cells, the *gonads*, which begin their differentiation very early, and in this way form a kind of chain from one generation to another. I was once a pupil of Giard, who pushed to the limit the distinction between *soma* (the body of each one in his

---

11 From this last stage on the virtue of the human generative act gives way to the definitive form, the rational soul. Cf. *Sum. Contra Gent.*, II, 89.

individual life) and *gonads*,[12] the histological elements that are destined for reproduction and which assure the good of the species. He considered them almost as parasites on the *soma*, or better as pseudo-parasites in symbiosis with the *soma*[13] I believe that this is a very important consideration (even as regards the psychology of the most unfortunate of human beings). The chain of gonads can be pictured as passing from one generation to another through the somas of the genitors, thus assuring the stability of the species, especially the one under consideration here, the human species.

12. *Second remark*, complementary to the first. Nevertheless, since primitive man and prehistoric times, there has been a development or an *expansive movement at the very core of the human species*. Since its appearance on earth, mankind has advanced (not without some accidental regressions surely) in its psycho-somatic constitution—I mean in the domain of racial differentiation—and in this particular domain such progress can be vast in its extension (as far as the multiplicity of races is concerned), but this differentiation remains at a *very elementary level* (it concerns solely those secondary characteristic affecting the specific basis which is identical in all).

A first question here: How should this development be interpreted? I think it has taken place (certainly very rapidly) on the one hand in a direct line *like an arrow*, and at the same time broadly in many directions *like a fan* toward those great racial families, so very diversified in our species. As a result we must affirm, on the one hand, not only the essential equality of all human beings as such (whether one is a model for Praxiteles and the other a pygmy), but also the human complementarity of the great racial families in the variety

---

12   The word *gonad* designates both the germinal tissue and associated tissues of the endocrine type. We know today that there is a period of embryonic life in which the original sexual cells, called *gonies* appear (as early as the 15th day) at some remove from the early developing gonadic structure—at the very heart of a somatic tissue—and then migrates toward that beginning gonadic structure. So during the period in question the germen-soma opposition has not yet been established.

13   See n. 14 on page 101. If Giard's ideas retain a certain importance for me, it is above all because they call attention to the fact that the gonads in each living being are ordained not to serve and perfect the individual life of that particular living being, but to work out in it those elements which will bring another living being into existence. When there is question of living beings belonging to a species in which the sexes are separate, the gonads are there to produce those "halves of a living being" I mentioned above (p. 97) apropos of the spermatozoon and the ovule, which by their union bring into existence another living being. It could be said that in such species, particularly in the human species, the male organism—the soma of the man—and the female organism—the soma of the woman—are, each in its particular case parasitically preyed upon by its eventual future child as by a stranger, but *from its own flesh*, which is being prepared in the new being. It seems to me that these are psychological elements which have far-reaching importance.

of qualities which distinguish them, each one having *more* than the others in certain respects, and *less* that the others in other respects. In my opinion, such a view favors cross-breeding and racial mixture. I might add that once this racial psycho-somatic differentiation of the human being has been established, it is in the intellectual and cultural order that its development has continued and will continue.

Second question: By what mechanism did the development of these diverse human racial families take place? Because of a kind of independence that is generally attributed to gonads in relation to the soma and because of a primacy accorded by geneticists to the role of the genes, the biologists of the western world, and especially of the English-speaking world, whether there is question of the formation of races or of species, generally deny any possibility of *inheriting acquired characteristics* which was Lamarck's grand idea. This idea has remained dear, if I am not mistaken, to Soviet biologists, and they accept the pitiful extrinsic Darwinian mechanism alone (natural selection of the fittest, that is to say, the one that by chance is in the best condition for survival). All of this, as we will see later, is a bit passé (from the nineteenth century), even though a contemporary biologist like M. Paul Wintrebert[14] has the highest possible esteem for Lamarck. It might be noted in passing that, in spite of the radical doubt to which many scientists[15] have resigned themselves today with regard to the possibility of finding a scientific explanation of the causes of

---

14   *Le Vivant créateur de son évolution* (Paris: Masson, 1963). This book, which a philosopher might well reproach for a certain number philosophically pretentious expressions which appear here and there, and for a certain outrageous choice of words, even if they are used to express ideas that are quite correct, but which, I imagine, were chosen to shock many of the biologists who pretend to be today's authorities, is, nevertheless, in my opinion quite a remarkable book. Let me note that it intends to revise and to clarify the views of Giard to which I alluded above. Mr. Wintrebert says again and again that the protoplasm "creates" or forms its genes. In this sense, then, the gonads are dependent on the soma, and this opens the way to the theory of neo-Lamarckian evolution ("the living being bequeaths to its descendents only what it has itself made"). It nevertheless remains that, once "created" in the organism of the begetter, these genes, by determining the development and the constitution of the begotten, at the same time determine, through its protoplasm, the formation of the gonads (germen and tissues associated with internal secretion) which will have its own proper life in this protoplasm, along with the impulsions that it brings to life in it, and which will live its individual life in a kind of parasitical way (even if in the evolutive stem, the protoplasm of the begotten, by modifying its genes, in the course of its life, in regard to the characteristics it will transmit, brings about to some degree a change in the chain of the gonads).
      On the subject of the illusions of certain geneticists as well as the difference between a living being and some machine invented by cybernetics, very apropos remarks can be found in the book already cited—A. Oparine, *L'Origine et l'évolution de la vie*, pp. 21–28 ff.

15   Cf. further on, n. 28, p. 114.

evolution, it would be an affront to the human spirit to give up all hope that such an explanation—always subject to revision, of course, as are all scientific explanations—will ever be found. But there are more optimistic scientists. And for my part, if a philosopher might dare to hazard an opinion on the subject, it is in the neo-Lamarckian line of thought (without excluding the support offered by the idea of the survival of the fittest) that in my opinion the hope expressed above has its best chances. If we suppose that this hope will one day be realized, the explanation (or rather the explanatory description) by science of the evolutive process, since science deals solely with the detail of the causal *material* involved, will not replace, but on the contrary will call for and make absolutely necessary, the more profound elucidations of the philosophy of nature. And these elucidations, for their part, can be no more than problematic, except for what touches on fundamental principles and the answers to certain fundamental questions, like the origin of man, which is the subject of our present reflections. (Poor philosophy of nature. We have to admit that in the course of the last few centuries it has, in general, cut a rather sorry figure).

On the other hand, let us note (and this brings us back to our subject) that the development which gave birth to different human racial families does not at all have the same significance as that on which the formation of the species depends: For these diverse human races all have the same specific nature. And as I already pointed out, these diverse races undoubtedly sprang up rather early—either by abrupt mutations or by adaptation to very different milieux. In fact, let us recall that, as Louis Bounoure says in his book *Hérédité et physiologie du sexe*,[16] species as defined by Linnaeus is not a simple homogeneous grouping of identical individuals; it is rather a collection of distinct types, "elementary species, lines or races which differ from one another by characteristics of detail"—so-called Mendelian characteristics—"added on to a common morphological foundation." I would say that this took place as the species spread into different geographical areas.

However it occurred, it must be admitted that the development of the human races (and this applies as well to the evolution of species, about which I will say no more) has been *directed*—hence, toward an *end*; and toward what end if not the actuation of the diverse perfections to which matter is in potency in the human generative cell, and all this through many accidents. In this way the élan of expansion, as it rose, became diversified, as I indicated in my first remark, by producing racial mutations deep within the human species.

13. Let us pass on to my *third remark*. The *direction* and the *finality* I just mentioned, operate *within the living being* (that is to say, in the case we are concerned with at present, within the *human being*), which, by its essence as a living being, is endowed with immanent activity; and this direction and finality operate, on the one hand, at the precise level of its *specific*[17] activity,

16   Paris, Flammarion, 1948, p. 36.
17   Concerning the difference of value that this word has in the vocabulary of the

where, on the other hand, this living being acts *as it is*, in the élan of *expansion* which permeates it, and which (again in the case we are concerned with) has given rise to the diverse racial families within the human species.

But it is clear, whether there is question of specific human activities, or of the human élan of expansion, that this finalizing direction depends, as I already noted in passing, on the motion exercised on the living being—exercised on the living being but attaining the very depths of that being—by a *higher causality*, absolutely primordial, the causality of that *subsistent uncreated Intelligence* which is the author of all being. It is God who is the first principle of the development of human expansion (as He is of the evolutive development of all life). His motion and His direction have operated, in the course of prehistoric time, in whatever concerns the expansive development of the human species, just as they have operated in whatever concerns the evolution of species themselves; but with this capital difference: that with regard to the expansive development of the human species, which has produced the diversity of races in the midst of this species, there have been no *substantial transformations*, as there have been in the course of embryonic development (according to the views of St. Thomas, to which I hold tenaciously) and as there have been in the course of the evolution of species.

14. My *fourth remark*, relative to embryonic development, according to the views I hold on the subject. In its evolutive development, the human embryo moves from a primitive stage in which it lives first of all a vegetative life and has a vegetative soul to a stage in which it will live a sensitive life and have a sensitive soul, then finally to a stage in which it will be informed by and intellective soul, making the child as it leaves its mother's womb capable of leading an intellective life which will then develop little by little.

Now what it is important to make clear here is the role of the *ultimate disposition* of the matter which conditions each of these two substantial transformations. By *virtue* of the human generative act, which causes the embryonic development to move up on the ascending evolutive scale (something entirely different from simple growth), this matter, at a certain moment, comes into possession of properties of such a kind that it can no longer remain informed by the substantial form that up till then gave it existence and life, and that it can no longer continue to be unless it is informed by a different substantial form, another soul of higher degree. This is the *ultimate disposition*, which is *disproportionate* to the substantial form, or the soul, which up till that time provided the form and is now *proportioned solely to another soul or substantial form*, which it calls for and requires. And under the informing power of this new substantial form, it will be—the same disposition—the prime disposition of the stage that follows. So the ultimate disposition is the bridge which facilitates the passage from one substantial form to another. In order to get a firmer grasp of these ideas, let us consider that at a given moment a kind of

philosopher and that of the scientist, cf. further on, pp. 111–112.

diffuse sensitivity, which requires an appropriate organ, appears and develops in the embryo that is still informed by a vegetative soul. At a given moment it is no longer compatible with that soul; it is compatible only with a sensitive soul, under whose informing power the nervous system will develop little by little in the embryo. At the *instant* when this ultimate disposition appears, the vegetative soul, which up till then had informed the embryo, will return into the potency of the matter and, under the virtue of the human generative act, under the form of the movement which (dependent, of course, on the general divine motion activating nature) rules the whole evolutive movement of the embryo, a sensitive soul will be *educed from the matter*.

What must be said now of the *ultimate disposition* which conditions the second substantial transformation in which at its final stage the embryo receives an intellective soul?

Let us note on the one hand that it would be absurd to attribute to the embryo that has arrived at its final stage any properly intellectual activity, any sort of abstract idea. We must not look for any actually exercised movement toward the intellectual life.

But let us recall, on the other hand, that the intellective soul is the substantial form of the body, and that it is not only the intellectual power that is proper to it but also, as act of the body, its vegetative and sensitive power as well. It is not an intellective soul alone, St. Thomas tells us, but also a vegetative and sensitive soul. It is not only the the principle of the intellective life in a man, it is the principle of the total life of his body, *vegetative life* and *sensitive life*. And that very life, in particular the sensitive life, whose formal first principle is the intellective soul, is of a much higher, a much more complex and refined qualitative degree than in beings endowed with no more than a sensitive or purely animal soul. So it is in the *sensitive* life of the embryo, and in the progress in that life, that we must look.

Finally, let us remember also that from the very beginning it is toward the intellective soul that the virtue of the human generative act, which controls the entire embryonic development as the rule of its movement, directs this development.

So I would say that at the highest point achieved in the sensitive life of the embryo in virtue of the human generative act, we find in that embryo, thanks to the affinity of the neurons and to the degree of cerebral development, a complexity and a ready disposition in the sensitive-motor capacity that corresponds to the level that this cerebral development *demands* in order for it to be ruled by a will capable of a freedom that it will exercise only much later on. We find also in the psychic life of the human embryo, however rudimentary it may be, a breadth of ready disposition such as is *demanded* by this purely animal psyche in order to emerge from its dream world, as well as higher powers (cogitative and intellect) such as it *calls for*, powers which will exercise their proper activity only much later on.

This is the ultimate disposition we are seeking. It is a very particular ultimate disposition, which does not condition the *eduction* of a new substantial form emerging from the potency of matter, but which *calls for* the *infusion* of a soul created and infused by God at that very instant. This means that the *ultimate disposition of the matter* now in question depends on the virtue of the human generative act precisely insofar as this biological act has as its first principle, in the human substantial being of the generators, a *spiritual and immortal soul*, and insofar as its virtue (always subject to the general divine motion) brings the embryonic development to a point—the ultimate disposition in question—that is *superior to anything that the biological universe with its laws* is capable of, *except the human microcosm at its peak*, which goes beyond the purely biological. In other words, human nature is not merely an animal nature. And, with the ultimate disposition we are talking about, which surpasses mere animality, this human nature requires its *formal* appearance in the embryo where up to that instant it was only virtually present. *At that very moment* God, who as transcendent first Cause directs the entire evolutive development of the embryo, infuses into it an intellective soul, *created* by Him at that very instant, for this particular individual who is from now on formally human. Let us note carefully that this intellective soul is a spiritual and immortal soul, not just the substantial form of the body; it is *spirit*, a spiritual substance informing a body, yet capable of surviving that body. This is why St. Thomas, who did not mince words, declares *heretical* the error of those who imagine that the human soul, the intellective soul, is not created by God at the instant that the human embryo receives it but is transmitted by the human generative act, or educed, by virtue of this act, from the potency of matter like all other substantial forms. (*"Haereticum est dicere quod anima intellectiva traducatur cum semine,"* I^a, 118, a. 2.)

15. Let us take note also of two important philosophical points. In the first place, it is quite evident that a spiritual soul cannot be educed from the potency of matter; this is a metaphysical impossibility. For every form educed from matter, before being educed, was only one of all the real possibilities implicit in the potency or potentiality of matter. Once educed, it has no existence *except that of the act* of that matter. It will return therefore to the potency of matter when the body which it informs decomposes. It is just the opposite with the spiritual soul. As I said a moment ago, a spiritual soul is the act of the matter, but it is also spirit; it is *a spiritual being subsisting* by itself (and communicating its subsistence to the body which it informs). In other words, even though a certain ultimate disposition of matter *calls for* a spiritual soul, the existence of this soul is independent of matter and will continue without it. This is why to say that it can be educed from the potency of matter is pure nonsense, for in such a case it could not *exist as spirit*, without the matter it actuates.

That spirit which is the soul of man does not depend *for its existence* on the body of which it is the substantial form; rather the body depends on it for its existence, and the body dies when its organization becomes so deteriorated that it can no longer be informed by this soul. The spirit which is the soul of a man, at the death of the body, does not take on *another "act of existing"*; rather it enters into another *state* of existence. But as to the "act of existence" which it exercised before death, it will simply continue to exercise it after death.

From the perspective of the evolutionist (whether there is question of the evolutive development of the human embryo or of the evolution of living species), only two conceptions have any intelligible value or philosophical coherence: either the conception which considers *materia prima* as pure potency, or the conception which affirms the existence of *spirit*; this latter is a conception illuminated by the two fundamental ideas of *potency* and *act*, and it is ours, with its special application to the case of the human being, about which I have just said a few words. The other conception, ignoring the division of being into potency and act and rejecting the notion of *materia prima* and of form, as well as the notion of spirit, from the very outset confuses reality and matter (here let us understand "matter,"[18] not as potency, but as *res extensa* which is perceived by the senses). Here matter includes everything that exists, man and the evolutive process alike. At first this matter was something or other dispersed throughout space, probably in the forms of rarified gas or cosmic dust, then on our planet, passing, of itself, to ever higher states of complexity and organization, ended up as the human brain, whose purely material activity is still called "intelligence," "reason," etc., without basing it on any higher form of life (since spirit as a distinct reality is considered a pure illusion). However untenable it may be, such a conception is philosophically coherent and, at least to a certain degree, intelligible. In this sense the word *matter*, even though it is based from the outset on a very serious confusion, nevertheless makes some sense. But when those who hold this materialist conception, declaring all the while that, of course, *spirit* exists, speak (we hear this every day) about an evolutive process in which *matter* is already *spirit*, at least virtually or implicitly, in which the *spiritual soul* emerges from *matter* (and this soul, of course, could perhaps have been created by God, and why not, if the word *creation* is enveloped in a thick enough fog, which is not difficult), and finally in which *spirit* is nothing but the sublimation and the glory of *matter*—then the word matter comes to mean absolutely *nothing*. It is not a word communicated from one thought to another, it is but a noise which pretends to be articulated and astounds the ear, a kind of booby-trap. The same can be said for the word *spirit*.

I mentioned that there was a second point which I hope I can lay out a little more briefly. Sometimes we hear people, even very cultured people, express their surprise that, in creating a spiritual soul for each human baby born into

---

18   The word *matter* has this meaning for us as well, but in this case we mean matter *informed* by a substantial form.

this world, God would put Himself out for an extraordinary intervention, taking no notice of the laws of nature—for a miracle. Those who speak in this way do not know what they are talking about. If God made a man out of a stone, this would be a real prodigy; but when He infuses a spiritual soul into a human fetus, there is no question of a prodigy. To receive a spiritual and immortal soul is certainly an admirable privilege for each of us, but there is absolutely nothing extraordinary or miraculous about this. Nothing could be more "natural," physically or metaphysically: *physically* because at a given point in the embryonic development, it is required or *called for* by the matter involved, as I just explained; *metaphysically* because this comes about by a metaphysical included in the creation of Man. As soon as He decided to create Man, and created the first man, God established this law. Let us not say that He is subject to this law! The necessity of this law has no bearing on the creative act; it has a bearing only on the effects produced by this act. The creative act is absolutely one in that limitless unique Instant which is the divine eternity. And it is absolutely free. It is not repeated or changed; it is the effects of this act which are repeated and multiplied in the course of time. It is one and the same thing for God to create Man, each man and each man's soul, from the first to the last. And it is an act of sovereign *freedom* whose effect is produced here below successively and *necessarily*, as soon as on the material side the conditions which call for that act are given, conditions which depend on a series of preceding individual events, each of which has been willed and permitted by God.[19]

But it is precisely to defend himself against such an aberrant phantasm being taken seriously that Rahner invented his "self-transcendence" and wrote for example that "parents are the cause of the human being in its totality and its unity, *and therefore of its soul*" (italics mine) "by virtue of the power of God, which is intrinsic to their action and which makes their self-surpassing possible, without being part of what constitutes them in their essence" (Karl Rahner, *Science, Evolution et Pensée chrétienne*, p. 117)—this is an explanation which would certainly not have been sufficient to appease the severity of St. Thomas which I pointed out earlier in this text. As regards the souls of their children,

---

19   I regret to have to point out my disagreement with Father Rahner on the manner in which he discusses this same question. (Karl Rahner, *Science, Evolution et Pensée chrétienne*, p. 115).

Is the world a whole that is so jealous of its unity that it demands that, to operate *"within the world,"* a cause must be *a part of that world*? If we hold that He who created the world *from nothing* also creates *from nothing*, or without making use of any secondary cause, a spirit, in the flesh that calls for it ("within the world," without the spirit itself being *born of the world*), is this the same as considering God "a demi-urge whose action takes place within the world" and "one cause among others *within* the world"? Irrational presuppositions which are no more than masked negations of God's transcendence: For the infinitely Transcendent is also Omnipresent; what is so surprising then that He should act within the world without necessarily being one of the agents which are in the world?

parents are no more than a *dispositive* cause, since the soul is created by God. And "to create" cannot now or ever mean to produce a new being by means of a creature which surpasses itself essentially; for either the creature in question plays no role whatsoever in this production, in which case its "self-surpassing" is nothing but words; or else the creature does play an active role (under God's action) in this production, in which case the word *to create* is nothing more than a mere word. Understood in the manner proposed by Rahner, the creation of the soul by God "becomes a case of God's action however it must be conceived. This action of God . . . brings about nothing that the creature does not do, because it does not operate along side the action of the creature, but brings about this action of the creature which surpasses and transcends its *possibilities*." (Karl Rahner, *Science, Evolution et Pensée chrétienne,* p. 119.) Such a statement is unthinkable, because an "action of a creature which surpasses and transcends its *possibilities*" is pure nonsense. A miracle-worker who raises people from the dead has the *power* to raise them).

16. My fifth remark, finally, is a parenthesis, but one which seems very important to me.

When he treats of the transmission of original sin, St. Thomas teaches that it is transmitted along with that (fallen) human nature which is communicated to the embryo by the human generative act (virtually at first, then formally, at the moment of the infusion of the intellective soul), and that original sin is contracted by the soul, the human, intellective soul, at the very instant of its infusion[20] but that if original sin is contracted from the very instant of its infusion, it is *by reason of the body* in which it is received.[21] The soul such as God creates it is pure and immaculate; it is by reason of its union with the body that, at the instant of its creation and its infusion, it is made to participate in the original transgression and receives the weaknesses and disorders that come from it.

Now this seems important to me from another point of view. For it also helps us to see how the child pays the price of the disturbances which have arisen in his hereditary line or in his own parents, whether there is question of purely physical disturbances due to pathogenic agents or to conditions of physical or social milieux (destitution, under-nourishment, etc.), or whether there is question even of psycho-somatic disturbances resulting moral transgressions.

In the first case, the child may be the victim of a burdensome heredity affecting his physical constitution, which may involve disorders of temperament exposing its soul to particular difficulties in its intellectual or moral activity.

---

20   Cf. *Sum. theol.,* Ia-IIae, q. 83, a. 1.

21   "Cum creatio importet respectum animae ad solum Deum, *non potest dici quod anima ex sua creatione inquinetur.* . . . Habito respectu ad Deum infundentem, *non potest dici quod anima per infusionem maculetur,* sed solum *habito respectu ad corpus, cui infunditur." Ibid.,* ad 4m.

In the second case, and this is the one which interests me, the child may be the victim of a burdensome heredity involving a sensitivo-affective disequilibrium which touches its very soul—that soul which God created pure and immaculate but which at the moment of its union with the body, at the very instant of its creation, and by reason of the dispositions of the body, is affected by this disequilibrium—a disequilibrium which sometimes can go so far as to produce in it dispositions and tendencies which incline it toward evil. In fact, certain moral transgressions of the parents, and certain profound moral disorders which upset their vital equilibrium, have inevitably in them, it seems to me, destructive psychosomatic repercussions, capable of attaining the gonads themselves, which thus become bearers, not of (progressive) "acquired characteristics" but of alterations which are then transmitted.

In such a case a certain particular individual disorder, added on the disorder which affects all human nature due to original sin, then passes through the human generative act and through the embryonic development in such a way that we must admit, it seems to me, that, hidden in the tissues of the body, the first germ, not only of neurotic or psychotic disturbances but also of dangerous or perverse moral inclinations, is present from the very formation of the embryo and develops along with it in the course of its intra-uterine life, but in a latent manner because it is merely somatic. This latent development will continue in the infant, in darkness, and manifest itself only much later. These considerations should make us indulgent toward many of the unfortunate.

IV. ON THE DYNAMISM OF NATURE AND HUMAN EMBRYONIC DEVELOPMENT

17. We come now to the fourth section, which will be short, concerning the dynamism of material nature and human embryonic development.

You remember the text from *Contra Gentes*, book III, chapter 22, which I cited in my first point. There St. Thomas says that, considered under the form of the mixed body, prime matter is *in potency* to the vegetative soul and that "in the same way the vegetative soul is *in potency* to the sensitive soul, and the sensitive soul *in potency* to the intellective soul."

It is important to understand that the assertion that the sensitive soul is *in potency* to the intellective soul is completely different from an assertion which would claim that the *dynamism of material nature*—a dynamism which surely always presupposes a general divine motion, universally activating all created things,—is capable by itself alone (under this presupposed divine motion) of *causing* the potency in question *to pass into act*.

Is the dynamism of nature capable on its own of transforming into act the potency in which the sensitive soul is found with regard to the intellective soul? Certainly not. It is capable on its own of transforming into act the potency in which the vegetative soul is found with regard to the sensitive soul, which itself was educed from the potency of matter, as we just saw concerning embryonic development. But it is incapable on its own of bringing about, at a given moment in its development, the emergence of an intellective soul, the *human* soul then replacing the sensitive soul which informed the fetus during the preceding stage. And this is so, not only because the intellective soul is spiritual and consequently cannot be educed from the potency of matter and cannot be created other than by God for each human being coming into the world, but also because the *ultimate disposition of the matter*, which requires the infusion into the fetus of this soul created by God, itself depends on a first principle, intrinsic to the being of the begetters, which as a spiritual substance *transcends the dynamism of material nature*: In other words, it depends on the substantial form from which the human generative act emanates, as from the formal constitutive first principle of the human being, and this first principle is the spiritual and immortal soul of the begetters. It is always under the general directing motion of God, Who activates everything that is created, in particular the embryonic development of man as that of the other animals, that the ultimate disposition in question is produced. But this time there is question of an animal endowed with reason, and in this case the general directing action of God activates a biological process intrinsically subject to the virtue of the human generative act, and of the first principle of this act—the spiritual souls of the begetters—which transcends the merely biological order and the whole dynamism of material nature taken in itself.

V. ON THE DYNAMISM OF NATURE AND THE EVOLUTION OF SPECIES

18. My fifth section—somewhat longer, alas!—will deal with the dynamism of nature considered this time, no longer in the domain of human embryonic development, but in an altogether different domain, analogous in a sense but fundamentally different, that of the evolutive movement proper to the entire living world, and in particular the world of animal life, so as at long last to tackle the problem of the evolution of species.

First of all, let us consider a case in which evolution is not involved—the case of the generation of some species which we have before our eyes, the bovine species, for example. In this particular case, the dynamism of nature is the *bovine generative act*, as well as the *virtue* of this act which determines the intra-uterine evolutive movement in such a way that at the term of the stage of vegetative life, however short it may be, a sensitive soul is educed from the potency of matter, and the definitely formed embryo of a little calf completes its intra-uterine development. The new being engendered in this way will be at the same specific level of its begetters.

But let us remember now that the world of living beings was subjected (I say *was*, because I think, and this is also the opinion of Jean Rostand,[22] as well as that of Albert Vandel,[23] that this immense adventure was a thing of the past, completely finished today), was subjected in primitive times, during the millions of years of the genesis of the universe, to a long evolution; and let us consider that a few anthropoids are supposed (and after all, this is more than doubtful)[24] to have foretold from very distant times the coming of the hominids (I prefer the word *hominians*)—let us say the *austriacopithecus*, which dates from the Miocene.

But before we go any further, as a preamble to our philosophical reflection, we should look for a rational imagery to help us focus our imagination.

Let us not picture to ourselves, for it would be a very unreasonable kind of imagery (but one which seems to haunt the unconscious of many readers of popular literature on the subject), all living beings as if they were carried along on the torrent of evolution, and each of the phyla (in which all living species would be engulfed) as a kind of funnel through which a continuous flux of mutations would pass, *without any intermediary stages*, ending up in one of those provisionary stages to which the evolutive movement tends—until it comes to its final term (if there is one). This is the imagery of a more than naive heracliteanism.

Instead, let us picture the phylum as a stem (in the midst of previously formed species which remain stable) among which (just as in its different branches) a series of ascending evolutive changes takes place which, like a staircase, before arriving at the terminal stairhead of the phylum in question, will necessarily include intermediary *specific landings*.

So! I cannot avoid using the words *species* and *specific* which cause so many problems for a philosopher who would like to question the experts. For nothing is blurrier, or has such a wide margin of uncertainty, as do these words in the vocabulary of the scientific expert, especially the biologist or the paleontologist, and this is perfectly normal for anyone who has any clear idea of all the different epistemological levels. I shall resign myself (this is annoying, but it's not serious) to using here the words *species* and *specific* in an *amphibiological* sense, in relation on the one hand (the object of our discussion requires it) to the *ontological* species of the philosopher (which connotes a single *nature*

---

22   *Le Figaro Littéraire*, April 20, 1957: "Shall we proclaim that evolution unfolds too slowly for our investigative means to be able to gather indications of it, or—*and preferably in my opinion*—shall we admit that evolution has run its course and that organisms today no longer possess, even to the slightest degree, those evolutive capacities that belonged to their ancestors?" (The italics are mine.)

23   "So the evolution of the animal kingdom appears today to be terminated," Albert Vandel, *L'Homme et l'Evolution*, 3rd ed. (Paris: Gallimard, 1958), p. 30.

24   The anthropoids and the hominids for a long time now have constituted two independent branches. On the *austriacopithecus*, cf. J. Piveteau, *Traité de Paléontologie*, 7 (Paris: Masson, 1957), p. 213.

common to a plurality of individuals), and on the other hand to the *empiriologi-cal* species of the scientific expert, which leaves the ontological species, even though presupposing it in an obscure way, in the realm of the unknowable. This empiriological species is limited to constituting one framework in a taxonomy that in no way pretends to coincide with the ontological species, which is unattainable through the criteria of science. The different taxonomic categories in fact are concerned solely with observable characteristics, considered more or less important, which permit individuals to be arranged in always more or less conventional and provisory groupings in the world of sensible representation. This world, however, set up by science as a distinct epistemological universe, can do no more than symbolize with [*sic*] the categories and objects of thought in the ontological order, but not reveal them. It is like a screen on which are drawn facts and measurements whose perfect precision is paid for at the price of the nebulous notions of common intelligibility[25] empiriologically recast.

We are sure that a chimpanzee and a crow belong to two different ontological species, but we are unable to separate them off and to say whether a chimpanzee belongs to an ontological species different from that of some other simian more or less close to it (even if it is classified in a different taxonomic species), or whether a crow belongs to an ontological species different from that of some other bird more or less close to it (even if it is classified in a different taxonomic species). There is only one ontological species which we are sure of knowing and encompassing, and that is the human species (which properly depends on the criteria of philosophy).

All this being understood, and I hope we will keep this in mind, let me return to my phylum or my evolutive stem. At the base of this stem there is a species (it is of little importance whether this be an ontological or a taxonomi-cal species, as long as the latter is not taken as an arbitrary substitute for the former), a species, that is, which is going to evolve.

Let us imagine, and this all seems probable, that at first we see appear living beings of a slightly higher level but still rather "weak," if you like, let us call them a sub-species or a line which possesses certain progressive characteristics, but which are insufficient to create a new specific type, such as it will eventually appear at a "strong" level to which the evolutive movement tends as toward an intermediate *landing* on the evolutionary staircase, where a certain new *species* will be found constituted, before mutating in it own turn.

When this new species is constituted (and it has to be, for it is through veritable *transformations* of living *natures*, and hence specific transformations,

---

25   By this I mean prephilosophical notions. Philosophical notions are of a higher
      order of intelligibility. For a more complete elucidation of the different remarks
      formulated here, I refer you to *Les Degrés du Savoir* (Oeuvres complètes IV, pp.
      309 f.; see the new edition published as volume 7 of The Collected Works of
      Jacques Maritain [Notre Dame, Ind.: University of Notre Dame Press, 1995]).

that the evolutive movement advances, more or less gropingly in the dark, as the phylum progresses), it is no longer included in the evolutive stem except by its nucleus; it is extended horizontally, outside the stem, like a leaf sprung from the stem, because, like a constituted species, it is stably perpetuated at its level of being. Indeed let us not forget what paleontology shows us: The great zoological groups appeared successively in the course of the earth's history (traces of invertebrates are found in the Pre-Cambrian era, which lasted about 2400 millions of years; invertebrates, fish, amphibians, reptiles appeared in the primary era (400 million years); mammifers and birds during the secondary era (150 million years); the primates during the tertiary era (less than 50 million); and man during the quaternary era (2 million at most, perhaps only 600,000 years).[26] And this historical succession of the appearances of zoological groups, paralleling the historical succession of the great epochs of the earth's history, is sufficient to suggest in an incontrovertible way the idea that life is a historical reality which developed evolutively. But at the same time paleontology shows us that the different species of the zoological groups, the greater part of which died out more or less slowly, before dying out passed stably through enormously long periods of time (the animal species of the quaternary era, including man, are still those of today). The permanence of certain species in the course of paleontological time was in certain cases even stupefying. A great specialist on termites, Thomas Snyder, found among immensely ancient fossils, a contemporary termite which he had at first described as new. According to Professor W. M. Wheeler, another famous specialist, 69 percent of the species of ants of the early Oligocene are living today—at least thirty million years later—and he found among them three species that were impossible to separate from modern species.[27] These are doubtless exceptional cases but informative nevertheless.

In any case, if there is an evolutive movement which is traversing or (rather) which has traversed the world of living beings, the fact is that the tableau presented by this world since the quaternary is one of genera and species that perpetuate themselves in a stable manner. And even, as Jean Rostand wrote ten years ago, "if we are obliged and as it were condemned to believe in evolution," the fact remains that in the eyes of today's science "living nature

---

26   Cf. C. Arambourg, *La Genèse de l'Humanité*, pp. 9–10; J. Piveteau, *Traité de Paléontologie*, p. 231.—Figures that are not very vigorous, but very significant in the order of grandeur. Recent research seems to indicate that the oldest of the lines foretelling the hominians from the far distant past (at the same time as the australopithicidae) appeared eleven and a half million years ago, and the hominians themselves nine million years later (already two and a half million years ago they were making primitive tools—with stone chips, sharpened bones, the pointed teeth of hippopotamuses, etc.).

27   Cf. W. R. Thompson, "The Status of Species," in *Philosophical Problems in Biology*, edited by Vincent E. Smith, St. John's University Philosophical Series, No. 5, 1966, p. 86.

appears even more stable, more fixed, more rebellious to transmutations" than it did to the science of a hundred years ago.[28] All of this must not be forgotten. We must hold tight to both ends of the chain.

But let us return to our evolutive stem. Before attaining the specific degrees I spoke of, let us admit in our imagery that the sub-species or the lines which led to this level—forms already higher but which still remained of the same specific nature as the living beings from which they emanated—were incapable, by reason of the cross-breedings which produced them, of stably reproducing themselves at their level of being and that they simply produced on the stem buds which were unable to leaf out. Except for the buds with no future, these forms remained enclosed within the evolutive stem.

After attaining the specific level in question, the stem continues its evolutive upward movement according to the same process.

19. This is the end of my long parenthesis on the kind of reasonable imagery our philosophical reflection needs. Let me return to my example: the anthropoid which would be part of one of the evolutive stems preparing the hominians from far back in time. In considering this anthropoid from a philosophical point of view, I must first of all consider it from an ontological perspective, whatever its taxonomical category might be. (And I will maintain this perspective till the end of my presentation.)

Whether it belongs to one of the sub-species or the lines enclosed within the evolutive stem, or to one of those species established at some level or landing along that stem but whose original nucleus remains included within the stem and subject to the evolutive movement (it is to just such a nucleus that I suppose the anthropoid I chose as my example to belong), this nucleus belongs, by hypothesis, to those like species which are subject to the evolutive movement within the stem.

Its case is different from that of the bovine which I looked at first. It is by means of the generative act of the anthropoid in question, or rather the anthropoid couple in question, that, under the divine motion whose precise nature I will try to describe in a moment, a specific mutation takes place within the evolutive stem. Then the dynamism of nature, or the *anthropoid generative act*, and the virtue of this act bring about in the embryo, at the end of the

---

28   "If we are obliged and as it were condemned to believe in evolution, we are nevertheless still waiting for a sufficient suggestion as to the causes of the transformation of species. We are still waiting for a supposition 'which could be accepted by anyone who reasons with prudence'" (Huxley). And I would add that we are perhaps in an even less acceptable posture than in 1859 for, after searching fruitlessly for an entire century, we have somewhat the impression of having exhausted the field of hypotheses. Besides, living nature appears even more stable, more fixed, more rebellious to transmutations, than it did before there was a clear distinction between hereditary variability and acquired variability." *Le Figaro littéraire*, April 20, 1957.

vegetative stage, an ultimate disposition *higher* than that which would have been on the level of the species of the generators and consequently causes a sensitive soul of a *higher specific degree* than that of its generators to be educed from the potency of matter, a soul which will inform an anthropoid nearer to an ancestor of man, though still very far from it.

But we must be careful here. Having arrived at this point, it is important to note the essential difference which exists between the evolutive development of the embryo I spoke of at length earlier and the evolutive development of the species I am speaking of at present.

In the case of embryonic development, we found—taking for granted as we did the directing motion of the first Cause activating all of created nature—a first principle of this development, which was the soul or the substantial form of the living being. It is from this formal intrinsic principle, which enables the living substance to be what it is, that the generative act emanates. This generative act, whose virtue orders the entire embryonic development and which causes the the specific nature of the being in question to pass into it, virtually, in such a way that the *ultimate disposition* which at a given point calls for a soul superior to the vegetative soul—the sensitive soul, that is—(and the case will be the same as regards the human embryo, for the passage of the sensitive soul to the intellective soul) found its sufficient reason in the soul or the substantial form of the generators (naturally taking for granted that divine *directing* motion which *generally or universally* activates all of nature).

In the case of the evolution of species, on the contrary, we do not find this formal intrinsic principle regulating the entire evolutive development. This is why the causality which we are always bound to consider first, no longer exercises a purely *directive* motion as in the case of embryonic development. This time, passing through all the evolutive stems, it is a *superelevating* and *superforming* motion (I would like to be able to say "creative," in the very wide and improper meaning that contemporary authors give to this word, insofar as there is question of *completing* the work of creation properly so called) which is exercised by God as the first of the mutations which will bring about the passage from one species to another.

Whereas in the typical embryonic development the divine directing motion moved the living generator to act *as it is*, and, if there is question of an animal, to bring about at a given instant in the embryo animated by vegetative soul the ultimate disposition calling for a substantial transformation, and a sensitive soul of the same species as that of the begetters, now, on the contrary, the superelevating and superforming divine motion (still general, but only as regards the world of life) moves a living being to become—at least in its descendants—*better than it is*, with the result that in the prenatal life of the being engendered by it (in every case if there is question of an animal) the soul, at first vegetative, then sensitive, educed from the potency of matter is of *a specific degree superior* to that of the living being in question.

But let us recall now what St. Thomas said in the text of the *Summa Contra Gentiles* which I quoted at the outset: prime matter, under a given substantial form, *tends* toward higher forms. Under the substantial form of an animal of a given species, matter, because it aspires to the actualization of all its potency, tends toward substantial forms of higher species. I pointed out that if to this metaphysical tendentiality is added the dimension of time, if it is spread out over time, it becomes an evolutive tendentiality. Let us remember also that the living being is endowed with *immanent* or *self-perfecting activity*. We are then led to distinguish in this self-perfecting activity of the living being two sorts of powers. In the first place there are the powers of self-regulation according to which it exercises its specific functions and perpetuates its species through reproduction, in short, it *acts as it is*. It is with these particular powers that biologists are concerned in their study of life functioning with that specific stability whose tableau it presents to us, and which Jean Rostand emphasized so strongly. In the second place there is a power of biological self-regulation of another order, a latent one, which does not awaken or is not awakened until the tendentiality of matter passes or passed over into act in higher forms, and until the superelevating and superforming motion of God, acting all along the evolutive stems, causes or caused living beings to become—at least in their descendants—better than they are or than they were.

This means that the living being itself and its immanent activity also played an active role in evolution, according to that general principle so dear to St. Thomas that God has given to beings created by Him the dignity of being themselves causes, under the motion of the primary Causality. The latent power I just spoke of can be conceived as a power of *finalized invention*, I mean to say in quest of actualizing forms, and hence of structures, under which matter aspires to find itself at some higher level of being, a power put into act when under the superelevating motion of God certain living beings (those on the evolutive stem) labor no longer simply to maintain their being and act as they are but also to cross the threshold of their own species or nature. I have pointed out from the very beginning[29] that this *transnatural* ontological tendency or aspiration exists among all the beings of the material world (even though they are actualized only where there is evolution)—which then tend *to become*—at least in their descendants—*better than they are*. I will come back to this perhaps in another seminar; today I wanted to give only a first indication and to note that in this line it is possible to disengage what is true in an all too abrupt formula, but a very significant one, of a contemporary biologist already cited, Mr. Wintrebert, who speaks of the "living creator of its own evolution" (it is the title of a book, *Vivant créateur de son évolution*, published by him in 1963); I would prefer that he used the word *sub-creator* or *sub-agent* of its own evolution.

And so, concerning the evolution of species, we have two different causali-

---

29   Cf. above pp. 90–91.

ties to consider: in the first place the causality of the Creator of being and His *superelevating* and *superforming* motion (whereas the divine motion is only a directing motion in the evolutive movement proper to typical embryonic development, which, under the regulation of the virtue of the generative act emanating from the substantial form or the soul of the genitors, is accomplished with a view to maintaining the specific type in its stability, such is not the case in the evolutive movement proper to the evolution of species).

And in the second place, we have to consider, at the level of a subordinate cause, still quite real and active, and which it would be a serious error to forget, the causality of the living being itself (the living being of the evolutive stem), whose immanent activity, under the superelevating motion of the first Cause, by the self-regulating process proper to that living being, invents or discovers something new which, first affecting the organism of the living being, passes into the gonads and into the virtue of the generative act. This living being (whose form seizes upon and actuates even the newly awakened[30] aspiration itself of matter toward some higher form of the same metaphysical level and to a form of a higher metaphysical level) takes part in this way in making itself

---

30   How does this awakening take place? Certainly for biological reasons, like, for example, the effort of living things to overcome difficult and changing conditions of milieu; but first and foremost because the superelevating and superforming motion of God, making instrumental use of the substantial form or the soul of the living being, first awakens and then brings about, through this form, the actuation and animation of the aspiration of matter *to pass over to something new* (an aspiration which up to that instant was kept latent by the substantial form as long as the divine superelevating motion did not make use of this form as an instrument).

I am only suggesting here summary indications as I perceive them. The tendency awakened in this way to mutate in a certain direction will take generations to bring about the completion, in a *specific* mutation, all the changes "invented" in the organism of the living being, changes which at first are extremely delicate. And this tendency itself will pass over along with the changes into the descendants, now by means of an embryonic development which is no longer "typical" (as a preserver of the type), but "transtypical" or "gradient" (raising the type and tending beyond it) which no longer has as object to maintain a type in its stability, but to maintain it in its movement toward better states, enabling it eventually to surpass the type.

The immense adventure of evolution, now completed, was based at one and the same time on *God's superelevating and superforming motion* and *the corresponding awakening, within the living being, of the transnatural aspirations of matter*. This is what has been completed. And it is not surprising that species today appear fixed in that stability on which Jean Rostand insisted (the sudden mutations which occasionally take place in today's world of living beings have no more than an accidental character, and one of low degree, which hold no interest for the theory of evolution). If it happens that science does provoke some experimental mutations, they seem to have significance only as aberrations with respect to the specific type, not as an evolutive movement bringing about progression in the species.

become—at least in its descendants—better than it is, and in making its life pass to higher specific levels, which are transnatural with respect to the nature of the living beings of the species in mutation.

20. In order to bring this section to an end, I would like to offer a few more precisions concerning the dynamism of nature in the case of *embryonic development* and in the very different case of the *evolution of species* (I am speaking of living species, in particular of the animal species, which are immersed in matter, by which I mean not endowed with an intellective soul, which is the unique privilege of the human species).

As to the *embryonic development* in all these species immersed in matter, *the dynamism of nature is sufficient by itself alone*, under the general *directive* motion of God, a motion that is absolutely universal in all of created nature. (But *it is not sufficient by itself alone* in the case of *human* embryonic development, which, of course, takes place under the God's general directing motion, but which is caused by a generative act proceeding from a formal principle intrinsic to the human being, the spiritual soul of the begetters, which is superior to the whole dynamism of nature).

As to the *evolution of all species* immersed in matter, once again the *dynamism of nature is sufficient by itself alone*, but this time, under a *superelevating* and *superforming* divine motion, which is still *general*, at least with regard to the world of life and species in mutation.

But concerning the case which we will now examine, the case of that evolution which is completed with the *appearance of the human being, the dynamism of nature under the general divine superelevating motion activating the world of life, is no longer sufficient* by itself alone. This is what we will see in our sixth and last point, to which I have finally come.

VI. THE DYNAMISM OF NATURE AND THE APPEARANCE OF MAN AT THE END OF THE EVOLUTION OF THE PRIMATES

21. Pardon me for all these preliminary remarks, but I still have a few more to make before beginning this last section.

The first concerns the opposition between the two terms *animal* and *man*, which is used constantly in ordinary speech and according to which the problem of the appearance of man is posed for the informed public, just as it is for scientists and philosophers. This choice of words is incorrect, for man is also an animal. We should say on the one hand an *animal not endowed with reason*, and on the other an *animal endowed with reason* (or, as the ancients did, *beast* and *man*). But let us pass over this and accept the ordinary manner of speaking, without forgetting that this may set us up for some nasty tricks.

The second remark concerns the meeting of science and philosophy, and the sphere of competence proper to each of them, when there is question of the two opposed expressions *animal* and *man*. The philosopher, on his own particular level, knows what an animal is as opposed to man. It is an animal with a sensitive soul but without that spiritual power which is the intellect. But if there is question of an animal inasmuch as its physical and psychic structure as well as its behavior are an object of observation, and offer, from the amoeba to the chimpanzee, an infinitely varied detail of differences (and of problems), the philosopher has no right to speak of this unless he first knows what the scientist thinks of it. Inversely, the scientist, on his particular level of observation and experiment, knows a host of things about man and about the human psychism as different from the animal psychism, but if there is question of man and his psychism considered in their ontological structure, he has no right to speak of them if does not first know what the philosopher thinks of them. These are epistemological rules true in themselves, indeed too true to be respected in ordinary practice—the difficulties due to human weakness and to the weaknesses of the different states of culture, ours included, are discouraging. Where the scientist would like to put some questions to philosophy, he finds the philosophers in total disagreement. Where the philosopher would like to know what science thinks on its particular level of competence, he sometimes finds scientists oriented in their scientific ideas, without admitting it, by a consciously or unconsciously accepted philosophy or prephilosophy, and also on occasion scientists of different schools who fight among themselves (this is not the privilege of philosophers alone), and sometimes too he finds scientists who on their own particular level (and precisely because they insist on it) share with him the uncertainties and hesitations of science along with the points that science has established.

My third remark, which is somewhat long, relates to the term *hominian*. This term signifies a living being of the order of primates situated in the phylum or group of phyla (monophyletism or polyphyletism, monogenism or polygenism, I leave these questions open for the moment) which ends up or end up in man. But this is a truly ambiguous term, which in the dialogue between the scientist and the philosopher leads to singular difficulties.

Let me explain. Point number 1: The scientists tell us that absolutely no *animal* (not one of the animals that the spectacle of nature spreads before our eyes) is capable of making the tools that the Neanderthals[31] made for example, or of attaining a "culture" (*pre-culture* would be a more exact word) like the one they achieved. Superior hominians such as these were not *animals*, simple animals (in the sense of the word animal in the two opposing terms animal-

---

31   According to the views prevailing in paleontology in recent years, the Neanderthals must be considered as a regressive form; it matters little to me for the moment, I cite them by reason of the signs of "industry" and of "culture" that they have left behind. I could have cited as will the Sinanthrope, which Piveteau regards as "having reached the instrumental phase" and "having crossed the threshold of intelligence" (J. Piveteau, *Traité de Paléontologie*, pp. 385 and 387).

man). This is what the scientists hold. And we should consider their authority on this point as irrecusable. The psychism of these hominians incontestably surpassed the capacity of all the animals which populate nature around us.

Does this mean that they were already men, primitive men? This is evident, is it not? This is what the pair of opposing words *animal* and *man* lead us to conclude immediately. Not being animals they must certainly be men. This is the conclusion naturally established by the paleontologists. Hominians of varying types, through whom the man of the later quaternary and of today was prepared, were *primitive men.*

And now for point number 2. To know what man is first and foremost the business of the philosopher, who (and I have in mind, of course, a philosopher worthy of the name) defines man as an animal endowed with an intellective, spiritual, and immortal soul: a concept foreign to the epistemological domain of the scientist.

Indeed, the philosopher knows that the intellect is spiritual and hence must emanate from a spiritual soul. He knows that between the soul of a simple animal and the soul of man there is an *absolute*, abyssal difference because the senses, enclosed in materiality, perceive only the particular, whereas the intellect perceives the universal and reflects upon itself (and this implies immateriality in both cases) so that *in its exercise* the intellect certainly does develop, as we see in the child; but as a *power* it is given, with the intellective or spiritual soul, from the very first instant when that soul is infused into an organism sufficiently elevated for an ultimate disposition of the matter to call for it there. To think (as some scientists and even some philosophers seem to do, what a pity) that what current speech calls animal intelligence, which is an interior sense (called estimative by the philosopher), can succeed, advancing step by step, in finally becoming intellect, is just as absurd as to think that an architect will one day reach the moon by building higher and higher towers, or that by dint of perfecting its scent a well-trained hunting dog will succeed some day, when his master has become an art dealer, in distinguishing a Rouault from a Vermeer or an authentic Picasso from a fake one.

Now that all this has been established, what is the philosopher going to think of our hominian who is a man, a primitive man? Well, the philosopher quickly perceives that all this is unthinkable. I hope to examine this more in detail in another seminar. Let it suffice for me to say at present that we are faced with a dilemma: *Either* our higher hominian *belongs* to a species (I mean an ontological species, the kind that interests the philosopher) different from the ontological species to which the man of the later quaternary or of today belongs, *or he does not belong* to an ontological species different from that of the man of the later quaternary and of today. There is no middle ground. But both hypotheses involve an absurdity.

Indeed, in the first hypothesis (primitive men belonged to an ontological species different from that of the man of the quaternary and of today) it has to be admitted that there are *several human species* which came one after the other, and this is absurd. An animal whose specific difference (having an intellective, spiritual, and immortal soul) separates him from *all* other animals, constitutes one single and unique ontological (and taxonomic) species—the only species, moreover, that we can perceive with certitude.

And in the second hypothesis (primitive men *did not belong* to an ontological species different from that of the man of the later quaternary and of today) it must be admitted that the human species—the unique human species which, in the hypothesis in question, began to exist much earlier, from the very beginning of the quaternary—did not arise at the term of an evolution in the course of which higher and higher forms of animals finally became *almost* men, in other words prepared man *until the ultimate disposition of matter called for an intellective soul*; on the contrary, it rose to a rung of still relatively low *animal* development on the hominian evolutive ladder; it was born of animal forms too low on that ladder for their cerebral and psychic development to produce in these beings *an ultimate disposition of matter calling for an intellective soul*. In short, the *animal* preparation necessary for the advent of the human species *was lacking*. Such a supposition is, in its turn, sheer philosophical absurdity—as if it could be imagined, no longer in the case of the evolution of living beings, but this time in the case of human embryological development, that an intellective soul could be infused at the very first stage of development, from the instant the ovule is fecundated. I might add that the supposition in question, which is an absurdity, is also directly contrary to any genuine philosophy of evolution (for which indeed it is necessary to recognize the essential importance of the ultimate disposition of matter which takes place at each substantial mutation required by the passage to a higher degree of evolution).

The philosopher notes that the two horns of the dilemma—the higher hominian regarded as a primitive man *belonged* or *did not belong* to an ontological species different from that of the man of the later quaternary or of today— are equally unthinkable. And as a consequence, he has to declare that the higher hominians regarded as primitive men could not really have been men. They were not *animals*, declares science. The were not *men*, declares philosophy. Now here we have a first-rate aporia.

22. Let me stop here for a moment, for I feel the urge once again to insert a parenthesis. This one will bear on two words which play a major role in the theories of the origin of man. First of all, the word *primitive man*. This word can involve two entirely different ideas. It can signify a man *not completely disengaged from animality* (or more exactly, from bestiality, for we must never forget that man himself is an animal). Then the idea signified by the word *primitive man* is no more than a pseudo-idea. From the instant that a being is established within the human species, from the moment he is a man, with his

intellective, spiritual, and immortal soul, that being remains, of course, immersed in *human* animality (and this says quite a bit), but it is completely disengaged from the animality of *beasts*. The word *primitive man* has only one intelligible meaning: and that is when it is understood as a man *still in the childhood of humanity*.[32]

The second word to look at is the word *hominization*, in which Father Teilhard took such delight, and which the best paleontologists also make use of. This word has a perfectly valid meaning: To say that an animal is hominized is to say that it draws closer and closer to man or that it *takes on more and more advanced humanoid characteristics*. But it is used in another sense which has no meaning except for the mentally lazy (like quite a number of words which slip from time to time into the vocabulary of scientists, doctors, and philosophers): a meaning that I will not call mythic (that would be too flattering), but simply magical—so magical in fact that it explains everything without requiring any thought at all. *To become hominized* then means to become more and more a man, all the while remaining—less and less—an animal (a beast, deprived of reason).

If we try anyway to include some idea or other under the word *hominization*, it becomes clear that we can include under this expression, used in this particular way, only three conceptualizations. The first conceptualization: The beings in question, which are animals, become more and more men in the sense that they are at first 75 percent animal and 25 percent human, then 50 percent animal and 50 percent human, and subsequently 25 percent animal and 75 percent human. In short, they are, not by juxtaposition end to end, but in their intrinsic constitution, *centaurs*; they are two different species at one and the same time. This is a concept all right, but a contradictory one, good for nothing but dazzling a befuddled mind.

Second conceptualization: The beings in question are already men, but they pass from a lower human species to a higher human species. This is an absurdity, as we pointed out a few moments ago.

Or finally, the third conceptualization: Perhaps the beings in question already have a *real human intelligence* which begins to operate but do not have an intellective, spiritual, and immortal soul, which only we will eventually receive. Another dazzling idea but difficult to digest. To possess a truly human intelligence, like the intelligence that after millennia of development an existentialist writer or a disciple of Michel Foucault would eventually possess, and still not have a *human soul*, what a pity after all.

Everything I just said does not diminish by one iota the value of the words *hominization* and *to hominize* as they are used by authentic scientists and eminent paleontologists. But there have always been here and there in the

---

32   I might note in passing that from the paleontological point of view, this appears to be the case for the human family called *Homo sapiens fossilis*, and which has the same anatomical characteristics as modern man.

world a few inauthentic scientists, and there is especially that great multitude of people who, without being either scientists or philosophers, today get their information about the fashionable theories through the mass media, a multitude with no defense against such confused ideas and exposed to many a low blow. This is why I consider my parenthesis not entirely useless.

23. Well that's over. So let me return to our aporia: beings which cannot be called animals and which cannot be called men either. What are we to do now? Abandon the whole matter here? A philosopher is not so quickly discouraged. There must be a way out.

Let me make two remarks about this: In the first place, and what could be more normal, the animal that the scientists and we too are talking about is the animal as we know it, such as the the spectacle of nature offers everywhere to our view. We must note, however, that this is the animal of the *historical ages*, from the later quaternary till today; but the animal involved in questions of the origin of man, the animal of the phyla in mutation of pre-historic times, was a part of that evolutive process which lasted so many centuries and is now completed. As a part of that process it showed a plasticity that we are far from finding in the animals of historical time. In the second place, I have noticed that at the peak of the development of the higher primates, more precisely of the hominians, at a given moment there must have appeared a more or less ephemeral series of animals which came *very close* to man and at the end of this series (I have already noted this) there appeared an animal which was *almost a man*, the kind from which man could be born.

Then the idea came to me that perhaps there was a way—the only conceivable way—out of the impasse in which our aporia seemed to imprison us. And this was to establish the hypothesis, breaking the dilemma *animal or man* which locked us into the aporia, that between "animal" and "man" a third term should be introduced, and that, at the peak of the more or less ephemeral series of higher primates I just spoke of—and during a relatively short and unique period in the history of life, justly so because it was the period in which the aspiration of matter toward its supreme actuation, by an intellective soul, would find its ultimate fulfillment, there were animals whose psychism, while remaining only in the sensitive order, surpassed the level of the psychism of all the other animals of prehistoric times, as well as the level of all the animals of our historical times. For the moment let us call them *overdeveloped animals*, or, if you prefer, *pre-men*. Then we no longer have to deal with the pair of opposed terms animal and man, but with a triplet or trio of terms: animal, overdeveloped animal, and man. This overdeveloped animal did not belong to the *animal kingdom* solely in the way that the animal endowed with reason belongs to it. Unlike man, who is informed by an intellective soul, it continued to belong to the immense category of living beings *informed by a sensitive soul or a purely animal soul*. But he was part of the last stages disposing these particular living beings to give birth to the human species. And because of a mutation of major importance, which prepared the final and definitive mutation, its psychism, while still remaining in the purely sensitive order, was already emerging (how? I have a little key in my pocket, but it is still too early for me to use it) superior to the mental capacities of all the other animals. In other words, this overdeveloped animal, or pre-man, was capable of producing tools and of attaining that "culture" (or rather pre-culture) in which today everybody believes he recognizes the characteristic signs of primitive men not yet set apart from bestiality.

The hypothesis I am proposing here is a philosophical hypothesis, but one which, I believe, might prove useful and fruitful in the hands of the paleontologists, even though on the level proper to science, it can appear no more than probable and is not susceptible to verification. But on the philosophical level it can be verified, and by this I mean established by a convergence of arguments which is compelling for the mind

For the moment I will be satisfied to recall that paleontology, when it comes to treating man and his appearance on earth, tackles a problem which, when inquiring into human nature, or *what* man *is*, does not depend on science alone but also and above all on philosophy. Are not the most eminent paleontologists aware of this when, having come to his point, they invoke the testimony of such and such a philosopher?[33] I will be satisfied too that between the primitive men they tell us about and the overdeveloped animals of my hypothesis the resemblance is so great that I have nothing to fear for the latter; here I am not referring to the mental habits and the philosophical presuppositions of the paleontologists but to the paleontological criteria of differentiation. This is why I feel free in the last part of this seminar to take my stand on this hypothesis (still unverified, but to be so later), as long as it is clearly understood that in our effort to verify this hypothesis we have the obligation to give our most careful consideration to the data of science, that is, of animal psychology and paleontology. This is what I would like to do in the next seminars, if God gives me the time and the strength to do so.

24. Now that my preliminary remarks are finished, let me pass on to my exposition, in which, by hypothesis, I shall maintain that the *hominians*, even though they are very high up on the evolutive ladder, even though they belong to the highest group of hominians, I shall maintain that *all these hominians* are overdeveloped animals and not men. (I would add that the very highest among these overdeveloped animals perhaps, no one knows, have left no

---

33   Thus, when they came to this point, J. Piveteau and A. Vandel refer to a great philosopher like Bergson. Cf. J. Piveteau, *Traité de Paléontologie*, p. 328; Albert Vandel, *L'Homme et l'Evolution*, p. 254.

I there is question of some other domain, animal psychology, for example, von Uexküll and Buytendijk, and many others, also make frequent reference to the *dicta philosophorum*, when looking into the differences between animal and man.

fossil trace; being still without intellect, and already groping in the vicinity of the spirit, they were undoubtedly less well equipped than the others with that innate knowledge which is a part of the instincts of animals without reason, and consequently were less fitted to defend themselves against their enemies.)

You may recall that in the preceding section (p. 111) I used as an example to clarify our discussion the case of an anthropoid, or austriacopithecus, giving birth to an animal of specific degree higher than that of his begetters, and a little closer to the hominians, although still very far from them.

Let me now take another example, this time from the group *at the highest degree of* the evolution of the primates, so that we can consider those animals which were the *immediate ancestors* of man and whose (sensitive) soul was by hypothesis at the highest point of the stem on which man would appear. I shall call these immediate ancestors of man (in conformity with the fundamental hypothesis on which I have just explained my position) animals overdeveloped *to the highest limit*, or hominians of the highest level, completely refined hominians, of the highest species. They reproduced themselves and propagated their species and, under the general directing divine motion which activates the whole of nature, gave birth to living beings of the same degree of being, hominians of the highest level like their begetters. All these animals, overdeveloped *to the very limit*, were the immediate ancestors of man, but only *in potency*. Their species was like a flower, full-blown at the top of the evolutive stem.

The nucleus of this species, however, continued to be included in the stem, and the living beings which composed it always tended to pass on to a higher degree of being.

Let us suppose now that among these hominians of this most highly developed level included within the evolutive stem, a single couple, or as many couples as you like (I am not a polygenist; but I already pointed out that for the moment I am leaving this question open. I will treat it in another seminar) engenders or engender, in fact, living beings of a higher degree of being, that is, the first human beings.

The soul of these particular beings will be a human soul created by God. This means that God, by an absolutely free act, chose the particular hominian couple or couples I just mentioned, with the purpose of infusing into the living beings engendered by them, in the course of the prenatal life of these living beings, an intellective, spiritual, and immortal soul, which will have been called for by an ultimate disposition of matter, produced in the hominian fetus or fetuses, at a certain instant of its or their intra-uterine development, and this soul will in a very particular way already be human (I will try to explain this precisely in a moment).

So we have here, as regards the intellective soul which is the substantial form of the human being, the *creation* of this soul by an act of God implying an absolutely free and gratuitous divine choice. And on the other hand, as regards the ultimate disposition to be produced in matter, a *superelevating and superforming* divine motion which is no longer a general motion with regard to the world of life but, this time, an *exceptional and absolutely unique* motion, depending on the same absolutely free and gratuitous divine choice, which at one and the same time includes that motion which calls man forth by an ultimate disposition of matter, and the act by which man is created by the fact that God has created the soul which is the cause of his existence.

25. It will be good for us to pause now (not too long, I hope) on this difficult notion of the ultimate disposition of matter.

This ultimate disposition takes place at an *instant of time*, at a single and identical chronological instant when the form that has been informing up till that moment—the sensitive or animal soul of the hominian fetus in the present case (and we should recall that this happens likewise in the case of human embryonic development)—returns into the potency of matter. At this same instant the newly informing form is either educed from the potency of matter, or else—in the present case (as in the case of human embryonic development)—not educed from the potency of matter but rather created by God and infused into the fetus.

Along with this, however, in the ultimate disposition there are two *instants of nature* to be considered. At a first instant of nature, precisely because it is the *ultimate* disposition—in the present case, at the *term* of the sensitive development of the hominian fetus which is going to become human—this disposition supervenes in a substance (in the present case, the fetus in question) which is still informed, for an instant of time by that form (in the present case, the sensitive animal soul) which is about to return into the potency of matter.

And at a second instant of nature, this ultimate disposition exists within the substance already informed by the new form (in the present case, it exists in the hominian fetus that has already become human, already informed by the spiritual soul created by God).

From this it follows that the ultimate disposition produced in matter under the exceptional and absolutely unique motion of God that I spoke of (and let us note in passing that this motion is exercised on the embryonic development of the hominian fetus, which is in the process of becoming human, from the very instant of the fecundation of the ovule), this ultimate disposition supervening at the term of the sensitive development of the fetus in question is, *at the first instant of nature*, already *virtually human*, I mean already human as far as the quality of the *sensitive life* of the fetus is concerned, already raised to the human *in this particular regard*, in other words, already raised, *in this particular regard*, to a level that is beyond the capacities of material nature and of life immersed in matter. This is the precision I wanted to make. (At the *second instant of nature*, the fetus has received the intellective soul, and the ultimate disposition is formally human: all this taking place in the same *chronological instant*.)

26. My digression on the ultimate disposition of matter is over now, and I hope it was not too dry. In any case, what is important is to understand that if a hominian couple or couples has or have given birth a child or to several children, this could not have come about except through a double manifestation of the absolute freedom of the first Cause: manifested on the one hand in the preparation of matter and its ultimate disposition, by an exceptional and absolutely unique motion,[34] raising an animal nature to a level of being which transcends animality and the entire dynamism that nature is capable of by itself, even under the general superelevating and superforming motion with regard to the world of life; manifested on the other hand, in the newly produced substantial form, the creation and infusion of an intellective, spiritual, and immortal soul.[35] So we can now understand how, with regard to the ultimate disposition of matter, the advent of man has been at one and the same time truly the *term of the evolution* of life in its ensemble and of the evolution of the primates in particular, but thanks to the final intervention of an absolutely free and gratuitous choice exercised by God the Creator, and transcending all the possibilities of material nature; and on the other hand (with regard to the new infused substantial form) truly an absolutely free and gratuitous *work of creation*, but thanks this time to a long presupposed history of living organisms, willed by God from the very beginning, and thanks finally to the transformation of an animal species into the human species.

The hominian couple or couples I spoke of has or have been, in the animal kingdom, our immediate ancestors *in act*. They are not the *father* and *mother* of the human race. There is no creature which is the father or the mother from whom the human race was born because it is from God, and created by Him, that man receives the soul which makes him a man, and that the first man received his soul—or in the case of polygenism, which I will not discuss now—that the first men received their souls. As St. Luke said in tracing the genealogical lineage of Jesus: "Cainan, who was the son of Henos, *qui fuit Seth, qui fuit Adam, qui fuit Dei.*" We are descended from Seth, who was the son of Adam, *who was the son of God*.

27. Let us conclude by returning to the text of St. Thomas that we began with, that the sensitive soul is *in potency* to the intellective soul just as the vegetative soul is *in potency* to the sensitive soul, just as matter in the form of the element is *in potency* to the form of the mixed body, and just as prime matter

---

34 This is why *Genesis*, which had no call to furnish us with scientific explanations but rather to instruct us on the most profound sense of the real from God's point of view, tells us that God formed man from the slime of the earth (from which the whole evolution of life has emerged). "Then the Lord God formed man out of the dust of the ground" (II, 7).

35 This is why *Genesis* tells us that God *breathed* a (*spiritual*) soul into the man He drew from the dust, "and He breathed into his nostrils the breath of life, and man became a living being" (*ibid.*).

is *in potency* to the form of the element; and that, consequently there is an *ontological* (metaphysical) *tendency or aspiration* of matter toward higher and higher forms, and finally toward the human soul as toward its ultimate form.

This ontological (metaphysical) tendency—since it is stretched out over time in a universe in movement and historical development, which is not the universe of the ancients but our own—is also a *physically efficacious* tendency (I mean "physically" in the sense that it is put into operation by powers proper to the world of material nature, the object of Physics in the Aristotelian sense or of the Philosophy of Nature). It is a physically efficacious tendency in that cosmic élan which, throughout the entire universe (the stars and the earth), causes matter to pass through all its physical and chemical transformations. It is physically efficacious too in the evolutive élan which, once it has crossed the threshold of life, causes matter to pass from the first living cells to more differentiated, though still very primitive, living beings, informed like the very first cells, with a vegetative soul. Then these most primitive and simplest vegetative living beings, formed in the bosom of the oceans which covered the crust of the earth, were transformed into aquatic, then terrestrial, living beings, informed by sensitive souls, would blossom into higher and higher species in the course of evolution (just as, after the continental surfaces had arisen, plants, born of the most primitive forms of vegetative life, would do in their turn). The dynamism of nature by itself alone is all that was needed in these two cases: in the first case (that of the cosmos) under the *directing and absolutely general* divine motion; in the second case (the case of the evolution of life and the crossing of the threshold of life) under the *superelevating and superforming* divine motion, still general, at least with regard to the world of living beings in evolution.

The tendency I am speaking of was physically efficacious up to this point. But once this point was passed, and if there was question of the passage from the animal living being to the human living being, then in this case the tendency in question was not *physically efficacious*; it did not remain solely an ontological (metaphysical) tendency; it always existed "physically" in matter but in this case *inefficaciously*. The dynamism of nature by itself alone, even under the superelevating and superinforming divine motion, general as it was with regard to the world of living beings in evolution, was not enough to make it efficacious.

There had to be the transcendent action of the first Cause and an absolutely free and gratuitous divine choice—on the one hand bringing living matter, under an *exceptional and absolutely unique* motion, to a disposition surpassing the capacities of material nature and life immersed in matter, and, on the other hand, creating *ex nihilo*, an intellective, spiritual, and immortal soul—in order to satisfy from above the tendency in question and to make it capable of attaining in the very bosom of the tangible and visible, "physical" (in the Aristotelian sense) reality of the world of nature, the final term to which it was ordered from the creation of the world and which is itself of the metaphysical order or beyond all material nature, since it is the intellective, spiritual, and immortal soul, the *human* soul.

POSTSCRIPT[36]

I was hoping to complete this article by another study touching on more particular points. I regret not being able to do so. I will try at least in this postscript to indicate, however imperfectly, the positions I believe correct concerning the problem of monogenism or polygenism.

1. First of all, in the sphere of science and of paleontology, I would point out that nothing enables us to decide by any sure criteria if we are concerned with a hominian or with a man.

If there is question of fossil remains, such as fragments of skulls or jawbones, the possibility is always there that they belonged to a higher vertebrate, very advanced in evolution but not yet a man.

And if there is question of primitive tools, we cannot, here either, put aside the possibility that higher vertebrates, who were not yet hominians, were capable of making them. Does not animal psychology show us generally in this regard that the resources of the imagination unaccompanied by reason clearly go much further than current prejudice inclines us to believe?

2. In the second place, if we take the point of view of philosophy, the most significant fact that confronts us is *the unity of the human species*. However profound the differences due to the diversity of races, of cultures and of conditions of life may be, it is always with a man that we have to deal, with his deep-seated psychological traits, good and bad, in the East as in the West, among the most civilized as among the most primitive peoples. Each individual possesses human dignity as well as human frailties.

In times past there were great civilizations of which only enigmatic traces remain today, as for example the giant statues of the Easter Isles and of Mexico (which clearly does not mean that those who made them were giants themselves but only that they wished to represent the power and sublimity of the gods they adored, in order to better render them homage). Without any doubt there have been great civilizations anterior to our own. But human species different from our own, this is impossible, for the possession of a spiritual and immortal soul not only separates the human species from all other animal species; it also assures the unity of that species. The titans, those "heroes of old, the men of renown" of whom the Bible speaks (*Genesis*, the second story of creation, iv, 1–4), and whose fathers were "the sons of heaven," who fell in

---

36   Written in 1972.

love with "the daughters of men"—the most probable supposition we can make about them is that they endowed with exceptional power because they came from the crossing of two different and complementary races, the lineage of Seth and of Cain. However renowned they may have been, they were, in their natures, men like us.

What conclusion can be drawn from this unity of the human species that I just insisted on? It is this: For the human species as for all other animal species, in the course of the evolutive process, it is by virtue of *biological lineage and hereditary transmission* that the *ontological reality* which is human nature is communicated to each new human being.

If we hold, according to Judeo-Christian tradition, that man was created in the state of grace, we must admit that if every new human being is born with a nature deprived of grace and wounded in its being, it is by reason of the hereditary transmission by which this human nature is passed on to him.

It certainly conceivable that by virtue of the divine superelevation of the evolutive process, an ultimate disposition of matter calling for the infusion of a human, spiritual, and immortal soul may have been produced in a plurality of hominian branches. But what is absolutely inconceivable for reason is that such an ultimate disposition would take place *at the same instant* in this plurality of branches. Each of them carried out its own evolution separately under different conditions. An interval of more or less long duration necessarily separated the arrival of each branch at the final stage in question. One of these branches then must have had priority in time.

But from the point of view of evolution, which concerns the material world, if one of the hominian branches, in which the disposition calling for the infusion of a spiritual soul was produced, had to have priority in time over the other branches, it is because, from the point of view of the first Cause, by virtue of the superelevation imprinted by Him on the evolutive process and of the exceptional and absolutely unique superforming motion causing the abyss between the human being and the purely animal being to be crossed, God the Creator willed that the ultimate disposition in question appear at a certain moment in time. There is nothing freer or more gratuitous than the creative Act. It is that "mad," boundless love of God for the being made in His image (demanding in response our "mad," boundless love for Him) which intervened here. And this love of God is *a love of choice, a love of election*, according to which one is taken and another left. Was it toward a single human couple destined, through the free and gratuitous divine superelevation, to be brought forth from that hominian branch we are speaking about (a branch which by this very fact would enjoy priority in time), that this love of election was directed, or was it toward a small group composed of the very first humans? I do not think it is the responsibility of the philosopher to settle this question (this depends on revelation). But the philosopher does know that a free divine choice was involved, and that all the other hominian branches were left aside. Whence it follows that he must hold that monogenism thus understood is based on reason.

3. Finally if we look at what we might call God's way of doing things, it seems to us that each time a historical change of immense importance took place, God willed that it be the work of one person alone (or of two alone). This was the case with Abraham becoming, by his acceptance of the sacrifice of Isaac, the father of all believers. This was the case with Moses bringing the people of Israel out of Egypt. This was the case with the Virgin in whom the Word took flesh. This was the case with him who must be considered the greatest of the prophets, charged as he was with the mission of Precursor of Christ. This was the case with St. Peter to whom the feeding of Christ's sheep was confided, or with St. Paul who, by the most decisive revolution in the religious history of humanity and at the cost of very difficult struggles, was charged with bringing the Gospel to the uncircumcised. And in the ages that followed the same divine way of operating is evident. It was because of two men, and only two men, Albert the Great as precursor and Thomas Aquinas as master, at one of the most troubled periods in the history of the Church, and despite seemingly insurmountable obstacles, that Christian intelligence put out to sea and its progress toward the truth was assured (to whatever peril it seems exposed today, if it is to survive, it will indeed have to follow the road on which the Common Doctor set it).

What is so astonishing about the fact that Revelation should teach us that the human nature of each one of us has its origin in a single human couple, or that this human nature should bear the mark of the tragic yet happy story of this couple (*O felix culpa*)?

In speaking of the divine way of doing things, my present remarks do not have the conclusive value, in my opinion decisive, of what was said in the preceding paragraph concerning the divine love of election. These remarks are nevertheless useful to enlighten our minds and to lead us to maintain that the monogenist position is the proper one and that polygenism must be rejected.

CHAPTER VII
ON THE PHILOSOPHY OF NATURE (II)

CONCERNING ANIMAL INSTINCT[1]

1. IN HIS *VOCABULAIRE TECHNIQUE DE LA PHILOSOPHIE* Lalande defines instinct: "A complex ensemble of hereditary, determinate, external reactions common to all animals of a species and adapted to an end of which the acting being is generally not conscious." Such a definition is acceptable only if, instead of saying "a complex ensemble of exterior reactions," one would say "a complex ensemble of coordinated mental operations of determinate ways of acting. . . . " Innumerable examples of animal behavior show how fruitless is the pretension to reduce instinct to a chain of reflexes. This was already made clear in Janssens's book *L'Instinct d'après McDougall*, published in a collection I edited in 1938.[2]

For many years now I have been interested in animal psychology, and this has permitted me to notice the admirable progress that this science has made in the past fifty years. Today I have a very special admiration for that eminent biologist M. Rémy Chauvin. His work,[3] as well as that of M. Thorpe,[4] have definitively swept away the mechanist theories formerly held in favor by so many.

2. When we speak of the psychism of the animal, it is normal to use the same words to designate the faculties possessed by its purely sensitive soul and the

---

1   *Editor's footnote*: Seminar given to the Little Brothers of Jesus in Toulouse on January 12, 1973. Cf. *Revue Thomiste*, 1973, no. 2.

2   E. Janssens, *L'Instinct d'après McDougall* (Paris: Desclée de Brouwer, "Questions Disputées" XX, 1938). McDougall and Janssens rightly maintain that *innateness* and *finality* are essential characteristics of instinct. When the word *finality* is used, it is certainly not understood that the bee says to itself: "Let's go build a hive!" Bees act in such a way as to construct a hive, and they do in fact make it, but without having the slightest notion of the end they are pursuing.

3   I am thinking of his epoch-making work on the migratory locust, and of such books as his *Traité de biologie de l'Abeille*, his *Physiologie de l'Insecte* or his *Vie et Moeurs des Insectes*.

4   Cf. W. H. Thorpe, "Learning and Instinct in Animals" and "Experimental Studies of Animal Behaviour," in *Current Problems in Animal Behaviour*, edited by W. H. Thorpe and D. L. Zangwill (Cambridge University Press, 1963).

sensitive faculties possessed by our spiritual soul but without forgetting that the words in question are applied with very different meanings in each case. This difference is extraordinarily striking with regard to the external senses, and notably the ocular apparatus, so that the diverse species of animals live each one in a world proper to it and altogether different from ours.[5] After taking account of this fact and of its importance, we can say that the faculties with which the souls of animals are endowed are: (1) *external senses* (with conscious sensations and unconscious sensations); (2) *memory* and *imagination* (with conscious images and unconscious images); (3) that faculty of basic learning or of *insight*, which as yet has nothing to do with reasoning properly so called but which, by mixing together only those things which come from the external and internal senses, "makes the animal see" in a purely sensitive way some particular object drawn from this source. The Scholastics called this faculty in man *cogitative* and in animals *estimative* (I will tell you in a moment why I reject this latter word); (4) *appetivity* and *affectivity* (conscious and unconscious) which in the case of the animal can be very strong but always remain strictly limited,[6] in short, *motricity*.

3. In regard to the words *estimative* and *cogitative*, it seems to me that in past times the idea men formed of the animal was far too summary and that, since in the case of man the cogitative faculty is at the service of the intellect, an effort was made to point out, by a different word to designate a different faculty, the

---

5   Cf. Vitus B. Dröscher, *Le Merveilleux dans le Monde animal* (Paris: Robert Laffont, 1968). Rémy Chauvin tells us, along with von Uexküll, that the insect and animals in general live "in a universe different from that of man. Their senses are very different from ours, and objects do not at all appear to them under the same aspect as they appear to us" (*Vie et Moeurs des Insectes* [Paris: Payot, 1956], p. 11). The biological universe, he writes again, "is a *world of signs* only certain of which are isolated by a particular species, which carves out its own universe in those particular signs. Other aspects of the cosmos are resolutely ignored or have no meaning. But it is precisely these aspects which turn out to be essential for another species. Encounters with sexual partners or with prey, the building of nests, hunting, etc., everything is carried out according to a *stereotyped ritual*, but the animal does not move about in a world of stimuli, as the disciples of Loeb believed, but in a world of objects. Its adaptability and its faculties of apprenticeship (early basic learning) may be very great, but they are exercised only at very limited moments, in the interstices of the ritual, so to speak" (p. 92).

6   A question arises here: Can an animal expose itself to danger or to death to protect another being to which it is linked by bonds of affection? This is certainly sometimes the case: first—and about this there can be no doubt—to protect its offspring; then, in the case of a dog, for example, to protect its master.
     But in order to help another animal? This seems to me rather doubtful. We must note, however, that jackdaws gather in groups to defend with their strident cries members of their own species when they are being attacked. Cf. Konrad Lorenz, *Il parlait avec les Mammifères, les Oiseaux et les Poissons* (Paris: Flammarion, 1968), pp. 74–76.

absence of any psychic determinant in the conduct of animals and to point out, in particular, their incapacity to learn or to "cogitate"—certainly in an area of purely and exclusively sensitive activity—in other words to fend for themselves among the things perceived by their senses (certain things, that is, which were of particular interest to their lives). As if in the case of man the external senses, as well as memory and imagination as "internal senses," were not at the service of the intelligence! And as if, on the other hand, the difference between the external senses in animals and the external senses in man was not as profound as (and more astonishingly profound than) the difference between the animal cogitative faculty and human cogitative faculty? The word *estimative* is one of very doubtful quality and modern studies in animal psychology no longer authorize its use. What must be said is that the cogitative faculty, a purely sensitive faculty, exists in both animals and man but in each case in an entirely different way. In man it serves the intelligence and possesses a vast range; in animals it remains in a pure and simple form, with a very limited range, but is still at the highest point of the animal psychism. This is why I would like to insist on it here and on the power of early basic learning, a kind of animal apprenticeship. On this point let us turn to that perfect observer Konrad Lorenz (cf. *Il parlait avec les Mammifères*, pp. 56–57, on the perplexed fish that "reflects") and to the great scientist Rémy Chauvin. The latter tells us that there exists in the insect a kind of *insight* (*Vie et Moeurs des Insectes*, p. 103)—indeed, without such a power no animal species could survive. He tells us also (p. 75), along with Kaeler and Van Holst, that "the organism is not a lazy donkey that needs the stimulus of a stick to make it move; it is rather like a high-spirited horse which ceaselessly seeks to leap over fences, but cannot do so as long as the relevant object, appearing in its sensorial field, does not open the lock," and he tells us too (p. 103) that in general, "this early basic learning, as perfect as it may be, takes place at lightning speed."

In regard to the higher vertebrates, there is the well-known story of the chimpanzee "which had at its disposal only the different segments of a fishing-rod in order to pull in a banana placed outside the iron bars of its cage. After a few rapid and incoherent attempts, these most gifted of subjects sit down in a corner, without taking their eyes off the fishing-rod; they seem to be reflecting. Suddenly, without any hesitation, seizing the separated segments, they put them together and pull in the banana; the problem has been solved." (*Ibid.*, p. 102.)

The animal has a thousand ways of protecting itself against it predators and its enemies. The insect disguises itself (as a twig, a pebble, or a dead leaf). Indeed, at the height of cunning, "Certain species are able to put on the aposematic livery of other uneatable or formidable species, and thereby gain the respect of their predators" (p. 196).

If a more detailed example is called for, I will limit myself to this one from ornithology. As Maria Koepcke has shown, birds in tropical forests have to protect their nests from all kinds of predators, particularly from bands of monkeys, even from pigs, from toucans, owls, snakes, and ants who would like nothing better that to eat the birds' eggs. A third of these birds hatch their eggs in easily defendable cavities in the ground and in trees. Parrots hollow out their nests in abandoned termite mounds. Other birds build their nests at the tips of very high branches where monkeys cannot climb without danger. Others see to it that the branches hang out over an expanse of water. Still others give their nests the form of a pile of dead leaves. Others again cover the holes they dug in the ground as nests with dead leaves, but wait for three months before laying their eggs so that the twigs and leaves completely hide the mound of dirt produced by the digging of the nest. The wren builds its nest in trees inhabited by ants, which, at the slightest shaking of the tree, come out in mass and cover the predator with with their painful bites. In the diverse forms of cunning used in this way, what has to be recognized is, not so much instincts in the strict sense of the word, but rather the work of that animal cogitative capacity and that power of early basic learning, which bring about the acquisition of habits transmitted by heredity.

4. Everything I have pointed out from the beginning confirms me in my long-standing agreement with McDougall and Janssens concerning what things make up animal instinct and concerning the faculty of early basic learning and also concerning questions about variations of secondary importance or concerning the normal interpenetration between innate and stereotyped instinct and acquired experience (which is also capable of engendering collective habits). Poorly informed people often attribute this acquired experience, in particularly striking individual cases, to what they mistakenly call "the intelligence" of such and such an animal—in any case this capacity must be called *cogitative*.[7]

---

7   Let us add that in certain cases it is the animals who teach us. Watching them function helps "healers" and naturistic doctors discover the medicinal qualities of plants. The work of Kayser on the hibernation of marmots, carried out for purely scientific reasons, showed themselves, in the order of practical application, to be of extreme importance to doctors, who can today, when it is necessary, have their patients hibernate or live at a much slower pace, as marmots do. And it can also happen that we might draw lessons of the moral order (if we are not too stupid) from the behavior of animals. Total devotion of parents to their offspring, the happy eagerness of the latter to obey. Unshakable respect (here the lesson surely goes too far) for social hierarchies and the rules of organized society . . .
      Contrary to those prejudices which would have it that in the love and marriage of animals, "bestial" (that is grossly sensual) movement predominates, we must insist on the fact that among the animals in whose lives love and marriage play an important role, betrothal almost always precedes physical union. Jackdaws become engaged to each other in the Spring following their birth, but are not capable of procreating until the next spring. The same is the case with wild geese.

In recalling that I was happy to concur in the general views expressed by McDougall and Janssens about fifty years ago, I have in mind especially that, in the course of evolution, it is always the psychic structure of the instinct which played the regulatory role with regard to the corporal structure itself.[8] But I insist on noting that what constitutes the object of my present reflections is not at all the study of animal psychology; it is above all the problem of that "knowledge" which animal instinct presupposes, but which the animal does not possess, that I want to touch upon.[9] It is very important here to make a

So in these two species, the normal duration of betrothal is exactly one year" (Lorenz, *Il parlait avec les Mammifères*, p. 83).

"One of the great pleasures of my life and of a work consecrated, as in my case, to pure observation in the midst of wild animals, is that these animals are magnificently lazy. The absurd activity of modern civilized man who can no longer find even the time to become a truly cultured person, is totally foreign to the animal. Even bees and ants, those symbols of diligent work, spend the greater part of the day in a 'dolce farniente'; but at these moments they are not seen, for when they are not at their work, they remain tranquilly at home" (*Ibid.*, p. 141).

8   "For McDougall, the somatic characteristics of each species are: 1. they serve the instinct; 2, they find in instinct their profound reason, as well as the cause of their evolutive development. 'The evolution of the animal world,' he wrote (*An Outline of Psychology*, p. 113), 'is primarily a process of differentiation and specialization of instincts; this much-neglected truth is obvious when we reflect on such facts as the following: Horned cattle or antlered deer do not fight *because* they are provided with horns or antlers; the species develops these weapons in the service of the instinct of combat. The carnivore does not prey on animals *because* he has large teeth; his teeth and claws have been evolved because his food-seeking instinct has become specialized in this direction. The seal did not take to the water *because* his legs were flipper-like and his body fish-shaped; he acquired these peculiarities of structure in consequence of his food-seeking instinct having become specialized for the pursuit of fish. The same is true of a thousand instances of shape and form and coloration, of bodily structure and function, down to the minutest details. The evolution of the animal world may properly be conceived as primarily and essentially the differentiation of instinctive tendencies from some primordial undifferentiated capacity to strive toward certain objects'" (Janssens, *L'Instinct d'après McDougall*, p. 22, n. 1).

9   If the specialists of animal psychology, only with the greatest reserve, touched upon the question of the origin of instinct and of the *knowledge* which the latter presupposes, it is because to tell the truth this question is the business of the philosopher and not the scientist. To invoke evolution in general terms is not sufficient, and to speak with McDougall of a "primordial undifferentiated capacity to strive toward certain objects" (cf. the preceding note) seems to cast very little light on the problem.

It is through the process of evolution of which He is the first Cause that God created the animal species. However undifferentiated "the capacity to strive toward certain objects" may have been in the first animal species or in a number of first species, there existed at least a tendency—a tendency to seek nourishment in some particular kind of food—which must have been there from the very beginning. And in order that the tendency in question be fulfilled, there had to clear distinction between what belongs to the realm of science and what belongs to the realm of philosophy.

In the scientific realm, the scientist is busy with the construction of syntheses concerning observable phenomena as such (always having, consciously or unconsciously, a latent ideal of general mathematization). And such a synthesis is of its very nature provisory; it prepares a new intuition and a new synthesis into which it will be absorbed.

"*The insect lives, not in a world of stimuli, but in a world of objects*," wrote Rémy Chauvin (*Vie et Moeurs des Insects*, p. 86). In proposing to science, as a general and fundamental theme of interpretation, what he calls *objectivism*, he has forced animal psychology to take a step forward which in my opinion is of fundamental importance. In addition he tells us (*ibid.*, pp. 222–223) that "everything has barely begun," and that even if "biology, and in particular the

---

be as well some innate discernment—due to some presupposed "knowledge"—which would permit the animal to distinguish in the immense variety of the productions of nature the kind of food which suited it. . . . This is the problem we bump up against, if, as we are convinced, McDougall and Janssens and the most eminent men of science today, are completely right to take sides against the behaviorists.

The question can be asked too whether or not among the behaviorists the obscure intuition of the existence of such a problem (one which has far-reaching consequences) did not have quite a bit to do with their tenacious desire to refuse to animal instinct anything at all connected with the mental or the psychic, and to reduce instinct to a chain of conditioned reflexes (which, to tell the truth, amounts to purely and simply emptying instinct of any meaning whatever.)

Now let us suppose that the first animal organisms descended, by means of some major mutation due to the evolutive impulse (or to a superelevating divine motion) from some hypothetical aquatic or terrestrial vegetables, ended up suckling, if I might use the expression, the juice or sap of these mother-plants. However complex and however high in its order may have been the vegetative souls of these first animal organisms, they were clearly incapable of providing these first animal seeds with the faculty of perceiving in the juice or the sap in question the nourishment toward which they were bound to tend; and they were even more incapable of conferring on this tiny animal, when later in the course of evolution it would begin from birth to lead its own life, the instinct to seek out in all the diversity of menus offered by the vegetable world (or the animal world for the carnivores) the particular food which suited it and which would specialize its general tendency to seek nourishment.

And if it can be said in a metaphorical sense that this little animal from that time on knew, innately, how to distinguish the food which suited it, the meaning of the word *know* in this case is entirely improper and philosophically inadmissible, since, being without an intellect, this animal is just as incapable as the plant of arriving at knowledge in the proper sense of the word. But it had to be able to distinguish the food that was good for it. But this depended on a knowledge in the proper sense of the word that was presupposed. The cosmos and its intelligibility demanded that there be such a knowledge; but it was not the animal that had it.

biology of insects, looks upon the living world with new eyes," it is neverthe-less still "waiting for someone who will cause a break-through to another level, by coordinating in a general theory, however provisory, that immense harvest of facts we can no longer control. Like the astronomy of old, it is waiting for its own Copernicus." Thanks to an intuition of genius, this Copernicus of biology will assemble these facts into a new explanatory synthesis, which will itself, by it its nature, remain provisory, in the sense I have just indicated because in its proper realm science works only with phenomena perceptible to the senses, and because scientific investigation is a hard struggle where everything depends on verified phenomena and on the synthetic power of the human mind and, hence, requires the freedom to advance without any limi-tation.

With philosophy it is a completely different kettle of fish. It works in an entirely different realm from that of science. It works on the intelligible being lying beneath the phenomena in that *reality* of which phenomena are no more than the manifestations which fall within the reach of the senses.

So if a philosopher makes a mistake, what he tells us is worth nothing; whereas to the degree that he attains to what is, what he tells us is purely, simply, and immutably true.

Since I had to touch on animal psychology, I had to stay as up to date as I could on the research and discoveries of science in this field, but this was no more than a prerequisite. This explains all the preceding pages. But from the beginning of my work, what I had in view were philosophical problems, particularly the one I alluded to above: Where does the *knowledge* presupposed by animal instinct (and also by its faculties of early basic learning—appren-ticeship) come from, a *knowledge* in the proper and intellectual sense of the word which the animal brings into play, but which it absolutely does not possess itself? This is the reason for the pages which follow, so I can now turn to the object I set for myself.

5. So let us pass on now to those unfettered reflections that Christian philosophy (it would be better to say philosophy in the fullness of it nature)[10] invites us to have no fear of proposing. They will bear particularly on that knowledge in the strict sense of the word, presupposed by instinct in the strict sense of this word, which is innate and common to all the individuals of a species, a knowledge which these individuals apply but absolutely do not possess.

If there is question of concrete cases suited for use as examples, there are only too many to choose from. Bees building their hive come to mind, or the macon wasp laying its eggs in a nest of mud which it has filled with caterpillars paralyzed by its sting, which it then closes up completely "in such a way that the caterpillars remain as a reserve of fresh animal food for the little wasps that

10   Cf. *infra*, Ch. XVII: "Along Unbeaten Pathways," p. 421.

the mother will never see and about whose needs she has no knowledge or even the slightest notion"; or again a young squirrel raised in captivity, who, "when he is given nuts for the first time, opens some and eats them, then buries others with all the movements characteristic of its species";[11] or "that izard wounded in the thigh which made itself a poultice of clay and herbs"; or "the weasel who, in preparation for doing battle with snakes, rolls about on the leaves of a plantain tree which are very effective against the stings of bees and the venom of snakes";[12] or the *death feigning instinct* that can be observed in many animal species, which is well known in ladybugs who roll up in the hand like little dead balls."[13]

Once again I will be satisfied to consider in detail a single particularly significant example: the swallow observed by the father of Maurice Mességué,[14] as he was stretched out on the grass, attentive to everything that took place in nature around him. One of the babies of this swallow was unable to open its eyes. The mother swallow went off to get a blade of celandine and began to rub the little one's eyes with it; with the application of this remedy its eyes were opened.

Everything happened *as if* the swallow *knew* that celandine is good for the eyes. But the swallow does not *know* this since it is incapable of any rational knowledge.

How can this be explained? Swallows do not eat celandine. Did some swallow by pure chance rub celandine on the still unopened eyes of one of its babies, after which they opened up, with the result that the cogitative faculty and the memory of this animal registered this fact, in such a way that it could be transmitted to the entire swallow species? This is patently absurd. There is absolutely no question here of a habit acquired by the faculties of apprenticeship. What is involved here is instinct in the strict sense of the word, of an innate instinct present in the entire species from the time of its origin. From the time that the species swallow appeared in the course of evolution, did the mother swallow have as a part of its motricity some blind mechanism by virtue of which, automatically, from conditioned reflex to conditioned reflex, when one of its young was unable to open its eyes, go to find a blade of celandine and rub it on the eyes of its little one? (This is a common understanding of instinct as a clock-like mechanism conferred "by nature" on all the individuals of a given species and causing them to act identically without any psychic operation.) All this is equally absurd.

So an intelligent solution must be found by reflecting on the fact that one of the essential characteristics of instinct is to be *innate* (even though, in certain cases, particularly the case of the migratory locust studied by Rémy Chauvin,

11   Cf. Janssens, *L'Instinct d'après McDougall*, pp. 5 and 6.

12   Maurice Mességué, *Des Hommes et des Plantes* (Paris: Robert Lafont, 1970), p. 20.

13   F. Buytendijk, *Psychologie des Animaux* (Paris: Payot, 1928), p. 127.

14   Cf. Mességué, *Des Hommes et des Plantes*, pp. 27–28.

it takes its definitive form after a certain period of time in which the psychic structure of the young animal matures as its corporal structure develops). From the moment that some new species appears on the earth, the individuals who make up that species are endowed with all their instincts as they are with all their organs and body parts. And it is the psychic equipment of the instincts that governs the physical equipment of the body.

6. But before going on to these reflections and proposing our hypothesis, it would be well to recall to mind some philosophical principles of a much more general and basic order and to meditate a bit on them.

Only God *creates*, that is to say draws, from nothingness whatever exists, He who made heaven and earth, *visibilia et invisibilia*: from the first instant that the angelic universe appears, just as from the first instant, in our particular epoch, when *prime matter* appears and all the first elementary corpuscles whose form actualizes this matter in a structuration of the lowest order in which our microscopes reveal to us the realm of indetermination. The creative Act embraces absolutely all things in the eternal instant in which Being *per se subsistens* lives; the creative Act is God himself in his free will (Cf. *Sum. theol.*, Ia, q. 45, a. 5).

But St. Thomas teaches also (*ibid.*, a. 3) that creation as received from God is "something in the creature," *est aliquid in creatura*, namely, a certain relation (real) to the Creator as the principle of its being." Let us be bold enough to try to comment on this text by asking if it is possible to draw some conclusions from it.

The way in which God, as the creative Act, *gives* being is evidently and from the very beginning of things always the same. But is the way in which the creature *receives* from God the being which it has entirely and solely from Him always the same, and does it not involve different modalities—I mean in the creature itself? I think that the way in which the creature receives its being from God implies two different modes.

Let us consider on the one had the case of the spiritual soul when, at that given moment when it is called for by the ultimate disposition of matter, it is created by God and infused by Him into the human fetus. Not only is the generative power of the parents absolutely incapable of producing it, but the soul itself, even though it is in the world, is in its essence independent of the world and all the world's productive powers; its spiritual and immortal essence is superior to that of the entire material cosmos. The being that the soul has from God, drawn by Him from nothingness, receives that being in a manner that is totally unconditioned,[15] immediate and instantaneous.

But after this let us consider the body of the child: This body was produced by the generative act of the parents, themselves having been engendered by

---

15   The ultimate disposition, which in the human fetus calls for the spiritual soul, itself presupposes an exceptional and absolutely unique motion of God. Cf. above ch. VI: "Toward a Thomist Idea of Evolution," p. 127.

other human beings in a continuous chain that goes back through the centuries. In the same way (this time for both body and soul) all the animals, whose souls are not spiritual, were produced by the generative power of their ancestors; and in a similar manner all the beings of the material universe were produced by the powers of nature. And yet all of this was also *created*, drawn from nothing by God, and by *God alone*: because all of these things are part of a whole which is the material cosmos, and which is itself *wholly created*, in its productive powers as well as in its being. Not a single one of its parts is independent of the whole; and it is this entire whole which must be kept in mind when any of its parts is under consideration. As far as the creative Act which proceeds from God is concerned, the soul of the animal is created *in the same way* as the spiritual soul of men, but in as far as we are concerned with the way in which the being, which it has entirely from God, is received by it, the animal soul does not receive this being *in the same way*. For this there had to be a long process that went back through all of time; the animal soul receives its being in a manner that is conditioned and mediatized[16] by the cosmos and by the productive powers, themselves created, at work in the cosmos—drawn in its totality from nothingness by God and by God alone.

This is why there is no opposition whatsoever between the ideas of universal evolution and of creation.[17] It is through the evolution of the material world in its entirety, and as a fruit of this evolution that (except for the human soul, which is spirit) everything appearing on the earth, especially the animals in the infinite variety of their species, has its being from God and from God alone; it is through evolution that each single thing exists, along with the entire world of matter, of which it is a part, drawn from nothingness by God, and by God alone, and is found in that very real relationship with God of having been created by Him—and of tending toward Him.

7. Finally, it should be noted that the world of matter is placed entirely under the sign of the opposition, one could almost say conflict, between two contrary exigencies or aspirations. On the one hand there is implied a radical tendency to maintain itself in being according to the degree to which it possesses that being,—from this comes the basic exigency of stability for the different species. On the other hand, by reason of the radical aspiration of the created to rejoin the Creator as much as possible and attain to the divine similitude, *divinam*

---

16 St. Thomas (*Sum. theol.*, Ia, q. 45, a. 5; q. 46, a. 3) considers it a grave error to believe that God created anything whatsoever *mediantibus* created ministers (q. 46, a. 3). But in this case he is speaking of the *creative act* and not at all of the way in which the creature *receives* the being it has from God.

17 "*In rebus naturalibus* gradatim species ordinatae *esse videntur: sicut mixta perfectiora sunt elementis, et plantae corporibus mineralibus, et animalia plantis, et homines aliis animalibus*" (*Sum. theol.*, Ia, q. 47, a. 2). All that has to be added is the dimension of succession in time and of development in time to have the notion of evolution.

similitudinem, there is implied as well a basic tendency to pass beyond the degree of perfection in which matter is found in this or that case; with the result that "in those things subject to generation and corruption the ultimate degree of the whole order of the movement of generation is the human soul," as St. Thomas says in the *Summa contra gentiles*.[18] This opposition between two contrary aspirations is at its maximum in the world of life and, above all, in the world of the animals other than the animal endowed with reason.

With the theory of evolution, which was unknown to the ancients, the metaphysical tendentiality I just spoke of became a succession of mutations which took place in the course of thousands of centuries.[19] However, from the opposite point of view, paleontology presents us with more and more examples of the stability of animal species through periods of time that are sometimes of stupefying duration.

How has nature, in actual fact, resolved the opposition between the two contrary exigencies or aspirations I just pointed out in the world of matter, above all once the threshold of life has been passed, most particularly of animal life? As I tried to show more clearly in a preceding work,[20] each phylum is like a mounting stem, from which grow leaves that spread out horizontally, and each of which represents a stable species. This stem, which may be very thin, is composed of different variations which come about deep within certain species and which, becoming more and more important, bring forth from the stem, at a higher level, a few new leaves that spread out horizontally. It is through the phylum that the evolutive élan passes and, by a transubstantial mutation, produces in the course of time, under the direction of the first Cause and under a superelevating and superforming motion exercised by Him, a new animal species endowed with the stability that it normally requires.

Here we see at work, under divine motion, the evolutive élan which from the very beginning God stamped into matter and which, in the vast multitude of phyla through which it passes, awakens in the living beings which compose them the transnatural aspirations of matter. What does this mean if not that the creature, while receiving its entire being from God, under the superelevating and superforming motion of the Creator, and through the activities that it receives from Him, contributes to its very own evolution. In this way God brings it about that, by means of the mutations, more or less infrequent and more or less spread out over time, which He brings about in it, the creature itself works at raising to a new degree of perfection a lineage which will, in its turn, have its whole being from God. The title which M. Paul Wintrebert, in a most improper choice of words, gave to his book *Le Vivant Createur de son*

---

18   Book III, ch. 22. Cf. above ch. VI: "Toward a Thomist Idea of Evolution," pp. 89–90, 116, 127–128.

19   I use the past tense because many biologists think that this long history came to its term in the animal world with the appearance of the human species.

20   See above ch. VI: "Toward a Thomist Idea of Evolution."

évolution[21] is very significant from this point of view. No! The living being does not *create* its own evolution; but in virtue of the evolutive élan which comes from God, the only Creator, the living being, under the superelevating motion which it receives from God, helps, in his role as a creature moved by the Author of being, to prepare and fashion new and higher structures for other living beings which will cross over the threshold of a new species, which, in its turn will also be drawn from nothingness by God, and by God alone.

8. So getting back now to the animal species and to the problem posed by the origin of their instincts, the hypothesis I would like to propose, and which I admit holds a particular attraction for me, is this: In their formation through the course of centuries, the mode in which the animal species received the being which, with all its so astonishingly varied structures they have from God and His creative Act, was not conditioned and mediatized, like everything else that preceded them on earth, solely by the evolutive élan which passes through matter and its productive powers, but that at the same time, and in order to control the long process of formation itself, another kind of conditioning and mediatization came into play, due this time to the role played in this affair by pure spirits.

I have been careful not to say that the angels were the instruments of the creative Act; I know that no creature can participate in it and that it makes use of no minister or instrument.[22]

But I know as well that the angels received the mission to administer the visible world: *"Creatura corporalis administratur per angelos."*[23] *"Omnia corpora reguntur per spiritum vitae rationalem,"* says St. Augustine (III. *de Trin.*). And St. Gregory: *"In hoc mundo visibili nihil nisi per creaturam invisibilem disponi potest."*

And when there is question of the animal world, of a world of living beings which instinct and an entirely sensitive power of knowing their environment make abound in all kinds of activities, what prevents me from supposing that the administration exercised over it by the angels goes so far as to control according to their wishes, under the direction and government of God, the entire mass of psychic and physical structures, which the evolutive élan of matter, according to its role, calls for and prepares in them?

We have just pointed out that the living being, and especially the animal living being, contributes in its way to its own evolution. Pure spirits too contribute to it in their way, as artists who, in the present context, are compa-

---

21   Paris: Masson, 1963.

22   *"Illud quod est proprius effectus Dei creantis est illud quod praesupponitur omnibus aliis, scilicet esse absolute. Unde non potest operari dispositive et instrumentaliter ad hunc effectum. . . . Impossibile est alicui creaturae conveniat creare, neque virtute propria neque instrumentaliter sive per ministerium." Sum. theol.,* Ia, q. 45, a. 5. Cf. above n. 16, p. 141.

23   *Ibid.,* Ia, q. 100, a. 1. Cf. *de Veritate,* q. 5, a. 8, and *Contra Gent.,* III, c. 78, 83.

rable to the great couturiers who in this country are the arbiters of fashion. Precisely because the angels are pure intellects, at the summit of the world of the spirit, is it not fitting for divine wisdom to associate them in some way in the progressive formation of beings which, even though they are endowed with psychic capacities, are at the lowest rung of the mental ladder, and exactly their opposite? I think that God has confidence in his beloved angels, in their sense of proportion and of beauty, as well as in their sense of the richest and most joyous fantasy, to the point of entrusting them, for His own pleasure and for theirs, with the care of generously dispensing in every direction all the resources and caprices of high fashion to deck out the great and the small in the fantastic world of the animals as their structures are being formed in the course of evolution.

The angels of heaven have neither disdain nor contempt for the beasts of the earth. While they are amused by them, they take care of them, as of the whole corporal universe, with a particular respect and solicitude. They thank God for having filled the world with them as numberless witnesses to His creative generosity in a spectacle both wonderful and amazing—and not only the slow preparation of that animal endowed with reason who would be created in His image and whom he would raise above the superior vertebrates, but also the abundant riches in beauty and ingenuity of a world filled with a marvelous variety of living beings still deprived of spirit, in which the progressive ascension of matter would unfold, but limited in this case to the possibilities of a purely animal soul.

And the holy angels thank God for having permitted them, invisible as they are, to satisfy at one and the same time their playful gaiety as lords of the spirit and their devotedness as faithful servants, in the wise administration of these visible creatures, by controlling their structures with fanciful delight, by taking part in their evolution, always under God's governing and superelevating motions, and by putting their art and their fantasy to work in furnishing all these specific forms, as varied as they are bizarre, with instincts which are themselves as varied as they are bizarre (there is a marvelous sense of humor in all of this).

This is the time to note that, generally, the multiple objects, which either consciously or unconsciously act upon the external senses, impressing *species* on the animal soul, in no way affect (any more than sensation does for the sense organs) the structure itself of the internal sensitive faculties ("internal senses": memory, imagination, cogitative faculty); and these *species*, solely as regards individual experience, make known to the animal such and such qualities of its milieu (these *species* or cognoscitive images, which are due to to a "spiritual immutation"[24] of the organ, indicate the very first beginnings of spirituality). But without the structure of the internal senses itself being in any way changed, it could nevertheless happen that certain more profound and

---

24   Cf. below ch. XVII: "Along Unbeaten Pathways."

general impressions, issuing from the faculties of basic early learning and registered by the infra-conscious of the subject, might bring about the appearance in one group or other of animals belonging to the same species certain habits which people lacking in critical judgment risk taking erroneously for new instincts. In this case there is no longer question of simple *species impressae* related solely to individual experience, nor is there question either of new instincts which would develop in this species; it is rather a question of what I shall call *structural characteristics*, characteristics which have been acquired but are transmitted by heredity,[25] and which engender, in domesticated animals for example, acquired hereditary habitual behaviors which are in no way instincts.

On the contrary, when, at the moment at which, in the course of evolution, a new animal species is going to be refashioned in its structures, in particular in its psychic structures, by a pure spirit, it is evidently not a question of characteristics acquired thanks to the faculties of basic learning engendering new habits; it is rather a question of the formative action itself by which a new species is fashioned, of genuine *instincts*, instincts transmitted to all the descendants of the first members of that particular species, and which will serve for the conservation of the species by directing the activity of each of its individual members.

The knowledge presupposed by animal instinct must therefore be sought for among the angels. They are the ones who know; they know that celandine is good for the eyes. And as they take delight in being the stage directors of God's great spectacle, they equip and "instruct" all the animals God created for the good of each species.

Each human being has a specific guardian angel because each one is a person whose soul is spiritual and enjoys free will. There is no guardian angel for each individual of the animal species. But there is an Angel for the species: an Angel for the swallows, one for the bees, another for the elephants. And each of these angels is commissioned to equip one species or another only at that moment when it appears on earth and at which he confers on it the instincts that the species will keep as long as it endures.

Among the instincts that he has imprinted in the depths of the swallows' infra-conscious, the Angel of this species inscribes the image of celadine and the tendency to rub, with a sprig of this plant, the eyes of the newly hatched bird, which have not opened on their own. When a mother swallow sees that one of her little ones has not opened its eyes, this (unconscious) image and this (unconscious) tendency come into play and make her act as if she knew what she does not know, but which the angel who has equipped the entire swallow species knows very well.

---

25   This is true, it seems to me, of the animal infra-conscious in man in certain more or less pathological cases, as it is, in a completely general way, of the animal infra-conscious in animals. This is why I think that the idea, so contested today, of the heredity of acquired characteristics should not be rejected.

And this image and this tendency are transmitted by heredity, in an immutable way, to all the descendants of the first swallows, and they will be *innate* in them as long as the species swallow exists.

Certain biologists think that it is the "education" received by the young (the imitation of the behavior of their parents) which establishes the instincts in question. It is clear, as McDougall[26] maintains along with many others, that such an explanation is worthless.

9. The views I proposed in the long preceding section are a sort of outline, summing up what I consider the essential point. In actual fact, things are far more complicated.

Instinct is, as I said, innate, common to all the individuals of a given species, and it presupposes a knowledge which others than the animals themselves are alone capable of possessing. As I noted above, there are in certain groups of animals (especially, but not exclusively, in the case of training and domestication) modes of behavior that are in no way due to instinct, but which—because of experiences undergone by the subject when a change of environment or some other factor adds something new to its way of life—come from hereditarily transmitted acquired habits.[27] This is the case, for example, with our domesticated dogs, wagging their tails as a sign of gratitude to their masters.

On the other hand it is important to note that in general, when the animal exercises the instinct on which its conduct fundamentally depends, it also exercises its individual psychic faculties in order to put into practical operation in a given case that instinct which it is obeying. And when it exercises its individual faculties of the perception of its environment, even of perspicacity (I did not say "intelligence"!), it is always in obedience to some instinctive impulse, in such a way that a specific instinct and individual power of experimentation are generally mixed together. So as we have already pointed out, it also happens (and there is no reason to be surprised at this) that quite often instinct, latent in the young animal, requires a certain time, usually rather short, to develop normally and become obvious to us.

Finally, it can happen that instinct itself becomes subject to variations, under the influence of conditions of environment and acquired habits. Among cows that live closed up in a stable there is a noticeable, definite weakening of the power of distinguishing—a power fully retained by cows left free in nature— between grasses which are good for them to eat and grasses whose ingestion is harmful to them (sometimes even seriously so).

It is this free kind of existence in which they move about as they wish, see these grasses, breathe in their scents, that is necessary for them to remain in

---

26   Cf. Janssens, *L'Instinct d'après McDougall*, p. 2.

27   I have already said (p. 145, n. 25) that in my opinion the Lamarkian notion of the "heredity of acquired characteristics," which is worthless as an explanation of evolution, is valid in certain cases.

full possession of this instinct. William James made a similar remark, from which he then drew erroneous conclusions, that baby chicks, young calves, and lambs, from lack of use, quickly lose the habit of following their mother or some person who for them represents her. These particular cases are exceptional, and the general rule is the stability of instinct. With many animals Lorenz made observations totally contrary to those mentioned by William James—particularly at his own expense, with young jackdaws which mistook him for their mother. "McDougall hasn't the slightest difficulty in pointing out numerous cases which establish the tenacity of instinct, despite prolonged disuse, despite totally contrary conditions."[28]

In any case, even supposing that the apparent variations of which I have just given examples might well be, in contradiction to what has been established by competent scientists, far more frequent than they are in actuality, it is important to distinguish between instinct such as it appears to the eyes of the observer in the external behavior of the animal and instinct such as it is rooted in the deepest levels of the animal psychism. Neither those cows who spend their lives closed up in a stable nor the other animals whose case William James generalized unduly *lost* instinct itself, that innate power, rooted in their psychism, with which they came into the world. It is the force of this innate power which has been diminished in them, to the point of becoming incapable of manifesting itself in their behavior.

Here let us point out a fact which at first sight seems a bit disconcerting. There are some animals (iguanas)[29] who, after living for a long period on land, changed to a half-terrestrial, half-aquatic life, plunging to the depths of the sea where they live on algae, remaining for long periods without breathing oxygen, and where they can stop the beating of their hearts. Does this mean that their instincts have changed and that, after coming into the world with instincts that fixed them in a terrestrial existence, they acquired other instincts that now fix them in their present half-terrestrial, half-aquatic existence? I

28   Janssens, *L'Instinct d'après McDougall*, p. 59. "This is the case with wild birds which, after being enclosed for a long period in narrow cages, far from their kind, as soon as they are set free, show evidence of all the activities of their species; this is particularly the case with wild ducks which, after being raised in a barn yard with their wings closely cropped, during half their lifetime, nevertheless search intensely for the slightest puddle of water and which later, when their wings are permitted to grow, do not fail to fly off and begin their life in the wild. . . ." The hedgehog has come through many centuries with astonishing stability.

29   These are prehistoric looking reptiles living on the Galapagos Islands. Equipped with lungs, they come up to the surface to breathe. In the sea their temperature falls and becomes almost equal to the water temperature; in absolute immobility (by which they burn up a minimum of calories) they are there in hibernation for a short time. Once they come back to the surface, they warm up in the sunshine which helps them recoup their energy. Biologists consider them amphibians not yet adapted to sea life. (It should be noticed that the dolphin too and the whale lived first on the land, before living in the sea as they do now.)

think not. In my opinion, what must be said is that we are in the presence of neither a change in the instincts themselves nor mere habits coming from hereditarily transmitted acquired characteristics. The instincts of these animals, inasmuch as they are powers rooted in the deepest strata of their psychisms, were made up of what I might call ambivalent possibilities: From the very beginning these ambivalent possibilities made them suited to the mode of life which is now theirs, but during a long time the tendencies which they held within them relating to aquatic life remained latent—the others relating to terrestrial life, operated with such force that they were capable, all by themselves, of directing the external behavior. Then, because of some change in the conditions of the environment or because of successful efforts made by a greater and greater number of members of the species, the two kinds of tendencies in question afterwards had enough strength to direct the exterior behavior and make it evident to the eyes of observers.

All of this brings up questions which I have no desire to discuss here. All that matters to me is the relation that I believe has been divinely established between angels and animals.

He who wants to act like an angel ends up acting like a beast, says a French proverb, which remains true in itself but which people often use to justify the baseness of their ambitions. Most Frenchmen today have nothing to fear from this proverb, for they are very far, except perhaps for the hippies, from claiming to be angels; what they want to be is "modern men," and modern man considers in poor taste, and wants banish from our language, the very word *angel*. But this in no way keeps the angel, under God's government, as I have tried to explain, from *making* or fashioning the animal in his own particular way.

APPENDIX
A Digression on Microphysics

I have been thinking for a long time about the problems taken up in the preceding pages and about more or less related problems. I take the liberty of proposing here, as an appendix, a few remarks that I made in December 1964 in an unpublished talk I gave to the Little Brothers in Toulouse.

Nuclear physics introduces us into a very special world, which is still the world of matter, but where matter is no longer anything at all like the matter within the experience of our senses. It is a domain in which matter itself shares in certain way the invisibility of the spirit. The photographs which the physicists offer us do not show us the atom or the electron itself, but rather their shadows, their fleeting images and their symbols. And the principle of indetermination shows us that it is impossible for us to grasp in a comprehensive way what is going on there: If we know precisely the position of the particle, we do not know its precise speed; if we know its speed, we do not know its position. There is always something which escapes us.

Well, I am not saying that this is a forbidden domain; I am saying that it is a dangerous domain. Naturally, in the West at least, we have gotten off to a bad start; we have begun with the atomic bomb.

The fact remains that in itself this guarded domain, this secret domain, has something sacred about it because, as I just said, here matter shares in a certain way and to a certain degree the invisibility of the spirit.

And the idea that I would like to advance now is that it is by intervening in this particular domain that the action of created pure spirits, the action of the angels is exercised on the material universe.

This action of the angels on the material universe is a general thesis taught by St. Thomas. God governs the inferior by the superior. Divine government makes use of the ministry of pure spirits to direct the material universe toward its ends, and this is not the exception but the general rule, according to the normal course of nature. It seems to me that a large place should be given to such a consideration in a sound philosophical theory of evolution, given the passage from the inferior to the superior that is implied in such a theory. If you consider in particular the evolution of organisms, are you not struck by a characteristic trait, the element of play, of humor, of wit, in the sense of that imaginative invention that makes one laugh, in short the element of the *amusement of the artist*, which appears, along with a host of other elements, luxuriousness, sumptuousness, beauty in the world of the evolution of species? Think of the perfectly useless drollery of the phenomena of mimicry or of the grotesque shapes of the giant animals of paleontology. In my opinion all of this means that God, who created things from nothing, without making use of any intermediary, but Who governs through created intermediaries, has directed evolution *through the intermediary of angelic intelligences*, who naturally took their tasks very seriously but not without having a little fun carrying them out.

But how can the angels cooperate in the government of the material universe? Is it by transporting continents and mountains, or by causing molecules to change places? No, let us rather entertain the idea that they act on matter (by instrumental motions which spiritualize it in some way) in the realm of microphysics—where that kind of invisibility which matter enjoys by reason of its indetermination with regard to our measures is in a relationship of propriety or affinity with the invisibility of the angelic motions.

I shall not say, as Bergson often did, that this digression "was necessary." I simply wanted to speak to you about this, and I have seized the first opportunity.

I might add that analogous reflections on micromatter (but this time leaving the angels aside) would perhaps not be useless to those who are interested in that area (very secondary, but still very real) of natural mysticism in which there is question of "powers" acquired for example by yogis. One is expected to look down one's nose at these powers, and yet they are there. And how? Also through penetration—this time by mental and cerebral artifices, that are more subtle and useful to man, and at times still more pernicious (tantrism) than those of our nuclear physics—through penetration into the guarded realm of the infinitely tiny, where matter shares to some degree in the invisibility of the spirit.

CHAPTER VIII
ON MORAL PHILOSOPHY (I)

LET US MAKE FOR HIM A HELPMATE LIKE TO HIMSELF[1]

1. WHAT I AM GOING TO SAY TO YOU may serve as a tiny interlude in the midst of all the work you are doing. For some time now, in order to get a little rest from my philosophical problems, I have taken to daydreaming and meditating on the Book of Genesis; and it seems to me that a fragment of my reflections, which are concerned with the creation of man and woman and with the expression, "Let us make for Adam a helpmate like to himself," as I think this expression must be understood, might perhaps have the good fortune to be of some interest to you.

I will begin however with a few preliminary observations. First of all, the perspective of my reflections is that of a *reading of the text* as would be done by *any Christian in search of intelligibility*, even though he may be a somewhat delirious old philosopher.

Next, the "literary genre" of what we read about the creation of Eve formed from the rib of Adam, or about the Earthly Paradise in general, is the language of myth, which, as Olivier Lacombe has so admirably shown, must be seen as a work of the creative imagination, of an imagination enlivened by the agent intellect in the supra-conscious of the spirit by which humanity has found nourishment in so many venerable archetypes and in so many grand and prophetic truths, proposed in a manner that cannot be verified and is mixed in with errors. The myth that concerns us goes back undoubtedly to ages and memories that are very ancient, but it has been purified by divine revelation. What is presented to us under an imagery that must not be taken literally, and with descriptive details which rise from that imagery, is an *essential content* of sovereign importance, a content of *divinely revealed truths* presented in hidden form, which we are asked to discover or, rather, but this is not what interests me at the moment, that the Church is asked to discover for us, as she has already, in particular at the Council of Trent. In short, what we are concerned with here is a *true* myth.[2]

---

1   *Editor's footnote*: An informal talk given at Kolbsheim. Cf. *Nova et Vetera*, 1967, no. 4, pp. 241–254. (Translations of this text have appeared in Spanish, Italian, and Czech.)

2   Cf. *Le Paysan de la Garonne*, p. 54 [OE C XII, p. 709].

This we know by faith; we know that the Bible transmits to us, through human instruments, the word of God revealing. Whatever the psychological or socio-cultural conditionings of these human instruments may be, the word of the God of truth is there. It is absurd to imagine that a Christian in quest of intelligibility should read the Bible *as if* he were one of his unbelieving brothers seeking by the sole light of his reason if and how the Bible might *lead* him to the faith. In his effort to understand, a Christian can read the Bible only as a man who already has the faith, just as a bird flies with its wings and does not try to imitate the walk of a quadruped. He knows in advance that where the Bible makes use of mythical language, there can be question only of a myth *which tells the truth*, however difficult it may be to decipher what is at once presented and hidden under its imagery.

2. I come now to my subject. There are, as you well know, two accounts of creation, notably of the creation of man. One is attributed to a priestly source, the other to a Yahwist source. This is interesting information, but how does it enlighten me? People who think they are quit of a text by merely explaining *from what source* it arose and *how* it was written are playing the shell game as far as I am concerned. The important thing is *what it says*. I can certainly draw some very profitable accessory precisions from the knowledge that it comes from a priestly source or from a Yahwist source. But for the moment, I could care less, as long as I know that the principle author, the Holy Spirit, willed that it appear in the Holy Book.

So let us read the two accounts of the creation of man. The first (Genesis i, 26–27): "Then God said: 'Let us make man in our image, after our likeness. Let them have dominion over the fish of the sea, the birds of the air, and the cattle, and over all the wild animals and all the creatures that crawl on the ground.'

> *God created man in his image;*
> *in the divine image he created* HIM;
> *male and female he created* THEM.

The second story (Genesis ii, 7, 18, 21, 23): "Then the Lord God formed man out of the clay of the ground and blew into his nostrils the breath of life, and so man became a living being." And further on, "The Lord God said: 'It is not good for man to be alone. Let us make for him a helpmate like to himself.'" (Father Mamie[3] suggests that according to the Hebrew it would be better to say: *I am going to make for him a helpmate as his vis-à-vis.*) And further on, after having made the animals appear on earth, all evidently unfit to fulfill such an office: "Then the Lord God cast a deep sleep on the man, and while he was asleep, he took out one of his ribs and closed up its place with flesh. The Lord God then built up into a woman the rib he had taken from the man. When he brought her to the man, the man said: 'This one at last is bone of my bones and

---

3   Who at the time was bishop of Fribourg, Lausanne, and Geneva.

flesh of my flesh; this one shall be called woman (*ishsha* in Hebrew), for out of her man (*ish* in Hebrew) this one has been taken.'"

Well, how are we to interpret these two accounts? The first is concerned with the unity of human nature and with the equality in nature and in dignity of man and woman, whose duality, "man and woman he *created them*," is synonymous with *Man* (with a capital letter), and constitutes his ontological fullness, "God created man in His image; in the image of God he created *him*." The other account is concerned with the relation between man and woman. Eve was formed from the rib of Adam.

As I see it, this last myth means two things: on the one hand woman is made to be the companion and helpmate of man. On the other hand, according to a remark made by Raïssa,[4] which she made with a smile and which is of major importance (this remark shows us how we must read from a mythic perspective—and also with a flash of poetic insight—a text written in the language of myth) Eve was not drawn directly, as was Adam, from the slime of the earth, but from from a more elaborate and more refined form of matter, from human flesh that was already living. What this means is that she received as her share the most delicate of qualities, those of the highest value for the human race. Those qualities which man received were at the same time more powerful and more directed toward action leading to a good end in the realm of the world as well as in the realm of thought, such as would by right of nature assure him the place of authority in the family community. I said *authority*; I did not say *domination* of a master over his slave, in other words, that just authority which respects the rights and liberties of those over whom it is exercised and which is indispensable to all social life. *Vir est caput mulieris*, this is a law of nature

---

4   Cf. Raïssa Maritain, *Histoire d'Abraham ou les premiers âges de la conscience morale*, pp. 61–62, ch. II, § 2: "In the progress of humanity which we try to read word for word in the Book of Genesis, whatever different interpretations may be possible, let us note that woman skipped a stage. She was not taken from the earth; she was not formed from the ground. She is dust, but through the medium of the flesh of man, as man is dust through the medium of animal flesh. She was made from human flesh; she was created within Paradise, whereas man entered Paradise only after his creation.

   And so according to the Bible, the physical origin of woman is more noble than that of man. The ransom for this privilege was that the demands of God and of men would be greater in her regard, and even, might it not be said, God's regard for her. It was Eve, who, by her own fault, it is true, but also by the boldness of her decision, which is a sign of adulthood, took the initiative which, when Adam accepted it, decided the fate of humanity. And it is also a woman who, with no human counsel, and by the fullness of her faith, compensated in a way for the failing of Eve, and brought back to its Savior and its God the whole of humanity which had gone astray. For the same reason God would permit that all the laws that men would make, on their own or under His inspiration, would always require of woman more abnegation, more purity, and more humanity. The traces, the memory of the earthly and animal stages, weigh more heavily on man. But Eve is very much like the better Adam."

(which, I note in parentheses, ought to make us consider matriarchal civilizations as abnormal, and which condemns as well the illusion of those who, in the name of the equality of nature between men and women, want priesthood in the Church to be conferred on women as well as men).

O.K. then as far as the exercise of authority being invested in man is concerned. It remains a fact nevertheless that, making excessive misuse of all this, man has persuaded himself, through the course of many centuries, that he is superior to woman by reason of the functions of authority vested in him. This is a mistake of the first magnitude: the functions of authority in a community are absolutely necessary and suppose particular qualities that are of particular importance, but which of themselves are not higher or more refined, and which indicate no superiority of nature whatever, except in the eyes of stupid, overweening pride. The pride I refer to reigned with unheard-of violence during pagan antiquity, and in Christian antiquity as well.

3. Let us insert here a philosophico-theological parenthesis: Aristotle gave an erudite philosophical form to this kind of mentality, considering woman as an *homme manqué*—a man that did not work out (see the *De generatione animalium*, chap. 3, where he says that *"femina est mas occasionatus,"* woman is a man that nature accidentally botched up). This seemed to go so clearly to the heart of the matter, alas, that St. Thomas thought he had to adopt this assertion of Aristotle and explains to us, with the support of the pseudo-scientific views of his time, that *"femina est aliquid deficiens et occasionatum,"* woman is something deficient and produced by accident, certainly not with respect to universal nature which requires woman for the perpetuation of the species, but with respect to *particular nature*, that is to say, with respect to such particular conditions that accidentally prevent the generative act from perfectly attaining its end (cf. Ia, q. 92, a. 1, ad 1m). It follows from this that in truth man alone corresponds perfectly to the definition of human nature (whose specific difference is to be endowed with intelligence and reason), for he is ordained *"ad nobilius opus vitae, quod est intelligere* (same article), whereas woman is ordained to breed. And again: *"naturaliter in homine magis abundat discretio rationis"* (ibid., ad 2m).

This conception of woman as a botched-up man, and of masculinity as the peak of human nature, is contrary to philosophical reason which, by the very fact that it proclaims the unity of human nature, proclaims at the same time the equal possession of human nature and, therefore, equality of value in the very things which constitute the specific human difference between the two *vis-à-vis* who confront one another in that nature and each of whom possesses a human personality. This conception is contrary as well to the text of Genesis which, in the first account of the creation of man, tells us that in creating Man, God made one human being male and the other female. But this notion of human nature culminating in masculinity, however aberrant it may be, does not cease to exert its power in our subconscious, even though the correct notion is evidently that of human nature as *shared between masculinity and femininity, while retaining the same value and dignity in the one as in the other.*

Far from accepting the idea that *"mulier naturaliter est minoris virtutis et dignitatis quam vir"* (Ia, q. 92, a. 1, obj. 2), and believing that what attests to the specific difference in the human being (the activities of the spiritual soul which, in point of fact, are not solely rational discernment) are naturally more abundant in man than in woman, what has to be said is that man and woman are equal in human value and dignity, but that they share differently in the qualities of that nature, in such a way that what one has in greater measure compensates for what the other has in lesser measure and that the *human being* finds its complete fulfillment only in *man and woman taken together.*

And I maintain for my part that in this distribution of qualities which characterize the activities of the intellective soul and which constitute the nobility of our nature, it is the share vested in woman which is made up of the keenest qualities, those which stimulate most the movement of life and of the spirit, qualities that are most precious for man. To say this is in no way to attribute to woman a superiority of nature over man. This would be to commit in favor of woman the error that has for such a long time been committed in favor of man. The advantage that I recognize in woman is dearly paid for by the contribution, far weightier than that of man, which nature imposes on her with regard to the propagation of the species.

Let me add that it is another capital error to seek in the sexual differences we have in common with animals, with beasts, the most basic foundation from which are derived and by which are explained all the other differential characteristics which distinguish these two human beings, man and woman. In other words, these differential sexual characteristics confer on a particular human individual that property of his individual nature, in its most intimate depths, by virtue of which *being-man* is his being, and on another particular individual that property of her individual nature, in its most intimate depths, by virtue of which *being-woman* is her being. Sex is the foundation of nothing more than the animal difference, however important and immediately evident that may be; it is not the foundation of the properly *human* differences between man and woman. Sex and the function of reproduction are in reality *for the species* and for the perpetuation of the species, and *in this sense* they are parasites on the person.

It is within the persons and the qualities which distinguish them as such that we find the foundation of the differential characteristics we are concerned with: On the one hand, there is authority and prudence, along with muscular strength, rational conceptualization, and execution which goes along with them; on the other hand, there are the resources of love and its untiring inventiveness, and the stimulation of its impatiences and alertness, along with the gratuitousness of the inspirations of the supraconscious, the quickness of insight and the readiness to be moved, and that incomparable jewel of human nature, the intuitivity of the spirit, which goes along with them, and a certain weakness in muscular capacity, in rational conceptualization and in execution which go along with them as well, but also a greater boldness and sometimes an even greater strength of soul than is found in man. All of this is not based on sex and the function of breeding, nor is it explainable by them. It is based on the division and distribution of those properly human differential qualities which, as is clearly indicated in the myth of Eve being taken from the rib of Adam and from his human flesh, God portioned out to man and to woman at the time of their creation as to equals in the same nature and dignity (by the complementarity of these differential qualities). Eve was created to be the companion and inspiration of man (inspiration—this was devilishly clear in the first sin. . .). It is not without interest to note parenthetically that the expression "let us make for him a vis-à-vis to help him, *faciamus ei adjutorium simile sibi*"—but do not forget the *simile sibi*, so vexing to tell the truth for a long tradition of commentators that held masculinity is such profound veneration, and which was so misunderstood—and do not forget that this expression is found consigned in a revelation made by God to a people that was living after all under a patriarchal regime.

4. I am going to have to stop here to try and make my thought more precise and also what I just said about the error of trying to find in sex the fundamental basis from which one can derive all the other differences which distinguish the two *human* (not merely animal) beings who are man and woman. This leads me to propose to you, in a kind of philosophic digression, views which I have not completely worked out, but which seem to me quite necessary to clear up our ideas on a question which today preoccupies everyone's mind and about which the most sincere good will cannot compensate for intellectual confusion. I am not thinking solely of our psychoanalytic explicators or of an attempt which, though praiseworthy in itself, trips and falls on a false conception of the person and of freedom, like that of Madame de Beauvoir. I am thinking also of a book like that of Madame Yvonne Pellé-Douël, *Etre femme*, in which the best and noblest of intentions are betrayed by the acceptance, as though it were self-evident, of the very error I pointed out.

First of all, we must go back to the text of Genesis. I think that the two accounts of the creation of man must be taken *together* and refer to two complementary truths both of which must be safeguarded: The first of these accounts has for object to emphasize the unity of human nature and the equality in nature and in dignity of man and of woman (from the very creative act by which man appeared on earth, human nature was male in one and female in the other); the second account, expressed in the language of myth—and, *according to the mythical conventions of this language*, presenting the creation of Eve as posterior to that of Adam—has for its object to emphasize the way in which God willed and brought it about that woman be differentiated from man.

The care with which the Sacred Book insists on all this in the two separate accounts seems to me very significant. The First Truth: Eve and Adam, whose duality ("man and woman he created *them*") constitutes man in his ontological fullness ("in the image of God he created *him*"), were created from the very appearance of humanity on earth, as the first account tells us—and as is suggested by a sound philosophy of evolution, which, in my opinion, ought to hold that, at the instant when in the embryo resulting from the generative act of a hominian couple under an exceptional and absolutely unique superelevating motion of God, an ultimate disposition calling for an intellective soul was produced, at that moment God created and infused this intellective soul into the embryo. And we can suppose that in this first appearance of a human being, it was either a set of twins, one a boy and the other a girl, born at the same time from the womb of the hominian mother, or else a first-born son and a second-born daughter, who were created in this way by God.

And now, the other truth contained in the second account. I have already pointed out that the symbolism of the story of Adam's rib signifies that while she has the same specific nature as man, woman was endowed with far more refined qualities, though less powerful. And now what are we to say of the expression *"ei faciamus adjutorium simile sibi"*? To what end? To bring forth children and to propagate the human species and, unlike animals, to continue to live together, as St. Thomas points out, as man and woman in domestic life to aid and comfort one another? Yes, certainly. But there is another and far higher end which the Ancients did not mention here because the dimension of time and of historical progress was not sufficiently clear and operative in their thinking.

What humanity was created for was to advance here on earth, to lead here an ever higher temporal and cultural life and at the same time an ever higher life of the spirit, and finally to enter into the Kingdom of God and of the beatific vision. This is the superior end in view of which Eve was created as an aid and companion to Adam, and in this regard the multiplication of the human species by human generation is no more than a necessary means. It is to better assure the progress of the human species toward this end that from the very beginning human nature was divided between two distinct subspecific types complementing each other. And this is precisely why from the creation of Eve it was necessary that the qualities which distinguish femininity from masculinity be different and complementary.

A parenthesis: If our first parents had not sinned, the progress of humanity—we cannot imagine such a progress—would have come about *solely in the line of good*. In the end, when man, still endowed with original justice and exempt from death, would have populated the earth and grown sufficiently in spirituality as well as in civilization, the world would have been found *disposed* for the transfiguration by which it would have entered into glory; and men would have entered, without passing through death (if not through death to self), into the vision of God. But original sin placed us under a totally different regime, in which the progress of humanity takes place *at one and the same time in the line of good and in the line of evil*, and with a generous measure of the latter. And so it is by a catastrophe, the thunderbolt of the end of the world, and by the resurrection of the dead, along with the separation of the good from the evil, that the final transfiguration will take place, and that the good will enter into the Kingdom of Heaven which Christ their Redeemer won for them. At the end of time, as Olivier Lacombe reminded us Monday—when Jesus returns, He will find little faith upon the earth. It will have almost disappeared from this world. It will still remain alive in the Church, thanks solely, perhaps, to a few small flocks, scarcely more numerous than those of the primitive Church, but living fully the life of faith and of the Mystical Body, and whose shepherds, like those of the primitive Church, will have that firmness in the truth and that heroic courage called for by their mandate. End of parenthesis.

5. Let us pass on now to my philosophical reflections. I mentioned a moment ago two *subspecific* types, masculine and feminine, which share the same human nature. To justify this expression, let me make use of a distant analogy, that of the races among which human nature is divided—they are indeed subspecific types, all having the same human nature in equal degree. But the diverse races come from an evolution, quickly produced no doubt, but which nevertheless took some time, and in which the accidental undoubtedly played its role. Whereas the distinction between the masculine subspecific type and the feminine subspecific type is linked to the very creation of man and of human nature.

In the second place it seems important to me to note that the difference between the sexes has an entirely different ontological meaning for the animal and for man. It is their sexuality, with all its biological and morphological repercussions, which constitutes the whole difference between the male animal and the female animal, between the deer and the doe. In other words, male and female typicity in the animal is a subspecific typicity of a *purely functional* order.

To the contrary, if all the preceding remarks are exact, we must say that in our case the sexual function, far from making all the difference between man and woman, is only one of the properties of a subspecific typicity of an essential order[5] which, deriving from the spiritual soul, embraces the entire

---

5   I mean a subspecific type which concerns the very essence (human) of the person under consideration. Perhaps it would be better to say "subspecific type *of a modal-essential order.*" (In saying *modal-essential*, I mean something that is a *mode* of the human essence itself.) All of this is in counterdistinction to the "subspecific type of a merely *functional* order" (when reference is made to the differentiation

nature, spiritual and corporeal, of the masculine or feminine human person. Masculine or feminine typicity is not a mere functional or genital typicity. It is a typicity *of nature* (of individual nature) ordered to the temporal and spiritual progress of the human species toward its end, and implying a differentiation in the qualities of the soul, and which includes as one of its properties, but only as one of its properties, however necessary it may be, the genital function related to human animality.

Consequently it can be said, it seems to me, that there is a bipolarity in the human being as to the differentiation between being-man and being-woman— a bipolarity ordered throughout the course of time to the general progress of humanity toward its end. There is a *carnal* pole, aimed at the propagation of the species, from the side of human animality and one of its functions; there is also a *spiritual* pole—in the order of the constitution of the human person— from the side of the spiritual soul which is the substantial form of the human being: I am speaking of the human soul *individualized in one direction or another from the very moment of its creation*, from the fact that God, in creating each soul, destines it to inform one or another particular body; I am struggling with words to designate this mutual complementarity at the very heart of human-ity—let us say, if you like, borrowing a metaphor from the chemists who tell us of dextrogyre or levogyre tartaric acid, that from its creation the soul of a man is *dextroversly* individualized and that the soul of a woman is *levoversly* individualized.

Let us remember here that the human soul is not individuated *by* matter (as is the sensitive soul of animals); it is, as I have just noted, and there is a world of difference between these two formulas, it is individualized *as ordered* to matter and to a determined body, male or female (whence it follows that it is masculine or feminine *by virtue of the typical form of its very being*). This is why the soul keeps its individuality, its masculine or feminine individuality, after death; and in the universe of the risen, where there will be neither marriage nor generation, there will still be men and women, whose differential charac-teristics will have nothing to do with a function of their bodies which will have disappeared. They will rather depend on the subspecific typicity due to each of their souls, which, from the time of their creation have been "dextroversly" or "levroversly" individualized *as ordered* to each of their bodies, but not individuated *by* them. And in their glorious life together, woman (no longer as spouse but according to her being-woman) will remain for man a vis-à-vis and a "helpmate," or let us say rather a companion in the activity of the blessed. In this way human nature will still find its ontological fullness through their mutual complementarity. These characteristic traits of femininity surely con-tinue on in the next world. Think of the care that the Virgin Mary takes of this world and of that impatience which impels her to appear to poor little children in order to rouse us a bit from our torpor . . .

---

between male and female in animals).

All of this means that Eve, created *to help* man, not just to bring forth his children, but together to move the human species toward its goal, was also created *as helping* man to realize along with her the complete ontological fullness of human nature—in other words, as being a person whose *being-woman* is complementary to the *being-man* of Adam. This evidently implies that, for his part, Adam is a person whose *being-man* is complementary to the *being-woman* of Eve, so as to realize along with her the complete ontological fullness of human nature: "God created man in his image; in the divine image he created *him*; male and female he created *them*."

So much for the spiritual pole of the differentiation between man and woman. When I use the term *spiritual pole*, I do not mean that those qualities particular to woman and those qualities particular to man, like those I mentioned above, all proceed from spiritual powers like the intellect, but they are all spiritual in their roots, as coming from the spiritual soul informing the matter and possessing powers such as the senses and the imagination, at the same time that it has powers of the spirit.

As far as the carnal pole is concerned, I have already indicated that sexuality creates for male and female animals a typicity of a purely functional order. This is not at all the case with man and woman, whose typicity is of an essential or a modal-essential order and includes the genital function as only one of its properties. This does not prevent sexuality from playing a very considerable role in the human being and in human life and from being the source not only of those sensible pleasures naturally associated with its act but also of magnificently human joys, like being a father or a mother and of giving rise to tendencies and activations so precious to our nature and also to frustrations, to psychic complications and distress, which, though having their origin in the body, affect the totality of the human person.

In addition let us note that the human person being that of an animal endowed with reason, and that the human soul being individualized as ordered to a determined body, sex and the function of generation and everything that is linked to the internal functioning of organic life—especially in the case of the woman, whether there is question of a kind of complicity established between her and nature, or whether there is question of gestation, in which the infant is in its mother's womb as in a naturally sacred nest—all these things create in human animality a kind of consonance or harmonic correspondence with everything which, at the spiritual pole, and on the side of the soul and its particular qualities, constitutes the human person in being-man and being-woman.

That idea in vogue today[6] which, by reducing the whole problem to a single carnal pole, considers sex and the genital function as the basic foundation from which derive and according to which are explained all the other differentials which distinguish the being-man and the being-woman is, as I hope I have

---

6   See the postscript, pp. 163–164.

shown, a basic error which vitiates our entire perspective on the human being. It's like trying to explain the genius of Mozart by the biochemical activities of his spleen or his liver.

Let me end this overly long digression by noting that everything I have said concerns solely the members of the human species, persons who at the same time are constituted by their soul and its particular qualities in their masculinity or their femininity, and both working in the service of the species through a certain function of the flesh. This is found neither in the world of pure spirits where each angelic person is a separate species, nor in the world of animals, where each individual is there solely for the species and for its propagation.

6. Taking up again—it will not take me long to finish—the thread of the unrefined reflections that came to my mind on reading Genesis, I recall that before beginning my philosophic digression, I had insisted on the person-to-person relation between Adam and Eve and had noted that in the distribution of the properly human differential qualities that God gave, from the moment of creation, to man and to woman as his or her share in the same human nature and dignity, Eve was created to be a companion and inspiration to man, and I mean in the entire work allotted to them both in this world.

I have not forgotten that Eve is also the mother of the human race but this involves us more than it does the person of Adam (who is also our father). And let us not forget either that it was *after the sin* that in Genesis (iii, 16) God said to Eve: "Your urge shall be for your husband, and he shall be your master." This *domination* of man over woman (which does not go unaccompanied by pride on the part of man) is entirely different from the authority I mentioned in my early remarks and which for long centuries has been expressed by the enslavement of women (an enslavement that continues today under other forms, thanks to the bestial idolatry of sexuality which depersonalizes women and leads them to consider themselves as nothing more than flesh destined for the pleasure of men, a condition which by its very nature leads to despair and leads some women to throw themselves into a kind of prostitution out of hatred for their own bodies). This *domination of enslavement* by men over women has absolutely nothing to do with the *nature* proper to the one or the other. It has to do uniquely with *the consequences of the first sin.*

I am sorry to have to add that if St. Thomas did not fail to condemn the enslavement of women—"*non debet a viro despici tanquam serviliter subjecta*" (Ia, q. 92, a. 3)—nevertheless the basic error that I have set out to attack, and which has played its role in the attempts to justify the secular enslavement of women—the basic error, that is, to consider the faculty of aiding man to breed as the sole privilege proper to a woman, and hence to consider sex and the reproductive function as the one characteristic to which, in the final analysis, her entire femininity is reduced; the Ancients were guilty of this error, and our most venerable doctors for their part as well, in accord with the mentality of their times, and from their particular perspective, which is at the opposite extreme (I would call it "procreationist") of the egocentric sexualism of our distributors of pseudo-Freudian philosophical drugs. This was actually in perfect accord with Aristotle's view of woman as a botched-up man. In their interpretations of Genesis we find some rather astounding assertions, like the following, which St. Thomas echoes in a *Sed contra* of the *Prima Pars* q. 98, a. 2): If it is said in Genesis that God made woman as a helpmate to man like to himself, well the help in question *is concerned uniquely with the work of generation*, and with no other work whatever "because (listen carefully to this) for any other work whatever man *could have been helped more suitably by another man than by a woman."* Or look again, at q. 92, a. 1, where St. Thomas teaches categorically this same flabbergasting *dicendum quod*. (After all, did he not find himself suitably helped in his convent by his secretaries and by the lay brothers . . . ? There is not a single word in Genesis to support such an assertion, which totally ignores the evident complementarity of the feminine and masculine types, as well as the fact that their differential qualities are those of the spiritual soul itself which informs the body according as it is individualized in one direction or the other.

St. Thomas did refrain in fact from pushing to its extreme limit this assertion which I find so scandalous, and he corrects it vigorously by noting in another article (q. 92, a. 2) that the work of generation is not the only one to consider and that there are also (which certainly does not go very far) other works for man and woman to do together in domestic life.[7] At any rate, if we pushed things to the very end in the perspective opened to us by the idea that the unique purpose for which Eve was made to complete man is procreation, we should in our male self-sufficiency (from which certain *bien-pensant* of the good old days were not exempt) see in woman no more than a prolific laying-hen who helps Adam reproduce himself, except for those accidental botched-up bungles in the work of generation, which produce a woman instead of a man. It is understandable that, rushing logically to the absurd, some pedants of the Middle Ages (of that time, on the other hand, in which the cult of the Virgin rehabilitated woman and in which the troubadours exalted her) asked themselves in all seriousness the question whether woman had a soul, a spiritual soul like her husband's. After all would not a purely animal soul have been sufficient for the job, since woman was created *in adjutorium viri* solely for the service of reproduction?

These old tales are good for nothing except to make us laugh, but what leads to very melancholy reflections is the idea that even the noblest thought of the

---

7   "Mas et femina conjunguntur in hominibus, *non solum propter necessitatem generationis* . . . sed etiam propter domesticam vitam, in qua sunt alia opera viri et feminae, et in qua vir est caput mulieris." Aristotle, to whom St. Thomas refers (*Eth.*, VIII) had made the same remark, to which I could just as well have made reference in what I said earlier (pp. 158–160) about the generative function in men and animals.

Angelic Doctor, in an area like the one we are speaking of, and in which the pressure of the cultural milieu exerts such force on the mind, was not able to free himself completely from the intellectual climate of his time, and from the prejudices which reigned there. This is one of the servitudes of our wounded nature, a servitude which no one escapes completely. If a mind so magnificently free as that of St. Thomas was unable to escape it on this particular point (femininity and the interpretation of *in adjutorium viri*), why should it be so surprising today to see a mob of servile minds consider it their first duty to adapt themselves and, if they are Christians (and animated by a kind of pastoral zeal), to adapt the Gospels to the unconditional demands of a mass culture and of a collective (excuse me, communitarian) mentality for which the love of metaphysical or religious truth is no more than an old piece of cast-off clothing unworthy of modern man.

Finally, to return to my original proposition, which concerned the reading of Genesis by any Christian in search of intelligibility, it seems especially important that the mind do this reading with the most complete freedom possible with regard to any prejudice whatsoever, whether it come from the human traditions of the ancients (Jesus had no soft spot for the doctors of the law) or from the intellectual fatuity of our dear contemporaries.

POSTSCRIPT[8]

This difference "of nature" between femininity and masculinity—according to which those characteristics, in both the man and in the woman, affect *human nature in its entirety* and relate just as much (and even more profoundly) to the psychic and spiritual order as they do to the corporeal order—is more and more misunderstood today and seems, as McLuhan shows (*Mutations 1990* (Maison Mame, 1969), pp. 9–34 for the French edition) to be in the process of completely disappearing from our social habits. Men and women are becoming totally indistinguishable in the depths of their individual natures and in the signs that manifest these differences, and it is the invasion of a kind of hermaphroditism in general behavior and in the very idea of what man is and of what woman is that has to be dealt with.

McLuhan does not judge; he neither approves nor disapproves; he simply states what he observes, and with what admirable lucidity. But without taking delight in useless verbal condemnations, a philosopher who makes use of any value criteria is certainly obliged from his perspective to note that this constitutes a very serious loss that must be chalked up against the civilization of the future. Such a loss carries in its wake an abject materialist biologism and the refusal to take into consideration, in the relation between man and woman, anything more than the function and needs of sexuality. After this, everything

8   *Editor's footnote*: This postscript was added in 1972.

is brought back in an absolute way to this single consideration, with the inevitable result that the world of tomorrow and one entire aspect of its cultural conditions will suffer an incontestable degradation.

Perhaps a more and more fervent cult of the Virgin Mary, more and more solidly founded in theology, within the Church and among Christians, will bring to this loss a kind of divine compensation.

CHAPTER IX
ON MORAL PHILOSOPHY (II)

LOVE AND FRIENDSHIP[1]
(A marginal note to the *Journal de Raïssa*)

IN THE PAGES WHICH FOLLOW there is a first part in which I will comment on and develop certain things which Raïssa expressed very clearly but very briefly. In the second and third parts I would like to propose my own views on several problems that trouble many minds today.

Let it be clearly understood that I am speaking here neither as a philosopher (which I happen to be) nor as a theologian (which I certainly am not). I am simply proposing a few reflections drawn from the experience of an old man who has seen many things, and who remembers what Aristotle said of the elderly, whose judgments it behooves us to take into consideration, even if they do not know how to present the reasons for their judgments (or if they present them wrongly). Raïssa had the wisdom of the Holy Spirit. I hope that a few of the privileges of the wisdom of old age will be granted to the thoughts expressed here. Naturally I have tried to put my reflections in some kind of logical order, but this is just an old habit of mine and you should not let yourself be taken in by it. It will be up to others to treat these questions in systematic form and with appropriate technical terms.

I. LOVE AND FRIENDSHIP

A Necessary Distinction in the Love of *Dilection*[2]

1   *Editor's footnote: Nova et Vetera*, 1936, no. 4, pp. 241–279. (Translations of this text have a appeared in English, Spanish, Italian and Czech.)

2   *Translator's footnote*: The French word *dilection* is very difficult to put into English. Even though the word exists in the English dictionary and is defined as "a loving, a preference," it is described as obsolete. In the translation of "Amour et amitié," which he prepared for *Notebooks* (the English edition of Jacques Maritain's *Carnets de notes*), Joseph Evans translated *amour de dilection* by "disinterested love" and in so doing he correctly emphasized one of the important connotations of Maritain's expression. His translation certainly indicates that this kind of love is an "unselfish" love whereby the immediate and primary preoccupation of the lover is the good of the beloved, not his or her own good, even his or her own life. But it seems to me that the English word *disinterested* has other connotations

I am referring here above all to page 149 of the *Journal*[3] (April 20, 1924); I refer as well to other related passages in which there are more or less noticeable echoes of what is said on this particular page.

Raïssa singles out at the very heart of love of *dilection* or love-for-the-good-of-the-beloved (which St. Thomas calls *amor amicitiae*[4] in opposition to *amor concupiscentiae*, that is to say love-for-the-good-of-the-subject, or covetous love), two kinds of love to which, in simply following the common and obvious acceptance of current speech, she gives the names *love* and *friendship*; but she gives to this common acceptance of current speech a rigor and a depth that go far beyond current usage. "The essence of love is in the communication of oneself, with fulness of joy and delight in the possession of the beloved. The essence of friendship is the deep desire for the good of one's friend that goes as far as giving one's life for that friend. God loves us with a love of friendship by taking care of all our needs and by dying for us on the Cross.[5] God loves us with this love in making us participate in His nature by grace—in making the sanctified soul His dwelling-place . . ."

Those words that are richest in meaning for human life are always the most difficult to encompass; they run the risk of either diminishing or overflowing our thought. Let us try then to be rather precise about a few things, even at the price of being somewhat tedious. All love of *dilection* is a gift of one's self. But the "gift" itself can be understood in two typically different ways. On the one had there is the love of benevolence or of devotedness, in which the lover gives himself to the beloved by giving him his possessions or what he *has*—and this is done more or less completely up to the perfection of devoted love in which one gives all that one has, all of one's goods, even the good of one's very life. This is *friendship*, and in this friendship the friend, in giving what he has, undoubtedly at the same time also gives, *in a certain way*, what he is, his own person or his very subjectivity (since what he is needs what he has, and since

---

(like "lack of interest" or "indifference") which do not fit Maritain's concept. It seems to me too that the French word *dilection* has other connotations that are not found in *disinterested*. *Dilection* is defined the French dictionary *Le Petit Robert* as "*un amour tendre et spirituel*." In addition, the Latin root of the French word is *diligere* (past participle: *dilectus*), and though this word in Latin does mean "to love," its basic meaning is to "choose," so that, "forsaking all others," the lover "chooses" and "cherishes" his or her beloved above all others. Because of the richness of all these connotations I have decided to keep the French word and use the expression "love of *dilection*."

3   *Journal de Raïssa*, Paris, Desclée de Brouwer, 1963.

4   The *amor amicitiae* is an *amor benevolentiae* or love of *dilection* (love for the good of the beloved) when it is mutual (*Sum. theol.*, Ia-IIae, q. 23, a. 1). From our persepctive it is this *mutua benevolentia* that we must take into consideration in our discussion; the expression *love of friendship* is the one that fits here.

5   Cf. Jn 15, 13: "There is no greater love than this: to lay down one's life *for one's friends*.

he can go so far as to give up his very life. There is not doubt that he does give himself, and in a very real way, but still *in a hidden manner and indirectly, through something else*, in other words by means and by the intermediary of other gifts which under signs conceal the gift of himself, and more or less parcel it out, permitting him to hold back in a greater or lesser degree the gift of his very own self as long as he has not given absolutely everything that he has.

But in *love* however, that is, love of truly human dimensions, in which the spirit is committed—I mean love considered in its most extreme and absolute form (for in its ordinary form the process I am talking about is indeed there, but only in a rough and primitive draft, as it were)—in *love*, the person or the subjectivity gives itself *directly, openly, and in complete nakedness*, without hiding under the appearance of some other gift less absolutely total. The person gives itself entirely and immediately by giving or communicating to the beloved, by whom it is enraptured, absolutely everything that it *is*. It is the very person of the lover which is the Gift, the simple, unique Gift without the slightest possibility of any reservation whatsoever. This is why love, in the extreme sense in which we are taking it here, is *absolutely and par excellence*, the gift of self.

The difference between love and friendship is not necessarily a difference in the *intensity* or the greatness of the love of *dilection*. This or that friendship can be just as intense as, or more intense than, this or that love. The difference between love and friendship is a difference in the *intrinsic quality* of the love of *dilection*, or in the *ontological level* at which it is found in the soul, in other words, in the power it has of alienating the soul from itself.

In God *love* and *friendship* are only two aspects of one and the same infinitely perfect love of *dilection* which is God Himself in His transcendence,—two aspects that we consider distinct from one another according to our human mode of conception and by analogy with what is apparent in human love of *dilection*, all of whose qualities and perfections are contained in their uncreated Exemplar.

In the creature (considering things in the natural order) *love* and *friendship* between two human beings are two different aspects of the love of *dilection* (since, in the case of *love* on the completely human level where the differences of the sexes enter into play, the flesh has its own claims to make, covetous or possessive love is joined to the love of *dilection*).

Different Kinds of Human Love

I specified a moment ago that in speaking of love I was talking about love in which the spirit is involved, love on the level of man and of human dignity—and that I was speaking of it in its extreme and absolute form.

The fact is that, if we take the word *love* in the common acceptance of current speech, according to the distinction it makes between love and friendship, there exists in man a kind of love that is of a merely animal and not of a properly human order, the kind of love which is the subject of many male conversations and of erotic literature, an exclusively carnal love, connoting exclusively sensual pleasure. This kind of love has reference *uniquely* to covetous or possessive love, and has nothing to do with the love of *dilection*. So we will spend no time on it here.

Love of a properly human order begins at that point where there is added to the attraction of the senses, at least in its primitive form, that gift of the person itself, direct and completely exposed, which we spoke about a moment ago, and which proceeds from the love of *dilection*. It can be said that at the moment when this threshold is crossed, and by the very fact of the gift by which the lover gives himself to the beloved, the word *exist* takes on a double meaning: the beloved alone exists fully and absolutely for the lover, the existence of everything else becoming afflicted with a kind of invalidity.

This love of the properly human order includes very many different forms, which we have no reason to analyze in detail here. Let us be satisfied with three typical cases.

First of all, there is what is called passionate love, which, in its most sublimated form, is also called romantic love. This kind of love plays a central role in human life; it is a mirage by which a certain nostalgia inherent in the human being lets itself be fooled; its entwined initials are carved on all the trees of the world. It feeds on a falsehood and on an illusion; it is the mirage or the simulacrum of *really true love* ("amour fou").[6] It considers itself eternal and it is ephemeral. In it the lover does give himself to his beloved (and the beloved to her lover), it is true, but in the imagination, in a kind of reverie rather than in reality; here it is possessive love or carnal desire which (without it being realized) holds the essential and preponderant place; the gift of self, which one can imagine oneself most sincerely to have given, is not real but is dreamed, and, as a matter of fact, is no more than a disguise by which our minds hide under royal adornments that sensual desire which, by deceiving the individual, the species makes use of for its own purposes. It is good for the human being to experience this state of exultation, which reminds us of the mating songs and dances of birds—but on condition that we do not pretend to remain in that state, for a man is not a bird.

In the second place, there is authentic love, into which it is rare (though not impossible) that someone would enter from the very first moment. Man achieves this love ordinarily only after a certain maturation in life experience and in suffering. It is the love in which someone really gives to the other, not

6   *Translator's footnote*: This is another expression that seems to have included so many connotations for Maritain that it defies simple translation. The word *fou* (crazy, mad, demented) in the expression *amour fou* seems to mean, at one and the same time, unconditional, unreserved, boundless, obsessive, exclusive, ecstatic, etc., as well as mad or crazy, and though in English we talk about being "madly in love" or "crazy about someone, "mad love," or "crazy love" would not work at all. So I have decided to keep Maritain's expression *amour fou*.

only what he has, but what he is (his very person). In the ordinary form of this authentic love (let us say very simply: in a *bel amour*) such a gift is given, but in a very elementary form, as in a rough sketch (which remains in rough form, at all the levels of more and of less); it is not given absolutely.

Finally, when this gift is given to the ultimate degree, we have, in the third place, authentic love in its extreme and absolute form. This love in which the very person in each case gives itself to the other in all truth and reality, is in the order of the ontological perfections of nature, the highest point of love between Man and Woman. Then the lover gives himself to his beloved and the beloved to her lover, *as to his or her All*, in other words is ecstatic in the other, makes himself or herself—even though remaining ontologically a person—a part which no longer exists except through and in that All which is his or her All. This extreme love is *amour fou*; and this name fits it very well because it does (in the special order or, if you like, in the magic and the spiritual "superexistence" of love) precisely what is in itself impossible and makes no sense in the order of mere existence or simple being, in which each person continues to be a whole and could not become a real part of another whole. This is the paradox proper to love; on the one hand it demands the ontologically unbreakable duality of the two persons; on the other hand it demands, and, *in its own way*, brings about a faultless unity, the effectively consummated union of these same two persons ("in a single spirit and love" As St. John of the Cross says of supernatural mystical union, but this is already true, on an entirely different level and in an analogical sense, of the natural union between man and woman[7] in *amour fou*). At the level of our present considerations, that is, the terrestrial level, (human) *amour fou*, unlike an *amour fou* for God, relates to the purely natural order; moreover, in this particular order, it is, as I noted above, an *ontological* perfection of nature—at the disposition, from a moral point of view, of the best and the worst of human beings. This is the source of its splendor and of its ambiguity. Its object is a created object. He who loves with an *amour fou* gives himself totally; the *object* of his love is a limited, fragile, and mortal creature. We would misconstrue the grandeur of our nature if we believed that this creature, loved with an *amour fou*, *necessarily* becomes an idol for the lover, and is *necessarily* loved by him more than God is. But we would misconstrue as well the wretchedness of our nature if we believed that the beloved *could not* be loved more than God by someone who loves with an *amour fou*, and *could not* become an idol for him. A human *amour fou* can be resplendent in a life that is morally upright and subject to the order of charity.[8] It can be just as resplendent in a life of sin (and not only outside of marriage, but within the state of marriage as well).

And now three remarks: 1. *Amour fou* implies and always presupposes (not necessarily having precedence in time, but necessarily having precedence in

---

7   "In a single spirit"—I said *spirit*, I did not say temperament, character, taste, etc.

8   Cf. further on, p. 187, n. 33, and pp. 189–191.

the order of being) the love of devotedness or friendship, all the while going far beyond the latter. 2. *Amour fou* goes beyond friendship because it is found at a more profound—at an absolutely radical—level of the soul, from the fact that it is a direct, unconcealed, and completely naked gift of the person itself, in its entirety, making itself *one in spirit* with the other. But by virtue of the very nature of the human being, who is both flesh and spirit, it entails by its very nature[9] union *in the flesh* as well, at least in desire, with all the carnal joy and pleasure of the senses *par excellence*, which are associated with that union. The human person can give itself to another, or find ecstasy in the other, to the point of making that other its All, only if it gives, or is ready to give, its body to the other at the same time that it makes the offering of its soul. 3. Nevertheless an *amour fou* is infinitely more than the desire of the senses. It is by its very essence, principally and primordially, a love of *dilection*; covetous or possessive love (for the advantage and joy of the loving subject itself, not of the thing loved) is secondary, and entirely subordinate to the love of *dilection*. Principally and above all the person is a spirit, and so it is as a spirit that it gives itself above all and principally when it gives itself in its entirety. To the degree that spirit surpasses the flesh, to the same degree *amour fou*, authentic love in its ultimate form, surpasses passionate love.

Love of Charity and Uncreated Love

In distinguishing *love* from *friendship*, it was especially of *amour fou*, of love in its most extreme form, that Raïssa was thinking in those notes of hers which I have entitled her *Journal*. And, in addition, she understood these words in and analogical and transcendent sense, for she was not thinking of that human *amour fou* which I have just been insisting on; rather she was thinking above all of the love of God for men (uncreated Love) and of man's love of God (the love of charity).

In the love of charity, whose *object* is Spirit self-subsistent in its transcendent infinity, the inscrutable Deity itself, the three uncreated Persons[10]—which is a gift of grace and belongs to the supernatural order—friendship and love

9   This does not mean that by an act of his free will a man could not—just as he can mutilate his own body, if he wants to—do violence by separating carnal love from his *amour fou*, either for some spiritual motive, or in renunciation of the flesh if the person he loves, or indeed would love forever with an *amour fou*, should ask it of him, or if both felt themselves called to this renunciation by God (we have seen engaged couples separate in this way to enter into religious life, or married couples take vows of continence) or for some other reason (if, for example, the woman whom he loves with an *amour fou* is married to another; as a matter of fact in such a case it is likely that he would bring about the separation in a completely opposite direction—by giving himself to a life of debauchery).

10   This is why the love of charity is known to our intellect only by means of an analogical knowledge, as the higher *analogate*, within us, of a reality attained first in the human world.

(*amour fou*) evidently are not two distinct species; they are two different degrees (not necessarily in intensity, but in their power to alienate the soul from itself)—inseparable in a certain sense—of one and the same love of *dilection*. In this kind of *amour fou* is there again implied, although in an analogical sense, a certain possessive love, this time of a wholly spiritual order, the desire, that is, to possess the Beloved and to let oneself become intoxicated by Him, to feel oneself loved by Him? Certainly there is; by its very nature this love demands the "fullness of joy and delight in the possession of the beloved." But then not only is this desire, having God for its object, absolutely pure of any carnal element; and not only is it subordinated to the love of *dilection*; but also it will have ceased and must completely cease to have as its justification (as is the case in covetous or possessive love properly so called) the good of the subject itself; it is not for itself, it is *for* God's *own sake*. loved first as He is, that the soul wants God *for* itself, or desires to possess Him, and the more He is possessed, the wilder this desire becomes. Here on earth this desire cannot be completely fulfilled. There will be dark nights to pass through, perhaps terrifying nights, and instead of joys and delights there may be times when agony and death will be offered as gifts to the lover, precisely because the love of *dilection* demands total and absolute sovereignty, and implacably tears up, one after the other, every single root that desire for the possession of the Beloved might have sunk in the soul of the lover to the degree that he loves himself naturally.

As to God's love for man, I have already pointed out that in God friendship and love are but two aspects, distinguished according to our human mode of conception, of a same single love, perfectly one, which is God Himself. In us the characteristics of what I call *amour fou* are found in God in a supereminent way, purified to the infinite and analogically transposed in conformity with what is compatible with His divine transcendence. In God there is absolutely no covetous or possessive love, because there is absolutely nothing that God needs. There is only the love of *dilection*: there is friendship of course, an infinitely generous friendship; but there is also *amour fou*, wherein He gives Himself to a whole (the created person) who is other than Himself and whom He has made capable by His grace of receiving it and of loving Him in return—with the result that, in this unrestricted donation by which it gives itself totally in return, the created person is capable of becoming one single spirit and love with that Love by which God loves Himself eternally, and in this way of bringing about in Him reverberations, so to speak, of that Joy in which He eternally exults in Himself.

And if God asks for our love in return for His love, it is purely in virtue of the love of *dilection* itself—not because He has a need to be loved by us but because He loves us. It is for us, not for Himself, says St. Thomas, that God seeks His glory.[11] It is for us, not for Himself, that He asks that we give Him

---

11   "*Deus suam gloriam non quaerit propter se, sed propter nos.*" *Sum. theol.*, IIa-IIae, q.

our hearts. *Praebe mihi cor tuum.*[12] "It astounds me to think of the value that the Lord attaches to our poor love. One is truly tempted to say that the object He proposed to attain was to possess our hearts: 'It is no laughing matter that I have loved you!' Is there not here a kind of metaphysical necessity? Uncreated love remains love, even while pouring itself out on creatures, and consequently it is not satisfied unless to its own expansion it finds the response of another expansion which makes union possible."[13]

Amour fou *for a Human and* Amour fou *for God*

Let us go back now to human love. We said that in us *amour fou* is present, emerges like Venus born from the sea, when the person gives itself entirely, completely exposed in its nakedness to another person as to its All, in whom it becomes enraptured and of whom it makes itself a part. The *Journal de Raïssa* in this connection shed a clear light on a central truth on which I must insist, in the language I am using here. It is a forewarning that I will point out this one time and then be finished with: In the following remarks a certain condition is presupposed, namely, that we are considering in the human being, not something that could well up in him momentarily from time to time—or, if it happens to be lasting, something that is subject to obstacles and contrarities— but rather something that for the human being is an habitual state, a way of life in which constant progress is possible.

So, taking into account what I have just pointed out, it must be said that it is possible for a man or a woman to have for the beloved whom he or she loves a perfect and complete *friendship* (devoted love), and an authentic *love* in its ordinary form, and to have at the same time an *amour fou* for God. But it must also be said that a human being cannot give itself at one and the same time, to the ultimate degree and in an absolute way, to two different objects as if each one constituted its All; in other words, if a soul has entered into an *amour fou* for God, then it must renounce any *amour fou* for another human—whether, as in the religious life, the soul renounces the flesh completely or, while remaining within the bonds of marriage, it does not renounce that unique and sacred love by which a man and woman become two in one flesh, but does renounce what, in the order of the ontological perfections of nature, is the peak and perfection of conjugal love, namely *amour fou*. Because an *amour fou de dilection* of such a kind that in it the Beloved becomes really and truly *the All* of the Lover requires absolutely that it be unique in the soul, and if such a love (*amour fou*) is given to God, it requires that it be given to no one else but Him.[14]

The human soul can have only one single Bridegroom, as the word is

---

  132, a. 1, ad 1m.

12 Prov. xxiii, 26.

13 *Journal de Raïssa*, p. 69 (June 18, 1918).

14 Cf. further on pp. 189–191.

understood in those highest of nuptials in which *amour fou* reigns supreme. This is why, if God happens to be this Bridegroom, His love is a jealous love. God must be, Jesus must be *the Unique Beloved*, the Only One loved with an *amour fou*.

"How shall I give Him proof of my love?—By giving myself to Him from the bottom of my heart, in such a way that no other love ever dwells there. . . . God is jealous of this special gift of the heart which is love, total and exclusive by its very nature . . ."[15]

II. THE MYSTICAL STATE

Love and Friendship in Charity

I said a moment ago that in the love of charity friendship and love (*amour fou*) are two different degrees (not necessarily in intensity, but in their power to alienate the soul from itself)—and, at least in a certain sense, inseparable—of one single and identical love of *dilection*. Let me try to explain my thought on this subject. By charity you love God "with all your heart, with all your soul, with all your strength and with all your mind."[16] It is evident that such a love implies not only friendship, by which the friend, as we said at the beginning, gives himself to his friend in a very real but in a hidden and an indirect way—in other words by means of and by the intermediary of the goods which he gives and which hide the gift of himself under signs and the piecemeal nature of that gift as long as he has not given absolutely all that he has; the love of charity also implies *amour fou* by which the lover gives his very person and his entire subjectivity, the very depths of his being, directly, openly and in complete nakedness, without any possible reservation, ecstatically losing himself in his beloved as in his All. An *amour fou* in which God is loved not only as a Friend, but as a Spouse.

Yet an important distinction must be made here. With regard to God there is no possibility, as there is with regard to the human being, of a simple friendship, excluding an *amour fou*. But there can exist with regard to God a love which *appears more like friendship than like amour fou*, a friendship in which *amour fou* is there, but buried within it, and not manifest except at certain moments. More precisely it is possible that, *in regard to an ordinary way of life*, that charity exist in the soul, *especially* at the level of friendship—in such a case a certain degree of *amour fou* may also be in the soul, but either in such a way,

15 *Journal de Raïssa*, p. 150 (April 20, 1924). The renunciation (of *amour fou*) in question here is what Raïssa in another passage admirably calls "to suppress or surpass the limits of the heart. (*Journal*, p. 221 ("Feuilles détachées," no. 38).

16 Luke x, 27 (Cf. Matt. xxii, 37; Mark xii, 28.) "You shall love the Lord your God with your whole heart, with you whole soul and with all your strength. Deut. vi, 5.

perhaps because of a kind of reverential fear, that the soul has no consciousness of or is scarcely conscious of it, or else in such a way that it is revealed by flashes of consciousness only at certain moments, even if only at the last instant of life. In this case, in order to simplify the language, let us say that this soul lives a way of life in which friendship (implicitly including *amour fou*) predominates. It is under this regime *at least* that every authentically Christian soul is found, every soul which has received and retains charity.

And it is possible too, in regard to its way of life, for charity to exist in the soul, *especially* on that level (which presupposes a level of friendship) of *amour fou* itself taking full possession of the human being and ruling his actions in a permanent and habitual way. In this case, in order to simplify language, let us say that this soul lives under a regime in which *amour fou* (implying and presupposing friendship) predominates.

The Regime of Amour fou *and the Regime of Friendship*

Now that these things have been posited, it seems that a definition of what is called the mystical state[17] is possible, equivalent to the definition which describes it as life under the regime of the Gifts of the Holy Spirit but less technical and more accessible to current language: We might say that a soul passes over to the mystical state when it passes under the regime of an *amour fou* for God.

It is the very nature of charity to tend to move in this way from the regime of friendship to the regime of *amour fou*. This is why it can be said that *de jure* every human soul, since it is called to charity, is called at the very same time, in either a proximate or a remote way, to the mystical life.

But this is a purely theoretical truth, in which only the internal exigencies of charity taken in itself are considered. On the other hand, if the concrete state of some particular soul or other is taken into consideration, then it must be said that those who cannot find a reason to exist except in an *amour fou* for God are called *de facto* to the mystical life, whereas those who can find their reason for existence either outside of God or, if they have charity, in a love for God in which the *amour fou* lies buried and concealed within friendship are not called *de facto* to the mystical life.

The perfection of human life or the perfection of charity considered in its purest and simplest sense, or even in all its general relationships, evidently supposes movement toward the predominant regime of *amour fou* for God or

---

17   The word *mystical* is the accepted term. In a sense it is an unfortunate choice (as is the case with many of our words) because it frightens off many ill-informed people. In reality it has nothing to do with any extraordinary privilege (*gratiae gratis datae*) but designates only a state in which human life and human conduct are usually helped by God's invisible and secret *inspiration* (a state which of itself, if everything had not gone awry in human beings since original sin, would be normal for those in whom the three Divine Persons dwell by sanctifying grace).

toward the mystical life. In this case the love of charity expands fully and freely in the soul, just as much in its power to alienate the soul from itself (because here the person or the subjectivity is given to God directly, completely exposed in its nakedness) as it is in intensity.

We pointed out above that in the love of charity the degree of friendship and the degree of love do not differ necessarily in their intensity. So now we must say that if a soul remains in the predominant regime of friendship, in which it does not cross the threshold of the mystical life, this soul can still attain on this earth a certain perfection of human life and of charity (perfection in a certain respect)—in such a case the love of charity expands without obstacle in the soul, as to its intensity[18] but not as to its power to alienate the soul from itself. It is in heaven that I know the perfection of charity in the absolute sense of the word.

In addition let us not forget that when it is living under the regime of friendship with its God, the soul already has within it, as does every soul in the state of grace, an *amour fou* for God, even though it is buried deep within the unconscious and does not make itself known except now and then by momentary flashes. This soul does not live in the mystical state or under the regime of *amour fou*, but in life it is brushed lightly by mystical inspirations and the *amour fou* of God. Does St. Thomas not teach that the Gifts of the Holy Spirit are necessary for salvation? So much the more are they necessary for the perfection of charity (even if only in a certain respect).

The Instant of Death

After this, what can be said of the preparation or the disposition of the soul with respect to the moment of death?

A soul which, after having entered into the mystical life or the regime of *amour fou* for God, has arrived at the end of its journey and attained, as much as is possible here below, the perfection of charity purely and simply in every respect, this soul is ready or disposed not only to be saved by passing perhaps through purgatory but to be united to Jesus at the very instant it leaves its body. Then if this soul perseveres in this disposition and crosses the threshold of death in a perfect act of *amour fou* for God, it goes straight to heaven.

18   We should understand that in such a case the intensity of charity is great enough for it to expand without obstacle in the soul, *on condition that* too crushing a trial is not imposed upon it. In the concrete perspective in which we find ourselves, we must, as a matter of fact, take into account the trials that God permits and the limit He assigns to them. God tempers the wind to the shorn lamb.

It is clear that under the regime of *amour fou* a soul, in the course of its progress, is capable of attaining a perfection of charity, in intensity as well as in the depth of the gift of self, *far greater* than under the regime of friendship. (Let us not forget that the perfection of charity that a person is capable of attaining in life is not an indivisible point. It continues to develop in size and includes many varied degrees.)

A soul which, having remained under the regime of friendship without having entered into the mystical life, has arrived at the end of its journey and attained here below the perfection of charity in a certain respect (as to its intensity, but not as to its power to alienate the soul from itself), this soul is ready or disposed not only to be saved by passing perhaps through purgatory but to be united to Jesus at the very instant that it leaves its body. If the soul perseveres in this disposition, the moment of death will also be the instant when *amour fou* proclaims its empire and sovereignty over the soul, and, in an act of perfect *amour fou* for God, it will cross the threshold of death and go straight to heaven.

Finally, a soul which does not have charity and lives in evil is unprepared or indisposed either to be saved or to be united to Jesus at the very instant that it leaves its body. Nevertheless we know that in a final sudden impulse of charity it can be saved at this last instant, and even more, that it can be united immediately to Jesus. *Hodie mecum eris in paradiso.*

Clearly Recognizable Contemplation and Masked Contemplation

What can be said of infused contemplation in respect to the perfection of charity? I know that this subject is a very controversial one—but this very fact gives each one of us the freedom to propose whatever opinion he thinks is true.

To begin with, I would like to point out that the expressions *mystical life* and *contemplative life* are not synonymous. The first is broader than the second. A mystical life exists when a soul passes under the regime of *amour fou* of God, but men who devote themselves to the active life can pass under this regime as well as men dedicated to the contemplative life. In other words, mystical life exists when a soul passes under the habitual regime of the Gifts of the Holy Spirit. Now among the seven Gifts it is on the two highest—the first two—the Gift of Wisdom and the Gift of Understanding (and also with regard to the knowledge of creatures experienced through union with God, or the Gift of Knowledge) that the contemplative life depends. The other Gifts more or less concern the active life. It is principally on them that the active life depends if it has passed under the habitual regime of the Gifts of the Holy Spirit; in other words, it is tributary to the mystical state and to mystical inspiration. Even so it must nevertheless be pointed out immediately that the Gifts of the Holy Spirit are interconnected and that the Gift of Counsel or of Fear of the Lord for example cannot operate without the Gifts of Wisdom and Understanding being involved as well. The difference will depend on the way in which the operation of one gift or another appears or is more manifest in the soul and in behavior. In a man engaged in the active life inspirations related to decisions to be taken will play a central role, while those related to the experience of divine things will perhaps play a merely marginal role as far as the field of visibility is concerned; the operation of the Gifts of Wisdom and Understanding will remain more or less concealed and go unnoticed.

From this it follows that those who have crossed over the threshold of the spirit, or of the mystical life, the grace of contemplation, the loving and heartfelt entry into the states of Jesus, will ordinarily take place differently, depending on whether they are contemplative or active. For, as I noted some way back, there is a *masked* infused contemplation, of an atypical, mitigated or discontinuous mode (with which "active souls" will have to be satisfied), just as there is a *clearly recognizable* infused contemplation, typical and manifest (more proper to "contemplatives"). Among those souls given over to the freedom of the Spirit of God, those "whose life style is active will receive the grace of contemplation, but more often of a masked, unrecognizable contemplation; perhaps they will be capable only of reciting the rosary, and mental prayer may bring them nothing but headaches and drowsiness. The mysteries of contemplation will not be present in their way of praying, but perhaps in the gentle touch of their hands, or in their way of walking, or in the way they look at a poor man, or at suffering."[19]

From these considerations let us conclude that to say on the one hand that a man is completely devoted to contemplation or that he leads a contemplative life, and to say on the other hand that a man is nourished, even though unconsciously, by more or less masked infused contemplation (and that he spreads about him, without knowing it, the fragrance and sweetness of this contemplation) are two very different things. But in either case, the man in question will have entered into the regime of the mystical life or of *amour fou* of God, and he will tend toward the perfection of charity, considered absolutely in all its relationships; and contemplation, under one form or another, even if in secret, will play an habitual directing role in his life.

And so, as Raïssa and I wrote in *Liturgie et contemplation*, it is understandable that "what seems to follow from experience is that, in the first place, higher states of infused contemplation always seem to be linked to higher states of perfection; but that in the second place, higher states of perfection do not always appear to be linked to higher states of infused contemplation, understood in the typical forms explained by the masters."[20]

While making progress toward the perfection of charity understood in its absolute sense and in every respect (in respect to its power to alienate the soul from itself and in respect to its intensity), one soul makes its way in one manner (the contemplative life in which the Gifts of Wisdom and Understanding are exercised in a predominant fashion and in which a more complete testimony,

---

19 "Action et contemplation," in my book *Questions de conscience*, pp. 145–146 [OE C VI, p. 721]. In this way all souls that have crossed over the threshold of the mystical life take part at the same time in *"typical or atypical, manifest or masked* contemplation, which is the multiform exercise of the Gifts of Wisdom, free and elusive and transcending all our categories, and capable of all disguises and of all surprises." (*Ibid.*, p. 47 [722])

20 *Liturgie et contemplation*, p. 47 [2nd part, chap. iv].

the sole absolutely necessary testimony, is rendered to the supreme source of all perfection among us: the *amour fou* of God for men and His desire that the soul become with Him a single spirit and a single love)—another soul makes its way in a different fashion (the active life in which the exercise of other Gifts is predominant, but in which the exercise of Wisdom and Understanding is certainly present, although more or less hidden, and in which a more complete testimony is rendered, let us not say to brotherly love, but let us say to the service of one's neighbor, both in body and soul, which is a *consequence* of this love, a love which demands that there be souls who devote themselves to this service).

Contemplative Life and Active Life in the Regime of Amour fou

Concerning the mission of contemplatives, both as regards the essential part of their lives as well as their role as witnesses among men, above all by their example, but also, when they have received the grace, by their word, I would be rather presumptuous to say anything at all after what Raïssa has said on the subject. Everything else depends on this mission.

Among those who live the active life, it seems clear to me that the greatest are those who, more attuned to the secret sources of energy in their own lives and more reverently attentive to the inspirations coming to them from above, have been raised, in the midst of all the exigencies of service to one's neighbor and of the apostolate, to a contemplation that is not simply masked but recognizable and typical[21] and, just as the contemplatives do, shed a particularly clear light on that very important observation made by Father Lallemant: "Without contemplation we will never make much progress in virtue . . . we will never break free from our imperfections. We will always be tied to the earth, and will never raise ourselves much above our natural sentiments. We will never be able to render a perfect service to God. But with it we will do more, for ourselves and for others, in one month than we would do without it in ten years. It produces . . . very sublime acts of love of God which are rarely made without this gift. And finally it perfects our faith and all the virtues . . ."[22]

This is absolutely true. And it is also true, however, that for a great number of those who are led by the Spirit, this blessed contemplation remains, as we remarked earlier, unperceived and hidden. And it is possible too, that a soul, devoted as it is, by the state of life it has chosen, to the contemplative or to the active life, might often believe (since contemplation can be *completely* masked, and since love, even *amour fou*—this is already true in the purely human order—is not necessarily conscious) that it has not crossed the threshold of the

---

21   This is the ideal characteristic of those who lead what is called a "mixed" life (in which action requires of itself that it overflow from contemplation), as was the case with Albert the Great, Tauler, Henri Suso . . .

22   *Doctrine spirituelle* (Paris: Desclée De Brouwer, 1959), pp. 347–348.

mystical state or of the regime of *amour fou*, whereas in reality it already crossed this threshold a long time ago. This is of very little importance; in such a case what is apparent to consciousness and what is not is quite secondary. The fact remains that for all those who have in reality crossed over this threshold there is but a single path. One soul, however, will tread this path in one fashion and another in a different fashion (*alius sic, alius sic ibat*, as St. Augustine said). And on this path toward the perfection of love in its absolute sense and in all respects, in the final analysis action in one way or another[23] overflows from contemplation—recognizable contemplation or masked contemplation whose sapiential savor passes secretly through those inspirations related especially to the active life, and through the exercise of the corresponding Gifts; in the final analysis, whether it leads an active or a contemplative life, and whether it receives the grace of open or masked contemplation in one or the other state of life, the soul, raised to the mystical state shares *habitually* in a contemplative influx. The soul finds refreshment at the springs of contemplation, whether it drinks long draughts there or whether this living water comes to it drop by drop through some intermediary or other. This is the path of *amour fou*.

The Regime of Friendship

In actual fact however, we have seen (it is a *de facto*, not a *de jure*, question) that there is another family—undoubtedly much more numerous—of authentically Christian souls who also make progress here on earth toward the perfection of charity but this time understood only in a certain respect. In their relations with God these souls are not under the regime of *amour fou*, but under the regime of friendship. Here below they advance on the path of friendship[24] toward the perfection of love, considered in respect to its intensity, not its power to alienate the soul from itself. By following this path they can, in the evening of their lives here on earth, enter directly into heaven. But it is at this instant only, and then through all eternity, that they will pass totally and fully under the dominion of *amour fou*. In their lives here below they do not enter

23   Whether *de jure* and by virtue of a demand of its very *nature* (as in the case of the preaching of the Gospel or of the teaching of *sacra doctrina*) or (in the case of any other activity) by virtue of the *mode* according to which it proceeds *de facto* under the regime of *amour fou*.

24   The two paths—of friendship and of *amour fou*—that I am speaking of here have nothing at all to do with the *two ways* about which certain authors made up a theory, and which they proposed as being distinct *de jure* and both leading to the *same ultimate end*, namely, sanctity and high perfection. The contradistinction between the path of friendship and that of *amour fou* is solely a *de facto* distinction. And it *should* open into and join the path of *amour fou*; and the perfection to which it leads is *not as high* as that to which the path of *amour fou* leads. And if in the evening of life a soul which has lived under the predominant regime of friendship with God can go straight to heaven, it is because in this case at the last moment of its life it made a perfect act of *amour fou*.

into the habitual regime of the Gifts; they do not cross the threshold of the mystical life. In the situations or the concrete circumstances in which they live out their lives, they are not called, *de facto*, to infused contemplation; they do not drink at the springs of contemplation.[25]

However we have also seen that these souls, who have *amour fou* within them, though buried more or less deeply in the unconscious and revealed to consciousness from time to time only by sudden flashes, are brushed lightly in their lives by the wings of mystical inspiration and *amour fou* of God. For if the inspiration of the Spirit from on high did not come, even only at certain particularly decisive moments, perhaps very rare (in any case there is always the instant of the first act of freedom in which man chooses his last end, and the last instant of his life in which he chooses or refuses to throw himself onto the eternal Mercy of God), if that inspiration did not come to raise our action above the powers of reason, even when it is enlightened by faith, there would be no salvation for any of us—and for all the more reason no progress whatever toward the perfection of charity.

Consequently we must say that the persons we are talking about are fleetingly *touched* in a more or less profound way by the Gift of Wisdom and at the same time in a more or less profound way by contemplation. This certainly does not mean they should spur themselves on violently and force themselves to achieve contemplation. It does mean that they must be faithful to vocal prayer and, if they have the time, to meditation, and keep themselves in constant readiness for passive recollection which some day may be granted to them. In fact, who knows whether or not some day contemplation will come, without their realizing it, and take up a hidden place within their vocal prayers, so that it may become habitual and spread its influence in their lives? Who knows whether or not some day, the *amour fou* of God will well up from the depths of their souls with an irresistible force and seize control of them, in such a way that they find themselves transported from the regime of friendship to the regime of *amour fou*? In these matters everything depends on the freedom of the Spirit of God, which is an *absolute* freedom—and is capable of bringing anyone at all, regardless of his state of life, under the regime of the Gifts, perhaps by changing at that moment (sometimes by turning completely

---

25   By the very fact that the love of God and the love of neighbor are two faces of one single charity, the two distinct predominant regimes of friendship on the one hand (in which the active life has not crossed the threshold of the mystical life) and of *amour fou* on the other (in which contemplation is *open and recognizable* in some—the "contemplatives"—and *masked* in others—those in the "active" life) should come together in the same state of mind toward one's neighbor. But how? It seems we can say that under the regime of friendship with God we love our brothers by trying *to love our neighbor as Jesus loved His neighbor*; and that under the predominant regime of *amour fou* for God it is ALSO (and first and foremost) *by seeing Jesus in our neighbor* that we love our neighbor ("I was hungry and you gave me food, I was thirsty and you gave me drink. . ." Matt., xxv, 35).

upside down) certain elements of the situation or certain concrete circumstances which, for a given soul, constituted an actual obstacle to the immediate
or distant call to the mystical life and to contemplation (overt or masked)—a
call to which, theoretically speaking, every human soul is subject, especially
every soul vivified by charity.

The fact remains that the obstacle I mentioned actually comes into play for
multitudes of souls, even authentically Christian souls. The particular situations and the concrete circumstances which constitute this obstacle may
sometimes be due to the soul's negligence, but as a general rule they depend
on the human condition itself, which means that Divine Providence accepts
the responsibility for them. And it is also a fact that all souls for whom the
Spirit of God has not removed the obstacle in question can—and should—advance toward attaining the perfection of love here below, even if only with
respect to its intensity and making their way solely under the predominant
regime of friendship.

And if many show themselves incapable even of this, and are too weak to
practice the law of God in all its precepts, at least they know, or ought to know,
that love is *the true face of God* and that this love will never cease to look on
them with pity and to ask for their love and to wait patiently for them admit
their wretchedness and turn toward the Divine Mercy.

Concerning the Word Contemplation

In the preceding discussion the word *contemplation* was used perhaps in a
somewhat too elastic way. But I really think that this elasticity was objectively
necessary. Why? Because the word *contemplation* must be used for want of a
better word, though in itself it is not a very good one. We have no word to
express something that takes place within man and at the same time transcends every human concept—that *passio divinorum*, that knowledge of God
which is more experience than knowledge and yet is supreme knowledge,
which comes about through love and the union of love and which is a
thousand miles form the *theôria* of the Greeks as it is from speculation and
philosophic contemplation. The word *contemplation* was kept by Christian
tradition because at least it saved the characteristic of supreme knowledge
proper to the experience in question. But in truth it has survived because it let
itself be overwhelmed by a meaning that was too heavy to carry and because
according to the terms of an unconditional surrender it agreed to become
ambiguous, in an ambiguity that turned out to be fortunate, by the way, and
fruitful and profitable for the mind, except for those minds who do not know
how to control the signs they make use of.

Exemplary Saints and Unnoticed Saints

Undoubtedly there are in heaven many more, immensely more saints than we can imagine. This is true first of all for saints in the ordinary sense of the word, I mean *exemplary* saints, heroes of the moral and spiritual life whose practice and example (even if only in the final period of their lives here below, as in the case of certain martyrs who before bearing witness by their blood had been guilty of serious faults, or as in the case of the Good Thief, who made his grand act of love just before breathing his last) went far beyond the life common to ordinary men and and tend to exercise on all humanity that sovereign *attraction* of which Bergson spoke. These exemplary saints do not live like everybody else, in the sense that even in their external behavior, which is the measure of their actions since it is the measure of the Gifts of the Holy Spirit, is higher than that of the infused or acquired moral virtues; they surprise us; in some way they always end up leading us confusedly astray; their heroism, however secret its sources may be, cannot go unnoticed in some way or other. These are the canonizable saints. A certain number actually have been canonized. Others, who make up an incomparably greater multitude, will never be canonized. All of them, at a certain moment of their lives, passed under the regime of *amour fou* and from that moment on advanced toward the perfection of charity understood absolutely and in every respect. At that same moment all of them, even if in the last moment of their lives, crossed the threshold of the mystical state and received the manna of infused contempla-tion (overt or masked). All of them became coredeemers with Christ because they became united to Him already here on earth, not only by belonging to the Mystical Body, but in an immediate relation as well, or in the immediate mutual giving of one person to another—as to the Bridegroom of their souls.

In saying that in heaven there are immensely more saints than we can imagine, I am thinking as well of those saints we might call *unnoticed or unrecognizable* because, except for the secret places of their hearts, they led lives among us like everybody else. If there was any heroism in their lives, and there certainly must have been, it is a completely hidden heroism. They deserve the name of saints nevertheless, in the sense that from this life in the world they went directly to heaven,[26] having made their way with perseverance along the path of friendship with God until they attained here below the perfection of charity (in respect to intensity). Then, as I have already pointed out, their last instant was an instant of triumph for *amour fou* which will continue for all eternity. I have no doubt that these "uncanonizable" saints make up a far greater multitude than the "canonizable" saints who will never be canonized. It is for them and especially for them that the Church each year celebrates the Feast of All Saints. Here we must think first and foremost of the immense mass of the poor and of the little people of God, I mean of all those among them who practiced to the limit abnegation of self, devotedness to others, and

---

26   I will be granted this definition, I hope, even though in a more general sense the name *saint* evidently fits any soul who is in heaven, even though to get there it had first to suffer the purifications of purgatory.

steadfastness in virtue. Throughout the centuries (and this is only one example among many) there have been peasant families in which work was sanctified by the sacraments, common prayer, and daily reading from the lives of the saints, and in which the fear of God, the virtue of religion, and a certain strictness in moral conduct served as a sanctuary or tabernacle for the theological virtues. Such families must have accounted for a considerable percentage of those saints who, after having lived their lives "like everybody else," went directly to heaven. Père Lamy, whom we used to call "the saintly Curé," never failed to insist on this. Undoubtedly the saints I am talking about here, for the most part, never crossed the threshold of the mystical state or had the experience of even diffuse or masked contemplation (unless they were perhaps *touched* by those fleeting experiences, more or less rare and generally unnoticed by them, that I mentioned above). However, if they did not do so with the full freedom and the supreme sacrifices of *amour fou* which are the privilege of canonizable saints, they certainly did, like them, carry their cross with Jesus, and, as members and parts of that unimaginably great human-divine Whole which is the Mystical Body of Christ, like any Christian in the state of grace, they did their part to fulfill the coredemptive vocation that baptism imprints on the soul.

Is it true to say that as the twilight descends and as the old Christendoms fall apart, it becomes more and more difficult, solely under the regime of friendship with the Lord, for the mass of men to retain the state of grace or charity and to remain faithful to the end, and to people heaven with saints who "lived like everybody else"? And can it be said at the same time that, in order to compensate or overcompensate for the losses, there is something growing, either in quantity or in quality, among those souls who live under the regime of *amour fou*, and that their role in the economy of salvation grows more and more important because (and this is especially true of those in whom infused contemplation blossoms freely, however small their number may be in comparison) their lived intimacy with Jesus, their complete renunciation of material things and of their very selves become more and more necessary in order to pay for the salvation of the many and in order to make present and readily visible to miserable men the depths God's goodness, innocence and love?

III. ON CHRISTIAN MARRIAGE

Marriage, Friendship, and Love

I have already offered elsewhere[27] a few more or less random reflections on marriage. As a beginning let me take up once again certain of these reflections in order to make them a bit more precise.

---

27   Cf. *Réflexions sur l'Amérique*, pp. 145–149 [OE C X, p. 871–874]; *La Philosophie morale*, pp. 443–444 [OE C XI, pp. 855–856].

I pointed out first of all that it would be a great illusion to think that marriage must be the fulfillment of *amour-passion* or romantic love. For passionate and romantic love, being nothing more in reality than animal desire disguised as pure love by the imagination, are impermanent and perishable in themselves, apt to pass from one object to another, and therefore unfaithful, intrinsically torn in the end between love for the other, which they have awakened, and their own essentially egotistic nature.

Undoubtedly sexual desire and passion, and romantic love too—or at least something of it—as much as possible should be present in marriage as an initial stimulant and starting-point. But far from having as its essential aim "to bring romantic love to its perfect fulfillment, marriage has quite a different task to carry out in human hearts, and that is to bring about, by a wondrous alchemy, an infinitely more profound and mysterious operation: I mean that it has to *transform* romantic love, or what was there at the beginning, into a real and indestructible *human* love, a love that is radically free of all self-centeredness,"[28] which by no means excludes sensual desire and passion, but which in itself and by its essence is principally spiritual—a complete and irrevocable gift of one to the other, for the love of the other.

The love I am speaking of here is above all a love of *dilection*. It is not necessarily an *amour fou*; but it is necessarily and primordially a love of devotedness and friendship—that absolutely unique *friendship* between married people one of whose essential ends is the spiritual companionship between a man and a woman in order that they may help each other fulfill their destiny in this world. And so it is a *love* (I am speaking of love in its ordinary form, which in the beginning I very simply called a "bel amour")[29] which is truly in the measure of the human person, in which the soul as well as the senses is involved,[30] in such a way that in this love, where sensual desire is present with all its power, a tenderness or *dilection* takes a very real precedence over any selfish considerations. Finally, actual carnal intercourse also is normally involved,[31] since the other essential end of marriage is the perpetuation of the human species. This is why each spouse has a right over the body of the other.

The essence of conjugal love consists in this unique and sacred friendship I just spoke of, along with love, a "bel amour," (when it is there) which is

---

28   *Reflections on America* (Garden City, N.Y.: Doubleday, Image Books, 1958), p. 80f.

29   A gift but still in the state of a more or less developed *rough draft* of what the person itself actually *is*.

30   This kind of love is *normal* in marriage, but it is not *necessary*; it is in fact missing in many marriages whose motive was above all of a social nature, not a personal one—obedience to parents, convention, not to speak of financial advantage or "great expectations" of "social rank" or of family pride. etc.—in brief, arranged marriages or "marriages of convenience."

31   Even in the loveless marriages mentioned in the preceding footnote.

equally unique and sacred and which is, and should normally be, a part of that friendship. By this friendship, marriage "between a man and a woman can be a true community of love, built not on sand but on rock, because it is built on genuinely human, not just animal, love, a love that is authentically spiritual, authentically *personal*—through the hard discipline of self-sacrifice and by dint of renouncement and purification. Then in a free and continuous ebb and flow of emotion, feeling and thought, each one really participates, by the power of love, in the deeply personal life of the other which is, by nature, the other's incommunicable possession. And then each one can become a kind of Guardian Angel for the other,—prepared as Guardian Angels have to be, to forgive the other a great deal," in short, someone "really dedicated to the good and the salvation of the other," and consenting to be "entrusted completely with the revelation of and the care for, all that the other *is* in his or her deepest human depths."[32]

To such a fundamentally and primordially necessary friendship, to such a love of complete devotedness, along with the carnal intercourse implied in marriage, and along with the love of the senses and of the soul, that "bel amour" which is implied or ought to be implied, to all this there can be added an *amour fou*, in which the unconditionally direct, overt, and naked gift of the person or subjectivity in its entirety is carried to its extreme form and absolute fullness—not only in the body, but in absolutely all that it is—so that it makes itself truly part and parcel of the All that the other is. It is here that *amour fou* is added on in full measure. But it is added on in response to a radical desire inscribed in the human being, since, as we have seen above, *amour fou*, in which the lover becomes ecstatic in his beloved and the beloved in her lover, and each becomes flesh of the other's flesh and one spirit with the other, this *amour fou* is the summit and perfection of love between Man and Woman, and hence the summit and perfection of love between spouses.

I do not think that this summit is often attained—far from it. But when it is attained, by virtue of some extraordinary good luck, which is a special and gratuitous gift, it is a glorious foretaste of heaven here below, in which a dream which has been a part of human nature from the beginning of time finds its realization, a dream of which all the wedding hymns of long ages past have revealed that nostalgia inherent in our poor humanity.

The State of Marriage, the Regime of Friendship with God, and the Regime of Amour fou for God.

After these considerations what must be said of the relation of marriage and conjugal love to the spiritual life and to the perfection of charity toward which every Christian has the obligation to strive, according to his condition and his possibilities?

---

32   *Reflections on America*, pp. 82, 83.

It is generally agreed that statistically speaking few human institutions are subjected to such social servitude under civilizations so different in time and place, to so many accidents, hazards, and misfortunes, to such habitual egoism and cruelty, indeed to such lying and hypocrisy, and exposed to so many failures as is the institution of marriage. This should not surprise us, since the married state is the condition of the vast majority of human beings. It is nevertheless a matter of fact that there are many very good marriages, in which human nature attains as real a happiness as is possible in this world, and through which, by providing God with the occasion to create immortal souls and by bringing into the world new human persons, man and woman accomplish the task of procreation which God entrusted to our race in such a way that this task itself truly becomes for them and for their children exactly what the Creator had designed it to be—the first and greatest of earthly blessings.

It is also a fact that the state of marriage, such as Christianity views it and such as the grace of the sacraments makes it possible to live, is neither that resolutely accepted *state of imperfection* to which a pseudo-theology at work in the imagination of certain laymen seemed to want to consign it, nor that caricature of a so-called Christian union in which the husband saw in his wife no more than piece of flesh destined for him so that he might reconcile his concupiscence with God's law. The state of marriage is a holy and consecrated state of life, in which, as companions on earth amid the afflictions and the joys of life, as in their duties toward their children, the two spouses (by the very fact of their differences, and of the rounding off of corners that such differences requirer) work out their mutual emancipation from the weight of those hereditary fatal flaws which their dead ancestors imposed on them. In this holy state they should normally help each other make their way, against all the winds and tides of life, toward the perfection of human life and of charity, with the result that for each soul, according to the degree of its faithfulness to grace, the state of marriage may finally flow not only into that antechamber of beatitude which the purifications of Purgatory actually are, but also directly into a blessed eternity and the vision of God.

If we go back now to what was said above about the regime of *friendship* in the relations of the soul with God, and if we keep in mind that, given the human condition, it is this regime that we should in fact expect to find most frequently in that great multitude of souls who possess charity and advance as best they can, then we should be able to say that it is under this regime of friendship with God that, in fact, the greatest number of souls who in the state of marriage advance toward the perfection of charity are to be found. These particular souls do not cross the threshold of the mystical life; nor do they find refreshment at the springs of contemplation, except perhaps by drinking a drop from time to time, even though it is a masked and atypical mystical life. If they experience fleeting touches of this life, it is in a way that is intermittent and goes unnoticed. But they do advance faithfully in love and can achieve its perfection here below,[33] if not with respect to the power of alienating the soul from itself, at least with respect to intensity (on condition of course that God spare them trials that are too crushing). These souls can furnish heaven with very many *unnoticed saints*.

Is this to say that in the state of marriage the human soul could not, in its relations with God, enter into the regime of *amour fou*? Come now! Not only is it possible, but the history of the saints shows us that in fact such was the case for many married people (and this history speaks of canonized saints, but there are also canonizable saints that were never canonized . . .).

How could it be otherwise, since all are called *de jure* to the perfection of charity taken in its absolute sense, with respect to the power to alienate the soul from itself just as in respect to its intensity—and hence to the mystical life and to contemplation whether overt or masked?

There may even be, in all probability, some particular cases in which—supposing that the two spouses, or one of them, are the object of a proximate call from God and respond to it—the married state, with the perpetual attention given to the other and all the daily sacrifices it requires, and with the human experience and the innumerable occasions of mercy and of fraternal help which life among men entails, might very well offer to this or that married person, at the same time that it brings greater risks due to the attractions of the world, even more propitious moral conditions for the entrance of the soul into the habitual regime of the Gifts of the Holy Spirit than the state of religion offers to some member of a religious order. And this remark could very well be true in a case where exceptional circumstances lighten ever so little the crushing material burden of being a father or a mother of a family, even with regard to the contemplative life, and I understand all this in relation to the renunciation and the simplicity of the "little way" of St. Therese of Lisieux rather than with those great typical signs described by St. John of the Cross and St. Teresa of Avila.

"In truth," wrote Raïssa in *Liturgy and Contemplation*, "contemplation is given not solely to Carthusians, to Poor Clares, to Carmelites. . . . It is frequently the treasure of persons hidden from the world, known only to some few, to their directors, to a few friends. Sometimes, in a certain way this treasure is hidden even from the very souls who possess it—souls who live by it in all simplicity, without visions, without miracles, but with such a flame of love for

---

33   Let us note here that, while advancing toward perfection under the regime of friendship, it is possible for someone to go very far along this path without any too serious conflict if he or she loves another human being with an *amour fou*, precisely because under such a regime the divine *amour fou* does not make clear the full extent of its demands.

But the case is not the same for those who make their way toward perfection under the regime of *amour fou*; then conflicts will arise along the way such as will require the renunciation of human *amour fou*, whether they like it or not; otherwise they will betray the demands of divine *amour fou*.

God and neighbor that good happens all around them without any noise or agitation.

"This is what our epoch has to become aware of, and of the ways by which contemplation is communicated throughout the world, in one form or another, to the great multitude of souls who thirst for it (often without realizing it), and who are called to it at least in a remote fashion. The great need of our age in regard to the spiritual life is to put contemplation within the reach of everyone."[34]

It is always necessary to tend toward what is higher. And so it is desirable that among young married couples who desire with all their heart to dedicate their souls to a Christian life, who are far more numerous than seems to be the case as a result of certain prejudices, and who, without harboring any illusions about the steepness of the path, aspire to the highest ideal of Christian marriage and to a life together in which both of them, advancing toward the perfection of charity, do not remain in their relations with God at the level of the regime of friendship, but pass over into the regime of *amour fou*.

The State of Father or Mother of a Family Is Compatible with Progress in Infused Contemplation and in Amour fou for God

Let us note here that, although Christianity recognizes bodily chastity as the indication of a more exclusive consecration to God, and even sees, as I will show further on, if not a necessary link, at least a particular propriety between it and specifically Christian contemplation, carnal intercourse between spouses is in no way an obstacle either to mystical life or to contemplation, even in its highest stages for either or both of the spouses who enter into the ways of the Holy Spirit. This is quite evident if we think of the fundamental and universal importance that the Old Law accorded to fecundity in marriage (and this is still the case in contemporary Judaism), or if we think on the other hand of those great and holy contemplatives, those contemplatives of enormous stature who lived under the Old Law, or also of those mystics of modern times who have not at all been lacking among the Jews, especially among the Hassidim. The great Muslim mystics (I am thinking here, as with the Hassidim, of those among them who went far beyond natural mysticism and experienced infused contemplation) could also be offered as testimony—we know that Hallâj, the most sublime and heroic of them all, who was tortured and hanged to death for having taught contemplation by the union of mutual love between God and man, was married and left behind two sons.

Nor is there any lack of examples among Christian contemplatives. They are relatively small in number among the canonized saints (it is not customary, it seems, to canonize simple lay people, with the exception of course of a few great political leaders). Nevertheless, holy widows like St. Bridgit, St. Frances

---

34   *Liturgie et contemplation*, p. 76 [part 3, ch. iv]. We both wrote this book, but Raïssa wrote this particular page.

of Rome, St. Jeanne de Chantal, the Venerable Marie of the Incarnation (Ur-suline), evidently did not wait to become widows before entering into the paths of infused contemplation; nor did St. Nicholas of Flü wait until he was a widower and became a hermit to do the same; all of them were great contemplatives beforehand. Blessed Anne-Marie Taïgi was the mother of a family. And the case of married persons who lived a life of infused contempla-tion, without being beatified or canonized because of it, is certainly far more common, as was the case in the sixteen and seventeen centuries (I cite Brémond at random): Marie de Valence and Madame Acarie, Marguerite Romanet, Madame du Houx, Madame Helyot and her husband, or in our day Lucie-Christine, Madeleine Sémer, or Elisabeth Leseur.

Married couples who entered into the regime of *amour fou* for God, and more particularly into that of contemplation, were certainly not obliged because of this[35] to renounce giving themselves to one another in the physical expression of their love and bringing children into the world.

Human Amour Fou *Is Incompatible with Progress in Infused Contemplation and in* Amour Fou *for God*

Still there is a certain renunciation (I have already touched on this in passing; I would like to insist on it a bit more at this point), a renunciation that, to tell the truth, is far more serious and to which a husband and wife are obligated. They are obliged to renounce, if they have ever known it, *amour fou* for each other. Living under the regime of *amour fou* for God, they cannot live, at the same time, under the regime of *amour fou* for a created being—at least they cannot do so without a contradiction and an interior wrenching that would keep them from advancing as God would like them to and would place obstacles in their path. In *amour fou* does not the lover give himself to his beloved as to his All, of which he then becomes a part? My All is my One Alone. Already in the natural order, in human *amour fou*, the total gift that the lover makes of himself entails and demands an absolute exclusivity. How much more is this the case in the supernatural order, in an *amour fou* that has God for its object! I have no doubt that it remains psychologically possible (for in this case we are concerned with two different, indeed incommensurable, orders) that along with this divine *amour fou*, to its detriment and in how irreconcilable a conflict with it, there should still subsist in the soul, at least for a time, an *amour fou* for a creature. But this would be all the more dearly paid for because then the Lover Himself, jealous of any other attachment, and for all the more reason of any other *amour fou* in the soul that loves Him, will Himself undertake to annihilate whatever still exists in the soul as an obstacle to an *amour fou* for Him.

---

35   The fact that certain persons decided on such a renunciation because of what they felt was a special and entirely personal call to follow at any cost, while they still remained in the world, at least one of the counsels of perfection, is an entirely different question.—Cf. further on p. 192.

If a human person gives itself truly and absolutely to another human person as to its All, to its One Alone because it loves that other person with an *amour fou*, it can certainly love God more than the other human person, as the order of charity requires—with regard to the sovereign lovability, the sovereign perfection and the sovereign rights which the soul recognizes in Him, and with regard to the obedience that the soul is ready to render to Him in spite of all else—in short, such a soul can love God with a love of friendship that is deeper than the *amour fou* it has for another human person[36] (in this case, we know very well that the soul loves God with an *amour fou*, at least with an *amour fou* concealed within friendship and perhaps with an *amour fou* that has already begun to blossom freely). However, it cannot go to the ultimate that an *amour fou* for God requires as far as the integrity of the gift it makes to God is concerned—and I am not speaking only of the gift of itself, but of the gift of whatever it loves more than itself.[37] And the perfection of charity considered under only one of its relationships is not such that with it the soul can completely surmount certain trials that are too crushing. We have pointed out above (p. 175, n. 18) that God limits trials to what the soul is able to bear and that under the regime of *amour fou* the soul is able to attain a greater degree of the perfection of charity, in both the intensity and the depth of the gift of self, than it is under the regime of friendship. There is certainly something that the soul will give Him, but holding back with regard to certain extremes in the divine demands, holding back with regard to an immolation:[38] the immolation precisely of that other to whom the soul gave itself as to its One Alone and to its All. The fatherly love of Abraham was not an *amour fou*. Mary's motherly love for Jesus—the tenderest and most perfect motherly love imaginable—was not an *amour fou*.[39] An *amour fou* is mad. If a man loves a woman with an *amour fou*, he will not consent to immolate her, even to God Himself. (He will struggle against God, and he will be broken.) If two spouses who pass under the regime of an *amour fou* for God know what they are doing, they realize that by this very fact they will have to renounce their *amour fou* for one another, that human

---

36   From this point of view human *amour fou* is under the control of charity.

37   From this point of view human *amour fou* could not be under the *perfect* control of charity. There is undoubtedly obedience, but one that is given reluctantly, perhaps even with anger deep down in the heart. This is far from *perfect* obedience.

   Nevertheless, is it not true that when the soul advances toward the perfection of charity solely under the regime of friendship with God, it is not required to give up its human *amour fou*? But in this case it does not advance toward the perfection of charity in the absolute sense.

38   Not every death is a death on the cross. "*Factus obediens usque ad mortem, mortem autem crucis.*"

39   What I mean to say is that Mary evidently experienced an *amour fou* for Jesus as *God* and man but that her *maternal* love for Jesus as *man* and God, being *perfectly* under the control of charity, was not an *amour fou*.

amour fou which in the natural order is the summit and glory of conjugal love, but which in the supernatural order is far less than the unique and perfect friendship rooted in charity and the grace of the sacraments. It can happen that a man or a woman who has made his or her All of another human being who is loved with an *amour fou* may enter into the authentic paths of contemplation. But a day will come, perhaps very late, when they will understand that an interior division makes progress in these paths impossible. They will then have to make the sacrifice, certainly not of their love, but their *amour fou* for this other human being.[40]

The Author of the Song of Songs

The *Song of Songs* is not a song of profane love, a human wedding hymn that has been plagiarized and applied to divine love. Its original purpose, as is maintained by the tradition of the Synagogue and by the best Christian exegetes, was to sing of the love between God and His People—and more truly still, in a prophetic light, to sing of the nuptial love, the *amour fou* between God and His Church, and inseparably from this, the *amour fou* between God and the soul that has attained mystical union with Him.

But it is clear, at the same time, that the author of the *Song of Songs* was a man profoundly versed, more so than even Dante himself[41] in matters of profane love, in the experience of human *amour fou* and the physical expression of love that normally accompanies it. When he wrote his *Song*, had he already renounced carnal love? I do not think anyone can say anything on this subject. But the one thing certain is that, at the time when, from his own personal experience (and what a marvelously unitive experience, in the rapture of a total gift), he sang his song of *amour fou* between God and His creature, he had already renounced human *amour fou*.

Even though Christian Contemplation Does Not Require Chastity of the Body There Is Nevertheless an Affinity between the Two

I pointed out a moment ago that if the contemplative life does not of itself

---

40   Saints make this sacrifice without hesitation. I am thinking of St. Elizabeth of Hungary, who loved her husband, as J. Ancelet-Hustache tells us in his beautiful book *L'Or dans la fournaise* (p. 44), with a profound love of both body and soul. The episode in the first years of their marriage, in which she passed the entire night in prayer, while Louis held her hand—and for such a long time that the two of them ended up falling asleep on the carpet (*ibid.*, p. 45)—does not signify solely that she wanted for a certain time to do violence to her flesh. But more profoundly still, I have no doubt, it signifies as well that during these particular nights she carried out a very definite sacrifice, and renounced for the *amour fou* of God, whatever physical expression there had been between these two spouses of their love for one another, the human *amour fou* she felt rising within her.

41   Shelley said that Dante understood the secrets of love better than any other poet.

require chastity of the body, nevertheless (whatever certain of today's Christians, more or less intoxicated with bad psychology and among whom chastity does not have a very good press, may think on this subject) chastity does have a certain relationship of propriety or of affinity to specifically Christian contemplation. In any case, Christianity recognizes in chastity the mark of a more exclusive consecration to God.

And it also happened in times past that couples, at a given moment in their conjugal lives,[42] not only renounced their *amour fou* for one another, but even in certain cases made a vow to renounce the flesh itself in order to give themselves more exclusively to Jesus. Such cases were undoubtedly quite infrequent and due to a very particular and clearly manifest vocation. No one was really surprised. It was known that they lived the sacrament of marriage all the more profoundly because one of the essential ends of marriage, the spiritual companionship between spouses for their mutual help in the journey to God, was strengthened and realized in a higher way by this *amour fou* for God. As far as procreation, the other essential end of marriage, is concerned, it was not denied but rather transferred to another plane; it was spiritual offspring that this couple expected from God, and it was to these offspring that they gave themselves. *Centuplum accipietis.*

After all, they had great examples, at the very highest point of creation—where humanity was borne to the confines of the divinity, in the humblest, the poorest, and the most hidden of lives among men. The love which reigned between Mary and Joseph was conjugal love in the purest plenitude of its essence. However, in this case, not only did the supreme *natural* perfection of love between Man and Woman, an *amour fou*, give way, according to the law of the cross, to an incomparably higher supreme *supernatural* perfection, the *amour fou* of both of them for their God; but it is still recognized that, whatever its particular appropriateness with regard to Christian contemplation may be, even if, of itself, chastity of the body is in no way required for contemplation, it does nevertheless retain primary importance with regard to the *state of life*—the state of perfection not only *to be acquired*, but also, in the case of Nazareth, already *acquired or possessed*, to which, by a unique privilege, Joseph and Mary found themselves raised in their married state.

The Merits of Chastity

Why this importance and these special merits of chastity of the body as well as of the soul?

---

42   On occasion from the very moment of the reception of the sacrament, which remained valid as long as the two married people took this vow, not before, but after the act of mutual consent in which each had given to the other full rights over his or her body, as an effect and a confirmation of this mutual consent. And to tell the truth, such things did not take place only in past times—I am thinking of two friends of ours who were married under these precise conditions. Raïssa and I were the witnesses at their wedding.

Let me recall in the first place that if it is possible to have carnal union without *amour fou*, on the other hand there can be no human *amour fou* which does not also normally entail carnal union as well, at least in desire. By renouncing all carnal union, even in desire, the religious who makes a vow of chastity does not sacrifice the flesh alone; at the same time he also makes a sacrifice which truly goes much further and attains the profoundest depths of man's natural aspirations, not only in his flesh but also in his soul and his spirit. Undoubtedly he does not renounce any form of feminine friendship, however strictly this friendship must be subject to interior vigilance (such a renunciation would be a great loss for the very progress and refinement of his moral life). But he does sacrifice every possibility of his attaining or desiring that earthly paradise whose dream haunts the subconsciouses of our race—*amour fou* between a man and a woman. The vow of chastity or of virginity is above all else the sign of such a renunciation.

Secondly, let me say that in mortifying the carnal instinct in himself, man does not simply come up against something which properly concerns only him as an individual person, such as would be the case when, to perfect himself, he mortifies his instinct of gluttony or of slander. He comes up against an instinct which is *first and foremost* the instinct of his species and far more than of his own individual person. It dwells in his person like a foreign despot and seizes upon him and torments him with an all the more tyrannical violence. Chastity holds in check a furious force immensely more ancient that the individual through whom it passes. Even in the purely natural order it is a kind of liberation—in one sense and in a certain way it delivers man from slavery to the species. It is a kind of victory, a kind of liberation which men in general, unless certain religious or naturalist prejudices make them believe it is forbidden or impossible, seem to have a tendency to envy, even if from quite a distance. Is not one of the reasons why virginity held a place of honor even among the pagans themselves? And is not why many pagan sages and I am not speaking only of the sages of India, whose testimony on this point is so striking—considered that when a husband (they said nothing of women for they were held too much in disdain) arrived at a certain age at which it was proper for him to devote himself more deeply to meditation by withdrawing into his interior liberty, it was also proper for him to cut off physical relations with his wife.

Thirdly, and more simply, it is clear that by the very fact that the mysteries of the Christian faith put particular emphasis on the importance of the flesh and the body, as well as on the metaphysical unity of the human person, whose soul is proper to a given body ("individuated" by its relation to that body)—it is only normal that, in a religion which teaches the Incarnation of the Word and the Assumption of the Blessed Virgin, those who wish to consecrate themselves to God, consecrate to Him not only their souls but their bodies as well. Did not Jesus give Himself entirely, body and soul, to men in order to save them? Those who love a human person with an *amour fou* give themselves to the other in their bodies and in their souls. Those who enter into a state of life dedicated to the *amour fou* of God must give God their bodies as well as their souls. The soul is given through love, the body through chastity. And even if we give no special consideration to the religious state, it must be admitted that in general, by insisting on the human person and its dignity, and by raising up and restoring the condition of women, and by teaching that the redemption of humanity depended on the consent of a little virgin of Israel, Christianity, with the help of the light of grace, at the same time raised chastity to a new level in the esteem of men.

Finally, there is a fourth consideration, which this time is concerned with contemplation itself, I mean, *Christian* contemplation. This final consideration with regard to Christian contemplation offers a certain nuance or attenuation to the statement (however valid it still remains) that the contemplative life does not, of itself, require chastity of the body. In reality Christian contemplation is indivisibly the contemplation of the uncreated Trinity and of Jesus God and man; the humanity of Christ—that humanity which belongs to the second divine Person, and all of whose properties are also attributes of this divine Person Himself—is always present in it in a manifest or a hidden way and cannot be detached from it. What the Christian contemplative keeps constantly and firmly in view is of course the one and triune God; but it is also a perfectly chaste man, born of the purest of Virgins, who Himself is God. It is He, it is Jesus who is the Spouse of his soul. How would a Christian who aspires to contemplation not feel himself attracted also to a life of continence or of chastity—once more, not as a necessary condition (except for certain persons because of their religious state) but as something that is more consonant with their desires.

Likewise, in Christian contemplation there is a certain innocence of approach, a gentleness and delicacy of touch, if I can put it this way, a certain candid demeanor and a certain matchless simplicity, as well as that light-winged liberty which familiarity with the Holy Spirit brings with it, and that intimacy with the divine Persons and with the heart of Jesus, for which, without perfect purity, the ardor of love does not suffice—all these things, without actually requiring it, are so to speak connatural with chastity of the body.

The Vows of Religion

These preceding remarks, I believe, can help us understand that the vow of chastity, and the two other vows which it accompanies, constitute for those who consecrate themselves to the religious state a veritable *holocaust*, by which in advance and forever they give themselves to God body and soul—and with what hope? if not the hope of making their way here below toward perfection, under the regime of *amour fou* for God and for Jesus.

The Promise of the Sub-deacon in the Latin Rite

A clear distinction must be made between the vow of chastity, which by its essence is destined for the easier and more rapid progress of the one who makes it toward the perfection of charity, and the promise which in the Latin Church the sub-deacon makes at the moment of his ordination.[43] When the bishop whom he has approached informs him that from now on he will have to observe chastity if he perseveres in his intention to receive the sub-diaconate, the ordinand simply takes a step forward (he takes *the* step). This promise[44] is of itself (like the priesthood), not for the one who makes it, but *for others* (so that, once ordained a priest, he who made it may be *better* able to carry out—with a complete devotedness that no other attachment and no other obligation would impede or diminish—his mission, his *ministry* in the service of the souls to whose good he is dedicated). The promise made by the sub-deacon is so far from being identical with the vow of chastity that when a man who is already a priest enters a religious order, along with vows of obedience and poverty, he also makes a vow of chastity (this is evidently because he has not yet made such a vow). The promise of the sub-deacon in the Latin Rite is not intended to be part of a holocaust of the human individual; it is a sacred *wound* accepted for the better exercise of his function in regard to others. And it is the responsibility of each one either to keep this wound open while putting up with it as best he can (in a difficult life in which he can undoubtedly become a "good priest," but a mediocre priest as well, or even a more or less defeated priest), or else heal the wound and transform it into a source of grace (for himself and for others) by giving himself freely, even though he remains in the world, to an *amour fou* for God. Only then will he be able to become a *"holy priest,"* through his personal response to the precept, which was addressed to all, to advance toward the perfection of charity and to the call which this precept contains.

ANNEX
Two Synoptic Tables

Those who do me the honor of reading what I write know that I have an immoderate penchant for drawing up synoptic tables and outlines. It seems to me that the matters in question in the (ninth) chapter of this book, and the

---

43   At the time when these pages were written the sub-diaconate had not yet been suppressed. Today the promise in question is made at the time of the reception of the diaconate.

44   Or this vow, if it is preferable to give it this name—the word is not important. In any case the reality designated by the word differs in nature from the vow of chastity properly so called, which is made with a view to acquiring interior perfection.

distinctions I have proposed in it are complex enough to deserve that an overview of them be provided in the form of a table. And so here are two synoptic tables[45] for this Annex—the first concerning the analogical notion of love, the second concerning the perfection of charity.

Table No. 1: On the notion of love

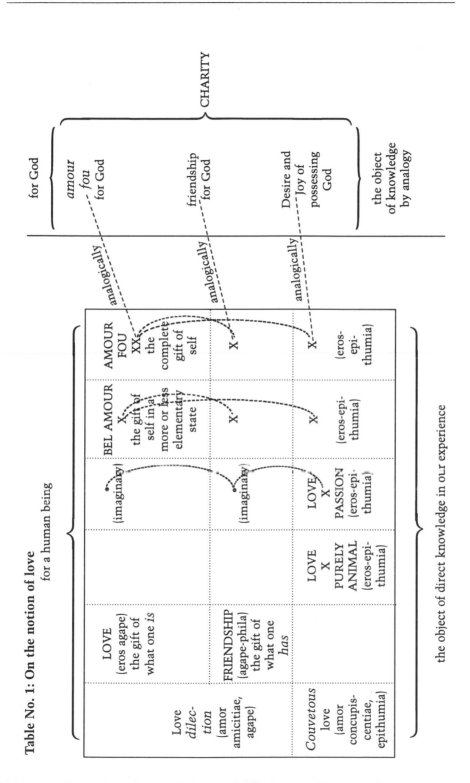

Table No. 2: On the pursuit of the perfection of charity

Regime of life	Mystical state	Type of life	Contemplation	Predominant practice of the Gifts	*Amour fou* for God	Mystical inspiration	The Perfection of charity (considered as already attained here below)
of *amour fou*	the threshold having been crossed	contemplative life (mystical)	more often typical and open	*Wisdom* and *Understanding* and *Knowledge*	habitually pre-dominant	in a habitual state	in all respects
(including friendship)		active life (mystical)	more often atypical and hidden	the other Gifts			
of *friendship* (in which *amour fou* lies buried)	the threshold not having been crossed	active life without habitual mystical inspiration		fleeting touches of inspiration			in respect to its intensity

Pursuit of the *Perfection of Charity*

as to the power to alienate the soul from itself — called *de iure* to cross the threshold

as to the intensity alone — this in fact remains the regime of many souls

CHAPTER X
ON MORAL PHILOSOPHY (III)

THE SPIRITUAL CONDITIONS FOR PROGRESS AND PEACE[1]

1. ON THE PROGRAM THE TITLE of my contribution to this session is: *The Spiritual Conditions for Progress and Peace*. I would like to change this title slightly and say that I will offer a few reflections on *The Role of the Spiritual with regard to Progress and Peace*.

Let me also make this preliminary remark. Peace and progress are things *of this world* or of *the temporal order*. For them the spiritual can furnish inspiration, light, and encouragement which men need in a very particular way, always more or less subject as they are to the temptation of despair—it can offer warnings as well, perhaps serious warnings which men need just as sorely; and in this way it can *help* them resolve the problems of this world and of the temporal order. The spiritual cannot *take upon itself the responsibility* of resolving these problems, and it can make no claim to do so.

If we are looking for a perfect model of the way in which the spiritual, deeply moved by disinterested love, can intervene to offer to the men charged with responsibility for the things of this world the help and ardent cooperation it is capable of giving without going outside its proper domain in doing so, even if by only a hair's breadth, we might look to the discourse that Pope Paul VI delivered before the United Nations Organization in New York.

2. It is in the perspective of *history* that the role of the spiritual with regard to the progress of humanity finds all its dimensions and reveals to us its capital importance. Of course, all this needs time, in some cases many long years. This is precisely why the action of the spiritual on men and on history is more vast and powerful by far than even the most violent and stormy temporal action, which exerts all its force at a moment in time and whose effects are then just as quickly borne away in the flux and fluctuations of time—and in addition, all of this, especially if it is of considerable scope, is radically dependent on what took place over time in the spiritual order. Marxism and the Communist

---

1   *Editor's footnote*: A speech delivered at the meeting of UNESCO on April 21, 1966. Cf. *Rencontre des cultures à l'UNESCO, sous le signe du concile oecuménique Vatican II* (Paris, Mame, 1966). Translations of this text appeared in German, English, Croat, and Italian.

revolution would never have taken place without Hegel, and there would never have been a Hegel without a Descartes and a Luther, and if we go all the way back, without the spiritual *élan* imprinted one day on the history of mankind, whatever deviations and falls from its potential it may have undergone *en route* since that day, by the preaching of a few Galilean fishermen.

The role of the spiritual as I see it here is essentially and above all a role of *inspiration*, in the broadest sense of the term. Technical discoveries have played an enormous role in the development of humanity. Spiritual discoveries have played an even greater role. It is thanks to this dynamic impulse, thanks to the *inspiration* born of these spiritual discoveries, that the history of man and of civilization has traversed its most characteristic stages.

We will never know the names of those men who stole fire and brought about the advance of humanity from the purely magic regime of primitive thought to the regime of the great metaphysico-religious myths. But we do have some idea of what Lao-tse and Confucius meant for China, the *Upanishads* and Buddha for India, Moses and the prophets for Israel, Socrates for Greece, and Mohammed for the Islamic world. We know too what Christianity meant for medieval civilization and its multiform continuations and finally for this modern civilization of ours which is about to become universal and whose technocratic regime, in order to become viable, requires the inspiration of the Gospels, either manifest or diffuse. There is nothing more striking than the astounding and ever-increasing acceleration of history set in motion by the spiritual revolution foretold by the recitation of the humble *Magnificat* of a tiny virgin of Israel.

3. I said that the role of the spiritual with regard to temporal history and its progress is above all a role of *inspiration*. It is essentially a role of *education* as well, of *cultural renewal* and, if I may put it this way, of mobilization of the intelligence and of the powers of knowledge. As a matter of fact, the inspiration and the spiritual impulse in act in the higher regions of the soul necessarily entail and require a *vast work of reason* renewing its perspectives and grasping in greater depths all the articulations of the real. It is on this condition alone that they are able to recast our ordinary system of thought and our behavior. No mystique, no faith is sufficient, however necessary either may be; it is indispensable that they be completed by a theology and a philosophy because man is man and because no inspiration truly inspires man if it does not come down to the point where the intellect and the senses wrestle with *what is*, and with the multiplicity of questions posed by existence.

4. Inspiration, education of the human being, cultural renewal—these, it seems to me, are the three aspects, the three major considerations according to which it is important for us to recognize the historic work accomplished by the second Vatican Council, and at this moment I am thinking particularly of

Schema XIII, of the Pastoral Constitution on the Church in the Modern World (*Gaudium et Spes*), and more particularly still of chapters IV and V of the second part. This historical work is of immense scope because it is the work of the Holy Spirit, and it must be pursued and continued because that Spirit which renews the face of the earth cannot be held back. The Council has provided the impulse and the inspiration; it has also provided the *teaching* which it is our duty to understand, to meditate upon, and to put into effect. And when we speak of the *application* of the teachings of the Council, we should think first and foremost of how necessary it is for us to *bring these teachings to life within our souls*, in such a way that it truly recasts our entire way of thinking; in other words we must concentrate on the deepening and the renewal of that theological and philosophical knowledge, which is a basic need of men, and to which in reality, despite appearances, so many minds aspire today, whether consciously or unconsciously, with an intensity that it would be very serious to misconstrue.

I would like to avoid the slightest ambiguity concerning the word "renewal" which I just used. What the present world needs so desperately is not pseudo-renewals in philosophy which betray reason in their effort to grasp being, nor pseudo-renewals in theology which claim to change those truths which came forth from the mouth of God. The authentic renewals we need so sorely—I am referring especially to Christians—are renewals in the ways we approach problems, in our methodology, in our concern for discovery and progress, in our way of posing questions and treating problems, more concerned with experience, and more intuitive, more attentive to the history of thought and to the development of the sciences, as well as to the different contemporary philosophies, and sophistries too, not in order to let ourselves as cowards be borne along in their wake but rather to understand and reinterpret everything in the light of a wisdom that is passionately faithful to reality and capable of growing endlessly because it lasts for all time. What wisdom do I have in mind? Of course, the wisdom of my old master in realism Saint Thomas Aquinas; and this wisdom is always young, for, as long as its disciples do not fall asleep, it is renewed from age to age in that mysterious fountain of youth which is truth.

5. I alluded a few moments ago to chapters IV and V of the second part of the *Pastoral Constitution on the Church in the Modern World* (*Gaudium et Spes*). I will limit myself here, for lack time, to calling to your attention two points upon which, from my point of view, it seems to me especially important to concentrate our attention.

In chapter IV, this constitution tells us that "in order that all citizens may be prepared to play their individual roles in the life of the political community, *great care must be given to civic and political education.*"[2] If we reflect on the

---

2   The Pastoral Constitution *Gaudium et Spes*, second part, ch. IV, no. 75, § 6.

accepted way of thinking since the time of the Renaissance, politics was considered as no more than a simple matter of intelligent cynicism, something essentially amoral, delivered up to the laws of deception and violence, whereas the Council teaches us that respect for the dignity of persons and their rights, a just notion of the common good, and the common good of the entire human family, consideration and recognition of the radical equality between individual human persons and between peoples, the elimination of racial hatred and discrimination, especially of anti-Semitism, as well as the instinctive feelings of hostility between nations,[3] all of these constitute the supreme rules of political life, especially for international politics. We can see to what an *immense task of education* we are called by the demands of such a revolution in our way of thinking. In this case it is a matter of bringing minds to recognize, in the long course of time, the truth of a political philosophy and a political ethic founded on reason enlightened by faith.

The fifth chapter (and this is my second point) treats of the safeguards of peace and of the construction of a community of nations. What I would like to emphasize particularly among all the teachings offered to us is the necessity, as is stated in § 4, for *a competent international authority with sufficient forces at its disposal*,[4] if we are to put an end to the nightmare of war. "It is clear," we also read in this chapter, "that we must make every effort within our power to prepare that moment when, with the general assent of nations, all war can be outlawed absolutely. Certainly this requires the establishment of some universal public authority, acknowledged by all, and endowed with effective power . . ."[5]

Here we are faced with a major problem which has long tormented this old philosopher: the problem—I will not say of a *World Government*, for this term tends to be too equivocal—I prefer to say a supranational political authority consisting, not of a world-wide empire or a world super-State, but of a real *political organization of the world*, based on the free consent and the free cooperation of nations and peoples. If you permit me to propose on this matter a few vintage thoughts that have been fermenting in my mind, I will point out first of all that in the present state of the world such an idea appears utopian. This is quite evident so that the problem for our time is not to bring into actual existence a world-wide political society, it is rather to work at the *distant preparations* for this society, by putting into motion the long effort of reason and good will thanks to which this utopia will end up becoming a realizable ideal. The hope of men in a temporal ideal, a dynamic ideal of peace on earth, must be preserved at any cost, even though it may seem utopian at the outset. And it is only too clear that today the absence of such an ideal has created a tragic void in the hearts of peoples and of rulers.

---

3   *Ibid.*, ch IV, no. 73, §§ 2 and 5; no. 74, § 4; no. 75, § 4; ch. V, no. 82, §§ 2 and 3.

4   *Ibid.*, ch. V, no. 79, § 4.

5   *Ibid.*, no. 82, § 1.

6. With regard to those distant preparations to which I just alluded, let me note in passing that two primordial considerations should be pointed out. The first—and this is a point I insisted on in a book published about twelve years ago[6]—is the decisive renunciation of the idea or of the idol of the sovereignty of the State, of the very idea of that mortal God, as Hobbes used to say, which sprang from the brain of Jean Bodin in the sixteenth century, and which is called the Sovereign State.

7. The second primordial condition is the awakening among all thinking men, governing and governed, of a very real concern, ever present and active in the depths of the heart, for the common good of humanity and for the good itself, the intrinsic good of each national community, and of the the very nations with which, on the level of political and economic interests, a given national community finds itself in competition.

Is this not what Schema XIII elucidated in several passages of chapter V, especially when it insists on the necessity of putting an end to "feelings of hostility, of contempt and of distrust,"[7] and when it tells us that "the firm determination to respect other men and *other peoples*, as well as their dignity, and *the assiduous practice of brotherhood, are absolutely indispensable* for the establishment of peace"?[8] And so peace is not the work of justice alone, "it is also," the same paragraph continues, "*the fruit of love which goes far beyond what justice can provide.*"

Love, this is the great evangelical word pronounced by the Church today, and it was long ago by Jesus as he announced the good news. And it is in relation to the temporal order itself and to what the peoples of the world are able to bring to reality among themselves that the Church pronounces this word. Nothing will be accomplished, even with the most ardent work of social renovation, even with the most generous efforts of apostolic action, absolutely nothing will be accomplished without charity, without that *agape* which certainly carries far more weight than the techniques of group psychology and other hobbies of the day, and of which St. Paul wrote: "If I speak with the tongues of men and of angels, and have not love, I am like a noisy gong or a clanging cymbal."[9]

Certainly, every one of us needs a change of heart,[10] the Council declared in the chapter I am speaking of. A great change of heart, by virtue of which primacy, even in such matters as politics and relations between peoples, where up till now cynicism generally held sway, true primacy will be accorded to an

6   *L'Homme et l'Etat* (OE C IX, p. 471 f.), (*Man and the State* [Chicago: University of Chicago Press, 1951]).

7   Pastoral Constitution *Gaudium et Spes*, second part, ch. V, no. 82, § 3.

8   *Ibid.*, No. 78, § 2.

9   I Cor. xiii, 1.

10   Pastoral Constitution *Gaudium et Spes*, second part, ch. V, no. 82, § 3.

authentic and efficacious friendship—and, as regards Christians in particular, that love which sees in every single man, to whatever religious or antireligious confession he belongs, exactly what he is intrinsically: a member of the Mystical Body of Christ, at least potentially—such a change of heart is the absolutely primary condition if the spirit and the teachings of the Council are to come to exist in reality.

8. And while I am at it, why should I not say everything that I have on my mind? In the last resort, what permits us to continue to hope is the fact that there is today an awakening, invisible in itself, but nevertheless recognizable in many signs, I will not say in the multitude, but in certain souls, less rare than one might think, an awakening of that life of contemplative prayer and union with God which is the hidden spring from which love flows in a thousand secret rivulets and which supports and sustains the work of men who devote themselves to the temporal action that is necessary so that the world may not perish. Did not Paul VI say in his discourse of December 7, 1966, at the close of the Council, that contemplation is the most perfect form of human activity, in respect to which, in the pyramid of human acts, the relative value of these activities, each according to its kind, can be properly measured? An invisible constellation of souls devoted to the contemplative life, I mean *in the world itself, in the very midst of the world*, this in the final analysis is our ultimate reason for keeping hope alive.

III

A LOOK AT SOME QUESTION OF A
PRIMARILY THEOLOGICAL ORDER

CHAPTER XI
FOR AN EXISTENTIAL EPISTEMOLOGY (I)

REFLECTIONS ON WOUNDED NATURE[1]

I. NATURE'S WOUNDS

1. IN A FUNDAMENTAL TEXT OF THE *SUMMA THEOLOGIAE*, St. Thomas tells us that in the state of wounded nature, man cannot, by his natural forces alone, accomplish all the good that his nature is capable of.[2] "By virtue of his nature," he can carry out many good individual tasks, like "build houses and plant vines," and alia hujusmodi (if the "house" he builds happens to be the Parthenon, or if the "vine" he plants happens to be a great philosophical system, the level to which he was able to raise himself in these goods which are connatural to him is certainly worthy of admiration), but he cannot, without failure, accomplish the *entire good* that is connatural to him, "*non tamen potest [agere] totum bonum sibi connaturale. . . . Sicut homo infirmus potest per seipsum aliquem motum habere, non tamen perfecte potest movere motu hominis sani, nisi sanetur auxilio medicinae.*"[3] If here and there, in what he does, a man arrives at the peak of his natural possibilities, it is because grace which raises him to the supernatural has also "cured" him in the order of his nature. So what is the situation in the case of that eminently human natural activity which we call philosophical activity? St. Thomas did not explain himself on this particular point. And it is precisely this particular point that I would like to address. In the state of nature where we find ourselves, the philosophy which reason is capable of *on its own* is incapable, even among the greatest of philosophers, of attaining *full* natural wisdom, or cannot avoid suffering some deficiency which hobbles it in its eager pursuit of the true.

---

1   *Editor's footnote*: A conference given at Kolbsheim, July 21, 1967. Cf. *Revue Thomiste*, 1968, no. 1, pp. 5–40.

2   St. Thomas *Sum. theol.*, Ia-IIae, q. 109, a. 2:"*In statu naturae corruptae etiam deficit homo ab hoc quod secundum suam naturam potest, ut non possit totum hujusmodi bonum implere per sua naturalia. Quia tamen natura humana per peccatum non est totaliter corrupta, ut scilicet toto bono naturae privetur, potest quidem etiam in statu naturae corruptae, per virtutem suae naturae aliquod bonum particulare agere, sicut aedificare domos, plantere vineas et alia hujusmodi; non tamen totum bonum sibi connaturale, ita quod in nullo deficiat.*"

3   *Ibid.*

Why is there this kind of impotence or wound in reason or, more exactly, why is reason hobbled this way in its highest speculative function, philosophical wisdom and metaphysical knowledge? This is a difficult question, on which, apropos of the famous[4] four wounds—*infirmitas, ignorantia, malitia, et concupiscentia*—inflicted on nature by sin, St. Thomas cast some very precious light as general principles guiding research,[5] but which, as far as I know, he has not discussed or treated explicitly. So we are obligated to make the effort ourselves and to risk a headache from applying to the matter at hand the principles of explication suggested by him.

2. When he treats of the wounds of nature, St. Thomas' perspective is a moral one, and it is from the point of view that they incline toward a moral fault, toward sin, that he looks on these particular wounds.

So he tells us that because the will is the principle of moral acts,[6] the inclination to sin is related primarily, *per prius*, to the will,[7] in such a way that the wound of original sin affects the will primarily, *per prius*,[8] before passing from it to those powers subject to sin because they are "moved to their actions by the will," or after being diverted from those actions, are "suppressed" by the will.[9] All this is proper, and uniquely proper, to the moral perspective, which, as I just said, is St. Thomas' point of view when he speaks of the wounds of nature.

But our present point of view is not the moral perspective or the inclination toward sin. It is a speculative perspective by which we will examine the wound inflicted on the intelligence.

Likewise we must not forget that when St. Thomas, from the moral perspective, tells us that *"per peccatum ratio hebetatur,"* because of sin reason is afflicted with a kind of dullness, he takes care to add *"praecipue in agendis,"*[10] "especially

---

4   I use the word *famous* because, as far as vocabulary is concerned, they are a more or less felicitous cliché in a long theological tradition whose origin after all seems quite uncertain (scholars have not yet found the text of Bede which supposedly is its basis).

5   Cf. Ia-IIae, q. 85, a. 1, 2 and 3, and the excellent *Cours de théologie morale* de M.-M. Labourdette, O.P.

6   St. Thomas, Ia-IIae, q. 74, a. 1: *"Cum autem proprium sit actuum moralium quod sint voluntarii . . . sequitur quod voluntas, quae est principium actuum voluntariorum, sive bonorum sive malorum, quae sunt peccata, sit principium peccatorum."*

7   *Ibid.,* q. 83, a. 3: *"Oportet ergo quod illam per prius respiciat quae primam inclinationem habet ad peccandum. Haec autem est voluntas. . . . Unde peccatum originale per prius respicit voluntatem."*

8   *Ibid.*

9   *Ibid.,* q. 74, a. 2: *"Unde non sola voluntas potest esse subjectum peccati, sed omnes potentiae quae possunt moveri ad suos actus, vel ab eis reprimi, per voluntatem."*

10   *Ibid.,* q. 85, a. 3.

in the practical order of acts to be accomplished"; it follows then that reason is also afflicted by this dullness, at least in certain cases, in the speculative order itself by the actual sins we commit.

Nor let us forget either that St. Thomas clearly indicates[11] that original sin—that is to say that privation of original grace which affects our human nature in its entirety,[12] the specific nature transmitted to each of us and which is the cause of the disorder from which our powers suffer—first has its seat in the very essence of the soul[13] before wounding by this disorder those powers of the soul which are the seat of actual sins. Then St. Thomas, when enumerating the powers that are wounded in this way by original sin, begins with *reason*, which includes prudence, and whose wound is *ignorance*.[14] To the extent that it suffers from this wound, reason is deprived of its being ordered to the true, *destituitur suo ordine ad verum*; let us accept this (according to the moral perspective that St. Thomas has taken) with regard to prudential judgment. But from our own present perspective we must still deal with the fact that reason is likewise wounded by original sin and deprived as well of its being ordered to the true in respect to speculative judgment itself, at least when there is a question of attaining the highest and most difficult truths. And the speculative judgment is certainly an act—but it is not a *moral act* (whose principle is free will).

The wounds that reason suffers from among philosophers, in our state of nature, can certainly be due to moral faults, to actual sins which dull their reason. I have in mind a philosopher who, preferring the world of dreams to reality, would give himself over body and soul to drugs out of love for pleasures of the senses—or perhaps to another drug, the drug of fashionable ideas or currents of thought sanctioned by public opinion because the hell he

---

11   Cf. *Ibid.*, q. 83, a. 2

12   *Ibid.*, q. 85, a. 3: "*Haec autem originalis justitia subtracta est per peccatum primi parentis.* . . . *Et ideo omnes vires animae remanent quodamodo destitutae proprio ordine, quo naturaliter ordinantur ad virtutem: et ipsa destitutio vulneratio naturae dicitur* [. . .] *quatuor sunt vulnera inflicta* toti humanae naturae *ex peccato primi parentis.*"

13   *Ibid.*, q. 83d, a. 2: "*Illud animae est principaliter subjectum alicujus peccati, ad quod primo pertinet causa motiva illius peccati.* [. . .] *Unde anima* secundum essentiam est primum subjectum *originalis peccati.*"

14   Then come: the will, which includes justice and whose wound is malice; the irascible appetite, which includes fortitude and whose wound is infirmity; the concupiscible, which includes temperance and whose wound is concupiscence. Cf. *Ibid.*, q. 85, a. 3: "*Sunt autem quatuor potentiae animae quae possunt esse subjecta virtutum . . . : scilicet* ratio, in qua est prudentia; *voluntas, in qua est justitia; irascibilis, in qua est fortitudo; concupisicibilis, in qua est temperantia.* In quantum ergo ratio destituitur suo ordine ad verum, est vulnus ignorantiae; *inquantum vero irascibilis destituitur suo ordine ad arduum, est vulnus infirmitatis; in quantum vero concupiscentia destituitur suo ordine ad delectabile moderatum ratione, est vulnus concupiscentiae.*"

has chosen to fear above all others is to be *mal vu*, considered of no consequence. But these after all are not real philosophers.

In the case of real philosophers, and this happens quite often, the wounds of reason may be due once again to the will, if you like, in those obscure powers to which it gives refuge, or to the unconscious pressures of affectivity, which determine their options. In such a case there may be some form of free consent, only God knows, at the very outset, but here we are concerned with human weakness much more than with a moral fault. And then these are not *great* philosophers.

And among these latter philosophers too, and this is what interests us, we find present those wounds from which reason suffers in our fallen nature. In this case there is question neither of moral fault nor of dominant inclinations of the will or of affectivity. It is not in this direction that the truly basic cause of these wounds must be sought.

Where then must we seek out the fundamental reason why our intelligence and our reason are more or less wounded by original sin in the *speculative order*, and wounded to the maximum in their power to attain *full* natural wisdom?

To find the answer to this question, all we have to do, it seems to me, is to transpose what St. Thomas explains to us from the line or the perspective of the *good* to the line or perspective of the *true*. What does he tell us in fact from his own perspective (the moral perspective)?

3. When he asks himself whether or not sin diminishes the *bonum naturae*, the good of nature, he distinguishes three entirely different meanings of the expression *good of nature*.[15] I am going to enumerate them in a different order than he uses. Let me say then that in the first place there is *the gift of original justice*, given in the first man to all of human nature; in the second place there are *the very principles of nature*, which constitute that nature; and in the third place there is *the natural inclination to virtue* (when we move over to our particular perspective, which is no longer a moral, but rather speculative one, we will no longer speak of a natural inclination to the good or to virtue but of a natural inclination to the *true*).

Through original justice human nature functioned in an entirely correct manner; this means two things: *primo*, reason *continebat* (held in check or regulated) perfectly the lower powers of the soul; *secundo*, reason itself, "*a Deo perficiebatur ei subjecta*," was subject to God, held in His hands and raised in perfection by Him:[16] and this *secundum supernaturale donum gratiae*, in virtue

---

15 *Ibid.*, q. 85, a. 1: "*Respondeo dicendum quod bonum naturae humanae potest tripliciter dici. Primo, ipsa principia naturae, ex quibus natura constituitur, et proprietates ex his causatae, sicut potentiae animae et alia hujusmodi. Secundo, quia homo a natura habet inclinationem ad virtuten . . . ipsa inclinatio ad virtutem est quoddam bonum naturae. Tertio modo potest dici bonum naturae donum originalis justitiae, quod fuit primo homine collatum toti humanae naturae.*"

16 *Ibid.*, q. 85, a. 3: "*. . per justitiam originalem perfecte ratio continebat inferiores animae*

of the supernatural gift of grace[17] (not the grace of Christ the Redeemer, but the original or Adamic grace, along with the three theological virtues.[18] Let us understand very clearly this *a Deo perficiebatur*: reason is "completed" or "consummated in perfection" by grace. This does not mean that through grace reason is completed or consummated in perfection *in its nature* itself; it means rather that grace creates in the supra-conscious of the spirit a *heaven of the soul*, a supernatural heaven where grace itself resides—it is this heaven of the soul which brings into consciousness the theological virtues (at least when they develop normally) and which by its radiance illuminates and fortifies reason *in its natural exercise*.

Since it is a gift *to human nature as such*, to the nature of all men to come, this supernatural gift of Adamic grace was indeed a part, and a capital part, of the *"good of nature"* from the very instant of its creation; it was the first good of nature (original justice).

This *first good* of nature (*"donum originalis justitiae"*) was completely taken away by the first sin (*"totaliter ablatum"*).

The *second good* of nature (*"ipsa principia naturae"*) was neither *taken away* nor *diminished* by the first sin (*"nec tollitur nec diminuitur per peccatum"*).[19] And again: *"peccatum non diminuit ipsam naturam."*[20] Human nature itself and its powers taken *in their essential constitution* are not diminished or intrinsically weakened by the loss of grace, which is a supernatural gift; they were not diminished or weakened by the loss of original justice; sin does not diminish nature.

And so the loss of original justice does not diminish either that natural inclination to the good inasmuch as nature is the root of that inclination, or inasmuch as it is contained in man's nature *at the radical state*. Let us be careful to understand this exactly. The non-diminution of this inclination to the good *in regard to its radical state* in nature itself does not signify anything particularly brilliant. In the ad 3 of q. 85, a. 2, St. Thomas tells us that the natural inclination to virtue remains even among the damned (otherwise they would have no remorse of conscience). And similarly, even in a blind man there remains the natural aptitude to see *"in ipsa radice naturae,"* inasmuch as he is, by his specific

---

   vires, et ipsa ratio a Deo perficiebatur ei subjecta."

17   Ia, q. 95, a. 1: *"Manifestum est autem quod illa subjectio corporis ad animam, et inferiorum virium ad rationem, not erat naturalis: alioquin post peccatum mansisset. . . . Unde manifestum est quod illa prima subjectio, qua ratio Deo subdebatur, non erat solum secundum naturam, sed secundum supernaturale donum gratiae."*

18   Cf. *Ibid.*, q. 95, a. 3.

19   Ia-IIae, q. 85, a. 1: *"Primum igitur bonum naturae nec tollitur nec diminuitur per peccatum. Tertium vero bonum naturae totaliter est ablatum per peccatum primi parentis. Sed medium bonum naturae, scilicet ipsa naturalis inclinatio ad virtutem, diminuitur per peccatum."*

20   *Ibid.*, a. 2.

nature, *"animal naturaliter habens visum,"* an animal having the natural capacity to see (all of this, of course, is not of much consolation to the blind man—but it does explain that he can be cured by a miracle).[21]

And all this is easily understood. What is diminished or weakened by the first sin in the *human nature transmitted to all men* is the *third good of nature, the natural ordering* toward virtue, not so much as regards its root in the essence of the soul, but rather as regards the state of its development and actualization in the powers of the soul, which make up precisely the center where these virtues should be formed and where the inclination toward them is found to be weakened. So if this inclination is diminished or weakened, it is not because of some weakness or diminution of internal origin[22] (which would then come from the very nature itself, whereas nature remained intact). It is because of an obstacle or hindrance, *"per oppositionem impedimenti,"*[23] according as, for example, having been moved by its proper object "the sensitive appetite inclines the reason and the will," in other words "according as the object acts on the power and according as one power acts on another, *"et deordinat ipsam,"* and causes it to deviate from its order or deprives it of its proper order.[24]

And so what has to be said is that the first good of nature (not in numerical order)—*original justice,* in virtue of which reason kept a hand on and regulated the lower powers of the soul and was in turn strengthened by the God's grace—having been totally lost (*"totaliter ablatum"*) by the sin of our first father, "all the powers of the soul remain in a certain way deprived of their order-ing—in other words, of their natural ordering toward virtue (the third good of nature)—and it is this deprivation that is called the wound of nature"[25]—the four wounds I just spoke of, which come from the *impedimentum,* from the constraint or the hindrance that one power suffers from another that acts upon it.

Here we find ourselves face to face with a *disordering,* a kind of dislocation or anarchy among the powers of the soul, and a resulting *inhibition* exercised by one power with regard to another, this disordering being the first effect of the loss of original justice; and this inhibition the second effect.

---

21   *Ibid.,* a. 1, ad 4: *"Dicendum quod etiam in damnatis manet naturalis inclinatio ad virtutem: alioquin non esset in eis remorsus conscientiae.... Sicut etiam in caeco remanet aptitudo ad videndum in ipsa radice naturae, in quantum est animal naturaliter habens visum; sed non reducitur in actum, quia deest causa quae reducere possit formando organum quod requiritur ad videndum."*

22   Such a weakness or diminution might little by little have an intrinsic effect, but its origin is the hindrance due to the disordering of the powers.

23   Ia-IIae, q. 85, a. 2, ad 1.

24   *Ibid.,* a. 1, ad 4: *"Et ex hoc causatur inordinatio, non quidem ita quod accidens agat in proprium subjectum, sed secundum quod objectum agit in potentiam, et una potentia agit in aliam et deordinat ipsam."*

25   *Ibid.,* q. 85, a. 3. This text was cited above, p. 209, n. 12.

II. THE WOUNDS OF THE INTELLIGENCE

4. We now have all the situations in which we have to make a transposition from the practical perspective or the perspective of the good, which was St. Thomas' point of view, to the speculative perspective or the perspective of the true, in order to find a response to the question before us. Through this transposition, we can now treat of those wounds inflicted by original sin on reason in its very speculative life and in its struggle toward natural wisdom, which is the supreme good of that life and which it was created to attain. However, in actual fact, as a consequence of the first sin, reason cannot attain that natural wisdom fully and without some defect, omission, or "irremediable" error at the very heart of any system elaborated by a philosopher, however great a philosopher he may be.

Since there is question of a disordering or loss of control in consequence of which speculative reason is more or less inhibited by the other powers of the soul in its drive toward the true, it becomes clear that wounds or *impedimenta* of all kinds can occur, from those which are the result of the most accidental of happenstances (you cannot philosophize when you are seasick) to those which result from the most fundamental of causes which no one can escape (and these are the ones we are looking for).

I said a moment ago that a philosopher who gives himself up body and soul either to drugs or to that sovereign fear of being *mal vu* is not a real philosopher. Still, in this completely accidental zone of morally disturbed behavior there is a kind of hindrance which, because the behavior in question is particularly frequent in our species, runs the risk of wounding the reason even of a real philosopher. I have in mind the miseries of passion and sex which afflict the human being—for example, a life which is constantly troubled by the great tragedies of love or a life which, out of defiance or anguish, has been voluntarily thrown to the anarchy of the flesh. In such a situation reason would find itself in a state of hebetude, according to the word St. Thomas chose. A certain chastity of body and soul is required of a philosopher who wishes to retain the purity of his vision.

At the same time I spoke of the pressures exerted on the intelligence by the affectivity and the obscure powers which haunt the will and which prevent many real philosophers from becoming great philosophers. I would like to add that there is a particularly typical case, one in which an *ego*, made all the more dominant the more it is entangled in its unconscious complexes, seeks to compensate for its frustrations by and in the system of concepts that it elaborates.

Finally I pointed out that, in the state of nature where we find ourselves, we must turn to the *great philosophers* in our search for what is truly fundamental and universal with regard to the wounds of speculative reason.

Here we have our task before us. I have done what I could, which is not very much, to move this research forward a bit. The views I am going to lay before you are no more than working hypotheses, but I must confess that I am very much attached to them because if we succeed in creating the tiniest amount of new light in a domain which borders on the upper ranges of metaphysics, this, in itself, would be more important than establishing a television relay station on the moon.

We are no longer in the perspective of the moral good but in the perspective of the true; we are no longer concerned with the inclination of nature toward virtue, nor with the wounds of nature in this respect, but rather with the desire or the love of the intelligence for the truth and with the wounds of philosophic thought in this particular respect.

It seems to me that we have to take two things into consideration here: in the first place, what I would call the cardinal qualities of the intellect; in the second place, the hindrances or impediments which, in the state of fallen nature, the intellect has to put up with because of something that, due to another power, most intimately concerns its functioning and the activity proper to it.

5. In the first place then, I would like to inquire what qualities in the intelligence correspond *analogically* to the four cardinal virtues in the powers of the soul. It seems to me that the quality of the human intellect which I will call *rational solidity* (here the philosopher is a great interconnector of concepts) corresponds to the virtue of *prudence* (which is found in reason). The quality of the intellect which I shall call *exactness of expression* (here the philosopher *declares* only what he *sees*) corresponds to the virtue of *justice* (which is in the will). The quality of the intellect which I will call *boldness of vision* (here the philosopher is a great intuitive and a great discoverer) corresponds to the virtue of *fortitude* (which is in the irascible appetite). Finally the quality of the intellect which I will call *limpidity of thought* (here the philosopher is free of the unconscious pressures and base desires of subjectivity) corresponds to the virtue of *temperance* (which is in the concupiscible appetite).

Here it must be noted that in order to have a *great philosopher* all four of these cardinal qualities are necessary, but what above all else makes him great— naturally supposing qualities number 2 (exactness of expression) and number 4 (limpidity of thought)—is the presence of qualities number 1 (rational solidity) and number 3 (boldness of vision).

And we must keep in mind too that under the influence of that disordering or loss of control produced in each of us by the first sin, it happens inevitably that these qualities of the intellect do not exist together in perfect equilibrium: one is there in excess with respect to another and vice versa. Why is this so? Because psychological temperaments (Be careful here! By "psychological temperament" I do not at all mean the unconscious pressures of subjectivity; I mean the *innate constitution of each individual*) not only vary considerably among the different individuals of the species, which is quite normal, but because, with the loss of original justice, for each of us, they maintain reason itself in a kind of dependency with regard to temperament and because even among the greatest of philosophers their intelligence is subject to the repercussions of their psychological temperament.

But we must look at this matter even closer, and this brings me to the second consideration I announced above: the hindrances and impediments which, due to fallen nature, the intelligence has to put up with because of something that most intimately concerns the activity proper to it. Here we come upon the relation between the intelligence and the imagination, insofar as the latter plays an essential role in the first operation of the mind, which is simple apprehension, and the abstraction of the form or idea, drawn from the phantasms with the light of the agent intellect. For us there is no intellection without "conversion toward images."

What I am trying to say here has nothing to do with the "imagining imagination" which, enlivened by the light of the agent intellect in the supra-conscious of the mind (let me refer on this point to the valuable elucidations of Olivier Lacombe) has created the great myths of humanity, frequently loaded down, no doubt, with errors, but more frequently filled with great truths (under forms that are rationally unverifiable).

What I have to say has nothing to do either with the imagination as "fancy" against which Malebranche inveighed and which he called the *"folle du logis"* (the family idiot of the human mind), and as a matter of fact, the wanderings of "fancy" play a completely accidental role in regard to philosophy.

What I will try to say concerns something far more difficult to express precisely and which touches on the very functioning of our intelligence, and which is going to burden my poor vocabulary with the anxious search for exact words.

Let us recall that the disordering or loss of control due to the first sin gave to the "lower powers of the soul," as St. Thomas said, a certain independence or autonomy freeing them from control of that reason which was proper to the state of original justice, and at the same time had a certain impact on reason itself. Well, from our speculative perspective, the same seems to be the case with that internal sense which we call the imagination in regard to the intellect which makes use of it.

The intellect, by an abstractive operation, draws its ideas from the images which it needs essentially. It needs them as simple matter to be illuminated by the agent intellect in order to bring forth the intelligibles which are potentially contained within that matter. This absolutely essential process *in itself* undergoes no alteration or diminution whatever. But now it is in a certain fashion *"parasitized"* from without. How so? Because these phantasms, while remaining the matter of the abstractive operation, at the same time retain, for their own advantage, in an anarchical way, an independent vital energy in the process in question, by reason of which the imagination attaches them to the *intentio intellecta*, to the idea which has been abstracted from them, like a lining or a doubling which reinforces it and hardens it from below, a kind of screen on which the intelligible as perceived by the intelligence takes shape. The intelligence also pauses on the luminosity of this intelligible, all the while fixing its gaze on its proper object (*intelligible*), and in so doing still remains turned toward the phantasm, and hence unconsciously subject to the vital pressure of the imagination.

Such remarks refer to a kind of transcendental psychology which has not been the subject of much study, but they are confirmed, I believe, by the experience of each individual, if he reflects attentively enough on the clumsiness from which intellection suffers in us; and they are especially confirmed by the analysis of how the mind operates, something which is discernable in the great philosophical doctrines.

And if these remarks are true, we must say that in the state of nature wounded by the first sin, the phantasms are no longer only a matter which, in its abstractive operation, the agent intellect illuminates in order to draw forth from it the intelligibles which it contains in potency. Rather by means of the idea or concept, once it has been formed—and which, having been parasitically infested by the phantasms, loses a little (sometimes a lot) of its intelligible transparence—these phantasms exert a certain impact on the intelligence (which has been wounded more or less in this way in its intuitivity). This impact is more or less forceful according to the situation, sometimes very forceful, and capable of producing aberrations (I have in mind idealism or phenomenology). Sometimes this impact is rather weak or even minimal but still real enough to be an obstacle to a supreme fulfillment of the work of the natural wisdom of the intellect, real enough to be responsible, I do not say for an error, but for an irreparable omission (here I have in mind the *Philosophus par excellence*, Aristotle).

How can I describe this impact? This is where I cannot find the right words. All I can come up with to propose to you is the expression: *impact solidifying the idea through the image, or else: impact notionalizing the exercise of the intelligence.*

Here is the point I wanted to get to. In the state of fallen nature the philosophical intelligence, when it sets itself with all its conceptual equipment to the work that is properly and uniquely its domain alone—I mean, on the one hand, without any help coming from above to cure this wound and, on the other hand, without repudiating itself and having recourse to the irrational, becoming irritated with this wound and by that very fact irritating the very wound itself—has a natural inclination to notionalism, to a notionalism that admits of the most varied degrees but by its very nature acts as an obstacle to the intellectual intuition of being. (This intuition is not the peak of philosophical wisdom, but it is the *indispensable condition* for attaining it; and this intuition is precisely what we lack to a greater or lesser degree because of the wound in our nature.)

Adam—that "primitive" of humanity's infancy who was endowed with original justice by supernatural grace—had this intuition of being as a gift of nature. There is nothing more natural in itself than this intuition—the intelligence is made for it. Yet it was more or less overlooked, in fact completely overlooked, by the philosophers, by even the greatest, in the course of their long history. Aristotle himself had it only implicitly or virtually,[26] he could neither become cognizant of it nor use it to give life to his doctrine. There had to be a theologian privileged with genius and with grace to bring this intuition of being into the light of day by transfiguring Aristotle and turning his gaze toward God no longer as the Prime Mover, but as *Ipsum Esse subsistens*, Being Itself subsisting by Itself (and hence creator of all that is not It). Thanks to this theologian poor urchins like us have been initiated into this intuition. There is nothing here that has anything to do with supernatural grace, as I pointed out; it is the fundamental, primordial natural light of the philosophical intelligence, when this intelligence in a flash breaks through the barriers of notionalism. But it was in a climate of grace and contemplation that the metaphysics of St. Thomas burst through these barriers and left to Christian philosophy—at least to that philosophy which is faithful to his spirit—the heritage of a great light, supremely natural in itself, and actually within reach of anyone who has the help of a good teacher.[27] It is probable however that a certain contemplative climate will always be necessary to maintain it intact. And it is very possible, I might add (Louis Gardet and Olivier Lacombe could enlighten us on this matter), that in the great non-Christian religions there may be some wise men (who are both philosophers and theologians at the same time) who, with the help of actual grace to heal their reason of the wound from which it suffers in the exercise of its most noble function, have attained on their own, without any help from the Angelic Doctor, in a formal way, as he himself did, the intuition of being.

6. A few clarifications are still needed, which, I hope, will help us make a little headway.

---

26   Hence really, but in a way that was capable solely of orienting his philosophical thought, incapable however of illuminating it and of leading it to take the decisive step. *Virtually* (really-virtually) as distinguished from *formally* (really-formally). *Virtually* means much more than "potentially."

    It also means "implicitly," but with the added idea of tendency. A grain of wheat is virtually a whole stalk of wheat. A foreigner who has all his loves and goods in France is virtually a Frenchman; he is formally so only when he has changed his papers. A man who knows that the Servant of Yahweh will save Israel believes virtually in the Incarnation of the Word, but this has not been revealed to him, nor does it illuminate his thought.

27   This light is received like a gift. And nature is not stingy with this gift when the intellect has not already been too captivated by abstract studies and when it is prepared by good beginning instruction.

In speaking a moment ago of the four cardinal qualities of the intelligence, I pointed out that, given the diversity of individual psychological temperaments and the condition of dependence in which, as a consequence of our state of nature, the intelligence is found in relation to the temperaments, these qualities do not exist in a state of perfect equilibrium in any single philosopher: if one quality shines in all its brilliance, it tends to obscure some other quality. *Rational solidity* (by virtue of which the philosopher becomes a great organizer of concepts, a great watchmaker of reason) cannot be manifest in all its fullness (Thomas Aquinas aside) except at the expense of *boldness of vision* (in virtue of which the philosopher is a great intuitive and a great discoverer). And vice versa.

I would like to pause here a moment to glance at a few typical cases. Take Descartes, for example, the father of modern philosophy in its historic age of conquest and glory (and which was ideosophic even at that time). In Descartes *rational solidity* was developed to a very high degree; his philosophy is the work of an admirable conceptual watchmaker. But he is the one who set modern philosophy on the path of idealism. This powerful Cartesian rationalism is linked to the theory of ideas, considered not as signs through which the mind seizes upon what there is in things but as the very objects of the knowing mind. This is what I call the theory of *idea-pictures*. I know nothing except my ideas, and it is because of the divine veracity that there are, behind these screens in front of which my intellect stops, things which resemble my ideas. With these idea-pictures, the impact of the imagination on the intellect took on a decisive force—an impact by means of the sensible phantasm, the parasitical doubling of the idea, and through which pass the vitality and the intentionality proper to the imagination. And at the same time there is a complete absence or deprivation of the intuition of being.

Or take Hegel, the father of modern philosophy (which has now turned into pure ideosophy) in his historical age of miserable consciousness and of disintegration. Hegel is also a great organizer of concepts and a great watchmaker of reason, he enjoys *rational solidity* to a formidable degree. But now there are no longer any idea-pictures masking realities which resemble them and through which divine veracity guarantees our intellect an indirect grasp on extra-mental things. The idea has completely supplanted the thing. This means that the impact of the imagination on the intelligence has become absolute: for if the idea has replaced the thing, it is because the phantasm, which parasitically doubles the idea, envelops and reinforces the intelligible brilliance of the idea with all the sensible brilliance due to the vitality and intentionality of the imagination. From that moment on the idea has completely lost its transparence as a sign; all the value of objectivity facing up to and imposing itself on knowledge has passed from the thing to the idea. There is no longer need for the thing; the idea is sufficient. And it is by means of *dialectics*, the universe of the life and movement of the idea, that the vast universe of a powerfully organized rational system is built up, comes alive and embraces all, the Hegelian universe of pseudo-wisdom. And at the same time the intuition of being is put under interdict. (When Marx put Hegel back on his feet,[28] in an astounding confusion, reality itself would come to live by dialectics. Here too the intuition of being would be put under interdict.)

Now let us turn to an authentic teacher of philosophic truth, our old master Aristotle. We will linger a little longer with him (not without the interruption of a long digression, which, to tell the truth, is more important to me than everything else). I am not looking at Aristotle here as the founder of a particular school (I dislike schools). Aristotle must be called the great forefather of the *philosophia perennis*. Here we are dealing with an authentically realist or ontosophic philosophy. In him that quality of the intellect which is *rational solidity* reaches its peak; with the exception of St. Thomas, there is no greater organizer of concepts. In him there is intuitivity, boldness of vision as well, but in this last case we still find a certain level of deficiency.

This is because the impact of the imagination on the intellect, by means of the phantasm which is that parasitic doubling of the idea, is still present, however feeble it may be—I would say *almost* at that limit or border where the intelligence might be freed from it. However, this border was never crossed. The immense universe of Aristotle's rational wisdom is a universe of essences grasped by the first operation of the mind, by simple apprehension, undoubtedly centered on being or existence, which, in fact, is there and imposes its primacy, but without being *formally* grasped; on the contrary it is present to his thought only in a way that is still blind or *virtual*, without having been perceived in its full light. In short—I shall return to this point—Aristotle had the intuition of being in an entirely implicit and *virtual* mode, as if implied without his knowing it in the fundamental élan of his realism. He was not able to disengage intuition of being itself from all the rest and to make of it the vivifying principle of his explicitly formulated doctrine.

III. A DIGRESSION ON THE INTUITION OF BEING:
THE CONCEPT OF EXISTENCE

7. How can this be explained? Here we must begin a vast digression in order to give closer consideration to the intellectual intuition of being. With it we leave the world of simple apprehension and enter the world of judgment. For there is a typical characteristic that is absolutely and uniquely proper to this intuition. It is produced *in and by an affirmative judgment* of existence: "I am,"

---

28   It is curious to note that Marx, as the *practical* theologian of the Revolution that would liberate humanity, played a transfiguring role for Hegel *analogous* to the role St. Thomas, as the speculative theologian of the redemptive Incarnation, played for Aristotle.

"things are"; but this judgment *like those others* in which a subject endowed with a certain essence is linked, by the copulative *is*, to some attribute or predicate grasped *by mode of essence*, that is, by means of an idea born of the abstractive operation. On the contrary, in the unique case I am talking about, the case of the intellectual intuition of being, the idea or concept (of existence) does not precede the judgment (of existence); it comes after the judgment and stems from it. In this case we are dealing with a judicative act (the second operation of the mind) which is *of a type different from all other judgments*.

Indeed, it does not apply an attribute to a subject. It is rather the subject itself that this judgment affirms or posits in the mind, as that subject itself is posited outside the mind, in extra-mental reality; and to produce this judicative act, by really *thinking* it, is, for the intelligence, in the very heart of the spiritual intimacy of its own operation, to grasp intuitively, or *to see*, the being, the existence, the extra-mental *esse* of that subject. This is what I call the intuition of being. By means of it I can plunge into the world of existence and escape from the world of essences and their relationships.

It is *after this* that a return of the first operation of the mind to what has been *seen* in this way (but not by means of this operation) will produce *an idea* of it, a concept or a mental word which will designate it and be manageable in discourse; then we will have the idea (of judicative origin following on the intuition of being) of the *esse* grasped as such or of the existence exercised in act outside the mind (as when I say, for example, "The soul communicates to the body its own *existence* or its own *esse*")

In other words, in the (unique) case of the intuition of being, *the concept, this concept* of *esse*, formed *after* I have *seen* this *esse*, is *second* with respect to the *judgment* of existence in which and through which, by pronouncing it in the intuition, my intelligence *saw esse*; this concept is due to a *reflective return* of simple apprehension to the judicative act in question. This is what I will call our second concept of existence.

It is of supreme importance to understand here that this concept is of an *entirely different origin* in the mind than the concept, expressed by the same word *existence*, which is produced in the mind, not from a judgment, but from the abstractive operation, in the same way as all the ideas drawn from phantasms by this operation: a concept of existence which in this case is of abstractive origin, not of judicative origin, and which I will call our first concept of existence.

It is most unfortunate that the words which signify two concepts of different origin happen to be the same: *existence* in the case of the concept of abstractive origin, *existence* as well (or *esse*, the act of existing) in the case of the concept of judicative origin; with the result that the two concepts themselves *seem* to relate to the same intelligible object, which is not true at all (when we say, for example, first concept of existence: "the existence of a spy in our services is indubitable"; or when we assert in an entirely different sense, second concept of existence: "the soul communicates to the body its own *existence* or it own *esse*").

Etienne Gilson seems to have been so fascinated by the intuition of being that he wrote, if I recall correctly, that there is no such thing as a *concept* of existence. Actually there are two of them,[29] which differ *according to their origin* in the mind, as I have just said (and, as I will insist on in a moment, they differ also *according to their meaning*, the one—the first, of abstractive origin at the first degree of abstraction[30]—belonging to the register of *Dasein*, the other of *Sein*).

There is a concept of *esse*, or of existence (our second concept of existence), which arises in the mind *after* the intuition of being, by a turning back of simple apprehension, or of intelligence as formative of ideas, onto that intuition; all of this happens on a certain level, the level of metaphysical intellection (even in the case of someone who does not realize what is going on, in the case of a poet for instance). And there is another concept of existence (our first concept of existence), which is formed in the mind *before* the intuition of being has welled up within it: I mean on the level of the first degree of abstraction, which is the level on which man's thought moves ordinarily and in the first place. This other concept of existence is of abstractive origin, not judicative, and, yes, it precedes the intuition of being. But such a concept plays no role in the intuition of being, and is in no way an integral part of it.[31] It remains completely foreign to it.

So it is understandable that in a multitude of judgments of existence, the concept of existence (previously drawn from phantasms by the abstractive operation) has, as long as the mind moves on the level of the first degree of abstraction, the sole meaning of *presence to my world*, as we shall see later on.

It is just as understandable that in the conversations of everyday life even those who have had the intuition of being also use, in the "vulgar" sense I just indicated, the concept of existence (based on the abstractive operation on the first level of abstraction), as for example when they say: "A visitor *is here*."

But when the threshold of a higher form of knowledge has been crossed and entrance has been made into the realm of philosophy, then some (even great metaphysicians, if they have not *formally* experienced the intuition of being) will make use of the concept of existence as of a concept due uniquely

---

29   In fact there are three (the third being the concept of existence, of abstractive origin like the first, but this time at the third degree of abstraction). Cf. further on, p. 233.

30   I am speaking here (and in the following pages) of the "pure and simple" first degree of abstraction, or the first degree of abstraction understood without any *participation* in metaphysical intellection—such a participation occurs only in the case of a philosophy of nature truly worthy of its name, and, at this stage of my exposition, this case does not yet interest us. Cf. further on, pp. 235–236.

31   The same is the case with the third concept of existence. Cf. further on, pp. 233–234.

to the abstractive operation, even if it belongs to the third degree of abstraction. In such cases, even if it remains a useful instrument in the hands of a good metaphysician, it remains of itself an instrument without sufficient power of penetration, and their metaphysics in some way or other will continue to suffer from a certain deficiency. This will be the object of our final considerations. Whereas others, who have formally experienced the intellectual intuition of being, will make use of the concept of existence as a concept of judicative origin, not abstractive, following upon the intuition of being—in other words, as designating (and this is undoubtedly what Etienne Gilson had in mind) an intelligible—*esse* or "the act of existing"—*which was not drawn from phantasms by the abstractive operation, like all the other objects of concepts.*

8. Let us be careful here, for none of this is easy. And in trying to scrutinize a bit the intellectual intuition of being, we find ourselves up against some new questions, which can be answered only by offering new views which will help, I hope, to make more precise the nature of this intuition.[32]

I just said that existence grasped by the intuition of being is an intelligible which is not drawn from phantasms by the abstractive operation. This is the intelligible *par excellence*, which the intelligence is made to see but which it sees only in the intuition of being, which is a metaphysical intuition. In the conversations of everyday life, the intelligence does not see this. It is satisfied with the concept of existence as it is offered, as are all other concepts, by the abstractive operation, and this on the level of the first degree of abstraction. The eye sees things; it does not know that they are. It is the intelligence which knows that they are, but as long as it remains solely dependent on the abstractive operation (even on the level of the third degree of abstraction), it knows this solely in a way that is properly speaking *implicit*, and still without having *seen* being, something that is the privilege of a metaphysical intuition unique in its nature.

Here we are face to face with a great problem: If the act of existing grasped by the intuition of being is an intelligible which is not drawn from phantasms by the abstractive operation, how does this act of existing, which is material in the things that our eye sees, become proportioned to the intelligence, and spiritualized, in such a way that the intelligence might come *to see* it, and *see it within itself* (in and by the judicative act I spoke of) just as it perceives the essences in the ideas, the *intentiones intellectae*, due to the abstractive operation?

A very delicate analysis is needed here, and this analysis is what I would like to propose to you in these rather hasty notes in which, no doubt, I express myself very imperfectly. But I think I am on the right path.

I think we must distinguish three stages, beginning with the perception of

32   The intuition of being was lived *in actu exercito* by St. Thomas and the Thomists (the good Thomists, that is), but I know of no treatise or *disquisitio* (and this is perhaps due to my ignorance) in which it has been studied by them *in actu signato.*

external sense (the source of the judgment: *things are*) or of consciousness (the source of the judgment: *I am*), a perception that is indispensable to the intuition of being.

The first stage then is the perception of external sense, of sight, for example (or the perception of consciousness; in order to simplify things I will speak only of the perception of external sense). The act of external sense brings within me (in the sense of sight), by means of a sensible *species* which it received from without, the color of a rose (seen by the eye). That is to say, the color of the rose enters the mind by means of an intentional form which transfers into the sense the particular way in which the surface of the petals reflects the light acting on the organ (retina and cerebral center). But at the same time and by the same reaction it brings into the sense of sight (without the sense of sight knowing what is going on) the act of existence on the part of the rose—not by a *species*, certainly, but by the intentional action exercised on this sense when it receives the *species* of the color of the rose.

And now for the second stage: My intelligence has no need of the imagination and its phantasms in order to know *that I see* at that moment when my eyes sees. The intelligence is present in the external sense; it envelopes and penetrates with its own life the life of the external sense, whose sensations (to tell the truth, true sensation always escapes us) it develops into perceptions which then fall under the grasp of consciousness. So the intelligence seizes upon this perception of the sense (of the *intelligenciated* sense in man); it becomes conscious, not only of the color of the rose (the sole object "perceived" by the sense of sight), but it also becomes conscious of its *seeing that rose*, in other words of the cognitive act itself of the external sense. At this moment the act is transported within itself, or enveloped by it, in a state of intentional doubling. It is there along with the *object* it perceives: the *color* of the rose, intentionally received by the sense thanks to the sensible *species*, and intentionally grasped by the intelligence thanks to the idea: *the rose* (which I see). And the cognitive act of the sense is also there along with the rose's *act of existing*, made present in the sense of sight (though not grasped by this sense) by the *intentional action* it undergoes in receiving the sensible *species*, and it is made present to the intelligence (in a *totally implicit* way and without being grasped by it as of yet) as implied in *the rose* (the object of an *intentio intellecta*) which it knows that *I see*: the thing that I see, a thing that is there.

Here the intelligence is found on the level of the first degree of abstraction, where it says, in its interior word: "That rose is there." "That rose is there" is the *Dasein*, such as a Thomist can and must understand this expression (I will explain this in a moment). It seems very important to me to note that this *Dasein* (which is no more than a substitute for the *Sein*) goes with the first degree of abstraction. At this point the intelligence says: That rose *is there*, or that rose is *present* to me; it does not say: That rose *is*. This is because the concept at this moment does not yet signify anything more than presence to my world. To be there means only to be declared *present, to be given to me as present*. And this is why a philosophy of the *Dasein* remains open to idealism. It is only with the intuition of being, with the *Sein* (understood in the Thomistic sense) or the *act of existing* seen through the intuition of being (our third stage) that metaphysical realism finds an invincibly solid foundation.

But we are still at our second stage, at the first degree of abstraction, and in the register of the *Dasein*. At this degree, what about the *Sein*, or the rose's *act of existing* itself? It is not perceived by the intelligence. At one and the same time the intelligence, on the one hand, *explicitly* seizes upon the rose as seen by the eye and, on the other hand, but in a *completely implicit way*, seizes upon the rose's *act of existing*, according as this is transmitted to the sense (without the sense having any realization whatever of the fact) by the intentional action that it undergoes, and according as the intelligence itself declares *that I see the rose* or *that the rose is there*. As of yet this is not to see the *esse* of the rose but only to know that it is present to me by means of a conceptual substitute (the conception of existence at this particular degree) which dispenses it from *seeing* in the fully intuitive sense of the word. The *esse*, or the act of existing on the part of the rose, is certainly, in an intentional way, in the intelligence, but in an entirely implicit state, according as it is implied, without the intelligence knowing it, in the rose which my intelligence knows that I see, or that the rose is present, in short, in the assertion: that rose *is there*. In this particular assertion, the judgment: that rose *is*, is not made. It is possible that the *Sein* may never be discovered; yet it is there, hidden, implied in something else, without the intelligence being aware of the fact. This means that at this first degree of abstraction, the rose's *act of existing* is already spiritualized but *in proximate potency* only, or as potentially contained in another intelligible; in short, as capable, but only capable, itself of becoming proportioned in act to the intelligence. It *can* be made visible to the intelligence and be seen by it. But it is not yet so; it remains hidden to the intelligence.

And now for the third stage. In the instant that the eye sees the rose and the intelligence says: "That rose is there," the intelligence itself passes, as if by a miracle—it's not really a miracle but a stroke of good fortune, a gift suddenly bestowed by nature—to a higher level which is not only at the third degree of abstraction, according to philosophical parlance, but also at a moment of natural contemplation in which thought is freed from abstraction. This can take place supra-consciously in a child, before any abstractive operation, and more or less supra-consciously in a poet, as it takes place consciously in an apprentice-philosopher or in a full-fledged philosopher in the midst of his work of meditation. At this moment the intuition of being suddenly flashes in the mind like a bolt of lightning, and the rose's *act of existing*, already intentionally present in the intelligence but only as spiritualized in proximate potency, or as implicitly and blindly contained in the "that rose is there" which the intelligence utters at the first degree of abstraction, is unveiled explicitly now as an object grasped, *spiritualized in act* and made proportioned in act to the intelligence. And this is brought about not by means of some *species* or *intentio intellecta* or other, but by means of an *intentio intelligens*, I mean by an act—this time a judicative act—which, positing the rose within the mind as it is posited in itself outside the mind, at one and the same time brings the rose's act of existing to a state of spirituality in act and makes the mind *see*. It is this very judicative act affirming the rose's act of existing outside the mind, which, inside the mind, makes it visible to and seen by the intelligence in the very instant when it says: that rose *is*, that rose *exists*, with the entire plenitude of (metaphysical) meaning in the word *to be* or *to exist*.

The intelligence *sees* being (the being of this or that) in the judgment of existence, unique in character, which it brings to bear at that instant. The affirmation of *Dasein* (on the level of the first degree of abstraction) in reality remains, as I have indicated in passing, a copulative assertion of presence to my world: Paul is there, Paul is present (in which the attention of the mind is concentrated above all on the subject as present: *"Paul* is *there"*). On the contrary, however, the affirmation of *Sein* (on the level of the third degree of intelligibility): Paul *is*, is a purely existential affirmation (in which the attention of the mind is concentrated above all on the verb). This is why in uttering this assertion the intelligence experiences a kind of revelation of the being pos- sessed by things, of extra-mental being, which sweeps away with a single stroke any temptation to idealism.

It is on the chance occasion when some individual reality is grasped in its singularity by the external sense—a tree, a bird, the calm ocean, a humble little hill, or the glance of a loved one, or a smile, or the gesture of the hand which passes in the instant, and will never return—or on the occasion when, at some privileged moment, my consciousness seizes upon the act of existing of that secret and hidden reality, but eminently mine, which is myself ("it has hap- pened to me on occasion," wrote Raïssa, "by a sudden intuition, to experience the reality of my being, of that profound principle, the very first, which places me outside of nothingness. A powerful intuition whose violence sometimes frightened me, and which was the first to give me some knowledge of a metaphysical absolute")[33]—it is, as I said, on the occasion of some individual reality grasped in its pure singularity that such an intellectual intuition of being is produced. But at the same time and by the same process (for in seeing that this rose *is*, I recognize at the same time that outside my mind there *are* as well, each one in its own particular way, a multitude of other things), it is being itself that is revealed to the intelligence, in the mystery of its limitless horizon, and of the irreducible diversity with which it posits before us each single existent. This is why it is precisely by the intuition of being, as *formally* given to the intellect, that the latter perceives the analogy of *esse* in the fullness of its meaning. What I want to say is that at this point the intellect perceives not only

---

33   Cf. Raïssa Maritain, *Les Grandes Amitiés*, p. 131, (Chap. IV, § [2]).

that the concept of being in itself is intrinsically varied (analogy of proper proportionality), just like the concept of all the transcendentals, but also that the analogy of being is *the reason and the key* of the analogy of the transcendentals and that this analogy crosses the boundaries of the infinite: If each one of the diverse existents is good in its own way or one in its own way, it is *because*[34] each one *exists*, or is posited for its own sake and in its own way,[35] outside the mind, and after all is said and done, precisely because there is a self-subsistant *Esse*—known to us analogically even though infinitely above our grasp—in which and with which all the other transcendentals, also raised to pure act, must be absolutely identified.[36]

Dasein *and* Sein

9. I would now like to propose some more general considerations on *the analogy of being and the concept of existence*.

We have seen that there are two concepts of *existence*, the one formed at the first degree of abstraction or intelligibility, the other at the third and in a mind that has experienced the formal intuition of being.

I have insisted on the difference in *origin* between these two concepts: the first being due to the abstractive operation and drawn from phantasms, through the light of the agent intellect (existence then is the object of an *intentio intellecta*); the second, on the contrary, being due to a return of simple apprehension on the intuition of being and the judicative act in which it is produced, which is an *intentio intelligens*: existence then becomes the object of this *intentio intelligens*, and it is by a return on the object grasped in this way that our second concept of *existence* is formed.

Next I insisted on the difference in *meaning* between these two concepts. Although the object of the first concept of existence is evidently not an essence (but then at this particular level the metaphysical notions of essence and existence have not yet been clearly separated out), it is nevertheless, like every concept of abstractive origin, grasped and conceived *by mode* of essence or *in the manner* of a *quid*, of an essence or of a quality.

---

34   By force of his basic realism, Aristotle certainly knew this, but he knew it only *virtually*, just as he had no more that a *virtual* intuition of being. He did not teach, after all, that being is analogous by an analogy of proper proportionality.

35   If each one of these did not exist, outside the mind, in its own particular way it is either because each one would be thought to exist outside the mind *but not in its own particular way, different from the way all others do* (in which case it would evidently be the same for all the other transcendentals, which would not be analogous either), or else because each one would be considered *to have no existence outside the mind* and that each one is no more than a mental representation (in which case all the transcendentals would be univocal, since they would all be representations of the mind *in the same way*).

36   Aristotle had no knowledge of this.

On the one hand it is formed on the level of the first degree of abstraction and subsequently remains enclosed within the sphere of sensible experience and of the world in which we live; it is its belonging to this world or its presence to this world that is designated here. It follows from these two facts that the assertion of existence here is in reality a copulative assertion in which a subject is declared *present to my world*.

When we speak of the existence of some thing on this particular level, it is to declare: "That thing (*subject*) is (*copula*) present or presently given (*predicate*)," in other words: That thing *is there*. We are in the register of the *Dasein* (Thomistically understood); we are in the register of the *Dasein*, which goes with the first degree of abstraction or intelligibility. And *to be there* is to be *present to our world*, to the sensible world (the word *there* being a predicate in a copulative proposition and *bearing by itself alone the entire existential meaning* that it communicates to the subject, whereas the word *is* has no more than a copulative meaning).[37] In other words, being (which is not considered in itself) is in this case *put in relationship* (to the sensible world), it is taken *in its relation* to the sensible world, to this *physis* which for the philosopher is the object of physics as understood by Aristotle and St. Thomas.

Consequently, and this is a point I want to insist on here: Being, or rather what holds the place of being in the mind, is conceived and used in discourse *by univocal mode*; the concept of existence is an analogous concept in itself (as the metaphysician well knows), but now it is no longer anything except the concept of *presence to my world*; and subsequently, remaining an analogous concept in itself (for the metaphysician, and according as it signifies the act of existing), it is now (on the level I am speaking of, and where it signifies no more than presence to my world) *taken univocally* and used univocally. When the greatest of metaphysicians says in the ordinary conversations of daily life: "Pass me my inkstand, *it is there*," or "Tell Reginald to come in, *he is there*," he is quite simply using the notion of existence as *Dasein* (in a copulative assertion, in which the word *is* serves only to link the word *there* to a subject), and he is using it in a univocal mode.

On the contrary, when we come to the second concept of existence, the one which precedes the intuition of being, we are in the register of the *Sein*, which goes with the third degree of intelligibility. Here the assertion of existence is not copulative but a properly existential assertion of the *act of existing*. Here being is grasped as such, in its own light which is a revelation to the mind within the mind of the extra-mental act of existing. It is no longer taken in its

---

37   I realize that the copula *is* is not a simple algebraic sign and that it signifies the subject as possessing a certain predicate in possible or real existence (I think I pointed this out in *Les Degrés du Savoir*). The copulative judgment therefore concerns or *implies possible existence or real existence*. This real existence then is possessed by the subject and the predicate. But when there is question of *real* existence, such as it is seized upon in the *intuition of being*, it is no longer the predicate nor the subject but *the verb* which bears the existential meaning.

relation to the sensible world; it is taken absolutely, in its limitless and intrinsically differentiated universality which embraces everything that *is* (and *is* in irreducibly varied ways).

Consequently (I will come back to this consequence shortly): Being, which is analogous by its nature and grasped as analogous, is now conceived and used in discourse *by analogical mode*. The concept of existence then is an analogical concept taken analogically. This is the privilege of the *Sein*.

In addition, it seems to me important to remark that what I have just said about existence must be said as well of *the existent* (*l'existant*) or *"be-ing"* (*l'étant*). It is fashionable today to oppose *"be-ing"* (*l'étant*) to *the existent* (*l'existant*); this is a mistake. A *"be-ing"* (*étant*) or an *existent* (*existant*) is quite clearly a subject which exists or possesses existence.

So there are two different meanings to the word *ens* or *étant*. In the first sense, it refers to the *Dasein* and to the level of the first degree of abstraction, where the assertion of existence is reduced to the copulative assertion "that thing is *present to my world*," "that thing *is there*."

In the second sense, the word *ens* or *"be-ing"* (*étant*) refers to the *Sein* and the level of the third degree of intelligibility; and as we have seen, the assertion "that thing is endowed with existence," far from constituting the primordial assertion of the act of existing, "that thing *is*," comes (for anyone who has experienced the formal intuition of being) *after* the primordial assertion of the act of existing. It is a return on this latter assertion, just as the concept of existence is a return on the judicative act in which the intuition of being occurs. But the assertion declaring that a subject is endowed with existence and is, in short, an *existant* or an *étant* is surely legitimate. Once I have had the intuition of extra-mental being and have formed the concept that corresponds to it—then evidently I can say that such a subject as I know *to exist* or whose *esse* I affirm is endowed with existence or that it is an *existent* (*existant*) or a *"be-ing"* (*étant*), an *ens*. I do not see how St. Thomas would have been uncomfortable speaking of God as uncreated *ens*.

10. I would like now to take up once again my remarks on the concept of existence on the level of the first degree of abstraction, which is also that of the *Dasein*.

On this level we find three distinct kinds of function of the intelligence, depending on whether we are concerned with the ordinary conversations of daily life or with the natural sciences or with the philosophy of nature.

In the ordinary conversations of daily life, the words *to be*, in such assertions as: *Paul is here*, that is to say Paul is present, are assertions in which the words *to be* is purely copulative; it is the *here* of Paul, or his presence to my world, that is meant to be affirmed and which bears the entire existential meaning. Here we see the equivocation from which the word *Dasein* must be purified. Such as it has been forged by contemporary philosophers descended from

Hegel. the *being-there* (Da-*sein*, here the *sein* upstages the *da*, and the meaning suggested by the word is *to exist*-there) appears as an inferior kind of *act of existing* which would be qualified by the *there* which diminishes and falsifies it, a pseudo *Sein*, a spurious or botched-up *act of existing* which tries to pass itself off for the *Sein* and would lead us down a misleading and fatal path in search of true being, toward the *Sein*. With such a pseudo notion of the act of existing, the mind cannot help but wander astray into the tinsel realm of cheap philosophic imitations and the illusions of lofty speculation. The *Dasein* does not offer a first approach to being, even a sorry and a deceptive one. It is a substitute for being, but not because it presents to the mind an *existence*-there, which would be a spurious, defective *Sein*. It is a substitute for being because it presents to the mind a "being-predicated-or-declared-*there*," that is to say a *there*, a *"Da" which all by itself bears the existential meaning*. In such assertions the word *Sein*, far from signifying "to exist" (to exercise the act of existing), is really no more than the verb *to be* used as a simple *copula*, applying the predicate *there* or *Da* to a certain subject. In other words, the *Dasein* is a substitute for being because, on the level of the first degree of abstraction, existence is no more than *presence to my world* attributed to a subject and connoting the act of existing *only by implication*, and because of this, *thought is dispensed from thinking "to exist,"* all the while designating it implicitly. Here we have, as I see it, the correct notion of *Dasein*, or of that "being-there," the word *being* in no way and on no account signifying the act of existing, and having no more than a copulative meaning. If, in the register of the *Dasein* (as correctly understood in this way), some other meaning comes along to reinforce the copulative sense by laying stress on the affirmation, the new meaning will be the inevitability of the *there* or of the presence in question. This presence imposes itself on me, takes its place irrevocably in my world. *Paul is there.* If I find this too annoying, I can always reply, on the same wave length: *I am not there* for him.

Hence the concept of existence, which is analogous in itself as well as for the metaphysician but which in this case is no more than the substitute-concept of presence to my world, is used *in a univocal way*. Whatever I happen to be talking about, I declare it to be *there* in this same way and with the same mode of signification.

The same is the case with the second type of the functioning of the intelligence on this level—one which is characteristic of the natural sciences. If I think, "The plesiosaurus no longer exists," I mean nothing more than that "the plesiosaurus is no longer a part of the terrestrial fauna; it is no longer *there* in the midst of this fauna." If a chemist successfully carries out the synthesis of insulin, at the end of the operation he can say: "Finally we have insulin; *there* it is." In this assertion what reinforces the purely copulative meaning of the word *to be*, is scientific certitude, and this has nothing to do with the ordinary conversations of daily life. The concept of existence or of being there is once again used *in a univocal way*.

Now what about the third type, which is characteristic of the philosophy of nature? What I have in mind is a philosophy of nature which, hypothetically, would be limited *purely and simply* to the first degree of abstraction, in other words, which would be accompanied by *no* metaphysical understanding *whatsoever* in the mind of the philosopher. And *in absolutely no way* would this philosopher experience the intuition of being, even if only virtually, or through some substitute for being which would then turn his doctrine awry. We would still be in the realm of the *Dasein*, but this time understood philosophically, that is to say, in an explanation or a knowledge which claims to be ultimate or fundamental in character.

In dialectical materialism we have an example of such a "philosophy of nature" (in a sense that is entirely different from the meaning Aristotle gave to this word). It seems interesting to me to bring two points to your attention. On the one hand, though Hegel has been put back on his pedestal, he is still there as the intellectual inspiration and doctrinal guide of Marxist realism (and, from the very outset, a prey as well to a parasitical idealism). Logic has become the soul of the real. Instead of being *ontological* as it should be, the philosophy of nature is now *dialectical*. And what reinforces, or, if I can put it this way, re-reinforces, the purely copulative sense of the word *to be* in the assertion of the being-there, is this very dialectical process, which is proper to *intentiones secundae*, to movement, to oppositions and syntheses in its interior discourse.

On the other hand, *praxis*, or (transitive) action, has taken on an absolutely primary and fundamental value in this philosophy, to the point of completely taking the place of speculative knowledge. And simultaneously as a consequence *to be* has become *to do* or *to act*. What does this mean, if not that, beside the dialectical, a second matter for thought, namely, *making* or *doing*, comes to reinforce the purely copulative sense of the word *to be*, in the "being-*there*" which goes with the level of the first degree of abstraction. With these two philosophical reinforcements, the dialectical and "making" (or "doing"), the assertion of existence remains more than ever the assertion of *Dasein*. And the concept of existence, which on this level is now no more than the concept of presence to my world, is used more than ever in a *univocal* way.

After this it can be noted that those philosophers, who, in their turn, have *absolutely no experience* of the intuition of being, can nevertheless, as they say, do metaphysics and think they are metaphysicians. (This can happen even to Christian philosophers, when they have more or less become infatuated with idealism or phenomenology.) Then such philosophers make use of concepts which by their nature belong to the third degree of abstraction, but the meaning of analogy has entirely escaped them. This means that, in their method of thought, they do not rise above the level of the first degree of abstraction, hence above the level of the *Dasein*. They can affirm the existence of God (and this is the case with the Christian philosophers I just alluded to).

Once again this existence is a *Dasein*, but this time alienated or extrapolated from the sphere propre to it, which is the world of sensible experience,—a sublimated *Dasein*. "God exists" now means "God is there in the invisible" (but He is now a datum of faith, which escapes any "proof" that reason can offer). These philosophers likewise use the notion of being or of existence in a *univocal* way.

Let me also remark that it is possible for a particular philosopher to be actually obsessed with the anguished desire to attain the *Sein* but without, in his case either, having ever had the slightest intuition of being, without ever having really understood just what metaphysics is, or taken the means to attain it. So he struggles within the *Dasein* and against the *Dasein* (which in the end he has misunderstood); he does all he can to escape it but without success. He has no desire to construct a philosophy of nature, yet it is in this very sphere that he stirs about in spite of himself with a dizzying display of concepts of his own invention, and without bringing any light to this sphere by the slightest degree of metaphysical understanding. (A kind of natural mysticism plays the part of a stand-in in a role that metaphysics ought to play for him.) And more than ever he uses the concept of being in a *univocal* way; in fact, what he really does, and this is his greatest error, is to mistake the *Sein* as *univocal in itself*. It seems to me that the philosopher in question is very much like Heidegger himself.[38]

38   This transcription will serve as confirmation: "The correct notion of *Dasein*, which belongs to the first degree of abstraction and designates 'presence to my world' (a notion that is univocal in itself and is used as such in the German language of everyday life), is expressly rejected by Heidegger.

"Heidegger gave the word *Dasein* a very special meaning. Translating his idea of *Dasein* into the language of the philosophy of being, it must be said that *Dasein* signifies the possibility for man to achieve an experience of the self (in the sense of a natural mystical experience). The possibility of such an experience is proper to man and for Heidegger it is this very possibility which defines man, that is to say, distinguishes him from all other beings (plants, animals,—God). Only man is *Dasein*.

This fundamental possibility in man to attain an experience of the self is ordinarily hidden from him (and blocked out for him by the fact that he is fixed in an 'intra-mundane' life). Man's first effort must be to rediscover this possibility.

"After rediscovering this possibility, he must reduce it, conquer it as pure possibility (it is in this first sense that Heidegger struggles against the *Dasein*,— *Dasein* as Heidegger understood it) by passing on to the act of self-experience. Since it is no more than a stage on the path of experience, the *Dasein* by its nature tends to be eliminated. At the end of this Heideggerian experience man becomes conscious of the *Sein*. But what is meant by this term, and what is inexpressible in itself (as experienced), has nothing to do with the perception of *Sein*, of being, in and by the judicative act which constitutes the intuition of being.

"Could not the Heideggerian *Sein* be called a sort of *Dasein*,—*Dasein* this time correctly understood? It would not be a question of a *Dasein* considered in its proper sphere which is the world of sensible experience (first degree of abstrac-

The Intuition of Being When It is Only Virtual

11. Everything I just said was related to the level of the first degree of abstraction, and to the perspective of the *Dasein*. Let us leave that behind and turn now to metaphysics; let us move from the *Dasein* to the *Sein*, from the level of the first degree of intelligibility to the level of the third.

This does not mean that the long proposals I am going to make will bear on the metaphysics of St. Thomas. No, I would like to consider metaphysical thought on another level (a level which is still imperfect and deficient but which has a special interest for us).

There are some philosophers who, without being St. Thomas or one of his great disciples, are *true metaphysicians* but who seem to be lacking in something. It is on them, and on the greatest among them, that I would like to pause for a moment.

These are real metaphysicians. In other words, not only are the concepts they use concepts of the third degree of abstraction or of intelligibility rather than of the first, but also, in order to think and to make use of these concepts, they themselves are placed within the third degree of intelligibility and metaphysical intellection, and they have a real sense of *the analogy of being*.

This being said, that very sense of the analogy of being, which they really do have, they have however in a way that is still incomplete and deficient. Why? Because they have not had *the formal intuition of being in its full light*. This was the case with Bergson, for example, who did experience the intuition of being, but in a *disguised* fashion, or by means of a substitute, *i.e.*, *duration*, from which subsequently his metaphysics suffered a doctrinal deviation; and his sense of the analogy of being too was just as much in disguise.[39]

And what about Aristotle? He's the one I wanted to get to. He's the one who had such an admirable sense of the analogy of being, and certainly not in the disguised way as was the case with Bergson; and yet in his case it was still

---

tion), but rather of a *Dasein* which expresses the presence of the self to the self, in the sense of pure presence, *pure Da*. Because we are dealing with this kind of *Dasein*, the Heideggerian *Sein* is purely and simply univocal. Perhaps the difficulty comes from the idea of *pure presence*. Here pure presence means a presence totally *without relation* to any other thing.

"When Heidegger opposes the *Sein* to be-ing (l'Etant), he is simply opposing one kind of *Dasein* to another. To the pure presence of the *Sein* (presence without any relation), to the pure *Da*, he opposes everything that is '*presence in relation to*,' that is, everything that can be present to my habitual world, to the world of my experience and my consciousness in the midst of my 'intra-mundane' life and as being in relation to the world."

39   What about Spinoza? I would say that he is a real metaphysician, but one that is completely off the track, and that he experienced the intuition of being (certainly not formally but at least virtually). But he immediately falsified this intuition in its entire conceptualization in such a way that his sense of the analogy of being was *completely* inhibited.

incomplete and deficient. For he too had a very real experience of the intuition of being, and not as Bergson did, in a disguised fashion. But he did not have that experience *formally and in full light*, he had it only *virtually*. Whence his metaphysics did not suffer from a doctrinal falsification or deviation, but it did suffer from a serious omission.

He was incapable of a *formal* experience of the intuition of being because his metaphysics was reined in, prevented from going the whole way by his notionalism or his mode of thought still riveted, in spite of his authentically realist élan, on the consideration of essences. And why was this so? I tried to indicate this in the preceding section, when I spoke of the impact of the image on the intellect in the state of our fallen and disordered nature. For the present I am taking this for an established fact.

Here we are face to face with an eminently interesting case, since we are dealing with the prince of philosophers. But this requires a difficult and very delicate analysis, of which I am capable of offering no more than an outline, and one that I hope is free of any serious errors.

Aristotle never got beyond the wall of essences. I mean that he conceived the *esse* itself in the same way that he conceived the other transcendentals, by an authentically metaphysical concept, or a product of the third degree of intelligibility, and which he used in an authentically metaphysical perspective, that of the *Sein*, but in a perspective that was still partially closed, or blocked by an inhibition, and not completely liberated or liberating, one in which the consideration is blocked at essences.

Let us be careful here and insert a parenthesis, but one of major importance. This Aristotelian concept of the *esse*, that I am speaking of now, is a *third* concept of existence. In the preceding section I spoke of two concepts of existence: the *first*, which is due to the abstractive operation at the *first degree of abstraction*, and which remains within the register of the *Dasein*, for it is no more than the concept of presence to my world; the *second*, which is due to a return of simple apprehension to the *judicative act* in which the intuition of being is produced, and which is the concept *par excellence* of being in the register of the *Sein*: a concept which, by means of that return in question here, which is carried out through simple apprehension, brings the latter to the summit of the third degree of intelligibility, but which itself is in no way of abstractive origin (its origin is judicative).

At present we are concerned with a *third* concept of existence, this time a metaphysical concept, *intentio intellecta* of abstractive origin, not judicative, but this time formed at the third degree of abstraction, not at the first. Let me remark in passing that if a child or a poet can have, as I noted above, each in a particular way, the intuition of being, nevertheless such concepts of abstractive origin, and formed at the third degree of abstraction, are proper to the metaphysician. But let us put this parenthesis aside and consider, among the concepts in question here, our third concept of existence. Its object is an intelligible, which in its notion implies no limitation whatsoever to the world of sensible experience from which it is drawn; so this intelligible, existence, stands in no relationship to the sensible world and is not reduced to the *Dasein* as in the case of the concept of existence (or of presence to my world) to the first degree of abstraction (my first concept of existence). This intelligible is the very *Sein* itself. Yes, but the concept of which it is the object is not due to a turning back to the intuition of being (something that is possible only when the intelligence has had this intuition in a formal way and in full light). This is a concept (of the third degree of abstraction) which here is still of *abstractive* origin, and which presents the intelligized object *in the manner of an essence*. In the mind of the metaphysician it can precede the intuition of being, with which it has nothing to do. And this is a stroke of bad luck for the metaphysician; for not only can the concept of abstractive origin—my third concept of existence— precede the intuition of being, but it can also, by this very fact, be an obstacle to the latter and prevent the metaphysician from breaking through the barrier of notionalism and arriving at the intuition of being, at least as it is received and possessed *formally* and in full light. In theory he will turn out to be a good, a true, and a great metaphysician, but all in vain, for his intuition of being will remain no more than *virtual*.

Now this is, I think, precisely the case with Aristotle. After this he will teach in vain that *esse* is distinguished from *essentia* just as act is distinguished from potency, since he continues to conceive *esse* itself (which is presented to him in that third concept of existence I just mentioned) *in the manner* of a *quid* or of an essence or *in the manner of essence or of quality*. He does not say that *esse* is an essence or a quality! But even though he contrasts it in a certain way to any order of essences or qualities, he nevertheless thinks of it in this way and cannot not think of it in this way—because it is presented to him by a concept of abstractive origin (and not by a concept, my second concept of existence, due to a return on the intuition of being formally received)—*from that same perspective* from which he thinks essences and qualities.

Visualized in this way, *esse* becomes an act just like any other, in the same way that *intelligere* is the act of the *intellectus*. And there is no doubt that Aristotle saw very clearly that there is an *analogy* between the statements *"esse* actuates the *essence"* and *"intelligere* actuates the intelligence." But what he did not see is that there is actually an abyss between these two assertions. In the second, "intellection is the act of the intelligence," intellection is said to be the act of a certain essence considered as existing;[40] whereas in the first assertion "existing is the act of the essence," there is question of an act by which an essence *which was nothing* is posited *extra nihil*, outside of nothingness; this is the assertion of an irreducible absolute, a kind of miracle of nature (which in

---

40   Even abstracting from existence: for in the same way one could say "making 4 is the act of 2 plus 2," or *"to arouse love which makes everything fruitful* is the act of Venus."

reality supposes the action of God the Creator, Who gives being to everything that is).

And so if it is visualized as it is by Aristotle, *esse* becomes a transcendental like the others, like the good, the one, the beautiful. Its absolute privilege, which is to be the king of the transcendentals, will remain hidden from view and will be known only *virtually*—a privilege which is but one with the fact which I recalled in a previous section,[41] and which in the same way will be known only virtually, namely, that the analogy of being is the reason and the key to the analogy of the transcendentals. To have known this only virtually, without being able therefore to make use of it in his explicitly formulated thought and his doctrine—this is one of the signs of Aristotle's limitations, and this shows, as I said a moment ago, that his perspective, even though it was that of the *Sein*, nevertheless remained partially obstructed.

And Aristotle might very well have known that *"ens et bonum convertuntur"* (the more being something has, the more good it has, and conversely); but he did not realize that the absolute identity between being and the other transcendentals (just as between being and the intelligibles, such as intellection and love, which of themselves imply no imperfection) is found only in an *Esse* of infinite transcendence, *"Ipsum Esse per se subsistens"*[42] Aristotle certainly knew that God is Pure Act and the Thought of Thought,[43] but Aristotle's Thought of Thought knows itself without at the same time knowing all other things (and this is surely so because it does not create them), and this Pure Act remains the Prime Mover of the universe. Aristotle did not realize that God is the creator of being because he did not realize that He is *Being itself subsisting through itself.*

In short, however nobly Aristotle speaks of God in his metaphysics, he does not reach Him in the constitutive elements of his metaphysics—analogically he does of course, that goes without saying, *"per speculum in aenigmate."* And as everyone knows, it is his *Physics* far more than his *Metaphysics* that revealed to Aristotle the proofs of God's existence. And this is all to the honor of Aristotelian physics: his philosophy of nature, like any philosophy of nature worthy of the name, is, to be sure, a knowledge founded on the level of the first degree of abstraction, but it is an *ontological* knowledge, which has escaped from the *Dasein*, and is concerned with the *Sein* itself. And this is so, because this knowledge, and the concepts it uses, are illuminated by the mind of the philosopher, and endowed with a meaning that is *participatively* metaphysical

---

41   See *supra*, pp. 225–226.

42   Before St. Thomas, St. Paul had already said: *"Credere autem oportet accedentem ad Deum, qui est,"* we must believe in God because He is (Heb. xi, 6).—And before St. Paul, the *Ego sum qui sum*, the revealed name of God, had been delivered by Moses to the children of Israel. "Then God said to Moses, 'I am who am.' Then He added, 'This is what you shall tell the children of Israel: I am sent me to you.'" (Exod., iii, 14).

43   Aristotle, *Metaph.* Bk. Λ, ch. ix, 1074b34–35; καὶ ἔστιν ἡ νόησις νοήσεως νόησις.

or significative of being, through the metaphysical intellection which the philosopher brings into play at the third degree of intelligibility (which supposes the intuition of being, even if it is there only virtually, as is the case with Aristotle).[44] The fact that the Aristotelian philosophy of nature is crowned by the demonstration of God's existence is the sign of its full philosophical authenticity. But this glory of his *Physics* was purchased by him at the cost of an irreparable omission in his *Metaphysics*, the omission of the intuition of being *formally* received and possessed; and by a defect in his *Metaphysics* just as irreparable (I mean in his very doctrine insofar as it has not been entirely recast). In his metaphysics, as I have just indicated, the analogy of being was seen, but only incompletely. It remains half hidden; it is not grasped in its full dimensions. To grasp it in its fullness was the achievement of St. Thomas, not of Aristotle.

This is what I wanted to tell you about the metaphysics of the greatest of philosophers, whose work was accomplished, in our condition of fallen nature, through the powers of human reason *all by itself*. My remarks undoubtedly remain quite imperfect; I would like to have gone back to all that Etienne Gilson has written on the subject of Aristotle's notionalism, but I did not have the time to do so, putting together these notes as hastily as I did. I hope these remarks are nevertheless sufficient for my purpose. And the same can be said after all about the whole of the present work that I am submitting to you. It is a work in draft form and very imperfect. But, as I said to you once before, I think it is on the right track.

12. To complete my exposé we must speak now of the *Sein* grasped in full light, and at the absolutely superior level of metaphysical thought, thanks to the intuition of being received in full light and *formally* possessed, and to a view, complete this time, of the analogy of being. Here I can do no better than send you back to the metaphysics of St. Thomas, that *nec plus ultra* of the human intelligence, according to the expression of Etienne Gilson, such as you can sort it out in his two *Summas*.

Let me note simply that this reading should be an attentive reading, because of the Aristotelian language that St. Thomas, in his humility, was accustomed to use, but which does not prevent his own thought from breaking forth in liberating flashes of light. This reading must be particularly attentive when there is question of the great Commentators, especially of Cajetan who, in spite of his genius (or because of the special characteristics of this genius), was more subject to the influence of the *Philosophus*, and was unable, as St. Thomas did so admirably, to free himself from Aristotle's notionalism.

44   So there is no longer question of what I called above (cf. p. 221, n. 30, and pp. 230–231) *the pure and simple* first degree of abstraction. In the mind that works (ontologically) on the level of the first degree of abstraction, there is in this case *participation* in the third degree, by virtue of the metaphysical intellection which, on another level, is in act in the philosopher and which illuminates his "physics" itself.

IV. THE EPISTEMOLOGICAL STATUS OF EXEGESIS

13. My first intention was that the reflections I just submitted to you would be the point of departure for a work of much greater scope, dedicated to the search for what might be called a "concrete" or "existential" epistemology, and at the end of which I would like to have tried, in particular, to define the epistemological status of exegesis. I am afraid that bringing such an undertaking to completion is beyond my strength. At my age one has to be resigned to bringing nothing to completion, to be content only with opening doors and taking a few steps down the path, hoping that others, better equipped, will continue to clear the way.

Let me however indicate to you briefly a few directing ideas, still in very rough form, of which I think I have gotten a glimpse or two concerning this subject. I do not think that the epistemology of exegesis has been considered or treated on its own account, as it should be, by the masters charged with teaching the critique of knowledge, in such a way that before getting down to work an exegete might receive from them an adequate and precise notion of the proper status, in the universe of human knowledge, of the work proposed for his intellectual research. This is a lack from which we all suffer and for which it is incumbent on our times to find a remedy.

It seems to me in general that exegetes today, according to an opinion commonly held but not critically elaborated, and simply taken for granted, conceive of their discipline as a kind of positive science which, as such, can and ought to become established in a valid and assured fashion, separate from theology, indeed, for some, separate from the faith itself. In my opinion, this is an illusion. Exegesis makes use of a scientific *apparatus or equipment* which it draws on from many varied disciplines of knowledge and erudition (linguistics, semantics, semiology, comparative grammar, paleography, archeology, etc., not to speak of history, which, inasmuch as it offers us a comprehensive image or tableau of the past, is not a science at all but which nevertheless offers us facts that are certain, at least more or less certain). This does not mean that exegesis itself would be—any more than history—a *positive science*, nor that it would be placed on the level of what we moderns call science. For science is what it is only because of the verifications of fact that observation and experience provide it; and it is clear that such verifications are outside the domain of exegesis, which cannot transport itself back into the past, to the times of the prophets of Israel or of Jesus, in order to test and verify in those times the value of its interpretations and hypotheses.

Is it an illusory idea, as I believe it is, that, with the information furnished by the equipment he receives from the diverse sciences and disciplines he makes use of (*plus*, in his own head, some explanatory hypothesis or other considered likely, and nothing more) the exegete has in his grasp an autonomous science capable of furnishing us with the exact meaning of a sacred text?

If such is indeed the case, one is led, it seems to me, after account has been taken of all the data on which the question depends, to the conclusion that exegesis attains its status as authentic knowledge only on condition that it make use of its scientific equipment in the light of higher truths, I mean in the light of the virtue of faith, and not only in the light of faith, but also in the light of an accurate comprehensive conception, founded in truth, of those divine and human realities to which the sacred text is essentially related when it states something in some particular instance; in other words, on condition that it *make use of its equipment in the light of the sapiential knowledge of theology.*

So I think that exegesis as an authentic form of knowledge (that is to say, insured against the accidental ascendancies of arbitrary and of subjective inclinations) is situated on the level, not of science (positive science), but on the level of *wisdom.* In other words on the same level as theology. And it is here that, presupposing theological knowledge and concurring with it as well, exegesis is able, in the conclusions that it proposes with the help of its scientific equipment and in the light of theology, to attain those certitudes that are proper to authentic knowledge, as well as to those well-founded hypotheses endowed with a sufficiently defined degree of probability which are likewise proper to authentic knowledge.

We have some excellent exegetes today. But everything leads one to think that most of them continue to believe (along with their less capable colleagues) or to admit more or less implicitly that their discipline is situated on the level of science (positive science) and not of wisdom. If we questioned them on the subject of their discipline, they would doubtless answer that in establishing the meaning of a sacred text they are making use of a positive science (basing their conclusions on purely factual research). And yet they are not really satisfied with this answer because at the same time they know very well, by their own work, that exegesis as they practice it is guided (but then by what authority? and how are they to avoid an epistemological contradiction?) by the habitus of theological faith that is actually present in their minds. And they would add, perhaps, either that exegesis ought to attain its end or be completed by and in theology—even though exegesis does not of itself presuppose the light of theology—or else that this positive science is an instrument of theology with regard to its initial data (just as philosophy is with regard to its doctrinal synthesis). All this is inadmissible in a healthy epistemology; for if a positive science has already determined by its own methods the meaning of a sacred text, it evidently could not be the instrument that theology would use in this way to establish its initial bases. In such a case one would have to say that the positive science in question furnishes theology with the initial bases, already determined by that positive science, on which theology will be established. In other words, it is this positive science which instructs the theologian in the first truths which the theologian *as such* needs to know. In short, far from being simply an instrument of theology, this positive science becomes its monitor and teacher. All the malaise from which the mind suffers here comes from the fact that *exegesis itself* and *the sciences* or scientific equipment that it *makes use of* have been unfortunately confused in a bastard concept so that it seems self-evident that in its task of determining the meaning of a sacred text, exegesis itself is no more than another positive science, which is not the case at all. The truth is that considered in its true nature it is a form of *wisdom* which *makes use of scientific equipment in the light of theological knowledge* and consequently presupposes that knowledge.

Why then are those to whom I made allusion excellent, first-rate exegetes? It is because they have in their hearts a faith so firm, so ardent that it animates and vivifies all the work they accomplish with the help of their scientific equipment, and which in this way compensates for their neglect of those theological lights normally required for such a work (a neglect that is in some cases more apparent than real, in other cases real but only more or less partial, and in still others real and total). It could also be said that, in the case of any exegete worthy of the name (regardless of what he may think of his own discipline), faith introduces more or less surreptitiously many rays of these lights[45] The exegetes I am referring to act in this very way, *in actu exercito*, or as regards the action or the operative vitality of their intellect in its actual operation, which is quite different from the way they think they act, *in actu signato*, or according to a theoretical idea accepted and commonly held by them. If my remarks are exact, they make only more manifest the need we all have for our conscious reflection on a clearly established epistemological status for exegesis.

The sole object of exegesis is not to establish critically, among its divers variants, the text proposed for our reading; evidently this is no more than a preliminary task (in which scientific equipment is king). The object of exegesis is to sort out for us the *meaning* which this particular text transmits to us, the *meaning of Sacred Scripture*. This is an entirely different matter. And it suffices for us to give the proper weight to this expression (to furnish us *the meaning of what God is telling us*, through the instrument of human language!) for us to see why I said a few moments ago that exegesis is to be placed on the same sapiential level as theology, in such a way that it presupposes and at the same time concurs with theological knowledge. What does this mean, if not that exegesis itself is—let us not be afraid to contradict commonly accepted opinions—*a part of theology*? It seems to me that as a consequence it would be to our advantage to renew our vocabulary with all due freedom (do not they say in current English "a biblical theologian" where we say "an exegete"?) and to

---

45   Lights of theology, either possessed in act and consciously brought into play (contrary to the presupposed theoretical notion), or possessed virtually, not consciously recognized. Father M.-J. Lagrange (whom I mention here because of the gratitude which Raïssa and I have always felt in his regard) had a solid theological formation, and he was very conscious of those lights.

recognize for an exegesis restored to its true nature the name of *scriptural theology*. This would lead to the distinction in theology between not just two parts (positive theology and speculative theology) but rather three constitutive parts: the first of these three parts being exegesis itself or "scriptural theology" (perhaps it could also be called "exegetical theology"); the second part, the theology which, since it groups two other sections of "positive theology" under one name, might be called by the abbreviated name patristic and conciliar (and its perspective would be historical); and the third, *speculative* theology (whose perspective would be that of the deposit of revelation as such).[46]

---

46   Traditional teaching, by distinguishing only two parts in theological knowledge, positive theology and speculative theology, in general divides positive theology into three different sections called *biblical theology* (or the positive theology of scriptural documents), *patristic theology* (the positive theology of the testimonies of tradition—this includes as well the study of liturgical tradition, and this is why in abbreviated form I called it "patristic" instead of "patristic and liturgical"); and the positive theology of the teaching of the ecclesiastical magisterium, which likewise in abbreviated form I designated by the name *conciliar*.

Two points, it seems to me, should be noted here. On the one hand, the distinction between exegesis and biblical theology appears arbitrary, for it does not rest on any difference at all with regard to their formal objects, and stems from empirical data with no epistemological import: namely, the manner in which, in their approach to a noetic domain which in reality is the same, the teachers, assigned to particular teaching duties, actually deport themselves according to certain mental habits, some tending toward an "exegesis" driven toward positive science by the very suspicions and prejudices opposed to it and which it has to overcome in order to gain recognition for the free use of its scientific equipment, others to a "biblical theology" which their particular perspective as theologians leads them to consider as as area of teaching entirely different from that exegesis which has been driven toward positive science and which has been erroneously presented as capable of doing without theological lights. In truth all this is no more than accidental.

On the other hand, the equipment used in the interpretation of a sacred text, when it is used correctly, offers factual information and verifications which all of theology evidently needs, but which are drawn from various empiriological sciences and disciplines; this is certainly not the case for the equipment that either the theology of the testimony of tradition and the theology of the teachings of the magisterium, or speculative theology have at their disposal.

And so are we not led to conclude that exegesis (according to its true epistemological notion) and biblical theology in reality make up one single identical discipline (which I have taken the liberty to call "scriptural theology"), and at the same time to distinguish this scriptural theology from the theology I have called "patristic and conciliar," whose perspective (historical in nature) is completely different, and in which I have grouped under one single title the two other sections (the theology of testimonies of tradition and the theology of the teachings of the magisterium) ordinarily recognized as distinct in positive theology? Hence the tripartite division I am suggesting here: *scriptural theology, patristic and conciliar theology, speculative theology*.

Each of these parts of the supreme sapiential knowledge makes use of a certain naturally and rationally ordered equipment, which should be good and valid and should "speak true" in its own order. The equipment of scriptural theology or exegesis is drawn from an empiriological type of science or discipline. I would say that it is "at some distance" from the sapiential knowledge which makes use of it, in the same way that the tool held in the hand of the artisan is at some distance from his head or his brain. Metaphorically it could be called a kind of "manual" equipment.

The equipment of patristic and conciliar theology is likewise an equipment "at some distance" or a kind of "manual" equipment insofar as there is a question of establishing historical data, but which on the other hand are directly concerned, as these forms of theology are, with the object or the contents of theological sapiential knowledge itself.

The equipment of speculative theology is an instrument vitally conjoined to the very elaboration of theology, and which, consequently, speaking in metaphors, I would no longer call "manual," but rather "cerebral." Here we now find wisdom, philosophical, metaphysical wisdom essentially founded in truth—which is instrumentally brought into play by theological knowledge.

It is not at all surprising that the three parts (if my suggestion of a tripartite division is acceptable) thus distinguished in theological sapiential knowledge develop conjointly, in a mutual interaction and sort of mutual involution, each presupposing the two others and each contributing to the growth and progress of the other two; this is the case with the parts of any living organism.

Finally, let me note that these three constitutive parts of theology (a sapiential knowledge of supernatural reason in its root) could be represented, as far as their continuity and their vital activity are concerned, by a circle closed on itself—the ancient symbol of the serpent biting its own tail. Suppose that in order to trace this circle our pen starts out at a point from which it rises toward the left then descends toward the right and ends up joining the beginning point. At the circle's point of departure we shall place scriptural theology—itself in a beginning state, and which will gradually rise to increasing levels of

Concerning the empiriological equipment used in the interpretation of the sacred text, I just said: "When it is used correctly." This is not the case when it is used in the light of some preconceived idea or other (garnered from the idols of the times) concerning the nature of exegetical work itself and giving direction to that work. Any intellectual apparatus is, in fact, always used in light of certain general principles, and it is important that these principles be good ones, that is, *true*, and *lofty and comprehensive enough* to direct the mind in its enterprise, as this particular case requires. From this it follows, it seems evident to me, that exegesis is capable of avoiding surrender to the arbitrary only if it uses its scientific equipment *in the light of the faith and of an authentic theology*, under which alone it can pretend to the status of authentic knowledge—I have particularly in mind a speculative theology at one and the same time founded in truth and always anxious to advance, and which the very findings of exegesis (or "scriptural theology") aid in its renewal wherever the need arises.

perfection at the same time as do the two other parts of theology. Higher on the circle, at a point of the ascending curve, we shall place patristic and conciliar theology; then, at a symmetrical point of the descending curve, we shall place speculative theology. And at that point where the circle closes on itself, in other words where the serpent bites its tail, we shall come back to scriptural theology, this time no longer as the point of origin, but as the ultimate end point of the entire movement. Meditation on the Holy Scriptures, in that devout turning inward of study which gradually changes into prayer, appears then as the fruit—*aliquid ultimum et delectabile*—of the entire sapiential knowledge of theology; and the work of the exegete or the scriptural theologian, which begins on an earthly level, finds its completion through the repose of the contemplative gaze, in the heaven of the soul, where the sacred text is not analyzed in its human letter but savored in its divine content.

All of this needs to be discussed, made precise, and carefully supported. This would be a new work, centered on the present state of exegetical research. I believe it necessary also to tackle vigorously the whole problem of hermeneutics and the philosophical bases involved. Today, let me be content to propose some avenues of approach, certainly not without complements and necessary modifications, by which a more profound reflection might be undertaken.

CHAPTER XII
FOR AN EXISTENTIAL EPISTEMOLOGY (II)

REFLECTIONS ON THEOLOGICAL KNOWLEDGE[1]

A BRIEF INTRODUCTION

1. THE REFLECTIONS I WOULD LIKE TO PROPOSE to you today are a kind of long preface to an essay that I want to write out (the fact is I have not yet got around to doing so). But with this brief preface we will be facing in the direction of some difficult problems, on which I will touch, being only too conscious of my own incompetence; nevertheless we must advance, all the while knowing full well that in what is said there will undoubtedly be many things that will have to be completed and put into proper perspective.

You will notice that the essay on which I am working is an essay on *existential* epistemology, which presupposes classical epistemology but which raises other questions and looks at them from a different point of view.

St. Thomas himself, in his question on *sacred doctrine* at the beginning of the *Summa theologiae*, which presents us with his thought on this subject in its most complete form—more perfectly laid out than in the *Summa contra Gentiles*[2] is

---

1   *Editor's footnote*: Seminar given with a number of Little Brothers of Jesus, at Kolbsheim, July 11 and 12, 1968. Cf. *Revue Thomiste*, 1969, no. 1 (pp. 5–27).

2   Cf. Michel Corbin, s.J., "La fonction et les principes de la théologie selon la Somme théologique de saint Thomas d'Aquin," dans R. S. V. R., LV (1967), pp. 321–366. The author brings to light the progress in reflection that *Sum. theol.*, q. 1, indicates with regard to the earlier writing of St. Thomas. On this point I am in complete agreement with him. On other points the case is not the same. In particular, I think that, if the function of theology is in truth to point out the intelligibility which, even though it transcends us, at the same time overwhelms us, and to show us the wonderful mutual coherence of the truths of faith, far more than to draw new conclusions from it, nevertheless the fact remains that the theological elucidation (and the Church is the sole authority to pass judgment in this regard) is either an *explication* in rational terms whose purpose is either to make more manifest the meaning of the revealed deposit (this is the case with transubstantiation, for example—in which case the theological elucidation can become the object of a definition by the magisterium), or it is an *interpretation* thanks to middle terms added by reason (this is the case with theological explications of the sacrifice of the mass): in this case, and this is not infrequent, there is question of a *theological conclusion* (which could not become the object of a definition). I would note also that the intuition of being, without which there is no authentic

concerned solely with what theology is *in itself or in its essence*: the knowledge of God and the deposit of revelation, which is a participation in the divine knowledge itself to which it is subordinate, and which, of itself, depends solely on the principles of the faith which contain virtually the entire subject to be known.[3] Thomas tells us nothing about the *existential conditions* which maintain *ex parte subjecti operantis*, on the part of the theologizing human subject: He barely alludes to them here and there. He had other and far more urgent things to do. We hold to and ought to hold to his infinitely precious teaching on *sacred doctrine* taken *in itself* as definitively acquired. But in these reflections, of which this exposé is no more than a preface, it is my intention later on to tackle a totally different field of considerations. And in these considerations the appearance of humility in theology—in complete conformity with the humility of St. Thomas himself—will be shown as complementary to the appearance of that supreme nobility and grandeur which theology gets from its object, and to its proper value—which must be maintained at any price—as a *science* or a form of knowledge completely authentic in itself, and indeed the most exalted of all forms of knowledge.

2. If we look at this matter from an historical perspective, we can hardly keep from asking whether or not the fundamental truths that St. Thomas had to establish concerning theology considered in itself have not gone a bit to the heads of theologians, however profound their personal humility may be.

Their personal humility is absolutely not called into question here. But it is no small matter to have to scrutinize and teach the queen of sciences. How could its sublimity not be reflected in some way on the theologian himself, certainly not with regard to his person, but with regard to his function, from the very fact that it is up to him to delve into the depths of this science and to teach it to other men. Or more exactly, how could the reflection of this sublimity not run the risk of masking, or of making the theologian forget a little, the stammering and all-too-human indigence of means by which this highest of all sciences is worked out and takes form in a human subject? Indeed does it not require poverty of spirit far more than self-assurance and self-satisfaction?

It seems to me that this is what has happened in the course of that magnanimous and candid epoch of theological imperialism, which is what the Middle Ages was, a theological imperialism which as a matter of fact, and despite all the burnings at the stake by the Inquisition, was a remarkable benefit to

---

metaphysics, has absolutely nothing to do with an intuition of God here below. To imagine that "to speak of the intuition of being runs the risk of leading to an intuition of God" ("altogether contrary to the letter of the *Summa*," to be sure !) only shows how certain theologians are a bit too neglectful of metaphysics and still have much to learn about the intuition of being.

3   Cf. *Sum. theol.*, Ia, q. 1, a. 7.

western culture. (The Middle Ages was dazzled by the object of theology; at least it had a sense of the object, and that counts above everything else.)

Whatever his personal humility might have been, the theologian as such sat enthroned over the universe of knowledge; he was the king of knowledge. And all the while he anathematized the doctors of the opposing schools; he had a very haughty and exalted idea of the profession exercised both by him and by them.

St. Thomas would not have wept so much if he had not known, for his part, what he had to cling to. He judged himself unworthy of such teaching authority because he realized all that it demanded of the infirmity of the thinking subject. Most of the doctors who appeared on the scene after him do not seem to have had any experience of this terror.

The Renaissance put an end to this theological imperialism in western culture but not in the heads of the general run of theologians, whatever ups and downs they may have experienced. And among some of our contemporary theologians who no longer have any faith in what gave theology its sublime nobility and sublime certitude, it is curious to note that the only common trait that they share with their confreres of the past is that they continue to deliver judgment as teaching authorities, even when, this time unlike their predecessors and under pretext of hypothetical research destined to make everything new, they hand down to us the most questionable products of the scholarly imagination.

3. All this gives us quite a bit to reflect upon. And it seems that the time has come to focus a bit of attention on this existential situation and on those existential conditions of theology in the human subject that have hardly been treated up till now.

As I already pointed out, St. Thomas had no reason to treat this type of questions, which relate to human subjectivity at work rather than to the term taken in itself and to its particularly lofty status—created participation in the knowledge of God and of the blessed—toward which it struggles. He was not ignorant of the existential situation and of the existential conditions to which the *opus theologicum* is subject in us; but his mission was totally centered on the term to be attained. He set out to definitively establish that, in itself and in its particular nature, theology is a science in the full sense of the word and the highest of the sciences, a form of wisdom and the highest form of wisdom of the rational mode. This he established in the *Summa theologiae* with incomparable mastery, basing himself on the principle of the subordination of the sciences (it is to the knowledge that God has of himself and to the knowledge of the blessed that theology is subordinate).

We will take our stand today from the same point of view that St. Thomas held; in other words there is question of theology considered *in itself and in its particular methods*. I repeat what I have already noted earlier: The views I am proposing to you in the present paper are no more than a long but indispensable preface to a very precisely limited subject I would like to treat later on, which concerns not theology in its essence and its proper methods, but rather the existential conditions in which it must be formed and exercised in a concrete way, and as a *habitus* or an intellectual virtue of the mind of the theologian.

ON THEOLOGY ITSELF AND THE METHODS PECULIAR TO IT

General Remarks

1. As I recalled just now, theology taken in itself corresponds fully and entirely to the concept of *scientia*, of knowledge, such as Aristotle understood it. It is a solid knowledge, capable of full certitude—formally natural (rational) or human, but supernatural in its root—in which reason scrutinizes and organizes the various truths of the faith or of the deposit of revelation and seeks to gain some understanding of them. Thus it has as its principles, and as its only principles, those of the faith, the revealed truths which are explicitly offered to our minds and which contain in an implicit and virtual state the whole of the *sacra doctrina*, which it is the business of reason to sort out in an explicitly formulated and ordered manner. And this science, which is wisdom as well, is the most elevated science or wisdom that reason can acquire, since it is subordinated, through the principles of faith (which believes and does not see), to the uncreated knowledge that God has of himself and to the knowledge of the blessed who see God.

This then is the very lofty idea that St. Thomas gives us of theology taken in itself, in the first question of the *Summa theologiae*.

But by what means is this incomparably noble and precious knowledge acquired, by what means does it take form, develop, and become established in us? By means that are as humble as its object is sublime. In fact human reason, which furnishes to theology taken in itself its proper means and to whom it pertains to unfold the divine principles of faith, is found on the lowest rung of the intellectual ladder: It is indeed spirit, but not pure spirit.

Ours is a discursive intellect, which progresses by the halting little steps of observation and reasoning. It composes and divides; it is obliged to parcel out the reality to be known, seizing on separate views and ideas of that reality which it later puts together in its judgments. And it is an abstractive intellect, which is not informed by *species infusae* as is the angelic intellect, but which draws its ideas from the senses, even those which bear on the purely spiritual, which is then known only through analogy.

Such are the means we must make use of in order to attain that science which has for its primary object that infinitely transcendent God Who on His own reveals himself to us, the Uncreated Whose essence is absolutely one and simple, and superior to every created intelligence.

2. To back out because of this would be cowardice and betrayal. To be a theologian demands a great deal of courage—the courage of faith and the courage of our incoercible need for intelligibility; and the courage of hope as well, and of confidence in Divine Providence—for the existential situation in which we find ourselves is far from a comfortable one. What we have before our eyes after so many centuries of history is not a single and unique theology which, while having to advance on its way through the course of centuries and comprising many diverse opinions due to individual points of view on questions of secondary importance, would constitute a body of doctrine and a general system on which all theologians would be in agreement, and thus would correspond, in the midst of the existential spectacle before us, to that theology taken in itself or in its essence of which St. Thomas spoke.

On the contrary we are face to face with a certain number of theological schools opposed to one another and with bodies of doctrine which are decidedly incompatible with one another even though they all invoke in the same way principles of faith which (I am not speaking here of the great schools traditionally involved in this enterprise) neither the Thomists, the Scotists, the Suarezians, nor even the Occamists and others have ever put in doubt. And nothing could be more natural, since it is human reason, with all its weaknesses, its shortsightedness, and its instability, which is busily trying to satisfy our thirst for intelligibility by organizing the truths of the deposit of revelation into a humanly developed body of knowledge. Where does theology taken in itself or in its essence come into the picture? Is it a daydream of our imagination? And is theology—instead of bringing us to a participation in the knowledge God has of Himself, busily occupied, as it is, with the pure Unknowable, concerning which we would hope to satisfy, at any cost whatever, our need for intelligibility by fabricating systems of purely human opinions in contradiction to one another, more or less plausible mirages—is all this theologizing equally vain? This would mean that *revelation* does not help us to *know* anything at all, which is absurd, and that the truths of faith are nothing but fictions or "myths" which the religion of Agnosticism throws out to us as food, to direct our actions. Or is theology considered in itself the ideal limit to which a certain given ensemble of rationally elaborated truths, supernaturally rooted in the truths of the faith, a genuine science and a genuine wisdom, existentially within our grasp, brings us closer and closer in the course of ages?

Here is where the courage of hope and confidence in the Providence of God enter into play. For could we possibly believe that in a work of such capital importance for that humanity which was redeemed by the Blood of the Incarnate Word, and for the nourishment and strengthening of faith in our souls, God left mankind entirely to itself, without His mercy intervening in history to succor and guide us?

Let us hope that the apprentice theologian, who has to make his choice among the diverse theological schools (along with, to take account of today, all the varied relativist gropings which some still call theology), will have enough confidence in the divine Goodness to think that, according to His customary way of acting as the entire history of salvation attests,[4] He has already seen to the birth of a privileged master charged with the elaboration of a body of doctrine which existentially corresponds (not without those lacunae to be filled in later and those good and bad strokes of luck which our order of existence inevitably involves) to theology taken in itself and in its essence, in order to bring us closer and closer to it through the course of ages. It will be up to someone who searches with a boundless love of truth to discover this master, with the help of the Holy Spirit. This constitutes a remarkable act of faith and confidence. I do not believe that anyone who aspires to be a theologian can do without it. This certainly implies more than adhering to particular traditions and to the particular Doctor of some Religious Order or other. And he who searches in this way will not be alone. To guide him in his search he has the preferences of the Church itself, since she has not failed to let us know that among all the doctors she has chosen one as her *Doctor communis*.

3. Let me go back now to those humble means I spoke of a moment ago which are the proper means—according to the measure of human reason—by which theological knowledge takes its form, grows and operates within us. They are good means, reason is made for the true, for what is most lofty as for what is most down-to-earth. But they are also fragile and exposed to error (as we know only too well) and to accidental mistakes. I mean that even when they are put to use in a doctrinal synthesis fully founded on truth, they still entail, for those of us who adhere to this doctrinal synthesis, risks that we must be very careful to avoid.

The great difficulty is the analogy or the superanalogy of the concepts which both the theological virtue of faith and theological knowledge make use of. Whatever the cost, all activity of thought must remain faithful to this analogy thanks to which we are able to lead our humble limited and parceled-out concepts along with our humble discursive processes across the boundaries of the infinite to draw closer in some measure to the infinitely transcendent One Whom we cannot grasp in Himself. It is a question of intellectual vigilance; for the knowledge of divine things is marvelously free in its handling of our poor means. And there is question not of analogy alone—I am referring

---

4   Cf. Jacques Madaule, Introduction to Paul Claudel's, *La Figure d'Israël*, from *Cahiers Paul Claudel*, vol. 7 (Paris: Gallimard, 1968), p. 17: "Every authentic love is a love of predilection, of choice. God began by choosing man, among all His creatures. Then He chose the lineage of Seth, to the exclusion of the lineage of Cain, then that of Noah, then Abraham, then Isaac and not Ishmael, Jacob and not Esau, Judah and Joseph among their brothers and so on . Incessantly we see choice at work: Moses, Joshua, the child Samuel, Saul, David among his brothers, Solomon among his."

above all to what is called analogy of *proper proportionality*[5]—there is also question of metaphor which it uses—and in large measure too, as Sacred Scripture leads us to believe[6]—to raise up our minds to some understanding of the Ineffable. However when there is question of *properly* applying a concept to the divine reality—and this is essentially what theology tries to do—it can make use of no purely metaphorical concept (unlike the Gospels, of course, which do not proceed theologically, but rather by direct revelation, presented by them under the form of parables).

I would like to point out here, in particular, two weaknesses or inconveniences inherent in the means our reason necessarily has to make use of: The one refers to *distinctions of reason* which theological knowledge has to make use of so frequently; the other to *certain concepts* themselves which it must use.

We are forced to distinguish from one another those divine perfections, which nevertheless are all absolutely identical in God's being itself. These are distinctions of reason: as, for example, between God's knowledge and His will, His love and His justice, etc. Nothing is more legitimate. But once these distinctions have been made, it sometimes happens that in a theological exposition we seem to make use of them *as if* there were a question of real distinctions. In other words, and this is unavoidable, it happens that we seem to treat everything connected with God's knowledge, for example, with everything connected with His will as if they were two domains just as fundamentally distinct and heterogeneous as those of knowledge and appetite in us. To tell the truth, this is not all that serious; for on the one hand, we know very well, all the while we are trafficking in this way with our rational discourse, that there is no real distinction among the divine perfections, nor between them and the divine essence; on the other hand, we know that the distinctions of reason that we use in this case are not only distinctions of reason founded *in re*, they are founded in a reality so much more real and rich with life than all created realities, that even *seeming* to treat them as if there were question of real distinctions is just a rather feeble way of paying homage to God's transcendence. Still it is necessary that our thinking activity never let itself be caught in this trap of "seeming." And it should never be forgotten that the One about Whom the theologian speaks is not a mosaic of different perfections glued to the wall of aseity, but the living God in His sovereign and transcendent unity, the same Being, subsisting in itself, in which we are obliged by our human means to consider separately each of the perfections in question, each

---

5   For the theologian the analogy of attribution plays only a secondary role—and this only on condition that it is accompanied by the analogy of proper proportionality.

6   Cf. *Sum. theol.*, Ia, q. 1, a. 9: "*Conveniens est sacrae Scripturae divina et spiritualia sub similitudine corporalium tradere. Deus enim omnibus providet secundum quod competit eorum naturae. Est autem naturale homini ut per sensibilia ad intelligibilia veniat. . . Unde convenienter in sacra Scriptura traduntur nobis spiritualia sub metaphoris corporalium . . .*"

of which is in reality His very *esse* and His very life, and cannot be truly known by us except by our taking account of all His other perfections. This would require, it seems to me, that in the teaching of theology the study of each divine perfection be completed by the consideration of its relation to some other perfection, as by "elevations" in which the mind would be made aware again and again of the infinite transcendence of the Uncreated.

The second weakness or inconvenience inherent in our halting, earthbound means is the one which pertains to certain concepts which theological knowledge is obliged to use. In fact, what it has to use are concepts that are manifestly not only analogical, and superanalogical, like that of being, goodness, intelligence and will, knowledge and love, which we recognize immediately, when applied to creatures, as embracing and circumscribing the object of intelligibility which they signify; but when they are applied to God, they leave *rem significatam ut incomprehensam, et excedentem nominis significationem*[7]. Theological knowledge must also use concepts whose original meaning is univocal *in current usage* but which can be, and are, raised by the theologian to an analogical level.[8] Some examples: "knowledge of simple intelligence and knowledge of vision," "antecedent will" and "consequent will," "absolute power" and "ordained power," "vindicative justice," etc. With such concepts we run the risk of falling unawares and by simple lack of attention into an unavowable univocity, and so having thoughts about God that are unworthy of Him. This particular weakness or inconvenience then is more serious than the first—but not too serious, for if the theologian's manner of expressing himself irritates our ears, he himself (if not someone who is listening to him) is always ready to regain control of the situation and escape from the trap of univocity, even when he is speaking of the vindicative justice of Him Who is Love, and Who has no desire or need to avenge Himself. In truth, I have nothing against the concepts themselves (we cannot get by without them); I dislike the *words* used to designate them.

---

7   *Ibid.*, Ia, q. 13, a. 5: *"Cum aliquod nomen ad perfectionem pertinens de creatura dicitur, significat illam perfectionem ut distinctam secundum rationem definitionis ab aliis: puta cum hoc nomen* sapiens *de homine dicitur, significamus aliquam perfectionem distinctam ab essentia hominis, et a potentia et ab esse ipsius et ab omnibus hujusmodi. Sed cum hoc nomen de Deo dicimus, non intendimus significare aliquid distinctum ab essentia vel potentia vel esse ipsius. Et sic, cum hoc nomen* sapiens *de homine dicitur, quodamodo circumscribit et comprehendit rem significatam: non autem cum dicitur de Deo, sed relinquit rem significatam ut incomprehensam et excedentem nominis significationem . . ."*

8   Because the concept in question, implying necessarily in reality neither limitation nor imperfection, was already in itself an analogical concept according to the analogy of proper proportionality. Each time we attribute to the uncreated Being one of our human concepts, drawn from creatures, it is this analogy of proper proportionality that we bring into play. And it is God who is then the *princeps analogatorum*, the sovereign analogate.

4. It was out of fidelity to and veneration for the Fathers and Doctors of the Church that the vocabulary of theology was set up, preserving, as if they were holy relics, those words which were themselves invented, on the spur of the moment, by our masters and ancestors in *sacra doctrina*. Attentive only to the mental construct necessary to solve some difficulty or to conquer some error, in order to translate this mental construct into words, with a freedom of spirit more to be admired than imitated, they seized upon whatever fell within their reach, even if they were expressions halfway metaphorical and heavily weighed down with obscurity.

I know very well that every science is obliged to have its own technical vocabulary and that it would be simply absurd to ask theologians to speak like everyone else, under pretext of adapting the divine mystery to the mental capacities of the general Christian community and making easy what is difficult by its very nature. The Christian community has need of theology— and what a need!—but of a theology that is science and wisdom, and this requires a mental effort on the part of everyone.

Still this effort must not be made almost impossible by the barbed wire behind which the routine of language takes refuge. It is not good that the loftiest and most universal branch of knowledge, because of a badly developed traditional vocabulary (not in its ideas but in its words), end up enclosed within a set of ramparts reserved for soothsayers who experience (this was certainly not the case for St. Thomas himself) a special kind of haughty delectation, typical of "people in the know" because they can be understood only among themselves. It seems most desirable that, without losing its veneration for the Fathers and holy Doctors (nor even for their language, which it would be sufficient to recall in footnotes), theology decide to elaborate a technical vocabulary whose only care would be to communicate in its strict intelligibility the meaning of the concepts used, all the while respecting the analogical perspectives involved which make them applicable to divine things. It is not worthy of theology itself to make use of the most poorly formed of technical vocabularies. It is also contrary to its role as nursemaid of the faith: For all Christians, in whatever secular tasks their lives may be engaged, ought *to be able*, if in other respects they are sufficiently educated,[9] to acquire, with the necessary time and effort, a genuine theological education. But the popular writing of excellent theologians is not enough for this. The technical vocabulary of theology itself, however technical it may inevitably become, must be a vocabulary more purely modeled on the intelligibility of the concepts to be translated into words than that of all the other sciences.

---

9   What must be said of those who are not sufficiently educated in other respects? They are just as intelligent as the others. It would seem to be the office of the priests charged with their instruction to translate for them in metaphorical language an authentic theological knowledge, and to do this, it seems to me, they must undertake to read with them and to explain the Gospels.

A Serious Problem

5. I tend to tremble a bit before the rather lengthy considerations I am about to begin because they will bring us to an immense problem which the theologians, as far as I can see, have done their best to push aside rather than to examine carefully. Let us start out with a few somewhat more thorough reflections that have to do with the means at theology's disposal with regard to the mystery of God, so unfathomable in its infinite intelligibility, to which the divine intelligence alone is proportionate, that even the highest of the blessed spirits who *see* God through His essence nevertheless remain forever incapable of *understanding* it.

Let me say first of all that when they are applied to God our analogical concepts do not push to their perfection only what they describe in creatures: God's goodness, or his wisdom, are not only goodness and wisdom *such as we know them here below but raised to the infinite* (something which after all would imply a contradiction). They are infinite, surely, but precisely because they are *essentially different* (this is the marvel of analogical intellection: *"non secundum eamdem rationen* hoc nomen *sapiens* de Deo et de homine dicitur")[10] from those perfections here below designated by the *same* concept which designates them in God. God is good; we know this because the goodness of creatures is an imperfect and deficient image or likeness of His goodness, but God is not good like the best of all men is good (this is why it is much better to know God by mode of unknowing than by mode of knowing); His goodness is not like ours, His wisdom and justice are not like ours (the "like" of the analogical concept *exceeds the signification of the latter*, as St. Thomas just told us). *Dolor*, St. Augustine pointed out, is much better than *stupor* and is closer to the divine condition;[11] in other words, impassibility as it appears to us in things here below (like the *stupidus, qui amisit sensus doloris*, or like the Stoic sage) is as far as it could possibly be from the impassibility proper to God. All this means that in reality each of the concepts by which we come to know God's divine perfections opens out, like a river does into the sea, into an infinity of splendors unknown to us. If it were not so, how would it be possible that things so different *for us* as goodness, knowledge, justice, mercy, will, intelligence should *in God* all be identical in the absolute unity of the divine *esse*? What does this mean, if not that we have an accurate view of the divine perfections only if at the same time our intelligence is in some way blinded by them? This blinding dazzlement has nothing to do with natural mysticism. It is proper to metaphysical knowledge and to theological knowledge; and when it seizes

---

10   *Sum. theol.*, Ia, q. 13, a. 5.

11   Here I am condensing into a few words some rather long texts: cf. St. Augustine, *Enarrationes in Psalmos*, Ps. lv, 6, P. L. , XXXVI, c. 650–651 (. . . vicinior est immortalitatis sanitas dolentis, quam stupor non sentientis): *De Civ. Dei*, XIV, ix, 2, 3, 6, P. L., c. 414–415, 416–417.

upon the intelligence to the point of fully absorbing it, it is characteristic of what can be called philosophic or theological contemplation.

Secondly, Aristotle says that in man there are virtues which remain "anonymous" and for which we have no name.[12] With what mysterious and infinitely more profound implication is a remark of this sort true of the Creator! Beyond what we know of Him, as totally true, by reason and faith, there are in Him perfections and splendors that remain *innominatae*, and not only *innominatae* but *innominabiles*, except metaphorically, of which we can have no idea to properly designate them and for which we have no name that is properly applicable to God.

This is what shows the limitations of our metaphysics and our theology, as well as the humility with which the highest accomplishments of the human intellect must fall prostrate before the Uncreated. And this shows as well, it seems to me (here I am touching on a particularly delicate subject) that, in taking account of these unnamed perfections, metaphysics and theology could impose on our minds less limitations due to the desire to attribute to God no more than what we can properly name thanks to concepts drawn from our human experience, and show itself much bolder in broadening the views it proposes to us, I mean in certain cases, rather rare, but in which there seems to be question of things we hold from the Gospels themselves, the teaching of which, even though it is in the form of parables, is beyond theology.

One more parenthetical remark: It is not enough to say that we can name the divine perfections solely by analogy. We must add that since our analogical concepts since they are drawn by abstraction, like all the others, from sensible experience, we cannot properly give a name to a divine perfection without our human experience first furnishing us with an analogical concept and an analogical name which we then apply to this perfection. Suppose that the language of a certain tribe has no name to designate what we call *love*, but to designate the human passion in question makes use solely of a name such as *lustful desire* or *libido*. A metaphysician or a theologian who speaks and thinks in this language would be unable to say, since he has no name for or concept of love, that *love* is one of God's perfections. Nor would he be able to say either that *lustful desire* or *libido* is one of God's perfections, since these particular names are not analogical and apply only to creatures. Because of this there would be an unfortunate irritating lacuna in the metaphysics and the theology of this imaginary tribe (whether it be primitive or ultra-modern) . . .

6. When St. Thomas teaches that God is merciful, he tells us that "mercy is sovereignly attributable to God: *tamen secundum effectum, non secundum pas-*

---

12   Cf. Aristotle, *Nicomachean Ethics*, II, 7, 1107b2 (πολλὰ δ"ἐστὶν ἀνώνυμα); III, 10, 1115b26; IV, 10, 1125b17 and b25; 11, 1125b26; 12, 1126b19; 1127a7 and a12; 13, 1127a14. Cf. St. Thomas, *In Eth. Nic.*, lib. II, lect. 8 (ed. Marietti, 1949, no. 341, p. 96); lib. III, lect. 15 (no. 551, p. 156): lib. IV, lect. 12 (no. 796, p. 219); etc.

sionis affectum," that is, in respect to the effect produced, evidently not in respect to the passion experienced. "For," he adds, "someone is called merciful because he is affected with sadness by the misery of another as if it were his own misery. He tries as best he can then to alleviate the misery of the other; this is the effect of mercy. Being affected by the misery of another then can in no way be said of God, but to dispel that misery (that is to say, whatever is lacking to the other, *quemcumque defectum*), this belongs to Him in the highest degree."[13]

All this is perfectly true, and it is quite clear that sadness and affliction, because by their very nature they imply dependence and imperfection, could not be attributed to God. Yet this leaves the mind unsatisfied, especially when it thinks back to the parable of the lost sheep (Matt. xviii, 10–14) and the parable of the prodigal son (Luke xv, 11–32) or to the command *"Be merciful, therefore, even as your Father is merciful"* (Luke vi, 36), proclaimed in exactly the same terms as *"You therefore are to be perfect, even as your heavenly Father is perfect"* (Matt. v, 48);[14] or when the mind thinks back to the sinful Magdalen kissing the sacred feet, and to the Samaritan woman, and to the woman taken in adultery (was not the human mercy of Jesus the living and fully accurate image showing us not only that what Jesus *does*, the Father *does* as well, but also that what there *is* in Jesus' heart in the human mode—in particular his marvelous compassion—*is* in the Father as well in the divine mode?). *Qui videt me, videt Patrem.* Moreover, if a perfection like love, to which mercy itself is so close, is properly attributed to God, it is not solely because of the effect produced. Love is attributed to God not solely because He is the cause of good in all things that exist, *creans et infundens bonum in rebus.* Love is a perfection of God, not only according to what He *does*, but also according to what He *is*. Indeed God is love itself.

Is it not the same in the case of mercy? God is Mercy[15] just as He is Love,

---

13   *Sum. theol.*, Ia, q. 21, a. 3: *"Misericordia est Deo maxime attribuenda: tamen secundum effectum, non secundum passionis affectum. Ad cujus evidentiam, considerandum est quod misericors dicitur aliquis quasi habens* miserum cor: *scilicet afficitur ex miseria alterius per tristitiam, ac si esset ejus propria miseria. Et ex hoc sequitur quod operetur ad depellendam miseriam alterius, sicut miseriam propriam: et hic est misericordiae effectus. Tristari ergo de miseria alterius non competit Deo: sed repellere miseriam alterius, hoc maxime ei competit, ut per miseriam quemcumque defectum intelligamus."*

14   Perfection is attributed to the Father not *secundum effectum*, but according to the intrinsic quality so designated. And when Zachary said: *"per viscera misericordiae Dei nostri"* (Luke i, 78), was he thinking of the mercy of God only *secundum effectum*?

15   This is just as true for Moslems as it is for Christians. Indeed to such a degree that for Islam Mercy designates God in His very own mystery. "The Merciful One" (*al-Rahman*), just like "Truth" (*al-Haqq*) is "a proper name for God." These two names "it could be said are synonyms for *Allâh*" (Louis Gardet, *L'Islam* (Paris: Desclée de Brouwer, 1967), pp. 59–60).

and precisely because He is Love. Should it not then be said of mercy that it is found in God, not according to what it *does*, but according to what it *is*, but in this case in a state of perfection *for which there is no name*: a glory or splendor without a name, implying no imperfection whatever, as distinguished from what we call suffering or saddness, and of which we have no idea at all, no concept, no name which might be properly applied to God. Indeed it is solely by reason of the effect it produces that in our mental baggage there is a concept and a name for mercy properly applicable to God, but this does not mean that we should be satisfied here and push on no further. Beyond the concepts by which we have a proper knowledge of God's perfections, the infinity of these perfections still remains *something unnamed and unnamable*, something properly unknowable by any single concept of ours. But in them there must exist that unnamed splendor to which what we call mercy in ourselves corresponds, not only according to its effect but according to its very essence. What must be said then, if not that there is question here of a perfection which cannot be properly represented by any of our concepts? This perfection, which in us is called mercy, exists, according to its essential element, in Him Who made us and loves us (that *passionis affectus* so clearly indicated by the biblical expression *viscera miseracordiae*). In us, however, mercy is but a reflection or a participation, sealed up in the darkness of our imperfection even as regards its very notion, which leaves us blind when we try to discern, except metaphorically, what its exemplar is like in God.

7. Here we find ourselves face to face with that unavoidable and formidable enigma upon which a great many minds who are dear to me have meditated, the enigma of that suffering which at one and the same time is the sign of our misery (and so unattributable to God) and the sign of an incomparably fecund and precious nobility[16] (and of which it seems impossible not to seek some

---

16   "*Je sais que la douleur est la noblesse unique*
          Où ne mordront jamais la terre et les enfers,"—
          (I know that suffering is the single nobility
          In which earth and hell will never sink their teeth)
          said Baudelaire. And Léon Bloy wrote: "I would never come to the end if I wanted to describe the marvelous effects of Suffering on the human faculties and on the human heart. It is creation's handmaid." "A heart without affliction is like a world without revelation, it sees God only by the feeble glow of twilight. Our hearts are filled with angels when they are filled with affliction."
          In *We Have Been Friends Together*, translated by Julie Kernan from the French *Les Grandes Amitiés* (New York, London, Toronto: Longmans, Green and Co., 1942), pp. 189–190, Raïssa wrote: "This question of suffering in Beatitude, and of suffering in God Himself, had already been raised by Bloy in *Le Salut par les Juifs*. This conjunction of suffering and Beatitude is allowed neither by theology nor by Aristotle. Beatitude means absolute fullness, and suffering is the cry of that which is wounded. But our God is a crucified God: the Beatitude of which He cannot be deprived did not prevent Him from fearing or mourning, or from

mysterious exemplar in God). All I dare to say on this subject is that suffering, a *privation of a good due* to our nature, can be described by the metaphysician as *what cannot be accepted*; and that what cannot be accepted in God—the sin of those beings He has created—God somehow does accept in His own way. By respecting with absolute magnanimity the free will of His creatures and their initiatives in nothingness,[17] and by permitting sin in view of a superior good which will over-compensate for it, it is to this this aspect of what *cannot be accepted in God*, that God does give his consent, *not in order to be subjected to it* (how could He be subjected to anything at all), *but rather to take victorious possession of it*. I will try to explain myself on this point in a moment. And by permitting men, the creatures of His hands, exposed in this life to the number-less proliferations of their misery (and their sins), all the fruit of the first sin, and by permitting the suffering of the innocent, again all this is something that is unacceptable in God, but which, for a higher end, God does accept in His own way. His incarnate Son could not look upon the sick without rushing to cure them. His heart found this particular misery of His creatures intolerable.

Let us try first of all to form some idea of the divine transcendence that might not be too unworthy of it. God's Beatitude is His very being; it would be the very same beatitude even if no created being had ever been made. But even though God decided from all eternity to make out of nothing beings other than Himself (so that there are more beings—in the plural—but not more *being*,

---

sweating blood in the unimaginable Agony, or from passing through the throes of death on the Cross, or from feeling abandoned. 'Every imaginable violation of what one is accustomed to call Reason can be accepted from a suffering God,' says Léon Bloy in *Le Salut*.

"For a created being, to be capable of suffering is a real perfection; it is the lot of life and of the spirit, it is the greatness of man; and 'since we are taught that we were created in the likeness of God, is it then so difficult to suppose, simply, that in the impenetrable Essence there must be something which corresponds to ourselves, *without sin*, and that the heart-rending epitome of human woes is but the dark reflection of the inexpressible conflagrations of the Light?'

"Because suffering implies in its very idea some imperfection, it cannot be ascribed to the 'impenetrable Essence.' But in some form which no human name can name, is it not needful that there be found in that Essence the whole element of the mysterious perfection which pertains to the suffering of the creature?

"These 'inexpressible conflagrations of the Light,' this kind of glory of suffer-ing, perhaps it is to this that correspond on earth the suffering of the innocent, the tears of children, certain excesses of humiliation and misery which it is almost impossible for the heart to accept without being scandalized, and which, when the face of this enigmatic world has passed away, will appear at the summit of the Beatitudes.

"I seek my excuse for what is obscure in these reflections by once more taking refuge in the words of my godfather and in saying with him: 'When one speaks lovingly of God, all human words are like blinded lions seeking a spring in the desert.'"

17   Cf. my book *God and the Permission of Evil* (Milwaukee, Wis.: Bruce, 1966).

in the singular, and the relation of creatures to God is in them, not in Him),[18] there is nothing to prevent God's "receiving" from them (and I am speaking metaphorically and according to our way of seeing) a certain joy, the pleasure with which He sees the goodness he has put in them,[19] the joy of that love by which so many creatures endowed with an immortal soul give themselves to Him, and of all their good actions, and the joy of our fidelity, and the even greater joy there is in heaven over our repentence,[20] joys which according to our way of seeing things might appear to be "above and beyond" what might be expected by nature but which in reality are in no way "above and beyond" God's beatitude and add absolutely nothing to it. This is so because, as Denis the Areopagite says, *"in uno, existentia omnia praehabet,"*[21] and because they were *already comprised and contained* in the absolutely one and supereminent infinity of His Transcendent Joy, to which nothing can be added.

Let us go back now to our consideration of evil. Each time that a creature sins (and in each case the creature takes the first initiative, the initiative of nothingness), God is deprived of a joy ("above and beyond" according to our way of looking at things) which was due to Him by another and which that other does not give Him, and something inadmissible to God is produced in the world. But even before triumphing over what is inadmissible by a greater good which will overcompensate for it later on, God Himself, far from being subject to it, raises it above everything by His consent: In accepting such a privation (which in no way affects His being but only the creature's relation to Him), He takes it in hand and raises it up like a trophy, attesting to the divinely pure grandeur of His victorious Acceptance[22] (ours is never such except at the cost of some defeat); and this is something that adds absolutely nothing to the intrinsic perfection and glory of the divine *Esse*, and is eternally

---

18   *Sum. theol.*, Ia, q. 13, a. 7. *"Cum igitur Deus sit extra totum ordinem creaturae, et omnes creaturae ordinentur ad ipsum, et non e converso, manifestum est quod creaturae realiter referuntur ad ipsum Deum; sed in Deo non est aliqua realis relatio ejus ad creaturas, sed secundum rationem tantum, inquantum creaturae referuntur ad ipsum."*

19   "And God saw that it was good," Gen. i, 10, 12, 18, 21, 25. "God saw that all he had made was good," Gen. i, 31.

20   *"Gaudium erit in coelo,"* Luke xv, 7; *". . . gaudet super eam,"* Matt. xviii, 13.

21   Denis, *De div. nom.*, V, 9—cited by St. Thomas, *Sum. theol.*, I, q. 4, a. 2.

22   This Acceptance is perfectly free and bears on things which God *permits*: first and foremost on the *nihilation* by which free creatures can evade God's "shatter-able motions." (Whether or not these shatterable motions are effectively shat-tered depends on the creature as nihilating first cause; and the permission for these nihilations—that is, *if* the free will withdraws from the divine motion by "making nothingness"—is implied in the very decision to create free beings.) And if the creature has freely caused a nihilation, the divine Acceptance carries over as well to any sinful acts due to this nihilation, which are the object of a permission of Divine Providence, insofar as the created agent remains engaged in the universal dynamism of being and process.

precontained in Its essential and supereminent infinity. For this is an integral part of a mysterious divine perfection which, even though it has reference to the privation of what is due to God by creatures existing at some particular point in time, is infinitely beyond the reach of these creatures. In fact, the creature, by his free nihilation, is indeed the cause of the privation in question in whatever concerns itself but in no way in what concerns some effect that might be produced on God by that creature. The only effect produced is to make the creature itself, in his relation to God, which is real only from his side, responsible for some privation or other of what is due to God. And such privations are presupposed from all eternity by that mysterious divine perfection I am speaking about. This divine perfection is eternally present in God and, by the infinite transcendence of the Divine Being, is the unnamed exemplar, incapable of being designated by any of our concepts, toward which like blind men we raise our eyes, and which corresponds in uncreated glory to what suffering is in us.

8. In the final analysis, does not the sin of the beings He has created constitute *God's evil*? Does not sin itself which stretches out over the long history of the world, and each of the individual sins committed by each one of us, "do something" to God Himself? In the act of contrition as it was recited in my time (I do not know what they say today), we said: "O my God, I am heartily sorry for having offended you because you are infinitely good and lovable and because sin is displeasing to you." This word *displeasing* is an ambiguous and really hypocritical word. A thing which displeases me can simply mean something that does not give me pleasure and leaves me completely indifferent. And it could mean as well something that displeases me in a *very positive way* and which consequently deeply affects me and wounds me in some way. And this second meaning is certainly present in the formula of the prayer (metaphorically, of course, but of capital importance); it is there, but carefully veiled by the first meaning.

In the formula of the act of contrition I think we would do much better if we had recourse to an expression that is frankly metaphorical, by saying for example "because sin cuts to the very heart of your love," and in the Our Father, a less defective translation perhaps would be "forgive us our betrayals as we forgive those who have done us wrong."

What sin "does" to God is something which reaches God in the deepest way, not by making Him subject to some effect brought about by the creature but by making the creature, in its relation to God, pass over to the side of the unnamed perfection, the eternal exemplar in Him of what suffering is in us, which I have just tried to explain.

"The entire humanity of Christ," wrote Raïssa, "is the mystery of Love. Jesus crucified is the image of the Father offended by sin; crowned with thorns by disdain for His will. . . . The pierced feet of Jesus signify that the offended heavenly Father was kept from running to our aid—Jesus whose pierced heart signifies that what we have offended was Love itself."[23] In speaking this way of the offended Heavenly Father, Raïssa did not have in mind some irreverent gesture made to the King as he passed in procession. She was thinking of a betrayal of love which "cuts to the very heart" (I am speaking metaphorically) of subsistant Love—in other words a betrayal by which (without producing any effect in Him) we make ourselves responsible for the privations of what we owe Him, privations that have been presupposed from all eternity by the eternal exemplar in Him, incapable of any designation by our concepts or our words, of what suffering is in us.

If we want to push logic to the limit (and attain some idea, necessarily disconcerting, but truer than what we are generally satisfied with, of the divine transcendence), then we must say that this mysterious perfection which in God is the unnamed exemplar of suffering in us, *constitutes an integral part of the divine beatitude*—perfect peace at the same time infinitely exultant beyond what is humanly conceivable, burning in its flames what is apparently irreconcilable for us. This peace exults at one and the same time in the eternal splendors of glorious Possession, for which (at least for many of which) we have names that properly designate them, and the eternal splendor of the glorious Acceptance as well, for which we have no name to designate it properly. This glorious Acceptance was made known to us in that image *par excellence*, the image of the flesh and blood of the Son of God dying on the cross—and then rising again (but He does keep for all eternity His five wounds which are glorious forever. And one day we are reminded of this Acceptance, as if by a living and holy "metaphor," by the glorious tears of Mary when she came to complain and to weap before two little shepherds chosen from among the poorest and least educated of the children of men. "From the time I have been suffering for all of you," she said at La Salette.

Is it necessary to add (it is so very evident) that the divine beatitude is unchangeable because the decision to create has been taken from all eternity and because the entire succession of time is completely encompassed within the divine Instant of eternity? God and His freedom, and all His free choices, and all His free permissions, *are* within that Instant which endures forever and to that Instant the final day of the world is as eternally present as the first.[24]

---

23   *Journal de Raïssa*, p. 35 (beginning of the entry for October 1916). And so the paradox which we are considering at this moment (namely, that among the perfections of the infinitely happy God must be counted the eternal exemplar in Him of all human suffering) concerns the uncreated paradigm which corresponds in some ineffable way, in God Himself, to those paradoxes which are the warp and woof of Jesus' life—the Son of God dying on the cross of infamy, His humiliations, His defeats, His anguish, His agony in the Garden of Gethsemane along with His authority and His beatitude in the heaven of his soul . . . "Philip, he who sees me sees also the Father" (cf. John xiv, 9). Here we are given a glimpse of one of the most profound secrets of the God's way of acting.

24   This immutable conjunction in God of the *de jure* (His being, His perfections, His

I do not want to get involved in overly technical explanations. Let me simply note that beyond the manifestly analogical concepts (of an analogy of proper proportionality), such as being, truth, goodness, and other concepts whose original meaning is univocal in current usage but which can be and are raised by the theologian to an analogical meaning[25] according to the analogy of proper proportionality,[26] there are concepts whose object not only implies

---

beatitude . . .) and of the *de facto* (the decision to create which was freely taken by Him from all eternity) is an immense and adorable mystery. Whether or not there are things other than He, the *very act* of free will deciding on the alternative is *de jure* and of necessity absolutely one with the divine essence. It is necessary that God exercise His freedom and just as necessary as His being. This is an integral part of Pure Act. But the *two terms* between which the choice is made, *one of which, as a matter of fact, has been decided from all eternity, the other not*, are on the one hand merely pure effect (that there be other things than He) and on the other hand no more than a pure absence of effect (that there not be other things than He). Neither of these two terms is necessary to the divine Goodness or the divine Being (which *"continet in se omnem perfectionem essendi," Sum. theol.*, Ia, q. 19, a. 4). Nor do they affect in absolutely any way God's being or His act of free will (which is not "specified" by them).

If there had been no other creatures, they could not have been, here below, the origin of those joys which their love and their merits might have brought to God (without exercising any causality in His regard). But like every possible joy, these particular joys are eternally precontained in God's infinite beatitude.

What must be said about the eternal perfection that I called the splendor of the victorious Acceptation as an integral part of the divine beatitude? If there had been no creatures, the privations of what is due to God for which the initiatives of nothingness of the created freedom would have been responsible here below (without exercising the slightest causality in His regard) would not have existed either. But the absence of a victorious acceptation taken *as presupposing existing creatures* and their initiatives of nothingness would itself have been a privation which God would have taken possession of as conqueror and which would have been presupposed from all eternity by the splendor of the victorious acceptation.

And, in an entirely different sense, the fact of not creating, in other words, of abstaining from producing a good which would in absolutely no way increase the Good, but which is one more good in existence, would have been for God—certainly not something incapable of being accepted nor a privation of absolutely anything necessary to His goodness, His being, and His beatitude—but rather a kind of renunciation of something which *befits* His goodness (*"condecet divinam bonitatem etiam alia ipsam participare"*;, Ia, q. 19, a. 2). And the victorious Acceptation of this kind of renouncement would have been, in this regard, the eternal, unnamed exemplar in Him, not of what is pain or suffering in us but of what can be the loftiest and noblest melancholy in a human being. (We know very well that a soul cannot possess true grandeur unless it is accompanied by such melancholy. . .)

25   Cf. above, p. 250.

26   This is so, as I have already noted above, because in these concepts univocally used in current language reflection discovers the *analogy of proper proportionality on which in reality they depend of themselves*, which, in such cases, is often joined

limitation and imperfection in its very notion, but which, in the reality to which they refer as it is experienced by us, designate no perfection *emerging* above the sensible. These latter concepts are univocal by their very nature and cannot be said of God except metaphorically ("God is my rock"). And finally there are concepts whose object also implies limitation and imperfection in its very notion and so cannot be said of God except metaphorically, but which in the reality to which it refers as we experience it, does designate a perfection *emerging* above the sensible, as is the case with suffering in the human person. Suffering is an evil and an imperfection, but by the fact that the spirit approves of it and consents to it and seizes upon it, it is incomparably noble as well.

Misery and nobility, evil suffered and grandeur of soul, heartbreak and illumination are all there together in one of those lived contradictions and in one of those indissolubly joined conflicts with which our psychology is not very content. And nobility of soul *emerges* to higher levels, all the while remaining bound to the misery that it drags with it toward the heights of the human spirit. A person who has not been taught by suffering knows nothing and does not amount to much, being as he is neither a true child nor an adult in the fullness of his truth.

From this we can understand that the concept and the word *suffering* can be used only metaphorically with regard to God and that nevertheless we ought to seek in an *unnamed* divine perfection the eternal exemplar of what in us is suffering with all its noble dignity. This supposes on the part of the spirit with regard to suffering (by reason of its nobility) a kind of double transfer: on the one hand, to an analogy of proper proportionality which we cannot isolate because we have no concept or word to bear or make clear its meaning and, on the other hand, to the divine Being Himself, in an eternal perfection which no human concept or name can properly signify.

From an entirely different perspective, this time historical, we can point out that it is Christ Who revealed to our consciousness this nobility of suffering. Before Him men were capable of seeing in suffering no more that the torments it imposed on them; it was nothing but an evil for them. Buddhism took for its object to deliver us from it by killing all desire. Stoicism pretended to triumph over suffering in a wisdom that annihilated it. As Raïssa wrote: "We do not role ourselves up 'into a ball' as Marcus Aurelius advised stoics to do, to offer to suffering the smallest possible target. Christians attach themselves to the Cross and expose themselves to any blows whatever."[27] It is only in a

---

to an analogy of attribution (which is only virtual, according to the remark of John of St. Thomas recalled in *The Degrees of Knowledge*, Appendix II). The most eminent example is that of the concepts of Father and of Paternity ("*Flecto genua mea ad Patrem Domini nostri Jesu Christi ex quo omnis paternitas in ceolo et in terra nominatur*," Eph. iii, 14) applied to the First Person of the Blessed Trinity. Cf. *Sum. theol.*, Ia, q. 27, a. 2 and q. 28, a. 4.

27   *Raïssa's Journal*, p. 188 (August 30, 1925).

Christian context, and by recalling the sufferings of the Son of God, that human beings—and the poets before the theologians—have come to understand little by little "what mysterious perfection there is in the suffering of creatures."[28]

9. If I spoke to you as I did, however clumsily it may have been, of a problem I would have preferred to keep to myself in order to mull it over and rework it again and again, it is because I think it bears on the very essence of Christianity.

And it is also because I think that this problem, with all its thorns, is at the darkest depths of the immense disorder from which the world is suffering today.

It is quite true that this disorder is the result of cultural and sociological conditions—the completely "scientific" and "technocratic" civilization in which we have been immersed. But there is question here, and much more profoundly so, of a kind of spiritual despair which troubles the deepest recesses of men's souls and turns them away from God, sometimes enraging them against Him. The pitiless face of reality and of the problem of evil has been uncovered to the modern world much more broadly than in past centuries. It is certainly a form of progress but one that is dearly paid for. In the face of this evil whose vision obsesses us everywhere, what can we make of the idea of an infinitely good God?

I know many Christians who prefer not to think about it and who, by a kind of dichotomy due to complete ignorance of theology and to the absurdities of a crippled "cryptogamic" rationalization, on the one hand have in mind a vague notion (at least this is what they were told) that God is Love and, on the other hand, think of Him, not as of a Father whose children, in that incoercible freedom which is their unheard of privilege, defy His will at every instant—whence the divine overcompensations—but who think of Him rather as Emperor of this world, a Playwright-Potentate who, by granting licenses to fail which *precede* our actual failings and by which He abandons the creature to itself, would Himself be the primary author of all the sins of the world and of all its misery and who would take pleasure in the dramatic presentation, under His own stage directions, of the long successive scenes of the human story in which evil flourishes in abominable abundance.

It is this absurd and intolerable idea of a Playwright-Potentate, insensitive in His heaven to the evil and suffering of the actors to whom He assigns the different roles in His theatrical production,[29] which is hidden at the bottom of the revolt against God by the great mass of non-Christians. I think that a metaphysical psychoanalysis of the modern world would uncover here the sickness which is eating away at their subconscious. If people knew (I am

---

28   *We Have Been Friends Together*, p. 190.

29   Plato (*Laws*, XII, 803b) thought that men are playthings in the hands of the divinity. He, at least, was a pagan, and this divinity for him was no more than the sacred power of Fate.

going to speak in metaphorical terms, but at the same time making reference, so I can use them, to the more elaborated points of view I just submitted to you), if people knew that God "suffers" with us and much more than we do from the evil that ravages the world, many things would certainly change, and many souls would be liberated. Then perhaps they would no longer find closed and devoid of meaning for them the words which tell them that because of His pity, in which we find so precious, even if it can be named only metaphorically, that *com-passion* by which He takes us to His heart and there makes our misery His own, He sent His Son, *factus homo*, to suffer and die for us—and that if in the world evil is found in abominable abundance, putting off from day to day the accomplishment of God's designs, the grace of Christ and its working in the depths of human hearts is indescribably more abundant, overcompensating for all this easily discernible evil with a view to those designs which God makes all the more lofty and beautiful, and in which the Christian believes because he believes in what is invisible—and that the passion of Jesus continues to the end of the world, in those friends of His whom He calls to cooperate in the work of redemption to "to fill up," as St. Paul says (Col. i, 24), "what is lacking in His sufferings" (with regard to their applications, not their merits).

"By declaring us members of Jesus Christ," wrote Léon Bloy, "the Holy Spirit clothed us with the dignity of redeemers, and when we refuse to suffer we are simoniacs in the true sense of the word and prevaricators. We are made for that, and for that alone" (and at the very same time for eternal life as well) . . . "The saints sought out the Passion of Christ. They believed the word of their Master when He said that he shows the greatest love who lays down his life for his friends."

And we who are not saints (yet we are called to become so), we can understand these things and do as best we can, advancing little by little, like cripples, along the same road, and counting on God's pity. To the problem of evil taken in all its dimensions, there is only one answer, the answer of faith in its integrity. And at the heart of our faith is the certitude that God, anyway Jesus said so, has for us the *feelings of a Father*.

Has it been left to an aged philosopher, good at most for trying to open a few doors, to dare in your presence to face up to—in an effort to show that we must not be leave it to the poets but must work to integrate it into theology—the great mystery of what, in an infinitely perfect and infinitely happy God, corresponds to what suffering is in us, not with regard to the frightening mark of imperfection it implies, but with regard to the incomparable grandeur that it also reveals? It seems to me that this great mystery opens up a singularly vast domain, over which the tyranny of words has too long cast its interdict, to theologians, who alone are properly armed to treat it by the strict methods of reason planted in the faith. If among them there are any in whom we place our trust who wish to enlarge their horizons, God grant that they put themselves to the task.

*   *   *   *   *   *   *   *   *   *

10. To bring to an end these lengthy reflections on theology as such and its proper methods, I would like to remind you of two texts of St. Thomas.

In the *Prima Pars* of the *Summa theologiae*, in which he teaches that the *sacra doctrina*, which is also called *theologia*,[30] is a science,[31] and the worthiest of all sciences,[32] and that it is wisdom *par excellence*,[33] he tells us that it is like a kind of stamp of divine knowledge within us, *"velut quaedam impressio divinae scientiae, quae est una et simplex ominum."*[34] Is there a more magnificent characterization of theology?

Now let us take the *Prima Secundae*, where he asks whether or not wisdom is the greatest of the intellectual virtues and then replies in the affirmative.[35] This article refers to wisdom in general, and above all, certainly, to that wisdom of a purely natural order which is metaphysics, but it is concerned also with a higher form of wisdom (otherwise why, in the *ad primam*, would St. Thomas refer, apropos of the wisdom he is talking about, to the words of St. Paul: *"spiritualis judicat omnia"*?). So the article in question does concern theology. And in the *ad secundam* St. Thomas tells us that man cannot perfectly achieve that wisdom *"ad quam pertinet Dei cognitio,"* in such a way that he might come into possession of something that is proper to God alone, as Aristotle says in the First Book of the *Metaphysics*. "Nevertheless" this knowledge which is only loaned to us, "this *very modest* understanding of God that can be acquired by wisdom, is preferable to any other knowledge." *"Illa modica cognitio"*—is there a more humble characterization of theology?

I remember my godfather Léon Bloy. "When we speak lovingly of God," he said, [and could we not say as well: When we try to speak exactly of God], all human words are like blind lions who were seeking a spring in the desert . . ."

Supreme elevation as to its object, extreme humility as to the means put at the disposal of human reason, this is the general theme of the epistemological reflections which, if I had the time and the strength, would follow upon this article.

POSTSCRIPT[36]

I have been granted neither the time nor the strength I had hoped for. Still I would like to propose here in as brief a postscript as possible (Alas! it will

---

30   St. Thomas, *Sum. theol.*, Ia, q. 1, a. 7.

31   *Ibid.*, a. 2.

32   *Ibid.*, a. 5.

33   *Ibid.*, a. 6.

34   *Ibid.*, a. 3, ad 2m.

35   *Sum. theol.*, Ia-IIae, q. 66, a. 5.

36   This postscript was written in 1972.

probably be much too long) three remarks to which I attach particular importance.

First of all, referring to chapter XIV ("No Knowledge without Intuitivity"), I would point out that the highest knowledge of the natural order, theological knowledge, evidently cannot have the intuition of its proper object, since this is the divine mystery itself. It follows from this that, in order to be properly constituted, theology needs the services of its *ancilla*, philosophy, and above all of metaphysics, which does have the intellectual intuition of its object—being—and that it too has need of higher illuminations which are those of the gift of Wisdom and of loving contemplation. It asks to be joined to these two kinds of knowledge, the one inferior by nature, and the other superior by nature, to theology itself which then finds itself caught between two other wisdoms.

On the other hand, St. Thomas teaches (*Sum. theol.*, Ia, q. 1, a. 8, ad 2m) "*quod argumentari ex auctoritate est maxime proprium hujus doctrinae.*" It is essential to theological argumentation to procede *ex auctoritate*, or to rely, in order to go forward, on the authority of what has already been declared, above all by the infallible word of God Himself ("divine revelation" and the "canonical Scriptures") but also, even though this authority is assuredly far less solid, and subject to discussion, by the Doctors of the Church—and even by the philosophers, "*ubi per rationem naturalem veritatem cognoscere potuerunt.*" It is by rational reflection on what God has said, and on what has been said by the Fathers and the great Doctors, trustees, and witnesses of the Christian tradition—indeed even by the philosophers themselves when they have spoken wisely—that theology fulfills its office, shedding light for us on the truths of the faith.

Does this mean that another sort of intuitivity, in no way implying intuition of the object of this knowledge, but which would enter into play apropos of this knowledge, and which remains only a natural quality of the thinking subject, would not exist among the theologians? *Absit*! However, in order to avoid any risk of confusion, I prefer to designate this other kind of intuitivity by the word *objectality*. It is useless for the theologian to argue *ex auctoritate*, and by referring to what was said before his time by the great Doctors; between him and the object (the particular question he is considering) a unique and personal relation is inevitably established. He has to know and to state *what he himself thinks* from his own individual perspective. If he does not remain a pure notionalist (a misfortune which is not very rare), the intuitivity as a psychic quality with which he is endowed by nature plays a capital role in such a case. In the sense I have just indicated every great theologian is a great intuitive. The objectality I am talking about is not required of itself by the knowledge (*ex auctoritate*) which is his. This objectality then must be regarded as something deeply desirable but "secondary" in theological elaboration.

On the contrary (and even when the object considered is too high for its intuition to be possible here below), this objectality is of "primary" importance for the philosopher and the metaphysician, for it is his knowledge itself which demands it. Metaphysics is in no way whatever a knowledge *ex auctoritate*. *The metaphysician finds himself face to face with the object he seeks to seize at his own risk and peril. He and his object must fight it out alone in single combat.*

Second remark. It will bear first of all on the word *Christian philosophy* which I mention with such lack of tenderness in Chapter XVII ("Along Unbeaten Pathways"). Such an expression runs the risk of being completely misunderstood, as if the philosophy in question were more or less reined in by confessional proprieties. The reality is quite different. Given the naturally high estate proper to philosophical problems and at the same time the limitations of human intelligence, as well as the wounds of nature which affect the human mind itself, we should not be surprised that even among the greatest minds philosophy *considered simply as such* might very well become a stumbling block. All the same we must feel sorry for those who have never felt the flame burn brighter in them on reading Plato or Plotinus. It is fashionable today to talk down "Hellenistic thought." I am convinced that it has played a providential role and that, just as in the realm of faith and salvation God gave a unique supernatural mission to the people of Israel, in the same way He gave to Greece a unique natural mission, which we have the duty to recognize. And when, thanks to the efforts of Albert the Great and of St. Thomas (and these two men alone were able to carry it off), Aristotle entered into the service of theology, in the midst of astonishingly contrary circumstances and at the cost of how many battles, an immensely important turning point in history was passed which saved the Christian intelligence and its entire future.

Whether there is question of a philosopher or of any man of faith, that faith impregnates the Christian intelligence completely. It deputizes philosophical reason to the single search for Truth, delivering it from its subjection to the world and from any form of servility to the fashions of the times. This is why what we call "Christian philosophy" is a philosophy set free, and ought to be called philosophy *understood fully* as such. This is no guarantee of course against any possibility of error, but it does permit this philosophy to move forward indefinitely and to maintain the integrity of the philosophical undertaking as it advances from century to century, even if, as in present times, it is encumbered with the frivolous and vainglorious declarations (but there is always some truth in them) of philosophical superstars to the enthusiastic delight of journalists.

St. Thomas said that when a philosopher begins to age he should turn to God. How could the work he was engaged in to the very end better conform to this wise exhortation than by the application of his philosophical reflection to the more lofty questions treated by that knowledge superior to his own which is called theology? This is what happened to me when I entered into old age, and this is what explains the content of this present volume.

That a philosopher, all the while remaining more than ever a philosopher and more than ever faithful to the perspective and the "objectality" proper to philosophy, should take on as the object of his reflection matters which of themselves depend on the science of theology, such an undertaking seems at first sight quite paradoxical and of such a kind as to scandalize both his philosophical and theological friends.

Nevertheless this undertaking is completely normal. It is in such a case, as a matter of fact, that what was, over a long period of time, and not without some arrogance, considered as the *ancilla theologiae*, best fulfills its true office with regard to theology, which is that of a *research worker*. For, since his perspective can in absolutely no way be considered a knowledge *ex auctoritate*, the philosopher in question, once he has set himself before the object that interests him (some particular theological thesis or problem), and finds himself all alone with that object, he can do no other than try to understand it as best he can. And so he finds himself actually freer than the theologian to perceive certain aspects about which nothing was said by the masters and doctors who followed upon one another since apostolic times[37] and to whose pronouncements theological knowledge must by its very essence make reference, as he argues in the faith his points with regard to those pronouncements, without neglecting to submit his arguments when necessary to interpretation and criticism.

Two points of evident importance are presupposed here. First, just as when he concentrates his reflection on questions brought up by forms of knowledge which are inferior to his own (new physics, biology, paleontology, etc.), the philosopher has the strict duty to educate himself ahead of time with the help of scientific scholars, in the same way and for even greater reason, he has the strict duty to educate himself as best he can through the teachings of theology, a wisdom superior to his own. Secondly, if he ever imagined that in expressing himself, from his particular point of view, on matters theological, he establishes on his own some theological thesis or other, the philosopher in question would be a fool and would fall into the worst kind of aberration. It is his ideas, his own paltry ideas, that he advances. It is the theologian's job to judge their validity or invalidity. The work of the *research worker* is evidently subject to the control of theology, with regard to which, by the very nature of things, a happy and beneficent docility is asked of him.

In order to educate himself as I just said through the teachings of the theologians, the philosopher in question needs to have recourse to only the

---

37   An example: In a book written in 1953 on *Creative Intuition in Art and Poetry*, I had to shed some light, apropos of poetry, on the concept of the "spiritual supraconscious," and to insist on its importance. Many years later (in 1967 in a book on *La Grâce et l'Humanité de Jésus*) I used the same concept with regard to a theological question concerning the human soul of the Incarnate Word. This was a new notion; and I had the consolation of seeing it accepted by the eminent exegete André Feuillet.

best among them. The Church herself had no fear of pointing to one of them as her *Doctor communis*. The philosopher anxious to instruct himself properly need feel no inclination to read Suarez, Scotus, or Occam. And when he reads the Fathers of the Church, it is in order to satisfy an entirely personal desire to find his joy in the light that emanates from them. It is not in the least way to construct with their help a *sacra doctrina*. In order to receive the instruction he needs in theological matters, he has need of no more than the Common Doctor of the Church and of the precious series—unbroken as it is—of his commentators (who do not hesitate to attack one another on frequent occasions—an excellent sign of the fact that Thomist thought is the freest of them all).

*   *   *   *   *   *   *   *   *   *

But it is not solely in order to fulfill as best he can his function as *research worker* in the service of theology that the Christian philosopher owes it to himself to take on from his own perspective and in his own "objectality" questions which concern theology. There is much more to this matter. That this should take place during the declining years of a poor old drop-out is no more than accidental. What is essential is that this is required by philosophy itself when it is free—in other words by philosophy considered fully as such—from the moment that it becomes conscious as quickly as possible of its true nature and of the journey it has to undertake. For it is a form of *wisdom*, and focuses on being itself, something that requires it to pass beyond the limits of its formal object, in order to include within its domain points to be scrutinized that extend as far as being itself. And, in order to find its completion as it should, philosophy is required to apply itself (tentatively) to the examination of those points according to its own methods, keeping always in mind that they derive from a higher form of knowledge. Here there is question of exigencies implied by the very nature of a philosophy that wishes to be truly and fully itself, in a mind in which reason has been raised up by faith. From the very outset, it is concerned to one degree or another, in one manner or another, with matters which belong at the same time to both philosophy and theology.

So the undertaking we speak of is paradoxical only in appearance. With an untrammeled extremism and proceeding on its own to the very end along the roads by which philosophical knowledge in its fullness as such makes its journey, it shows in all its simplicity just what this knowledge is. It is of itself, and considered as philosophy—and even considered as philosophy set free by faith, something that is perfectly *normal*.

And not only is it normal. It has become *necessary*, since today we must hold the line against a theology of the death of God that has been aborning for some time and which, under the guise of philosophy, has invaded the culture, corrupts a great number of clerics who are as presumptuous as they are ignorant, and sets itself to troubling or destroying the faith of a Christian people whose duties of state do not permit them to study under the great professors of theology (there still are some around) and acquire some of the very specialized knowledge that they dispense.

On this whole question, Ernst R. Korn, in whose competence and gifts my life which is about to end has put all its hope, expresses himself much better than I can in his preface to this book, toward which I strongly suggest that the reader turn his attention.

*   *   *   *   *   *   *   *   *   *

In 1960 Etienne Gilson published two important books in which he gives considerable attention to theology: *Introduction à la philosophie chrétienne* (Paris, Vrin) and *Le Philosophe et la théologie* (Paris, Fayard). One might reproach him for having played a little too much the schoolmaster for the theologians, and what is more serious, for not having consecrated a more thorough discussion to what is the key to our needs, I mean the *knowledge by analogy* of divine things, which are beyond the capacities of our intellect. As for me, what I see above all in these two books is the way in which the author shares with us, with his customary total loyalty, the progressive discoveries made by him since he came to the Sorbonne, culminating in the unshakeable convictions he has finally come to. Nothing is more moving and more instructive than the experience and the indefatigable personal research of a great mind thirsting for truth.

On the other hand, I feel obliged to tell Gilson how much I was moved by what he said of me in far too generous terms. As a matter of fact, I do not give a tinker's damn for what *La Société française de philosophie* and dear Mr. Bouglé thought of me in 1936, for what I think of myself is hardly less flattering. (I must admit, however, that I believe my long labors have opened a few doors; so that, having come to an age when death may come at any instant, and will prevent me from seeing what I had hoped for here below, my concern is that there be a few others to cross the thresholds of the doors I have left ajar.

Finally let me say that what appears to me most significant with regard to my present proposal is the fact that in Gilson's eyes as in mine (and he was following the paths of his cherished lovely Clio, while I preferred those of Minerva, and had the temerity to feel my way along her paths at my own risk and peril) there could be no Christian philosophy that is not led eventually to raise its eyes toward theology, and to propose *tentatively* its own views on matters whose *knowledge* (Christian philosophy knows this) depends, not on philosophy, but on a superior wisdom to which the *opus theologicum* is dedicated.

A third remark. This one concerns that philosophical and theological pluralism considered today to be just as normal as the variety of dishes on a good menu by all the past masters of various systems of thought who want to be up to date and consider themselves the intellectual elite of Christianity. One might ask if they are not the innocent victims of a confusion that is so general and so insidious that it goes undetected: a confusion between the *exercise of authority* in the Church and the *demands of the intellect* in each one of us.

If we look at the exercise of authority in the Church, it is quite clear that the decisions of the magisterium cannot strike anything except those doctrines that are manifestly contrary to the Christian faith. For many centuries this exercise of authority was carried out with cudgel and cane, a system that made the work of the Holy Office quite easy and set up a kind of reign of terror; in spite of this, the principle was always maintained that those doctrines opposed to one another, in which (however violent the conflict between them might be) the Church discerned no opposition to faith in the deposit of Revelation, had a perfect right to be expressed and taught freely within the Church.

In our times, there is no more question of solemn condemnations or consignments to the Index, etc. Yet, on the other hand, our superstars find in any theology or fantastical exegesis whatever, in any more or less camouflaged Hegelianism, and in any atheistic philosophic system, something or other to freshen up the apostolic faith. However the magisterium evidently always maintains the right (which it is careful not to abuse)—and the duty as well—to point out from its point of view, as best it can, that this or that philosophical or theological position is not incompatible with the faith. And the principle still remains firm, at all times and more than ever now, that any philosophical or theological doctrine which is incompatible with the Christian faith, retains the complete freedom to be expressed and taught within the Church. This is the sound pluralism that must be recognized in what concerns the exercise of authority in the Church.

But at the same time, this is where things become singularly complicated. For the fact is that today such large account is given to this pluralism, such vast proportions are attributed to it, and the practical largesse dispensed by it shines with such brilliance, that everyone is ready to extrapolate and to conclude that not only in what concerns the exercise of authority within the Church but also in what concerns the very exigencies of the intellect as well, this philosophical and theological pluralism is required as such as the normal and necessary condition presupposed by the work of thought to which our mind is called.

There is no greater mistake. In fact, as soon as there is question of the work of the intellect to be accomplished by each of us at our own risk and peril, the point of view changes entirely. What is involved here is the personal relation between each of us and the truth which our mind must serve. What the intellect seeks is the Truth, and there cannot be two Truths.

If one philosophical or theological doctrine is true in its basic principles and in its essential structure, then all others must be considered more or less false. I must reject them, not assimilate them. I certainly know very well that in the falsest of doctrines and in the wildest ones (especially the wildest) I can find something for my instruction and put my hand on some pearl of great price which is offered to me by pure chance. But between this realization and the thought that these doctrines themselves are interchangeable, or that they generously complement one another in an uplifting dignified cacophony, there is a veritable abyss.

A rational explication of the deposit of the faith is worthless unless it is provided with a true theology; and a theology cannot be true unless it is sustained by a true metaphysics. Let each one accept his responsibility. To make of philosophical and theological pluralism the presupposed condition for the good accomplishment of the work in which anybody and everybody who professes to be a thinker is engaged is an outrage to the intellect and a betrayal of the truth. There was a wondrous assortment, a rich pluralism of thorns in the crown forced down upon the head of Christ by the soldiers of Caesar.

CHAPTER XIII
FOR AN EXISTENTIAL EPISTEMOLOGY (III)

THE SUBSTITUTE FOR THEOLOGY AMONG THE SIMPLE[1]

I. PRELIMINARY REMARKS

1. *THE SIMPLE*—THIS WORD THAT I AM USING is a word of yesteryear. Do simple people still exist today? Perhaps I should speak instead of unsatisfied, complicated people, if not of people with complexes. Yet there is a certain progress here but one which, like any progress, is dearly paid for. The progress I am referring to is a general awareness of the truth that every man, as such, has the right to culture. For the moment we are at a rather discouraging cultural level, for the "culture" generally offered today is the culture dispensed by newspapers and even more by television, radio and films, along with the random reading of some fashionable book or other. But this is a pseudo-culture, infinitely inferior to the old popular wisdoms—the wisdom of the peasant or of the artisan—which are in the process of disappearing. I think that as far as the problem of general access to culture is concerned, things can only improve, if, at least with regard to schooling and public instruction, the decision is made to give a liberal education to all.

But in my presentation I will use the word *simple* in a very particular sense, entirely different from the ordinary sense of the word. As I use it this word has a precise and well-defined meaning; for me it signifies those *who do not have* those habits of mind called the intellectual virtues, and in particular those who do not have the *theological habitus*. It is extremely desirable that by any means possible the Christian people receive a certain theological education, in other words a certain more or less elementary communication of what they need to know among all those things known to the theologian (a theologian worthy of the name, of course). But, however desirable and necessary it may be, this simplification of theological truths for the general public will never go very far and will never engender in the minds of this audience what can be properly called *knowledge* or *science*. They will remain, and this will be the case for the vast multitude of people, unequipped with the *theological habitus*, unpossessed of the knowledge *of divine things*. So my idea is that, considering the manner in which they live out their lives, we ought to be able to find, on an altogether

---

1   *Editor's footnote*: Seminar given to the Little Brothers of Jesus, at Toulouse, May 5 and 6, 1969. Cf. *Nova et Vetera*, 1969, no. 2, pp. 81–121.

different plane, something to take the place of this *habitus* in the great majority of faithful souls.

2. I would add further, as far as these "simple" and unlearned people are concerned, that among them, just as well as among the intellectuals and the scholars, there are saintly souls raised to very high levels by the gift of wisdom and by infused contemplation, and who will appear on the last day as pillars of the Church. But when I use the word *simple*, I do not have these special souls in mind—they have already passed over the threshold and rest in the shelter of Jesus' wounds. I have in mind rather those souls who, while they are steadfast in prayer, follow a "little path" in the realm of the mystical life itself and belong to the ordinary run of Christians.

One last preliminary remark, called for by what we are going to treat today. Aristotle (or someone else, I do not remember who) speaks of what is known *inter sapientes*. It is also *inter sapientes*, is it not, that we philosophize, when we do so in a seminar with the Little Brothers of Jesus.

II. THE PRACTICAL EXPERIENCE OF THE LIFE OF PRAYER WITH ALL THE KNOWLEDGE IT ACCUMULATES ALONG THE WAY

3. In common sense there is a "substitute for philosophy," which is a kind of prephilosophy, a first and entirely spontaneous and still formless approach to what philosophical knowledge is in someone who has acquired the philosophical *habitus*. And whether it is through valid reasoning even though without any critical context and of insufficient depth, or through some instinct of the intelligence in contact with life experience, this prephilosophy can attain certitudes which philosophy alone establishes by mode of a fully elaborated system of knowledge.

There is likewise a *substitute for theology* among the simple but of a kind entirely different from the common sense substitute for philosophy because in this case there is no question at all of some kind of pre-theology or of a first approach, however formless it may still be, to what theological knowledge is in someone who has acquired its *habitus*. There is question here—I am thinking, for example, of devotion to the Rosary, or the exercise of the Way of the Cross, or the reading of the lives of the saints, or above all of the constant attention (without egocentrism, but in view of union with God) to what takes place within the soul and to what is given to that soul—there is question, not of some knowledge, however rudimentary it may be, within anyone's grasp, but rather of the entirely personal practical experience of the life of prayer in each soul along with that knowledge in the order of experience which each one accumulates in this way little by little.[2] And the certitudes that this

---

2   "Such a high, such a purely supernatural reality as theological faith, cannot come into the mind without profound consequences for its life and for its intimate

"substitute for theology" can attain in the light of faith have nothing in common with those that a science or any rational discipline can establish. They are certitudes of a completely individual and private order—for example, the certitude of having been called to a particular state of life, or, if we stay in the secular realm, the certitude of the obligation before God to accept or refuse some employment, or to participate in some social movement (or if one is married someday to make a very serious decision with regard to one's child in view of the good of the soul under one's responsibility), or again the certitude that a prayer has been heard in the course of a pilgrimage, or of having been unfaithful to grace on a particular occasion, or of having been helped and strengthened by one of the Blessed who is particularly loved—all of which make up the varied warp and woof of contingent and more or less decisive occurrences which constitute the spiritual experience of the Christian. The practical experience of the life of prayer, with all that it teaches us, with the entire weight of concrete knowledge with which it enriches the soul, this is what I call the substitute for theology among the simple.

Whereas theological knowledge plays an essential role in the intellectual life and in the forward progress of the Church itself, this substitute for theology, the completely personal experience I am talking about, with all the knowledge it accumulates along the way, plays an essential role in the moral activity and the forward progress of individuals who, as members of the Church, try to be faithful to its spirit.

The analogy that can be pointed out between the substitute in question and theology itself is that in both cases there is an expansion of the faith in some thing of which it is the principle within the human intelligence and a progression in knowledge in which, in one case by deliberate purpose, in the other by instinct and by feeling one's way, the *fides quaerens intellectum* is at work. But in the case of theology this is brought about by a work of research and a demonstration effectuated by reason, thanks to a *habitus* of knowledge which develops within the reason and is the highest of all forms of knowledge. In the case of the substitute for theology among the simple however, this is produced by the experience of the life of prayer along with the treasure of knowledge that it enlarges little by little, and in which, undoubtedly far more generously than might be admitted today, lights and personal inspirations intervene (I will come back to this point later), which presuppose theological faith and extend its domain over our lives, but which remain distinct from it, in the same way that theological knowledge depends on and derives from theological faith but remains distinct from it.

4. "*Confiteor tibi, Pater, Domine caeli et terrae, qui abscondisti haec a sapientibus*

psychology," said Father Labourdette (in his mimeographed course on faith given at the Dominican House of Studies in Toulouse, p. 150, apropos of II-II, q. 7). "A whole phenomenological description could be given of the concrete attitudes of the believer."

et prudentibus, et revelasti ea parvulis."[3] It seems to me these words of the Gospel are applicable here if we understand by "the wise and the prudent" those whose vision is obscured by self-satisfaction; in such a case this wisdom is but self-sufficiency and their prudence miserly precaution.

To tell the truth, the most learned and the most educated of men, if they are Christians, are and ought to be *parvuli* everywhere except in their scientific labors and in the domain of their competence. And if in this presentation I use the expression "substitute for theology among the simple," it is because, in actual fact, these simple souls have nothing to replace in them the theological *habitus* which they do not have. But in their personal lives the greatest theologians are also *parvuli*, simple souls. I have known and do know several in whom there dwelt and dwells now an admirable spirit of childhood and among whom the best and purest of what replaces theology among the simple was and is humbly at work in the blessed experience and work of sanctification each day, more so and better than among the generality of simple souls.

Here I must depart a bit from my subject, for what I call the substitute for theology among the simple is entirely different from "popular piety" or has only a very distant relation to it. But the fact remains that certain theologians are tempted, under pretext of protecting the simple from illusions and superstitions (which in fact are not all that rare), to entertain such a rigorous distrust of popular piety[4]—in this case misunderstood as to its true nature and confused with love of the miraculous—that by dint of mistrusting anything that might risk polluting their theological faith and in order to preserve that faith in a perfect state of asepsis, they would keep popular piety locked up in some castle-keep, like a captive princess who is too beautiful to let run free. If he gives in to this temptation the theologian risks becoming one of the *sapientes et prudentes* mentioned in the Gospel. Even his smile of condescending scepticism will be partly responsible for the etiolation of spirituality among so many Christians who think it normal to separate their lives from their faith and to lead an upright existence (as much as is possible), completely deprived of any personal religious experience while their faith, locked away in its castle-keep, adheres—sometimes rather arrogantly, sometimes half asleep—to the universal truths listed in the Credo.

The attitude of the Church itself toward popular piety is entirely different. It never ceases to encourage such piety. It rejoices with people in the feasts they continue to celebrate annually in their local sanctuaries and recommends many popular devotions. Even the attraction exerted by unusual supernatural occurrences causes it no fear. It recognizes, after examining the witnesses,

---

3   Matt. xi, 25. Cf. Luke x, 21.

4   Or toward private assurances received from above. To her learned friend Father Ybanez, who, "on two sheets of paper full of theological reasons," tried to turn her away from the reform of the Carmelite order, St. Teresa in her answer "begged him to spare her his science." *Vie*, XXXV, p. 427.

Apparitions of the Blessed Virgin, including the messages she sends us by means of simple children, at La Salette, at Lourdes, at Fatima, at Pontmain, and at other places. It blesses the crowds who come in pilgrimage to places where miracles took place. It protects stigmatics from their detractors (even when their partisans are a bit too zealous). And above all, the Church makes the canonization of its saints, which is a mark of its glory, an occasion in each case to renew the piety of the faithful.

5. It is quite clear that in the experience of the life of prayer or the life of faith,[5] and in all the practical incidences it implies, both reason and the moral virtues, especially prudence, under the light of faith play a fundamental role which ought to be examined through a complete "phenomenological description of the concrete attitudes of the believer."[6] But are reason joined with faith always sufficient to cause the soul to act in every case according to the requirements of a life of faith, and to make it act in God's sight always as it should?[7]

Nor, for the same reason, have I dealt with the role which is played, in the "substitute for theology among the simple," by the virtue of prudence and by the discernment which is proper to it, as it is to the other infused and acquired moral virtues. The reader can easily fill in this lacuna. Or does the soul not need, in certain cases at least, to be helped normally by some form of support which, however different it may be from theological faith itself, is still in some way superior to reason?

A few pages back, I spoke of *private certitudes* that can be part of the experience of the life of faith. This is a point I would like to insist on now.

It is undoubtedly clear that in the course of our spiritual lives as in the course of our lives *inter homines* we take a course of action, guided by probabilities that are purely a matter of opinion. But it is impossible to commit our lives absolutely based solely on probabilities and opinions; for this we need certitudes.

So the concrete experience of the life of faith at certain more or less frequent moments must include such certitudes—certitudes which do not imply, as theological faith does, that here we *cannot be* mistaken, but which imply that here in fact we *are not* mistaken.

---

5   Prayer being a direct consequence or a direct effect of faith, which is an act commanded by the will under the light of faith (*orate semper*), I am using the expressions "life of prayer" and "life of faith" as synonymous.

6   Cf. above, p. 274, n. 2.

7   The essential role of the gifts of the Holy Spirit in the supernatural structure of the soul comes into play here. If I have not treated this subject in my text it is because I had another subject in view (closely related, as a matter of fact) and which was enough to take up an entire seminar all by itself. Concerning the gifts of the Holy Spirit, one might refer to what is said about them in the Postscript.

In the experience of the life of prayer, do we attain these certitudes by means of rational demonstration, as happens with the certitudes of theological knowledge? Certainly not.

By what means then? For, from the side of reason, those things to be believed and to be done on which in the course of his spiritual experience a man commits his life in a fundamental way, undergoing the worst of agonies if necessary, are things of an absolutely singular and contingent order. Undoubtedly nothing is required above and beyond the equipment provided by nature and by the acquired and infused virtues to furnish their subject with certain judgment when they offer a grasp of verifications on the natural level[8] or when they are the object of an unconditional command of the moral law or of an unconditional demand of a theological or moral virtue. But, except in the case I have just mentioned, even with the different virtues which perfect our powers, reason leaves man disarmed for making any *certain* judgment concerning things of an absolutely singular and contingent order which depend on the life of faith. Such things cannot involve a rational proof that leaves no room for doubt. The most laborious reasoning may very well show someone with a high degree of probability; it will never show *with certitude* that God has called that person to a particular state of life, or demands a particular sacrifice (did not the sacrifice of Abraham set the standard for us all), or exacts the risk of one's skin by testimony against some iniquity, or gives assurance of some help sent from heaven. In such cases, if reason alone were involved, to take the leap into certitude would be to sin against intelligence.

The conclusion to which we are necessarily led is this: Except when something verifiable on the level of nature or an unconditional command of the moral law or of a virtue is imposed on reason, certitudes in matters of a contingent nature which play a role that cannot be overlooked in the concrete experience of the life of faith are certitudes of private inspiration of the supernatural order[9] and to which the soul *adds* faith.[10]

---

8   This is the case, for example, when a miracle is rationally established because we know that the fact in question surpasses all the possibilities of nature.

9   The inspirations I am thinking of here are aids *passively received*, called for by the gifts of the Holy Spirit in certain circumstances. Of themselves, the gifts move the soul by divine inspirations *actively received* (to which, in other words, the soul opens itself freely), as is the case for everything that is received in virtue of the supernatural structure of the soul and of its life divinized by grace and charity; the gifts of the Holy Spirit are *habitus* which dispose souls to follow carefully the divine inspiration and to open themselves to that inspiration in its free activity ("*homo sic agitur a Spiritu Sancto quod etiam agit, inquantum est liberi arbitrii*," Ia-IIa, q. 68, a. 3, ad 2m). Further on see the Postscript.

10   Let us illustrate the considerations I am proposing here by an example which greatly transcends them: the absolute certitude that Joan of Arc had that her Voices spoke to her in God's behalf. "If I said that God has not sent me, I would damn myself" (Olivier Leroy, *Sainte Jeanne d'Arc, Les Voix* [Paris: Alsatia, 1956], p. 96. "For what is to be believed in my revelations, I ask no advice whatever

III. THE ANGELS AND THE ORDER OF THE UNIVERSE

In order to explain all this we have to begin from very far back, I mean from the consideration of the order of the universe as St. Thomas sees it. There is but one universe, he tells us, produced by the creative act of God—a single universe which at one and the same time includes pure spirits and the material world along with us who are spirits in flesh so that the first law of the universal order is the *convivium* of angels with men.

What he teaches on this point is at the very center of his philosophic and theological thought concerning created things; for him there is question here, not of truths that are important though accessory, but rather of fundamental truths. And one has the impression that what he says about them is in his eyes better established and more obvious—and more fundamentally normal—than Brother Reginald's presence next to him or than the sunrise we can look at each morning. The *invisibilia*, the angels in their vast multitude, along with those animals endowed with reason that we are, and all the other *visibilia* here below, constitute one and the same universe. The *invisibilia* were created because they are *necessary to the perfection of the universe:*[11] if man with his feeble intelligence tied to his senses is the head of material creation, how would there not be above him, since the universe is a divine work, the immaterial splendor of pure spirits, of "separated substances," at the head of the entire creation? Anyone who knows what intelligence is should understand this.[12] Although mistaken on many points concerning their nature, Plato and Aristotle did not doubt the existence of separated substances.[13]

Created in the state of grace, as Adam and Eve were later, the angels within an instant made their free choice, some, waiting on God's gratuitous generosity for their supernatural beatitude, received it immediately, others, choosing to depend entirely on themselves and solely on the power of their nature, were immediately cast down.[14] As ministers of God, the holy angels (and these are the only ones who interest us here) are charged with the care of everything here below, and very specially with the care of men, whose spiritual and immortal souls are, like them, the images of God, and one day will be raised up, in the state of glory, to become their equals. Every single man, wherever he may be born on this earth or under whatever religious regime, has an angel appointed to watch over him.[15] Without the help of the angels and the light

---

from bishop, priest, or anyone else." (*Ibid.*, p. 76).

11   Cf. *Sum. theol.*, Ia, q. 50, a. 1.

12   "*Antiqui autem* ignorantes vim intelligendi. . . *existimaverunt quod nullum ens esset nisi corpus.*" *Sum. theol.*, Ia, q. 50, a. 1.

13   Cf. the first chapters of the opusculum *De subtantiis separatis*.

14   *Sum. theol.*, Ia, q. 63, a. 3.

15   Cf. *Sum. theol.*, Ia, q. 113, a. 1, 2, 4, 5.

received from them, human reason cannot bring man's knowledge to its perfection, even his knowledge of a purely natural order.[16] According to an exigency of the universal order—from which our freedom certainly can withdraw us (and how!)—the regulation of our activities in the realm of intellectual knowledge depends on the government of the angels, "*cognitio humana ad intellectum pertinens a Deo mediantibus agelis ordinatur. . . Oportet ergo quod nostra intellectualis cognitio reguletur per angelorum cognitionem.*"[17] The angels watch us; they are very closely involved in human life. All this is fundamentally normal and corresponds to *a basic law of nature*, as well as to a requirement of grace.

7. St. Thomas teaches likewise that in knowing things pure spirits receive nothing from those things. It is from God, from the supreme Intellect subsisting in itself, that they receive all their knowledge, thanks to infused ideas, to *species innatae* which from the moment of their creation equip their intellects and maintain them continually in act, whether these infused *species*[18] relate to what is naturally knowable—in which case they are innate and connatural—or whether they bear on the mystery of divine things, which can be known only supernaturally—in which case they are innate by a gift of grace so that these infused *species* make it possible for angels to penetrate into this mystery from the very beginning (since the angels were created in the state of grace), and then by successive revelations[19] to penetrate it more and more profoundly, enriching those *species* in their objective content itself.

As participations by pure spirits, from the instant of their creation, in divine knowledge constantly derived from God, these angelic *species*, contrary to abstract *species* like ours, cause the angelic intellect to know—and this not only as to their essentiality, *but as to the very existentiality* of the thing known—all the more particular objects of knowledge, even to the singular itself[20]

---

16   "*Inter alias intellectuales substantias, humanae animae infimum gradum habent. . . Unde oportuit quod habeant organa corporea, per quae a rebus corporalibus cognitionem haurirent, ex quibus tamen,* propter debilitatem intellectualis luminis, perfectam notitiam eorum quae ad hominem spectant adipisci non valent, nisi per lumen superioris spiritus adjuventur." *Sum. contra Gent.*, III, c. 81.

17   *Ibid.*, c. 91.

18   *Species* could be translated by the word "representation" which I hesitate to use since modern idealist systems have made it ambiguous.

19   Cf. *Sum. theol.*, Ia, q. 57, a. 5, and q. 58, a. 1.

20   Cf. *Sum. theol.*, Ia, q. 57, a. 2: "*Modus quo intellectus angeli singularia cognoscit, ex hoc considerari potest, quod, sicut a Deo effluunt res, ut subsistant in propriis naturis, ita etiam ut sint in cognitione angelica. Manifestum est enim, quod a Deo effluit in rebus non solum illud quod ad naturam universalem pertinet, sed etiam ea quae sunt individuationis principia. . . Sicut igitur Deus per essentiam suam, per quam omnia causat, est similitudo omnium, et per eam omnia cognoscit non solum quantum ad naturas universales, sed etiam quantum ad singularitatem: ita angeli per species a Deo*

How are we to understand the existential scope of angelic *species* and the knowledge that they give of the singular and the contingent, except by admitting that (since things flow from them into angelic knowledge as they flow from Him into existence, and since the divine knowledge, of which these *species* exist as images, is itself sovereignly existential—*secundum quod causat, sicut et cognoscit*, Ia, q. 57, a. 2) angelic *species* cause new elements to appear in their objective content as these elements rise into existence in their dependence either on contingent encounters or on free volitions? An angel does not know the secrets of the heart, but he does know a particular event at the origin of which was the free choice of Julius Caesar or Herod at a given moment of our time (just as one angel knows some thought or other which at a given moment in the *aevum* another angel freely chooses to communicate to him).

Likewise Isidore (lib. I *de Summo Bono*, c. 12) says that the angels know many things by experience, and St. Thomas does not hesitate to affirm as well—in referring precisely to Ia, q. 57, a. 2, on the angelic knowledge of the singular—that the word *experience* can be applied to them: "*experientia angelis attribui potest per similitundinem cognitorum et non per similitudinem virtutis cognoscitivae*, experience can be attributed to angels with regard to what is—existentially—known to them, not in regard to a faculty of knowledge which would be other than the intellect," Ia, q. 54, a. 5, and to the contingent itself, embraced or subsumed in the universality proper to each one of them.

And the more universal an angelic *species* is, the richer it is in intelligible content grasped in this way, and all the higher too is the angelic intelligence in its capacity to make use of this more universal *species*. (Let me note in parentheses that, by the very fact that they were created for the perfection of the universe, there is an order or scale of perfection among the angels,[21] and that the only order that can exist in this case—that is, between individual persons each of whom is a separate species—is an order of greatness in intellectual power and in the grasp of truth.)[22] It is the most universal of *species* then that are infused into the intellects of the highest angels. So here we are face to face with the great question of angelic illumination.

---

inditas res cognoscunt non solum quantum ad naturam universalem sed etiam secundum earum singularitatem, in quantum sunt quaedam repraesentationes multiplicatae illius unicae et simplicis essentiae."

21   Here I am applying views that St. Thomas put forward concerning the vastness of the angelic multitude.

22   Such is the order to which we are referred in a wholly symbolic and poetic fashion by that arrangement of angelic hierarchies which served as an imaginative background for Denis the Areopagite and for the description of which he used such beautiful names—a kind of Dionysiac tableau which is proper not only for consoling us a bit about our own human hierarchies, but which was for St. Thomas and for Denis the occasion for more profound metaphysical considerations.

IV. ANGELIC ILLUMINATION

8. When they *consider in act*[23] something or other that is shown by angelic illumination, angels can see one another[24] in their infused *species*, and all of them, from top to bottom and from the bottom to the top of the scale, can speak to one another—that is to say, manifest their thought to one another—each time that the will of one of them orders a concept or mental word to be made manifest to some other angel.[25] Then this angel sees the mental word in the angel who is speaking to him, and whom he himself then sees as angels see one another, since the infused *species* make each angel intentionally present in the intellect of the others.[26] And so the angel who speaks exercises no action whatever on the angel to whom he is speaking. He merely opens himself up to that angel.

Finally, every illumination among the angels is a form of locution, but every locution is not an illumination. For truth is the light of the intellect, and to illuminate is to make known to another what is in one's mind *because it is a truth* by means of which the other will be instructed; whereas to speak is simply to make known to another what is in one's mind because of a desire to open oneself to the other. To illuminate means to manifest a truth,—and hence to know it better than the one to whom it is communicated. Now God is the principle of all truth.[27] From this it follows that it is up to the most powerful of the pure intellects and those closest to God to illuminate the others.

So angelic illumination moves in one direction, it descends from the highest to the lowest of the degrees of perfection among the pure spirits,[28] the higher angel illuminating the angel below him with regard to things of nature, of grace and of glory.[29] And this is done with total generosity, for an angel reveals to the one he is instructing everything he knows—although of all the things he has transmitted he inevitably retains a more perfect knowledge: *"sicut unam et eamdem rem plenius intelligit magister, quam discipulus qui ab eo addiscit."*[30] (Among the angels, master lectures are nothing but a delight for the students, and they are delivered in a manner worthy of the nature of those students. . . .)

---

23   Cf. *Sum. theol.*, Ia, q. 58, a. 1—An angel speaks to himself then by forming a concept, a *verbum mentis* (Ia, q. 107, a. 1).

24   Cf. *Ibid.*, q. 56, a. 2.

25   Cf. *Ibid.*, q. 107, a. 1 and 2—see n. 23.

26   Cf. *Ibid.*, 1. 56, a. 2, ad 3m. It is when he *considers in act* (as indicated a few lines above) a particular *species* in which another angel is shown to him that one angel sees another.

27   Cf. *Ibid.*, Ia, q. 107, a. 1 and 2.

28   Cf. *Ibid.*, q. 106, a. 1, 3 and 4.

29   Cf. *Ibid.*, q. 106, a. 1, ad 2m.

30   Cf. *Ibid.*, q. 106, a. 4.

9. Among the angels how does the illumination of one by another actually take place?

By turning his thought toward the angel he would illuminate—which means, metaphorically speaking, to draw closer to him—the higher angel, St. Thomas tells us,[31] fortifies the intellect of the other angel. On the other hand, and above all, with regard to the object proposed to the mind, the higher angel, who knows by means of more universal *species* and who embraces in his more universal conception a richness of content too vast for the capacity of a less powerful intellect, divides his own conception into a multiplicity of more particular conceptions proportioned to the capacity of the less powerful intellect he wants to illuminate. It is these more particular conceptions, prepared within himself in consideration of the other, that he presents to the other while speaking to him, that is to say, as he opens himself up to the other. The other sees these conceptions in the higher angel. And nourishing his own thought with them, he is instructed by them in truths which he knew only in an imperfect mode adapted to his native capacity, or, if there is question of things revealed, that he did not yet know. He is illuminated by the higher angel.

10. But do angels illuminate only other angels who are lower than they are? Angels also illuminate human souls.[32] What can be said about the manner in which this illumination takes place? St. Thomas is not very explicit on this matter. It seems to me that with the psychological data at our disposal today it is possible to push the analysis of this question a bit further. This is what I would like to take the risk of doing now.[33]

Let us keep in mind first of all, following St. Thomas' example, that it is important to avoid at all times the slightest shade of Platonism. In my opinion, this requires that here we must posit that the illumination of a man by an angel takes place in an essentially different manner from the illumination of one angel by another. For a man can in absolutely no way whatever see in the angel who illuminates him anything at all of the *species* which are in the angel and of the conception that the angel wishes to transmit.

But without being a pure spirit the human soul is still a spirit. And since the human intellect, however spiritual it may be, is open from below to the *action*

---

31   Cf. *Ibid.*, q. 106, a. 1.

32   Cf. *Ibid.*, q, 111. a, 1.

33   On this point I would like to distance myself from the classical Scholastic views, which hold that the human mind,—which, since it is not a pure spirit but a form informing a body, is subject to the action of the material world and receives from it (through the senses) certain determinations (*species impressae*), nevertheless enjoys (and this is what I contest) the same kind of intangible interiority to itself as an angel does with regard to the world of pure spirits and cannot receive from any action exercised on it by an angel any intelligential determination whatever, even if it were, unlike our *species impressae*, in complete act of intelligibility.

which material things exercise on it by means of the senses, why could it not, however closely it may be linked to matter, be open in the same way from above—I mean in the *supraconscious* of the spirit—to the action excercised on it by a pure spirit? Hence the only satisfying explanation, in my opinion, is to admit that under the motion of God (as a special motion directed toward some individual person) the angel imprints on the supraconscious of the human spirit an intelligential determination which, without being a *species impressa* like those that come to us through the senses, is also *received* under an action from without.

The angel has not only divided his conception in order to proportion it to the capacity of a less powerful intellect. He has also reduced it and whittled it down still more, to the point of making it a tiny spark of intelligibility in act—let us call it an unformulated intuitive apprehension fecundating the intelligence. And this time (under the divine motion) exercising an *action* on another spirit in the order of efficient causality, it is this germ fecundating the intelligence that he imprints on the higher part of the human spirit which I call the supraconscious, from which it passes down into the conscious under the form of a mental word expressing an intuition.

At the same time, the human intellect finds itself strengthened by the very fact that a higher spirit acts on it under the divine motion, instrumentally, in the case that concerns us here,[34] and in this way causes a light whose source is God to pass into it. "An idea" which derives from a knowledge by instinct or by supraconscious connaturality and gushes up unexpectedly in counciousness to enlighten the mind and lift a veil from it—that is to say, on the one hand, from the point of view of the object, something presented to consciousness in an imaginative or conceptual *species*, from the point of view of the subject, a *lumen* which enables the intellect to seize upon the truth of what is shown to it in this way, and all of this in a flash—this is what is generally called an *inspiration*, whether it is born naturally in us as in numberless cases (and not among poets alone),[35] or comes from on high as in the case presently under consideration.

V. PRIVATE INSPIRATIONS AND THEOLOGICAL FAITH

11. Now I have not forgotten that the subject of the present seminar concerns the experience of the life of prayer or the life of faith in each of us.

---

34   This by reason of the *lumen propheticum* which will be taken up later on. Cf. *Sum. theol.*, IIa-IIae, q. 172, a. 2, ad 3m.

35   So the *lumen* I am speak of in the text is the completely natural light of the intuitivity of the spirit, when the flash of a knowledge by connaturality, too high and too pure to be consciously grasped, wells up in the supraconscious, before descending into consciousness, where it will take form in ideas or in images, then in words.

If I have spoken of angels and angelic illumination, it is because the assistance of the angels and the illuminations which come from them play a role that is absolutely normal in Christian life, regardless of how often it is forgotten. It is to this *convivium* with the pure spirits that we must have recourse to account for those passively received supra-rational certitudes without which, at certain moments or at especially serious turning-points in the adventures which Providence arranges for him, the Christian would not commit his very being and all that is vital to him.

As I noted, such certitudes[36] pose a particular problem which I would like to consider now, and on this subject here is the analysis I propose.

I think that at the moments I speak of an inspiration coming from an angelic illumination intervenes.

According to what we have just seen, it comprises an action by which an angel (or one of the blessed) imprints on the human supraconscious a germ fecundating the intelligence, an unformulated intuitive apprehension which, once it has passed into consciousness, takes form in a *species* or a conceptual statement expressing something intuitively perceived.

And at the same time it comprises a *lumen* (of the supernatural order in the case under consideration) which causes the intellect to grasp the truth of what is shown to it in this way, and through which an assent which is not just a more or less probable opinion, but a certitude—that supra-rational certitude which is the subject of our present reflections.

This *lumen* is not the *lumen* of theological faith which bears on those truths which have been revealed and proposed by the Church. This is why we can slip away without being guilty of any transgression against theological faith (I will return to this in a moment).

What must be said of this *lumen* from on high which is not a *lumen* of theological faith and which concerns a certitude of a private order?

Just as the germ received into the supraconscious is a reduction, a whittling down, to fit our feeble capacity, which the illuminating angel made its own *species* undergo, in the same way the *lumen* in question must be considered a diminished form, a minimal participation of that *lumen* which attains its fullness in the prophets. Let me note in passing that according to the teaching of St. Thomas prophetic revelation takes place through the intermediary of angels. By reason of a basic exigency of the natural order *"manifestum est,"* writes St. Thomas (IIa-IIae, q.172, a. 2), *"quod prophetica cognitio fiat per angelos."*

Is there any reason to be astonished that the most ordinary of Christians, if they live by the faith, should receive through the intermediary of pure spirits, in the decisive moments of their existence, a minimal participation in what the

---

36   Cf. Thomas Merton, in *The Seven Storey Mountain*: "I suddenly found myself filled with a vivid conviction. The time has come for me to go and be a Trappist. Where had the thought come from? All I knew was that it was suddenly there. And it was something powerful, irresistible, clear."

theologians call *lumen propheticum*? As I affirm this, is my aging brain wandering astray in an outdated kind of supernaturalism? Many of our contemporaries are happy to admit that the prophetic spirit has been very generously passed around, at least among the avant-garde of the most zealous proponents of renewal, in the sense that men are aroused by the sacred élan of the cosmos to announce great marvels like the Death of God for example or the duty of priests to abolish the sacred. But what I am talking about is something entirely different. The diminished form of the *lumen propheticum* I am speaking about does not bring about the announcement of anything at all. It is concerned only with humble private certitudes in private conduct. It might be compared to a healing hand laid on the forehead of a sick person. It has nothing to do with the soul or the élan of the cosmos. It is supernatural and received from the Holy Spirit through the ministry of the angels. This is why what I have to say may perhaps have a chance of interesting a few *sapientes*, but is certainly a comic incongruity in relation to the spirit of our times. Still my old brain remembers what St. Peter wrote: "*Vos autem genus electum, regale sacerdotium, gens sancta, populus acquisitionis.*"[37] These men to whom St. Peter spoke, these Christians who live the life of faith, this mass of *parvuli* crowding about Jesus—a chosen race, a royal priesthood, a holy nation, the people God formed for Himself—I am not at all astonished that the least among them could be guided at certain moments (more frequent than is thought) in their personal lives by inspirations coming from heaven and by however tiny a ray of the *lumen propheticum*.

12. Let us be careful to avoid any misunderstanding and point out that not only do we often act, as I mentioned above, according to simple probabilities, but also that angelic illumination and the inspiration it brings are far from always bringing certitude. Even the prophet in the full sense of the word cannot always distinguish between what he says from his own mind and what he says through the spirit of prophecy (IIa-IIae, q. 171, a. 5). Sometimes he acts, as St. Augustine says, "by some instinct to which human minds are subject without knowing it." For all the more reason we ordinary Christians often do not know if the inspiration which we obey is purely natural or comes from heaven.[38] This is why often in our life of faith the interior movement which makes us take some stand or other is incapable of engendering certitude, even if in actual fact it does come from heaven. So we guide ourselves by what is simply probable, a matter of opinion, not by certitude.[39]

---

37   I Peter ii, 9.

38   "*Non quicumque intelligit aliquam veritatem, cognoscit quid sit intellectus, qui est principium intellectualis operationis; et similiter non quicumque illuminatur ab angelo cognoscit se ab angelo illuminari.*" *Sum theol.*, Ia, q. 111, a. 1, ad 3m.

39   *Natural* inspirations can bring certitude in natural matters. But we are talking about the *life of faith*: and here, for the reasons indicated above (pp. 275–277) there

If in my present reflections I insist on the certitudes that private inspiration sometimes brings us, it is because such certitudes pose a special problem for me which I am trying to elucidate.

This said, let me get back to my subject.

After a long period of self-interrogation, a man suddenly sees, in a flash of light, that he must leave all, his father, his mother, the hope of starting a family, and all the promises of this world, to become a wandering beggar.

It is God Who asks this. He decides to follow this calling. To the inspiration he has received, he *adds faith* (which presupposes a sufficiently strong illumination from above). This "faith," as I just pointed out, is not theological faith. If he had refused the *lumen* in question, he would not have sinned against theological faith.[40] A certain man brings his wife, who is suffering from cancer, to Lourdes; and when she is immersed in the bathing-pool she is instantly cured. On seeing this he is certain (which supposes a sufficiently strong illumination from above) that his prayers have been answered by a miracle, and he would put his hand in the fire to attest to the fact. However, on his return home, the mockery he encounters troubles him deeply and one day he says to himself, "After all, it is important for me to follow my reason. A medical diagnosis is not always entirely trustworthy. What is more, I understand enough about psychology to know that a powerful emotion can have surprising effects on the organism. My friends make fun of me when I tell them of the miracle I witnessed. And did not my parish priest tell me that it is childishness for a good Christian in modern times to put more faith in the invisible than in the visible? What I really did was give to a moment of weakness. This entire story is an affair of the imagination." In refusing to believe in something about which he received certitude from above, this man in no way sins against theological faith.

And yet the private certitudes which concern us at present evidently have

---

cannot be (at least when something verifiable on the level of nature or an unconditional command of the moral law or of a virtue is not imposed upon reason) any *certitude* with regard to things to be done or believed by a given individual, except a *supra-natural* certitude (even though it is non-theological).

40   Joan of Arc disobeyed her Voices on two occasions (once when in an attempted escape she leaped from the top of the castle-keep of Beaurevoir; and again when, in the cemetery of Saint-Ouen—*out of fear of the fire*, "I prefer to sign rather than be burned"—she signed the statement of abjuration—really a pseudo-abjuration, for she did not understand the formula that they had her sign), and she repented for having done so as for a serious sin: *a sin of disobedience*, yes, certainly (to a formal prohibition in the first case; the second is more mysterious—her saints had warned her in advance that she would commit this fault, which, by her repentance and subsequent revocation, served to cast this eighteen-year-old girl into the heroic acceptance of martyrdom, the true "deliverance" which had been promised her). Was this *a sin against theological faith*? Evidently not (Cf. Olivier Leroy, *Sainte Jeanne d'Arc, Les Voix*, Ch. XI).

a very close relation to theological faith, which even plays a major role in such cases. This is the problem we have to elucidate.

13. As a matter of fact, these certitudes in private matters and the inspirations on which they depend are part and parcel of a context which embraces everything that is at work in the Christian soul: first and foremost theological faith (would a man go to Lourdes and ask for a miraculous cure, or would another abandon everything for God, if they did not have this faith?)—and the two other theological virtues as well, and the gifts of the Holy Spirit, and the moral virtues, and the experience of the life of prayer with all the graces and trials which accompany it, and the lessons that can be learned from someone else's experiences, and everything that can be derived from the use of reason. But it is theological faith which, in the vast synergy of concurrent causalities, is the primordial *cause*, as the cause which presupposes everything else, of that certitude whose ultimately determining cause—even though subordinate—is only private inspiration.

Just as the notion of some particular thing to be done or believed which translates into consciousness what has been imprinted on the supraconscious by the action of a pure spirit differs from the content of theological faith, in the same way the humble ray of the *lumen propheticum* which causes one to hold to the truth of something that is shown in this manner differs from the light of theological faith. Here there is question of certitudes of an entirely singular and contingent order *added on* to the incomparably superior universal truths of theological faith, and of a charismatic *lumen added on* to the incomparably more lofty *lumen* of theological faith.[41]

Looking for a pencil I have lost, I search about the room, and with the help of a flashlight finally find my pencil in a corner. The light which all the while illumined my search is the bright light of day, without which I could have done nothing. The feeble ray of my flashlight was a supplementary light, added on at a particular moment, which finally helped me see the thing I was looking for. This thing belongs to me, it does not belong to the art gallery. It is entirely different from the things that decorate the walls. In the same way, the ray of electric light that comes from my flashlight is entirely different from the light which illumines the gallery and which comes from the sun.

The fact remains however that theological faith is present in the soul at the very origin of those certitudes in private matters that we are talking about. It is the great light of theological faith which, along with the tiny supplementary ray of a diminished form of the *lumen propheticum*, is the cause of the certitudes in question. These particular certitudes are in no way a part of theological faith. They are essentially distinct from it. But in given souls in given circumstances, they are particular and contingent *consequences* or *effects* of theological faith.

---

41   By way of a very weak analogy, we might think of a great hall—an art gallery, if you like—whose windows let in a generous amount of daylight; it is by means of this light that we see the paintings on the walls.

This is why, supposing that a man has received from above a private inspiration strong enough to bring him certitude—in other words, supposing that (with regard to what he himself perceives) in a private matter he has received an inspiration bearing with it the sign of its truth and being one with all his lived experience of confidence in prayer—this is why such a man, without committing the slightest fault against theological faith, could turn away from such a certitude and such an inspiration and refuse or cease to add faith to what for him is, or has been shown, indubitably to be done or believed. However, if he does this, he withdraws his life to the same extent from the dominion and the causality of theological faith. He does not shake his faith, he does not even weaken it, but to a certain extent he does emancipate himself from that faith.

I think that those men whom the Gospel calls men of little faith, *modicae fidei*, were men who had theological faith, but who—at first undoubtedly with regard to the private inspirations received from angels (because this is what is easiest to withdraw from) and then, little by little, with regard to all those practical actions under the command of the will, especially concerning lack of confidence in prayer—had gradually emancipated their lives more and more generally from the dominion of theological faith. This faith was always present in the soul, as firm as one might want to consider it (but present in a soul that is more and more *ill-disposed* toward it). This faith had but *little*, indeed very little, *effect* on the soul. This is a danger against which all of us must be on our guard. "Is a faith which does not act a sincere faith?" our old Corneille asked. Those men who have the faith, but whose faith does not act, Jesus called hypocrites.

VI. CONCERNING FAITH-CONFIDENCE

14. To the preceding considerations might be added the question of "faith-confidence" about which I said a few words in one of my books.[42]

But let us note, before entering into this matter, that there is a certain confidence—a confidence in God and in the Son sent by Him—which is an integral part of theological faith itself. I believe because it is God who speaks; in this act of self-surrender I encounter God and I encounter the Christ, God made man: Such a total filial confidence in God who speaks is at the very root of the option of the will moving the intelligence to adhere freely to the truths of salvation which surpass it. This is a theological confidence, addressed directly to God, and which is the very motive of theological faith, inseparable from it and inherent in it. This theological confidence in the absolute Truth of the Word of God, as well as in the Good which it promises, had to be mentioned from the outset. With what I am calling faith-confidence we are up against an

42   *On the Grace and Humanity of Jesus*, p. 85, n. 26.

entirely different question. And it is only the third kind of faith-confidence which I will distinguish, as we shall see, that can be identified with the theological confidence I just mentioned.

15. What I call "faith-confidence" is a *faith* by which a soul puts its trust in a divine assurance concerning some singular and contingent object—*confidence* in the granting of a prayer, for example or, if we think of so many cases in the Gospel, confidence in the Savior's power to perform a miraculous cure. Once the miracle has been performed, Jesus says to the man or woman whose prayer has been granted: *"Filia, fides tua salvam te fecit*: Vade in pace";[43] "*Vade, fides tua salvum te fecit*, your faith has cured you.[44]

It is important here to make a careful distinction between three essentially different kinds of faith-confidence: the kind Jesus possessed to a supreme degree; the kind that we Christians who are not the contemporaries of Jesus possess; and the kind possessed by those, mostly the sick, who had the privilege of seeing Jesus and of listening and speaking to Him.

Jesus, the Incarnate Word, who in the heaven of his soul enjoyed the vision of God and the state of beatitude and the fullness of infused knowledge, evidently had neither theological faith nor theological hope. However, St. Thomas teaches that, without having theological hope, He did have hope *respectu aliquorum quae nondum erat adeptus.*[45] We must also think, it seems to me, that without having theological faith He had in His soul here below a sovereignly exalted faith-confidence, an absolute confidence in the help of His heavenly Father in any particular circumstance whatever and in any trial, however formidable it might be. This is the first kind of faith-confidence, totally independent of theological faith: a faith-confidence proper to Christ alone.

On the contrary, the second kind of faith-confidence is a *consequence* or an *effect* of theological faith, *essentially distinct* from this faith but *presupposing it* and closely dependent upon it—in particular confidence in the power of prayer and confidence by virtue of which we *add faith* to a private inspiration or concerning some singular and contingent thing to be done or believed. It is to this kind of faith-confidence that my preceding remarks referred and the kind that the Christian experiences in his prayer life.

A third kind is the faith-confidence of the contemporaries of the Lord—especially of the sick—who had the privilege of seeing Jesus and of listening and speaking to Him. The cause of this faith-confidence in them was not theological faith, it was not its consequence or its effect, *it was theological faith itself*, insofar as it was expressed in the soul and then professed by that soul in a given case.

---

43 Luke viii, 48.

44 Mark x, 52.

45 *Sum theol.*, IIIa, q. 7, a. 4.

The multitudes to whom Jesus spoke had theological faith, they believed all the truths that came from the mouth of God which He had revealed to Israel through Moses and the prophets; the Centurion too had theological faith, we can be certain, at least, with regard to the first truths pointed out in the Epistle to the Hebrews, *"credere oportet accedentem ad Deum quia est, et inquirentibus se remunerator sit."*[46]

16. For Jesus Himself, it was a question of being there, the Word Incarnate, and of announcing to them (in parables, the explanation was reserved for the disciples) the good news confirmed by miracles performed in humility, as He Himself had come in humility. For the divine plan willed that His passage among us, even to His death on the cross and His resurrection, should be enigmatic, and destined above all to touch and to test human hearts in the very depths of their mystery (it was after Pentecost that its meaning would be publicly unveiled for all).

And the *parvuli* to whom Jesus addressed His words, it was sufficient for them that, in seeing and hearing "that man" through Whom God spoke to them, they believe in Him and the "good news" He announced to them. More or less obscure for their understanding, this good news contained virtually all the divinely revealed truths which through Jesus were destined to complete the credo of Israel. All these men *already had theological faith*, which was *constantly presupposed* by Jesus' teaching, a theological faith still wholly implicit in who the promised Messiah would be and when He would come. And then it was *in Jesus too* that they believed—in Jesus who was in fact the Incarnate Word! And for a number of them the faith of Israel already became more or less explicit concerning the person of the Messiah who had now arrived and who was now present before them, the Son of God (still in an imprecise sense) in whose word, with all the inscrutable depths that it concealed, they believed, even if they did not understand, as in the truth that came from God. (And this was sufficient for them to adhere virtually, without knowing it, in the supra-conscious of their souls, to the mysteries of the Incarnation and the Redemption.) In any case, this was theological faith itself, faith in the divinely revealed truths, which a man professed when with complete confidence he said to the Incarnate Word: Yes, you have the power to cure me if you want to. Jesus did preform the miraculous cure, but He did it as a sign of the salvation brought by this faith.

Fides tua salvum te fecit. Whether they are Latin or Greek, Aramaean or Hebrew, these words contain a blessed ambiguity. Directly, in most cases, they mean: *your faith cured you*, and they mean no more than that.[47] But in the

---

46   Heb. xi, 6.

47   The synoptic texts to which I give the references here concern the cure of the body: Matt. viii, 10–13; ix, 22; ix, 29; xv, 28; Mark vi, 56; x, 52; xi, 5; Luke viii, 50. But in other texts there is question of the forgiveness of sins and of salvation:

background, like an echo, there is also the sense: your faith has saved you; it has saved you for eternal life. It is through this *faith that saves* that all the sick mentioned in the Gospels were *cured*.

In the Gospel the word *faith* has an eminently concrete and existential meaning: *at one and the same time* and with one single external appearance *faith* means both *theological faith* and *faith-confidence*. If in general the emphasis is put on faith-confidence, it is because theological faith is always presupposed and presupposed above all else—was it not to the flock of Israel that Jesus was sent first of all? (And undoubtedly it is also a hypothesis which I have already risked making,[48] because this faith-confidence, the first kind of faith-confidence I distinguished a moment ago, is the only "faith" that Jesus experienced within Himself.) With regard to ourselves, the word *faith* in the Gospel in every respect designates *theological faith* (which is required above all else), faith in the divinely revealed truths which the apostles proclaimed and to which they bore witness—*the Spirit will teach you all things*—then transmitted to us and proposed by the Church, and also the *consequences* and *effects of that faith* (essentially distinct from that faith but caused by it), in other words that practical confidence, that faith-confidence engendered by it[49] when theological faith "acts" in the soul and maintains the entire life of that soul under its dominion. With regard to the contemporaries of the Lord who had the privilege of seeing Him with their eyes, in the Gospels this word *faith* designates *theological faith itself* (already possessed by the children of Israel and more or less explicitly with regard to the person of the Messiah who had now arrived, and in a virtual manner with regard to all that this entails)—theological faith which, inasmuch as face to face with the Incarnate Word, it was professed and attested to by an absolute confidence in the power of this man to command nature and perform miraculous cures, itself appeared as faith-confidence: that is, the third kind of faith-confidence, in which there is found at work that theological confidence itself which is the motive of faith, and which is inseparable from faith.[50]

17. It seems particularly important to me to insist on this point so that we may avoid misreading the Gospels and creating in our minds an aberrant conception of faith itself. There is no shortage today of sacred orators or of

---

Mark ii, 5; Luke vii, 50 (in addition cf. Matt. xvi, 25; xxiv, 13; Luke xix, 10, etc.).

48   Cf. *On the Grace and Humanity of Jesus*, p. 85, n. 26.

49   This was the case for the disciples. It is this faith-confidence and the *effect* (and sign) of theological faith to which such texts as Matt. xxi, 21; Mark iv, 10; xi, 24; and Luke xvii, 5–6.

50   Theological confidence which is at the root of theological faith (cf. above, p. 289) is evidently, by this very fact, at the root of the attestation or profession of that same faith and because of this what I have designated as the third kind of faith-confidence should be identified with it.

theologians who, under the impact of anti-intellectual prejudices nourished by the ideosophies of the times, like Lutherans without realizing it, try to reduce *theological faith itself to faith-confidence*. For Luther faith was the confidence I personally experience within me of my own salvation. These people base themselves on a great truth which I recalled at the beginning of this section, namely, that faith implies *as its motive* an encounter with God and a total confidence in Him; but what they are actually saying is something entirely different. They are telling us that, in absolutely every respect, faith *consists essentially* in this person-to-person encounter, this dazzlement of the heart, this gift of oneself to Jesus as Savior and this total confidence in Him and in His love. And at the same time we must relegate to the old, outdated routines of our ancestors and throw on the trash-heaps of the past whatever might lead us to consider "God's revelation" "as a vast system of ready-made truths," as the Dutch Catechism puts it, and as it says elsewhere, "a collection of things to be known."[51] Let us have no *ready-made truths*! In proclaiming this what are they asking for? Truths which are *to be made*, truths which I am to discover myself? Changing truths perhaps? This is a strange notion of *revealed* truths . . .

If Truth does not come first; if revealed truths do not make up an ensemble of things *to be believed*, today just like yesterday (and which it is theology's duty to organize into a science), then the person-to-person encounter, however true it may be in reality, and all the other expressions, exact in themselves, whose repetition is so pleasing to the ear, become no more than sentimental rhetoric. It is quite true that a conversion is a dazzling encounter—but *with the God of Truth*. It is quite true that the life of faith is a more and more profoundly personal experience of the terrible and gentle love of Jesus—but one in which *all the unfathomable truths of the Credo* are lived out and meditated upon again and again. It is quite true that Revelation is a light given to each one of us to guide our steps, a message sent to each of our hearts so that we might live out that message. But if this revelation is not a vast ensemble or, if you will, "a vast system" of holy *truths* come from God, *and which like Him transcend time*, and for which after the example of Christ we must be ready to die, and which the Church of Christ, His Spouse, the flesh of His flesh, has the mission to transmit to men and to preserve in their purity, then there is no light, and no message for us to live out.

"Haec oportebat," dicere, "et illa non omittere."

VII. DIFFERING DEGREES OF RECEIVED INSPIRATION

18. Let us take up once again the thread of our ideas. Before this digression on faith-confidence and theological faith, we were busy with those certitudes

---

51   *Une Introduction à la foi catholique: Le Catéchisme hollandais* (1968), p. 375.

in singular and contingent matters which in their prayer life Christians happen to receive from private inspirations due to angelic illumination. I still have to touch at least summarily on a final point in this subject, namely, the differing *degrees of strength* of the inspirations and the illuminations in question.

In the first degree—a very feeble one—what has been imprinted on the supraconscious (and which then passes into consciousness just like anything else grasped intuitively in the heaven of the soul by a natural process) bears within it nothing that might in any way reveal its origin. All we know is that an idea arrives by surprise or that we are seized by an intuition, in short that "that we have an inspiration": of natural or supernatural origin? Impossible to tell.[52] What conclusion can we reach from this, if not that we often take for a natural inspiration one that in reality comes from above? It is by reason of this first and feeble degree of strength in angelic illuminations that—given the fact that our *convivium* with heavenly spirits is something *absolutely normal*—I maintain that illuminations and inspirations received from angels are *frequent* in reality, at least on the level in question, even though we do not recognize them as such. A practical conclusion: more confidence than we ordinarily have in the help of our guardian angels. When we have a sudden inspiration, it can certainly have a purely natural origin. But it is probable that more often than we suspect our guardian angel has whispered in our ear.

At the second level, the illumination and the inspiration received have much greater strength. They bear within them a certain mark, experienced yet ineffable, which distinguishes them from a purely natural process. The light which illuminates the soul is different. And it is in such cases, when the ray of the *lumen propheticum* is sufficiently strong, that the soul, with an authentic certitude, adds faith to what it has been shown by such an inspiration, particularly (but not necessarily) when it is in response to a prayer made in an ardent spirit of faith and when it is intimately related to a long experience of the life of prayer.

If it happens that words are heard, I think it is by virtue of psychological mechanisms through which what is present in the supraconscious is expressed

---

52   Cf. above pp. 285–287.

Medicine has recently made considerable progress with the discovery of a preventive method for overcoming the scourge due to the "RH incompatibility factor," to which many newborn babies fall victim every year. When the wife of the biologist C. A. Clarke woke him up in the middle of the night to tell him: "Give them the anti-RH," she was evidently acting under the impulse of a very vivid intuition or "inspiration." Was this completely natural? Or was some angelic illumination involved? Impossible to tell. All that can be said is that if an angelic illumination did take place in this particular case, it was by virtue of a very general disposition of the order of the universe (cooperation between angelic and human intellects). In addition, the case in question conforms to another disposition of nature, just as general (cooperation between the feminine intellect, by nature more intuitive, and the masculine intellect, by nature more rational). (Cf. *Le Monde*, February 27, 1969.)

in the verbal imagination as they pass into consciousness—I do not believe that in such a case a pure spirit whispers human words into our ear. But what does happen at this second level is in fact entirely different from what happens in a purely natural inspiration. In the case of a purely natural inspiration, the subject "speaks to himself" under a subconscious motion of his own. In the case of an inspiration of supernatural origin, it is no longer exact to say simply that the subject "speaks to himself"; for here, in reality, a pure spirit illuminates him under a special motion of God: it should be said, rather, that it is a pure spirit that speaks to him in God's name, using our psychological mechanisms as instruments. And it is this which, by an effect produced in the soul under the primordial light of theological faith and the added ray of *lumen propheticum*, makes the soul certain that the words it has heard come from heaven.[53]

In a very beautiful recently published book,[54] André Frossard, after pointing out to us that at the age of twenty he was a perfect atheist and entirely ignorant of anything about the Catholic faith, tells us how he was suddenly turned completely upside down, converted in two minutes, when, in search of a friend, he entered by chance into the chapel of the Sisters of the Atonement on the rue d'Ulm (where the Blessed Sacrament is always exposed). Let us listen to his testimony, which, precisely because up till that moment he had absolutely no idea or no experience of the Christian faith, tells us with total ingenuity what took place.

"First of all, these words were suggested to me: *spiritual life*.

"They were not said to me, I did not form them myself, I heard them as if they had been pronounced close to me in a low voice by a person who saw what I did not yet see."[55]

Here then are two words heard in exactly the same way as I have just

---

53   The locutions I am speaking of here can be compared to what St. John of the Cross calls "formal words" (*Ascent of Mount Carmel*, Bk. II, Ch. 30). He distinguishes (ch. 27–31) three categories of words: *successive words* (which the subject actually says to himself, even though they can be inspired by God—cf. in my exposé, the few words I just said about "inspirations of the first level"), *formal words*, and *substantial words*.

      Formal words "occur without the mind making any contribution of its own" and "sometimes they come to it without in any way being garnered from what is being said to it while it is thinking of something entirely different"—"sometimes it is just one word, sometimes two or more"—"I call them formal because a third person communicates to the mind, without adding anything of his own" (*loc. cit.*, *Les Oeuvres spirituelles du Bienheureux Père Jean de la Croix* (Paris: Desclée de Brouwer, 1949), pp. 294 and 293).

      Concerning the difference between the general subject of my present reflections and the general subject that St. John of the Cross had in mind, see further on p. 299.

54   *Dieu existe, je l'ai rencontré* (Paris: Fayard, 1969)

55   *Ibid.*, p. 165.

indicated, with the single difference that this time they were heard, not under a ray of the *lumen propheticum*, but under a ray of the *lumen fidei*.[56]

Let us return to his account. "The last syllable of this murmured prelude had scarcely reached the shore of my consciousness when a reverse avalanche began. I am not saying that the heavens opened up; they did not; rather it rushed forth, it rose up like a silent fulguration in that chapel beyond all suspicion within which it was mysteriously enclosed. How can I describe this with words that recognize their own inadequacy and refuse me their help, and which threaten to intercept my thoughts and consign them to the storehouse of fanciful delusions? If a painter had the gift of seeing colors as yet unknown, what would he paint them with? It is an indestructible crystal of infinite transparence, of an almost unbearable luminosity (one degree more would have destroyed me) and a *kind of blueness*, an entire world, another world of a brilliance and density that pushes our world back into the fragile shadows of unfinished dreams. This is reality, this is truth, I can see it from the darkling shore where I am still detained."[57]

Note the words: "almost unbearable luminosity"; this is the *lumen fidei*. And note too that it possessed an inexpressible nuance which the author, forced as he was to make use of our poor human language, translates by the words "a kind of blueness" which he underlines in his text. I would like to read you the entire following page in which he recalls the unheard of richness of content which the illumination he received bore within it. But what I just read is enough to make my point. Still I would like to point out just these words: "There is an order in the universe, and at its summit, beyond this veil of resplendent mists, there is the evidence of God, an evidence that becomes presence, an evidence become the very person of Him whom I would have denied an instant before. . . ."[58] The illumination he received bore the mark of its author. It came from God.

---

56   The very exceptional character of such a case is due to the fact that the *lumen fidei* takes on the appearance here of a thunderbolt passively received, even though it is essential to faith that it be voluntary. In reality the theological virtue of faith is given to the soul instantly at the very same moment because at that moment, and even without being aware of it, the soul in its turn, under the effect of grace, adheres voluntarily and freely to everything that is shown to it by this light, and to this extent receives it actively: "Credo, Domine."

57   André Fossard, *Dieu existe, je l'ai rencontré*, p. 166. There are many other examples of sudden conversion, from the conversion of St. Paul in the apostolic age and which still sheds its light on the universal Church, to those in modern times, of Louis Ratisbonne, for example, of Claudel and of Massignon. But they were not characterized beforehand by a total ignorance of religious matters as was the conversion of André Frossard. One might say that this particular conversion was a challenge to our time thrown down by a Providence that had no particular fondness for sensitivity and discretion.

58   *Ibid.*

The case of André Frossard is an extreme and exceptional one, but it is a magnificent illustration, at an incomparably less elevated level (where in the light of theological faith, mediated this time, a ray of *lumen propheticum* enlightens the soul) of what I think is characteristic of the private inspirations that any Christian in the course of his existence, if he is faithful to the life of prayer, is capable of receiving from angels, when the strength of these inspirations is at the second degree I just spoke of—and at the third degree as well, which I will turn to now.

At this third level, I would say that the mark or sign I just mentioned, which remains ineffable even though it has been experienced, and which is the bearer of the fecundating germ imprinted on the supraconscious, is like the "signature" of the blessed spirit (either an angel or a glorified soul) who is acting on us in this case under a special motion of God. Does not the tone of voice of someone who is speaking to us make us recognize who it is? Similarly, in the illumination received there is a mysterious but very precise nuance (remember the "kind of blueness" mentioned by André Frossard?) which is the sign of the individuality and as it were the "name" of the one by whom this illumination and this inspiration come to us, and which enables us to recognize him.[59]

---

59   For Joan of Arc, St. Catherine, and St. Margaret were named; but not St. Michael. Yet she knew perfectly well the identity of St. Michael. She had seen him "with her very eyes, and she was as sure of it as she was of God's existence" (Quicherat, K, p. 93: Olivier Leroy, *Sainte Jeanne d'Arc, Les Voix*, p. 32). Olivier Leroy wrote: "Joan was certain that the apparition was St. Michael, but she could not say how it was she knew this, because she did not know how to explain that her knowledge was intuitive. She felt that to say: "I know that it was St. Michael because it is a truth communicated to my mind without words," would be to draw the fire of new questions and create new difficulties. It was exhausting to converse with men who did not speak her language" (*Ibid.*, p. 33). And he points out (p. 35) that St. Teresa of Avila, "speaking of the visions of saints that she had, remarks that she understood many things that they expressed without words, beginning with their identity. When she saw them she recognized them as very intimate friends: she knew who they were without being able to say or to understand how she knew this" (cf. *Château intérieur, sixieme demeure*, ch. v, p. 403, Bouix translation). Concerning the vision of Jesus Christ that she had during mass on the feast of St. Paul, Teresa wrote again: "It was evident to me that this was Jesus Christ Himself; this was due to the degree of clarity with which He deigned to show Himself to me" (*Vie*, ch. XXVIII, pp. 302–303).

We are still faced with a very difficult problem here which surpasses our limited capacities. But I will risk a few reflections on it. I think that a certain absolutely unique quality of emotion, of spiritual joy ineffably experienced by the souls of Teresa and Joan, with supreme sweetness made them connatural to the *very being* of the one whom they saw and who spoke to them. In addition, if this person was someone on whom in their everyday existence and in their simple life of faith, their thoughts and their love had been concentrated in the past, then the emotion that they were accustomed to experience at the very mention of the name (for St. Teresa the name of Jesus! or for Joan of Arc the name of the angel who had said *quis ut Deus*) already had the same absolutely singular

From this, I think, comes the feeling that in very different cases and in very different ways, prayerful souls can experience the *presence* of someone from heaven, and this can be the Lord Himself, or Our Lady, it could be a guardian angel with whom the soul in question feels a habitual relationship, it could be one of the Blessed who has been invoked, it could be someone now in heaven that the soul knew and loved on earth and by whose help it is sustained, in such a case it is not at all surprising that this someone should be known by name.

In my *Carnet de notes*[60] I mentioned that our sister Vera often heard Jesus speaking to her (in the depths of her heart, without any material sound) and that starting from a certain date (September 1939, when the horrors of the war were about to begin) He permitted her to confide this secret to us: She transcribed the brief messages she received in this way on scraps of paper which she gave us. She knew very well who spoke to her in her prayers; and nothing was simpler, or humbler, or more lacking in self-interest and less surprising than these messages confided to us to keep us from losing hope, and which were a treasure for Raïssa and me.

19. The three degrees of strength that I just mentioned in angelic illumination and the inspiration received depend on what can be called the ordinary supernatural,[61] the level of the supernatural at which the ordinary Christian who perseveres in the life of prayer is involved.

At an entirely different level, much higher—and rarer by far—there are angelic interventions which depend on the *extraordinary* supernatural: those in which a pure spirit takes on a sensible form by assuming all the visible and tangible appearances of a human body (cf. *Sum. theol.*, Ia, q. 51, a. 2 and 3). It is not surprising that in such cases the pure spirit pronounces words that affect the external sense—like the angels who conversed with Abraham, or the one who spoke with the holy women at the tomb of the risen Christ, or the angel Gabriel who conversed with Mary on the day of the Annunciation. I have no reason to be concerned here with this extraordinary supernatural.[62] I would

---

tonality, though with an incomparably lesser intensity, as the emotion which would penetrate them before the apparition. This is why they intuitively gave a name, with complete certitude, to the being that each saw and who spoke to them. We could say that they *recognized* this being.

60   Pp. 285 ff.

61   In conformity with current usage such illuminations and inspirations are often called "extraordinary graces" (I have often used this term myself): but in my opinion this is a very ill-chosen expression. These are charismatic graces, surely, but graces which are not necessary for salvation and are relatively infrequent (at least with regard to the second and third degrees of the inspirations in question). I am persuaded however that they are in themselves ordinary graces, or graces which conform to the common order established by Providence for those *parvuli* who are faithful to the life of prayer.

62   Joan of Arc's Voices and visions were dependent on this extraordinary supernatural. I referred to them in the preceding notes only because they shed light

simply point out parenthetically that what took place on the day of the Annunciation was a sublime response to what had taken place with Eve in the earthly Paradise, and that—here I am advancing an opinion contrary to that of St. Thomas[63]—the fact of having been deceived by the Father of Lies did not, in my opinion, presuppose any sin at all for Eve who had no experience of evil or of lying (and to whom I imagine he presented himself as an envoy of Elohim). She sinned only when she *consented* to do what the bad angel was suggesting to her.

---

from a higher region on the considerations I have proposed in this essay on the level of the ordinary supernatural. Joan's Voices were auricular words; the saints whom she saw and who said to her: "Daughter of God, go, go, go; I will be there to help you, go!" appeared to her in bodily form. (She had her first vision at the age of thirteen; at that time she made of vow of virginity, but she had not yet committed her faith. She still needed to weigh these matters. It was only at the time of her third vision, when she found out the identity of the angel, that she had, as she said at her trial, "that will to believe" (cf. Olivier Leroy, *Sainte Jeanne d'Arc, Les Voix*, pp. 122, 130). "She repeated untiringly that her Voices came from God, that she heard them every day, several times a day, that she saw them with her eyes and heard them with her ears: just as I see you, judges, and as I hear you. 'You can believe me or not!'" (*Ibid.*, P. 133–134). She fell to her knees before St. Catherine and St. Margaret, "kissed and embraced them—putting her arms around their knees. She could smell their fragrance and feel their form, which did not vanish at her touch." (*Ibid.*, p. 132).

Concerning the questionable historicity of St. Catherine of Alexandria and of St. Margaret of Antioch, see the very apt remarks that Olivier Leroy makes in his precious little book (*Ibid.*, pp. 134–139). Edmond Richer, an seventeenth century specialist at the Sorbonne, thought that it was angels who appeared to Joan under the form and figure of these two saints, and I concur in this opinion. As I pointed out in my text, Angels can "take on bodies" (*Sum. theol.*, Ia, q. 51, a. 2) presenting all the appearances (visible, tangible, olfactive, etc.) of a human being. And not a single saint—except the Lord Himself and His Mother—is in heaven with his or her body.

"Whether these two saints are historical or not," writes Olivier Leroy, "Joan had no more than a very limited knowledge of their lives. However, what she knew of them, what she honored and venerated in them had a permanent truth about it, a truth that was outside the grasp of History past or present. In the persons of Catherine or Margaret, she venerated virginity, the love of God, Christian wisdom and the abnegation of martyrdom, and she honored them by imitating them to the point of dying as they did. These are not realities that can vanish like an historical fiction." (*Ibid.*, p. 138)

63   Cf. *Sum. theol.*, IIa-IIae, q. 163, a. 4, ad 1m: "*Seductio mulieris ex praecedenti elevatione subsecuta est.*" Was not the eating of the forbidden fruit the *first sin*? How could it have been preceded by another, by reason of which Eve was deceived by the serpent? It was not out of pride but out of naïveté that she believed the serpent ("you will be like gods, knowing good and evil") who was more cunning than she. It was out of pride that, instead of replying, "What difference does that make? God has forbidden us to do it, so I will not do it," she instead took the fruit of the tree of the knowledge of good and evil and ate of it.

Since I have named him, let me add that the demon too can send inspirations of his own, false inspirations and pseudo-illuminations in which he does not act under the special divine motion mentioned above, but only under that general motion under which everything in the universe acts, and which he made use of this time as the principle agent taking the very first initiative of nothingness, as happens every time in the case of moral evil.

VIII. FINAL REMARKS

20. To conclude this long exposé I would like to indicate clearly that the perspective within which the reflections I have proposed to you have always been placed is entirely different from that of a great master like St. John of the Cross. In principle, and rightly so, he shows himself quite severe toward whatever relates to the charismatic order, sensible graces, private illuminations and inspirations, locutions heard (even when they come authentically from heaven), visions, etc.—because he is speaking to privileged souls, set out toward the summits of the contemplative life. From this point of view, whatever is not God and the pure experience of God is accessory or parasitic and runs the risk of delaying the ascent or leading the soul astray down dead-end paths. Such souls are like wives whose husbands overwhelm them with flowers and jewels. "Do not send me any more of these things. It is you alone that I want." This is what the holy Doctor tries to have them respond to God. In other words, what he is concerned with from his perspective is to have them climb, often by the most dizzying paths, the mountain's highest peaks.

But the paths of such heroic mountain climbers are not the only paths there are. There are also footpaths across the plains and over humble little hills, and walks through woodlands and trails that have to be blazed through the underbrush. These are the paths open to the generality of Christians, to the simple souls that we all are outside the sphere of our special competences and the *habitus* that go with them, the paths of those who, living in the world (without being of the world), try to live, and make progress in, a life of prayer. And it is in this particular perspective that all the reflections I have submitted to you should be placed.

They are definitely not concerned with those high levels of knowledge which risk distracting us from the one thing necessary, or with the scaling of the highest peaks to which the wisdom of the Holy Spirit can lead. They concern only those who are engage in "contemplation on the way" (*in via*) and their humble secrets in *the practical conduct of their lives.*[64] Are not charismatic graces bestowed above all *ad directionem actuum humanorum*? And do not the

---

64   "*Quandoque enim illuminatur intellectus hominis ab angelis ad cognoscendum solum quod aliquid est bonum fieri. . . . Quandoque vero per illuminationem angeli instruitur etiam quod hoc sit bonum et de ratione quare est bonum.*" C. Gent., III, c. 92.

faith, the reason, and the prudence of those who are committed to contemplation along those paths that lead through the very midst of this world need to
be *aided* from on high with support that is perfectly normal in itself? What I
would like to point out is that today more than ever it is of primary importance,
it is more important than anything else, that they be told this, and that they be
assured that along with them, and better than they do themselves, God and
His angels take care of the practical conduct of their lives.

We know very well all the ambushes that the world has prepared in advance
for a Christian life. We know very well that more are called than are chosen
and that good seeds can fall on rocks or be smothered by weeds. But we know
just as well that the common run of Christians compose the people of God,
that royal and priestly people that St. Peter just mentioned,[65] and that all are
called to the perfection of the love of charity. They must fight their way, more
or less blindly, through the immense throng in which vice and virtue, heroism
and cowardice, generosity, perfidy, and cruelty, a thirst for true love and
abominable egoism are tangled together pell-mell, in which wandering astray
is more frequent than right action and in which pretense and disguise reign
everywhere supreme. For in this melee things do not happen as they do in
books, and the atheism or the lack of perseverance of some is at times no more
than the disguise worn by an unsatisfied desire for the absolute which hides
a lingering nostalgia for the faith, a faith that in certain cases is buried in the
misery of the senses or in bitter disillusionment with self; whereas the edifying
conduct of others is sometimes no more than a disguise in the pursuit of the
vilest self-interest.

In this world we are very well situated to learn never to judge the deep
recesses of souls and, if one is sufficiently open-hearted, to "admire everywhere and to understand as much as possible the freedom, the breadth and
the variety of God's ways."[66] But pitfalls lie everywhere. We are not concerned
here with a procession of monks following the Blessed Sacrament. We are
concerned with the complete confusion and disorder of a fair or a vast carnival
in which each one wears a mask which disguises him from his own eyes even
more than from the eyes of others, and in which each one nevertheless goes
his way under the attentive control of the justice and pity of the Father, and
under the merciful gaze of Jesus and of Mary, and also under the gaze of the
angels of heaven and the blessed, whose *convivium* with us, let me repeat it
one more time, is something absolutely normal. And in order to make their
way through this carnival, do not souls need, at particular moments and in
more or less serious particular circumstances, illuminations and inspirations
that come from the angels and the blessed souls in heaven?

21. Here a short rather general digression seems to me in place. I would like

---

65   Cf. above, p. 285.

66   *Journal de Raïssa*, p. 154.

to say a few words about what appear to me to be laws in the realm of nature and the realm of grace.

God has a boundless respect for nature and for the order of the universe He created; His own honor is involved here, as well as the honor of his free creatures. This is why He sends His rain on the just and the unjust, and lets the free will of men, as they willingly choose to nihilate (or cause nothingness) take the first initiative in evil: not only to choose sin for themselves, but also, as a consequence of that same freedom, to torture, to debase, to pervert, to assassinate others, to pour out over the world crimes against the body and against the spirit. This is the law, the terrible law of the realm of nature. This realm is not abolished; it is transfigured by the boundless overcompensation which the realm of grace pours out over human history, by virtue of the Blood of Christ.

For at the same time that He leaves each creature endowed with reason free to sin, even though that creature may not have asked for anything except through the fact of his existence, God sends to each and every one of them the immaculate snows of his grace. But only those souls who do not turn away from God's loving attentions enter into what can be called the normal regime of grace. And among these particular souls there are some who have the privilege of being helped and protected all along their way—I do not mean that they are protected against suffering and persecution, against failures, nights of interior desolation, their apparent abandonment by God, the holy and cruel Cross (on the contrary, all this is their lot, for they are co-redeemers). I mean that they are protected against their own misery, and in addition against whatever comes from without—temptations of the devil, the pitfalls of this world and of suffering itself—and threatens to make them fall, in such a way that all things, even the worst, contribute to their progress toward God.

Why such a privilege? Because these souls ask without ceasing. Let us recall what is said in Luke xi, 9–13: "Ask and you shall receive, seek and you shall find, knock and it shall be opened to you. *Omnis enim qui petit, accipit....* Your Father in heaven will give to those who ask him, *dabit spiritum bonum petentibus se.*" Ask, ask above all else, and it will be given to you. This is no counsel of piety; this is the proclamation of the law of the normal regime of grace. A request from below (itself inspired by grace) must rise toward heaven if heaven is to answer. *To ask* is the presupposed condition.

So if we aspire to be helped and protected *without ceasing*, it is not enough to believe in the divine goodness, nor to have that confidence I spoke of a moment ago in our guardian angel; we must pray *without ceasing* to our heavenly Father and to the Lord Jesus, and pray *without ceasing* (in one sense this is easier) to the angels and the blessed in heaven. And so if we succeed in asking like this *unceasingly*, then we can and we must be sure of never receiving a stone instead of bread, sure of being helped and protected *unceasingly*. If we did not have this certitude we would be men of little faith.

Father Osende explains that it is within reach of each of us to pray always, thanks to what he calls *prayer of the heart*, which is "unconscious" or rather supraconscious.[67] In actual fact, however, there are very few who pray always and ask without ceasing: perhaps, above all, because most give in to fear, a fear that after all is not without its cause. Indeed a corollary to the law we are concerned with here is undoubtedly that the more you ask, the more you will receive, but along with it the more you receive, the more will be asked of you. *"Omni cui multum datum est, multum quaeritur ab eo"* (Luke xii, 48). It is not possible that in the case of those who ask without ceasing and receive without ceasing one day or other the "question of the Chalice" should not be put to them, as it was to James and John:[68] *Can you drink the cup that I will drink?* (Matt. xx, 22) In other words, it is impossible that one day or other the call to be a *disciple* should not be addressed to such a person. And it has been said: "If anyone comes to me without turning his back on his father and mother, his wife and his children, his brothers and sisters, indeed his very self, *he cannot be my disciple*" (Luke xiv, 26).

"The demands of Christ with regard to his *disciples*," writes Raïssa, "are absolutely inhuman, they are divine. There is no doubt that whoever wishes to be a disciple of Christ must hate his own life . . ."[69] And she is right to add: "But such demands are for disciples *alone*. With regard to the general community of men Christianity is quite *human*, in the sense that it accepts men in their weakness and inconstancy, as well as in their nature, attached as it is to natural goods (father, mother, etc.). They will never hear within them a call as severe as the one recounted by Luke.

"All that is asked of them is to believe and to continue to hope even after their wildest aberrations.

"Nor is it the sinner, the 'worldly,' who fear God the most,—it is rather those who, having been chosen as disciples, know that they will be more severely treated. Of them *everything* is demanded."

But the others, the vast multitude of all the others, all those who, caught in the maelstrom of the regime of nature and of a fallen nature such as ours, "will never feel within them the call" addressed to the disciples, what must be said of them concerning the privilege of being protected without ceasing which we were just discussing? It must be said that since they have not received *much*, *much* will not be asked of them. The privilege we spoke of is not for them; since they do not ask without ceasing, they are not protected without ceasing. So are they abandoned? Those who never, or almost never, ask, are they abandoned? Though they make their way stumbling often and wandering astray among the shadows, they are far from being abandoned.

For there is another law of this normal regime of grace, a law which

---

67   Cf. *Liturgy and Contemplation*, p. 37–39.

68   *Raïssa's Journal*, p. 154.

69   *Ibid.*, p. 369

expresses a fundamental exigency of the communion of saints. This is the law which states that prayer is not only for oneself, but also for others, for all the others; and from this prayer for others, also prescribed for each one of us, God forms an immense storehouse of grace from which, at the request of the angels and the blessed, He distributes His riches in every corner of the earth. This is what aids and protects, undoubtedly not without ceasing, but at particular moments and in particular circumstances, and in innumerable crucial situations, the souls we are speaking of at present.

And these souls have their own particular privilege, which bear witness to the way the divine transcendence operates and stems from the scandalously paradoxical ways of God's mercy.

On the one hand, concerning the evil into which the souls in question fall through their own fault, they have the word of Jesus: "There will be more joy in heaven over one repentant sinner than over ninety-nine just who have no need of repentance" (Luke xv, 7). How fortunate the Good Thief was! And how fortunate those great sinners who repent!

On the other hand, with regard to the infinitely multiple and limitlessly distributed forms of evil they suffer from the miserable conditions of this world and from the swarming cruelty of the wicked, they have these words of Our Lord: "Blessed are those who weep, for they shall be comforted." (Matt. v, 5). The murder of the innocent! They are in heaven sooner than those who survive them. The suffering of children, the debasement and perversion of the weak and defenseless, who in God's sight are also the innocent! When they cross the threshold, God's gentle pity will make them equal to the angels. Happy the innocent who have been trampled underfoot; happy those who have been tortured who, if they had any debts to pay, will already have paid them here below . . .

22. "This digression was not altogether useless," an expression which those who followed Bergson's courses at the College de France heard quite often. Getting back to my subject, let me say this once again in conclusion. In the order of the intelligence faith alone is not sufficient for the human intellect to attain the highest knowledge of divine things it is capable of in this world (it will be fully satisfied only by the beatific vision). Theological faith must extend its domain in the intellect by means of consequences and effects that are distinct from faith but depend on it, which are the truths organized among themselves by theological knowledge and wisdom, thanks to a long and difficult labor of reason rooted in the faith. And for this a special *habitus* is needed, one that is reserved to the small number of those who are capable of acquiring it.

Similarly, in the case of those who are not capable of acquiring this *habitus*, whom I call here the simple, faith alone is not sufficient for them to lead the life of the spirit to which the Christian people is called, or to lead those who really want it toward the perfection of charity, to the extent that the one or the other can get there by fulfilling his duties of state and according to the extreme diversity of conditions to which human existence is subject. Theological faith must extend its rule over the entire soul, by consequences and effects that are distinct from faith but depend on it, which depend certainly on reason and on the cardinal virtue of prudence, but where, in the long and difficult experience of the life of prayer and of the search for intimacy with God, prudence and reason need to be helped and enlightened from above, above all by the gifts of the Holy Spirit but also by angelic illuminations and inspirations, which is the subject I wanted to speak about today. Everything that has been acquired in the course of this experience, each one of all those truths that have been lived out from day to day in this experience and brought into play by it so as habitually to enlighten the spirit, all of these things play a role with regard to the practical conduct of truly faithful souls among ordinary Christian people (and they are more numerous than one might tend to believe). And this particular role is analogous to the role which the theological *habitus* plays with regard to the intellect and which, making them capable of leading lives worthy of their vocation, alone makes them capable, each in his or her own way, of proclaiming to this poor world the Kingdom of God (*to come*, though it has already begun *within the Church*).

That Christian laypeople are called to bear witness to their faith and to participate in the apostolate of the Church (under forms that are far from always having to be organized) is quite evident. The same is the case for fraternal charity. But is it not necessary that first and foremost they themselves have the experience of an authentic life of faith? That in addition, with regard to the body politic, they are called to a social and political action that is also worthy of their vocation is no less evident. But it is not this additional activity in the temporal order which will furnish them, except by accident, the slightest help in their life of prayer and faith which is their first vocation.

What they need first of all is good instruction and guidance in that life. It seems to me that the masters of the spiritual life and the theologians have hardly treated the numerous questions concerning the life of faith as it relates, not to people who have vowed themselves specifically to the life of prayer, but to the common run of Christians, questions which contemplation in the midst of the world raises for theological reflection, and apropos of which the first and immediate need is to have a solidly founded doctrine that can be readily applied to particular cases. For the experience of the life of faith, with all the lived truths that it brings to light, is a very individual thing which each person acquires for himself, in an ensemble of circumstances which is particular to him; but this same experience of itself presupposes a body of universal truths which it is the theologians' job to sort out, in order to set up a domain accessory to his area of specialized knowledge (a tiny province indeed, far away from the big cities of learning)—a body of truths that he should be able to teach to ordinary Christian people. I have a dream of a school of wisdom open to anyone who would want to study there. The teaching I am talking about is not at all what I have called the "substitute for theology among the simple," (the substitute I refer to is the experience of the life of faith itself with all that it brings with it). The teaching I have in mind would present general truths presupposed by this experience, and such teaching is necessary because human beings are endowed with intelligence and have the need to recognize everywhere the primacy of truth.

May our friends in theology consecrate a little of their time to exploring from a doctrinal point of view the domain I have just alluded to.

As for myself, today I have done no more—with some temerity, for I know what I lack here—than try, in a somewhat desultory way, to draw a little attention to this problem.

POSTSCRIPT

Throughout the preceding essay the whole question of charismatic graces or graces *gratis datae* is involved, for, as I see it, angelic illuminations and inspirations are part of these graces *gratis datae*.

The question of these graces needs to be treated in a systematic fashion by someone more competent than myself. Nevertheless I am going to take the risk of proposing, in a hypothetical manner, my own views on the question, which are no more than a philosopher's groping about in the dark (and which will, I am somewhat afraid, stir up some controversy).

Let me point out first that today the notion of charisma is put to immodest and aberrant use, behind which can be found, like a *panic-stricken* idea, drunk with the dreams of the "anti-establishment" imagination, the classical idea of graces *gratis datae* in the tradition of the great theologians.

It is this particular idea which interests me and which, in my opinion, should be examined closely—and reworked—in a meditation evidently in strong opposition to the cheap prophetism of today.

It seems to me that the great theologians who established the theory of *gratiae gratis datae* have concentrated their attention either on the great prophetism of Israel, or on the *great charisma* at work in the primitive Church (cf. Mark xvi, 27–20; I Cor. xii, 8–10). These great charisma (which, once the Church was founded, rather quickly ceased to shine out in all their brilliance as divine signs) were clearly destined *ad utilitatem aliorum* (*Sum. theol.*, Ia-IIae, q. 111, a. 1; the word *aliorum* is added by St. Thomas; St. Paul in I Cor. xii, 7 says simply *ad utilitatem*) or *ad utilitatem Ecclesiae* (in contrast to sanctifying grace or grace *gratis faciens*, by which God, the ultimate supernatural End of the soul, is already here below present in the soul and unites it to His love).

I would say, however, distancing myself on this point from my master, that if graces *gratis datae* considered generally are defined by this characteristic, such a definition leaves aside a vast domain which also depends on the graces *gratis datae* (but this time stripped of the external brilliance of the great charisma).[70] Moreover, it is not without a certain amount of awkwardness and without having to turn to exercises of high-powered acrobatics that eventually the notion of charismatic graces or graces *gratis datae* had to be extended to "extraordinary graces"—visions, revelations, etc.—of which the lives of the saints offer us many examples. Such charisma can certainly be destined for the edification of others; but they can also, and probably far more frequently, be given by God as a testimony of His love to encourage and help the saint (though the prudence of a St. John of the Cross and of a St. Francis de Sales made them a bit suspicious of this) in his own personal life of union and immolation. The fact remains, again undoubtedly, in memory of the great signs at work in the primitive Church, and also as a justification of their extension to the particular case of visions and revelations (or the diversion toward it) of the notion of graces *gratis datae* defined as given *ad utilitatem aliorum, ad utilitatem Ecclesiae,* that it is then the *extraordinary* supernatural that classical theology has in view when it takes under consideration those charismatic graces received by certain friends of God, in reality and primarily, for the benefit of their personal sanctification and of the lofty contemplation they so ardently desire.

So I make bold to think that it is very important to recast and broaden the whole idea of charismatic grace or graces *gratis datae* in order to give it the breadth and balance that it requires by its nature, which classical theology seems to me to have elaborated in a rather constrained and artificial manner beginning with a definition that is far too narrow.

It would become evident then, it seems to me, that the essential characteristic of graces *gratis datae* is not their relation *ad alios* as is evident in certain of these graces but rather their function as *means* of a supernatural order granted with a view to the practical conduct of life, through a gratuitous effusion of divine generosity, *in addition to* the means which all those who are in the state of sanctifying grace have at their disposal because of this state, and which all of them must make use of. The supplementary or additional means in question here can play a major role with regard to the apostolic work of the Church, and they did so above all with regard to its founding (it was for the utility of the Church then that such charismatic graces were received by particular individuals); but they can, at least in certain cases where special help is required, play their role as well—a minor role, though more extensive by far—with regard to the completely interior and private work to be accomplished by each individual person who would make faithful progress amid the shadows of this world toward the perfection of charity.

---

70   After all, a good definition should tell us what a thing is and not simply the end to which it is ordered.

From this new perspective how are we to define *gratia gratis data*? As I see it, in the following fashion: It is a gratuitous means or help (gratuitous above all)[71] given, in addition to what is necessary for salvation, *ad utilitatem Ecclesiae vel animae*, for the good of the Church *or of the soul itself* (for is not each individual soul, though in a state of imperfect similitude, like a Church in miniature?). Let us remark that the help in question is what I shall call a *passively received* help (as might happen to someone asleep whom someone else awakens by ringing a bell or shaking him in order to assign him a task that later he will have to carry out of his own free will). Such is the case with angelic illuminations and inspirations which from without imprint an intuitive germ in the human supraconscious. Such helps passively received are supplementary or additional graces, exterior to the supernatural structure given to the soul by the grace of the virtues and the gifts, and incapable of sanctifying on their own, even though they are means in the service of the life of grace.

Just as the Church, holy in the image of Christ her Bridegroom, needs these extra graces to make its way amid the fortunes of this world that she has the mission to evangelize, in the same way the soul who truly wishes to lead a life of faith normally, at least in certain circumstances, needs such extra graces— which undoubtedly at times can depend on the extraordinary supernatural, but which generally depend on the *ordinary* supernatural and bring their help to the *ordinary run of faithful souls*. According to the particular conditions and difficulties of each soul, these extra graces are sent so that each soul may make its private way in the midst of the contingent, singular, and changing situations through which its spiritual life must pass. In this way, with the help of such assistance conferred through the ministry of the angels as a complement and even as a surplus to the grace of the gifts and the virtues, the soul finds itself encouraged and strengthened, and even enjoying a very particular intimacy in those moments when the path it is following seems to disappear in the sand.

I think it is this way for two reasons. First of all, as St. Thomas shows us so admirably (Ia-IIae, q. 68, a. 1 and 2), the theological virtues being infused into us without our ever attaining their full and perfect possession (*"imperfecte enim diligimus et cognoscimus Deum"*), reason, even though it is informed (*"imperfecte informata"*) by these virtues, is not enough to move us as we need to be toward our ultimate supernatural End without the help of the Gifts of the Holy Spirit. On the other hand, it is quite true that it is the particular office and the lofty privilege of these Gifts to place man in a condition to be easily moved by divine inspiration. Yet it must be noted that, precisely because they are part and parcel

---

71   I say "gratuitous above all" because the graces in question are given *over and above* the gift of sanctifying grace—supposing of course that the subject is in the state of grace—and depending on the use that his freedom makes of the gifts of this grace. We know that *gratiae gratis datae* are sometimes received by those who are not in the state of grace; in such cases they are received for others (and why not, in certain cases, for that person's conversion?).

of the dynamism of grace *gratum faciens*, whereby they move us in the very exercise of our freedom, it is in that interior heaven in which the soul dwells with the divine Persons present within it—in other words it is in its very life, in its immanent activity of grace and charity tending toward its ultimate supernatural End, that the Gifts of the Holy Spirit complete the supernatural structure of the soul and move it from above. The inspirations which come through them are inspirations *actively received*; by this I understand that the Gifts, by the very fact that they are *habitus*, lead souls to obey divine inspirations promptly, not as if they were mere instruments *cujus non est agere, sed solum agi*, but rather as instruments who, being endowed with free will, are acted upon in such a way that they themselves act at the same time (Ia-IIae, q. 68, a. 3, ad 2m). When St. Thomas wrote: *"homo sic agitur a Spiritu Sancto quod etiam agit, inquantum est liberi arbitrii,"* he did not have in mind a *passively received* incentive, following which the soul acts freely; his thought is that it is within the very instant in which it is acted upon by the Spirit that the soul itself acts, opening itself freely, under the influence of grace, to the inspiration received. This is what I call an *actively received* inspiration. Such inspirations fulfill their simple office of insuring the growth of our life of grace without anything else being required.

But I do not believe the same is the case with certain particular and contingent occurrences that take place within us or from without and regarding which we must take a stand, and which are related, sometimes to a very high degree, to our progress in our life of grace and of charity. In such situations we can make our decision in one way or another without necessarily cutting ourselves off from the life of grace (for example, must I take or refuse before God some political option or other? Shall I enter into religion or remain in the world? Is some change or other, particularly important in my eyes, that has come about in my spiritual life in conformity or not with Gods plan for me?). In such a case, the Gifts of the Holy Spirit, in order to enable us to judge suitably and obey a divine inspiration, will themselves often include—and this is the point I would like to make—a call for gratuitous forms of assistance which are *passively received* because they make the soul see an objective datum, a truth to be known or applied which, once known, will enter into the life of grace and charity to feed and strengthen it. These gratuitous forms of assistance, these gratuitous lights received passively, are *gratiae gratis datae*, in the humble sphere of the personal life of faithful souls.

Secondly, it is important not to forget that great general truth on which I insisted in my essay, and which concerns the divine plan itself, namely, that the *convivium* between pure spirits and human beings is in conformity with the disposition of the universal order and is in fact required by it.

For the two reasons I have just pointed out, I believe it must be concluded that it is *normal* that, in certain circumstances where the inspiration received is complete only when something is made evident by means of a passively received impulsion, the Gifts call for reinforcement by some form of angelic illumination and some ray of the *lumen propheticum*, or graces *gratis datae* conferred in this way, which help the faithful soul lead its life of faith unfalteringly amid the vicissitudes of this world, certainly in a sufficiently great number of cases in which the soul must for example make an absolutely decisive choice which involves it own destiny or the destiny of those in its charge.

The Gifts of the Holy Spirit are, of course, far superior to graces *gratis datae*. However, it is not because of indigence, but rather because of their superabundance that in such cases as I mentioned the Gifts make use of these graces *gratis datae*.[72]

---

72   Cf. *Sum. theol.*, IIa-IIae, q. 172, a. 2, ad. 2m: "*Dicendum quod gratiae gratis datae attribuuntur Spiritui Sancto, sicut primo principio; qui tamen operatur hujusmodi gratias in hominibus mediante ministerio angelorum.*"

CHAPTER XIV
FOR AN EXISTENTIAL EPISTEMOLOGY (IV)

NO KNOWLEDGE WITHOUT INTUITIVITY[1]

I. INTELLECT AND REASON

1. REASON, SAID HEIDEGGER, is the most implacable enemy of thought (or rather of thinking, of *Denken*).

This is a kind of blasphemy against human intelligence (with which the Heideggerian *Denken* is, after all, far from being synonymous); for human intelligence, bound as it is to the body and to the senses, is at the lowest rung on the ladder of spirits; but it is spirit, and certainly it has to reason, but it is an *intellect* which reasons. Precisely as an intellect, it is capable of grasping intuitively: by becoming some thing *intentionaliter* it sees that thing, or "reads in it" (*intelligere*, that is, *intus legere*); and precisely as reason, it advances by means of a discourse which gathers concepts together in order to have the evidence of the first principles pass through them. Wiser than Heidegger, the ancients distinguished between discursive reason and intuitive reason, as Milton (cf. J. Milton, *Paradise Lost*, Book V, ll. 486–488) said after Aristotle.[2] Rational discourse is a chain or tissue of conceptual statements (judgments) strung together by logical connections (necessary if the reasoning is demonstrative) leading to necessary conclusions. To the contrary, the intuitive functioning of the intellect is characterized by a certain immediacy.

2. In order to make my vocabulary precise, I shall reserve the word *intuition* either for the intuition of the external sense, for the creative intuition proper to the poet, or for purely intellectual and cognitive intuition—here of course I am thinking of those intuitive judgments which govern all logical connections and which, joining together immediately a subject-concept and an object-concept, themselves still fall under the jurisdiction of the notional order, like the principle of identity and the other primary assertions which we owe to the *intellectus principiorum*, but I am also thinking, and especially so, of the metaphysical intuition *par excellence*, the intuition of being—that privileged judica-

---

1   *Editor's footnote*: Cf. *Revue Thomiste*, 1970, no. 1, pp. 30–71.

2   Cf. Aristotle, *Nichomachean Ethics*, Book VI, ch. 6, 1141a2–8 (translated by W. D. Ross).

tive act by which, "seeing" without putting together concepts, the intellect seizes directly upon the real.[3]

II. ABSTRACTIVE OPERATION AND INTUITIVITY

3. Let us look at the first operation of the mind, in which the agent or illuminating intellect draws from the sensible real, which has been grasped by the perception of the external sense, and then interiorized by the imagination, the determination (*species impressa*) of the intellectual faculty which enables this faculty to know, to utter within itself, always under the action of the illuminating intellect, a *species expressa*, an idea, a concept or mental word by means of which it perceives the intelligible, then seizes it in exercised act.

This process is an abstractive process but one which envelops an intuitivity.[4] For the concept or mental word is in no way the *object* known by our intelligence in the first operation of the mind; it is the *intentio intellecta* which makes it possible to become the other immaterially; it is the bearer of the *thing to be seen* thanks to which the identification with that thing takes place in the mind, and by means of which the *object* (an intelligible nature discerned within the thing) is *known*: "*in quantum dicit verbum, anima cognoscit objectum.*"[5]

So in its relation to the intelligible (universal) object drawn by abstraction from the sensible real, the concept, because it makes us perceive or "reveals" this intelligible to us, entails, however abstract it may be, a certain element of intuitivity. And once it is stored in the mind, it will always keep this kind of intuitivity which is proper to it. When we handle our concepts like signs to be organized and put together, they continue to bear the signified within them, that is, the intelligible object we have attained thanks to them—and which they show us directly or, if it is of the metaphysical order, which they present to us analogically, as if in a reflection. It is only through the reflection proper to logic that the concept is known as such and itself becomes an object of thought.

4. I would add that the *verbum mentis* I just spoke of is the concept spontaneously and *naturally* formed by the intelligence. There are also *artificially* formed concepts, as is seen in the conceptual vocabulary of the sciences or of philosophy. These always presuppose natural concepts with their element of intuitivity and refer to them in a more or less distant manner. But it can happen

---

3   Cf. above, chapter XI: "Reflections on Wounded Nature," pp. 207–242.

4   Cf. Jacques Maritain, *Creative Intuition in Art and Poetry* (New York: Pantheon Books, 1953), pp. 75–76; paperback edition (New York: Meridian Books, 1955), pp. 55–56).

5   Cf. St. Thomas, *De Veritate*, q. 4, a. 2; *Sum. theol.*, I, 34, 1; *Sum. Contra Gentiles* IV, c. 11. Cf. also *Bergsonian Philosophy and Thomism* (New York: Philosophical Library, 1955), pp. 104–106.

that they are wrongly formed, when the object they present to the mind has itself been formed by the mind according to a system of ideas that is not founded in truth (let us say, for example, the "a priori forms," the "noumenon," the "phenomenon," or the "categorical imperative" of Kantian philosophy). In such a case, what is presented to our mind is not an intelligible nature existing in reality, and undoubtedly grasped and handled by the mind, but without any intuitivity in the strict sense of the word on the part of the mind (except for the natural concepts presupposed from afar).

An analogous remark can be made about definitions. Certain ones share in the natural intuitivity of the abstractive operation (and also in the intuitivity of a more or less extensive sensible experience, which is itself controlled by a more or less extensive knowledge): This is the case, in particular (but I do not mean to say that these are the only good definitions), for many of the definitions that come to us from the Ancients and whose accuracy is due, if I might put it this way, to the natural candor of the intelligence: for example, when man is defined as an *animal rationale*, art as the *recta ratio factibilium*, prudence as the *recta ratio agibilium*, or evil as the *privatio boni debiti*. Other definitions, then, which do not share in any way in the intuitivity of the abstractive operation, can have no value for the mind, either because they are badly constructed or because they refer to a conceptual object that has been artificially formed and wrongly so.

III. JUDGMENT AND INTUITIVITY

5. Let us now consider the second operation of the mind, judgment. Without referring to the intuition of being or of the first principles, it is the intuitive character of certain judgments that I would like to take note of—above all, those that are at the origin of the great scientific reforms.

For a long period of time the mind had made progress by following the paths of a commonly accepted system of ideas. Beginning at some given moment, usually following upon the discovery of new facts, the rational explanations that had been proposed in this way met with greater and greater difficulties and became more and more complicated. At the same time a certain disquiet or malaise slipped unconsciously into scholarly thought. So it came about that in the minds of research scholars totally new ideas sprang up which completely overturned the long accepted notions and demanded the elaboration of a new system of ideas. Think, for example, of the Copernican revolution in astronomy, of Einstein's introduction of the physics of relativity, of Freud's introduction of the psychology of the subconscious, or of the arrival of the idea of evolution, especially in biology, but also in cosmology.

How can we describe what happens in such cases? The description I am going to propose will undoubtedly need quite a bit of retouching, but on the whole I think it is a true one. It seems to me that in the minds of such scholars (uneasy both about reality itself and about the explanations of that reality, and trading off, if I can put it this way, one against the other) a kind of toppling of the old regime took place from the very start. Instead of first turning their gaze toward those conceptual constructions that they sought to set up (with greater and greater difficulty) and toward those rationally satisfying conclusions that would be drawn from a sequence of rational arguments (now more and more complicated) by which an effort is made to take account of phenomena following accepted methods, it was instead *toward reality, toward what is*, that scholars turned their gaze exclusively—looking at things in a new way, forgetting for the moment the accepted explanations. Each one looked at the world (or more exactly *his particular world*, the one which is the proper object of his particular science). And, of course, he did not, and does not, "see" it, either with the eyes of his body or with those of his mind (he is a man, not a pure spirit endowed with infused *species*). When I say that he looks at reality, I mean that, leaving aside in the area of his interest the system of commonly accepted rational explanations, he asks himself: *What is actually taking place in reality? How do things behave in concrete existence?*

To answer such a question he puts aside, as I said, the commonly accepted system of rational explanations, but he keeps in his head everything he knows from other sources and considers as certain, and he concentrates his thought on the ensemble of facts related to his field of interest—an ensemble of facts which, as characteristics of reality or of that world toward which he is turned, he *looks at* but cannot *see*. These facts become for him a kind of masked substitute for that vision refused to the human intellect and turn into so many enigmas to which he must find the key.

With regard to the agent or illuminating intellect lodged in the supra-conscious of the mind, it seems to me that all the factual data considered in this way play a role in some ways analogous to that of the *species impressa* received from the imagination, under the action of the agent intellect, through the faculty of intellectual knowledge (*intellectus possibilis*, according to the vocabulary of the Ancients). I do not mean that the agent intellect, after having drawn from those facts on which the scholar has concentrated his thought some kind or other of *species impressa* informing the intellectual faculty, would bring about the production by the latter of a mental word. Certainly not. What I think is that, under the action of the illuminating intellect, it comes about that from the simple rapprochement of certain of these facts, and *without any rational or discursive process*, there spring up like sparks, first a new image in the creative imagination toward which the mind turns and then a new *assertion* in the intelligence which changes the entire system of ideas accepted up to that time.

6. This is a judgment which, far from being a conclusion drawn from reasoning, is due to the mind's intuitivity and bursts forth in a flash of

intuitivity. Even though it might bring certitude to the mind of the man in which it is produced and because of which everything that once troubled his intelligence now suddenly receives complete satisfaction, that certitude remains hypothetical with regard to science as long as factual observations have not confirmed it. It is in this way that the observations carried out by Galileo on the satellites of Jupiter, the rotation of the sun on its axis, and the phases of Venus established the necessity of replacing the Ptolemaic system of the world by the Copernican system.

I think that in the mind of Copernicus himself, the assertion that the earth revolves about the sun started out as one of the intuitive judgments I just mentioned, which brought its own certitude to the mind in which it burst forth—and for which the legendary expression attributed to Galileo after his forced abjuration: *Eppur si muove*, seems like a typical formula.

IV. REASONING AND INTUITIVITY

7. Finally let us move on to the third operation of the mind. What I would like to point out above all is a paradox which it seems to me is not ordinarily given sufficient emphasis, namely, that for *a science* to be established and developed in the human mind—a science that is destined to make continual progress—the intuitivity of the intelligence and the discourse of reason must not cease to control one another, under different relationships.

Let me first have recourse to one of those more or less limping comparisons I am so fond of. However much they may limp, they help me to think.

If you like, suppose we imagine an explorer who has to travel through a strange country. He prepares the first stage of his journey in his head by determining with the help of his compass and of the stars the direction he is going to take. Perhaps he has in hand too some rather inaccurate map or other drawn up long ago by his predecessors. This preparation is a work of the rational order.

But before committing himself and his party to the chosen direction, he sends ahead a few members of his expedition to reconnoiter the terrain. They discover that by following the direction he has decided upon they run up against a mountain lake or a vast swamp; there can be no question of going ahead without the whole troop with, its vehicles and baggage being lost in that lake or bogged down in the swamp. The explorer receives, let us say by field telephone, the information discovered by the reconnaissance team, information which depends on the external senses and is of an experiential-intuitive order.

So he sends out a group of cartographers to join the reconaissance team. Their job is to determine rationally and verify the information furnished by the reconnaissance team, by transcribing signs marked down exactly on paper according to the laws of cartographic projection: All this as a rational rectification which, on the one hand, completes the ancient imperfect map which the explorer perhaps has at his disposition and, on the other hand, permits him to establish a map which later on anyone else can make use of, thanks to the notional signs that it provides.

So naturally he decides to change direction in order to bypass the obstacle in question. In this way at the end of his expedition he will have traced out, by means of cartographic signs, the entire route he followed and which others will be able to follow after him. To my way of thinking, this route traced out on the map is the symbol of what, in some area of its research, any science at all, at a given point in its development, will have won from the land of the unknown.

Let us note in passing that the completed sketch of the route, which from now on can be viewed in its entirety on paper, could be considered by those who later on make use of this map as due solely to the work of cartographers. But in reality the mapmakers would not have been able to carry out their work of a "rational" order, except for the work done beforehand by the reconnaissance team that explored the terrain. This work of an "experiential-intuitive" order, in a certain respect, was determined and verified rationally by the cartographers. On the other hand, let us not forget the work (of a rational order) of the explorer, when he determined the original direction, and when later on each change in direction was clarified and verified, in another respect, by the work the reconnaissance team carried out with the help of its physical senses and its intuitivity. A completely abstract epistemology too often forgets or neglects, on behalf of rational discourse, those aspects of the constitution of a science which depend on the intuitivity of the mind. An existential epistemology owes it to itself to give both intuitivity and reason their due. In addition we can say that both intuitivity and reason play an essential role in *established* science (when that science is a *habitus* that is truly exercised and lived in act and capable of making progress) just as they do in science *when it is in the process of being established*; but that the role of intuitivity is more apparent in this latter form of science, and the role of reason more apparent in established science.

8. So then, in the work by which any science is elaborated and lived out in act by the mind and by which it advances, the intuitivity of the intellect is controlled by reason in a certain respect—i.e., with respect to the exactness or correctness of its conceptualization and the rigor of its logical inferences; and the discourse of reason is controlled by the intuitivity of the intellect in another respect—i.e., with respect to "reconnoitering the terrain," in other words, with respect to changes in direction to which, at certain junctures along the path of its progress, rational discourse is obliged to make by the glance that the mind's intuitivity constantly casts on reality.

It is in this sense that, in my opinion, the law enunciated by St. Thomas must be understood: *"Discursus rationis semper incipit ab intellectu et terminatur ad intellectum."*[6] For it is certainly not enough to say that the discourse of reason begins with the first self-evident principles and ends up in those conclusions which a well-conducted rational discourse has made evident in their turn: as if one could elicit an entire philosophy, as Parmenides tried to do, from the principle of identity, which in itself undoubtedly presupposes the intuition of being but which, like the other first principles, is essentially concerned with the logical connections among concepts which have these first principles as their ultimate rule. Let us say rather that the discourse of reason always (*semper*, says St. Thomas) begins with something seen by the intellect (either in a previously established conclusion or in a rationally controlled judgment of intuitivity) and always ends up with something intuitively seen by the intellect (in a correctly established conclusion).

I just mentioned those junctures of rational discourse in which the intuitive glance cast by the mind on reality obliges reason to change direction along the path it is following. How can I best describe a little more precisely what I understand by this and which is an entirely different intuitive process than the one concerned with the second operation of the mind and those discoveries which bring about the reform or renewal of science? I would say that if reason is attentive solely to its own constructive power, to the pursuit and development of the logical sequences of its concepts, and to the growing multiplicity of conclusions which, if I may put it this way, it is its job to breed, it may very well, once rational discourse has headed down a certain path, find itself at some point in time, tempted to ignore some fact or some existential datum which it would indispensably have to take into account in order to arrive at the truth and which would oblige that rational discourse to branch off in a new direction. It is at such a moment, at such a juncture in its discourse, that reason—in order to catch its breath, as I just said, with "something intuitively seen by the intellect"—really needs a warning coming from the mind's intuitivity, which in this particular respect is in control of reason.

If this intuitivity is unceasingly on its guard, as it should be, then the intellect, as it advances rationally step by step, at the same time keeps its glance ever turned toward reality, which it would like to see, but cannot see, as our eyes see it. It is by means of the imagination that the intellect endeavors to picture reality to itself, to "see" it. In this way the role of the imagination from then on appears to be essential in a process which I consider primarily negative. While the discourse of reason unfolds and in accord with the conclusions posited by reason, the imagination, illuminated like the intelligence by the agent intellect, constantly creates representations and images—however schematic and barely sketched out they may be and, when there is question of completely spiritual matters (whose concept is analogical), how-

---

6   *Sum. theol.*, IIa-IIae, q. 8. a. 1, ad 2m.

ever purely symbolic they may be. By means of these representations and images the intuitivity of the mind *looks at* reality which it also cannot "see" as our eyes see it. The fact that at a given moment the image thus created finds itself in conflict with a fact, an existential truth which we know in some other way—either by sensible experience or by some science or other or by some connatural knowledge, even if this were still unconscious (or by theology, by an article of faith or scriptural text)—a fact which reason neglects to take into consideration, the intuitivity of the mind, turned toward this image in order to look at reality by means of that image (*"nihil sine phantasmate intelligit anima)"*[7] immediately confronts that image with a categorical *no*. No! It is not possible that things happen in this way. And at the same time it opposes a categorical *no* to the conclusion that reason has posited or is about to posit, and which is expressed by the image in question.

There is no logical inference here; there is a refusal of the intuitive order, a judgment of intuitivity, which—once under the control of reason in a fitting relationship—obliges reason to take account of the existential truth which it took the risk of ignoring, and so forces rational discourse to take another direction. It is as if, before permitting the positing of a conclusion toward which rational discourse seems to be leading, the intuitivity of the mind sets out ahead, thanks to imaginary models through which it looks at reality, on a sort of *trial run* of this conclusion on some concrete existential reality . . .

9. Shall we look for an example to illustrate what I just said? Here is one that comes from metaphysics and concerns the agent intellect. In showing that in order to take account of the human intellectual operation, which supposes an abstract *species impressa* of the data of the imagination interiorizing the data of the external senses, it is necessary to posit an actuating cause, a cause that is above the knowing intellect (*intellectus possibilis*), which is capable of becoming all things, which is itself above the imagination, which in turn is above the external senses—an actuating cause, that is, which makes the intelligence become the thing known, and which is the illuminating intellect ever in act by itself, *separatus, et impassibilis et immixtus*,[8] Aristotle had imprinted on rational

7   St. Thomas, *Sum. theol.*, Ia, q. 84, a. 7, sed contra.—*Ibid.*, corp.: *"Hoc quilibet in seipso experiri potest quod, quando aliquis conatur aliquid intelligere, format aliqua phantasmata sibi per modum exemplorum in quibus quasi inspiciat quod intelligere studet."*—*Ibid.*, ad 3m: *"Cum de hujusmodi (sc. incorporeis) aliquid intelligimus, necesse habemus converti ad phantasmata corporum, licet ipsorum non sint phantasmata."*—Cf. q. 85, a. 1.

8   Aristotle, *de Anima*, III, 5, 430a17–18, ed. P. Siwek (Rome: Gregorian University, 1933), "Textus et documenta, 8," pp. 254–255): χωριστὸς καὶ ἀπαθὴς καὶ ἀμιγής St. Thomas in his commentary *In Aristotelis Librum De Anima*, III, lect. 10 (man. ed. Rome: Marietti, 4 ed., 1959), nn. 728ff and pp. 173ff.) explains that the *intellectus possibilis* already possesses these three properties (and all the more reason for the acting intellect to have them too since it is nobler), and that *separatus* signifies separated from matter and not separated from the soul of the

discourse a direction toward what is higher, toward the transcendent, which according to Avicenna and Averroes (who read Aristotle from the perspective of his Greek commentators) reason continued to pursue by positing the existence of a separated intellect which is the same for all men.[9]

Whence, pursuing its flight into the sublime, reason must conclude that this separated and universal intellect is God Himself, who by his universal radiance causes the act of intellection in the human intellect and, in making of this human intellect the place or the mirror of the intelligibles, leads it back little by little to the land of the pure spirits to which it belongs by nature.

Well then let us put ourselves for the moment where reason is all set to posit the existence of a single identical separated intellect common to all men. What image will reason make use of to express this eventual conclusion? With my taste for naïve sketches I would have imagined, for example, an immense sheet of light formed by the rays of the Sun of all intellects falling upon and penetrating each individual of the human race so that, inside his head, it might unwrap the intelligible from its sensible packaging and cause the act of intellectual knowledge to take place within that man. Now suppose that such an image is presented to my intelligence which is turned toward reality,

---

individual subject. Here let us transcribe these lines of St. Thomas, *In Aristotelis Librum De Anima*, III, lect. 10, n. 739, p. 175, which concern Avicenna: *Si intellectus agens haberet in se determinationem omnium intelligibilium, non indigeret intellectus possibilis phantasmatibus, sed per solum intellectum agentem reduceretur in actum omnium intelligibilium, et sic non compararetur [intellectus agens] ad intelligibilia ut faciens ad factum, ut Philosophus hic dicit, sed ut existens ipsa intelligibilia. Comparatur igitur ut actus respectu intelligibilium, in quantum est quaedam virtus immaterialis activa, potens alia similia sibi facere, scil. immaterialia. Et per hunc modum, ea quae sunt intelligibilia in potentia, facit intelligibilia in actu. Sic enim et lumen facit colores in actu, non quod ipsum habeat in se determinationem omnium colorum. Hujusmodi autem virtus activa est quaedam participatio luminis intellectualis a substantiis separatis. Et ideo Philosophus dicit quod est sicut habitus vel lumen: quod non competeret dici de eo, si esset substantia separata.*"

9   Cf. Louis Gardet, *L'Islam, Religion et Communauté* (Paris: Desclée de Brouwer, 1967), p. 221: "For Ibn Sînâ . . . the human soul belongs by nature to the world of the Intelligibles to which it will return. . . . Human knowledge is an illumination of the individual possible intellect by the separated acting Intellect. But it is no longer, as in Fârâbi, a unification of the intellect and the intelligible: the human intellect does not become the intelligible, it is its place, the receptacle (*mahall*), and, when it is purified, the 'mirror' in which all lights are reflected."

What did Aristotle himself think of this question? However good may be the reasons invoked by St. Thomas (cf. *Sum. contra Gent.*, II, c. 78) to show that the Philosopher expressly rejected the idea of an agent intellect separated from the individual soul, it can be asked whether those reasons do not leave us in the realm of the probable and whether on this point Aristotle did not remain hesitant, in other words, whether, in reading Aristotle from his own perspective, Thomas Aquinas was not more firm than Aristotle himself in his fidelity to Aristotelian principles and Aristotelian realism.

looking at reality, and making use of the imagination to represent this reality to itself because it cannot see the way my eyes see. I say that the response will be immediate: *No!* That cannot be. I am the one who produces my act of intellection. That God may move me to cause this act, so be it; but I am the one who causes it within me. I am the one who does the thinking. It is impossible that the intellect by whose action and light I think should be separate from myself.

This *no* like a flash of lightning envelops a judgment of intuitivity which reason will control in the relationship which concerns it, and it will transform it into a rationally established assertion ("Each of us is a human person, master of his actions, and consequently equipped to produce them"). And it is this judgment of intuitivity which obliges rational discourse to change direction, to reshuffle its cards and fall back on the human subject and its individual soul, instead of continuing to ascend toward heaven. It is in the heaven of each individual soul that the agent intellect is lodged. It is not the individual soul that it transcends; it is all the other powers in that soul which are concerned with knowledge. It is not the Sun of all intellects. It is a light continuously in act within the mind of each one.[10]

Why am I persuaded that a judgment of intuitivity of this kind arose in the mind of St. Thomas himself, concerning the question of the agent intellect?

Because, on the one hand, we know that this question is centrally important to his entire thought. By making the illuminating intellect come down into each individual soul, he affirmed in a very decisive way his aversion for all Platonic or Plotinian idealism, as well as his realist conception of the human person, and in general of the creature in its relationship to God, Who moves it to act but gives it in creating it the complete equipment required by its nature[11] (and He has such respect for His creatures that when there is question of a free creature, it can turn away from Him by a first initiative of nothingness).

And because, on the other hand, there is nothing in what St. Thomas expounds on the subject of the agent intellect that makes the central importance of this question in the Thomist synthesis stand out, except perhaps in the eyes of someone who is already aware of it. If we read the Commentary on the *De Anima* (III, lect. 10) and the *Summa theologiae* (Ia, q. 79, a. 3, 4, and 5),[12] we see only the rational discussion and demonstration unfold with regard to this particular problem as with all the other problems—a tapestry of

10   Cf. St. Thomas, *Sum. theol.*, Ia, q. 79, a. 5, ad 3m.

11   Cf. St. Thomas, *In Arist. Lib. De Anima*, III, lect. 10 (nn. 728ff).

12   Cf. St. Thomas, *De Spiritualibus Creaturis*, q. 1, a. 9–10 (man. ed. Marietti, *Quaest. disp.*, II, pp. 400–411); *Compendium theologiae*, 83 (man. ed. Marietti, *Opusc. theol.*, I, pp. 38–39); *Quaest. disp de Anima*, q. 1, a. 4–5 (*Quaest. disp.*, II, p. 294–300); *Contra Gent.*, II, c. 76–78 (man. ed. Marietti, II, pp. 221–230); *Quodlibet*, VIII, a. 3 (man. ed. Marietti, p. 161–162). We can see in the very number of texts, and in the insistence with which St. Thomas treats this question, an *indirect sign* of the

arguments which is woven continuously stitch by stitch. Nevertheless St. Thomas was certainly conscious of the central importance of the position he was defending on this particular point. So it must be that St. Thomas himself saw this importance in a different way, a way that is hidden from us in the letter of his texts, but which it is up to us to discover—I mean by a judgment of intuitivity. But the pure objectivity which the Angelic Doctor considered as requisite for his function as teacher of theology forbade him to carry such a judgment over to his texts before it became, once it was under the control of reason, a rational truth. Here (as is the case with all our old masters) it is like a trick which "cartography" played on what I just now called the "reconnoitering of the terrain." It would be too naïve to let ourselves be taken in by this trick.

V. THREE GREAT PHILOSOPHIC MINDS

10. A few more words concerning the reciprocal control of intuitivity by reason and of reason by intuitivity.

I suggested in another essay[13] that we give the name "boldness of gaze" to that cardinal quality of the intelligence which corresponds to intuitivity and which is the basic property of the intellect as *intellect*; and that we give the name "rational solidity" to that quality which corresponds to the constructive power of the intelligence in the logical handling of concepts and the discourse of reason—here we have to do with the characteristic property of the intellect as a *human* intellect.

It happens naturally that in the case of one or other of the philosophers one of these two qualities takes predominance over the other (but without ever obliterating the other completely).

From this point of view what must be said of the father of modern philosophy? He had some powerful intuitions (relating especially to the work to which he was called), he preferred "good common sense," or reason in the state of nature, to scholarly reason, and he took clear ideas for sorts of quasi-angelic atoms of evidence; yet it was rational solidity, the power of constructivity and the ardor of reason to set up assemblages of clear ideas which predominated in him. *Cogito, ergo sum*: the intuition of being is not present at the beginning of his philosophy but rather one of those assemblages, a condensed argument of reason: a fact attested by consciousness—"I think"; and an inference—"therefore I am." He deduces his existence from his thought.

With Descartes reason is not controlled by the intuitivity of the mind turned toward the real, since the mind is turned solely toward itself. The philosopher remains shut up within his thought, clear ideas suffice for everything, it is at the level of reason that what is held to be true must be "adjusted," reason is

---

importance it held for him.

13   Cf. above chapter XI: "Reflections on Wounded Nature," pp. 214–215.

controlled only by itself: by its own power of constructivity, its own ease and satisfaction in putting together conceptual clarities, its own fecundity in conclusions linked one to the other and forming a system, to such a point that they constitute *the* universal Science. It is no wonder then that the greatest of the sons of Descartes (however displeased he was with his father) should dream, as he wiped clean the lenses of his spectacles, of constructing a purely deductive metaphysical wisdom.

Nor is there any reason to wonder at the errors and illusions which proliferate within Cartesian philosophy itself: the theory of innate ideas (idea-pictures which are the objects of knowledge and whose divine veracity guarantees their resemblance to the real that is hidden behind them; the dualism which divides man into subsistent Thought and subsistent Extension, and which makes the soul "an angel dwelling in a machine and directing it by means of the pineal gland,"[14] the theory of the animal-machine, the theory of time as a succession of discontinuous instants, the theory of judgment as function of the will, the ontological argument which claims to prove the existence of God solely by the idea of the Perfect or of the Infinite, and all the rest, and above all the idealist prejudice in which this philosophy has fixed modern thought.

11. And what about Hegel? He had a primordial intuition, the intuition of the mobility and anxiety essential to human life, the intuition of the tragic becoming of a living being who is obliged unceasingly to contemplate death and negativity and to overcome their power by the energy of thought. But at the same time he carried idealism to the absolute by denying all extra-mental reality and by making of reality—of nature, of history, of the world—a manifestation of Thought within itself, or of Spirit discursively thinking itself. In such a way that, to tell the truth, the *magnum opus* of Hegel was to bring about the violation of the concept and of reason by reality such as he perceived it in his primordial intuition and to introduce becoming into the concept itself and contradiction into reason itself.

"Reason seeks out its Other, knowing full well that there it possesses nothing more than itself, it is solely in quest of its own infinity."[15] The concept, which is no longer a sign making a nature, discerned in the thing, known and intelligible, but the self-affirmation of thought, envelops and engenders the other to what it posits; the "no" is present in the "yes" and the "yes" in the "no," as Jacob Boehme put it, with this difference that for Boehme it was a question of a mystical experience, for Hegel an axiom of reason: the identity of identity and non-identity.[16] It is as if all of Heraclitus, distilled into a

---

14   J. Maritain, *The Dream of Descartes* (New York, 1944), p. 179.

15   G. W. F. Hegel, *The Phenomenology of Mind*, tr. by J. B. Baillie, 2nd ed., (New York: Macmillan, 1931; London: Allen and Unwin, 1931), p. 281.

16   Cf. J. Maritain, *Moral Philosophy: An Historical and Critical Survey of the Great Systems* (New York: Charles Scribner's and Sons, 1964), p. 140.

powerful alcohol, passed over into Parmenides to intoxicate and overpower him—let me use another expression of Hegel regarding truth—in a "bacchanalian revel where not a single member is sober."[17] At the same time dialectics becomes knowledge, the only authentic form of knowledge; and reason is freed of absolutely any control by the intuitivity of the mind turned toward reality: since there is no longer absolutely any extra-mental reality to which thought has to conform. As a matter of fact, Hegel remained in communication with the extra-mental being whose existence he denied, with everything that experience, knowledge, and history brought him and which he preyed upon with a superb power of poetic intuition. But this was not at all so that the intuitivity of the mind turned toward reality might control rational discourse. On the contrary, it was in order to transport all that into the world of pure thought and re-engender it there, in order to drag all that into a bacchic revel of dialectics transformed into metaphysics, leading oppositions and logical self-mutations in the assault on heaven and the earth.

From then on reason was controlled only by itself, by its own power of constructivity, carried now to the infinite, by its own satisfaction in raising ever higher the ambition to lay hold, in its élan toward the supreme affirmation of itself, on the entire universe of knowledge, and by accomplishing this to foster the illusion of having transferred to universal wholes the singularity, the personality, the liberty which, in the dialectic of the Logos, have been torn away from their proper place in the individual.

And in this way absolute Knowledge, in which divine thought and human thought are identical, is consummated in the Sage, whereas God, after having alienated Himself from Himself in the world, reintegrates Himself there in Himself and there brings all things back to Himself through man and human thought. Thanks to a shell game which shifted all of reality into the dialectic movement immanent to Thought, and integrated the irrational into reason, Hegel has led us to the absolute triumph of rationalism—and at the same time to its ultimate bankruptcy—in which we see Philosophy as the third essential stage (after Art and Religion) in the development of the absolute Spirit, actually to be nothing more than a Grand Sophistry passing itself off as supreme Wisdom.

One final, and parenthetical, remark about Hegel. When we hear him rise up in protest against the distinction between the spiritual and the temporal, and tell us that in its finished form "secular life is the positive and definite embodiment of the Spiritual Kingdom,"[18] or when he declares that "God must be conceived as *spirit in the community*,"[19] (for it is only there that He knows

---

17   G. W. F. Hegel, *The Phenomenology of Mind*, Preface, p. 105; cf. my book *Moral Philosophy*, p. 135.

18   G. W. F. Hegel, *The Philosophy of History*, tr. by J. Sibree (New York: The Colonial Press, 1899), p. 442.

19   G. W. F. Hegel, *Enzyklopadie der philosophischen Wissenschaften im Grundrisse*

Himself), or that "the march of God in the world, that is what the state is,"[20] or that "since the state is mind objectified, it is only as one of its members that the individual himself has objectivity, genuine individuality, and an ethical life";[21] when he explains to us that man must take possession of his divinity in this world and in this life at the end of the work of history, Jesus being the first among us to realize that he was God because God and man at the same time become God in man; in such a way that Christianity does not succeed in being what it really is, in truly realizing itself, except by ceasing to be Religion (or represented in myths) in order to become Philosophy (in the sense of absolute Knowledge) by understanding that there is no world beyond, no afterlife, and no other world than this World;[22] and again when he explains to us that the men who have been the instruments of history, even if they had "necessarily to trample down many an innocent flower,"[23] are justified in the end because History is the judgment of God, the history of the world the tribunal which judges the world, *Weltgeschichte ist Weltgericht*, Hegel then appears to us as the prophet of many of the aspects of our age and its mentality.

The fact is there are two kinds of prophets: those who like the prophets of Israel are connatural with the Spirit of God and His freedom (and who in general are not very easy on the world), and those who are connatural to what Hegel himself calls the Spirit of the world. And how is this so? Because of an intuitivity which, with its ear cocked for anything which at a given epoch moves history and culture deep down and which in reality turns thought, enslaved to time, even when that thought thinks it can attain absolute Knowledge on its own, into an echo of the siren-song which leads their age astray, a song which is imperceptible to ordinary ears. All that has to be done to make clear what I am trying to say is to recall these few words of Hegel: "*Napoleon ist der erscheinende Gott*, Napoleon is god manifesting Himself."[24]

From the higher regions of the universe of the spirit comes the inspiration of the first kind of prophet; from the dark regions of this universe comes the inspiration of the second kind: for these latter prophets, however brilliantly they may fill the stage with their own presence, have made themselves the

(1830), ed. by F. Nicolin and O. Poggeler (Hamburg: Felix Meiner, 1959), #554, p. 440.

20   G. W. F. Hegel, *Hegel's Philosophy of Right*, tr. with notes by T. M. Knox (London: Oxford University Press, 1952), p. 279.

21   *Ibid.*, p. 156.

22   All of this is made quite evident by Alexander Kojève in *Introduction à la Lecture de Hegel* (Paris: Gallimard, 1947); cf. my book *Moral Philosophy*, pp. 179–181.

23   G. F. W. Hegel, *The Philosophy of History*, ed. cit., p. 32 (cf. my book *Moral Philosophy*, pp. 197–199).

24   G. W. F. Hegel, *Die Phänomenologie des Geistes*, IV (Ed. G. Lasson—J. Hoffmeister, 4 ed. (1937), p. 472; French trans. *Phénoménologie de l'Esprit* by J. Hyppolite (Paris: Aubier, 1934–1941), II, p. 200).

servants and worshipers of the Emperor of this world. But there is something even crazier this time in the world of human futility; I have in mind the case of a Christian theologian who, instead of studying Hegel with the greatest of critical care and making use of him, of his prophetic instinct, of his ambitions and his errors, to better understand certain aspects of our historical age, would undertake the renewal of theology itself by submitting it to Hegel's inspiration and to his metaphysics, with Hegel as his guide and teacher.

12. Finally, what must be said of Heidegger? With Hegel there was question of reason turned away from reality and controlled by itself alone. With Heidegger, on the contrary, it seems to me we are concerned with an intuitivity which is enamored of reality and renounces reason, an intuitivity which also wants to be subject to no control but its own.[25] Moreover, we are not concerned here with that intuitivity of which I spoke at length a few pages back, an intuitivity which, with its gaze fixed firmly on things was in quest of that pure objectivity characteristic of the intellect operating according to laws that are strictly its own and committed to the ways of knowledge. Heidegger is concerned with poetic intuitivity, as is Hegel, and also with an intuitivity that depends on natural mysticism. In both cases intuitivity plays an essential role, whether, as in the case of poetry, the other and the self are grasped indissolubly together in an experience which proceeds from affective connaturality and is essentially creative or, as in the case of natural mysticism, the soul empties itself of everything to attain the existence of the self and to be enraptured by it.

This is the kind of intuitivity which, I believe, comes into play with Heidegger and refuses any control by reason in this connection and in relation to the exigencies which are proper to reason. But because Heidegger is a philosopher, whether he likes it or not, the intuitivity in question is passionately in search of being, even though it is foreign to the intuition of being, which is of the purely intellectual order. And because, even as he deposes reason, Heidegger still remains under the influence of and in allegiance to Hegel, and holds fast to his ambition to attain, if not an absolute Knowledge like Hegel's, at least a Wisdom which fulfills the aspirations of the mind, intuitivity in his case takes on the whole work of conceptualization which, beginning with the very first operation of the mind, follows its course normally in that more and more ample constructivity in which discursive reason has its domain.

I think that here we are at the root of the Heideggerian tragedy. For if poetic intuitivity (and undoubtedly also the intuitivity which comes from natural mysticism) is wonderfully profound in him, the fact remains that to expect from poetic intuitivity the elaboration of philosophic concepts and their

---

25 I hope I am not mistaken in thinking that the interpretation I propose here is justified by the remarkable studies of Heidegger published by Louis Gardet and Ernest Korn in the *Revue Thomiste* 68, 1968, pp. 381–418; 69, 1969, pp. 164, 320–324.

organization into a formal body of knowledge is to ask the impossible. This is so, on the one hand, because of the pure objectivity required of philosophic concepts; on the other hand, because poetic intuition is a creative intuition and because the expression that it demands is by its very nature a work of art, not of knowledge. It is essential for this expression to manifest the self and the other together, and this thanks to the creative imagination; the other cannot be shown in this form of expression except in the experience of the self who undergoes that experience and knows it through affective connaturality. If someone wants to turn the expression of a poetic intuition into a philosophic expression, which implies its detachment both from the experience of the self and from the primacy of the creative imagination, that expression will by the very fact become relatively weightless, or rather lose that intimate and living norm which constitutes its exactness and its truth.

If such a metaphysical conceptualization is demanded of poetic intuitivity itself, its ideas will be blind and its words will be irremediably disappointing; not only will they be diverted from their original meaning or be hammered out in an artificial manner, but they will not end up saying what the philosopher wants to say. Far from working on intelligible natures grasped in a mental word, thought (Heidegger's obscure *Denken*) concentrates on what it can still hold on to of the fleeting content of its intuition when it tries to desubjectivize that intuition before (and for the purpose of) conceptualizing or intellectualizing it in metaphysical terms. It stays put and stirs about in the darkness of night. Indeed, it is inevitable that, once this conceptualization has been carried out, the philosopher should resent it as a betrayal of what had been perceived intuitively by him and had moved him in the depths of his being. This is why in the end he must despair of philosophy and of metaphysics. We know that now—and if what I tried to explain is exact, we could have expected it— Heidegger has turned toward the poets themselves and the theogonic powers of their language, hoping to find in them the kind of prophetic revelation the desire for which seems to have obsessed his mind from the very beginning. Myth is his true native land.

VI. FINAL REMARKS

13. Not a single one of the three philosophers I just spoke of[26] experienced, either formally or virtually, the metaphysical intuition of being. Bergson had it in a virtual manner. He left the tracks a bit in his critique of intelligence and of the concept, but he himself was too intelligent ever really to deny reason. That intuitivity which was the very life of his thought was not poetic intuitivity

---

26 To tell the truth all three belong to what I call ideosophy, the first two in the most explicitly voluntary way, the third despite himself and contrary to his deepest aspirations.

put to work in order to satisfy the desire for a metaphysical wisdom which is natural to our minds or in order to nourish the daydreams of a dialectic which would lead us to absolute Knowledge. Nor was it fully liberated philosophic intuitivity either, such as a pure intellect would require. But it was an effort of the entire soul toward this intuitivity, and its beginning. This is why Bergson was truly a metaphysician, and this is why we are indebted to him for having cried out for all to hear, in the metaphysical desert of our times, the call for that basic renewal which philosophy had been awaiting for three centuries.

14. To conclude all the reflections I have proposed in this essay (after all is said and done, maybe I have only battered down doors that already stood open), let me advance three formulas that I consider to have the force of principles.

First: All by itself, and without the control of the intuitivity of an intellect that is turned toward reality, the discourse of reason will inevitably go astray either by failing to branch off when it should or by heading down the wrong path. All by itself, and without the control of reason over the exactness of its constructions and the rigor of its logical connections, intuitivity will inevitably veer off toward something other than the pure objectivity of the intellect, and consequently conceptualize awry.

Secondly: The intuitivity of an intellect turned toward reality is not just some simple individual quality giving an advantage to some thinker or other among all the others; it is *necessary* to the validity of thought as *knowledge*.

Thirdly: *There is no knowledge without intuitivity.*

POSTSCRIPT I
ON THE THEORY OF SETS

1. We should face up right away to an objection. Does not the theory of sets give the lie to what I have just affirmed? This theory represents an extremely important step forward in contemporary science. And it involves no intuitivity whatever.

My answer is this: It is quite true that the theory of sets involves no intuitivity. But it does not constitute, nor does it claim to constitute, a way of *knowing*. It is an instrument of science, not a science.

In other words it consists essentially in the construction of a *new language*, signifying and regulating the *logical operations* carried out in the process of reasoning. This new language is at once both perfectly coherent and purely conventional.

And what seems quite remarkable to me is that the words which make it up and which are concerned with the logical categories subsuming our thought contents in order to apply their laws to them, do not come, as do those of classical logic and its *intentiones secundae*, from a reflection on the concepts already formed by the mind through abstraction and the different kinds of knowing in which the mind is engaged; it is rather *a priori*, by gratuitously posited conventions, that they have been chosen and that the system of laws which their grammar implies has been elaborated, like an algebraic system invented for its own sake, in an arbitrary, but at the same time a rigorous, manner; all this in such a way that—after the simplest possible first conventions have been chosen—the words or logical categories of the new language so constructed, and the laws of its grammar, are capable, or at least they are considered capable of subsuming any thought content whatever in order to assure or verify its rational correctness.

Let us add that, at the very beginnings of the theory and in the first conventions that were posited, these words themselves (proper to the theory of sets), as a matter of fact, undoubtedly derive from sensible experience by way of abstraction. But this is not what matters, and this is not what gives them their meaning. As a consequence of the conventions posited at the beginning, they impose themselves from above with that kind of gratuity and freedom which is characteristic of a mathematician's way of thinking (especially of the mathematician seduced by the great modern developments in axiomatics). And because of an exigency of the nature of human thought, they are undoubtedly accompanied in us by concepts (for example the concept of "set," of "element," of "union," of "intersection," of "complementation," of "relation," of "graph," of "lattice," etc.). But those concepts which underlie them in our minds, evoke them and use them along the way without having as their purpose to examine them and signify them. In other words, the meaning is attached to these words directly, not through the intermediary of concepts, in such a way that although they are present within us, nevertheless of themselves (I mean for those operations to be carried out according to the laws of the new language in question) they are not at all necessary (an electronic machine can do perfectly well without them).

It is often said that with the theory of sets we have a new form of logic. This is undoubtedly so, but only if we add that this new logic has nothing in common with classical logic[27] (which focused its gaze on the functioning of thought, the operations of the mind, the *intentiones intellectae*, the univocity and analogicity of the latter and the words that express them, etc.). It has nothing to do with traditional logic other than to point out and regulate the operations to be carried out. The theory of sets is not a *science* at all (even if only of *intentiones secundae*, like classical logic, which is both science and art);

27   A. J. Ayer says this very clearly (*Language, Truth and Logic* [London, 1946], pp. 80–81). Since he wanted to continue betting on radical empiricism, he could do nothing other than reject traditional logic, "concerned," as it was "with the working of thought," and substitute for it a logic that was completely formalized, concerned solely with the relations of sets and susceptible to an *a priori* presentation.

it is uniquely an art, an *ars grammatica-logica*,[28] and it is on this basis that it plays such an important role in modern mathematics—without being itself in any way part of the mathematical sciences: It is strictly an instrument, a logical grammar that these sciences make use of (and which other systems of knowledge can make use of as well).

If this logical grammar is used today with such great success by the mathematical sciences, and if it renders them priceless services, it is above all else in what is concerned with the organization, the systematization, the ever broader applications of the sciences, the methods of teaching the sciences, and the extraordinary rapidity with which, thanks to electronic machines, they can carry out immense calculations. In this sense the sciences are indebted to it for their great progress. But can it be expected of the theory of sets that it be sufficient to lead the mathematical sciences to the discovery of new horizons and new speculative domains, in other words to help them grow and be renewed in their intrinsic structure and *precisely as systems of knowledge* (I have in mind, for example, discoveries such as analytic geometry, or differential calculus and integral calculus, or non-Euclidean geometries, or hyperspatial geometries, or topology . . .)? Bringing about discoveries is not the business of logic, especially not the kind we are talking about, from which, because it is entirely conventional, all intuitivity has been eliminated. A mathematician of genius who uses the theory of sets as an instrument and as a logical grammar may very well bring mathematical knowledge to new heights and open new empires to it. But it will not be by virtue of the logical instrument he made use of, but by virtue of his own powers of imagination and intuitivity.

2. As I just indicated, it is not only to mathematics that the theory of sets brings a new logical instrument, a new *ars grammatica-logica*.[29] Since it is independent of the nature of the propositions that it brings into play, in other words since the thought content which the theory of sets submits to the laws of its logical grammar is, as far as that grammar itself is concerned, entirely

---

28   "A method resting upon the employment of Symbols, whose laws of combination are known and general, and whose results admit of a consistent interpretation," G. Boole, *The Mathematical Analysis of Logic* (New York-Oxford, 1847; 2nd ed., Oxford, 1948). Text cited by William and Martha Kneale in *The Development of Logic* (London-Oxford: Oxford University Press, 1962), p. 405.

29   Cf. G. Boole, *The Mathematical Analysis of Logic*, p. 405. "They who are acquainted with the present state of the theory of Symbolic Algebra, are aware that the validity of the processes of analysis does not depend upon the interpretation of the symbols which are employed, but solely upon the laws of their combination. Every system of interpretations which does not affect the truth of the relations supposed, is equally admissible, and it is thus that the same processes may, under one scheme of interpretation, represent the solution of a question on the properties of numbers, under another, that of a geometrical problem and under a third, that of a problem of dynamics or optics . . ."

indeterminate, it is not at all surprising that this theory should consider itself universally valid. The content in question can be furnished by any science at all, no more necessarily mathematical than physical, astrophysical, biological, etc. In short other systems of knowledge than mathematical knowledge can pass over or be tempted to pass over into the logical realm of the theory of sets, can make use of or be tempted to make use of this grammar for their own account (I shall come back to this point). Nevertheless the fact remains that there are two clearly privileged domains of the theory of sets: on the one hand, the mathematical sciences, and on the other hand, and especially so, their application to procedures in the construction of electronic machines, of computers and calculators, for the use of various scholars, in particular of physicists (these machines have many other uses in banks, in big business, etc., but it is the scientific use that interests us here).

At this point let us note, as a quite remarkable fact, that if in the practical order electronic calculators constitute such a triumph for the theory of sets that one might be led to believe that the latter had been invented in view of the former, nevertheless its birth preceded them in time: "symbolic algebra" founded on the purely speculative level by George Boole (who died in 1864) is quite anterior to the invention of electronic calculators, which would have been impossible without Boole's algebra along with the study it made possible of the chains of contact of electrical circuits, and along with its binary language—0 or 1, open or closed, etc.

Here we have one of those singular encounters or convergences which are not rare in the history of science, and which can be explained, I believe, because the speculative theory, which comes first, and then its practical application both depend, in the unconscious of the mind, on the same intellectual climate (in the present case on a fundamentally nominalist intellectual climate).

In this way the theory of sets appears to us as predestined to man's creation of that new species of slaves, henceforth indispensable to civilization, electronic machines, calculators, computers, logic machines—in other words, a new species preadapted to the *"thought" of a machine*. This form of thought remains absolutely incapable of any intuition whatsoever and of any universal idea formed from the world of experience. It operates exclusively with words, with signs, with orders for the opening and closing of circuits, which human intelligence alone can prepare and transcribe, after long, patient, and meticulous labor, on punch cards (or magnetic tapes) which it offers to the machines as food on which the "electronic thought" of the machine—the prodigiously rapid operations carried out by it—depends, and which are "read" by the electric reader which is a "peripheral" part of the machine. And the response furnished by the machine likewise appears under the form of signs, this time to be deciphered by man, as they are inscribed on punch cards or magnetic tapes, or in the form of typewritten statements which are typed out automatically.

It is quite clear that a treasure trove of intuitivity put to work by some science and translated into formulas can be changed into the food of "words" and operative signs which at the start man offers to the machine through the punch cards he has prepared. But it is equally clear that in the entire work accomplished by the machine, or in the entire "thought" it is capable of, not the slightest intuitivity can enter into play. More and more perfected electronic machines may be invented, which may imitate the human brain by registering sensible data ("sensible" to animal and man in the proper sense of the term, "sensible" to the machine only in a metaphorical sense) coming from the external world, which may electronically trigger information or conclusions at the end of the operation carried out by the system of circuits. Any resemblance to the human brain will remain illusory in the sense that such machines will still be lacking in any intuitivity just as they will be lacking in any perception or sensible knowledge and in any thought in the strict sense of the term.

3. I pointed out at the beginning,[30] that those notions, and above all the fundamental notion, on which the theory of sets is based, undoubtedly derive, like all our ideas (all the ideas that we form naturally, and all those as well which, consequentially and indirectly, we form artificially), from sensible experience by means of the abstractive operation (which, as I remarked, implies a certain intuitivity); but it is not because of this that the notions we are talking about have meaning.

Far from being an absolutely universal notion and one that is analogical in itself like the notion of being, the notion of set is a univocal notion that is as general as possible. At the outset, and abstracted from sensible experience, on the level of common everyday knowledge, it refers to an object of thought: some collection or other, some group or other, so indeterminate and so poor in content that the intelligible that is grasped in this particular notion interests the mind only because of the concrete things embraced by it (a group of *researchers*, a collection of *stamps*, or of *paintings*, etc.). When the change is made to logical algebra and to the level of scholarly knowledge, abstraction is made of such concrete things; and we leave aside the level of common everyday knowledge, we leave aside as well that intuitivity which on the level of common usage determines the meaning of the words *group, collection, set*. And the word *set*, which will govern the entire vocabulary of the algebra to be created, will become a purely conventional term, arbitrarily chosen and posited.

But we must dig a bit deeper. I hope I am not mistaken when I say that there is a considerable difference, from the point of view we are taking, between classical mathematics and the algebra of Boole. In classical mathematics, the primary notions, arithmetical and geometric, were still based on *entia realia*

---

30   See *supra*, p. 327.

(preliminary to *ens rationis,* which is the true homeland of mathematics), and they were directly drawn by abstraction, like all our other naturally formed notions, from sensible experience. But from the outset they belonged to the second degree of abstraction or of intelligibility: in such a way that in this respect they retained the kind of intuitivity that is proper to the abstractive operation. To the contrary, the notion of set (or, if you wish, of collection or group), inasmuch as it is drawn, like our other naturally formed notions, from sensible experience by the abstractive process, is an empirical notion which depends on the first degree of abstraction. And the meaning or intelligibility that it possesses here, on the level of common everyday knowledge, is in no way scientific; it is totally different from what logical algebra itself requires and remains foreign to it; the mind does not stop here;, rather it is at this point that it gathers its force before moving on, and in order to move on, to the level of scholarly knowledge. At this instant it makes the leap from the first to the second degree of abstraction. And by taking this leap into the universe of beings of reason, it cuts every link with the direct and natural abstractive operation and with the kind of intuitivity which it involves. The word *set* is then posited by arbitrary authority, or as if by a gratuitous decree, and implies and brings with it a notion that no longer has anything to do with the direct and natural abstractive operation.

Let me note in passing that on the level of common everyday usage, where the notion has retained its experiential meaning and the kind of intuitivity that is linked to the direct and natural abstractive operation, any "set," any "collection," any "group" essentially implied a plurality of elements. At this level it would be nonsense to speak of a collection of stamps or of paintings which would contain not a single stamp or painting, or of a troop that would be made up of one single soldier, or of a flock in which there would be only one sheep or no sheep at all. To the contrary, once the notion of set has passed over into scholarly usage and to the second degree of abstraction, it is necessary, and perfectly legitimate, to speak of zero element sets ("empty" sets) and of sets with only one element. This is a sign that the sense of the word *set* in ordinary usage (where intuitivity is still involved) *is not* the sense in which the word is used in the theory, in which there is no longer any intuitivity, but an *a priori* position.[31] When an attempt is made to describe what a set is, human nature

---

31   In Gaston Casanova's book on *L'Algèbra de Boole* (Paris: Presses Universitaires de France, 1967), p. 7, we read: "The simultaneous consideration of several objects of the same nature or of different natures constitutes *a set.*" (In speaking this way one takes a position in reality on the level of common consciousness, for which a set implies by definition *"several* objects.") Further on (p. 8) the same author mentions "sets formed of a single element," and *"empty sets* which contain none at all." (Here we have moved to the level of scholarly knowledge.)

It is important to note that the meaning of the word *set* is not the same in the two cases. If this were not so, we would be faced with the very considerable contradiction of affirming that "the *simultaneous* consideration of *several* objects"

and the human intellect demand that we begin with the common everyday notion at the first degree of abstraction, with its meaning that is completely inappropriate to mathematics. Boole's algebra (a logical mathematics that is strictly nominalist and is constructed from one end to the other in a purely conventional manner, whose guarantee is its success and fecundity) requires that in its scholarly usage the word *set* and the notion of set be posited conventionally, without any appeal to intuitivity and leaving aside the fact that at the beginning of the abstractive operation we acquired them from experience. All that they entail in the way of evidence comes to them from what the notion of set meant in current language. But this notion was foreign to scholarly knowledge and to the particular and proper meaning that the word *set* has in the theory of sets.

Finally, what about the meaning of the primary notion put to use in this theory? It has nothing at all to do, as I said a moment ago,[32] with the direct and natural abstractive operation. It does not refer to an "intelligible nature" perceived in a concept. It would therefore be fruitless to seek to manifest it by stating the intelligible notes possessed by such a nature. I think this is a totally *operational* sense,[33] and that what the word *set* designates are the possibilities

---

can be the simultaneous consideration of *one single object* or of *no object at all.*

32   Cf. *supra,* p. 331.

33   The purely operational meaning of the symbols used in any sufficiently formalized symbolic logic clearly comes from the definition of the logistic method proposed by C. I. Lewis: *"By the logistic method, the principles of logic are not antecedently presumed as rules of demonstration. Instead, the rules in accordance with which proofs are given are rules of more or less mechanical operations upon the symbols, such as rules allowing certain substitutions to be made in the postulates or in the theorems previously proved,"* C. I. Lewis and C. H. Langford, *Symbolic Logic,* 2nd ed. (New York: Dover Publications, Inc., 1959), p. 118.

The operations envisaged by C. I. Lewis along with the rules that govern them do not concern the immanent workings of the intelligence which constitute the object of classical logic; they are rather *manipulations* carried out on symbolic structures. The complex operations are the result of the ordered combinations of elementary operations, defined *a priori* and independently of any logical interpretation, in the manner of quasi-mechanical processes. In the system proposed by Lewis, these are operations of substitution, of conjunction and of detachment: *"It is to be observed that the performance of these simple operations is independent of their logical significance. They could be carried out 'mechanically,' according to the rules, by one who had no interest in the interpretation of the symbolism,"* Ibid., p. 126.

If C. I. Lewis insists so much on the purely operational character of the symbols and of the generative operational steps in a completely formalized symbolic logic, it is because he has in mind in this way to establish the possibility of founding *a priori* a logic of propositions exempt from the vicious circle. The calculus of propositions perfected by Schröder and derived from the algebra of Boole is in fact "circular": for the laws of deduction, admitted as data at the beginning of the system, are the object of demonstration as well: for example, in

of operation. Perhaps it could be said that it is also a prospective meaning which is unveiled to the degree that the development of the theory gradually makes known the different properties of the sets. In any case, if one would like to propose a definition of the word *set* with the help of intelligible notes, one would have to go back to the abstractive origin of the notion of set, and hence to what this notion is for common everyday knowledge, by leaving in the implicit what that notion becomes when it takes on its proper meaning as it passes over to scholarly knowledge and to the second degree of abstraction:[34] a way of defining that I find a bit silly; it would seem far better, by agreement, simply to pose a "set" as containing zero, one, or several elements, and possessing well-defined properties which will become apparent as the theory develops.

the elaboration of the chains of theorems it is admitted that P and Q being two propositions, 'P implies Q' gives: if Q is false then P is false, and this same law—logical—is established in one of the theorems of the system whose symbolic formulation is: $P \supset Q . \equiv . -Q \supset -P$. (Cf. *ibid.*, p. 117. Read: "P implies Q" is equivalent to "not Q implies not P.")

The possibility of establishing *a priori* a logic of propositions exempt from the vicious circle rests on the possibility of constructing a symbolic system whose rules of development are not the laws that govern the deduction of propositions since the object of such a system is, precisely, to establish these very laws. The stakes here are very important, as much so for the thinkers of the school whose initiator was Bertrand Russell (Cf. B. Russell, A. N. Whitehead, *Principia mathematica* (Cambridge: Cambridge University Press, 1910–1913, 1926–1927) as for philosophers who care about epistemology.

For the former, it is a question of showing the nature of mathematics by establishing that mathematics are not the exemplification—by means of the addition of postulates of interpretation—of a symbolic system that is universal in its scope. (C. I. Lewis, *Symbolic Logic*, p. 23).

For the latter, Lewis' project rests on an *a priori* view of the nature of intelligence, a view that is all the more "dogmatic" because it remains implicit. In fact, when one proposes to interpret the symbolic system in question by assigning to primitive symbols the task of representing propositions, account is not taken of the fact that the propositions are not "objects," but signs. Whether they are written or oral, propositions are by their very nature the signs of the judgments of the intelligence, and their relations signify the operational steps of the intelligence engaged in the elaboration of ifferent systems of knowledge. To admit *a priori* the possibility of the transcription of symbolic algebra in terms of the relations between propostitions in the final analysis comes down to assimilating the operational steps of the intelligence to the mechanical operations whose possibility is represented by the symbols made use of in the symbolic system. An epistemology careful to recognize, to analyze, and to justify the different fields of the activity of the intelligence would, on the contrary, take pains to delimit (and to limit) where the new logical grammars are concerned, their sphere of validity by reason of the specific type that the proper object of the different kinds of knowledge assigns to the operations of the intelligence. Cf. further on, p. 334.

34   Cf. *supra*, p. 331, n. 31.

4. One more remark to bring this digression to an end.

Indirectly, and through reflection on the work of the mind, classical logic was fundamentally referred back to being, and to the intuition of being, presupposed in actual fact by the principle of identity. This is why it had an absolutely universal value. To the contrary, being and the principle of identity are foreign to the algebra of Boole. His perspective is that of a radical nominalist empiricism. And Boole's stroke of genius was to choose for the construction of a new logical grammar a generic notion so simple, so common, and so general—the notion of sets and their elements—that it could be slipped on like a garment to envelop in all their expressions—which are univocal in themselves—the ideas and the rational elaborations which the mathematical sciences make use of at what we call the second degree of intelligibility and which the innumerable so-called positive sciences make use of at what I call the "pure and simple" first degree of intelligibility.[35]

This logical grammar is supremely abstract. But let us be careful! The word *abstract* in this case refers only indirectly to the abstractive process that begins with sensible experience; it signifies: *which makes abstraction of all content, whatever it may be,* of the sciences I just spoke of however abstract they may be in themselves. This is why the logical grammar in question is applied to all the sciences in an absolutely general way. As I have already noted,[36] being independent of the nature of the propositions it puts into play, it is not surprising that it should consider itself universally valid.

If this is not surprising, it still entails an ambiguity of the first magnitude. It is in no way universally valid in an absolute sense or in a pure and simple way, as is classical logic. It is universally valid in a relative sense and in relation to all those sciences *for which it was made* (and which for the nominalist empiricist are the only ones that deserve the name of science). It would be unpardonably careless to consider that logical grammar just as valid for systems of knowledge like philosophy and metaphysics, where thought functions according to laws over which that grammar has no control and to which, unless they are willing to accept the violation of their very nature, it would have no recourse but to refuse to such thought the very right to exist.

5. Metaphysics is totally centered on being, on the *Sein*, it lives on the analogy of being, and thanks to analogical concepts (according to the analogy of proper proportionality) it is established as a system of knowledge. And to the extent that it is an authentic form of philosophy, the philosophy of nature,

---

35   Cf. *supra*, Ch. XI, "Reflections on Wounded Nature," p. 221, n. 30. I call the "pure and simple" first degree of abstraction or of intelligibility that first degree of abstraction understood without any *participation* in metaphysical intellection (a *participation* that is implied by all philosophical knowledge belonging to the first degree of abstraction).

36   Cf. *supra*, pp. 328–330.

even though constituted at the first degree of abstraction, is likewise concerned with the *Sein* itself, since the concepts it makes use of are illuminated in the mind of the philosopher and are endowed with a sense that is *participatively* metaphysical or significative of being, through the metaphysical intellection that the philosopher brings into play at the third degree of abstraction or intelligibility.[37] *Mutatis mutandis*, the same can be said of moral philosophy.

But the new logical grammar invented by Boole has chosen for its part, and for its only part, the *Dasein*. From the very outset, in other words, from the very instant that it posited as its first foundation a generic notion like that of set, it chose to ignore the *Sein*; from the very start it excluded the intuition of being, decided to ignore the analogy of being and to work exclusively with univocal terms and concepts. It was made for the *Dasein* and for the univocal. This is its domain, and it is with regard to this particular domain—the mathematical sciences and those sciences which stand at the pure and simple first degree of intelligibility—that it is a valid instrument for the mind, and a very precious one. This is to say that, by the first convention that this grammar itself decided to posit, metaphysics and all sciences that are properly and authentically philosophical are strictly foreign to it and in their regard can do no other than declare itself incompetent.

Now we can see how what I pointed out above must be understood,[38] namely, that other sciences besides the mathematical sciences might cross over or be tempted to cross over under the logical regime of the theory of sets. Those that are able to cross over under this logical regime are those sciences constituted at the pure and simple first degree of abstraction. Those that might be tempted to cross over—at their expense—are those sciences of ontological orientation. In giving in to such a temptation philosophy would be guilty of betraying itself.

Alas! We know a little about human nature and we know a little about the temptations to which our dear philosopher colleagues are exposed. For many of them what is new, just because it is new, has an irresistible charm. Face to face with a new logic which is admirably successful in its own domain, will not certain among them be led to believe that it is purely and simply *the* New Logic, that scientific Logic which according to the modern mind must replace the old Logic, classical Logic, and take absolute control of thought in every domain? They will then want to have philosophy pass under the logical regime of the theory of sets (or, in other words, to "axiomatize" philosophy), and the only result of this would be incalculable damage; on the one hand, with regard to the philosophical sciences, the human sciences especially, which are already disoriented by idealism, or phenomenology, or empiricism and nominalism, will be decidedly confirmed in their refusal of the *Sein* and bound by chains

---

37   Cf. *supra*, Ch. XI: "Reflections on Wounded Nature," pp. 235–236.

38   Cf. *ibid.*

to the univocal; on the other hand, with regard to metaphysics, which "Logic" will put under interdict.

6. In particular the idea that God can be known by reason would be considered as excluded on principle by "Logic." Indeed, it is quite clear that an infinitely transcendent being, who is the cause of all things and is self-subsistent Being itself, could be neither a set, nor an element in a set. God is above and beyond any set, and such an assertion is pure and simple absurdity in the eyes of the new logic, which works solely on sets and the elements of sets, recognizes the univocal alone, and hence excludes *a priori* any term or concept which by analogy would put within reach of the mind something that is beyond all creation, that is, beyond whatever is defined by a finite number of properties.

Moreover it is the reversibility of operations which in the new logic replaces the principle of identity; the idea of a being which is the cause of all things without itself being caused is therefore sheer nonsense, like the idea of a relationship by which things are really related to God on whom they depend for everything, whereas God is absolutely independent of things and that between Him and them there is no real relation, only a relation of reason. In the eyes of a philosopher for whom the logical algebra of Boole from now on is Logic itself, all this does not even deserve an examination, it is simply unthinkable, it is a language devoid of meaning.

Must we add that the philosopher in question is himself victim of the most impudent vicious circle? In order to make his declaration that the knowledge of God through reason, and any proofs of God's existence, are incompatible with Logic and condemned by Logic, he makes use of a logic that has been expressly fabricated in such a way as to be incompatible with such proofs and such knowledge, since it was fabricated for the single unique domain of the *Dasein* and the univocal, and with those sciences, like mathematics, and like those sciences which stand at the first degree of intelligibility, has nothing to do with philosophy (at least with a philosophy worthy of the name) or with metaphysics or with any possibility whatever of leading the mind beyond what falls under the senses or the imagination.

I have absolutely nothing against the algebra of Boole or against the theory of sets considered in itself. I admire them and in themselves I have no reason to criticize them. I have done nothing more than try to situate them. But for the naïve and the infatuated who take them out of the proper domain in which they are valid, and who, in considering them as the only real *Logic*, look down their noses at philosophy, for such people I feel no pity. And I thought it might not be inopportune to be on guard against them, for a number of these new masters are already at work; and considering the state of philosophy today, it is not impossible that they will be accorded a certain respect for some time to come.

POSTSCRIPT II
ON THE THREE DEGREES OF ABSTRACTION

1. What I would like to note here rather rapidly is that at each of the three degrees of abstraction or intelligibility recognized by classical logic, we find present and verified that law of intuitivity on which I insisted as necessary for knowledge, but under extremely different forms and modalities.

At what I call the pure and simple first degree of abstraction (from which any participation in metaphysical intellection is excluded) stand all the sciences—empiriological and empirio-mathematical—which hold sway over civilization today and make up, along with the mathematical sciences, what current parlance calls Science (a good number of our contemporaries, under the influence of positivism and nominalist empiricism, consider them the only form of knowledge that man is capable of). What contributes to their prestige is the enormous practical power they dispense. Concerning the rules to be put in place by human beings in the exercise of such enormous power, they have, in the final analysis, nothing to tell us and do not claim to tell us anything. As a matter of fact, in each nation, the only things that regulate the use of this power are fear of another and avidity for power, along with an unnatural haste, for the importance of *time* for any kind of maturation—even (and especially) in the human and moral order—is completely misunderstood by them. What is involved here, let us not forget it, is as it were the basic barbarism, due to a loss of spiritual center or direction, of the actual social condition of humanity, and not at all the sciences in question taken in themselves and in their proper dignity as forms of knowledge.

In the daily labor and the patient, indefatigable research of men who consecrate themselves to the empiriological and the empirio-mathematical sciences, the intuitivity put into play depends above all on good sense enlightened and refined by the intelligence, let us call it intelligentiated sense. The cogitative power or the *ratio particularis* is equally involved. Thus a kind of flair is developed, along with a kind of connaturality with the world of experience and with the different levels of the material world, which fosters the capacity to perceive signs for the mind in enigmatic form and to guess at new avenues of approach, and all of which is controlled by admirable habits of exactitude and rigor. In brief it is through the intuitivity of understanding then that the mind looks at reality and is turned toward the real.

If there is question of the great epoch-making discoveries which from age to age renew or revolutionize science, then we must think of something else, of that *judgment of intuitivity* I tried to explain above.[39]

Finally let us not forget that at the term of scientific reasoning, verification by fact, thanks to observation and experimentation, plays an absolutely indispensable role. Without it the most astute conceptual constructions remain

---

39   Cf. *supra*, pp. 312–314.

hypothetical; it is this factual verification which, by confirming the well-founded hypotheses and rejecting the others, establishes science in its proper rank as a form of knowledge. Here once again the intuition of the intelligentiated sense is at work, this time in a decisive declaration whose conditions have been prepared by the intelligence, and which the intelligence has carried out by means of the intuition of understanding which has utilized the more and more richly and subtly developed instrumentation of scientific equipment.

2. Those sciences which stand at the pure and simple first degree of abstraction and the techniques to which they give birth have set out along the road to making the world subject to man. But the highest horizons of the mind remain closed to them.[40]

Other sciences—in this case philosophic, and especially the philosophy of nature—stand also at the first degree of abstraction, but they are at the first level inasmuch as they are *participatively* illuminated by metaphysical intellection and the intuition of being, which depend on the third degree. More purely speculative than the sciences of nature, the philosophy of nature makes us able to penetrate into the domain of primary truths. It is already a form of wisdom, or rather it is a door that opens on to wisdom. Its object is still the world of nature and of matter at its different levels, but it looks at this world from an entirely different angle, with a method of approach and an intellectual equipment that is entirely different, which are not shut up within experience, the observable and the measurable, but which stand at the level of being and of the quest of being as the first principle of intelligibility of what we see acting and stirring in the world around us. This is why the philosophy of nature knows man and the things of man in a more perfect and more comprehensive way than do the empiriological sciences which are concerned with the human being. This is also why, at the end of its search, it is led, as was already the case for the Physics of Aristotle, to posit the question of the First Cause and to make it clear that in considering nature human reason naturally and necessarily comes to the question of the existence of God.

Nevertheless the philosophy of nature and the philosophical sciences which depend on the first degree of abstraction[41] remain and should remain closely

---

40   I am speaking of the empiriological sciences as such. But the scholar himself is a man whose gaze rises, more often than one would think, beyond the proper object of his science. And so it happens that certain physicists give in to the need for absolute mathematization, but, on the other hand, it also happens that other physicists (and this has great significance for philosophy) give in to a more or less unconscious metaphysical need; and so a certain quest for being, however poorly formulated it may be for lack of philosophical equipment, animates and renders fruitful their research and their teaching.

41   By this I mean such sciences as physics if one day it should decide to philosophize, according to the wish of J. R. Oppenheimer (without stopping at the more or less unconscious need mentioned in the preceding note); and biology too (cf. the work of Hans Driesch and of Dr. Maurice Vernet); and likewise and above

linked to their sister sciences, the sciences of nature, whether purely empiriological or mathematicized, not in order that they conform servilely to their
type of explanation which is not philosophical, but in order to understand
what it is they bring to us and then include it in some way in their own
philosophical light. The philosophy of nature has a strict obligation to take
account of the results and the progress made by the sciences of nature, to
whatever type they belong.

I have noted elsewhere that on this point the current teaching of the
philosophy of nature for a long time now has incurred a considerable amount
of reproach and that the Thomist philosophy of nature has urgent need,
certainly not to be doctrinally changed, but to be renewed and brought up to
date by a much closer contact with a scientific universe which has been
completely transformed since the days of St. Thomas.

What a lacuna, for example, when we come to hylomorphism and the
theory of corporeal substance, to find in most of the classical expositions no
reference whatever to the corpuscular structure or to the quantum structure
of matter which today play such a fundamental role in the science of the
physical world! For us the great challenge is to give a *philosophic interpretation*
to this corpuscular and quantum structure with the imagery that they entail,
all of which does nothing to change the philosophical truths recognized by
Aristotle and St. Thomas. But this does demand a serious effort at critical
elaboration, for which the majority of the most deeply meditative, the best
informed and the freest minds among scientists and among writers deeply
interested in science lack the necessary tools. And this challenge inevitably
poses for us difficult and complicated problems.

I shall limit myself to noting here that since the advent of quantum mechan-
ics the physicist knows very clearly (just as the philosopher ought to know)
that what mathematical physics arrives at "is not the 'thing itself,' but rather,
if you wish, the modalities of our relations to those things"[42] (these relations
which things maintain with the observer being expressed by a more and more
formalized science in the pure terms of mathematical regularities, while the
"models" or imagery from which they are drawn are put aside as inadequate).
In short, what our physics arrives at is an "empirical reality," whose "objectivity" is "weak." The fact remains that in "non-empirical reality," behind the
physicists' symbolic entities and presupposed by them something else lies
hidden which is not the concern of the physicist as such: so that in listening to
the physicist, the philosopher is free to turn his thoughts not so much to what
he is talking about, as to the hidden implications of what he is talking about.
And so he will say, from his particular point of view, that the different entities

all the human sciences, if they were what they should be.

42   Cf. the invaluable study of Bernard D'Espagnat, "Orientations actuelles de la
      physique théorique," in *Acquisitions récentes et tendances actuelles en physique*
      (Paris: Aubier-Montaigne, 1968).

of physics necessarily presuppose an "objectively strong" ontological foundation: implied by the quantification of energy as far as the activity of matter is concerned, by the particles which appear on the screen of scientific imagery as far as its substance is concerned.

From the point of view of the corpuscular structure of matter, it seems reasonable to say that the individual species water is the chemical particle itself,[43] the molecule H_2O. On the other hand, in the world of biology, it is the entire living organism which constitutes the *individual*. Here the micro-particles described in scientific imagery as composing the genes, the chromosomes, the cells are, just like the different tissues and organs, ontologically integrated into the unity of a whole, the *individual organism*—infusoria or elephant—informed[44] even to the smallest corpuscle discernible in its constitution by a single substantial form, a vegetative soul or a sensitive soul (intellective soul in the case of man).

3. But let us get back to the subject of our concern, the intuitivity which accompanies knowledge. In the case of the kind of philosophic knowledge we are talking about, this form of knowledge does not enjoy the fruits of the intuitivity that is peculiar to the sciences of nature alone. It has its own peculiar intuitivity: philosophic intuitivity which belongs to the very intellect itself. Regarding the human sciences—which in reality are philosophical sciences and demand to be treated as such (something denied them today)—perhaps it could be said that here too, by reason of that knowledge by connaturality due to our experience of men—and of ourselves—a kind of intellectual flair is developed which plays a very important role in research and discovery.

At any rate, it is to the philosophy of nature that I want to give particular attention. Here we are in the domain, long under consideration, of that intuitivity of the mind that is turned toward reality and which "looks at" that reality without being able to "see" it as our eyes do. As I noted, it is by means of the creative imagination, illuminated like the intelligence, and along with it by the light of the agent intellect, that the mind "looks at" reality in this way. Let it suffice for me to insist here on the importance of a text from St. Thomas

---

43   Concerning the world of elementary particles (proton, electron, neutrino, for example, which conform to Fermi's statistics; or photon, for example, which conforms to the statistics of Bose and others) it does not seem that research is as of now far enough advanced for the philosopher from his own position in the same domain to risk considering the question of ontological individuality.

44   In more precise terms, it is the *materia prima*, which, in each of the cases in question, is informed by a *forma substantialis*, so that, together, they constitute in being, the material individual.

I wonder if some expression like "form of first ontic determination," for example, might not be preferable to the expression "substantial form," in the case in which certain particles—or system of particles—should be considered as simple phases due to an essentially unstable form.

that I cited earlier in a footnote: "*Quando aliquis conatur aliquid intelligere, format aliqua phantasmata sibi per modum exemplorum, in quibus quasi inspiciat quod intelligere sudet.*[45] In these phantasms of the creative imagination, the mind "in a certain way sees" the real which it strives to understand with the help of the over-arching universal concepts that philosophical intellection makes use of. He looks at the real and cannot see it in the way our eyes see it, but he *sees it so to speak* thanks to the imagination.

In regard to that intuitivity peculiar to the philosophy of nature, to which our present reflections are directed, here we are concerned with the intelligentiated imagination and no longer with the intelligentiated external sense as we were with regard to the natural sciences. And it is in order that we might intellectually lay hold on the *real*, to look at and "in a certain way to see" the *real*, that we make use in this way of this noble and marvelously precious "internal sense."

With regard to the things which the philosophy of nature wants to scrutinize, the imagination does not present us solely with examples formed from what we already know about those things, either by means of previously acquired philosophical truths or by means of our philosophical interpretation of scientific data. With images it has created, the imagination constantly reinforces the notions and explanations gradually elaborated in proportion as we make progress in our rational discourse, without ceasing, at the same time, to be turned toward the real; and it is in confrontation with these images that at certain moments, as we have seen, the intellect perceives intuitively that rational discourse has wandered astray into a false theory, or risks doing so, and must be put back on track, so that from a certain point of view intuitivity is in control of reason. Apropos of this role of the imagination, we might think for example, not only of Copernicus and Galileo as we did earlier, but also of the discoverers of the idea of evolution and of those who first denied the fixity of species; the image of a living world traversed throughout the ages by the movement of a "creative" duration underlay their original intuition, however poorly conceptualized it may have been in the case of Lamarck with his notion of adaptation to environment or in the case of Darwin with his notion of natural selection and the life struggle.

Everything concerning the essential role of the intuitivity of the mind (and of the intelligentiated imagination), which is already true for the philosophy of nature, must be said *a fortiori*, and in an incomparably richer and broader perspective, when, moving to the third degree of abstraction, we turn our attention to the case of metaphysics. Metaphysics is the highest form of rational knowledge in its purely natural use, and it is the highest form of knowledge by intuitivity, that knowledge in which the intuitivity of the intellect finds its fullest and most perfect exercise. We know that at its very beginning is found that intuition *par excellence*, the intuition of being, and that

---

45   *Sum. theol.*, Ia, q. 84, a. 7; cf. above p. 317, n. 7.

as it advances rational step by rational step, it is constantly animated and illuminated by this primordial intuition. It is not surprising that because of it intuitivity and reason control one another each in a different respect, according to the general schema I have indicated, but with greater amplitude and in a fashion more imperiously imposed than in any other form of knowledge. For thanks to the basic analogicity of being, and to the analogical concepts that nourish it, metaphysics is concerned not only, as is the philosophy of nature, with the realities of the sensible world, but it breathes the air of the higher regions, finds its life in the invisible universe of the mind, and has as its task to come to a knowledge there of those realities which escape the senses and enable us, already even in the purely natural order, to cross the frontiers of the eternal and the divine. (At the same time the images which serve as instruments for its intuitivity are constructed with more freedom, the freedom of the creative imagination in purely symbolic figuration.) And the higher the truths which such a knowledge strives to conquer, the greater the risks involved. And they demand that here intuitivity and reason be always on the alert.

But there is another matter, and it is very important that it be discussed. When the metaphysical *habitus* has been developed in man, and when, in particular, it tends above all else toward God and divine things in proportion as the natural forces of human intelligence are capable of gaining access to them, metaphysics opens out on a kind of contemplation that must be called *philosophical contemplation*, and which, like any contemplation, entails a certain superior kind of intuitivity. I would like to spend a few moments on this matter. I am afraid I may not be up to this task, the vocabulary that must be used will certainly cause us many a headache. But we must try.

Let us note immediately that this philosophical contemplation borders on two other kinds of contemplation—that contemplation proper to supernatural mysticism and that proper to natural mysticism—between which a careful distinction must be made. These three types of contemplation may very well, in certain individual cases, be subject to some mixing together. In themselves and by their essence they are totally different. The contemplation proper to supernatural mysticism is an entry into God's depths by the knowledge of connaturality which is due to the love of charity and to the gifts of the Holy Spirit, above all to the gift of Wisdom. The contemplation proper to natural mysticism is a purely intellectual experience of the *esse* of the Self, obtained through the void, the abolition of concepts and a turning back toward un-knowing. Philosophical contemplation is likewise a purely intellectual contemplation, but a positive one, one without any turning back of the natural drive toward knowledge, due, when the mind is fixed on them so that it may be absorbed into them, to those analogical concepts thanks to which we know God *per speculum, in aenigmate.* How can such a knowledge by analogy pass over into a state of contemplation? And how can it at the same time imply a certain higher element of intuitivity? I shall try, as far as I am able to, to answer these questions.

Let us recall two assertions by St. Thomas that I had the occasion to cite in an earlier chapter.[46] In the Summa theologiae, he tells us apropos of the analogical intellection and the analogical concepts which we use to name God: *Non secundum eamdem rationem hoc nomen* sapiens *de Deo et de homine dicitur.*"[47] We are using one and the same analogical concept: *sapiens.* But it is definitely not according to the same *ratio,* or with the same intelligible extension, that this concept designates what is in God, divine wisdom, and what is in the creature, so that the wisdom of man is indeed the mirror or the resemblance by which we know the wisdom of God, but this mirror is so enigmatic and the resemblance so distant and deficient, that the wisdom of God is something entirely different from—infinitely other than—man's wisdom, thanks to which we are able to know and name it by analogy; in other words our concept of wisdom and our name for it, when they are applied to God, leave *"rem significatam ut incomprehensam, et excedentem nominis significationem."*[48] They leave the signified reality deep within its unfathomable mystery, beyond—infinitely beyond—our understanding, and exceeding or surpassing—infinitely surpassing—the signification of the word.

It seems to me that these two assertions, if we reflect on them with sufficient attention, furnish us the keys we are looking for.

The created analogate is the mirror in which we come to know—but enigmatically—the uncreated analogate. When a philosopher is not satisfied simply to name some uncreated perfection or other and gives it a hasty tip of his hat before passing on to the next, but instead he sets himself to meditate on it and what he knows of divine things, he comes to realize that his intelligence and all his ideas are completely outstripped by them and prove totally disproportionate to them. The more he focuses his mind on the ideas that help him come to some knowledge of God, the deeper experience he has of the devouring power of that outstripping and of that disproportion, as well as of that dark night in which, at the very instant here below when the signs that proceed from Him enable us to utter His name, God hides Himself from our human eyes.

The experience I am speaking of does not refer to the object, to God Himself; it refers to something created, to what goes on in the mind of the philosopher, on the outstripping of all his ideas, and on the disproportion which affects them with regard to the divine reality. He has no experience of the depths of God as St. John of the Cross did; he has rather the experience of his own congenital infirmity as a creature before his Creator whom he seeks to know. And the deeper this experience is for him, the greater value and splendor it gives to the analogical concept he has of God's grandeur. But he knows that this concept too is completely inadequate; and all the more inadequate the more his mind is absorbed in this concept.

---

46   Cf. above chapter XII: "Reflections on Theological Knowledge," p. 243 f.

47   St. Thomas, *Sum. theol.,* Ia, q. 13, a. 5.

48   *Ibid.*

Here is how I picture knowledge by analogy becoming philosophical contemplation: a completely intellectual form of contemplation, which may certainly be accompanied by a feeling of natural love for God, but which in itself is not a contemplation of love. It would rather be a contemplation of fear and trembling, which seems to me to be very close to adoration. Let me note parenthetically that adoration, which is also related to the grandeur of God and to the mystery which envelops Him, has its origin, it seems to me, in natural religion, which undoubtedly has never existed among men in its pure state but which, like in filigree, shines through all the religions of humanity. Adoration is not a theological virtue like charity. I believe that it is an essentially human and natural virtue, of which man will never completely rid himself, even when he turns it toward false gods (which are always at hand), or even when he turns it into blasphemy.

Now what must be said of that element of intuitivity which is as inseparable from philosophical contemplation as it is from any other form of contemplation? I just noted that the experience which constitutes philosophical contemplation does not have to do with God Himself but rather with what takes place in the knowing subject and with the disproportion of his concepts with regard to the very object that he knows. This is exactly how it is with the element of intuitivity we are speaking about at the moment. And yet in this case we must go much further, for the intuitivity of the mind, in some way or other, always has some relation to the object known. So in this case it must have some kind of relation to God Himself. How can this be? I say that it is in an indirect manner and by a sort of reversion onto the object—where there is a change of sign—of a negative datum present in the knowing mind.

Inasmuch as it designates a certain created analogate, wisdom in man for example, the analogical concept embraces and circumscribes this created analogate. But this perfection in God is altogether different from what is found in man. And just how it is entirely different in God, or by what splendors it is so, or the way in which in the divine reality it escapes our understanding, and outstrips—infinitely outstrips—the signification of the name, all of this remains strictly unknown to us, and in this respect we can do no more than stammer out concepts that are equally disproportionate and outstripped by their object. Over the very thing that is properly divine in the divine perfection that we come to know, there is cast a veil of unknowing. In other words, the analogical concepts by which we know God and divine things bring us at the same time both knowledge and nescience. And the better we come to know God, the more we realize that our lack of knowledge in His regard remains far more profound and vast than our knowledge.

But then, is not this gnawing negativity, this unknowing which accompanies and invincibly overflows the knowledge of the knowing subject by the very fact a reverse image of something infinitely positive in God; is it not the negative image in us of the *divine sublimity*? As I see it, this is what the intuitivity of the mind seizes upon immediately, in an instantaneous perception. Through this instantaneous perception, which brings about a change of sign, the negative datum, or that invincible nescience which remains in the knowing subject and of which he is conscious, is turned back onto the divine object, and in this way makes manifest the eternal perfection in God of which the reverse image I spoke of is the sign in us.

Undoubtedly we already have the idea or the analogous concept of the divine sublimity, but the intuitivity of the spirit, by means of the reversion that it brings about, illumines this idea and makes it all the more resplendent, in such a way that the dazzled intellect plunges into it as into a luminous abyss which overflows in all directions.

In my opinion, this is how that element of intuitivity linked to philosophical contemplation in a certain way bears on the divine object itself, by fixing our mind on the divine sublimity and absorbing our mind in that sublimity—and despite all this philosophical contemplation does not prove unfaithful to its nature as a purely intellectual contemplation by means of ideas, and it does not enter into the depths of God by supra-conceptual experience or the connaturality of love, as is the case with supernatural mystical contemplation. It could be said that at its highest point philosophical contemplation is also an apophatic contemplation, at least in the sense that the concepts which bring about this knowledge always play an essential role but admit to being vanquished, just as the intellect in adoration admits to being vanquished when it fixes its gaze and attention on those concepts. Be silent, poor human mind.

I would add that the element of unknowing I spoke of as presupposed by the intuitivity proper to philosophical contemplation, being as it is the supreme fruit of the knowledge of God by analogy, evidently has nothing to do with that form of unknowing by means of the abolition of all concepts and by the creation of the void within the soul which we come across in the typical forms of natural mysticism.[49]

5. Finally with regard to the second degree of abstraction, the one that is proper to the mathematical sciences, I have a prefatory remark to make first. Up to the present, when I spoke of the intuitivity of the mind, I always added: the intuitivity of the mind *turned toward the real* because what I was first and foremost concerned with was philosophical knowledge. But in the case of the mathematical sciences, it is not toward the real but toward beings of reason that the mind and its intuitivity are turned. Separated from corporeal sub-

---

49   The remarks just made concerning the intuitivity of philosophical contemplation apply as well, it seems to me, to the intuitivity of *theological contemplation*, with these essential differences that in theological contemplation the central concepts concern articles of faith—and that the light used by the mind is not only the light of reason but also, and primarily, that of faith—and finally that what accompanies this contemplation is not the natural love of God, but the love of charity, not a natural adoration, but a supernatural adoration inseparable from charity.

stance and from the world of sensible experience by an abstraction which, this time, isolates its object from the real and recasts it in an idealist manner, extension and quantity actually constitute for thought a multiform noetic universe apart, which infinitely overflows the conditions proper to the world of matter such as it exists in reality and such as our senses and our intellect lay hold on it at the first degree of abstraction.

This multiform and teeming universe, not of existing things, but of pure objects of thought, on the one hand is constructed by the mind with regard to the manner in which it takes form beginning with the abstraction which draws out the first principles of things, and at the same time is independent of the mind with regard to its properties (some basic quiddity or basic definition or other having been first freely posited, constitutive of some branch or other of the mathematical sciences) because this is a universe of pure rational necessities. The ideal entities which compose them have their own consistency and their own structures that are just as firm, and their own laws which are just as inflexible as those of the real world; so that if it is true to say that the mind freely causes them to appear before it, it is equally true to say that they unveil themselves to the mind that explores them. It is as if from the ocean of the imagination, the intellect, with a wave of a magic wand, causes islands to emerge or archipelagos or mountains covered with eternal snows, which have no existence except as ideals or as pure objects of thought, which the mind sets itself to scrutinize. There are no sciences freer than the mathematical sciences, which in a sense create their own objects (as is the case with art), but they are not forms of art, they remain sciences, whose truth consists in conformity, if not to existing things, at least to pure objects of thought which, once their ideal existence has been posited, depend solely on that ideal existence for their entire logical development and all their properties. This is a type of knowledge that is completely foreign to physics (since it is concerned with a purely ideal object), but which is a marvelous instrument of physics.

It could even happen that some sector or other of this universe of beings of reason (non-Euclidean spaces, for example) would have to be considered, I do not say as presenting us with characteristics of the real world—I do not think that by confusing geometry and physics one can declare that what is called, at the first degree of abstraction, the extension of corporeal things, of the plains, of the seas, from all of which, at the second degree of abstraction, geometry draws forth the primordial notion of space by the natural process of the formation of ideas, constitutes a Riemannian space. I would say rather that Riemannian space can and ought to be considered as ideally applicable—according to the needs of the physical theory—to the real world, and as permitting a more satisfactory explanation of certain aspects of that real world.

6. But let us leave all that aside. What I consider essential to notice here is that, at the second degree of abstraction, the intuitivity of the mind—turning

its attention this time not to reality (even if by means of the imagination), but to this or that system of ideal entities which the mathematical imagination gives rise to—here too, plays a fundamental, indispensable role in knowledge.

And since there is question here of ideal systems which, however consistent they may be in themselves, are created by the mathematical imagination, is not our concern here above all with an intuitivity of the artistic or aesthetic order? *Integritas, consonantia, claritas*: integrity, consonance or harmony, splendor or clarity, is it not because he is in search of these three elements typical of beauty, to which his soul is interiorly attuned, that the mathematician suddenly sees a principle of intelligible fecundity and intelligible organizing power open up to his particular science new horizons and new avenues of approach to a higher synthesis?

Here I find perfectly sufficient the testimony of an eminent scholar in a mathematical area for which, despite my incompetence, I have a particular reverence: topology, which Leibniz, who conceived the idea, called *analysis situs* (much later Riemann won for it its scientific status), and which studies the relative positions of geometrical entities, not by means of number and measurement, but solely in their qualitative properties or their "ordered relationships."

"The first essential bond between mathematics and the arts," wrote Marston Morse,[50] "is found in the fact that discovery in mathematics is not a matter of logic. It is rather the result of mysterious powers which no one understands, and *in which the unconscious recognition of beauty* must play an important part. Out of an infinity of designs a mathematician chooses one pattern for beauty's sake, and pulls it down to earth, no one knows how. Afterwards the logic of words and of forms sets the pattern right. Only then can one tell someone else. The first pattern remains in the shadows of the mind."

Apropos of these shadows of the mind, and the sparks of intuitivity which flash forth from them, Morse cites the examples of the discoveries made by Henri Poincaré and by Gauss.

"Gauss tells how he came to establish a theorem which had baffled him for two years. Gauss writes: 'Finally, two days ago, I succeeded, not on account of my painful efforts, but by the grace of God. Like a sudden flash of lightning, the riddle happened to be solved. I myself cannot say, what was the conducting

---

50   M. Morse, "Mathematics and the Arts," in *The Yale Review* (Summer 1951), pp. 607–608 and 605. Here is another passage worth citing: "Often, as I listen to students as they discuss art and science, I am startled to see that the 'science' they speak of and the world of science in which I live are different things. The science that they speak of is the science of cold newsprint, the crater-marked logical core, the page that dares not be wrong, the monstrosity of machines, grotesque deifications of men who have dropped God, the small pieces of temples whose plans have been lost and are not desired, bids for power by the bribe of power secretly held and not understood. It is science without its penumbra or its radiance . . ."

thread, which connected what I previously knew, with what made my success possible.'"

"Mathematics," Marston Morse continues, "is the sister, as well as the servant of the arts and is touched with the same madness and genius.

"The creative scientist lives in 'the wildness of logic' where reason is the handmaiden and not the master. I shun all monuments that are coldly legible. I prefer the world where the images turn their faces in every direction, like the masks of Picasso. It is the hour before the break of day when science turns in the womb, and, waiting, I am sorry that there is between us no sign and no language except by the mirrors of necessity. I am grateful for the poets who suspect the twilight zone."

You will notice that mathematical intuitivity is not poetic intuitivity, for in the latter it is the subject and the object, the self of the poet and the world which are revealed together to the mind, whereas the intuitivity of the mathematician is of a wholly objective order, as is the case with the intuitivity of the mind in any knowledge properly so called.

This is why when he speaks of "mysterious powers which no one understands" and on which mathematical discovery depends, Marston Morse is perfectly correct to add that "the unconscious recognition of *beauty*" must play a major role here. Fascination with the beauty within the object—an object that is completely ideal—and not that creative emotion, that secret depth of connaturality between things and that subjectivity which makes the poet a "dreamer of what is true" as Aristotle put it. In the same article, the interest that M. Morse shows in Albert Dürer seems to me quite significant in this regard. "In his younger days, when he was preparing the engraving *Adam and Eve* (1504), he had hoped to capture absolute beauty by means of a ruler and a compass. Shortly before he composed the *Melancholia I* (which was for him the portrait of Geometry), he was forced to recognize: 'But what absolute beauty is, I know not. Nobody knows it except God.'"[51] Marston Morse remarks that "Dürer was a creative mathematician as well as an artist. He wanted his geometric theories to measure up to his art," and "his discontent on this account was unique among artists of all time."[52]

---

51   Erwin Panofsky, quoted by M. Morse, "Mathematics and the Arts," p. 606.

52   M. Morse, *ibid.*, p. 606. Georges Béné, professor of experimental physics at the University of Geneva, who kindly consented to read these pages, thinks that the remarks of Marston Morse are valid for a great many physicists as well, and that in their regard it would be necessary to speak, not only of "intelligentiated sense," but of "intelligentiated imagination" as well.

On the other hand he writes to me: "For many of the fundamental discoveries in physics, one notes that the scholar 'felt' the result, acquired the conviction of its exactitude before having tried it out or before having been in a condition to demonstrate it: the well-known case of Galileo is an example of this: at a very young age he acquired the conviction of the heliocentric movement of the earth (from his observations), but he had the bad luck never to be able to offer convincing proof of his conviction. He thought he had found it (in the tides) when in 1632 he published the work which was to bring about his condemnation. Unfortunately the tides are not caused by the movement of the earth, but rather by lunar attraction, something that Galileo never believed.

"On the other hand, after a more or less important work of experimentation, the researcher is led to make a judgment concerning the degree of confidence he must place in the different measurements he has made. This judgment is essentially the result of a global 'feeling' which is rarely mistaken, even if the researcher cannot give objective reasons for his choice.

"The role of experiments. and this is exact, is principally a choice between several hypotheses, but often an experiment offers more than was expected of it and in its turn poses new questions. I have personally had occasion to verify this fact."

These observations of an eminent scholar, to whom notes 40 (p. 338) and 44 (p. 340) are also due, offer proper nuances, at the same time as they confirm in what is essential, the philosophical views I have proposed here, especially with regard to physics. For this I express my deep gratitude to my friend Georges Béné.

CHAPTER XV
A LOOK AT THEOLOGY (I)

THE SACRIFICE OF THE MASS[1]

I. THE PROBLEM

1. I JUST READ TWO NOTES on the Mass in which Brothers, for whose knowledge and competence I have a very special appreciation, have proposed, from the perspective which theologians take, some points of view which are very interesting but which nevertheless leave me a bit dissatisfied. And this reminded me of some things I have been thinking about for a long time but which I had never formulated in an articulate manner. So now I have tried to write out my reflections, in spite of the fatigue I have been suffering from these past few weeks; I offer you this working paper then with a certain apprehension, certainly not because of the substance it contains, but rather because of the expression of that substance and a vocabulary which I fear I have only imperfectly mastered. At any rate, the approach and the perspective that I am going to propose are very different, I think, from the different explanations advanced by the theologians (including even our dear Abbé[2] Journet who set me on this path, and whose book on the Mass is rich in so many truths. I shall come back to this book shortly). Perhaps the difference here is due to philosophical habits of thought, which give direction to a philosopher's thought even when this philosopher, who has taken quite a bit of his intellectual nourishment from theology (he has some very close friends who are theologians) takes the risk of reflecting on matters theological from a theological point of view.

It must seem rather presumptuous on my part to propose a new idea on a subject as venerable as the Mass, a subject on which theologians have been working for such a long time. Nevertheless one is faced with such a diversity of opinions among these very theologians that one is tempted to ask if this diversity is not due to the fact that the perspective from which they look at the problem does not entail certain inextricable difficulties.

---

1   *Editor's footnote*: A seminar given to the Little Brothers of Jesus, in Toulouse, May 15, 1965. Cf. *Nova et Vetera*, 1968, no. 1, pp. 1–35.

2   When I gave this conference to the Little Brothers, he had already been Cardinal Journet for several months.

In an appendix to his book on the Mass (Appendix II, pp. 333–335), Msgr. Journet in this regard traces out a quite edifying historical resumé:

1. Certain theologians seek in the Mass a sacrificial destruction distinct from that of the Cross. For *Bellarmine*, and for the *Salmantincenses*, it is the communion of the priest consuming the glorious Christ which constitutes this destruction. For *de Lugo* there is a sacrifice because in the consecration the (glorious) Christ is destroyed in respect to His human mode of existence. For *Lessius*, the double consecration *constitutes* a mystical immolation of the (glorious) Christ.

2. In the eyes of *Suarez*—the only logical one in this august assembly, but at the expense of St. Paul and the absolute unity of Christ's Sacrifice—the Mass is a sacrifice "specifically and essentially" different from the Sacrifice of the Cross.

3. For *Father de la Taille*, Christ is in heaven in the state of victim, of immolation and of perpetual host, and it is the Church who, by her act of offering, appropriates this perpetual host. For *M. Lepin*, the Sacrifice of the Mass is simply the offering that the glorious Christ makes of Himself under the representative signs of His immolation.

4. For *Cardinal Billot* and *Father Garrigou-Lagrange*, the invisible offering of the glorious Christ in the sacrament, joined to the exterior sign of immolation, is sufficient to constitute a proper and real sacrifice.

5. For still others, like *Dom Vonier* and *Cardinal Lépicier*, the presence of the glorious Christ on our altars represents and applies the Sacrifice of the Cross which is thus found present in a certain manner.

Finally let us note the very just criticism made by Msgr. Journet (footnote, p. 106) of the opinion of *Bellarmine*, who attributes to the glorious Christ a sacrificial act, which, after all, since it is no longer, properly speaking, either meritorious or atoning but only impetratory, is something quite different from the sacrificial act of the Cross.

Well, it might be thought that such a variety of opposed opinions—and apparently quite arbitrary ones—is the sign that we have not started down the road in the right direction, in other words, that from the outset we may have placed ourselves in a false perspective if we look for the explanation of the Sacrifice of the Mass in the direction of the *glorious Christ*, such as He is in heaven and on our altars. Would we not do better to look at the question from another perspective? Since there is question here of a *sacrifice*, are we not, in reality, in the perspective of the *passible Christ*, such as He was on Calvary, in that absolutely unique Sacrifice by which He redeemed the human race at one time and for all time, *semel*? Is it not in this perspective that we must seek the solution we need?

The position of Abbé Journet goes well beyond the saraband of theological opinions I just mentioned, and it is situated on completely different level. For the central intuition and the directing idea of the author is that the Sacrifice of the Mass *is identically the very sacrificial act of Calvary*. It is from Abbé Journet (in conversations that date way back, long before his book) that I got this central idea; and this is one reason, among so many others, why I am so grateful to him.

And yet it seems to me that (in order not to base his position on a philosophical thesis proper to the Thomist school—the thesis that all moments of time are *physically* present to the divine eternity—and which to my way of thinking is the point on which the whole question hinges, but which is not accepted by many theologians)[3] our friend and master has not yet gone far enough in his theological systematization.[4] According to this systematization, the Sacrifice of Calvary itself is made present to us, at each Mass, by its *operative application* to a new moment in time and by the *contact of its redeeming spiritual power*). The sacrificial act of Calvary is then seen to be "above time" by the spiritual power "of the unique sacrificial act of Christ."[5] (in other words by the contacts of its redeeming spiritual power)

But is there not a real distinction between the contact of a spiritual power and the ontological act itself from which that power proceeds? So that if terms are used in their strictest sense, regardless of what we might prefer, it is not the spiritual act of the Cross itself but only the *spiritual contact of its redeeming power* that, from this point of view, would have to be declared present at each Mass? This is why I think we must go further and say that the Sacrifice of Calvary is, through the intermediary of its "physical" presence to the divine eternity, itself made present to a particular moment in our time, on each occasion that a Mass is celebrated.

It seems to me that when there is question of the Mass, we are faced with a problem, with respect to *time*, analogous to the problem of the Eucharist, with respect to *space*. In the case of the Eucharist, how can the Body of Christ, while remaining in heaven, be present as well on all the altars of the world? In the case of the Mass, how can the Sacrifice of Christ, having taken place in moment of time that is definitively past, be present at every single instant of time when a priest pronounces the sacramental words? Evidently one answer cannot be modeled on the other.

It is preferable, on the other hand, that the proposed solution be simple (I mean at least in its essentials). I do not believe that those solutions which require subtle considerations from the very outset are generally good ones. It is necessary too that a solution that has been effectively realized in a single case, be valid as well in all other similar cases imaginable—and so it is that in the case of transubstantiation, other cases can be imagined in which a body

---

3   In the eyes of these theologians (whom I find to be but timid metaphysicians), it is only inasmuch as they are *known* by God that they are present to His eternity. But how can an event be known to creative Eternity—for whom there is neither past nor future—without it being *ontologically* present to Him?

4   Cf. Charles Journet, *La Messe* (Paris: Desclée de Brouwer, 1957), pp. 93–97.

5   *Ibid.*, p. 99.

that is present in one place, through transubstantiation, would be made miraculously present as well in some other place.

The solution I am about to propose to you appears to me well-suited to satisfy human reason when it tries to get some glimpse of a mystery of faith that is infinitely beyond it. I like it because it is based on the crudest realism. But I am not going to try to convince you; I will be content simply to expose to you as best I can the way I see it.

2. But before doing so, it seems to me that we might find some advantage in a brief consideration of the difficulties that are encountered in reading the ordinary exposés of the theologians on the subject of the Mass, difficulties which seem to me to force us to seek a more radical solution. Without getting involved in any particular theological controversy over this subject, I would like, before beginning my presentation, to make three very general remarks concerning the distinction, quite just and necessary in itself, but formulated in an unfortunately equivocal manner, between the *bloody immolation* (on Calvary) and the *un-bloody immolation* (at Mass).

1st remark. When an immolation or a sacrifice is qualified in a certain way, the qualificative used may refer to the word *immolation* in a double way.

On the one hand, it could refer to the *the very act of immolation, to what constitutes* immolation in itself; it could be called *physical*, for example, if it consists in the putting to death of the victim; or it could be called *purely spiritual*, if it consists in an act of perfect abnegation.

On the other hand (I am getting a bit ahead of myself on what I will have to explain in my presentation), the qualificative used can refer to the manner in which the immolation is present at a certain moment of time—that is, to its *mode of presence* at a certain moment in time. On Calvary, the immolation of Jesus was present at a certain moment of time in history when the Jews were subject to the Roman Empire. In the Mass, this same immolation, as I will insist in a moment, is made present—through a miracle—at a certain moment of our own particular time.

2nd remark. It is evident that an immolation consisting in the *death* of the victim (that is, if the victim is an animal, in the simultaneous destruction of its body and its soul, or if the victim is a human being, in the destruction of its ontological unity, the separation of its soul from its body), such an immolation is *by nature or by what properly constitutes it as such* different from an immolation which does not consist in the death of the victim.

How is it possible to say that an immolation that consists in the putting to death of the victim and one that does not consist in the putting to death of the victim are different only by mode? Death is not a mode.

3rd remark. When, in the discussions of the Sacrifice of the Mass, there is question of *"bloody immolation"* and of *"un-bloody immolation,"* the qualificatives "bloody" and "un-bloody" can be understood as referring either to the immolation *itself*, or to the manner in which it is present at a certain moment in time (and just as well to the manner in which it is offered), that is, referring to its *mode of presence at a given moment in time* or to the mode of oblation.

3. In the first case (that is, if the qualificative refers to the immolation itself), to say that there is only a difference of mode between the *bloody* immolation on Calvary (an immolation *consisting in the putting to death* of Christ by the separation of His soul and His body) and the *un-bloody* immolation of the Mass, an immolation *which would not consist in the putting to death* of Christ (which took place only once, under Pontius Pilate, and is not renewed on the altar)—to say that between these two kinds of immolation there is no more than a difference of mode would be an entirely ineffective verbal artifice. Let us repeat, death is not a mode. To be or not to be, to die or not to die, there is no more essential difference. A bloody immolation in itself or consisting in a putting to death differs essentially from an un-bloody immolation in itself or not consisting in a putting to death.

Now suppose that we use the words *bloody* and *un-bloody* to qualify the immolation itself. Then, from such a perspective, if we insist above all else that the Mass is a *real sacrifice*, it will follow that this real sacrifice is *other* than the sacrifice on Calvary; we would have to say that following upon the unique bloody sacrifice carried out on Calvary there has been on our altars through the course of ages a continuous series of un-bloody sacrifices which differ in nature from the Sacrifice on Calvary.

Or else if (always from the same perspective) we insist above all else that the Sacrifice of Christ is an *absolutely unique* sacrifice (that is, the one on Calvary), and therefore that on Calvary and in the Mass there is question of the same absolutely unique sacrifice (the one on Calvary), it will follow that this same unique sacrifice, carried out in the past, was real on the Cross but is not real in the Mass; then we will have to say that the only *real* sacrifice was the one on Calvary, and that the sacrifices which follow in succession on our altars are only *symbolic and figurative* sacrifices, in which the death of Christ (whatever may be said about its spiritual virtue, whose efficacy, whether sacramental or not, extends through all moments of time until the end of the world to redeem and to save us) is merely *represented* and *commemorated*.

4. The Catholic faith nevertheless asks us to profess in the same breath that the Sacrifice of the Mass is a sacrifice that is *real* and *properly so called*.

Are we then required to reconcile the unreconcilable?[6] Between one position

---

6   It seems to me that this is what is being attempted when it is said that the application, today, of the spiritual virtue of the sacrifice carried out in the past is that very sacrifice itself newly present, or again that the glorious Christ bearing with Him His redeeming act is, by the fact of His eucharistic presence on the altar, a Christ Who is actually sacrificed.

which affirms the *reality* of the Sacrifice of the Mass but implies the negation of the absolute unicity of the Sacrifice of Christ, and another position which affirms the absolute unicity of the Sacrifice of Christ but implies the negation of the reality of the Sacrifice of the Mass, the mind can flit back and forth, as a bird with wings flapping goes from one corner of its cage to the other; there can be no genuine reconciliation.

The more one reflects on the difficulty formulated in terms that are not just simplified but actually *denuded* like those I just used, the more it becomes apparent that there is only one conceivable solution: The words *bloody* and *unbloody* refer, not to the immolation itself, but rather to its *mode of presence* at any particular moment in time.

The immolation as such is the immolation, and *uniquely* that immolation, of Christ on Calvary, under Pontius Pilate, consisting in the putting to death of the victim or an immolation that was *bloody* in itself. But the *mode* according to which that immolation *is present* at some particular moment in time is itself, this is quite evident, *bloody* in the case of Calvary and, as we will see, *un-bloody* in the case of the Mass. So it is a miraculous mode of presence, due to that sign "with its existential implications" which is the double (separate) consecration of the host and the chalice, and which signifies the death of Christ—His bloody immolation—by an *un-bloody* action that the priest carries out before our very eyes.

And let us note immediately that the mode of the oblation (bloody or un-bloody) follows the mode of presence of the immolation. Such is the kind of presence at a given moment in time, and such too is the kind of oblation. There took place, carried out by Jesus on the Cross, an oblation (of Himself and of His sacrifice) which was immanent to the immolation itself and was one with it. This oblation was bloody, like the immolation itself and like its presence at a given moment in the history of the world. And there takes place, in the Mass, an oblation of the bloody sacrifice carried out on the Cross (this bloody oblation being inseparable from the sacrifice itself) which is—today, at Mass—an un-bloody oblation, just as the miraculous mode of presence in our time of the immolation itself is un-bloody. This is an un-bloody mode according to which, on our altars, that same unique immolation—the immolation on Calvary that is bloody in itself—is now, at each Mass celebrated here below, offered to God[7] by the glorious Jesus and by His minister, the priest, who serves

---

7   This oblation takes place on earth. There is another oblation, *in heaven*—and with no rite that is visible to our eyes—made eternally by Jesus.

This oblation by Jesus of the sacrifice accomplished on the Cross did not cease with the death of Christ; it continues for all time. But from the very first instant—bringing to a close the *ultimum tempus* of the life of Jesus here below—of that state of separation, which was the condition of His soul before the state of definitive reunion which is that of the resurrected Christ, this oblation ceased to be bloody. And un-bloody as well is that oblation by which, after the Resurrection and the Ascension, the glorious Jesus continues in heaven to offer that

as an instrument of His all-powerful will (and it is also offered—in a manner that is equally un-bloody—by the community united to the priest, just as long ago at the foot of the Cross, the oblation of the dying Jesus was made to the Father by the Virgin, St. John, and the holy women, who united themselves spiritually to the act by which Jesus gave His life).

The Mass is a *real* sacrifice *in the proper sense of the term*. And in order that the Sacrifice of the Mass be identical to that of Calvary, it is not sufficient that there be one single victim in both cases; in both cases there must be the same single identical putting to death. Since the bloody immolation of Christ on the Cross at a given moment is made really, though invisibly, present, in an un-bloody mode by the priest acting before our eyes, each single Mass must necessarily bring about a coincidence between some given moment in our time and *the very moment of Christ's immolation on Calvary*; in other words, it must transport us in some fashion, make us present at that moment in time past when the real and bloody Sacrifice of Christ took place—at which, however invisible it may remain for us, for an instant, the priest really makes us spectators. This is the heart of the mystery.

How is this possible? This is the important question we must put to ourselves in our reflections on the Mass. And it is only in this way, I believe, that we have any chance of getting a glimpse, to the extent that it is possible for us to acquire some obscure knowledge of such things, of that "most radical solution" I spoke of a moment ago. Now you can see why I said at the beginning of our colloquy, that the essential question which both philosophers and theologians must put to themselves when they try to get some notion of the mystery of the Sacrifice of the Mass must be formulated in terms of presence *in time*, just as the essential question concerning the mystery of the Eucharist must be formulated in terms of presence *in space*.

II. BY MEANS OF THE SACRIFICIAL SIGN THE DIVINE OMNIPOTENCE MAKES US PRESENT AT THE SACRIFICE OF THE CROSS AS IT IS ETERNALLY PRESERVED IN HEAVEN

5. Now let us get to work on our problem. The principle on which I am

---

immolation of His which was accomplished at one time and for all time on the Cross.

But how is it possible to *offer* what *no longer exists*? If the oblation of the sacrifice of the Cross continues eternally in heaven, it is because, like every single moment and event of time, the immolation of Calvary, past with regard to time, is immutably present to the divine eternity.

As far as the oblation *on earth* of the immolation of Calvary is concerned, it is through the Mass that it continues here below; and the glorious Christ is undoubtedly the principal agent of this oblation, inasmuch as He makes use of the ministry of a priest himself acting at the altar.

basing myself above all others is what might be called the principle of St. Peter Damien, a royal principle fearlessly affirmed by him and to which the Thomist school has remained faithful (here there is question of that divine transcendence which by its light in a certain way blinds the human intellect): All instants of time together are *physically* present to the divine eternity. I recalled this doctrine in *Existence and the Existent* (pp. 86–87) and also in *God and the Permission of Evil* (pp. 77–79). Each moment of time is present to the divine eternity, not only as being known to it, but physically; this is the word used by the theologians, that is, in its very being, ontologically. On this point see John of St. Thomas, *Cursus theologicus*, volume II, q. X, disp. 9, a. 3. All moments of time are present to the divine eternity—in which there is no succession, but which is one single instant which continues on without beginning or end—because the creative ideas embrace according to their own measure, which is eternity and which infinitely transcends time, all the material things that those ideas brought into existence and whose measure is the succession of time. According to the text of St. Peter Damien,[8] "the divine today is the incommutable, indefectible, inaccessible eternity to which nothing can be added and from which nothing can be taken away. And all those things which here below happen and come one after the other, flowing progressively into non-being . . . stand in the presence of this today and continue to exist motionless before it. Within this today and still motionless there is that day when the world had its beginning. And nevertheless, that day on which this world will be judged by the eternal judge is present as well."

This is what St. Peter Damien has written. The entire passage of time, all its successive moments, the whole flock of days at once and all together, is held and possessed by the supreme Instant of the infinite Being. For us this is completely unimaginable; it is the proper mystery of God's infinite transcendence.

Well, the same is the case for the central event of human history, the death and sacrifice of Jesus Christ under Pontius Pilate. That event took place at an instant of time in the history of the world. And, as St. Peter Damien says, *it stands in the presence of this today and continues to exist motionless before it*; it is eternally present to the eternal instant of God.

The Mass transports us, so to speak, into the presence of this event that is *eternally present* to the divine duration and which in its own proper duration is a thing *of the past* (yet preserved in heaven), and it makes present to that event *other moments*, other *todays* on earth than the one which was proper to it here on earth. It is *through the intermediary of eternity* that on earth today we are really, physically (and not just by memory or by thought) put miraculously, at a certain moment, in the presence of the past, in the presence of the past event of the immolation of Christ on Calvary. At the most solemn moment of the Mass we are made really present at the Sacrifice of the Cross such as it took

8   Ep. IV *De Omnipotentia*, cap. 8, P.L. 145, col 607 B.

place in the past. But if this is so, it is because, by the (miraculous) effect of a ritual sign ("with existential implications") accomplished on the altar, we are made really, physically present at this same Sacrifice of the Cross such as it is eternally preserved in heaven, such as it stands immutably present to the divine eternity.

And let us understand clearly that it is at this past event in its entirety, in its full and total reality, that we are thus made mysteriously present, such as that event has been preserved in heaven. It is not only the final act of the love of Christ delivering Himself up for us, it is not only His interior oblation which are there before us; it is also the physical event of His final act of oblation, by which His soul effectively left His body; it is the very consummation of his sacrifice, His death on the Cross. Whoever says sacrifice says death and immolation at the same time. There is no way to avoid it. At the celebration of the Mass, Christ dies each morning before our very eyes; He dies the death that He underwent voluntarily on a single unique occasion on Calvary. We are mysteriously brought face to face with this event always present to the divine eternity, such as it is, in its full reality, through the action of the priest as instrumental cause when he carries out (I will come back to this in a moment) the sign of the double consecration. And our eyes, at this special moment, look upon the death of Christ in Whose presence they have been placed, but what those eyes see is only the sign carried out on the altar.

6. In all of this, as I just indicated, the *principal agent* can be no other than the glorious Jesus, the eternal Priest, miraculously causing, by an act of His all-powerful will, the "presentiality" of new moments in time at the past event such as it is preserved in heaven, immutably present to the divine eternity. But in order that such an effect be produced, a certain operatory process, if I may put it this way, is required on the part of the earth. For it is not possible that the event on Calvary be produced once again—just as it was in the past—as an event of our time. In order that we be once again in its presence, another event has to take place—event no. 2—which takes place in our particular historical time and by means of which we are placed, without seeing it, in the presence of event no. 1, the sacrifice and death of Christ.

So we need *a man from among us*, the priest, who is the *instrumental agent* of the all-powerful causality of Jesus and who produces this event no. 2 at a certain moment in our time.

And this event no. 2 produced by him in our time must itself be *miraculous*—as the means of the miracle through which the past event, eternal in God, is reactualized for us.

And this event no. 2 produced by the priest must be a *sign* behind whose veils event no. 1, the event of Calvary, is before us now, at a given moment in our time, in a mode of *un-bloody* presence: since it affects our time now, not in the mode of presence which was proper to it at a given moment in history, but in the mode of presence proper to the *sign* produced in our time and by means of which it is now before us.

Event no. 2, produced by the priest, is the double consecration, by two separate acts, of the host and the chalice, by which figuratively, or in the *sign* produced, the Body and Blood of Christ are represented as separated, and this separation *signifies* the death—the real death—of Christ. This double consecration is the *instrument* here below by which the all-powerful will of the glorious Christ puts us miraculously in the presence, today, of that event, eternal in God, but definitively past as far as human history is concerned, which took place on Calvary.

7. But let us pay attention and understand this clearly! Here I am not speaking of the *thing* done by the priest; I am speaking of the duality of the *action* he has done. I am not speaking of transubstantiation itself, of the change itself that the words of Consecration bring about, and by which, when he says, "This is my Body" and "This is the Chalice of my Blood," the Body of Christ is there in place of the bread and the Blood of Christ in place of the wine. All of this refers to the *sacrament of the Eucharist*. In this case the end attained by the divinely efficacious sign which consists of the sacramental words is actually the Body of our Lord present right there before us, under the species of bread, which will be eaten by the priest and the faithful, and the Blood of our Lord present right there before us, under the species of wine, which will be drunk by the priest and (in the Eastern rite and by certain particular arrangements in the Latin rite) by the faithful.

On the contrary, what I am talking about, and which concerns the *Sacrifice of the Mass*, is the act of consecration itself under its double aspect or as it is done at two separate moments, first the consecration of the bread and, immediately afterwards, the consecration of the wine. It is in that interval of time between the one consecration and the other that the Sacrifice of the Mass as an immolation is accomplished. The immolation begins with the consecration of the bread and ends with the consecration of the wine. The sign, by whose instrumentality the Sacrifice of the Mass is accomplished, is the very duality or the division, the separation inscribed in the act of consecration,[9] so that

---

9   This is why the two consecrations are necessary for us to be present before a
     completed immolation or the death of Christ on the Cross. I have indicated that
     as far as the sacrificial sign (with its existential implications) is concerned, the
     immolation begins with the consecration of the bread and is completed with the
     consecration of the wine. This means that even the sacrificial sign itself is
     completed or consummated only with the consecration of the wine so that the
     death of Christ, which was instantaneous, is made present to us only at that precise
     moment of our time. The interval which separates the consecration of the bread
     from that of the wine is the brief *fieri* which has as its term the death of Christ—the
     final gift He made of Himself on the Cross and the *consummatum est* and the *Pater
     in manus tuas commendo spiritum meum*—which, it seems to me, is made miracu-
     lously present to us.

making the glorious Christ present on the altar *as if* (figuratively and not in reality) His Blood and His Body were separated one from the other, the act of consecration *announces* and *signifies* the death of the passible Christ, that same immolation and death which took place in time, on Calvary, and to which, by a miracle of God's omnipotence, our own particular time is made present for a short moment—that interval between the two consecrations that I just mentioned. With regard to the permanent thing that space is, I mean making present, behind impenetrable veils, the Body and Blood of the glorious Christ within our own space, it is perfectly normal that the sign which produces or effectuates the eucharistic transubstantiation have as its term some thing—the consecrated host or the consecrated wine—which is with us and remains with us for a certain time.

On the other hand, with regard to the fluid thing that time is, I mean making present at some given moment of our time, behind impenetrable veils, the immolation and death of the passible Christ, it is perfectly normal that the sign which causes that sacrifice which took place once and for all *sub Pontio Pilato* really *to be*, and to be *now*, today, present to us, in an invisible way, have for its term as well some thing—Jesus' final gift of Himself on the Cross—who is present to spend a few brief moments with us, two minutes perhaps.[10] This some thing which passes away so quickly is the absolute center of the Mass.

In other words, what the double sacrificial sign makes present to us is an event which took place in time. Once this event—the death of Christ on the Cross—has been made present to our time, the sacrificial sign (which refers to the passible Christ) has finished its work. What goes on afterwards on the altar[11] has nothing more to do with the passible Christ, but with the glorious

---

And so we can understand why if the Mass is interrupted after the first consecration, the sacrifice of the Mass may very well have begun, but it is not *completed* as an immolation. (Besides, it is, as we shall see later, *finally consummated* as an act of religion only by the communion of the priest.)

10   I realize that since the relation of the sign to the signified is of a purely intentional order (in as much as the role of the sign is to *make known* something other than itself), it is quite possible that a very brief sign relate to a thing that endures much longer. But the sacrificial sign is also a sign with *existential implications*. And in this respect it has for object to make a moment of our time coincide with a moment of time past. This is why it seems to me that the duration of the moment in question must be the same with regard to the sign as it is with regard to the signified—on the altar just as on the Cross: namely, the brief interval in time during which, within a particular historical reality, there took place *the final moments* properly so called of the life of our Lord, the final acts of thought, of will, of love—of *too great* a love, surpassing all human capacity here below—by virtue of which His soul was separated from His body and He died on the cross.

11   I am thinking here especially of those rites which, after the double consecration, continue as far as the *Pater*. These are rites which have value only as signs and no longer have any "existential implications" as did the sacramental signs and the sacrificial sign. Their obvious signification has as its object the oblation which

Christ whom the transubstantiation has made present ("locally" but not as "in a place" or circumscribed by a place) among us and which will become our nourishment through communion.

8. I hope I have shown how, in the solution that I have proposed, the Sacrifice of the Mass is a miracle *like* the transubstantiation, which takes place *at the same time* as the transubstantiation but is *another miracle* than the transubstantiation.[12]

By reason of the same sacrificial action or the same sacrificial sign of the double consecration, we have to do here with two distinct miracles accomplished at the same time and inseparably joined to one another: the miracle which makes us present, for a moment, at the immolation of the passible Christ, at a time in the past (but eternally preserved), and the miracle which makes the Body and Blood of the glorious Christ present on the altar, in a certain place in space where we ourselves are. By the institution of the Eucharist as Christ wished it, a double miracle is simultaneously produced by the same ritual action and the same ritual sign, which, inasmuch as duality or division is entailed in the act of consecration, is the *sacrificial sign* and, inasmuch there is a transubstantiation of the bread and wine, is a *sacramental sign*. The miracle of the reactualization of the immolation of the passible Christ (*vera sacrificatio*) and of the changing of bread and wine into the Body and Blood of Christ by the priest (communion) consist so totally of one and the same mystery that if the communion of the priest happened to be missing Mass would not really be celebrated: for the Mass is *consummated* (in the sense of being brought to its final term) only when the immolated victim itself is *consumed* (its flesh eaten and its blood drunk).

How can we try to understand this? I would say that from the Canon of the Mass on, the sacrifice is already *fully accomplished and fully pleasing to God*—it

---

the Church makes to God of the immolation of His Son; one could think that they also signify symbolically, the Passion of Jesus continuing on in His Mystical Body.

12   Let me make myself clear. The two distinct miracles I am speaking of (the one by which, at a given moment in time, we are made present at an event that took place on Calvary in the days of Pontius Pilate and Caiphas, and the one by which the glorious Body of Christ is made present on our altars, and in a given place—without being circumscribed by it—of our space) are so closely joined and united that they could be designated rather as two distinct faces of one and the same miracle: for it is in the very act, and by virtue of the very act of transubstantiation that both of them are accomplished: the first inasmuch as the priest, in order to carry out the transubstantiation, proceeds to two different consecrations—of the bread and of the wine—whose very duality signifies the death of Christ, and thus makes us really present (yet without our being able to see it) at His death itself on Calvary; the second inasmuch as the proper *effect* of the transubstantiation is to make the body and blood of the glorious Christ really (although invisibly) present under the species of the consecrated bread and wine.

is the same sacrifice as the one on Calvary, fully accomplished *by the Man-God* and fully accomplished *with regard to its acceptance by the Father*: the sacrifice of the Son of God dying on the Cross to redeem the world, and whose infinite merits and the final gift of self in an infinite act of charity satisfy in all plenitude divine justice and divine love. But even if it is already fully accomplished *with regard to God*, nevertheless it is only with the communion that it will be carried to the final term to which it is ordered *with regard to the Church and the sacred rite* which she carries out while she advances on this earth. It is important to note that, at the moment when he communicates, the priest no longer acts as minister of Christ, as he does during the consecration, but rather as minister of the entire Church, taking her place before God.

Let us recall that God does not take pleasure in the destruction as such, in death considered as such; He takes pleasure in them only insofar as they are necessary for a transformation into a higher life: immolated on the Cross on Good Friday, after three days Christ "rebuilt the Temple" and rose from the dead, entering into the life of glory that befitted His divinity. And, with regard, no longer to the Word incarnate but to simple men, God makes souls pass through death and destruction only to bring them to divine life. The immolation of the victim was pleasing to Him, in the sacrifices of the Old Law, only because they prefigured symbolically, through the eating of the victim, that other eating by which He now nourishes with Himself the creature that He made and wants to lead to eternal life.

On the other hand let us consider the marvelous changes that the New Law, in moving from symbol to reality, has introduced into the universe of the sacred. The sacrifice of Christ on the Cross was an act of religion (*Holocautomata pro peccato non tibi placuerunt. Tunc dixi: ecce venio*)[13] which infinitely transcended the virtue of religion.[14] So at the center of the Mass, of that supreme

---

13   Heb. x, 6–7.

14   Heb., vii, 26–27: "For it was fitting that we should have such a high priest, holy, innocent, undefiled, set apart from sinners and *become higher than the heavens*. He does not need to offer sacrifices daily (as the other priests did), first for his own sins, and then for the sins of the people; for this latter he did once for all in offering up himself"; ix, 11–14: "But when Christ appeared as high priest of the good things to come, he entered once for all through *the greater and more perfect tabernacle, not made by hands (that is, not of this creation)*, nor again by virtue of blood of goats and calves, but *by virtue of his own blood*, into the Holy of Holies, having obtained eternal redemption. For if the blood of goats and bulls and the sprinkled ashes of a heifer sanctify the unclean unto the cleansing of the flesh, how much more will the blood of Christ, *who through the Holy Spirit offered himself unblemished unto God*, cleanse your conscience from dead works to serve the living God?" All that is said here infinitely surpasses the proper domain of the virtue of religion.

In my text I speak of an act of religion which infinitely transcends the virtue of religion. To use a distant comparison, St. Francis of Assisi and St. Benedict Labre both had the moral virtue of prudence, but did not the acts of paradoxical

act of religion that the Church carries out at the moment of consecration when the unique Sacrifice, hidden under veils, is renewed, there is an act of religion—that of Christ Himself, in whose presence we find ourselves, which infinitely transcends the virtue of religion. And if the immolated Victim, now glorious, is finally eaten by the priest, and after him by the faithful, it is not in order to make agreeable to God a sacrifice which, since it is that of the Redeeming Lamb, God has already fully accepted from the moment of consecration; it is so that with regard to men and their act of religion, which likewise transcends the order proper to the virtue of religion, the immaculate Spouse be maintained and strengthened in her life and unity, and fill up in herself, throughout all time, "what is lacking"—as to its application, not as to its merits—"in the passion of the Savior." This is why the sacrifice of the Mass is carried to the term to which it was ordered only when, already carried out by the words of consecration and already fully accepted by God, the Church herself partakes in it in the person of the priest who eats the Body and drinks the Blood of the Lord, the faithful people taking part also when they receive Communion after the priest in that final consummation of the sacrifice of the Mass (cf. below, section 20).

Now a final remark on the "sacrificial sign" of the double consecration. If

prudence which characterize their lives transcend this virtue?

I am not unaware that an act elicited by a moral virtue (which like all *virtutes humanae*, perfect man inasmuch as he is *moved by reason*, cf. *Sum. theol.*, Ia-IIae, q. 68, a. 1) may be commanded by charity, and by that fact even rendered heroic: does not St. Thomas tell us (IIa-IIae, q. 124, a. 2) that martyrdom is an act of the virtue of fortitude commanded by charity and by this fact carried to its ultimate perfection ("*martyrium est actus maximae perfectionis*," ibid., a. 3)?

However I maintain that the act in question thus commanded *transcends the proper order of the moral virtue of the same name*, especially if it is the effect of the movement and inspiration of God, which is better than reason; in other words if it emanates (which is certainly the case with martyrdom, for the Gift of fortitude is there) from one of the Gifts of the Holy Spirit "which dispose men to be *divinely moved*" (Ia-IIae, q. 68, a. 1).

How much more is this so if the act under consideration is the execution of the Uncreated Divine Will itself deciding on the redeeming Incarnation from all eternity—in heaven, it is the will of the Father, as in absolute identity it is also the will of the Son, the Second Person of the Blessed Trinity, and on earth, it is likewise the divine will of this Second Person descended into the flesh: Christ's divine will, which an incomparable effusion of the Holy Spirit, into the human soul and the human will of Christ, makes Him obey even unto death—in this way making Him accomplish *an act of religion which infinitely transcends the virtue of religion*.

However, might one not say, *ad contrarium*, that it is the moral virtue of religion that *elicits* the act in question? It is not elicited by this virtue; it is rather *drawn forth from it*, under the supreme regulation of charity, by that breath which, divinely carrying away the entire soul, carries this *virtus humana* to the point—in the oblation of God made man dying for love on the Cross—where all the means and measures and motion of human reason are surpassed.

by efficacious sign we understand a sign which *causes or produces what it signifies* (as is the case for the sacramental words "this is my Body," which are the cause of the transubstantiation), what I call the sacrificial sign—the duality or separation which is manifest in the action by which the priest makes the Lord present on the altar—is not an "efficacious" sign. But if we understand by efficacious sign any sign which of itself causes an effect in the being (whether it produces what it signifies, or, if the signified took place in the past, makes it present again at a given moment in time), then we must say that the double consecration is an efficacious sign, which brings it about that the thing signified (the sacrifice of Christ) and which took place at another time *is present now*, once again, at a given moment in time. However, to avoid any risk of confusion, I prefer to use the expression *with existential implications* to characterize the sign of the double consecration.

The sacramental words "this is my Body," "this is the Chalice of my Blood," change the substance of the bread into the substance of the Body of Christ and the substance of the wine into the substance of His Blood, in such a way that the glorious Christ, without ceasing to be in heaven, is also *here (hic)*, I mean at a particular point in our space. The double consecration brings it about that the immolation of Christ, without ceasing to have taken place, is also *here (nunc)*, I mean present at a given moment of our time. By the divine omnipotence, there is added to the proper function of the sign, the power to make the signified really and existentially attainable.

The sacrificial sign of the double consecration is a sign with existential implications which the glorious Christ uses in order to reactualize for us, by a miracle of His omnipotence, that sacrifice which, when He was passible here below, he accomplished under Pontius Pilate, and which at each Mass, is once again *there*, as present at a certain moment of our time.

III. MIRACULOUS PRESENCE AT AN EVENT WITH REGARD TO THE TIME (NOT THE SPACE) AT WHICH IT TOOK PLACE.

9. Having arrived where we are, all that I have just indicated with broad strokes should now be considered more closely to test its truth and furnish the necessary precisions.

Let us begin with the notion of *presence*. This is the idea we are working with. Let us say more precisely: The idea we are concerned with is that of *presence at an event itself "situated" at a given moment of time or duration.* Let us see if we can look into this a bit more profoundly.

To be present at some event (that is to say, at a certain spatio-temporal complex)—does not this mean to be situated oneself in space and time in such a way as to be able either to touch, to see, or to hear the things which are then occurring? I do not think that *presence* can be defined without appealing to the senses. The notion of presence is undoubtedly analogous (we say, for example, "to put oneself in God's presence," just as we say "to keep oneself close to God"); but in its first signification or its first analogate, the word *presence* refers to the material world, to the world of space-time. And naturally, in that particular world, we are *present* to something only when for us there is a combination of all sorts of conditions relative not only to time, but also to space, to the possibility of exercising our senses, in brief to the entire physical and historical context of the event. I am present at a play when, at a given time that I can read on my watch and when the actors are actually presenting the play, I am in a certain place in a theater at a time when I can or could see and hear what is taking place on the stage. (I said, "I can or *could*" because if, for example, it is played behind the curtain or if the lights are not turned on or if I am blind or deaf, I am physically quite present at the play and the play is quite present to me, even though I cannot enjoy it.)

And so, what is essentially implied in the notion of presence is a condition of space-time, *to be there* (*Dasein*) in time and in space at the same moment when and at the same place where the thing or the event to which one is present *is there* as well.

This being given, the presence with which we are concerned, that presence which brings it about that during the Mass, at a certain moment, I become really present at the Sacrifice on Calvary (and by the same token the Sacrifice on Calvary becomes really present to me), but this time without my being able in any way to attain that event through my senses, that essentially mysterious and supernatural presence is an analogate of the sensible presence I just mentioned.

10. Well, what it is important to take note of in the presence we are considering is a disjunction—which only the divine omnipotence can effect[15]—between presence in time (*Dasein* in the sense of *esse nunc*) and presence in space (*Dasein* in the sense of *esse hic*); between presence at a certain moment in time and presence at a certain point in space. It is solely the first sort of presence, presence *to time* (our presence *to time*) that comes into play here.

The priest and the faithful are themselves made really and miraculously present *at a moment in time* when an event—the immolation of Christ and His death on the Cross—took place at a certain definite spot on the earth, even though they are in no way themselves *situated* at the point in space where this

---

15   In the natural order we find something which resembles such a disjunction but from an infinite distance. As a matter of fact, with the help of a telescope I can observe in the world of the stars an event that takes place at an enormous distance, and to which I am apparently "present in time" without being present to it "in space." But in fact the telescope, by prolonging my vision, makes the organ of my sight physically or spatially present to the event in question, whereas this same event can be very distant from me temporarily—in fact it may have disappeared long before the light by which I see it reaches me.

event took place. The place in question is the one at which the Sacrifice of Christ was accomplished, and where, outside time, it is always accomplished inasmuch as it is physically and ontologically present to the divine eternity. We ourselves are situated there in space only in thought and in spirit, not in reality.

In the same way, due to the fact that I am made present at the moment in time when the sacrifice was accomplished, we must say that the sacrifice is made present at a certain moment of my time. But no more than I myself am made present at the place where the sacrifice was accomplished (in other words, no more than I myself am *situated* in this place) is the sacrifice made present to the place or situated in the place where I exist. It is not placed on our altars

The sacrifice of Christ is present before the eternal Instant of God and "remains motionless before Him." But it is not to the place where it was produced that the divine omnipotence so to speak "transports" us, makes us miraculously present ourselves through the double consecration, by making a moment of our time coincide really and invisibly with that particular moment.

11. Considering then the proper time of the event on Calvary and the proper time of that other event which is the Mass I am attending, let us imagine the actual day of the condemnation and the immolation of the Lord, the actual day of the first Good Friday, as a sphere on the surface of which a tiny segment, almost no more than a point, marks the very brief moment when Jesus consummated His sacrifice and delivered up His soul to the Father. And let us imagine the actual day on which I attend Mass as another sphere on the surface of which a tiny segment, almost no more than a point, marks a very short moment (two minutes perhaps) during which the priest carries out the double consecration.

In order to form for ourselves an image of that miracle by which the Sacrifice of Calvary is made really though invisibly present at each Mass celebrated here below, we will say then that the divine omnipotence brings it about that the actual day in time past which was the first Good Friday itself—and which as far as duration here below is concerned no longer exists, is now nothing, but which is forever present to the divine eternity and imperishably preserved before it—happens to touch the sphere of that day in time present which is the actual day on which I attend Mass. These two spheres touch at one point which, on the sphere of the first Good Friday, marks the moment of the immolation of Christ, and on the sphere of the actual day on which I attend Mass, marks the moment of the double consecration. By the fact of the contact that has been established in this way—in other words, by virtue of a kind of ecstasy, one miraculously produced, of a moment of our time in the divine eternity—the two points in question coincide, they are a point common to both spheres; the two moments in question, that of the consummation of the sacrifice (marked on the first sphere) and that of the double consecration (marked on the second) make up only one single moment, a temporal envelope of the event signified by the double consecration: I am, in my own particular time really simultanized with the moment of Jesus' time when He delivered up His soul to the Father.

And so it is that by the double consecration we are made really, though invisibly, present at the Sacrifice on Calvary, and the Sacrifice on Calvary is made really, though invisibly, present to us. It *is there* (*est nunc*),in order to be offered today on earth, in an un-bloody mode, by the glorious Jesus and by the priest, His instrumental agent here below, and by ourselves united spiritually to the priest[16]—just as it was offered in a bloody mode on the first Good Friday, by Christ nailed to the Cross.

The moment I just spoke of is like a window through which, just as I see the altar, I would also see Calvary and the Cross if the coincidence in question— which concerns only a brief slice of time and which is enough for the invisible, intangible, and miraculous presence which results from the double consecration—were extended to all the other spatio-temporal conditions required by *sensible* presence, that is, in the very place where I actually exist—in other words, if I were a contemporary of Christ and found myself on Golgotha at the time of the crucifixion. (But then I would have no need of this miraculous window.)

During the Mass, at the moment of the double consecration, I am present at the Sacrifice on Calvary *as if* I were there (in the order of space and all the above-mentioned conditions) because *I am there* really in the order of the unique moment miraculously made common to the time when Jesus lived and to the time during which I myself am living.

12. We can now see how, in my opinion, we must picture these things. The sign which is produced on our altars and occupies a brief moment in our time—the double consecration—signifies, in an abridgment of extraordinary plenitude, all that took place in the soul and body of Christ when, in a moment that was just as short, He consummated His sacrifice and death on the Cross. And, as a sign *with existential implications*, it makes all that present to our time, by the very fact that it makes a moment of our time *present to all that*, situating us in this way, for a moment, in the same time as all of that.

In fact, to say that the Sacrifice on Calvary is reactualized for us in the Mass is to say that by means of the sign (with existential implications) which is produced on the altar, the divine omnipotence places us, during that moment

---

16   For all this, it cannot be said that the faithful "concelebrate" with the priest! The priest alone, by reason of the sacrament of Holy Orders that he has received, carries out the *sacrifice* of the Mass, he alone offers it up *sacramentally*. The community of the faithful carries it out in no way whatever and does not offer it up except by *uniting itself spiritually* to the sacramental oblation at the moment of consecration. Cf. below, section 20.

of our time when the double consecration takes place, before something that transcends time absolutely: the signified event itself as it *is eternally present to the divine eternity*. And at the same time, through the intermediary of the presence of this event to the divine eternity, we find ourselves placed in the presence of this same event as it took place according to its proper nature as an event in time—in other words as it took place in a moment of time past under Pontius Pilate; here we find ourselves definitively situated for a brief moment in the same time as that event. And so, by virtue of the divine omnipotence making use of the sacrificial sign as an instrument, we ourselves are miraculously made present, at a moment of past time, to an existential reality which that moment contained. From then on we are permitted to say as well (this is really the same result, expressed in other terms, like a simple corollary) that this past moment and the existential reality it contained are now miraculously present to us, in an invisible manner, and under the visible sign of the double consecration.

At this point, let us remark that as present to the divine eternity, the Sacrifice of the Mass exists under two different aspects. On the one hand, it is present there under a mode that is *foreign to its nature as an event in time*, the mode of the divine eternity and of divine ideas. On the other hand, it is evidently there as well under the mode which is *proper to its nature as an event in time*, posterior to one event and anterior to another: in short, speaking of it today, we must say that in its presence to the divine eternity we find it, on the one hand, under the aspect of an *eternal* event and, on the other hand, under the aspect of a past event. Eternal and past at one and the same time, in two different respects— this is not very easy to grasp. Yet this is what St. Peter Damien says. Let me read his text again: "In the divine today in which beings remain motionless before him, still motionless there is that day when the world had its beginning. And nevertheless, that day on which this world will be judged by the eternal judge is present as well." The day when the world *took* its beginning is evidently past with respect to the day when it *will be* judged, and yet both the one and the other are *eternal and motionless* before the divine today.

To use a metaphor which, though completely inadequate, is still somewhat useful, I would say that we can imagine the entire course of time in a solid state, like an *immense space* present to the divine eternity and in which any part at all is spatially situated *before* one part and *after* another. This is the image of a *preserved past*.

It is clear, on the other hand, that if abstraction is made of the presence of the event to the divine eternity, we would be dealing with a *past* that has not been preserved. And it is equally clear that the sign effectuated on the altar does not signify the event as purely and simply past, in other words, as no longer existing. How can we put ourselves in the presence of what is not there?

What the sign effectuated by the priest signifies, and what it makes present to us, is the *past* event as it is *preserved* in God. So then it is indeed in what is eternally present to the divine today that we are put in the presence of the Sacrifice on Calvary, but there it evidently still keeps its connatural mode of and event (past for us) taking place at a certain moment in time, under Pontius Pilate.

So therefore, while through transubstantiation the glorious body of Christ is placed on the altar at a certain point of our space, on the contrary, through the double consecration, the slice of our time during which it takes place coincides with a certain moment of past time, of a time that is not our time but the time of the contemporaries of Jesus so that for an instant it is *we* who are miraculously made contemporaries of Jesus the viator and of Pontius Pilate; and we then have before our eyes—invisibly, in and through the sign produced on the altar, and under the mode of this sign—what took place in the soul and body of Our Lord on Calvary and in the historical context of the time of Pilate. A better way to express this might be to say that by virtue of the sacrificial sign, a certain moment of our time is miraculously made *participant in the divine eternity in order to be merged with a certain moment of a certain past time that has been preserved within it*. This is the kind of *ecstasy of a moment of our time in the divine eternity* that I just mentioned.

IV. THE MODE OF PRESENCE, BY WHICH THE SACRIFICE THAT IS BLOODY IN ITSELF IS REALLY AND INVISIBLY BEFORE US, IS A BLOODLESS MODE

13. Let us sum up. We have seen that what the double consecration, the separate consecration of the host and the separate consecration of the blood, signifies is an event which took place in the past and which is present to the divine eternity. The sacrifice that took place on Calvary is absolutely unique. At a given moment of our time, by a miracle of the divine omnipotence and by means of and by the power of a sign produced on the altar, we are face to face with that unique Sacrifice which we cannot see, hidden as it is under the veils of the sign by which we are made present to it.

Let us say that for an instant we are *made contemporary to that past event* taken in its full reality as the sacrifice of the passible Christ giving His life for us, whereas the *mode of presence* under which He comes in touch with our own time (or, to be more exact, He occupies one of these brief moments, He passes through it) is not the same mode of presence He had in history. It is the *mode of presence* of the *sign* which signifies it on our altars. In other words we do indeed assist at that *bloody sacrifice* through the power of the sign, at that real sacrifice without any alteration or diminution, which took place under Pontius Pilate; we are present at the death of Christ, at the *Pater, in manus tuas commendo spiritum meum*.

But under a *mode of presence* that is *bloodless* because it is the mode of presence of the *sign* which in our own time signifies this sacrifice and which brings it about that at some moment of our time we are miraculously made contemporary to the thing signified.

To say that the Sacrifice of the Mass is bloodless is to say that there is no victim on the altar for the priest to put to death by lance or by knife. Nevertheless I think that the expression "bloodless sacrifice" has been the source of terrible confusion.

Brains were racked in an effort to make the *sacrifice itself*, the sacrifice in its very structure, a *bloodless* one, the result being to deprive it of a quality that is essential to its reality.

But it is in no way the sacrifice itself—the thing signified—that is made bloodless; it is rather its *mode of presence* to our time—through and in a sign—which is *bloodless*. The Sacrifice of Christ is reactualized at Mass, by a bloodless mode, which means that the sacrifice, bloody in itself, is signified on our altars, and—by the power of the sign—invisibly attained by us in its reality, under a *mode of presence to our time* which is that of the sign—bloodless—by means of which and under whose veils we are made contemporary to it.

There is no blood flowing before our eyes on the altar, as there was blood flowing on the Cross before the eyes of the holy women and the Roman soldiers, but that blood which flowed on the Cross is an essential part of the reality to which, for a brief moment, we are miraculously made contemporary, and before which at the same time we are miraculously placed, without its having anything to do with our particular space. The Precious Blood shed for us is an essential part of all that took place in the immolation of Christ on the Cross (the bleeding wounds in His hands and feet, the bleeding wounds caused by the crown of thorns, and, just after the death of Our Lord, the stroke of the lance piercing His heart), even though everything that takes place *on our altars* takes place under a *bloodless mode*, the mode of the sign with existential implications, the mode according to which the double consecration takes its place in our times.

14. This is the essence of what I wanted to propose to you. There are still a few remarks to add.

I said that the solution proposed in the case of the Mass must be valid in any other imaginable analogous case.

Let us imagine that there was question of reactualizing another past event, the resurrection of Lazarus. Here the same principles are valid. This event is physically present to the divine eternity. The omnipotent will of Christ can bring into being, before our eyes, at some moment of our time, this particular past event eternally preserved in the divine today. For this His will would make use of a human instrumental cause which in our time would produce an event number 2, itself miraculous, which is a sign with existential implications, with the result that through the power of this sign we are for an instant made contemporary to the resurrection of Lazarus such as it took place in its own time.

Any past event at all can be imagined to which we are for an instant made contemporary, in the same way, by the divine omnipotence making use of an instrumental human agent and a sign that this agent produces in our time.

The physical or ontological presence of all instants of time to the divine eternity; the divine omnipotence; a man serving as instrument of that omnipotence in order to produce at a certain moment of our time a certain sign of existential implications—this is what is needed for any past event, if God will it, to be made, in its very reality, invisibly present, not to our space, but to our time, under the veils of a sign produced in our time.

And certainly the mode of presence under which the event in question is in this way reactualized for us in our particular time is not the same mode of presence under which it existed in the past. For the mode of presence is the mode of the *sign* by which it is signified in our time.

15. Here we have come back again to the bloodless mode that I spoke of a moment ago in its relation to the Mass. This is a mode of presence proper to the *sign* by the means and the power of which, at a given moment of our time, we find ourselves contemporary to the Sacrifice of Christ on Calvary.

It is a mistake that would spoil everything if an attempt were made to put this bloodless mode *in the sacrifice itself*, which is the *thing* that is invisibly reactualized for us by means of the sign that fills an instant of our time. The bloodless mode is the mode of the *sign* on our altars. But the sacrifice itself to which we are made present by means of the sign is the sacrifice in its *existential integrity*—that sovereign act of charity, that interior oblation, that exterior oblation, that death, such as it was on Calvary and such as it is forever in the divine eternity. Nothing can be changed in it, nothing can be taken from it, not even by God Himself. This is the event just as it took place in the past—blood and pain included—and to this *past* event, for a moment of our time, we are miraculously made contemporary. Therefore Christ suffering and dying, in His own time, the time of Calvary, is the object in whose presence the sign of the double consecration, produced in our own particular time, places us in an invisible manner. Whereas, on the contrary, by means of transubstantiation, the glorious Christ, such as He exists *now* in heaven, is present on the altar.

It would be useless to seek in this presence of the *glorious* Christ the slightest element to explain the Mass *as a sacrifice*, as perpetuating the Sacrifice of the Cross (except insofar as this presence of the glorious Christ under the sacramental species is itself ordered to the communion of the priest, by which the sacrifice is definitively consummated). This communion in the flesh and blood of the glorious Christ is what comes *after* the immolation, what crowns it, so to speak. It is with the eating of the immolated victim that the transubstantiation has to do as such. It is wonderful to think that at Mass we are first in the presence of Christ suffering and dying (*immolation*), and then, for the eating of the immolated victim, it is the glorious Christ, the eternal King of all creation, who is given to us.

V. AUTHORITATIVE TEXTS AND THE INTERPRETATION THEY REQUIRE

16. In conclusion, I think it would be quite easy to show how the point of view I have proposed is in complete accord with the texts quoted by Denzinger, and above all and in particular with the classic declarations of the Council of Trent.

Let us point out a certain number of essential texts:

First text (Council of Trent, Denzinger-Schönmetzer, 1740): Christ offered "Himself once (*semel*) to God the Father on the altar of the Cross, a death thereby occurring that would secure an eternal redemption."

"At the last supper on the night He was betrayed" [I Cor. xi, 23] He left "to his beloved spouse the Church a visible sacrifice (as human nature requires), by which that bloody sacrifice carried out once and for all (*semel*) on the Cross by the shedding of blood would be represented . . . and the saving power of this sacrifice would be applied to the remission of the sins we commit every day."

Second text (Council of Trent, 1743): "In this divine sacrifice which is carried out in the Mass, this same Christ is contained and immolated in a bloodless manner (*incruente immolatur*), who on the altar of the Cross 'offered Himself once and for all in a bloody manner, *semel se ipsum cruente obtulit*'[17] (Heb. ix, 14–27)."

The words "immolated in a bloodless manner" or under a bloodless mode (*incruente immolatur*) can be understood, as we have seen, either in regard to the very nature or the formal constitutive of the immolation or else in regard to its mode of presence to our time. In the first case one is exposed to insurmountable difficulties. It is therefore in regard to *the mode of presence to our time* that these words must be understood. The *incruente* refers to the *sign* of the double consecration, which represents in a bloodless way and under a *visible* mode on the altar (in a sign with existential implications), the bloody immolation of Our Lord on Calvary which by the sign in question is itself made *really and visibly* present to a moment of our time. The immolation is visibly on the altar only in the sign which represents it under a bloodless mode.

This is what is said in the third text that I would like to call to your attention

---

17   The formula *semel se ipsum cruente obtulit* "offered Himself once and for all in a bloody manner," condenses three passages from the *Epistle to the Hebrews* (ix, 14, 27, and 28). In fact the word *cruente* (in a bloody manner) which might possibly lead one to expect some allusion to another oblation—this time bloodless—does not appear in the epistle.

(Council of Trent, 1741): Christ, after having celebrated the ancient Passover, "instituted a new Passover, namely, Himself to be immolated *under visible signs* by the Church through the ministry of the priests, *se ipsum ab Ecclesia per sacerdotes sub signis visibilibus immolandum,* in memory of His own passage over from this world to the Father, when he redeemed us by the shedding of His blood."

This immolation under visible signs, carried out by the Church through the ministry of the priests, can be a real sacrifice, a *true* sacrifice *properly so called* (*verum et proprium sacrificium*) (Denz., 1751), only if, in its essence and in its proper constitutive, it differs in no way from that absolutely unique sacrifice ("by one offering He has perfected forever those who are sanctified," Heb. x, 14) by which "Jesus appeared once and for all (*semel*) for the destruction of sin" (*ibid.* ix, 26) and "offered Himself once and for all (*semel*) in order to take away the sins of many" (*ibid.*, ix, 28)—in other words, only if it is the immolation of Calvary, that absolutely unique immolation which redeemed us all once and for all, and in the presence of which we are placed, through all time, through the *visible signs* produced on the altar, each time the Mass is celebrated.

Fourth text (Council of Trent, 1743): "In fact there is but one and the same victim (Jesus) offering Himself today through the ministry of the priests as He offered Himself then on the Cross, the only difference being in the mode of oblation, *sola offerendi ratione diversa.* The fruits of this bloody oblation on the Cross are gathered in all abundance by the bloodless oblation."

I would point out here that the word *oblation* can be considered a synonym for the word *immolation*; in this case the text I just cited can be explained in the same way as the preceding one.

But the word *oblation*, as I already indicated at the beginning, can also be taken in the strict sense of *offering*, whether it is one with the act of immolation or whether it is distinct from it. In this case, it must be said that there are indeed two different oblations: the bloody oblation which the suffering and dying Christ made of Himself on Calvary; and the bloodless oblation which the glorious Christ, and the priest who acts in His name, as well as the faithful who by prayer unite themselves to the Mass, together today make on our altars thanks to the visible sign of the double consecration. Yes, but a bloodless oblation of what? It is the offering of the victim immolated on Calvary, the offering of the Sacrifice of the Cross whose reality (*past* yet *preserved* in the divine eternity) is made really though invisibly present to us at a given moment of our time, by means of a visible sign with existential implications.

Fifth text (Encyclical of Pius XII, *Mediator Dei* on the Liturgy, 3847): "The sacrifice on the altar is not a pure and simple commemoration of the crucifixion and death of Jesus, but a true and proper sacrificial act (*vera et propria sacrificatio*)[18] in which by His bloodless immolation the Sovereign Priest accomplished the same thing He did long ago on the Cross, offering Himself to the eternal Father as the perfectly acceptable victim . . ."

---

18   Cf. above, *verum et proprium sacrificium* (Denz., 1751)

Sixth text (*ibid.*, 3848): "The mode according to which Christ is offered is nevertheless different." And after having recalled that this mode was bloody on the Cross, but can no longer be so today, by reason of the state of glory in which the human nature of Jesus now is, the Pope adds that on our altars "the sacrificial act is made strikingly manifest by external signs which are indications of His death (*sacrificatio per externa signa, quae sunt mortis indices, mirando quodam modo ostenditur*)." For "through the transubstantiation of the bread into the body of Christ and of the wine into His blood," the eucharistic species "represent the bloody separation of body and blood (*cruentem corporis et sanguinis separatio figurant*)." So that by means of these distinct indications Jesus Christ, in the sacrifice on the altar, is "signified and shown in the state of victim (*in statu victimae significatur et ostenditur*)."

Let us be careful to note these *externa signa quae sunt mortis indices*. The double consecration is a *sign of death and immolation*. But it is only a sign, with nothing more than figurative or symbolic implications? No, it is a sign *with existential implications*, in the same way that the words of the sacraments are *efficacious signs*. The double consecration is a sign of death and immolation with *existential implications*, which make us, for a short instant of our time, miraculously present at the Sacrifice on Calvary.

Seventh text (*ibid.*, 3852): "This bloodless immolation, in which through the words of consecration Christ is made present on the altar *in the state of victim*, is carried out by the priest alone, inasmuch as he represents the person of Christ, but not inasmuch as he represents the person of the faithful (*ab ipso sacerdote perficitur, prout Christi personam sustinet, non vero prout Christi fidelium personam gerit*)."

17. Just as in the texts of the Council of Trent, and in a language that is perhaps a bit more stern, we find again in the texts of Pius XII the expression *bloodless immolation*, and at the same time the unfortunate equivocation in this expression that I pointed out at the beginning. There is a similar equivocation too in the expression "in the state of victim."

Indeed it could be understood that on our altars an immolation is carried out that is bloodless in itself, in its very nature and in its proper constitutive, that is, an immolation which on the one hand would be a true and proper sacrifice, a *vera et propria sacrificatio*, and which, on the other hand, would consist *solely* in the fact that Christ is *signified in the state of victim* because the eucharistic consecration *represents* (is a figure of) the bloody separation of flesh and blood. It seems so difficult to hold both these affirmations together as valid that there might be reason to fear that one would end up with the contradictory notion of a "true and proper sacrifice" that would be only a *figurative* or symbolic sacrifice.

In my opinion, the correct interpretation is entirely different. It consists in saying that the Sacrifice of the Mass is "a true and proper sacrificial act" in which—by virtue of the "visible" sign (with existential implications) of the double consecration "representing" (*figurant*) in a bloodless fashion "the separation of the body and blood," in such a way that in it Christ is signified "in the state of victim"—the only and unique sacrifice accomplished once and for all, the bloody immolation itself of Christ on the Cross *is now*, by a miracle, reactualized for us, that is to say, *made really though invisibly present under a bloodless mode, at a certain moment of our time.*

18. Finally I would indicate that in the point of view that I am proposing it is quite clear that the Last Supper was the *first* Mass—*and celebrated by Christ Himself*—that first Mass is no different from the Masses celebrated today except that there the Priest visible to the eyes of men was Jesus in person and because, in that transubstantiation, it was into the body and blood, not of the glorious Christ, but of the still passible Christ, that the bread and wine were changed.

As far as the sacrifice itself is concerned, there is no difference: for the presence of all the events of our time to the divine eternity is just as valid for the future as it was for the past; therefore it is that very sacrifice on the Cross—the bloody one—still in the future[19] on Holy Thursday, and pre-actualized on that particular day, but eternally present to the divine eternity, is made really though invisibly present in our time, by the visible bloodless sign with its existential implications of the double consecration.[20]

---

19   Notice the use of the future in the Vulgate (Math. xxvi, 28): "*Hic est enim Sanguis meus novi testamenti, qui pro vobis* effundetur . . ." which *will be shed*. The Greek participles in Matthew, like those in Mark and Luke, are present participles, but a present participle, as an adjective, remains indeterminate with regard to the time *implicitly signified*, and may very well refer to the future ("when he leaves us, his departure, *celebrated* with joy by some, will be regretted by many": *celebrated* means "which will be celebrated"), or it may refer to the past ("when he left us, his departure, celebrated with joy by some, was regretted by many": *celebrated* in this case means "which was celebrated") or even to the present ("he is leaving us; his departure, *celebrated* with joy by some, is regretted by many": this time *celebrated* means "which is being celebrated").

And is it not by virtue of the meaning traditionally recognized in the Christian community that the Vulgate, in the most complete gospel account of the Last Supper, uses the future (*effundetur*)? It is out fidelity to this Vulgate *effundetur* that the Roman canon of the Mass has kept it: "qui pro vobis et pro multis *effundetur* in remissionem peccatorum," *which will be shed* . . .

Moreover, the Jerusalem Bible, which was translated from the Greek, also uses—in Mark and Luke as in Matthew—"which will be shed."

20   The sacrifice of the Last Supper was a bloodless sacrifice (with respect to its *mode of presence*) like the sacrifice on the altar. And not only was the sign of the double consecration, which made the Sacrifice of Calvary present at a certain moment in time, a bloodless sign; but it was the sovereign High Priest, Christ *still living on this earth*, who, on Holy Thursday, was the first priest to offer the sacrifice of the Mass, when by the double consecration, on that particular day, in the course of His last meal with His disciples, He made, invisibly present at a certain

The fact that the Last Supper was the first Mass was affirmed, as we have seen, in the most explicit manner by the Council of Trent (Denz., 1740)

VI. THE TWO ESSENTIAL MOMENTS OF THE MASS

19. There are two moments of capital importance in the Mass: the absolutely central moment of the sacrifice, which is also (even though there is question of two distinct miracles) the moment of the transubstantiation; and the moment of communion, when the priest, and after him the faithful, proceed to the eating of the victim immolated on Calvary and now in glory "at the right hand of the Father."

The absolutely central moment, the moment of the sacrifice as immolation, is the very brief interval of time which extends from the consecration of the bread to the consecration of the wine, or from one elevation to the other. If at that particular moment we bow down in both soul and body, it is because, for a few moments, our time opens onto eternity in order to become one with the time when Christ was immolated in the midst of the cruelest sufferings.

By virtue of the visible signs which, while making Jesus present on the altar, make his bloody immolation invisibly present as well, under a bloodless mode, for a brief interval of our time, we are placed, without our being able to see them, on Calvary before Jesus bleeding on the Cross.

During those few instants which separate the consecration of the bread and the elevation of the host from the consecration of the wine and the elevation of the Precious Blood, let us understand clearly, in the faith, just what miracle these sacred rites have made us witness to, let us thank Jesus for His immolation *reactualized* before us, let us make ourselves one with this immolation, from which our poor love and our poor and painful little crosses receive their co-redemptive power.[21] And would that we could inject into this act of union all our love and the total gift of ourselves! This is the moment when we participate in the Mass in the most profoundly active way and at the same time it is for us a moment of absolute silence.

For this moment is pierced by that cry alone which only they can hear who

---

moment in time, the Sacrifice on Calvary which was to take place the following day.

21   It is important to understand as well that while the priest (and through him the entire Church) is offering to God the redeeming sacrifice at which the double consecration makes us present (and which the dying Jesus offered on the Cross, and which the glorious Jesus offers in highest heaven each time the Mass is celebrated here below)—at this very same moment the priest (and, through him the entire Church) also offers to God the co-redemptive sacrifice carried out by the Mystical Body *in via*, throughout all time, in its pilgrim and crucified state (a sacrifice which was also offered on the Cross by Christ our Head and is now offered by Him in glory).

were there at a special place in space and at a special moment in time, a cry which makes all creation bend its knee, that great cry of Jesus commending His spirit into the hands of the Father.

It is fitting that the faithful raise their voices at other moments of the Mass. And the moment *par excellence* when it is most fitting to raise their voices and sing together in the joy they share is that moment when, after the holy reality of the sacrificial immolation, the Mass draws back the veil on the holy reality of the *agapé*. It is the moment of eucharistic communion, the moment of the feast that has no equal, in which, taking their nourishment from the Blessed Sacrament of Jesus Himself, the faithful are not only assumed in some fashion into His very own human-divine life, purified and strengthened like His own members in whose veins the grace and blood of His heart are flowing, but they are, through Him and in Him, mysteriously united to one another, each time in such a way as to make the unity of the Mystical Body more intimate and more profound. It is during the Communion of the faithful, and right after it, that sacred song at Mass should resound with the greatest brilliance, sweetness and purity, in unanimous exultation.

20. Perhaps a few explanations are needed here. At the moment of the double consecration, the priest carried out the sacrifice of the Mass and offered it sacramentally (by virtue of the sacrament of Holy Orders), in an oblation which, as he asked just before the consecration, God, who cherishes his Church, made perfectly pure and acceptable—*quam oblationem, tu, Deus, in omnibus, quaesumus, benedictam, adscriptam, ratam, rationabilem, acceptabilmeque facere digneris*—and by which the Church presents to God, so that He might accept it again from the hands of his Spouse, that same offering which Jesus made of Himself once and for all time on the Cross. And, later, when he has taken communion in the Body and Blood of Christ, the priest has consummated the sacrifice and brought it to the final term to which it was ordered.

This is enough for the Mass to be really and completely celebrated. But it is not yet enough as regards the intentions of divine love, which wants the faithful too to take communion in the Body of Christ. Here there is a kind of superabundance[22] in regard to the celebration because of which the sacrifice that has already been carried out, offered and consummated, overflows, so to speak, onto the community of the faithful, and which corresponds to what the Lord Jesus prescribed. It is His express will that those who follow Him receive this sacrament: *"Take and eat: this is my body. . . . All of you drink of this:* this is my blood of the new covenant . . ."[23]

---

22   It is perhaps because of this aspect of superabundance that in the course of history the customs prevailing in the Church with regard to the communion of the faithful have varied so much, until, after the Council of Trent, the importance of frequent communion was asserted more and more forcefully. Cf. Charles Journet, *La Messe*, p. 313.

23   Matt. xxvi, 26–28. Concerning communion under one species, cf. Charles Journet,

At the moment of consecration, let me remind you, the faithful in no way carry out the sacrifice of the Mass, or the oblation that is inseparable from it, along with the priest (indeed under the same title or right as he, as some seem drawn to believe out of sympathy for their Protestant brethren). But when the Body of the Lord is given to them, the faithful participate in this sacrifice by their act of personal piety, they are one with it, they enter into it—in the sense that when the faithful people receive the fruit of the sacrifice, after the priest, as he did, they too consummate the sacrifice (bring it to its final term) by consuming (eating) the sacrificial Lamb, now glorious in heaven. Pius XII, in his encyclical *Mediator Dei* expressly pointed to this role of the faithful.[24] Like the priest (but not under the same title as he, that is, the one through whom the Church acts), they bring the sacrifice (that is already carried out) in the end back to the creature, when they receive the sacrament of life, the Christ of the sacrament Who unites them to Himself and among one another in the deepest recesses of that intimacy which is accessible to God alone. This is the blessed reiteration of the Last Supper,[25] at which Jesus gave His disciples His flesh to eat and His blood to drink and made Himself the sap of the mystical vine which, as it passes into the secret depths of the being of each member in order to transform him, through the centuries gives nourishment to the Mystical Body, so that it may live by divine and by fraternal charity. "He who eats my flesh and drinks my blood abides in me and I in him."[26] "He who eats me, he also shall live because of me."[27] "The cup of blessing that we bless, is it not the sharing of the blood of Christ? And the bread that we break, is it not the

---

La Messe, pp. 272–273: "We know 'that Christ, having risen from the dead, dies now no more, death shall no more have dominion over him' (Rom. vi, 9), that His body and blood are no longer separated, that, wherever His body is, His blood is there as well, *and that consequently in receiving them under the single species of either bread or wine, we receive Him in His entirety.* such as He is in His glory. We eat His flesh and drink His blood.

24   "Each time, indeed, that the people renew what the divine Redeemer accomplished at the Last Supper [by giving His body to eat and His blood to drink], the sacrifice is truly consummated." Cf. Charles Journet, *La Messe*, p. 125.

25   Let me remark in parentheses that the new liturgy, as attached as it is to the spirit of community, is nevertheless singularly lacking in outward signs that recall the eucharistic meal. Outwardly, nothing distinguishes the file of the faithful going to receive communion standing up from a file of people who are strangers to one another waiting in line before a ticket-window. In order to recall in their exterior demeanor the memory of the Last Supper, would it not be sufficient (as was done in the eighteenth century) for them to kneel, elbow to elbow, before a communion cloth held by two acolytes and receive the sacred species from the hand of the priest, like table companions at the same meal? (This note was added, February 1968.)

26   John vi, 56.

27   John vi, 57.

partaking of the body of the Lord? Because the bread is one, we though many, are one body, all of us who partake of the one bread."[28]

21. To someone attending Mass with the same conception of things as I have presented them here, the Mass would seem to include three large distinct parts.

A first part extends from the *Confiteor* to the beginning of the Preface. The readings and the prayers in this entire part are directed toward the *preparation of the faithful gathered in the church*—who are but a tiny portion of the Christian people as a whole, even if they make up a huge throng—for the sacrifice which will be carried out before their eyes and in which they will be united as one (this preparation for the sacrifice and orientation toward it being especially noticeable beginning with the Offertory).

The second part extends from the Preface (included) through the *Pater*. In this part it is not solely the faithful assembled in some particular place of worship, it is the entire universal Church that we must see as gathered mystically around the priest; it is *in the name of the universal Church* that—as the minister and instrument made use of in heaven by Jesus in His glory—he offers up the sacrifice or the immolation of the *eternal Victim*. This second part of the Mass, the holiest and the principal part, is essentially dedicated to the reactualized sacrifice or immolation of Jesus, at which a moment of our time is made miraculously present; the absolutely unique sacrifice is present once again, for a few instants, *actually* put back again before the eyes of our faith.

And after a few moments, still in the state of victim, but this time only in regard to the symbols offered to our eyes, Christ is *signified*, no longer, as at the moment of the double consecration, the passible Christ dying on the Cross, but rather the glorious Christ, *to all appearances* delivered up defenseless, under the two holy species, into the hands of the priest, raised, lowered, moved here and there on the altar (and later, before the *Agnus Dei*, broken). All this is purely symbolic of course, but how rich in profound meaning.[29]

Finally the third and last part of the Mass is the part that begins after the *Pater*. Here the perspective changes once again: now all is directed toward the

---

28   I Cor. xx, 16–17.

29   It is at this point that the consideration (on which Father de la Taille insisted) of *the state of victim* in which the glorious Christ is signified under the species of consecrated bread and wine takes on its true value. This is definitely not what constitutes the sacrifice of the Mass; there is no question of a real state of the glorified Christ but only of a signified state. The fact remains that such a signification has a very great importance, inasmuch as it refers to that reality which is the passion of Christ *continued in His Mystical Body* of which, in heaven, He remains the Head, vitally joined to His members. (And the fact remains too that if Christ in this way is signified in the state of victim under the eucharistic species, it is by virtue of the real immolation of the passible Christ to which the Sacrifice of the Mass makes us miraculously present, and of which it is a reiteration under the bloodless mode of the double consecration.

preparation for receiving the sacrament of the Eucharist and toward an appeal for divine mercy on *the individual persons* whose nourishment the immolated victim, now glorious, is about to become.

In the first place it is the priest himself who, on the one hand, as the celebrant (whatever the interior state of his soul may be), is about to bring the sacrifice to its final consummation by his communion in the Body and Blood of the Lord and who, on the other hand, as an ordinary human person, should be in the state of grace to receive the sacrament for eternal life.

In the second place, it is each of the faithful who, as guests invited to the eucharistic supper, are also going to participate, as we have seen, in the final consummation of the sacrifice, but for whom there is question first and foremost—if they are as they hope they are, in the state of the grace of the One who loved them first—of receiving the life of their life, from communion to communion, until they reach the fullness of their years.

CHAPTER XVI
A LOOK AT THEOLOGY (II)

APROPOS OF THE CHURCH OF HEAVEN[1]

I. OUR ATTITUDE TOWARD THE CHURCH TRIUMPHANT

IT SEEMS TO ME THAT ON THE SUBJECT of the Church of Heaven an extreme negligence prevails among Christians so that considerable progress has to be made on this point, not in dogma or doctrine of course, but in increased awareness.

1. The Church Triumphant and the Church Militant make up one single Church, one single unique Mystical Body in two essentially different states: the Church Militant is *in time*, as Abbé Journet tells us, in a pilgrim and crucified state; the Church Triumphant is *in eternity*, in the state of glory.

The living bond and the living relationship between the two are made manifest in the public life of the Church here below through the liturgy. The entire liturgy is turned toward heaven. And heaven listens to it. However, the feasts of the temporal cycle are centered first and foremost on the different states of Our Lord during His earthly life; and in the feasts of the saints, each one is commemorated only once a year. The prayers we recite are always prayers of petition for what we consider our good here below, and for the intentions of the Church Militant (and this is the way it should be; it is absolutely normal in the prayer of the Church Militant, which is like a beggar vis-à-vis the Church Triumphant). In this way the liturgy and the breviary assure and maintain a continuous communication between earth and heaven.

But what about our private prayer, our personal spiritual life? Heaven seems so far off, so abstract, so impersonal. Naturally I am not speaking of the Holy Trinity or of the Blessed Virgin. Certainly we think of them, in a habitual, even profound manner. But the Mystical Body, the angels and the innumerable saints, the whole of that humanity which peoples the heavens and which makes up the Mystical Body of which Jesus is the head, all of this remains hidden, as if behind an azure curtain. This is undoubtedly due in part to the fact that heaven is *unimaginable* and that Revelation teaches us but a bare

---

1   *Editor's footnote*: Seminar given to the Little Brothers of Jesus, at Toulouse, May 28, 1963. Cf. *Nova et Vetera*, 1964, no. 3, pp. 205–228.

minimum about *the other world*. Why? Because we would never understand. We do not have a single guidepost. (We are like primitives from an uncivilized tribe, led aimlessly through a world's fair or before some electronic machine, without a single point of reference or any common measure. They are not astonished by all this; they just do not understand. I think it is pretty much the same with regard to heaven and the afterlife). But it is also due to our stupidity and to our repugnance to attach ourselves firmly to the *invisible* and there seek our daily bread.

I am going to insert a parenthesis here: I just said that Revelation teaches us only a minimum of details about the other world. This is true. However, even though nothing there is accessible to our imagination, I believe we still know a bit more than we think we know, though not enough attention is paid to this.

We think naturally that the cause of the beatitude of the blessed is the vision of the divine essence; evidently this is the essential; but it is not the whole of their lives.

Just as the Incarnate Word on earth led a human and a divine life at the same time, in the same way the blessed in heaven have entered into a life that is divine in itself and into a joy that is divine in itself because of the Beatific Vision, but there they also lead, outside the Beatific Vision though penetrated by the rays of its light, a glorious and transfigured human life.

From the moment they see God, they love Him, by the necessity of their nature, without their having to exercise their free will in this regard. But with regard to all the rest, with regard to the entire universe of creatures, they continue to exercise their free will; they act freely without being able to sin. On the other hand, among themselves, and with the angels in whose midst they are like equals, there is an intellectual communication (without words, of course) that depends on each one's free will. The blessed are, all of them, masters of the thoughts of their hearts and lay them bare to whomever they wish. And they are all citizens of the Heavenly Jerusalem, over which the Lamb reigns supreme.

So there is a very real *human life* of glory and very real human interactions of glory for separated souls, just as there will be after the general Resurrection for those human persons raised from the dead, who certainly will not be satisfied to walk up and down the avenues of Paradise carrying palm branches. They will be masters of a human nature that will be forever without any sighs or tears, and which they will actively involve in the great human life of the Holy City as well as in the adoration of God.

Even before the Resurrection of the Dead, an immense and perpetual conversation goes on in heaven. (And I believe that in this conversation the angels will tell us stories about our poor little world, for how can we think that everything that happened within the flux of time, all filled with so much beauty, with so much love and distress, will all be lost forever? The angels remember.)

And in heaven, at each instant of discontinuous time which is the time of pure spirits, *events* will take place: New blessed souls arrive constantly from the earth to be born to eternal life, they are welcomed by the others, friendships are established; and from Purgatory too newly freed souls arrive ceaselessly; and each time that a sinner converts on earth, there is joy and thanksgiving among all the saints of heaven. All this creates a fabulous history, within a span of time entirely different from that of our history here.

And the blessed will have complete knowledge, without any deficiencies, of the world they left behind and of its relation to God and His eternal designs, and of the modes of participation of each creature to its Uncreated Principle. And the higher spirits, whose knowledge is simpler and more perfect, will illuminate the other spirits. And they will teach one another about what God expects of them and about the role of their prayer in the great struggle for the salvation of souls. And in the world they left behind in order to dwell in the world where the glorious bodies of Jesus and Mary are found (outside and beyond our entire universe of space), the blessed are able to intervene; they are still present there by their love and by their action, by the inspirations they give us, and by the effect of their prayers. And the love they had for those they loved on earth, they still have in heaven, transfigured now, not abolished, by glory; and if this was a love of charity, then that love was already on earth what it now is in heaven. You remember the words of St. Teresa of Lisieux: "I want to spend my heaven doing good on earth." These words have a singularly broad extension—in the sense of what one might call the humanism of the saints, even in heaven.

This all comes down to saying that the creature and all the reflections of uncreated Goodness have their role too in the beatitude of the blessed. They are added on without adding anything themselves; they add absolutely nothing, not by the thickness of a hair, to that beatitude which comes to the saints in heaven from the vision of God and which deifies them, transfers them into the very order of the divine Transcendence, but those spiritual riches which come from what has been created are something *above and beyond* which is integrated into the joy and into the supreme actuation of the blessed, without in any way increasing them. In a somewhat similar fashion, from the very fact of creation, there are *beings* in addition (numerically) to uncreated Being, without any (intensive) increase in *being* itself by as much as the thickness of a hair.

I have come to the end of my parenthesis. You will have to forgive this digression, which I hope was "not without some use" as Bergson liked to put it.

Before this long parenthesis I was saying that in our spiritual lives heaven, the next world, the Church Triumphant are all too far removed and ignored and that this is due in great measure to our negligence about turning our attention in this direction and our repugnance to latch on to what is invisible.

2. And yet *the other world* is present in our own world; it penetrates our world like a lightning bolt—invisibly. In each tabernacle Jesus is present in glory, in His humanity and His divinity. And heaven is there as well, inasmuch as in the Eucharist, the Body of the Lord, is itself the sign of His Mystical Body.

They are all there, crowding behind Him, not sacramentally present, of course, but still present by their attention, their adoration of Jesus, and their love for Him, and also by their love for us. "Where the body is, there the eagles gather." In a virtual manner, all the saints of heaven are in your chapel, around the tabernacle. And, actually, in a very special manner, all those who love you and whom you love in a particular way, and who adore Jesus along with you.

And if we cannot imagine them, we can at least love them. And if there is a terrible curtain between the invisible world and the visible world, love can take us behind it. The same love of charity is in them and in us; by our love we come into contact with them as they with us, and by our prayer as well.

From this point of view we can get a clear understanding of the importance, disregarded by liturgists who focus more or less on the far distant past, of the exposition of the Blessed Sacrament and of the hours of adoration consecrated to it. This is the gate of heaven open on earth. And we look through this gate with the eyes of faith.

3. Formerly, with a more or less primitive and superstitious mentality, there was a great and profound familiarity between the saints and the Christian people. As you know, each saint had his own specialty, generally a specialty as a healer of some sickness and infirmity or other of either humans or animals. One had recourse to them in determined circumstances of one's life. Today hardly anything of this remains except devotion to St. Anthony to find lost objects.

This familiarity with the saints was, after all, terribly selfish. We drove them to distraction with our miseries and our needs. We turned to them only to beg them to bring about what we *wished* here below, to see to it that *our* will was done. Even so the saints put up with us. In this at least a kind of permanent contact was maintained with them.

This more or less primitive mentality has been drastically purified. We should certainly not miss it. But it has been replaced by a self-styled rational mentality—really an anemic and aseptic mentality—in which for all practical purposes there is no living contact with the saints.

And this seems disastrous to me.

For at a lower level, certainly, and *below* the liturgy, *popular piety* plays an essential role in the life of the Church because it expresses the direct and spontaneous movement of souls, with respect to their daily lives and their special lot in the world,

and varies according to the different periods of time just as the life of the world itself does.

In this sense one could say that the liturgy, while absolutely necessary, is nevertheless insufficient. First of all, because lived participation in the liturgy, whatever may be done about it, will always be limited to a relatively small number of the laity.

Next, and especially so, because in liturgical prayer (am I going to say something heretical here), it seems to me that its grandeur and its superiority come from the fact that as a general rule *my own particular* prayer *becomes effaced* in the universal prayer of the Church—the Church not only of all places in this world but also of all times, along with its enormous memory. This is why the Old Testament holds a position of such capital importance in it. Each one is there as a *part*, each one prays the prayer of a whole which covers the entire earth and all times since Abraham and before.

Surely there are moments—Christmas, Holy Week, Easter—when *my own particular* prayer is fully involved in liturgical prayer and nourished by it. Surely in the daily Mass there are prayers that correspond to *my own particular* needs. Surely there are psalms which on occasion become *my very own* life of flesh and blood. But in the final analysis I do not think this is the general rule. And when I recite the divine office, not only does the astounding bad taste of certain hymns remind me of relatively recent epochs that I would prefer to forget, but even in the psalms themselves, that's right, I have no particular desire to smash on a stone the newborn babes of Babylon, or to see the sons of the impious reduced to beggary and chased from their homes, or to annihilate a bunch of kings whose names mean nothing to me at all.

Whereas popular piety, the piety of the Christian people, the piety of the little people of God, has to do with requests and initiatives that spring spontaneously from the very heart of people, in particular circumstances and particular undertakings and the entire temporal context of their existence, and it has to do also with the stirrings of the Holy Spirit which pass through all of this. This is an indispensable part of the life of the Church Militant. And as I just said, it is more and more neglected. There is Lourdes and the great places of pilgrimage, and some particularly famous saints like the Curé of Ars or St. Teresa of Lisieux, and also, and especially, that kind of para-liturgy of popular piety, the adoration of the Blessed Sacrament. But with regard to the immense throng of people that make up the Mystical Body in the state of glory, popular piety has turned to dust. It could be said we stupidly believe that this entire group of people has dozed off in the Beatific Vision, no longer wants to bother looking at us, and has forgotten us. And for our part, we seem to be doing everything in our power to foster this kind of thing.

4. The idea I would like to propose to you is the following: Since the Church Triumphant makes up but one single Church with the Church Militant, and since the saints continue to be busy about the things of this world and be interested in them (they see all of this in the Beatific Vision itself), well then,

they certainly must have their own idea and their own intentions about these matters, about the life and the behavior of each of us, about what goes on in this world, and about the progress and expansion of the kingdom of God.

And undoubtedly each of them has particular ideas as well of whatever concerns, in a more special way, the *mission that he or she had here below*, and those whom they loved and were individually charged to protect here below. The holy founders certainly have their ideas about the religious orders they founded, the various patron saints have their own ideas about the countries or cities under their protection. St. Thomas Aquinas has his own ideas about the advance of theological truth and those special truths which he himself established and defended here on earth; St. John of the Cross about the progress of the contemplative life; Father de Foucauld about the vocation of those who witness for Jesus without preaching or teaching but through brotherly love, and who should be, like de Foucauld, universal Little Brothers.

So then, the real way in which we ought *to exist with them* and maintain a living communion with them, is it not—far more than to pray to them for *our intentions* and to lay *our* needs and *our* desires before them (all of which is very necessary and will certainly continue)—is it not rather to pray to them for *their intentions*, theirs not ours, for the accomplishment of their own particular designs and their own particular desires concerning things here below, so that in this way the will of heaven might more readily be accomplished here on earth? In the Our Father we say, "Thy will be done," and in this sense we are praying to God in God's behalf; well, I say that we should pray to the saints of God in their behalf as well, so that their will may be carried out by idiots like us.

If the Dominicans throughout the world offered thousands of masses *for the intentions of St. Thomas Aquinas*, the intellectual state of affairs here below would perhaps be much better off. And the same for the business of the apostolate and Catholic Action—what if all the priests said their masses *for the intentions of St. Paul?*

5. I have been speaking of the canonized saints.

But there are lots of other saints in heaven—not only canonizable saints who have not yet been, or never will be, canonized—they are, all of them, *exemplary* saints, who are beacons for humanity and who have lived under the habitual regime of the gifts of the Holy Spirit so that it can be said (and here I again take up a theme from "Love and Friendship") that they did not live like everybody else in the sense that, at times even in their exterior comportment, the measure of their acts, being that of the Gifts of the Holy Spirit, is higher than the measure of the moral virtues, whether acquired or infused. This is why they surprise us, disconcert us in some way; their heroism, however secret its sources may be, cannot help but become manifest in some way or other for all to see.

So, and this is what I would like to insist on, in addition to the exemplary saints, canonized or canonizable, in heaven there are, not only all the elect who have passed through and been delivered from the pains of Purgatory but also all those elect, whose number I believe to be enormous, who on this earth were saints *who went unnoticed*, I mean that, except for the secrets of their hearts, among us they led lives like the lives of everybody else. If there was any heroism in their lives, and undoubtedly there was, it was a completely hidden heroism. And they went directly to heaven because they died in an act of perfect charity. It is for them also, and especially for them, that each year the Church celebrates the feast of All Saints. It is here above all that we must think of that immense mass of the poor and of the little people of God, I mean of all those who went to the limit in the practice of abnegation of self, of devotion to others, and of steadfastness in virtue.

And it is these saints who touch each of us most closely, in the sense that among them are those who were close to us on earth, among the departed members of our own families, in the long line of our ancestors, among our friends and among the people we met. Surely some of them are from among your deceased Little Brothers. God is not stingy with His grace; it is we who do not have enough practical faith and who are not attentive enough to the glory of those whom we no longer see. I remember that the Curé de la Courneuve, when he told us the story of Notre-Dame des Bois, and how he had carried a statue of the Blessed Virgin through the woods as far as the little old house he wanted to turn into a chapel, told us that the saints accompanied him in procession through the trees—the saints, that is to say, not St. Peter and St.Paul, but the holy souls, now departed and in their glory, whom he had known, peasant men and women who had belonged to his family and to his village. Can we believe that these saints who touched us and whom we have known have forgotten us? that they do not want to help us, and that they do not have a better idea than we do about what is best for us, or that they do not have their own particular intentions with regard to the things of this earth and to the friends they have left behind here?

II. THE DEPARTED

The second part of my presentation, which follows naturally from the first, is about the departed and what we think of them.

6. I would like to begin here with a little parenthesis about language—something that scandalizes me is the way Christians speak of their departed. They call them the dead. They have not been able to renew their miserable human language on a point which nevertheless touches on the essential doctrines of their faith. The dead! We attend masses for the dead! We go to the cemetery to bring flowers to the dead, we pray for the dead! As if they were not a million times more alive than we! As if the fundamental truth proclaimed in the

Preface of the Mass for the departed, *"vita mutatur, non tollitur,"* life is changed, not taken away, were itself a dead truth, incapable of making fruitful and of transforming the ordinary routine of our way of thinking and speaking.

Villier de L'Isle-Adam used to say that death was an invention of the undertakers.

I think that the word *death* or *dead* does indeed have its proper use to designate that terrible moment when the soul is separated from the body—then for sure, we are face to face with death, that death which horrifies our nature, to such a point that it is actually unthinkable, and we can say that a man "is dying"; and after that we can speak of that man as "dead" on a civil death certificate or a police register, whose vocabulary is not a vocabulary of truth, but only of sordid appearances.

But those who have left this world to enter into another are not dead. If they are in heaven and see God, they are the living *par excellence*; if they are in purgatory where they are suffering, but with the certitude that they are the elect and will see God, then they are, by that very certitude, and by the very pure and ardent love with which they accept and even bless their sufferings, far more living than we. And even if they are in hell, in that abyss of a second death, at least they have done with the mutability and the tergiversations of earthly life and with the dark hidden recesses of the unconscious; they have made a definitive choice of their own free will and deep down within themselves they see clear. These are perverse and chastised living persons; they are not dead.

7. That's the end of my parenthesis, now let us get back to our consideration of the comportment of Christians in regard to the Church of heaven.

The second thing which scandalizes me is the sinister, lugubrious trappings of the ceremonies with which Christians surround their funerals; all this black and the signs of mourning in which we deck out our churches, their walls, the pews, the altar (I am told that this is beginning to change in some parishes, so much the better, but it is still not very noticeable), and even the black vestments that the priest puts on to celebrate the Mass.

This is not the way things were in the first centuries of Christianity. As is pointed out in de Martimort's remarkable *Introduction à la Liturgie, L'Eglise en prière*—"the spirit of the Christian funerals was profoundly different from that of the pagan funerals. On the one hand, Christians did not, as did the pagans of the ancient world, attach to their funerals an absolutely decisive importance for the afterlife of the departed; above all, the certitude of salvation and of the resurrection of the dead led Christians to proclaim that Christ had conquered death and that their hope and their joy were stronger than their pain. Early Christianity manifested this reaction in different ways, in their funeral inscriptions, in their costumes, dressing in *white, the color of immortality* instead of in lugubrious black; and above all in the liturgy of the funerals itself, in which the dominant note was faith in the resurrection rather than mourning. This note, covered over in part in the present Roman liturgy by later additions or exterior details [it would be interesting to find out at exactly what time these additions were made] is expressed in a dazzling fashion in the Eastern liturgies, for example the Byzantine funeral liturgy, which in these circumstances makes use of the *alleluia.*"

We might add here that, in France, the way in which for several centuries the Roman funeral liturgy has been carried out goes way beyond the reservations expressed in the passage I just read. How can we explain the frightful invasion of mourning and affliction into those rites in which faith in the redemption and the resurrection ought to be the dominant note? There is ample matter here for erudite historico-sociologico-theological studies. If you ask my opinion (as a simple working-hypothesis, for I am not much of an erudite), I would tell you that I recognize here, first of all, a kind of naturalist revenge taken against supernatural faith by the *social component of human nature*, with its demands and its traditional customs. It is considered an obligation of etiquette toward the deceased, a duty that the social and family group would consider a dishonor to shirk, if for a few days they did not give way to shrill wails of lamentation or at least show their sorrow by their black clothes and outward signs of mourning. To tell the truth, what would we not need in the way of ashes and mourning to express, if it could ever be expressed, the true, authentic sorrow we feel in being separated from someone we loved more than our own life? *Et Rachel noluit consolari*, Rachel would not be consoled.

Well, it is this sorrow, so natural to our heart and this blackness of human mourning that people want at any price to find in their funeral rites and which they have succeeded in imposing on Christian rites, at least as far as the color is concerned—even in the priest's vestments—and the exterior details of the ceremony. And this phenomenon of *naturization* has such a hold on man and his social side as such that it is found not only in bourgeois parishes where the flash of silver tears sewn onto tenebrous draperies shows off and magnifies the sorrow of the rich but also in poor country parishes where the faithful, with all the strength they can muster, force their parish priest to celebrate all year long requiem masses, all humbly and uniformly lugubrious, with that parody of a coffin, draped in black and surrounded with cardboard candles, on which, accompanied by a bewildered altar boy, he sprinkles the holy water of absolution.

It would seem the height of incongruity to think that the poor departed soul for whom all this sadness is required has any chance to exult in the joy of Paradise and become a part of the Church Triumphant.

8. But I think there are still other reasons for this prevalence of mourning and blackness and of a kind of somber apprehension in the common attitude

toward the deceased and for the common practical indifference shown toward the Church of heaven—this time reasons that are specifically religious.

Just before the arrival of rationalist and anthropocentric humanism and the enthusiasm it brought with it for the material conquest of nature, infallibly necessary progress, prosperity, and all the other nonsense, there was a period of distress and despair at the end of the Middle Ages which makes us think a little of existentialism today. If I remember correctly, it was in the fifteenth century that the great vogue for Dances of Death had its beginning. And this state of mind made its way into religious sentiment. In de Martimort's book we are told that the *Dies irae* is an Italian composition of the twelfth or the thirteenth century (I would have thought it more from the fourteenth). This central part of Catholic funeral services today, which rattles the congregation a bit, in which the members of the choir take pleasure in bellowing false notes to imitate the final thunderclap, de Martimort's book assures us, is "the only hymn of the mass which deviates from ancient Christian piety" because it is completely "absorbed in the fear of the last judgment."

As a matter of fact, though, the *Dies irae* is one of the most beautiful poems in the world, a work of extraordinary and admirable poetry, indeed of admirable Christian poetry—think of the stanza *"quaerens me sedesti lassus"* and what follows—yet it is a Christian poetry which turns ambiguous and is engulfed in terror. Even so, I would like to come somewhat to the defense of the *Dies irae* because terror, as Moses felt it too, is also essential to Christianity, and to all religion, even in the purely natural order. It is terror at the infinite majesty of God, fear and trembling in the Presence of Him Whom no name can name, before the divine transcendence which upsets all our limits, before the *Deus excelsus terribilis.*

But the ambiguity slips in at the point where this terror descends into the human universe—terror before the unveiling of all the secrets of our miserable hearts on the day of judgment, the terror of the judgment itself, the terror of human destiny, of chastisement and of hell.

So it is quite true that to describe the second coming of Christ and the Last Judgment as a day of wrath, of calamity and misery, a day of tears and unfathomable bitterness, *dies magna et amara valde,*[2] *lacrymosa dies illa,*[3] is after all a strange way to sing of our Christian hope. God's mercy has not been forgotten, but it seems to consist in His drawing forth those who are its object from a lake of perdition to which all men seem destined.

Now is there some theological idea behind this terror of the Last Judgment—and of human destiny—that I just mentioned? In my opinion, yes: the Augustinian idea of the massiveness of iniquity, of wrath and of death, and

---

2   *Dies illa, dies irae, calamitatis et miseriae, dies magna et amara valde*: these words of the *Libera me*, in the absolution, which begin in the same way (but inverted) as the *Dies irae*. Recall and still accentuate the somber grandeur of that day.

3   *Lacrymosa dies illa*: in the 18th stanza of the *Dies irae*.

above all the idea which seems linked to *the small number of the elect*, which, in later centuries, was to grow even worse with Jansenism.

Here, I come across a difficulty which comes from St. Thomas himself. St. Thomas (cf. *Sum theol.*, Ia, q. 23, ar. 7, ad 3m) seems to accept the interpretation, which in my opinion is very contestable, of Jesus' words about the tiny gate and the narrow path (Matt vii, 13–14) as referring to eternal salvation; in my opinion what is being talked about here is the earth: on the one hand those who *on earth* set off down the wide and spacious road of sin and perdition (this does not mean that they will be lost); on the other had those who *on earth* take the narrow path to eternal life in which *they already have a share here below*. In other words, St. Thomas seems to follow the pessimistic views of St. Augustine and seeks to justify them by arguments drawn from what takes place in nature. The good proportionate to the *common state* of nature is found, he tells us, in the greater number; for example, sufficient understanding to get through life, only imbeciles are without sufficient understanding. But on the other hand, if there is question of a good which *surpasses the common state of nature*, for example, a profound knowledge of intelligible realities, this is reserved for a comparatively small number. In the same way, since the vision of God exceeds the common state of nature—which in addition and above all bears the wounds of original sin—*pauciores sunt qui salvantur*, the elect will be far less numerous than the damned.

Well, let me tell you that these arguments seem extraordinarily unconvincing, and indeed can be turned back on themselves. For salvation is not, like the profound knowledge of intelligible realities, a high point of *natural perfection* which surpasses the common state of nature, it is rather something entirely supernatural which belongs to an order entirely different from the order of nature. And the law of nature is not abolished by grace; instead there is *another law*, proper to the supernatural order—in this case the law of the redeeming mercy and salvific will of God—which overcomes and drags in its wake the law of the tiny number of those who succeed in surpassing the common state of nature and which must, by a relationship of propriety, make the number of the elect correspond to the victory of Christ's redeeming Blood over evil and to the generous measure required by the boundless mercy of God.

And added to this, the wounds of original sin have less force to deteriorate our nature than the wounds of Christ do to raise us by grace to the friendship of that God who pardons.

I am convinced that the idea of *the greater number of the elect* is dominant and will become more and more dominant in Christian consciousness. First of all for doctrinal reasons. On the one hand, there is God who "wishes that all men be saved" and who sends His Son to redeem them by His death on the Cross. On the other hand, there is man who, by those nihilations of which he is the first cause, escapes from God's love. Who is going to be persuaded that man with his attempts at evasion is *stronger* than God with His love? This does not mean that hell is not crowded; it simply means that for sure the crowds in Paradise are much bigger.

Secondly, there is something that stands in *practical* contradiction with the exigencies of Christian life: I mean with regard to the unity of the Church Militant with the Church Triumphant as it ought to be lived out by us, something that just cannot be true. The idea of the much smaller number of the elect translates itself, not among the theologians, of course, but among the faithful people, by the domination of fear over hope and by the more or less confused, but irresistible feeling that hell is, *in actual fact*, the place of destination that most befits the *common state* of humanity, that is, the greater number, and from which one escapes only through the good luck of an exceptional act of mercy. These are the terrors of the *Dies irae*.

But then, if there are without doubt canonized saints to whom the Christian people continue to turn, but as if toward kinds of supermen, strangers to the destiny of ordinary human beings, then what about the rest of the elect—in far smaller numbers than the damned, we are led to believe—what about this tiny number of the elect who with the canonized saints make up the Church Triumphant, the Mystical Body in heaven? The Christian people will end up considering them too as escapees, separated off from the common lot, and who have nothing more pressing to do than to turn their backs on us and forget us in order to take refuge in eternal beatitude. The sense of unity and of living communication between the Church on earth and the Church in heaven will be irreparably broken and eventually lost.

9. Finally, it seems to me that we can single out a third cause for this prevalence of mourning and blackness, for this kind of somber apprehension in the common attitude toward the departed as well as that kind of practical indifference toward the Church Triumphant that I have been speaking about for some time now, actually far too long, please pardon me.

This time there is no question of the latent and more or less confused idea that the common state of humanity destines us for hell, an exception being made for a relative small number; there is question of the latent and more or less confused idea that the common state of humanity destines us *normally* to spend a more or less long period of time in purgatory, so that those souls who go directly to heaven enjoy a supra-normal privilege.

This latter idea represents a great step forward over the first. For all those who are in purgatory are already among the elect who will one day be in heaven. And this idea is not incompatible with the belief in the greater number of the elect.

However, we might very well ask if since the time of St. Catherine of Genoa (end of the fifteenth century) common Christian consciousness regarding the departed has not been so fixated on the thought of purgatory that it has not somewhat lost sight of other truths.

Here I am not going to argue about the question of *numbers*. It would require a good deal of presumption to ask whether the elect who are waiting in purgatory are more or less numerous than those who are enjoying the beatific vision. I am arguing about what is or is not *normal*. And you know very well that between the notion of what is *normal* and what is *more frequent in point of fact*, there is an enormous difference. The comportment of human beings that is *more frequent* tends to be rather sinful. But this is not the *normal* comportment of human beings, the comportment that conforms to the law and the demands proper to his rational essence.

So, what I am saying is that even if the chosen who must pass through purgatory may be more numerous than those who go straight to heaven, nevertheless it is the latter who are to be considered *normal* in a humanity redeemed by the Blood of Christ. It is not the saints alone, the great heroes of normal life, both exemplary saints and those who went unnoticed; it is the ordinary run of sinners too, like us, who, even after wandering very far astray, go straight to heaven if before their death, or at the moment of death (or even perhaps at the very instant when the soul leaves the body) they make an act of perfect charity. Because they have had confidence in the infinite merits of Christ. Let us remember the *commendatio animae* of the ritual; let us remember the Good Thief: *This day thou shalt be with me in paradise.* What is normal for the Christian is to go straight to paradise, to meet our Lord. Not only the reprobate in hell, but even the soul who passes through purgatory as well, whatever question there may be about number or frequency, both represent *abnormal* cases, the first because it supposes revolt against God, the second because it indicates that the soul has not let the redemptive work come to completion within it here below.

This remark seems to me important with regard to our relations with the Church Triumphant because it is of such a kind as to fortify the ardor of our hope for the souls who leave this world. Because of the terrible transcendence and the inscrutable majesty of God we have an absolute obligation to pray for the souls of the departed, never will our compassion for them be great enough. But because of the infinite mercy of God and the infinite merits of Jesus, we do not measure up in a practical way to the loftiness of our faith if our hope for their eternal destiny does not go almost to excess. But then, as a matter of fact, this hope is generally no more than a tiny, timid vigil light whose sputtering flame is half buried in the ashes of indifference.

In paradisum deducant te Angeli sings the Church at the end of the funerals for the departed; she incenses their bodies: "May the angels lead you to paradise, on your arrival may the Martyrs receive you and conduct you into the Holy City Jerusalem. May the choirs of angels welcome you, and along with Lazarus, who was once a pauper, may you find eternal rest." In paradise, with Jesus; not only is it normal to show not the slightest hesitation in believing—with our human faith, of course, and without forgetting the mystery of the divine transcendence—that such is the lot of those whose sanctity of life is known to us, to the extent that we have been able to know it; but we should boldly hope also that the same is the case for all those who at some moment or other showed some sign of response to the attentive kindness of God's grace. And even for those in whom no sign of this kind was discernible, we ought to hope too, so that our hope for them, more or less strong according to the situation, and however anxious it may be, in spite of all remains far stronger than our fear.

Why am I speaking to you like this, especially of those we have known? It is because of a certain idea I have in my head concerning the Church Triumphant. It seems to me that in turning our attention to the Church Triumphant we must think first and foremost, evidently, of Jesus and Mary, of the Holy Angels, and of the great saints whom the Church proposes for our veneration; but there is also a certain role to be recognized for the un-canonizable elect, for the saints who went unnoticed but whom we have had the opportunity to know and who have known us here below. They took the memory of their friends with them to heaven. They continue to love them as they used to love them. I mean that they love them not just with the supernatural love they derive from the beatific vision—as St. Paul for example loved St. Thomas Aquinas, or as St. Thomas loves Abbé Journet—they love them also with human love, raised up and transfigured by supernatural love, and with the love of charity they had for them here below. It is experimentally, if I can put it this way, that, both humanly and divinely, they take an interest in the affairs of their friends and have their own points of view regarding them. In brief, in the beatific vision they maintain the care they devoted to them on earth, and they continue the prayers they used to say for them.

And on the other hand, inversely, we who continue to live here below, and who here below knew these un-canonizable elect who are beginning their eternity while we are still here on earth, we remember them, and we can call upon them. Since they are inscribed in no martyrology, who is going to remember them when we have done with this planet? They will fall into anonymity; no one down here will tug at their sleeve for a helping hand.

And all this is to indicate that the blessed I am talking about, the un-canonizable blessed who are in a certain way our contemporaries, form a kind of fringe by which in each generation the Church of heaven is kept in contact with time that passes away, and in physical continuity, so to speak, or, if you prefer, in psychological continuity, with the Church Militant.

It seems to me of very practical importance to be as attentive as possible to this. And for example, if you permit me to make an allusion to what is of concern to you, it is important to place great confidence in your departed Little Brothers, of whose death I just recently read a beautiful and moving account.

In order to indicate to you how extensive may be the applications of the remarks I have made in this second part, it will be sufficient, I think, to pose the following questions:

Does it not seem that after apostolic times there occurred, as for as the common attitude toward the destiny of souls is concerned, a kind of slippage which after the fifteenth century turned into a kind of progressive collapse of the practical exercise of the virtue of hope—on the one hand under the weight of the consciousness of human unworthiness and misery, on the other hand under the weight of all the formulas and contorted affectations of the ready-to-wear humility and of the overwhelming self-accusation that the Christian people were fed in the manuals of piety whose authors ordinarily were persuaded that outside the religious state (or more generally, with the French School, outside the ecclesiastical state) one is in very great danger of losing one's soul?

But in reality, is it not precisely because we are all radically unworthy of eternal life and have, *all of us*, except the Virgin Mary, a "hollow heart full of filth," as Pascal put it, that for each and every one of us hope founded not on ourselves but on the Blood of Christ, which is *divine*, ought to be far greater than the fear due to our straying off which is only *human*?

In particular with regard to Christian laity, whose role and whose action in the Church Militant are now the order of the day, and certainly very justly so (but not without some misunderstanding at times), in order to have a clear understanding, in theory and in practice, of this role and this action (which since it is of the Church can bear no fruit except by the power of the Holy Spirit) is there not a condition that is definitely not prerequisite, I mean the fact of understanding that the laity in question, if they die in the state of grace, are in fact seriously exposed, like everyone, and perhaps in even greater numbers, to the obligation of making a more or less lengthy detour through the purifications of purgatory? Is it not rather that, as they lead lives that are frankly and openly the lives of lay people, and even if they are not a part of official Catholic Action, they are *normally* called, just like those who have left all to follow the evangelical counsels, when they leave this life to pass directly into the Church Triumphant? In other words, that the Christian life of the laity is, by the very fact that it is Christian, in virtue of the merits of the Blood of Christ, normally ordered to end up directly in paradise?

III. ON PRAYER

10. In the third part I would like to offer you a few reflections on prayer. That is to say that I would like to turn back to discuss a bit more a point I have already made.

I said at the very beginning that we should pray and celebrate Masses for the intentions that the saints have with regard to us and the things of this world. A question comes up immediately: Do the saints of heaven need this? They are with Jesus. Through the beatific vision, they are a part of the very family of the Holy Trinity; and for their intentions with regard to the earth, do they not have at hand the weapon of prayer, the prayer of the blessed, far more powerful than ours? Do they need, so to speak, the reinforcement of our weak little prayers?

Well, I would remind you that I spoke not only of our own particular prayers, but of masses to be offered, in which here on earth we have the prayer of Christ Himself in His final act of oblation.

And in addition, I maintain that our own particular prayers are required, and it seems to me that the entire treatise on prayer is involved here.

For it is quite clear that God does not need our petitions to wish our good and to know infinitely better than we do just what our good consists in, or to exercise His power to bring about that good. And yet, He, the Almighty, wants us to present our petitions to Him: and not only for ourselves, but also for Him, for His own intentions, as is the case in the first three petitions of the Our Father, when we ask that His Will be done.

Evidently, He has no need of us or of our prayers for this. But as St. Thomas explains (cf. IIa-IIae, q. 83, a. 2), just as in the things of nature, God has arranged that a certain effect is produced because according to the laws proper to the essences involved some cause or other has brought it about, so too in human things, in the affairs of the *free* agent that every human being is, He arranges that certain effects will come about *as a consequence* of certain acts freely carried out by humans, in particular as a consequence of their prayers. "It is according to the disposition of Divine Providence, not only that certain effects happen, but also that they come about from certain causes and a certain determined order. Now among created causes, human acts are also the cause of certain things; whence it follows that human beings ought to accomplish, not in order by them to change the divine ordering of things, but rather so that certain effects be produced in conformity with the order set down by God. It is the same with natural causes. And it is also the case with prayer. We do not pray in order to change the divine disposition of things, but rather in order to obtain what God has ordered as having to be brought about through the prayers of the saints . . ."

There is then *an order set up by God* according to which certain things come about here below because we have prayed to God concerning them.

It is very clear, is it not, that among these certain things that God wishes to have happen on condition that we ask those things of Him, there are things which correspond not only to our own desires and intentions but things which correspond as well to the desires and intentions of God Himself (think again of the first three petitions of the Our Father)—moreover, this is the case with everything that is good—therefore there are clearly other things that correspond to the desires and intentions of the saints in paradise.

There is a mass of things, which are concerned not only with our desires and intentions but also with the desires and intentions of the saints with regard to God's work on this poor earth of ours, things which come about only because human freedom here below turns toward God in prayer.

11. This is something that is absolutely certain, and is no more than a repetition in different form of some very general truths taught by St. Thomas.

But it seems to me that we must try to be a bit more precise, and here I am entering the field of certain hypotheses that I would like to propose to you and which require more profound consideration.

In the *ad tertium* of this same article 2 (IIa-IIae, q. 83) that I just read to you (I have quite a number of things to say about this *ad tertium*, but this is not the time), St. Thomas writes: "There are a great number of things that we receive from God's liberality without even asking for them. But there are certain things He wants to give us at our request, this is *for our own good*: namely, in order that we might acquire a certain habit of confidence in having recourse to God—*ut scilicet et fiduciam quamdam accipiamus recurrendi ad Deum*—and in order that we come to recognize that He is the author of all our goods."

Yes, this is undoubtedly quite true. But is that all there is? Is there question, as we might risk thinking if we remain on this level, only of a kind of educative and pedagogical ordering by Divine Providence, destined to assure the equipment of our moral life, like those rules that a good father of a family lays down for the proper moral formation of his children?

My idea is to go much further. Did not St. Thomas himself, in the body of the article, take care to note that in the things of nature God established a similar order between the effect He wishes to bring into existence and the cause which produces that effect, according to the very laws of essences or the laws of nature? What I think is this, that, as far as prayer is concerned, what we are involved with is not solely a disposition of God's paternal Prudence aimed at the moral formation of human beings, but rather a genuine *law*—I would gladly say an ontological law—not just of nature, but of the entire universe of the spirit and of freedom, and more especially of the supernatural order.

I do not know exactly how to put this. One might say, it seems to me, that with regard, certainly not to all things that depend on this universe, but to a certain ensemble of things which depend on it, the intentions of heaven are carried out here on earth only by means of certain conditions, certain enticements or certain initial steps which have their origin in God's dispositive causality and which depend on the prayer of spirits turned toward Him. But this is not all: Why is it necessary that the Sacrifice on the Cross which took place at a given moment in time, but with an infinite efficacy that is valid for all time, why is it necessary that the same sacrifice—this time under a bloodless mode—be made present once again, throughout the entire course of ages, each time a Mass is celebrated on earth, if not because it is necessary that, from this earth throughout the ages—this time through the supplication and immolation of the God-Man Himself, the head of humanity—an appeal should rise up, a cry, an abyss dug deep into human freedom, which in the impermanence of our fleeting length of days corresponds to the eternal merciful will of God?

This is what I would like to propose to you, without being very sure of what it is worth.

It seems to me that in the laws established by Providence regarding the behavior of created things, there are three orders, or rather three *regimes*, to be considered:

In the first place, the *ordinary regime* of creatures without intelligence, or of material nature. Divine Providence looks after the good of all these creatures, it nourishes the tiny birds, it clothes in beauty the lilies of the field, through the exercise of natural causalities and forces, without any prayer or demand being addressed to God, unless it is by the very existence and needs of these things—little birds certainly open wide their beaks, and how!

In the second place, there is the *ordinary regime* of intelligent creatures inasmuch as they are *free agents*. These intelligent creatures, because they are intelligent, know that God exists and that everything comes from Him. Here then, it is the law, a law necessary for this regime, that those goods which the divine liberality wants to dispense to such creatures be received through the causality of *their prayers*, according as their freedom turns toward God and, by having recourse to Him, opens up in the soul—and not only in the soul that does the praying but at the same time in that invisible universe in which all souls exist in intersolidarity—the way along which the intentions of God's generosity will pass to their realization here below. It is as if there were at the summit of the soul a window facing heaven, a window which depends on the soul's freedom for the opening and closing of its panes and its shutters. As long as the shutters are closed the light cannot enter. When in a free act of recourse to God the soul opens this window and its shutters, light floods in, and with it an avalanche of heavenly gifts which all along were pressing against the panes to gain entrance.

Let me note parenthetically that when there is question of human beings, who make up a part of both the world of nature and the world of freedom, the exercise of their freedom by having recourse to God in prayer also has an effect on their natural life itself. We can find our own nourishment and nourishment for our families without praying to God, as is the case with a multitude of human beings, just like all the animals in nature. But Jesus told us to pray for our daily bread, *our* bread, the bread of all our brothers as well as our own; and if there were a greater number of people making the fourth petition of the Lord's Prayer, and a greater number of Christians doing it *better*, there would be less famine in the world.

Finally in the third place, there is the *extraordinary regime* of intelligent creatures inasmuch as they are *free agents: and receive without having asked*. Certainly not extraordinary as far as God is concerned because He is always the first to give, but extraordinary as far as created spirits are concerned because it is according to the *nature of things* that created spirits present their petitions to Him who is the author of all good—that they ask before they receive. And fortunately this extraordinary regime is there and produces its effects with great frequency! So, by exceptions, which at times can be miraculous, but mostly just outside the ordinary course of things—by exceptions to the laws of the *ordinary* regime—the goods that free agents need are given *without having been asked for*, without the free agent's having recourse to the first Cause of all good. This is an extraordinary regime because in this case the gifts from heaven, instead of entering into the soul and into the world by the ordinary way, by the freely opened window I spoke of, enter instead like a thief in the night, if I may put it this way, without the soul opening up of its own accord and asking God for what is good. The word *effraction* that I just used metaphorically turns out to be a seriously limping metaphor because in reality there is no violence whatever involved because the causality of the Almighty never does violence to the creature. It would be truer to say that heaven weighs so heavily that with its gifts that it penetrates right through the walls of the soul.

Then the soul receives without having asked. This is the case, for example, with certain natural or supernatural inspirations, with attentive grace that anticipates need, with a multitude of benefits that escape our consciousness or our attention and which are at times due to fortuitous encounters—and due above all to that sovereign work of God which is the "justification of the impious."

Let us add right away that if the one who is impious, by the very fact that he is impious, has not turned toward God to ask that he be healed, there are other souls who have prayed and suffered and have perhaps been put on the cross and have perhaps given their lives for this. St. Teresa of Lisieux prayed for Pranzini. And there is that enormous mass of prayers by the saints that God makes use of at His pleasure for the benefit of some individual or other. So finally what I refer to in the strict sense as the *extraordinary regime*—unless it is understood as those goods given to a single specific person without their having been asked for *by that particular person*—is reabsorbed in large measure (and even entirely if there is question of the supernatural order and of salvation) into the *ordinary regime* which is proper to free agents as such, in this sense that the goods they receive from God *have already been asked for* if not through their own prayers, then at least through the *prayers of the saints* and of the entire Mystical Body, and above all through the prayers of Jesus and Mary.

12. I would like to make one more remark: If everything I just said is exact, then we can see that what constitutes the *ordinary regime* for material nature (to receive without having asked) is the *extraordinary regime* for free agents (for some particular free agent); and inversely, what is the *ordinary regime* for free agents as such (to receive after having asked and because one has asked) is an

extraordinary regime for material nature, which is the case, for example, when a natural occurrence takes place because of the prayer of a free agent—the cure of a sick person, the deliverance of a person escaping from his persecutors, the end of a war, the fall of a tyrant, a bounteous harvest of the fruits of the earth, etc., without forgetting the petition for our daily bread.

What is especially important in all this is to understand that prayer is not just something good, which it undoubtedly is, or something to be recommended or something pious, but *more or less optional*; it is a *necessity* in the world as God made it. It is just as necessary to pray as it is to sow in order to reap or to use some source of energy to make a machine function. Even in those natural things destined to serve human beings, a humanity that does not pray may very well achieve by science and technology a formidable mastery over matter, but if it does not pray all this could end up to its harm. It is humanity which will become enslaved to matter instead of using it for its own liberation, and in splitting the atom will become enslaved to dust. This is why a great nuclear physicist I knew said to me one day that a few lines of Baudelaire foretold all that disturbing work on the atomic bomb and its true meaning. I can still see him going off to find *Les Fleurs du Mal* in his library, and showing us these line from the poem entitled "L'Imprévu":

> *Et puis, Quelqu'un paraît que tous avaient nié,*
> (And then, Someone appeared whom all had denied)
>
> *Et qui leur dit . . .*
> (And who said to them . . .)
>
> *Reconnaissez Satan à son rire vainqueur,*
> (Now acknowledge Satan with his conquering sneer)
>
>> *Enorme et laid comme le monde . . .*
>> (Enormous and ugly like the world . . .)
>
> *Je vais vous emporter à travers l'épaisseur,*
> (I will carry you off through the dense thickness,)
>
>> *Compagnons de ma triste joie,*
>> (As companions of my sad, miserable joy,)
>
> *A travers l'épaisseur de la terre et du roc,*
> (Through the dense thickness of earth and rock,)
>
> *A travers l'amas confus de votre cendre,*
> (Through the chaotic heap of your ashes,)
>
> [These were the lines that so struck the physicist]
>
> *Dans un palais aussi grand que moi, d'un seul bloc*
> (Into a palace as enormous as myself, from a single block of
>   stone)

Et qui n'est pas de pierre tendre,
(which is not soft, but hard as flint,)

Car il est fait avec l'universal Péché,
(For it was built of universal Sin,)

Et contient mon orgueil, ma douleur et ma gloire!
(To house my pride, my suffering and my glory!)

After this I would like to read you the end of the poem, first of all because, in my opinion, it contains some singularly beautiful lines of poetry, and then because it has a precise relation to the Church Triumphant:

Cependant, tout en haut de l'univers juché,
(And yet, perched on the very peak of the universe,)

    Un ange chante la victoire
    (An angel entones a hymn to the victory)

De ceux dont le coeur dit: "Que béni soit ton fouet,
(Of those whose hearts proclaim: "Blessed be thy whip,)

Seigneur! que la douleur, ô Père, soit bénie!
(O Lord! May my pain be blessed, O Father!)

Mon âme dans tes mains n'est pas un vain jouet,
(In thy hands my soul is not a useless plaything,)

    Et ta prudence est infinie."
    (And thy prudence is infinite.")

Le son de la trompette est si délicieux,
(The trump sound is so delightful,)

Dans ces soirs solennels de celestes vendanges,
(In the solemn twilight of this heavenly grape-harvest,)

Qu'il s'infiltre comme une ecstase dans tous ceux
(That it infiltrates like an ecstasy into all those)

    Dont elle chante les louanges.
    (Whose praise that trumpet sings.)

Well, what was I saying myself? That if we do not pray, we may conquer empires and become extremely wealthy, but we will never become the consumers of those things that are the most important for us as human beings. If we do not pray, we may be great painters or great musicians, but there will always be something dead in that grandeur. If we do not pray we may become great philosophers, but we will betray philosophy and walk right by the truth—we may be remarkably erudite and more or less daft experts in theology, we will never be great theologians or exegetes. If we do not pray we can make no progress in the Christian life, nor receive any of the really good things, true fraternal charity, interior peace and joy, or even the dunghill of Job with its vermin, through which here below we enter into eternal life.

In conclusion, if I were to sum up in a single sentence what I would like to have been able to show in this "seminar," I would say that to a degree far, far greater than we think, the intentions of heaven with regard to the earth and its goodness for us are frustrated or paralyzed by our neglect of prayer, especially prayer to the saints of the Church Triumphant—exemplary saints and those who went unnoticed—and very especially prayer *for the intentions* of these saints and for the purposes of the Church of heaven.

CHAPTER XVII
A LOOK AT THEOLOGY (III)

ALONG UNBEATEN PATHWAYS[1]

I HAVE ENTITLED THE REFLECTIONS I am going to present to you today "Along Unbeaten Pathways." What I mean by unbeaten or untrodden pathways are certain marginal questions which ordinarily are not insisted upon very much, but which in truth open out onto very great problems.

In this present little talk, I will propose to you two attempts I have made as best I can—which does not mean that they are very brilliant, for they treat very difficult things—to go with you down two of these little untrodden ways.

I

1. My first attempt has to do with what the greatest of realists tells us about the condition of the blessed after the resurrection of the body. It was to the *Supplement* to the *Summa theologiae* that I went for help. This was not written out by St. Thomas himself; it was Reginald or someone else who put it together with texts taken from works by Thomas that were anterior to the *Summa theologiae*; and so the different points treated there were taught in the *Compendium* and in the *Summa contra Gentiles*;[2] there is no doubt then that the *Supplement* presents us with what is very surely the thought of the Angelic Doctor.

Perhaps I will be told that the subject I propose to speak about is so far beyond anything we can know about it here below that it would be more prudent to say nothing. If it turns out that one day we are included among the just, then when that time comes we will get to see just how things are. Meanwhile, let us be sure we do not dirty the immaculate fingers of our science by running them over questions that arouse suspicion, and let us be sure we do not give the impression of descending to theology-fiction.

The Angel of the School did not retreat from one single question. I would

---

1   *Editor's footnote*: A seminar with the Little Brothers of Jesus, Toulouse, February 28, 1972. I hope the reader will excuse the somewhat familiar language I am accustomed to use with my Little Brothers. Cf. *Revue Thomiste*, 1972, no. 2, pp. 233–252.

2   Cf. in particular regarding the questions we are going to discuss, *Comp. theol.*, I, c. 151–184; *Contra Gentiles*, IV, c. 80–90.

like to follow him in his discussion of certain questions, a few of which may seem a bit bizarre, but concerning which, when his mind recognized something true, he responded without blanching. There is no question at all here of theology-fiction. There is question of theology through the work of the imagination, which is something entirely different, and besides it is great fun. If I have chosen to spend quite a bit of time at this, it is first of all because I get a kick out of doing so. And it is also because I think this is the way we should go about thinking.

In the resurrection, affirms St. Thomas—and this is a capital point—in the resurrection, the soul takes on once again the same body it had here on earth. The conditions will be entirely different, of course, but for each of us it will be the same body that is living and breathing here right now, *"idem corpus numero."*[3]

"In carne mea," says Job (xix, 26), *"videbo Deum Salvatorem meum."* In my flesh I shall see God my Savior.

To understand this it is enough for us to recall that the soul, which is spirit, is also the substantial form of a living body, and each individual soul the form of a determinate individual body. (Again it is necessary to have a precise notion of prime matter, that *pure potentiality* which as such has no nature and no existence as long as it is not actualized by some form, but which metaphysics discerns in every material being as radically implied by the latter.) If my own soul once again informs matter, it will be my body that is there. If the soul is glorified, the body will be glorified as well, living an immortal life, a body that will not increase, will never wither away, and will obey laws of a physics we know absolutely nothing about except that it is different from ours.

So that individual who passed simply and naturally among us is the very same person who will rise for eternity. *"Est idem numero homo qui resurget."*[4]

And it is with all his limbs and all his organs that he will rise. The man who has risen is a man who has come to his final perfection and who finds himself integrally restored forever. *"Oportet quod omnia membra quae nunc sunt in corpore in resurrectione hominis reparentur."*[5]

Absolutely nothing that made up the structure of our perishable body or that made it beautiful will be lacking. It will have its own hair and fingernails.[6] The intestines will be there too, as will all the other organs. Since they will have nothing more to do in the way of digestion, they will be filled, certainly not with foul superfluities, but with the most noble of fluids, *"plena non quidem turpibus superfluitatibus, sed nobilibus humoribus,"*[7] destined, I suppose, to maintain the entire body in pure, sweet freshness. Because of a scruple of intellectual

---

3   Sum. theol., Supl., q. 79, a. 1.

4   *Ibid.*, q. 79, a. 2.

5   *Ibid.*, q. 80, a. 1.

6   Cf. *Ibid.*, q. 80, a. 2.

7   *Ibid.*, q. 80, a. 1, ad 2m.

honesty—I do still have bit—I might point out that in the case of the noble fluids in question we are actually up against a case of theology-fiction, for it could just as well be said that the intestines will simply remain empty, along with the rest of the stomach and the urinary tract. But this is the single little license granted to fantasy that will be encountered in my résumé, and however futile may seem the questions to which they reply, all the other assertions reported by me are assertions that St. Thomas held to be founded on reason.

And for him it was a general truth of the greatest importance that in our risen bodies all the functions of animal life will have disappeared, but not those things which served them and which from then on will be subject to the laws of a radically changed physics. So the blood which once circulated in our bodies and wonderfully kept us alive here on earth will continue to circulate within it and carry into all its parts the radiance of its glorious state. Do we not have an evident sign of this? For each time the Mass is celebrated the wine is changed into the Blood of Christ in His Glory. In short, everything in our bodies that was *humanly true* will be present in the bodies of those who have risen from the dead, if it be clearly understood that, while preserving in this way, as the *Supplement* to the *Summa* maintains, everything that here below was *truly human* in the ontological structure of their bodies, the life they lead will be a completely different life—new and eternal—totally and supremely *truly human*, in which their souls will be divinely delivered from the slightest subjection to the body it informs and will exult for ever in beatitude.

St. Thomas tells us many other things about those who have risen from the dead. He tells us that they will all be of the same age, which will be the time of youth, since they will live for all eternity "in maxima perfectione naturae [humanae]"[8] and it is in the time of youth, at the age when Christ laid down His life, that human nature is in its most perfect state; full growth has been attained and decrepitude has not yet begun.

They will all be there like people in their thirties, all beautiful this time without a doubt. But they will not all have the same height, since height is an individual characteristic.[9]

Finally, as I noted a moment ago, the functions of animal life, of nutrition and generation, which play such an essential role in the human body here below, will completely cease in the bodies of the risen,[10] even though all the organs destined for these functions remain present within them. Likewise, eating, drinking, engendering, all this was very necessary for the human species, but the pleasures found in them remain far removed from perfect joy, "*solae enim delectationes spirituales . . . sunt simpliciter delectationes et propter se quaerendae.*"[11] Perfect joy, even here on our earth, is limited to what comes from

8   *Ibid.*, q. 81, a. 2.

9   Cf. *Ibid.*, q. 81, a. 2

10   Cf. *Ibid.*, q. 81, a. 4.

11   *Ibid.*, q. 81, a. 4, ad 4m.

heaven, along with persecutions, anguish upon anguish and the torments of the Cross. What is there so astonishing in the fact that for a human being who has attained ultimate perfection in the state of glory, there should be no other joy but perfect joy, this time in all its purity?

2. The question posed in this fashion concerning the organs of the body which will be present in the next life—restored, as they will be, in their tiniest parts with an absolute fidelity, even though their functions have disappeared and they no longer serve any purpose at all—that question is still worthy of a moment's reflection.

In the state of the way (*in via*), which is where we are right now, they were made in such a way as to be functional; and this is the case in all of nature, and with all the beings it contains. Yet in its very first finality nature was created, not *to do or make*, but *to be*, and thereby render glory to its Creator. God is not an industrialist who manufactures more or less workable typewriters or automobiles to sell at the highest marketable price to bring him a substantial return on his investment. God is an artist, the supreme *artifex*, who in making nature and all it contains, wanted first and foremost, even as far as this present mode of becoming is concerned, to squander being and beauty in the most lavish fashion.

Today we think that humanity issued from the slow evolution of an animal series. In no way does this negate the fact that through all this long history of evolution it was the First Cause who started it and that the human body, the body that one day would become the body of the Incarnate Word, was the distant aim of the Creator, and was formed, sculpted, and adorned by Him—formed by Him in His own image (I shall get back to this shortly)—with the love of an artist for his work, and what an artist! and with what love! He certainly had in mind that this body should function, but also and above all that it should *be*, and that it should be beautiful. The beauty of the human body, even in this miserable world of ours, is something that God cherishes.

Maybe because among those around us there is considerable ugliness and deformity, or perhaps because our way of looking at things is too stupid and too dulled by habit and we scarcely think of this beauty, that in the end there is almost no one who is conscious of it except the great poets, the great painters, and the great lovers. Yet it does exist. And when time will have run its course, and the world of becoming will have come to an end, and when the human bodies of the risen find themselves in the supreme perfection of human nature, then their biological functioning will no longer have any importance at all. What will matter is their beauty and the perfect integrity of these animated statues living a life of beatitude for all eternity.

3. When we are told that with the resurrection the flesh itself will be *spiritualized*, I think this must be understood in two different ways: in the first

place, as I just tried to explain, inasmuch as the body with all its organs, even those which have forever ceased to function, has from then on become the sign through which the sublime dignity of our beatified spirit appears; by its visible and tangible beauty, it is the physical manifestation of the splendor of a soul which now sees God. From the biological order proper to the state of the way, it has passed over to the aesthetic order. And whereas it is transcendental Truth which shines forth in the souls of the blessed, it is transcendental Beauty which shines forth in their risen bodies.

In the second place, when we are told that at the time of the resurrection the body will be spiritualized, I understand it—and here the functions that it exercised continue to exist more fully and effectively—in the sense that in the body the organs and the activities of a supra-biological order will all be at the service of the beatified soul and so will share in its pure spirituality. How is this so? Here we must think of the organs and the activities of the senses—of the external senses first and also of that internal sense which is the imagination.

From the beginning of the state of the way in which we now find ourselves, the imagination, within the emanations of the different faculties of the soul, proceeds in us from the intellect; and in the service of our intellectual life, it does not gather up only all the things which issue forth and rise within it from the exercise of the external senses, it acts too as an instrument of the intellect and as descending from it, as a creative imagination or intelligentiated imagination, playing an immense and indispensable role in humanity: for we do not think without images, and the universe of imagery due to the creative imagination is an inexhaustible treasure of essential importance for culture in all its forms among all peoples. As Olivier Lacombe pointed out, it is the creative imagination or the imaginative intellect which is at the origin of the myths of the great religions in which so many precious intuitions mingle darkly with error. And when it is in the service of divine truth, the creative imagination bestows incomparable benefits on us. The creative imagination has contributed as much as theology has to the formation of Christianity. Amid the noblest and most beautiful of images, and thanks to them, the people of the children of God, the little people of Christ have been educated. Architecture, statuary, stained glass windows, illuminated manuscripts, liturgical chant were all radiant with a beauty through which the doves of the Holy Spirit everywhere passed into the everyday life of the people. Modern man has changed all that. Because he esteems himself superior in intelligence, he despises images and asks no more of them than to stimulate his bestiality. And as far as religious art is concerned, for two centuries now he has taken it upon himself to offer to the faithful a spectacle of the worst kind of sentimental mediocrity and conventional pious ugliness. And today jazz is not going to offer a cure for a liturgy that has been handed over to all-powerful experts who think of nothing else than, by dint of vulgarization, to get a flock of sheep, whom they consider underdeveloped, to bleat in chorus.

Well, in the land of the risen the creative imagination will be at work in the service of beatitude with a sublime beauty we can only dream about. But I mention this only in passing for fear of going on too long. The question of the external senses seems to me primordial, and this is what I would like to insist on.

4. The bodies of the risen just will be incorruptible, as St. Paul tells us ("*seminatur in corruptione, resurget in incorruptione,*"[12] I Cor. xv, 45), and at the same time impassible and unalterable because they will be subject *in a fully perfect manner* to the rational soul, just as the soul will be subject *in a fully perfect manner* to God. "And thus in the glorified body no change at all can come about that might be contrary to the disposition by which it is found perfectly under the rule of its soul,"[13]—although according to the degree of sanctity of the blessed souls, the *cause* of such an inalterability (namely the beatitude their souls enjoy) is more or less elevated in degree.

No action from without therefore can harm or alter the glorious body or the dispositions of matter within it. But St. Thomas adds immediately that the activity of the five senses will be exercised in them in all fullness, since the organs of the senses, just like the body as a whole, are then in the highest state of perfection possible to human nature. So when the eyes see and the ears hear, when the other external senses enter into the act of knowing, it will not be because the body has been subjected to some alteration which would modify its nature; it is by virtue of an immutation of the spiritual order received by the organ of sense and which is connatural to it; here there is question of a *spiritualis immutatio*[14] with regard to which whatever comes from without to affect the organ physically plays only a purely instrumental role. The sensible quality, the sound, and the color, whose substratum exists materially in the external milieu, are received by the sense "*secundum esse spirituale*"; in other words, it is not the sensible quality as it proceeds from outside that will come to affect the body and modify it in its being. It is its *species* or its *intentio* which pass through the organ of sense. *Species, intentio*? these are difficult words to translate: Let us call it the immaterial impression produced in the material organ which the soul informs as it informs the entire body, and which is the instrument of a faculty of knowledge: "*sicut pupilla recipit speciem albedinis et tamen ipsa non efficitur alba.*"[15] The pupil of the eye receives the immaterial impression of whiteness without itself being made white. For, just as is said in Aristotle's *de Anima*, lesson 24, the sense is receptive of such "*intentiones in*

---

12   Cf. *Ibid.*, q. 82, a. 1, sed contra.

13   *Ibid.*, q. 82, a. 1: "*Corpus humanum et quidquid in eo est, perfecte erit subjectum animae rationali, sicut etiam ipsa perfecte subjecta erit Deo. Et ideo, in corpore glorioso non poterit esse aliqua mutatio contra dispositionem illam qua perficitur ab anima.*"

14   Cf. *Ibid.*, q. 82, a. 3.

15   *Ibid.*

materia praeter materiam," it receives impressions in matter that are beyond matter, to the exclusion of the matter which, in the exterior milieu, the sensible quality, whose *species* they are, included in its physical substratum.

And so, it is with the senses that in every animal immateriality has its very first beginning. But in all of them it stops there, except in that animal endowed with reason, in whom this immateriality which begins with the senses is destined in our case to come to full bloom in the higher faculties because our soul is spirit. Sensation is an *immutatio spiritualis.* We must not let all the evil that the majority of moralists tell us about the senses and sensuality lead us to forget the great dignity of these senses in us.

It seems to me that in reflecting on this we notice that many things are changing. Ascetical and mystical writers do well to put us on guard against the senses and their pleasures, which are not *"delectationes propter se quaeren-dae,"* pleasures to be sought for themselves. But would they not do well also to teach us first of all to understand and respect this spirituality in the rough which begins with the senses? To respect the senses is not a bad way to learn that it is stupid to abuse them.

5. The five senses will find many occasions to exercise themselves fully in our risen bodies,[16] even the sense of taste, though the risen neither eat nor drink; some slight moistening of the tongue will be enough. Do not pipe or cigarette smokers here below experience the taste of tobacco without having to ingest anything? A little smoke is enough.

It is clear that when the risen put their senses to work, they will put their imaginations to work as well. Concerning the relation of the senses and the imagination to the intellect, the *Supplement to the Summa,* as far as I know, has nothing to say. With the help of our senses and our imagination will we be able to form concepts in the afterlife? I would like to be able to answer no, out of spite for those against whom I have spent my too long life in battle. Moreover, will not the glorified soul, once it is reunited to its body, continue to receive, like the angels, a swarm of infused ideas thanks to which it will have full knowledge of the universe? In reality, however, since, after the resurrection, human nature will be restored to the peak of its perfection, and since it will enjoy a very high level of experimental knowledge, it must be admitted that it will draw from the senses and the imagination abstract concepts that will double so to speak those infused ideas and will well up in the minds of the blessed with marvelous facility for their human mode of knowledge and for their conversations together, as well as for their common song and for the praise of God.

And the fact remains, as I just mentioned, that the imagination does not serve solely for the formation of ideas. Like the intellect it is a royal faculty, whose activity descends form the heights of the spirit down to the voice or the

16   Cf. *Ibid.,* q. 82, a. 4.

hand; in man creative imagination gives rise to a whole world of his own invention, whose riches and fecundity in the world of the risen will be without limit. St. Thomas teaches that in heaven they will retain the habits of knowledge acquired in their earthly life,[17] and this is true for the many other habits that ennobled their intellects. I envision them continuing in their divine manner the immortal labors of a Bach, a Mozart, a Dostoïevski, a Giorgione, prodigious artists and artisans, multiplying with full and sovereign liberty many and varied reflections of the Creator's work, and revealing to one another something of the innumerable possibilities which actually have not passed into being and still rest within created nature and created beauty. But these are my personal daydreams on the question, and no doubt are not worth very much.

6. Let us get back to St. Thomas and what he tells us about the bodies of the just who have risen.

He teaches us[18] that they will move about at their pleasure. The brightness which shines forth in them will be the redundance in their flesh of the glory of their souls.[19]

The world in which they live will be a world made new.[20]

And in this world made new there will be neither plants nor animals.[21]

Here is something that, at first glance, seems surprising, even disappointing, a paradise that is not a garden! No beech trees, no oaks, no prairies, no gentle sheep, no tame lions, no wild flowers, no roses, no lilies more gloriously clothed than even King Solomon!

But on reflection, we come to see that nevertheless the Angel of the School was right once again. The image of the paradise of pleasure which haunts our subconscious is an image of the earthly paradise, where everything began for us, but which it would be absurd to transfer to the end of all things and to make of it an image of the human world in the state of glory, where there will no longer be any becoming, any evolution, or any continuous time. "*Quidquid remanebit post mundi innovationem, in perpetuum erit, generatione et corruptione cessante. Ergo plantae et animalia penitus post mundi innovationem non erunt.*"[22] This world is strictly and absolutely unimaginable. A philosophy which would attempt to form even the slightest idea of it with the help of what we know here below would be fit for Bedlam. At any attempt by analogical thought to do so in regard to this world we must shout: Stop right there, there is no way

---

17   Cf. Ia, q. 89, a. 5.

18   Cf. Suppl., q. 84, a. 3.

19   Cf. *Ibid.*, q. 85, a. 1.

20   Cf. *Ibid.*, q. 91, a. 1.

21   Cf. *Ibid.*, q. 91, a. 5.

22   *Ibid.*, sed contra.

through! Because here we have come the final point beyond which the transcendence of divine things alone holds sway.

But then with this paradise without plants or animals will not creation suffer an enormous loss, the loss of all the wonders of nature which speak so magnificently of God to anyone who knows how to look at them and love them?

My answer is: Creation will suffer no loss, for all of it, the verdant countrysides we love, the forests we cherish, our beloved menagerie of huge and tiny animals, gracious and fearfully powerful, all of this will continue to live eternally in the memory of the blessed.

Now let us put aside any particular questions and turn our eyes toward the great high truth to which our little bypath has led us, and which is implied in all that has been noted up till now. This truth concerns nothing less than human nature itself and the conception we must form of it.

You may have noticed that on several occasions, when he speaks of the condition of the risen just, St. Thomas teaches that human nature—I repeat human *nature*—will come to its perfection only in the world of eternity, in other words once it has arrived at the height of the supernatural, *after the resurrection of the body*, in the risen just whose bodies will be completely subject to the soul, which in its turn will be completely subject to God. The rational animal will attain perfection only when the functions of animality have forever ceased in him. At that point the entire truth of human nature will be in him. What a paradox! This is the way it is because the soul which informs our body is a spirit, and because our body exists for this spirit, and also because (and this is how we must understand the "spiritual body" that St. Paul speaks of, *"seminatur corpus animale, surgit corpus spirituale,"* I Cor. xv, 44) the body will be perfectly and absolutely at the service of the spirit only in the world of the risen, after it has suffered here below through all the not very funny exigencies and the good and the malicious tricks of animality, and through all the labors and torments of the world of becoming and of evolution—then all this will be behind it and over for good.

But every nature aspires naturally toward its perfection. And if we consider human nature as such, and only human nature, we have to say that of its very self it envelopes, essentially, a *natural* aspiration toward something which is infinitely above it and about which it knows nothing (what we do know we know only through faith), a natural aspiration toward a state that it can in absolutely no way attain by its own powers, nor by any conceivable progress in the world of becoming. Aristotelian because of the hylomorphism it supposes, such a notion of human nature is, with respect to what I just pointed out, more Pascalian than Aristotelian; it presents us with an image of man that is at once grandiose and pathetic. And it explains many things, notably the fact that the natural aspiration I just mentioned is at the origin and the heart of all the great religions of humanity, however foreign they are to the Judeo-Christian revelation, with all their famous myths full of enigmatic truths as well as vast illusions.

It also explains the fact that if we try to wrench from our hearts this aspiration toward what is *naturally impossible* which is as essential to us as our skin, to that same extent we bring about the degeneration of our nature, and in so doing we lose the very idea of nature (this is the very path down which the fashionable philosophies of the day are sending us).

7. Here I am at the end of my first little untrodden way. What we have seen along this path is not without interest for us, for it is about our last end. May I be so bold as to suggest that if our parish priests dared speak of these things, there might perhaps be somewhat fewer young men and women looking for an artificial paradise in LSD and marijuana. Whatever the case may be, all the troubles and worries that this consumer society of ours creates can look forward to a great future.

My first tentative approach is over now, but I would like to say a few words about a question that still torments me.

It is written in Genesis (i, 26): *Let us make man to our own image and likeness*, in the image and likeness of the One and Triune God. The whole of question 93 of the *Prima Pars* is a commentary on these words, and I have no intention of going back over what St. Thomas said on this subject. But cannot a poor old philosopher be permitted to dream about this text of Genesis in his own fanciful way, without discussing it solely in the light of what the wisdom of the Fathers tells us about it?

According to St. Gregory, as article 3 of Ia, q. 93, reminds us, it is in the angels that the divine image is best expressed. This is true, replies St. Thomas, if in the image of God we look only at the degree of intellectuality and spirituality. But, he adds, this image is more faithful in man inasmuch as man proceeds from man in the same way as God proceeds from God in the Trinity, *"in quantum homo est de homine sicut Deus de Deo."* Well, it seems to me that we might emphasize still other considerations, in trying to understand that it is about men and not angels that the astounding assertion of Genesis was made.

It seems to me that if the image of God is more faithful in man, it is precisely because man *is not* a pure spirit: not in the sense that the slightest trace of materiality would be attributable to God, but in the sense that He created matter as something good and that He takes pleasure in seeing it. So just as He made the world from matter, and from the slime of the earth made that great masterpiece of art, the human body, in the same way man in his turn, with his creaturely hands, makes great and beautiful things out of matter, an entire universe that is all his own.

I would like to go further still. How can we not ask ourselves if among all the divine perfections there is not—in a way that knowledge by analogy can give us absolutely no inkling of (here again it must stop short, blinded by the light, with its hand to its mouth)—how can we avoid asking ourselves if there is not in God something which corresponds in a supereminent way to that reality, which in actual existence implies a lack or imperfection, but rich with what treasures, to that reality which here below we call suffering, and which the Son of God became man in order to assume?[23] For human freedom God has an unheard of, almost stupefying, respect; and by this freedom man can withdraw himself from the God's love; in fact he spends quite a bit of time doing just that. And when love is betrayed is there not in the one who loves a suffering that is all the greater because his love is greater? God is Love itself. And we constantly betray this love. What does the expression "offense against God" mean, if not that our betrayals pierce to the very heart of subsistent Love?

It is clear that to suffer in act is incompatible with the perfect beatitude of God. But the divine beatitude is a mystery just as incomprehensible to our mind as the divine essence itself. And to pretend to exclude from that essence the exemplar, about which we can form no idea at all, but which is infinitely true in itself, that is, the exemplar of all that is beautiful and good, noble and generous, pure and tender, and exquisitely refining in our human sorrows and in our tears, and is found only there—in short to see in the divine beatitude nothing more than our human happiness carried to the limit—would be to treat our living God as a lifeless idol. In other words divine beatitude and divine love imply in them, as Father Dehau often reminded Raïssa, what the theologians—they have a word for everything—call *virtual suffering*, which, in a mode that is infinitely more true than suffering in us, exists in God but with no imperfection because in Him it is but one with His love—one with His love in as much we reject it and turn away. Virtual suffering exists in God; it exists in the angels too. But it is in man alone that suffering wounding an intelligent being exists formally and in act. So this is what man has in act, and what God in His deepest truth has too, but only virtually; with the result that the Incarnation of the Word was necessary so that in the human nature that He took on suffering could end up touching a Divine Person. The blessed sufferings of the Redeemer were the sufferings of God, just as His death was the death of God. They give us an inkling, in my opinion the truest and the most terribly real inkling, of how it must be understood that when He endowed with an immortal soul a being made from the slime of the earth, God created that being in His own image, a kind of wretched mirror in which He recognizes Himself.

II

8. I pass on now to my second attempt. The subject is a difficult one, but it is well worth a headache or two. At first sight, the question posed seems to

---

23   I have already touched on this point in chapter XII, "Reflections on Theological Knowledge," pp. 253–258.

make no sense at all; but if we look more closely, we see that it is of considerable importance; and still the answers we give to that question, however true they may be, cannot satisfy our minds completely—and this is precisely what is good about it.

The question here is about the relation between the pure spirits, angels or separated souls, and their place in space or, more exactly from my point of view, in a space that is not our space.

At this point, I am going to stop for a long parenthesis, with implications that are far more general, and which will take us a bit afield of our subject, but on which I am going to insist because it relates to a possible recasting of the idea by which philosophers and theologians conceive of space.

I would like to propose a new idea here, one that is entirely hypothetical. Let us remember that scientific progress has relativized for our cosmology the very notion of space. From the ordinary representations spontaneously imposed on us all by natural appearances—from Ptolemaic cosmology and Euclidean geometry with its three dimensions—down to the divers theories of space-time coming from the discoveries of Riemann, of Einstein, of Heisenberg, the idea of the space to whose laws our universe is subject, we can say, in brief, that the idea of *our space* has undergone formidable changes. Now these very changes themselves in the conception of *our space*, in my opinion, authorize the philosopher and the theologian to see in this new space no more than one of the possible forms of space, and to form, in their own particular domains, the hypothesis of the existence of a space with totally different properties, which I will call *the other space*, tributary not to time, like ours, but to eternity, and which would co-exist invisibly along with our own space. So that we can now think what it was not yet possible to think at the time of St. Thomas—namely, that the space in which the pure spirits are involved is not a place in *our space*, but a place in that *other space* that is absolutely irrepresentable to our imagination and absolutely unknown to our science, in relation to which high and low in our space have only a metaphorical meaning. My hypothesis then consists in this: that such a place is infinitely beyond our universe, *not* in the sense that to attain it we would have to traverse our universe and pass beyond it, but in the sense that the place in question belongs to a space *totally different from ours* where everything exults in the absolute: It is a place in *the other space*. Think about it; we are not talking just about a Copernican revolution in an astronomy which is still in relation to our space, in whatever way we may conceive of it. We are talking about a kind of mental triggering or a revolution in our mind concerning the very idea of space, a mental trigger that quick-releases us from our space as being "the Space," the one and only space, a release that leads us to admit that there is—inaccessible to our imagination or to our science (though, of course, perfectly intelligible to the blessed)—a space entirely different from ours, infinitely more vast, *that other space*, which is proper to the other world, the world of glory.

So I would say that it is in this other space that the glorious bodies of Jesus and Mary are found. When Mary appears to little shepherds, she does not appear to them as she is "in heaven"—in *the other space*. On the other hand I would say that at the instant of His resurrection Christ immediately found Himself—glorious—in that *other space*, from which He passes again into ours where, scarcely letting His glory even be guessed at, he appears to Mary Magdalen, to Peter, to Thomas (with His wounds, trophies of his victorious Passion which will remain forever in His body): In short, when He showed Himself to his disciples during forty days so that they might become witnesses to His resurrection, He was making Himself seen in our space such as He had once lived there. And I would say too that on the day of His Ascension,[24] when the disciples saw Him rise up toward heaven and disappear from their sight into the clouds, it was not then that He made is entry into the other space—He had entered there at the moment of His resurrection—it is rather that then He gave us a visible sign of the fact that He *was going back* there after His appearances here below and that from then on He would remain there, to sit at the right hand of the Father. From this place of glory where He dwells in this way He will not return among us except to the new earth, itself glorified, where the risen just will reign with Him forever.

And like the place of glory where—in *the Other space*—the bodies of Jesus and Mary are now found, in a similar place—in the Other space—in my opinion, are those pure spirits, the holy angels and the holy separated souls who await the resurrection of the body.

Finally I would add that it is also in *other spaces than ours* that, according to my hypothesis, we must conceive as existing, on the one hand the separated souls who are purifying themselves in purgatory, and on the other hand those who are suffering the pains of hell with the demons.

9. The new idea I just expressed, however clumsily, seems to me both exact and important, above all to help us, I will not say to arbitrarily reinterpret (I would be ashamed of this), I would say rather to purify, while maintaining it in its original fullness, the meaning of many things which the sacred texts tell us about the hereafter.

The fact remains that, whatever kind of space is under consideration, the question of its relation to the pure spirits is always there confronting us. I said just now that at first sight this question seems to make no sense. The pure spirits, as a matter of fact, are part of the world of the *invisibilia* and of immateriality; and to imagine that they possess dimensions commensurate to a place in which they would be enclosed like passengers in a bus or fish in a net would be patently absurd. It is "ridiculous," says St. Thomas, to treat a

---

24 Cf. the excellent article by Father Pierre Benoit, "L'Ascension," in *Revue Biblique*, LVI (1949), pp. 161–203. I was struck by how close my hypothesis on "the other space" is to the views expressed by the author in the last pages of this article.

separated soul as having corporeal dimensions and for this reason assign it some kind of receptacle.[25] Incorporeal things cannot be in a place in the way we habitually understand it, *"modo aliquo nobis noto et consueto,"*[26] according as when we say that a body is properly in some place.

However our holy Doctor hastens to add: "But they are in a place according to the mode which is proper to spiritual substances, which cannot be fully manifest to us, *qui nobis plene manifestus esse non potest."*[27]

This is because we are animals endowed with reason who cannot think without images, without spatial images. When we think of a pure spirit, we inevitably ask ourselves: *where is it?* as if it were a body in a place. It is stupid to ask the question: where is it? but this is what we do naturally at first. And this imbeds a little thorn in our mind which we cannot pull out very easily.

The question: where is this pure spirit? is nevertheless a perfectly legitimate one, provided that it is not asked as if it were a matter of a body with its dimensions in extension. For here place must be considered according to an entirely different mode. This place is not simple, extensive quantity. It has its own qualities; and with respect to pure spirits, place must be conceived according to the qualities it possesses, qualities which are known to us only imperfectly. And, if the hypothesis I just formulated is correct, this is valid for any spaces that the philosopher or the theologian can think of. And so now, following the *Supplement* to the *Summa*, we are once again back to the idea that the ancients formed of space, in conformity with the conceptions of their cosmology, and in conformity too with the spontaneous (non-scientific) representations imposed on each of us by natural appearances, which remain in play in our *daily lives*, whatever our scientific bent may be elsewhere: spontaneous representations according to which common parlance continues and will always continue to express itself, and according to which I shall express myself from now on in all that remains of my exposition.

I note in passing that every agent is present where he is acting, in such a way that if the guardian angel of a Little Brother acts on him at El-Abiodh to give him some good idea, the angel himself is at El-Abiodh by the action that he exercises in this way, but this is not the question here. In this case there is question of the place where a pure spirit resides or dwells in his very being or his very substance. This place is rich in many, many qualities, and it is according to the suitability of or the *congruentia* between the qualities of this place and those of the pure spirit in question that it has its abode. This means that it dwells in a particular place where his own nobility or his own unworthiness is in accord with those of the place in question. By the moral value which affects his being, and by everything that, in virtue of his freedom, is pure or impure in him, this angel or this separated soul is more or less close

25   Cf. *Sum theol.*, Suppl., q. 69, a. 1.

26   *Ibid.*, q. 69, a. 1, ad 1m.

27   *Ibid.*

to God or more or less removed from Him. Its dwelling place will itself be more or less agreeable or disagreeable; hell far down below us, and heaven very high, infinitely far above us.

To make my thought on the relation between place and pure spirits, let me have recourse to a rather far-fetched metaphor. Let us imagine immaterial beings whose spirits live in an interior harmony and beauty as perfect as the greatest masterpieces of music and poetry. And let us imagine a place in space where the plays of Claudel or Shakespeare are presented, the melodies and symphonies of Moussorgski, of Erik Satie, of Arthur Lourié are played in a marvelous fashion, unique in all the world. Well by virtue of a suitability or a correspondence, itself unique in all the world, a natural and indissoluble link is established between such spirits and such a place. It is *here* that for their joy they will take up their abode, even if the place itself were no more than a point in space and the spirits numbered in the thousands. And it would be exactly the same if the place were as vast as the Pacific Ocean and the spirits numbered only two or three. They are not there like birds in a cage, each is *there* as a pure intellect in the midst of poems or of songs which enrapture it.

The Psalms speak to us unceasingly of the place where God dwells. *Why should the pagans say, "Where is their God?" Our God is in heaven; whatever He wills He does* (Ps. ciii, 10).[28]

Separated souls are not in places which confine them spatially, but this does not keep them from being in places and residing in dwellings whose delights and beauties or painful purifications or infernal flames are not proportioned to their interior state. About these dwellings we can speak only in general; anything that could describe them for us in clear and precise detail is inaccessible to us. And when we set out to form some clear idea of them, we have at our disposal no more than the most rudimentary of images with which we would be only too naïve to be satisfied.

Poets perhaps can help us out a bit. Is there not a kind of imperfect presentiment of a universe better than our own in Baudelaire's sonnet *La vie antérieure?*

> *J'ai longtemps habité sous de vastes portiques*
> *Que les soleils marins teignaient de mille feux*
> *Et que leurs grands piliers, droits et majestueux,*
> *Rendaient pareils, le soir, aux grottes basaltiques.*
>
> *Les houles, en roulant les images des cieux,*
> *Mêlaient d'une façon solennelle et mystique*
> *Les tout-puissants accords de leur riche musique*
> *Aux couleurs du couchant reflété par mes yeux.*

---

28   The Psalms also declare Him *above* the heavens (or *beyond* the heavens)" cf. Ps. viii, 2; cviii (cvii), 5; cxiii (cxii), 4.

C'est là que j'ai vécu dans les voluptés calmes,
Au milieu de l'azur, des vagues, des splendeurs
Et des exclaves nus, tout impregnés d'odeurs,

Qui me rafraîchissaient le front avec des palmes,
Et dont l'unique soin était d'approfondir
Le secret douloureux que me faisait languir.

Long since, I lived beneath vast porticoes
By many ocean sunsets tinged and fired,
Where mighty pillars, in majestic rows,
Seemed like basaltic caves when day expired.

The rolling surge that mirrored all the skies
Mingled its music, turbulent and rich,
Solemn and mystic, with the colors which
The setting sun reflected in my eyes.

And there I lived among voluptuous calms,
In splendour of blue sky and wandering wave,
Tended by many a naked, perfumed slave,

Who fanned my languid brow with waving palms.
They were my slaves-the only care they had
To know what secret grief had made me sad.[29]

As I said at the beginning, what we know for true about the relation between pure spirits and place, however metaphorical it may be, is of considerable importance, but is still incapable of satisfying our mind because, as St. Thomas says, this requires a mode of presence totally different from the kind of presence we know here below and to which we are accustomed, a mode of presence, "which cannot be sufficiently manifest to us." And this is precisely what is good about it, for with only our own actual experience as a starting point, there is no way we can penetrate the secrets of a universe completely foreign to ours.

10. *Our Father who art in heaven.* How could a true son of Israel, and in general how could an authentically religious man ever be astonished at this formula used by Our Lord. It is like raising our heads to look at the stars when we turn to God and speak to Him.

The heavens which are the abode of our Father have nothing to do with the astronomers' heaven. They are not the empyreal heaven.[30] It is an absolutely

---

29   Charles Baudelaire, *The Flowers of Evil: A selection,* translated by F. P. Sturm, edited by Marthiel and Jackson Mathews (New York: New Directions, 1955), pp. 15–17. Used with permission.

30   St. Thomas and our old masters were more on their guard in these matters than

unimaginable place, where the glorious bodies of Jesus and Mary are found, along with the good angels and the separated souls of the blessed awaiting the resurrection—an absolutely unimaginable place outside of and beyond the whole of our universe (in the sense I just indicated, supposing, of course, that my hypothesis is accepted). And what these heavens are a sign of, and what they proclaim to our minds in metaphors, is the infinite transcendence of God.

We announce that God is infinitely transcendent as calmly as we state that two and two make four. Yet such words are explosive and much more than explosive. They are crushing and terrifying. God infinitely above us, infinitely distant from us, in heavens that are totally inaccessible to the highest of created beings considered merely according to their natures, God in His limitless grandeur, His omnipotence, His infinite holiness which makes us tremble, His majesty before which we are nothing. But these same words contain an ineffable tenderness and sweetness, since He has willed that by His grace dirty little worms like us should be united to Him where He is and be themselves deified by the vision of His essence if they do His will on this poor sad earth where their bodies will one day decay.

Let us recall the veneration and ardent love with which Jesus speaks to Him. *"After He had spoken these words, Jesus looked up to heaven and said: 'Father, the hour has come! Give glory to your Son that your Son may give glory to you . . .' (John xvii, 1) 'I have given you glory on earth by finishing the work you gave me to do. Do you now, Father, give me glory at your side, a glory I had with you before the world began. I have made your name known to those you gave me out of the world. . . . Now they realize that all that you gave me comes from you . . .' (xvii, 4–7) 'As long as I was with them, I guarded them with your name which you gave me . . .' (xvii, 12) 'I gave them your word, and the world has hated them for it; they do not belong to the world any more than I belong to the world . . .' (xvii, 14) 'Father, all those you gave me I would have in my company where I am, to see this glory of mine which is your gift to me, because of the love you bore me before the world began . . .' (xvii, 24)."*

It is to His Father Who is in heaven that Jesus speaks in this way. He was with Him before the creation of the world. And to the same heaven from which He, the Son of God Himself, came down, Jesus, as man, took His body back after His death and resurrection. And where He is, He wants to have along with Him those whom He loved and who returned Him love for love. All of Christianity is here. We are lost if we do not understand that in the first line of the Lord's Prayer the words *who art in heaven* are inseparable from the words *Our Father* and are just as essentially important.

As Raïssa wrote in her *Notes sur le Pater*,[31] "heaven or *things on high* (Col. iii, 1–2), is also and above all, essentially the other world where God is loved and

---

we tend to believe. Cajetan considered the empyreal heaven a fable.—Cf. P. Benoit, "L'Ascension," p. 202, n. 2.

31   Raïssa Maritain, *Notes sur le Pater*, pp. 33–35. *Notes on the Lord's Prayer* (New York: P. J. Kenedy & Sons, 1964), pp. 34–35.

obeyed in an absolutely perfect way by the blessed and the angels, where *the sons of God are revealed* (Rom. viii, 19), and where creation enters *into the freedom of the glory of the children of God* (Rom. viii, 21),—'heaven is where sin has ceased, heaven is where the wound of death exists no more';[32] it is the *inaccessible light* where *the Blessed and only Sovereign* dwells (Tim. vi, 15–16); it is the universe of the beatifying vision, the Church Triumphant and Heavenly Jerusalem, which existed from the very beginning with the holy Angels fixed in their choice of God, and which will attain its fullness with the resurrection of the bodies of the just, from then on 'spiritual,' conformed to *the likeness of the heavenly man* (I Cor. xv, 44, 49), and when Christ has *put beneath His feet the last enemy* which is Death. . . . Then *He will say: henceforth all has been subjected* (I Cor. v, 26–27).—It is the world where, because it is a divinized world, the Father dwells—still better than He already dwells in the souls of the saints here below—completely *at home* and pleased, finding there not the slightest obstacle to His love. A world whose existence we know from revelation, but whose nature and laws are impenetrable to us. A heaven whose azure is a veil beyond which our gaze cannot pass. At night it glitters with stars, but we have no telescope to bring close these stars of the night of faith."

11. Now let us picture a historical process in the course of which men who for generations still considered themselves Christians, and who, perhaps (it is not for us to judge the depths of the human heart) in the beginning had a high degree of theological faith, but who committed the worst of theological errors, they actually rejected the *who art in heaven*—first in their interior experience, then by insisting openly and explicitly, in their systematization, that this is no more than a myth.

Let us suppose also that there may have been among them men of genius. But they were all imaginative individuals gone astray, I mean that instead of obeying the proper demands of the intellect for thinking and forming their concepts with the help of the intelligentiated imagination, they used the imagination itself, which they mistook for the intelligence, to think and form their concepts; whence it followed that their concepts, being no more than masked images, were considered all the more profound as they were obscure, and they stirred about in the darkness with all the more energy in a language that was furiously hermetic and ultra-"intellectual"; here let us render homage to Hegel, to the master of masters, before whose mind *modern man* falls to his knees. In reality all these people considered reason their enemy and called on imagination to send it packing, all of which ended up in corrupting reason by inflating it beyond all measure.

So they have done with the Father Who is in heaven. Their god is no longer in heaven; he swims about in the ocean of immanence, where the faithful come face to face with monsters of the deep which alternately terrify and enchant

---

32   St. Ambrose, *de Sacramentis*, lib. VI, no. 20, P. L., XVI, col. 451.

them. And this god now is underneath everything; It is a kind of indeterminate divine prime matter as vast as the world itself, which takes its form within each one of us, especially in the consciousness of those thinkers who venerate it, and for whom contradiction itself is the sign, certainly not of the truth, since they no longer believe in truth, but of the power and mastery of man over himself and over things; with the result that terror seizes them when they feel this power escaping their control or a dionysiac joy exalts them when they feel it welling up.

Well, this god from below has his name; he is the *Ungrund*. And this *Ungrund* has been the life secret and the sacred mystery of German philosophy for three or four centuries. It is also the object of a malefic form of natural mysticism, which slams shut and solidly bolts the door against divine mysticism. (A little parenthesis here: I just used the expression "natural mysticism," and I have used it often because, when we are under the pressure of research, we use the words we have at hand. But however worthy of attention the thing might be, the words in question are not worth a tinker's damn. I have racked my brains to find a better expression; what I would like to propose is "the mysticism of gazing at oneself" or, more briefly, "mirror mysticism," in opposition to "the mysticism of loving union with God" or "mysticism of fire." The same problem arises with the expression "Christian philosophy" which I have often used as well, and which is just about as worthless; What I propose in its place is "philosophy considered fully as such" or "philosophy forging ahead" as distinguished from "philosophy considered simply as such" or "stumbling philosophy.")

End of parenthesis, now back to the subject. What I affirm as a fundamentally central truth is that in this regard a decisive choice is absolutely necessary. Men of today must choose between the earthbound *Ungrund* and the Father Who is in heaven; there is no middle way.

12. These thoughts came to my mind following a conversation with Heinz in which he told me about his study of the Reformation. He also spoke to me at length of Jacob Böhme, that amazing, frenzied shoemaker who was so persecuted by the Lutherian authorities of his day and who, precisely because of his spiritual experiences which he coarsely and realistically described, actually exercised an enormous influence, and not only in Germany, and because of which he can be considered the great prophet of the *Ungrund*.

All this has set me to quite a bit of daydreaming, but it is Heinz who will shed some light on these great problems.[33] I would like, though, to note here just how much I was struck, as he was too, by what Nietzsche said—that all German philosophy in reality has been *theology in disguise*. "*Larvatus prodeo*, I move ahead wearing a mask," said Descartes, but in a very different sense, as if by deliberate ruse, whereas it is with complete good faith, believing that they

---

33   Brother Heinz publishes his work under the name Ernst R. Korn.

were high-flying metaphysicians that the great German thinkers threw themselves body and soul into this contraband theology, even if they ended up in
the poetry of despair, which is the only way out after denying the Father Who
is in heaven.

French philosophy, at least what there is of it today, has nothing to do with
fraudulent theology. It is rather a fraud perpetrated by cold objective reason,
marketing by-products of scientific imagery, for the nourishment of minds, all
the while pretending to send the imagination packing, all of which ends up
corrupting the imagination, which takes its revenge by creating the void in
reason itself. As Pierre Emmanuel wrote in his recent book *Pour une Politique
de la Culture*, "[W]hat we need is a complete history of rationalism—or, if you
like, of the colonization of the imaginary by reason, in order to show the
intellectual terror and tortures inflicted on the imagination that modern 'reason' has made use of to establish its empire. The imagination has been chased
from the real, its eyes have been poked out to deprive it of the light of the
intelligence, it has then been exiled into the darkness of illusion, where often
it is tracked down like a witch just for the crime of existing. . . . She, the Mother,
the begetter of every invention, the educator of universal sensitivity, holy *Ratio*,
the wet-nurse of the cosmos, has had to submit to a spiritual humiliation
without parallel in the history of thought, at the hands of niggardly, perverted
'reason,' indeed, of an *a-raison* privative of the complete man, and consequently of reason itself in man."[34]

---

34   Pierre Emmanuel, *Pour une Politique de la Culture* (Paris: Ed. du Seuil, 1971), p.
      148f. To continue: "What this ambitious, arrogant and avaricious 'reason'
      wanted was, at the least expense and as rapidly as possible, to secure its *power*
      over the world and over man, by bringing them back to the "peau de chagrin"
      of appearances that were better and better controlled and more and more
      'de-realized.' From everything that by nature escaped this control even the right
      to exist had to be removed: and to accomplish this nothing more was necessary
      than to divide man into two parts, the luminous part—which, of course, was
      reason itself—and the blind part, the 'irrational' part, progressively reduced to
      a vestigial state, soon destined to disappear forever. This is how 'reason' came
      to be what it really is, a totalitarian cancer, the sole definitive Utopia, whose
      fanatic followers, with supreme imprudence, accuse the imagination of those
      unreal connections which are the incurable vice of generalized abstraction.
          "Worst of all, in this void-machine which knowledge is in the process of
      becoming, the laws of this pseudo-reason, invented by an imagination that has
      become enslaved, are applied more and more strictly to those things which will
      not spare man himself, if he does not succeed in escaping from it by freeing and
      reunifying the imagination. For the moment, each of its *disjecta membra* lives out
      its own particular alienation. The scientific imagination, cantoned off in labora-
      tories, furnishes its technically expert 'reason' with the theoretical means to its
      power; poetry, the only one of all the arts tolerated in the schools up to a certain
      age, like a kind of verbal calligraphy which is good for nobody knows exactly
      what, and which the adult hastens to forget; however, in the depths of the
      collective psyche, in those areas of sensitivity which have returned to savagery,

With some regret I put aside this long quotation. It is a great help to us in understanding that what we call philosophy today in France is just literature—the serial novel of the erudite who are very intelligent and informed about everything but have no idea whatever about what philosophy is. And since, in spite of everything, even without being conscious of the fact, we are always dependent on a philosophy, all this literature is in fact in the tow of German philosophy.

Let me conclude with this thought: If my remarks are true, as I think they are, I must admit that they are not of such a kind as make easily accessible and attractive to the intelligence that easy-going and pacifying universal ecumenism which is so dear to our shepherds.

---

a demented force wanders restlessly, a force which all the therapists and all the police are less and less capable of repressing. And so the most urgent question, which must be posed globally, in order to examine it exhaustively in each of its aspects (urbanism, demography, education, mass media, etc.), is, bluntly stated, to find out how to save man from his own excesses, from his own madness: and this, it must be stated again and again, is a philosophical question."

CHAPTER XVIII
A SUPPLEMENT TO THE BOOK *ON THE CHURCH OF CHRIST (I)*

APROPOS OF THE FRENCH SCHOOL[1]

1. THE FRENCH SCHOOL, to which Henri Bremond gave the name that quickly became classic,[2] offers a vast and complex field of study that in many respects still has to be cleared for production. Reading the learned works published on this subject raises many problems in the mind. The reflections I am going to risk proposing to you today from my simple perspective of an aging philosopher have to do with only one of them, the one which concerns the notion of the priesthood that has been imposed for a long time now by the French School.

By way of introduction, a few preliminary remarks about a word in current use perhaps would not prove useless. I mean the word *state* as it is used in ordinary parlance. In current usage this world has two very different meanings. Sometimes, as in the expression "duties of state" it refers to a function that a man acquits himself of in the community and to the particular mode of behavior that it entails, in other words to what I might call his *functional state* (military state, diplomatic state, medical state, etc.). Sometimes the same word *state* designates what I might call an *existential state*, that is, the typical mode in which the person himself faces up to existence—this is a state which affects the sources of action of his very being and of his entire ethos: "married state," for example, or the "state of a man dedicated to the solitary life (hermit)" or "vagabond state" or again "state of servitude" or again, in Marxist vocabulary, "state of a man of property" or "proletarian state."

But we must now recognize a third meaning for the word *state*. For the existential state I just spoke of was an existential state in the world and before men. Whereas what we must consider here is the existential state of a human creature *in the Church and before God*, in other words, in his relation to the divine transcendence. And it is for just such an existential state that in theological vocabulary the name *state of life* ought to be reserved—whether it is the state

---

1   Cf. *Revue Thomiste*, 1971, no. 2–3, pp. 463–479.

2   *Editor's footnote*: Cf. Henri Bremond, *Histoire littéraire du sentiment religieux en France, depuis la fin des guerres de religion jusqu'à nos jours, III: La Conquête mystique, l'Ecole française* (Paris, 1929).

in which the human condition places Christians in general or whether it is the state that has been set up especially for those who adopt it as a help to progress toward union with an infinitely transcendent God and the perfection of charity.

It becomes immediately apparent that on this level the difference between *function* or functional state and existential state or *state of life* becomes one of major importance. On the one hand, when we speak of the "sacerdotal state" we do so in order to designate a "functional state," the holy "function" of the priest who transmits to us the grace of the sacraments, as distinguished from all the other functions that people can exercise here on earth; on the other hand, when we speak of the "religious state" or the "state of perfection" (still to be acquired, of course), it is in order to designate the "state of life" of those who by a single act at a given moment give their lives to God forever, having left all behind for Him; and this is distinguished from the state of life of those who, equally members of the people of God and striving as well, if they are faithful Christians, to order all that they do during their passage here below toward the love of God above all else, nevertheless have not renounced those goods to which a human being naturally and with perfect right is most closely attached.[3]

2. However different the notion of the holy function may be from the notion of the state of a consecrated life, it easily happens that the mind slips from one to the other, especially when it is under the absolute sway of some end it is pursuing, namely, of an end in which one's love of God is totally committed. This slippage was constant in the mind of the founder of the French School.

This can be explained, in my opinion, not only by the prestige which Denis the Areopagite and his hierarchies always exerted on the mind of Bérulle but above all by the lofty practical finalities he pursued and by the very excellence of the work to which he was totally dedicated and to which his holy death itself—while he was celebrating Mass—bore witness: to reform, or rather to sanctify, the life of the clergy (which in his day was in dire need of restoration) in their consciousness of the holiness to which the priest is called, as indeed is every Christian, but in a very special way in the case of the priest by virtue of his office or mission in the Church. The Oratory was conceived and founded by Bérulle as a seed-bed or nursery of priests who would devote themselves to a lofty spiritual life and the pursuit of sanctity and who would shine forth by their example on all the clergy of France. This holy Cardinal (who was also, and this is a rather fearful thing, a confused, mystical Platonist) would have needed a theological rigor which historians in general do not recognize in him in order not to slip from the notion of the exigencies of the sanctity of the sacerdotal *function* to the notion of the sanctity of a *state of life* in which the

---

3   On the discussions going on presently (often very futile ones) and on the studies in depth (the work of Father P.-R. Régamy) of the healthy teachings about the religious state, see the remarkable study by Father M.-Michel Labourdette, "La vie religieuse" in the *Revue Thomiste*, 1970, pp. 442–455. I touch on this question here only to recall certain elementary truths and primary points of evidence.

priest would be constituted by the ordination he received from the hands of a bishop.

What effect did such a slippage have on the thought of Bérulle? On the one hand he was right, and magnificently so, in his insistence on the holiness toward which the priest ought to strive. *Domum tuam decet sanctitudo, Domine, in longitudinem dierum* (Ps. xcii, 5). And is not the perfection required of the bishop, according to St. Thomas,[4] higher than the perfection to which religious are called by their vows? We must not forget that the simple priest, whose situation is not the same as that of a bishop or religious, should, because of the demands of his holy function, be chosen with particular care and is bound because of his very special office, by the same obligation to pursue as best he can the search for interior perfection to which the religious is vowed by his state of life.

---

4   Cf. St. Thomas, *Sum. theol.*, IIa-IIae, q. 184, a. 5 and 7. It is quite certain that the perfection required of a bishop is higher than of a religious, but there is some obscurity in article 5 because here there is question of state of perfection of both the bishop and the religious together ("*Utrum praelati et religiosi sint in statu perfectionis*"), whereas the episcopal state (the state of one who has received the fullness of the priesthood) is manifestly a *functional state* like the ordinary sacerdotal state (of a simple priest), whereas the religious state is a *state of life*: an essential distinction that must be maintained at all cost; that a bishop is delegated to the highest perfection is so, not because of the *state of life* in which he has been constituted, but because of the holy function he exercises in the Church in all its fullness and its highest degree (a *functional state* that is certainly higher than the religious *state of life*).

I imagine that it is Denis the Areopagite and his hierarchies that are responsible for the obscurities I just pointed out and for certain disappointing formulations. In *Eccles. Hierarch.* V (cited by St. Thomas in the *sed contra* it is said that the bishop is *perfector*: he perfects all the others (including the religious, who in his *status perfectionis acquirendae* is *perfectus* or made perfect by the bishop): a thing which might lead one to believe (as I regret having done when I wrote in *Primauté du spirituel*, Paris, 1927 [*The Things that are not Caesar's*, New York, 1930]) that the bishop, in the office of *perfector*, finds himself already in a state of *acquired perfection*, something that is hardly confirmed by experience. (These remarks are made only in opposition to the Platonism of Denis the Areopagite. It is quite evident that as successor to the apostles and as shepherd of all of Christ's sheep in his diocese, the bishop is the dispenser of the goods we receive from the Church in our progress toward God.)

According to St. Thomas (*ibid.*, a. 8) the simple priest, as distinct from a bishop, is not in a state—the (functional) state of *perfector*—higher in perfection than a religious. Yet the demands of the holy function that he exercises in the Church imply in him, in a very special way, the will to give himself completely as well, to acquit himself of his function in the best way possible, to the search for interior perfection as is pursued in the state of life of the religious in virtue of a calling to which he or she has vowed to respond. (Religious without fervor certainly respond less well than the simple priest responds to the demands of his function when he is given over completely to the Spirit who turns men into saints.)

On the other hand Bérulle was mistaken, and seriously so, in exalting the sanctity of the state of life in which the sacrament of Holy Orders places the one who receives it. From affirming the eminent perfection to which the priest is called to exercise his function in a manner that is in complete harmony with what that office demands, to affirming the eminent perfection of the state of life which is conferred on him at the same time as the sacramental powers, there is no more than an imperceptible step for Bérulle, and he was happy to take that step.

This is the source of the assertions that the state of the priesthood (and not just the state of the bishop) is superior to the religious state, "and is even the source of all the sanctity which is in the Church of God";[5] that the priesthood contains in totality what religious congregations divide up among them;[6] that by becoming a priest one enters into the order of Christ Himself.[7] Even though they do not give up all for Jesus by the three vows, the Oratorians, far from being the religious of a certain Ignatius like the Jesuits (who found all this a bitter pill to swallow), or of a certain Dominic or a certain Francis, they themselves were *the religious of the Word incarnate*. As a consequence their spirituality must consist above all in losing their own subsistence in order to live solely in the Person of Christ, who never ceases to draw them "into the unity of the divine Person."[8]

In short if the priest is called to sanctity, it is because the sacrament of Holy Orders has turned him into a superchristain. This word comes not from Bérulle, but from one of the erudite who in our day have studied him with the greatest care and best understood him. Michel Dupuy did not hesitate to write this astounding sentence: "He cannot be defined as a superchristian. *For he is not just that. But it is urgent that he be at least that.*"[9] He is not just a superchristian; What is he then and what veneration must we pay him? By the very fact of the state of life in which he is constituted and which imposes on

---

5   Cf. Paul Cochois, *Bérulle et l'Ecole française* (Paris: Ed. du Seuil, 1963), "Maîtres spirituels" 31, p. 26 (who cites the *Correspondence of Cardinal Pierre de Bérulle*, ed. J. Dagens (Paris-Louvain, 1937–1939), I, p. 118, under the siglum CB, I, 118. For the meaning of these sigla see *ibid.*, pp. 183–184).

6   Cf. Michel Dupuy, *Bérulle et le sacerdoce, Etude historique et doctrinale, Textes inédits* (Paris: Lethielleux, 1969), "Bibliothèque d'histoire et d'archéologie chrétienne" 7, p. 182 f.

7   Cf. P. Cochois, *Bérulle et l'Ecole française*, p. 26 [Fragment IV, 1618]: "But then, is it possible that Our Lord would have desired so great a perfection from all the religious orders, and not have demanded it from His very own order, which is the priestly order?"

8   Cf. M. Dupuy, *Bérulle et le sacerdoce*, p. 195. n. 1 [OP, 87, no. 2. The meaning of the sigla is explained on pages 19–20 of this work]. As the author says in summing up Bérulle, the "priest 'enters' into the unique Person of Christ which is that of the Word." (p. 118). Cf. further on p. 1122.

9   M. Dupuy, *Bérulle et le sacerdoce*, p. 190.

him the ideal toward which he must strive, must we say that among us he is, if not Christ Himself, at least the *hand* of Christ,[10] under the appearances of a poor human creature who is to annihilate himself unceasingly to the point of losing his very own subsistence but who in receiving the sacrament of Holy Orders was assumed into a participation of the divine Personality of the Word incarnate? This would be waxing a bit too lyrical.

3. Each time there is a slippage from the *function* to the *state of life* of which I have pointed out a few consequences, there are signs of the presence of Bérulle.

"He energetically underlines," writes M. Dupuy, "that the priesthood is 'functional,' to use the contemporary vocabulary."[11] But Bérulle adds immediately that "our priesthood is a state"[12] incomparably firm and stable because the sacerdotal anointing emanates from that of Jesus,[13] who (and this is the thesis dearest to Bérulle) is a priest because of and as a direct consequence of the hypostatic union: so that the character of the priesthood is the mark *par excellence* of the superiority of the priesthood over the religious life.

"Most of the time Bérulle mentions the priestly character only to show the superiority of the priesthood over the religious life. The priest is consecrated to God by the sacerdotal character, whereas the religious is so by his vows. So one gets the impression of the character as a divine action, whereas a vow is a human action; the priesthood is a sacrament, whereas a solemn vow is no more than an ecclesiastical institution."[14]

"Our priesthood is the result not of a vow like in the religious state, that is to say, not as a result of our action (indeed a vow would be an action of ours), but of the action of Christ, that is to say that it draws its stability and its very being from the consecration by Christ."[15]

"[And so] the priesthood is not just an effort toward perfection, like the religious life, but a state of perfection."[16]

Bérulle explains to the Oratorians that what characterizes priests is their being "instruments of the Son of God to work out his glory in souls, cooper-

---

10   As Michel Dupuy wrote, *ibid.*, p. 195 and n. 1: "The priest is united to Christ more than as an instrument, he is conjoined to Him, he is not only in His hand, he is in a sense His hand itself; he is a member of Christ. Bérulle reminds the Oratorians of this [OP, 87, no 2: 'The Son draws them . . . into the unity of His divine Person, making them His members']." "He makes them his members"; this does not mean that He makes them members of His Mystical Body, like other Christians. For Bérulle this signifies that He makes them *members* of His divine *Person* itself.

11   *Ibid.*, p. 190.

12   *Ibid.*, p. 191.

13   Cf. *ibid.*, p. 189.

14   *Ibid.*, p. 191.

15   *Ibid.*; cf. Bérulle himself, *ibid.*, p. 289 [OR, 15, no. 2].

16   M. Dupuy, *ibid.*, p. 199.

ating in their salvation,"[17] and M. Dupuy notes again in this regard: "The priesthood could not be presented in a more 'functional' manner."[18] But Bérulle does not miss the opportunity also to explain to the Oratorians that the priesthood is a "state of sanctity."[19] And as we just saw he attaches the firmness and stability of this state to the priestly character: incomparable firmness and stability, since they are the result of the absolutely indelible nature of the priestly character. How can such a conception not appear rather bizarre when one recalls that the indelible mark that the character imprints on the soul of the priest is no other than the power with which he is invested to transubstantiate bread and wine and to absolve, even if he happens to make himself personally unworthy by the loss of grace. "There is no common measure," writes M. Dupuy, "between the indelible character of the priesthood and the stability of the religious life."[20] I should think so! The indelible character remains even in hell.[21] This seems even more doubtful for the state of sanctity linked with the priesthood.

Everything seems to me to suggest that Bérulle confused in one single unthinkable idea (and so all the more intoxicating) the indelible sacerdotal *character* and the sacerdotal *grace* received along with the character (as if it were a new modality in which sanctifying grace blossomed) at the time of the priest's ordination (a modality unique in its kind, for the sacrament of holy orders is the only one which has for its aim above all else, not the sanctification of the subject, but of others through his ministry).

Does he not hold as certain that the anointing which consecrates priests here below is the radiance on them of the priestly consecration received from the Father by the Son which in his eyes is the hypostatic union itself?

Does he not think that if priests, when celebrating Mass and administrating the sacraments, are the instruments of Christ, it is as conjoined[22] instruments of the Son of God that this is so.[23]

---

17   *Ibid.*, p. 198; cf. p. 408 [OR, 75, no. 6].

18   *Ibid.*, p. 198.

19   *Ibid.*, p. 192; cf. p. 313 [OR, 22, no. 3].

20   *Ibid.*, p. 191.

21   Such a thing was no embarrassment to the faithful disciple Bourgoing when, carried away by his eloquence, he wrote this curious sentence (cf. *ibid.*, p. 189 and n. 10): "Our priesthood shares in all these exalted and excellent conditions [of the priesthood of Christ], for it is a state, a firm and permanent state, which gets its firmness and stability from the very consecration of Jesus Christ and which adores by this firmness the eternity of His priesthood. *For it imprints on the soul a character which is its own image and resemblance, which will never be effaced, which will persevere and endure forever, into eternity itself, even in hell.*" (Italics mine) Preface to the *Oeuvres complètes du Cardinal de Bérulle*.

22   A *conjoined* instrument is what the humanity of Christ was with regard to the divine Person and is the proper effect of the hypostatic union.

23   Cf. P. Cochois, *Bérulle et l'Ecole française*, p. 31 [AO, 1 bis]. Cf. also M. Dupuy,

And is all of this not one with his thesis of predilection: "The Son draws them every day into the unity of His divine Person, linking them to His deified humanity and making them His members";[24] the priest then must "enter into the Person of Jesus, not only to celebrate Mass, but during the whole of his life"?[25]

"His own person must give up its place so to speak to the Person of the Son of God, as was the case with the humanity of Jesus: the humanity of Christ subsists in the Word; in Jesus there is no human person. For Bérulle this 'deprivation of human subsistence' is the realization of the perfection of abnegation and constitutes the closest union with God possible to a creature."[26]

This then is the perspective in which Bérulle represents the indelible character received by the priest, or rather this the illusory amalgam which he effectuates between the character imprinted forever on the soul of the priest (*but* which, and by that very fact, can continue even without grace) and the grace of the priesthood such as he conceives it, emanating from the priesthood of Christ into the soul of the priest like a ray of the hypostatic union (*but* which, by the fact that human beings are free, can be lost). With the help of a bit of oratorical imagination and a good deal of complacency with vagueness, such an amalgam is not difficult to put together. All that has to be done is that the mind modestly abstain from fixing its gaze on each *but* and on the parenthesis which in each of the two cases mentioned contains a truth essentially inseparable from the statement that preceded it.

4. The least that can be said of Bérulle's theology of the priesthood is that, as M. Dupuy points out,[27] it remains "woolly" and sentimental, along the line of affective theology.

Concerning the priesthood of Christ, the great Thomist theologians, Cajetan, John of St. Thomas, the Salmanticenses teach that it is because of His capital grace, which constitutes Him head of the Church, not, as Bérulle believed, because of the substantial grace of the hypostatic union, which made Him the Incarnate Word, that Jesus possesses the supreme priesthood.[28]

Bérulle et le sacerdoce, p. 118 [OP, 87 no. 2].

24   Cf. Dupuy, *Bérulle et le sacerdoce*, p. 118 [OP, 87 no. 2].

25   *Ibid.*, p. 119.

26   *Ibid.*

27   Cf. *ibid.*, p. 103 (especially apropos of the idea, inspired by Denis the Areopagite, that like an angelic choir, priests will form the "choir of Jesus"). Speaking of Bérulle's thought: "Let us recognize the fact," writes the author, "it lacks coherence. If a theological balance sheet were drawn up for it, the entries would be quite sparse. It presents the priesthood in a way that is no more than 'floue' (woolly, vague, hazy)." Cf. also, in the conclusion to the same work, pages 243–244 and 248–249.

28   Cardinal Journet holds faithfully to this great doctrine of the Thomist school on the priesthood of Christ. The same is the case for the ministerial priesthood of our priests (*non-conjoined* instruments), the priestly character, sacramental grace. Cf. especially *L'Eglise du Verbe Incarné*, 1 (Paris: Desclée de Brouwer, 1941), pp.

Other theologians of great renown, among them my dear teacher Father Garrigou-Lagrange,[29] like Bérulle, hold that what formally and directly constitutes the priesthood of Christ is the substantial grace of union with the uncreated Word; it is then by reason of the hypostatic union itself, by reason of the Incarnation, that Christ would be Priest as He is Mediator.

I think that this theological thesis must be flatly rejected. It forgets that Christ IS first Mediator *in His very being* as the Incarnate Word, or as Man-God, before ACTING as such; for "to be a priest" is to have the power to exercise a mediating *action* and, above all else, to offer sacrifice. Hence it is *radically* by reason of the substantial grace of the hypostatic union, by reason of the fact that through this grace He is man, but it is *proximately* and formally by reason of His capital grace—of the grace of the virtues and the gifts (understood in as much as He is head of the Church) which is present in His soul in limitless fullness—that Christ is the priest of the new and eternal alliance, just as it is proximately by virtue of this grace of the virtues and the gifts that He does all that He does.

Christ is mediator *in His very being* by reason of the substantial grace of the hypostatic union. And He is mediator *in His action* by reason of the infinite sanctifying grace that reigns in His soul; it is in virtue of this personal grace—which is also His capital grace[30]—that He carried out that work, which is adorable above all others, for which He was sent: The sacrifice of the Cross is the *mediating* act *par excellence* and in an absolutely transcendent sense. And it is also the *sacerdotal* act *par excellence* and in an absolutely transcendent sense, inasmuch as He who is the priest of all the good things to come and *"sacerdos in aeternum secundum ordinem Melchisedech"*[31] (Ps. cx, 4; Heb. v, 6) made to the Father, in the bloody liturgy of the cross, and in a homage of cult and ritual that was superterrestrial in its grandeur, an oblation of Himself as victim and Lamb of God, taking upon Himself the sins of the world, to reconcile humanity to God and open to it the gates of eternal life: a sacrifice of infinite value by

---

68–71 and p. 116; and the long footnote no. 2 (criticizing Scheeben), pp. 121–123. (*The Church of the Incarnate Word*, Vol. I, London and New York, 1955, pp. 50–53, 88–89, and the long footnote 2, pp. 93–94.

29   Cf. Réginald Garrigou-Lagrange, *Le Sauveur et son amour pour nous* (Paris, 1933), pp. 190–193. To tell the truth, Garrigou-Lagrange presents this thesis rather like a theological opinion to which he rallies not without some hesitation, for the pages in question are not lacking in expressions like "it seems to me" and "therefore it appears."

30   There is only a distinction of reason between the personal grace of Jesus and His capital grace.

31   This *sacerdos in aeternum secundum ordinem Melchisedech*, it seems to me, ought to be interpreted: according to the order of the Church of heaven, in other words as eternal Mediator and as eternal Priest, who was made such by the personal grace (capital grace) received by the incarnate Son from the Father from the instant He was conceived in the womb of the Virgin.

reason of the infinite merits of the Savior and which abolished all the ritual sacrifices of former times.[32]

5. *There is only one Mediator between God and men, Christ Jesus, Himself a man* (Tim. ii, 5). Christ is the only Mediator, inasmuch as He *is* the Word incarnate uniting in His very being the human nature He received from Mary to the uncreated Son consubstantial with the Father, and inasmuch as He alone was able to accomplish the mediating and sacerdotal *work* of infinite value and transcendence by which He saved the world by dying on the cross.

But this work, which He alone could carry out, He did not wish to carry out alone. As the only one capable of carrying it out, He did not wish to reserve this unique privilege, as if by some kind of jealous selfishness, for Himself alone. In His infinite love, He wishes, through "the superabundance of His merits, growing and multiplying in His living members,"[33] to associate in this unique privilege all those who answer His love with love: in the first place Mary, that immaculate creature whose perfect oblation of a pure creature that she alone as Mother of God could make of herself as she stood beneath the Cross (so that Mary is the only one to participate in the redemptive act itself);[34] in the second place all those who live in faith and charity and participate through the grace of Christ, not, of course, in the act of the Redeemer Himself, but in the effects and fruits of that act.[35]

In my flesh I fill up what is lacking in the sufferings of Christ (Col. i, 24). What exactly is lacking in the sufferings of Christ? "As the Passion of God it is forever gathered up into the eternal. What is lacking in it is its *development in time.*"[36] "What was lacking in the sufferings of Christ," wrote St. Thomas, "was to have been suffered by Him in the body of Paul and the other Christians."[37]

In other words, the redemptive work accomplished by Christ once and for

---

32   Cf. Charles Journet, *L'Eglise du Verbe Incarné*, pp. 71–76.

33   Cajetan, cited by Ch. Journet in *L'Eglise du Verbe Incarné*, 2 (1962), p. 225.

34   Cf. the admirable study of Father Marie-Joseph Nicolas, "La doctrine de la corédemption dans le cadre de la doctrine thomiste de la rédemption," *Revue Thomiste*, 1947, no. 1, pp. 20–44, citations from which can be found in *Le Paysan de la Garonne*, pp. 358–359. (*The Peasant of the Garonne* [New York: Holt, Rinehart, Winston, 1968], pp. 248–249).

35   This is a *secundum quid* and "dispositive" mediation (St. Thomas, *Sum. theol.*, III, q. 26, a. 1). Only the mediation of Christ is "perfective," or brings about as its proper term the union of man with God. "All other mediations are called either "dispositive" because they produce only dispositions toward union with God which Jesus alone can bring about, or "ministerial" because as instruments of Christ, they apply to men, in time and place, the proper effects of the mediation of Jesus." Marie-Joseph Nicolas, *Théotokos, Le Mystère de Marie* (Paris, 1965), pp. 189–190.

36   *Journal de Raïssa*, p. 228 ; *Raïssa's Journal*, p. 246.

37   St. Thomas, *in Col.*, c. I, lect 6 (I, 24).

all, in order for it to extend throughout all ages, requires that not only in heaven those who have been saved by Him love us and pray for us and be continually at work in our behalf, but that on earth too all those in whom He dwells by His grace love and pray and suffer the pains of the cross as He himself did.

As they complete in this way what is lacking in the sufferings of the Savior, they add absolutely nothing to His infinite merits, compared to which their merits are but small change. What they do is *apply* them (under the motion of the Spirit of Christ). They apply them little by little for the salvation of their poor brothers, who spend one moment after another in the history of this poor earth. They apply them inasmuch as the whole weight of their sufferings and their love, assumed by the Church, the Spouse of Christ (whether they belong to it visibly or invisibly), is integrated into the work of salvation by which this work itself *applies* to men, the infinite merits of Him who accomplished this work in its fullness.[38]

This is the co-redemption to which all Christians are called. It does not at all ask them to be superchristians but simply to be (and this involved God know what agony for the most saintly among them) *Christians to the end*. This is what St. John of the Cross had in mind when he repeated the words of Denis the Areopagite: "Of all things divine, the most divine is to cooperate with God for the salvation of souls."[39]

Placed in its entirety under the sign of the redemptive cross, in whose power all members of Christ are to participate, in the deepest recesses of their hearts, in the love and the pain of each day, applying the merits of Christ wherever God pleases, this co-redemption continuing from age to age is the work *par excellence* of the *royal priesthood* of God's people, of that immense throng which lives in the grace of Christ—men and women, clergy and laity, great saints and old stragglers, all of them "priests" in the broad analogical sense, and as mysterious as the hidden corners of the human soul. This is the work which is directed toward the ceaselessly renewed miseries of history, by the torments all these people undergo and by the charity that is in their hearts, by the effects and the fruits of the adorable Mass, bloody as it was, which Jesus, the eternal priest, alone, once and for all, suffered before the eyes of men and angels on the day of His passion and death.

6. The priest is called in a very special way through his holy function itself to take part in the mediation of co-redemption I just spoke of, but he is called

---

38   Cf. Paul VI, *Profession of Faith* (*The Pope Speaks*, XIII, 1968, p. 279): The Church "is the seed and the first fruits of the Kingdom of God, through which the work and the sufferings of Redemption are continued throughout human history . . ." Cf. also *Dogmatic Constitution of the Church* (*Lumen Gentium*) I, 7, in (*The Documents of Vatican II*, ed. Walter M. Abbott, s.j. (New York, 1966), pp. 20–22).

39   Testimony of Elisée des Martyrs, "Avis sixième" in *Obras de San Juan de la Cruz*, 5, ed. Silverio de santa Teresa (Burgos, 1931), p. 351.

to it along with all those who live in faith and charity, and not called more forcefully than they are (it may well be that certain laypersons, a St. Benedict Labre, a St. Monica, a St. Elizabeth of Hungary, "fill up" far better than many a priest "what is lacking in the Passion of the Savior"). As we have seen, the state of life of the priest is the same as that of most ordinary members of God's people.

The mediation which he is called to exercise as a priest is of a completely different order: This is a "ministerial" or functional mediation which he exercises in the hierarchical structure of the Church, in which he is endowed with the canonically fixed authority to transmit to men the truths of the faith, to celebrate in their midst the sacrifice of the altar, to give them the body and blood of Christ, and to confer on them the graces of the other sacraments—without his having in any way to be a superchristian in order to acquit himself of these holy functions as such.

So let us now consider the priesthood of the priest in its relation to the priesthood of Christ. If, according to the thesis that I hold as true, the priesthood of Christ, which evidently presupposes that He be a man, radically depends on the substantial grace of the hypostatic union, but is derived directly and formally from His capital grace, then it is not difficult to see how a priest participates in the priesthood of Christ. The anointing received by the priest confers on him at one and the same time both the grace of the priesthood, as a particular modality of habitual grace (calling for the appropriate actual graces), and the priestly character as well, along with the powers it implies. By his ordination he is a priest in completed act (a priest in all its fullness in the case of episcopal ordination). And he participates in the priesthood of Christ as an instrument (non-conjoined) which Christ (and, in a certain sense, the person of the Church)[40] make use of in the whole sacramental order.[41]

But if one holds that the priesthood of Christ comes formally and directly from the substantial grace of the hypostatic union, and is one with His being as the Divine Person Incarnate, one is almost inevitably led to think with Bérulle that the anointing received by the priest at the time of his ordination makes of him a *conjoined* instrument of Christ, and His own *hand*, the hand that the Divine Person makes use of to act among us.

How can any clear and precise theology of the priesthood be constructed

---

40   Cf. my book *On the Church of Christ* (Notre Dame and London: University of Notre Dame Press, 1973), pp. 145–146.

41   With respect to Preaching the Word: What, in itself, and above all else, makes of a man a priest is the power of transubstantiation. But this itself presupposes that the community in which he receives Holy Orders was itself born from the preaching of the Gospel. "Announcing the good news of the Gospel"—teaching the truths of the faith—is thus (cf. the *Decree on the Ministry and Life of Priests [Presbyterorum ordinis]*, ch. II, 4, [*The Documents of Vatican II*, ed. Abbot, pp. 538–540]) the first *in time* of the functions of the priesthood in the strict sense of the word, whereas in a broader analogical sense, it is to this same thing that the entire "priestly people" is called—in bearing witness to Christ.

on such a basis? Will it have to be declared that the priest is a man whose person, by the very fact that he is a priest, cedes it place to the person of Christ in such a way that, if in his spiritual life he must annihilate himself to the point of losing his own subsistence, it is because his lived experience must bring to his consciousness the fact of what he has been made in reality by his ordination? He has been *transpersonalized*, and this is the reason for which the sacrament of Holy Orders has constituted him in a state of sanctity. The grace of the priesthood in him will produce its effect in completed act only when he has reached eminent sanctity; up till that moment he is no more than an incomplete priest. And if he happens to fall into a life of mortal sin, he becomes a monster; he ceases entirely to be a priest, all the while retaining the sacramental powers conferred along with the indelible mark imprinted on his soul, and which from then on marks him out for the wrath of God. . . . A whole treatise could be worked out in this style: a piously delirious theology.

7. The point here is certainly not to attribute such a theology to Bérulle. He was saved from this by his lack of precision and by his very manifest aversion (and a very intelligent aversion at that, for he was quite suspicious of the difficulties of such an undertaking) an aversion for any effort to put his own thinking about the priesthood into some systematic form by giving it a solidly reinforced structure.

The same must be said of his famous disciples, Condren, Bourgoing, M. Olier, and of the French School in general. Above all else they wanted to look more deeply into his spiritual doctrine. I imagine that these men, whose eminent piety was joined to a vast culture and to a humanism that was exceptionally open (even to the extent of encouraging good Monsieur Descartes in his philosophical reform which they thought destined for the service of religion) found it repugnant to submit to the control of theological reasoning, out of some strange sort of humility, the sacred ideal of priestly holiness that they devoted themselves to living and propagating. The intelligence is a good thing since it loves and seeks the truth. But if one begins by accepting its despotism and proposes to satisfy its demands before all else, does one not run the risk of pride? This is possible, however one also runs the risk of illusion . . .

The French School did an immense service to the Church by insisting with admirable zeal on the sanctity toward which the priest has the duty to strive. This service however could be of only limited duration because it was ambiguous and because to promote a great good it sought the help of a number of false ideas. The great reproach that can be made against it is that it promoted an illusory sublimation of the priesthood through a misunderstanding of its true grandeur.

8. *Illusory sublimation*: Shall I repeat the many remarks I made on this matter above? The belief that "God took on flesh" is absolutely and strictly the very same thing as "God made Himself a priest"; the belief that the priest is a

superchristian, and even more than that; the belief that he is a conjoined instrument of the Savior; that he enters into His divine Person; that by his ordination he is constituted in a state of perfection and sanctity; finally the belief that through this very state all those things that he happens to do *in the exercise of his functions* are marked with the seal of the sacred. . . . The French School went so far in this direction that, at least in more recent times, many of those it formed believed that the priest communicates a higher dignity to and actually sanctifies whatever he happens to do *in his ordinary life*. Some even thought (contrary to Bérulle) that any act at all accomplished by a priest—trimming trees, fixing a watch, turning or soldering a piece of metal, indeed even scolding his altar boy or eating a meal with friends—is a sacerdotal act.

Let us put aside this last pious excess as unattributable to the venerable masters themselves. In any case, the point of convergence of the great Bérullian themes mentioned above is still there: We were to believe that from the moment that he does something in the exercise of his functions, the priest, *because his ordination, in making him the hand of Christ, constituted him in a loftier state than that of the ordinary Christian*, then acts as being *of Christ* by privileged right and brings to men a ray, sometimes a bit obscured (but in such a case we shed a furtive tear and then quickly pull the veil), a ray which emanates from Christ—and from the Church; we were to believe that from the moment that he acts in the exercise of his functions, *he commits them both by his own behavior* and that for whatever he happens to do or say, the divine Person of Christ and the holy person of the Church are in some way responsible. *Sacerdos alter Christus*—is this maxim, which is valid for the priest at the altar or in the confessional, just as valid for whatever, in the exercise of his functions and in the sphere of the office confided to him, he may happen to do (like the judges of the Holy Office condemning Galileo) or happen to say (like Bossuet proclaiming in the cathedral of Metz that the Jewish people is a monstrous people whom God has preserved as an enduring example of His vengeance)?[42] Was it *Christ* or the *Church* who through them did and said these things?

If we reflect on the fact that for a long time now the moral and spiritual climate under which our future priests were formed has been the climate of the great sublimating themes I just mentioned, we find it less difficult to explain why young people today, suddenly discovering what is so illusory in these themes—and no longer able (so much the worse for poor Denis the Areopagite) to see in priests *the religious of Christ*, gathered around Him like an inspired heavenly choir through which all His graces come down to mankind—turn in a natural reflex, one that is only too natural, toward the opposite extreme.

After this, two other remarks can be made about the French School.

In the first place, we should state that in general, when an ideology capable of inflaming the human heart is used in the service of some practical end, it

---

42   Cf. my book *On the Church of Christ*, pp. 200–211 and 166–167.

has all the more chance of seducing people the more that ideology itself remains vague. Now in this case it is in the service of an eminently noble practical end, one dear to the hearts of all Christians—the sanctification of the priest—that the central ideas of Bérulle and the French School concerning the priesthood are to be found. It is not astonishing that, far from being unfavorable to these ideas, the very absence of any rigorous systematization helped to give them a preponderant influence during three centuries. Nevertheless, even though the will is a good thing in itself, any trace of wishful voluntarism is a dangerous thing for theology and the sign that one day or other it will have to breathe its last sigh.

In the second place—here we come across a far subtler phenomenon and at first glance more surprising. How is it possible that a great number of Churchmen remain under the sway of the French School while at the same time they have doctrinal positions on the priesthood that are totally different? We can only believe, it seems to me, that having been more or less formed by this School in their youth, they received unforgettable graces from heaven through the lofty spirituality they were taught there, and whose Platonic blemishes they were all the less capable of recognizing as it was presented in a vague theology that escaped any rigorous intellectual systematization (and consequently any critical examination). The intellect may later have been able to repudiate the imprecise theology undergirding this spirituality; its imprint nevertheless remained deeply engraved in the soul's sensitivity—in short the French School has continued to exert its influence in *the affective order*. And so it happens that the great Bérullian themes have been integrated into what they hold most dear in their spiritual life, even without their knowing it, by servants of God who are among the best and the holiest; at the same time there are others, equally among the best, who hesitate to meddle in any way with these themes because for a long time now—as if illusion could ever find lasting protection!—the way in which they sublimate the priesthood was considered the guarantee *par excellence* for maintaining the respect we owe to the Church's ministers. (And not only are we supposed to respect them, but to love them as well.)

Here we can understand what an immense influence the French School has enjoyed and in fact still enjoys (but for relatively few years, we can be rather sure), an influence which is exerted first on its own disciples, but which extends to a great many minds in whom it is no more than affective, and to which we find tributary, by excesses in the opposite direction to which their violent reaction gives rise, those adversaries who today dream of putting the sacerdotal function by means of any ideology at all in the service of the socio-temporal. Blest be that great theologian who, to extricate the clergy from the crisis in which it is struggling so painfully, will one day develop a sound theology of the priesthood, made new with the help of the theology of the old masters! He will have answered to one of the most pressing needs of our time.

9. Illusory sublimation of the priesthood *by a misunderstanding of its true grandeur*, I wrote above. As a conclusion to this article I would like to take the liberty of saying just how I see this grandeur, I who in self-flattery can find nothing else to say about myself except that after too long a life I have at least acquired a little bit of experience. In my view the grandeur of the priesthood is a grandeur of a purely functional order, but I have no doubt that the function of the priest is the highest—and at the same time the most exposed and the most heavily burdened with crosses—that a man can be called to fulfill.

Let us repeat once again: the *state of life* in which the priest is placed is no different from that of the ordinary Christian. It is because of the *function* conferred on him that the sacrament of Holy Orders makes of the priest someone "set apart" for God (set apart by his function, not by his state of life). On the one hand, the sacerdotal *character* leaves on his soul an indelible imprint: by it he becomes a sacred object, in a way like the paten or the chalice he uses at the altar—and this is there for all eternity, even in hell, where undoubtedly such an imprint brings down on him a number of supplementary discomforts. On the other hand, and especially, the *grace* of the priesthood makes his function a holy function; henceforth he is the mediator between God and mankind, he is charged with the celebration of the Mass, the sacrifice of God the Savior for all mankind; he is charged with transmitting the grace of the sacraments and, in union with his bishop and the Pope, with teaching them the divine Truth.

I show respect for the consecrated hands of the priest; I like to kiss them as we kiss a crucifix; and I show respect for the person of the priest, whatever he may be as a man; I bow my head when I see him. This is why I cannot help missing the quaint, outmoded external signs that reminded us of this function, the threadbare cassock, the shoes with buckles, the wide black shovel hat . . .) I know that the priest like the rest of us, only in a very special way, has, in the midst of all his sometimes miserable tasks and all the often crushing worries that they entail for him, the obligation to strive for the perfection of charity and for the union of love with his Master. I know that he can succeed in this, and that a holy priest, at once because of his function among us and because of what grace and sorrow have led him to become, is what is best in all the world. And I thank divine Providence for having let me know several such priests: living examples of a magnificent freedom of spirit joined to an inflexible love of the truth and of the attention that must be given to "expanding our hearts enough to admire everywhere, and understand as much as possible, the freedom, the breadth and the variety of God's ways."[43]

The fact remains that the conditions of existence and the state of life of the priest are in themselves (unless he has chosen the religious life, which is not required of the priesthood, nor is the priesthood required of it) the same as the conditions of existence and the state of life of ordinary Christian people. Like

---

43   *Raïssa's Journal*, p. 154.

all the others who make up these ordinary people he retains the disposition of all he has here below, and he retains as well the most precious good in nature, the disposition of his conduct as he decides of his own free will. It is true that the Church, at least in the Latin rite, which extends through the whole of the West, demands of him that he give up the right to found a family, but this is not because of the state of life in which one leaves all for God; it is only to better satisfy the demands of a function—working for the salvation of souls—which demands total devotion of him who exercises that function. However, for other reasons, many find it desirable today that a regime which, while maintaining this general discipline, would permit marriage for priests in certain determined cases.[44]

From the very fact, the marriage exception apart, an exception which perhaps some day will lose some its rigor in the Church of the Latin rite, that the state of life of the priest is that of ordinary Christians, it should be considered normal that he earn his living by his own work—manual or otherwise—on condition of course that the time required for the exercise of his priestly functions is not found drastically reduced. This would seem possible through a cooperative organization that would permit part-time work. Then too, work in the midst of men, his brothers, who share their existence with him each day, holds the possibility of very considerably enlarging his contacts with them and of making them feel, however obscurely, that he is in the service of a God of love.

But the point I am insisting on here—namely, that it is solely the holy function exercised by him, and in no way a more perfect state of life, that distinguishes the priest from the common run of Christians people—has other consequences that should be pointed out as well. If the function of the priest confers on him authority *in the order of the means of salvation* that the Church uses to announce the divine truth to mankind, to transmit to them the grace

---

44   As the example of the Eastern Churches (including the Eastern Catholic Church) shows us, celibacy is not linked to the priesthood in any absolutely necessary way. Suppose for example that one day permission were given to men who had been living in the married state for a sufficiently long time, and in a sufficiently irreproachable manner, to receive priestly ordination (as long as their wives were in agreement). We might well ask if the time has not come when the existence of such married priests is desirable, I would even say advantageous, for the priestly ministry itself. Is it not the case that in a multitude of good works—catechism, church clubs, study groups, etc., collaboration between priests and lay Christians is required more and more? And especially in the period of a civilization that is prey to so many crazy ideas, and morally corrupt, does such a collaboration not entail grave risks if it takes place among young people all equally immature in their adolescent mentality? It would seem that such risks would be far less if it were only with married priests—and as much as possible with their wives, less ready now than they ever were to give up keeping an eye on their husbands— that devoted (and sometimes sentimental) young Christian women give themselves to a common apostolic work.

of the sacraments, on the other hand it confers on him *in the order of the social-temporal* absolutely no superiority over lay people as such, by reason of which he would enjoy in this particular order some privilege of government, as if he were in a more perfect state of life. It is certainly the job of anyone, cleric or lay, who is sufficiently versed in theology to formulate and develop a social doctrine founded on Christian principles; but it is not the job of the priest to organize and direct lay people in their political and social activities. Such activities depend on their own responsibility. And the priest is certainly free to make his personal political choices as he sees fit; but as a priest he must show the same fraternal welcome to all those whom God places in his path, to whatever political party they belong (as long as that party does not involve them in sin).

10. And so, what makes for the grandeur of the priesthood is not a more perfect state of life than that of the ordinary people of God, it is the holy function exercised in the Church for the salvation of souls. The priest is the *sacrificer*, it is he who as instrument of Christ and of the person of the Church, re-actualizes invisibly before us the sacrifice in which the Lamb of God once and for all gave His life to wash away the sins of the world, and which the Church, and we along with it, offer to God so that at that instant in time He might pour forth the effects of His mercy in answer to our supplications. And in a completely different sense the priest is sacrificer—inasmuch as he brings God's sword into souls by faithfully teaching them the Gospel and all that it demands of them, as well as by demanding a "firm purpose of amendment" as a condition for the absolution he gives to sinners ("Go, and *sin no more*," said Jesus to those whom He pardoned).

And the priest is *sacrificed* as well. God exposes him to every kind of blow in the midst of the world, with unparalleled responsibilities since they are responsible for souls—betrayed by the ingratitude or the futility of the greater part of those for whom he wears himself out, and often by the negligence and mediocrity of his superiors. To make his way toward the sanctity to which he is delegated in a very special way by his holy function, he does not have, except in those relatively rare cases in which he has chosen the religious state, the help of a rule and the vows of religion. He must make his way alone, at his own risk and peril—*singulariter sum ego donec transeam*—toward God Who does not fail to send him His grace, but Who respects in him, as in every man, the freedom each of us has to escape Him. In other words, God gives more importance to the common good of His people and to the function the priest exercises in their regard than to the personal good of the priest. This is precisely—and this is what the French School does not see—because the priestly function is of such immense and absolutely capital importance for the Christian people and for humanity as a whole, that not only the earthly happiness of the priest, but also the help he would receive if by his ordination he were placed in a more perfect state of life than that of ordinary people, is sacrificed to this holy function. Does not one single Mass, with its infinite extension, have an incomparably greater value, in the order of intercession for the world, than the entire life of sanctity of a pitiful human being? On the other hand—in the order of the union of love, which is so dear to Him Who is Love itself, between Him and this pitiful human creature (but who was made in the image of God)—is not a bit of true sanctity and of the ardor of grace in a single person worth far more than the attendance at Mass of many others who have their minds on nothing but their business and their pleasures? Let us, however, never forget the absolutely transcendent mystery to which the function of the priest is attached: *at each Mass Christ dies for us*, not that His death is repeated or continues there, but because at all the Masses which follow one upon the other throughout time an *eternal* sacrifice is carried out: while having taken place at a unique moment in time, it is gathered up into the eternal, since it is the *human* death of a *divine Person* incarnate.

Finally the priest is himself constantly *eaten up* crumb by crumb by the miserable flock he is charged to lead to eternal life and which demands of him the perpetual gift of himself. It may happen that parish structures change, in such a way that by working in teams the priests of one particular section in a diocese find themselves freed from an isolation that is only too cruel. Still it will always be demanded of the priest who is responsible for souls to know *nominatim* each one of them who may need him and to maintain with each of them person-to-person relations that end up devouring his own person. And then there is not just the flock confided to his care. His function as a mediator makes him a witness of the Gospel among us; it demands of him—he has become more conscious of this today—to open his heart to all the misery of the world; he hastens to find out about it, to keep himself informed about what it is like in far-off countries, to become involved in it as much as he can when it is near him, to cultivate a taste for it: He feels the obligation to consecrate to it a good part of his prayer. He tries to remedy it a bit by those initiatives of fraternal charity which have never been lacking and which humans will always need. And certainly it is not his business to wage political and social battles to make a decadent civilization less inhumane, nor to let himself become involved in any kind of dissident and rebellious propaganda whatever, but it is his business to bear witness with his words by proclaiming the truth for all to hear when he has before his eyes some injustice or cruelty. All the requests and the supplementary forms of anguish I just mentioned end up tearing him to pieces and causing his life to be devoured by his neighbor.

Let us say that both as sacrificer and as sacrificed and eaten—as was our Lord Who gave Himself in the supreme generosity and the ultimate accomplishments of His priestly work—the grandeur of the priest and of the priesthood is by its essence a *eucharistic* grandeur.

CHAPTER XIX
A SUPPLEMENT TO THE BOOK *ON THE CHURCH OF CHRIST* (II)

THE SONG OF SONGS[1]
An unauthorized translation for private use
FOREWORD

1. NO TEXT HAS EVER BEEN SUBJECTED to such a multitude of discordant interpretations as has the Song of Songs. Those that catalogue it as a song of carnal love, a hymn dedicated to the charms and duties of conjugal life (why not a libretto for family theater, as Renan would have it), or as an erotic poem, indeed one of the most obscene, all these should be thrown into the trash, for the simplest and most evident reason: No song of carnal love could ever have attained the extraordinary splendor of this most beautiful of all poems.

André Chouraqui[2] calls our attention to the fact that the Song of Songs, which belongs to the sapiential *Scriptures* whose content was definitively fixed, after much discussion, during the period of the second Temple, has been venerated ever since then in Jewish tradition as the sacred song *par excellence* and chanted in the synagogue every Friday at the evening service. This same author points out as well that "the authorized exegetes are not at all embarrassed at the importance given to the flesh and blood of the Sulamite; for them there is question here *of nothing else* than the mystical union of Israel with its God. The *Targum*, the Midrash, and the rabbinical texts see in the Song of Songs *nothing else* than an exposition of the historical drama of Israel in its three great acts, the departure from Egypt and the biblical period extending to the destruction of the Temple; the exile, and finally the messianic redemption. . . ." From the Christian position, this same interpretation (cleansed of the results of rabbinical imaginations that were at times strangely arbitrary) is followed by modern exegetes, at least by the rather small number of them who do honor to their science.[3] In the eyes of these masters whom I love and admire, without

---

1   *Privately published* in Toulouse in 1971 at the Imprimerie du Centre.

2   Cf. A. Chouraqui, *Le Cantique des Cantiques, suivi des Psaumes* (Paris: Presses Universitaires de France, 1970), preliminary remarks, pp. 6, 7, 12; and André Feuillet, *Le Cantique des Cantiques* (Paris: Editions du Cerf, 1953), especially the priceless pages of Chapter III.

3   "If the facts we emphasize are correct," writes André Feuillet (*Le Cantique des*

thinking that it is only with their learned explications that we can read and cherish the Song of Songs and find nourishment in it, this Song, which has all the appearances of a human love song, in reality sings of the mystery of Israel's election and of God's marvelous love for His people. It is an "allegorical poem" which *beyond its immediate signified,*

at the same time as it refers to this love, refers to the great episodes in the history of the Jewish people, in such a way that it requires commentary and interpretation in terms of these episodes and of parallel testimony about them found in the Old Testament.

Evidently the precious explanatory value of this interpretation must be recognized. However I maintain that this interpretation presupposes a *first completely open reading* at once much simpler and much more fundamental, and whose importance is decisive: For it is certainly praiseworthy for the commentator, taking the point of view of the science of exegesis, to give the Song of Songs an allegorical interpretation like the one I just mentioned. Nevertheless, in itself and by its essence, this is not an allegorical poem. Like every great poem, it is an enigmatic poem, in which there is no question of evoking ideas, but rather a question of obeying, in order to give it voice, a spontaneous impulse of the soul that is completely intuitive and supra-conceptual, and in which the resonances of words reverberate endlessly, but which nevertheless goes straight to its object: And this object is "absolute love."[4] *As its immediate signified,* this poem sings of love *in its pure essence.* This is why, while it uses images of carnal love projected with rays of glorious light as its verbal signs, the admirable realism of these images cannot shock or give an instant's pause to the most chaste of souls. The pure essence of love, in fact, is in itself independent of the raptures of the flesh and the senses, which in man are naturally though not necessarily linked to it, and it infinitely transcends them.

And this is also why the Song of Songs is a poem of the pure essence of love at the point where, free of any foreign element, it exults in its full and supreme expansion—the poem of the virgin love between God and His creature. This Song has cosmic import; it offers the entire world to God. But it is essentially a poem of the love between God and the beings He has chosen for himself. So there are three ways—each one true—of reading this Song. If it sings first, and for those to whom it was addressed at the very beginning, about the love between Yahweh and His chosen people, it also sings, prophetically, it sings *above all,* for those who have knowledge of the mystery of the Incarnation, about the love *between Christ for the Church.* And for these last it also sings, as

---

Cantiques, p. 8), one is led to conclude that the modern exegesis of the Song of Songs has almost always wandered off the straight path." However, notes the same author (*ibid.* p. 18), the effort to put things back on track has finally been accomplished by a number of commentators (Father Joüon, Father Buzy, Ricciotti, A. Robert, and, I would add, above all André Feuillet himself).

4   A. Chouraqui, *Le Cantique des Cantiques, suivi des Psaumes,* p. 7.

if in echo, about the love between God and the soul that has abandoned itself completely to Him in the secret of mystical contemplation.

To read it as the song of Christ's love for the Church is to give a *specifically Christian reading* to the Song of Songs. Before being pushed into the background by modern or "scientific" exegesis (whose sole object is to establish the meaning that the authors of the inspired texts consciously had in mind themselves[5] and consciously proposed to communicate), this specifically Christian reading was dear to the heart of the ancients. Even though they multiplied explanatory glosses (of a theological and "parenetic" kind) which were not always called for by the text of the poem,[6] and cultivated a use of allegory that was more or less arbitrary, it was to this Christian reading and to the eminent truth of its essential theme that the Doctors of the first century held fast, Origen, Theorodet, St. Ambrose, St. Gregory of Nyssa, Procopius of Gaza, Justus of Urgel, the *Synopsis Scripturae sacrae* attributed to St. Athanasius,[7] St. Jerome, St. Augustine, like St. Bernard in the twelfth century, and much later, at the beginning of the seventeenth century, Cornelius à Lapide, who took up their rather free interpretations in a tiresomely systematic and rationalized form. Our poor beloved Baudelaire is at the exact opposite extreme of the Canticle. He desperately sought a supernatural ecstasy in carnal love. The Song of Songs lives, in the pure ecstasy of love, by a supernatural ecstasy, in the service of which, in order to sing of it, all the power and beauty of carnal love is enlisted as a pure sign and means of expression, as a reflection without proper consistency on the living waters of poetry.

2. We have just seen that the Canticle can be understood in three different ways, all of which are authentic (and the only ones that are authentic).

In each of these three ways of understanding it, our reading of the Canticle to start with is a *quick, fresh first reading* done in the light of that meaning and

---

5   Did the inspired author himself know what he was saying? Put in this way the question smacks a bit of impertinence. However, it is not impertinent, but simply and certainly true, to affirm that he did not know *everything he was saying*. We know more, in the light of Christ who came to us, about what the author of the Song of Songs tells us than did the author himself. This is why the kind of reading devoted to this text during the Patristic age was not only well founded but necessary, even if such a reading enveloped the text in commentaries as fruitful in themselves for Christian thought as they were futile as exegeses of the Canticle itself and as interpretations of the meanings that the text bears within it.

6   See below, pp. 449–450.

7   Cf. A. Robert and R. Tournay, *Le Cantique des Cantiques*, translation and commentary (Paris: Lecoffre, 1963), pp. 45–47; and A. Feuillet, *Le Cantique des Cantiques* p. 128.
     Like the Fathers, the author (Gilles of Rome?) of the second Commentary on the Canticle attributed to St. Thomas sees in this *melodia spirtualis* that the Canticle is a dialogue between Christ and the Church.

this reading is determined by the answer to a single simple question: From the perspective we have taken, who are the speakers in this dialogue?

To say that this first reading is exact and correct is to say simply and solely that it is legitimate to attribute to each of the two speakers the identity with which this reading invests them.

After these few precisions in our vocabulary, I have two remarks to offer.

First remark. According to meaning no. 1 (the Old Testament meaning, which can also be called the *original* meaning), the first reading (which sees in this inspired poem *the love song between Yahweh and Israel*) is an incontestably exact and correct reading; and the primordial idea that it offers to the mind (the house of Israel is the beloved bride of Yahweh) is an idea that is true in itself (which we Christians however call an idea that is *basically* or only initially true because the first reading from which this idea is derived is the reading that was the original *aim of the human author of this inspired poem*.

From the time the Canticle was composed about the middle of the fifth century before our era, Israel has faithfully held to this original authentic meaning.

According to meaning no. 2 (the New Testament meaning, which can also be called the *prophetic* meaning), the first reading (which sees in this inspired poem the *love song between Christ and the Church*) is an incontestably exact and correct reading; and the primordial idea that it offers to the mind (the Church is the beloved bride of Christ) is an idea that is true in itself—and this time we can say that it is true *par excellence* or *supremely* true because the reading from which the idea is derived was the *aim of the divine Author* (and of Him alone) *of this inspired poem, through the Holy Spirit who made the human author say more than he knew he was saying.*[8]

This is the authentic (prophetic and Christian) meaning to which the Christians of the first centuries and their great doctors were so deeply attached. Naturalist commentators, of course, consider meaning no. 2 as purely mythical, just as they do meaning no. 1, which, in their hypotheses about what the author had in mind, they replace with fictions of their imagination, and a rich variety of more or less ingenious absurdities. The same can be said for a number of Christian exegetes. As far as the eminent men of learning who have renewed the modern exegesis of the Canticle are concerned, they do not of

---

8   As regards meaning no. 3 (according to which St. John of the Cross understood the Canticle), I would say that this is an authentic meaning but a meaning by *derivation* and not, as in the case of meanings no. 1 and no. 2, *purely and simply*. According to meaning no. 3, the first reading (*the love song between God and the soul that has entered into mystical union*) is an exact and correct first reading, but *by analogy*, and not, as is the case with meanings no. 1 and no. 2, *by direct signification*. And the primordial idea that this reading offers the mind (the soul that has entered into mystical union is a consecrated altar for Christ and His bride) is an idea that is true in itself, but first *in an experimental way*, then finding confirmation in the Canticle by way of *analogy* and resemblance.

course hold meaning no. 2 in disdain, as the naturalist commentators do, but (because the commentators of the patristic era had nothing to do with scientific exegesis) they put that meaning aside to devote themselves entirely to meaning no. 1, as Jewish commentators were accustomed to do, though in a completely different spirit than the latter. The Rabbis in fact sought a kind of theological elucidation which would reveal the broad and mysterious implications of the Canticle; whereas modern exegesis proposes above all to establish the most rigorous possible literal meaning—and this, at least among the best of their representatives, excludes in advance a swarm of sometimes delirious fantasies to which the rabbinical interpretation of the Canticle finally surrendered.

3. Second remark. I said above that in itself and by its essence the Canticle is not an allegorical poem but a work of the most *genuine* poetry inspired from above, singing in a spontaneous impulse of the soul, about absolute love, about love in its purest essence: originally the love between Yahweh and His chosen people; prophetically the love between Christ and His Church; mystically the love between God and the soul that has entered into contemplative union.

Nor is the first reading we give to the Canticle in any one of its authentic meanings an allegorical reading. In each of the three meanings, the reader grasps directly, and through the primary signification of the poem, just who the speakers are in this dialogue, as what was directly aimed at by the author (human or divine).

However, there is nothing to prevent, on the level of purely intellectual research, a first reading coupled with a *reflexive reading*, in other words interpretative commentaries and learned explications of the general movement of the poem and the particular signification of various verses.

According to meaning no. 1, whether there is question of rabbinical interpretations, careful above all to bring to light the broad implications of the Canticle in all its fullness, or whether there is question of modern exegesis, careful above all to give the precise literal meaning, this reflexive reading is concerned with *the history of the chosen people in its unfolding in time in the midst of the nations*, with the cruel trials, the infidelities, and the miraculous splendors it involved. We know this because this is clearly shown through the biblical context of the Canticle (thanks, in particular, to the method of parallelisms used by the best of the modern exegetes), as well as through consideration of the ambiance in which the man who composed it was situated. His head and his heart were filled with all that—I mean filled with all that made up the history of his people. But we have to be careful! In a general fashion it was in the unconscious part of his poetic soul that he was filled with all of this. There is nothing to indicate that he thought of these things consciously and deliberately; and it was from the unconscious part of his soul that the allusions his imagery makes to all of this emerged and burst forth in flashes of light.

According to meaning no. 2, our first reading leads us to see in the two speakers of the Canticle the Church and the Incarnate Word. It is Christian revelation that tells us this, by what it makes known to us of the mystery of the Church; the Church is the Bride, *sine macula, sine ruga*, of Christ the Savior. And the love which gives her completely to Him is so strong and so ardent that, while she still makes her way here below, this love leads her to fill up "what is lacking in the sufferings of the Redeemer,"[9] and then in heaven, in the perfect consummation of the union between the two, it will equal the love which burns for her in the human heart of the Incarnate Word.

When we read the Canticle according to meaning no. 2 (just as when we read it according to meaning no. 1, but perhaps even more so), the first reading is evidently what is most important of all. Can this be coupled, as is the case with meaning no. 1, with a reflexive reading which on the level of rational knowledge tries to give an interpretative and explanatory commentary on the text? I am far from certain, but I hope so. I hope that some day a good specialist in mystical theology will attempt to provide us with such a commentary.

But, in any case, it is clear that this reflexive reading could not be the same as the kind that is fitting for meaning no. 1. In the reflexive reading proper to meaning no. 1, to a certain degree, recourse may be had to the notion of allegory because in this case the commentary refers to a whole series of things and events in this life which help us understand the lines of the poem. Recourse to the notion of allegory, on the contrary, is in no way possible for meaning no. 2 because, for this meaning, the reflexive reading must go as directly as the first reading to the sacred mystery which dwells in the deepest depths of the person of the Church. While according to meaning no. 1, the reflexive reading would be concerned with the temporal history of the chosen people in the midst of the nations and in its relation with the world, the reflexive reading which would take place at the level of meaning no. 2 would be concerned with *the lived spiritual experience of the person of the Church, the Bride of Christ, in her innermost self, in her relations with her Spouse*, with the stages of the progress of her indefectibly holy love, together with the vicissitudes, the purifying dark nights, the renewals of more profound union with the Beloved and the exalting joys which such a progress involves. And so the commentary on the Canticle, in order to get some glimpse of the doctrinal explanation to give it as a song of love between Christ and His Church, to this end would have to make use of the mystical theology of St. John of the Cross,[10] by bringing

---

9   With regard to their application throughout the ages, not, of course, with regard to the merits. Cf. Col. i, 24.

10   I am alluding here to the *reflexive reading* of the Canticle made by St. John of the Cross. Concerning this reflexive reading and the theological commentary involved I must repeat what I said earlier (p. 446, n. 8) about the "primordial idea" due to a first reading and of which the commentary in question (the mystical theology of St. John of the Cross) is an admirable development. It was by relying on states which he actually lived through that this Saint worked out the great

the lower analogate, the object of meaning no. 3, so to speak, up to the level of the supreme analogate, the object of meaning no. 2.

4. The various authors, however great they may have been, who commented on the Canticle during the patristic age, could hardly speak about the progress of the Bride in her spiritual experience and in her indefectibly holy love through the course of centuries because at the time when they were writing, the progress in question had itself only begun. How could they even attempt to discern the various phases of this progress without there being a history of the Church putting before their eyes, in the world of visible appearances, the factual data from which theological reflection can rise to the invisible world of purely spiritual realities and inquire about the different states through which the person of the Church passes in its relation to the person of its Spouse, and in the progress, the purifications and the wonders of her love for Him?

As little as I know about patrology, I think I am safe in saying, at the same time, that the Fathers and Doctors of the Church were quite annoyed and felt constrained to pass beyond the Canticle in what they said about it, since, even though they saw in it the song of the love between Christ and His Church, they nevertheless could not limit their commentaries to this *single* object—the love of Christ and His Church—which is proper to the specifically Christian meaning of the Canticle, a love whose phases they were in no condition to treat, given the period when they were writing.

They were obliged then to extend their commentaries broadly in vast and free digressions in which, according to the whim of each one's particular genius, there was question, not just of the Church but sometimes, and still more vastly, of the Christian soul in general, sometimes of the entire human race, sometimes of the Church before the Incarnation as it passed through the centuries since the time of Abel, sometimes of the very Church of Christ to come as it would enter into its final stage with Abraham, Isaac ,and Jacob.

These were fortunate digressions, after all. For no doubt they departed from the Canticle itself (each of the three authentic meanings shows the presence of a *bride*: the bride who was the house of Israel—meaning no. 1; the Bride who is the Church of Christ who has come—meaning no. 2; finally the bride— meaning no. 3—who analogically has become, however poor it may be, an individual soul when the loving attentions of the Holy Spirit and the soul's docility to these loving attentions make it worthy of the name of bride). At any rate, when the commentators of the first centuries considered these souls, they did so, not as St. John of the Cross did, solely with regard to those who had crossed the threshold of mystical union, but rather with regard to *the Christian soul in general*. They treated at length those truths which govern the life of every baptized soul in that combat which the soul must wage—despite its own weaknesses, its repeated falls, and its infidelities—in order to follow the call

---

themes of his mystical theology, and it was in confirmation of them that he situated them in the reflexive reading of the Song of Songs.

of grace and remain in God's friendship. They thus established for all centuries to come the doctrinal foundations of Christian spirituality. Let us say that these priceless teachings of the great Doctors of the patristic age were *occasioned* by the Canticle, but not as a strictly valid interpretative and explanatory commentary on the text of the Canticle. And it is in this way that the Song of Songs has in fact played a unique and very eminent role, even though it was indirect, in the admirable theological elucidations from which all later development of Christian thought on the matter of spirituality was to proceed.

5. If it were to be considered impossible to produce a strictly valid interpretative and explanatory commentary (of the theological order) on the song of love between Christ and His Church—in other words a *reflexive reading* of the Canticle according to meaning no. 2—or if no theologian could be found to undertake the project, nevertheless we still have that first reading, more important now than ever; and by itself this reading would be enough to enlighten us in a decisive way on a point I would like to discuss for a moment in order to complete what I tried to say elsewhere about the person of the Church.

Now the person of the Church—that supernatural personality which, as a collective whole, she receives from God because of the image of Christ imprinted in her and which transcends the personality of the multitude of her members—this person of the Church is revealed to us in its most brilliant aspect as the Bride of Christ. But we can envisage this person of the Church from two different angles.

Whereas, on the one hand, from the point of view of the work accomplished by her, the most important aspect for us humans is her mission with regard to us (she is there to help us understand her voice and that of her Spouse, and to give us the grace of the sacraments in order to bring us to eternal life); on the other hand, this time from the point of view of what she is in relation to God and of her very life as a person, there is in the Church something that is just as essential but far more profound in itself that is no less important for us to look at very carefully, and on which we must look with open eyes.

What the Song of Songs actually reveals to us is that the Church must not be considered solely as carrying out on earth the work of her Spouse, and faithfully transmitting His word, and helping Him through the course of ages by her love, her prayers, and her co-redemptive sufferings to accomplish His work of salvation. It is not solely the *work* accomplished by the Church that it is important to consider; it is just as important to consider what is at the very heart of her subjectivity as such. For every person has its *subjectivity*. Now it is the Canticle which introduces us into the most intimate core of the Church's subjectivity.

Whatever is related to this subjectivity itself in its very own life, its particular traits, its characteristic beauty, the experiences in which it is involved and the contrasting states through which it passes, well that *first reading* I am talking about here gives us a glimpse of all of this. This first reading has nothing to do with discursive knowledge; it is thanks to the insightful and discerning emotion of the heart awakened in us by the poet; it is musically, if I may put it this way, and not conceptually that it reaches us and enlightens us and that it is enough, for it is in this way, as if by an admirable symphony, that it introduces us into the secret of the living relation between the created person of the Bride and the uncreated Person of the Bridegroom, into the secret of the mysterious, gentle advances of their love and of the progress here below of the love of the Bride until their union is totally consummated.

The Canticle reveals to us that everything within the subjectivity of the person of the Church—this living relationship between her and the Incarnate Word—is totally given over to a whirlwind of love which through adventures of anguish and of delights that are too exalted and too beautiful for our feeble understanding, carries the earthly Beloved and the divine Lover off toward the radiant summits of the eternal hills.

*   *   *   *   *   *   *   *   *   *

6. It is important to notice that with the chosen people, or the house of Israel, the multitude we are speaking of is a multitude so profoundly rooted in the same faith in a God who reveals Himself and in the same Law received from Him that this people is addressed *as if* it were one single person in the strict sense of the word: "Hear, O Israel . . ." I have not forgotten that Israel considered as a nation was only a "moral person," as is the case with any nation. However what was far more than a simple moral person was the religious Israel—what I mean by this is the ensemble of the just of Israel, an ensemble visible to God alone, let us say *the true Daughter of Sion, the real Israel.* Because this was the Church of Christ to come, "without blemish" and "all beautiful," which had now at last arrived at its final historical stage,[11] this real

---

11   The Church of Christ to come (which is substantially the same—*eadem numero*—as the Church of Christ Who has come) began to exist *ab Abel*, or beginning with the repentant Adam and Eve who had re-entered the state of grace. At the various cultural and religious stages of humanity, as she herself passed through a succession of different states, she was made up of the ensemble of all those souls living in the state of grace and charity; an ensemble which, as such, remained invisible to the eyes of men, and in which elements of visibility were manifested only in a very fragmentary way, through certain formulas of adoration or certain rites of offering which, even in the midst of an environment of error, nevertheless by their nature were directed toward the true God (I am thinking of the altar "to the unknown God" which Paul praised in his letter to the Athenians, Acts xvii, 23–24). It was not the Church of Christ which was acting then as a visible social body offering sacrifices to the unknown God; it was rather a certain number of men who—even without knowing it—by carrying out in the midst of a pagan environment an act of religion addressed as such to the true God, gave a fragment of visibility to the Church of Christ Who was to come. It was only in the last stage of its development—that of faith in the revelation made to Moses—that the

Israel tended toward a personality in the full sense of the word in a particularly forceful way, all the more so as it was the heart of a people itself set aside by

Church of Christ Who was to come (the ensemble of just of the house of Israel) found itself placed in a religious regime freed from any environment of pagan error. Even though it was emerging into a higher unity still only in a way characteristic of an exceptionally coherent collectivity, and into a people that the true God had made His very own, it still tended toward its ontological personality much more forcefully than before. At the same time, thanks to a book in which it read the word of God, and thanks to a body of institutions of divine right, it received a still imperfect general visibility, which was not the visibility of the Church as a social body acting among men, but rather a visibility of religious acts prescribed by these institutions and the teachings of the Bible, which the just of the house of Israel, with the help of the Holy Spirit, made the very life of their souls, and somehow in this way, they already served the Christ whom they did not yet know.

As I indicated in the text it is fitting to distinguish, on the one hand, that ensemble of the just of Israel, who make up the Church of Christ Who is to come—all beautiful and without blemish from the start—which has arrived at its final historical state (this was the Bride of the Canticle according to meaning no. 1, if it is understood by its most mysterious, its most profound, and its most secret content: Bride in a sense that is not yet the full sense but a strictly proper sense, a Bride who in the just of Israel never knew a blemish or committed an infidelity).

On the other hand, and properly distinct from this unspotted Bride, there is the chosen people in its totality, which, because it is linked to God by divine contract, might also by extension and in a broad sense be called the bride of Yahweh. This bride however was indeed far from being unspotted. She was guilty of serious infidelities, and in her head there were many errors which contended with one another, like those of the Pharisees and the Sadducees. And yet she too is the Bride of the Canticle, according to meaning no. 1, but a Bride all of whose faults and infidelities are then entirely forgotten. (See below, p. 455)

If, after this, it is said along with St. Thomas (*Sent*, IV, d. 27, q. 3, a. 1, qla 3) that "the Synagogue" should also be called the "bride" of Christ (*uxor, non concubina*), it is in an improper sense, for in this case the word *Synagogue* is used equivocally, to designate in a general way the religious regime under which Israel was living, whereas if it is strictly understood, it designates only those men who, in the name of the Law of Moses and of the Holy Book, exercised their authority over the people of Israel, and who in the very exercise of that authority were exposed to error and to sin. They are the ones who sent Christ to His death.

It should be added that among the just who made up the Church of Christ Who was to come, once it had arrived, in Israel, at its final historical stage, many converted on hearing the preaching of the Apostles and in this way became visible members of the Church of Christ Who had come; whereas, other just souls, who for one reason or another remained attached to the Synagogue in good faith, keeping themselves in the state of grace, from then on found themselves invisible members of that same Church of Christ Who had come, as would be the case in the course of centuries for all men who without embracing the Christian faith or without ever knowing of it, nevertheless live in a state of grace and charity.

God, and which God consecrated for Himself, with the result that it could already be considered *virtually* and *tendentially* an ontological person (the Church of Christ who has come can alone be considered so *formally*). The Daughter of Sion, carrying within her womb all those souls who, in Israel, were invisibly sanctified by grace and charity, could, with a perfect right, and *in a proper sense* (even though in a sense which is not the full sense of the word, implying the full possession of an ontological personality), be called "bride"— the bride of Yahweh.

Furthermore, by the very fact that it was chosen by God to be His people, and by reason of the Covenant of Sinai, that Israel which was visible to the eyes of men, the chosen people in its entirety, could *by extension*, but with full right, and *and in a broadened proper sense*, receive the name of bride, and be called the bride of Yahweh.

After this, when there is question of the Church of Christ Who has come, we then have to do with a person in the truest sense, in the full sense of the word, for it is no longer just virtually or tendentially, it is formally that this Church is an ontological person, embracing all the members of God's people within one supernatural personality which transcends the natural personality of each one, and which God gives to His Church by reason of the image of Christ that she carries within her. It is in this way that the Church is the Bride of Christ in the most strictly proper sense and in the most fully personal sense of the word *bride*. And it is quite clear that in the Canticle understood according to meaning no. 2, there could be no question, in the mind of any commentator, of the infidelities of this indefectibly holy Bride.

It is quite different in the case of meaning no. 1. The prophets of Israel severely reproached the chosen people, and with good reason, for the faults and infidelities by which, after having been raised to such heights, they betrayed the love and the holiness of the ineffable God by falling again and again into the self-complacency with which they covered their stiff and obdurate necks. What reason is there for surprise if we remember these faults and infidelities in an allegorical interpretation of a reflexive reading of the Canticle understood in the sense which interests us here, according to meaning no. 1?[12]

Yet there is something quite astonishing, something which, by what miracle? determines the completely proper and singular character of the Canticle; I mean that this Song of Songs contains *absolutely no reproach* with regard to the chosen people, with regard to the bride.[13] Here the word *infidelity* is *never*

---

12   Cf. A. Feuillet, *Le Cantique des Cantiques*, p. 18: "The Canticle is at once a lyrical and a dramatic allegory from the middle of the fifth century; this allegory sings of the merciful love of Yahweh for his bride Israel and the return of that bride to grace despite numberless infidelities which were the cause, not only of the miseries of the captivity, but again of the disappointments and sufferings of community after the exile."

13   René Laurentin makes a similar remark in his *Court traité de théologie mariale* (Paris: Lethielleux, 1959), p. 91, n. 12.

pronounced, and there is *never* any question of the faults that bride was guilty of and which brought her misfortunes down upon her. What does this mean? Is it because, according to meaning no. 2, there could evidently be no question of infidelities committed by the indefectibly holy Bride of Christ? Undoubtedly so, and we can see here a sign of the extraordinary power and the extraordinary implications of the inspiration of the Holy Spirit, which make of the Canticle a book that is unique in every way in the Old Testament: a book in which, while making use of the human author of the poem to have him speak of the house of Israel, of the bride of Yahweh, the Divine Author makes him speak as well in a prophetic way of something that the human author had no idea he was speaking about, namely, about the Church, the Bride of Christ. But it is still very striking to note that right away with meaning no. 1, in which there is question solely of Israel and its God, the human author of the poem gives the impression of being completely ignorant of these faults and infidelities of the chosen people which our exegetes, instructed by the prophets, know so well. For his part he certainly knew of them, and better than they perhaps. But his poem does not know them.

When he wrote his poem they remained buried in the underground of his soul like things which absolutely do not emerge in the memory. It is as if they had never existed. Under the omnipotent hand of the Spirit which seized on him, *he forgot them*. Perhaps in this case we can understand Psalm xliv in an accommodating sense: "*Audi, et vide, et inclina aurem tuam, et OBLIVISCERE POPULUM TUUM.*"[14] Forget your people, at least forget all its faults. Lift your eyes only to the bride *who has returned to grace*. Why? Because in the poem everything belongs to love and is for love; because what he is singing of is absolute love, the love of Yahweh for the bride He has chosen for Himself. And God Himself, in His love that is stronger than death, and who asks no more than to pardon, do not His saints make Him forget the sins of men?[15] All the pains and agonies of the Bride are the pains and agonies of love. The failings

---

In the discussion that follows, it is *the entire people of Israel* that I regard, along with our best exegetes, as the "Bride" of the Canticle understood according to meaning no. 1. But let us not forget in the deepest most mysterious depths of the Canticle this same "Bride" is also, and above all—strictly speaking—solely the ensemble of *the just of Israel*, who constitute, in the midst of the chosen people, *the Church of Christ to come which has arrived at its final historical stage*. Cf. p. 451, n. 11.

14 Verse 11.

15 Speaking about the prayer of the saints and their "stammerings of love," Father Dehau writes: "God is sufficient for them," and God is fully satisfied with them. "God does not need anything else. . . . God forgets all the blasphemies, all the iniquities which deserve that the earth be crushed. One asks sometimes why God does not chastise. . . . Ah! It is because God is with His saints, and near them. He forgets. He does not see, does not hear anything else but this stammering of the saints which wins us His mercy."

which are there in the background of history are totally forgotten. How could we doubt this? The Spouse Himself, Yahweh Himself proclaims that His Bride is completely *without stain*:

> *You are all beautiful, my beloved,*
> *There is not a single stain in you* (IV, 7)

7. It seems to me that this is a point that has escaped the attention of our best exegetes and that this constitutes a serious omission. By the fact that they have dedicated themselves to a completely reflexive and expressly allegoric reading of this inspired poem, without seeking (this was not their business) to enter into the personage of the inspired poet himself, as poet, they filled their heads, and consciously so, with the entire historical background of the faults and infidelities committed by Israel. But they put all this in the head of the inspired poet as well, at the precise instant when carried away by divine inspiration all this had gone out of his head.

They tell us that the sleep of the bride is a blameworthy torpor, due to the fact that she has left her Bridegroom and must return to Him; and that this torpor is a proof of the infidelities and betrayals she has committed. Apropos of the first sleep (*Cant.*, II, 7), we read in A. Robert and R. Tournay (*Le Cantique des Cantiques*, p. 108) that "its precise signification is revealed by the parallelism with Isaiah li, 17, and lii, 1, which the author surely seems to have aimed at intentionally. The turns of phrase in Isaiah are closely related to those in the Canticle: 'Awake, awake, get up, O Jerusalem' (li, 17); 'Wake up, wake up, O Sion!' (lii, 1). Furthermore, in Isaiah, the personified Jerusalem is in exile; she is represented as stretched out on the ground in the dust, deep in sleep after having drunk the cup of giddiness which symbolizes the divine anger (li, 17b, 21, 22). An energetic call that comes from God invites her to rise up now . . ."[16] And further on (*ibid.*, p. 110), it is a case of the sleep of the bride being compared to "imperfect repentance," or to "imperfect conversion"—to that piety which is "like a morning mist, like the dew which evaporates in the first daylight hours."[17]

The turns of phrase in Isaiah are described as "closely related to those of the Canticle," except that they happen to say just the opposite of what the Canticle

---

16   "An energetic call that comes from God invites her to rise up now, to shake off the dust of her bonds, the signs of her captivity, to dress herself again in festive garb and to regain her splendor of former times. The two passages, which pertain to the same development, correspond closely to the general situation which forms the background of the Canticle and to the images it uses to translate it." A. Robert and R. Tournay, *Le Cantique des Cantiques*, p. 108—"to the images that it uses . . ."? It must be said that here they have wandered away from the truth.

17   Another thing that should be noted here: it is perfectly true that there is no real conversion without a free act of the will. But "the teaching of this verse" (*ibid.*, p. 111) does not consist in such a trite commonplace. There is no question at all here of a conversion, but only of love.

says, *Wake up! wake up!* says Isaiah. I beseech you, says the Spouse in the Canticle, *be careful not to waken, not to stir up love again* . . . (Cant. ii, 7). And who can see in this verse of the Canticle the slightest trace of an allusion to an unfaithful bride, "stretched out on the ground in the dust, deep in sleep after having drunk the cup of giddiness which symbolizes the divine anger"?

Then too, if in the sleep of the bride is seen the historical background of her infidelities and betrayals which reappeared time and again (ask Exechiel and Isaiah about these infidelities and betrayals), how could Yahweh beg that she not be awakened, He who sent His prophets precisely to arouse Israel from its sleep? And one has to be aroused too from imperfect repentance and from imperfect conversion, that morning mist which evaporates at the first light of day. From this Yahweh never ceased to arouse Israel.

In chapter II of the Canticle, it is immediately after having said: "I am faint with love, his left arm is under my head and his right arm embraces me" (vs. 5 and 6) that the bride falls asleep. She falls asleep in the arms of her Spouse; no doubt he is the one who lays her on the bed where she will continue to sleep. And it is precisely at this moment that the Spouse cries out (vs. 7)

> *I beg you, O daughters of Jerusalem,*
> *By the deer and the hinds of the fields*
> *Take care not to waken, not to rouse love again*
> *Until she wishes it.*
> (let us translate this last line:
> *As long as she gives herself up to rest.*)

Here there is nothing but tenderness. And if instead of saying: "Take care not to rouse my beloved again," the Bridegroom says: "Take care not to rouse love again," it is because the bride, asleep or awake, is totally love itself. The Bridegroom knows that this love has not yet reached its full perfection; it must grow, it must progress toward the eschatological glory that Israel was waiting for, and toward that eternal consummation whose ultimate truth will appear in meaning no. 2 of the Canticle. In that love on the path of progress and increasing perfection (however great the cost) the repose of sleep after the fatigues of the day is still necessary. The Bridegroom contemplates her lovingly in this state of repose, he knows that her heart is awake, he knows that on her own she will open her eyes and rise up to be delivered totally into his blessed hand, working and suffering for him in the burning heat of the sun. He is pleased to wait for this moment of his own sweet will. His earnest entreaty to the daughters of Jerusalem is a cry of confidence, one more gesture of tenderness toward his Beloved.

The second sleep of the Bride (Cant. iii, 5) calls for similar observations.

8. Let us move on now to the reading of the Canticle according to meaning no. 2, as singing of the love of Christ and of His Church.

Earlier I mentioned (pp. 448–449) a few words about the way in which, in my opinion, a reflexive reading of the Canticle in this sense should be done, supposing that this is possible.

I have not the least intention here of undertaking such a reading, which could be the job only of a theologian. The point of view I am taking is that of a first completely open reading. But from this perspective itself, it seems to me that the Canticle can at times, like a flash of lightning, bring to light in the mind, which does not stop here, some question or perception, which, if an attempt is made to look at it more profoundly in the light of theological knowledge, would end up in a reflexive reading. This makes me a bit uncomfortable. I hope that in naïvely forging ahead I will get myself out of this difficult strait, even if I have to touch with reverential fear on some problem that is difficult and new for me.

This said, let us try to get started and make a little headway.

A first point to notice is that the Church of Christ Who has come is endowed, as I already remarked, with a supernatural personality received from God by reason of the image of Christ imprinted within her. She is then—and this is the very mystery of the Church—an ontological person properly so called, a created person made up of a multitude which embraces in its perfect unity the lambs and the sheep of whom, in His own name, Jesus appointed Peter the shepherd. "*Pasce agnos meos. Pasce oves meas.*"[18] This is the Bride of Christ, indefectibly holy,[19] "*sine macula, sine ruga,*"[20] which advances in charity through the course of ages until that final consummation of the love of the Bride and the Bridegroom in the glory of eternity.

Next—this is a second point to note—a distinction must be made between the person of the Church, in its proper mystery and proper reality, and "churchmen" or the "personnel of the Church," that is to say, "those men who by the fact that they belong to the secular or religious clergy, are the officially recognized servants of the Church, and in particular, those who, from the top to the bottom of the hierarchy, have been granted authority with regard to the Christian people."[21] The person of the Church is indefectibly holy, its personnel is not—no more so than are its other members. When the personnel speaks or acts *as the instrumental agent* of the Church (the extraordinary and ordinary magisterium, and the entire sacramental order), we can be sure that it is the person of the Church who speaks and acts through this personnel, with its holiness and its infallibility. When it speaks or acts *as proper cause*, it represents the Church to the degree that it is faithful to grace and to the assistance of the Holy Spirit; it can be mistaken, and clumsily mistaken, and this has been far

---

18   John xxi, 15, 17.

19   *Indefectibiliter sancta*: Vatican II, Const. *Lumen gentium*, chap. V, paragraph 39.

20   Ephes. v, 27: "*Non habentem maculam aut rugam, aut aliquid hujusmodi, sed ut sit sancta et immaculata.*"

21   *On the Church of Christ*, pp. 140–141.

from lacking in the course of history. For all these errors, it is not in any way the person of the Church, but only its personnel which bears the responsibility.

When we think of the exactions imposed by the Crusaders, of the iniquitous treatment of the Jews in the latter half of the Middle Ages, of the Inquisition, of the role the temporal power played in it, of its burnings at the stake, of its habit of considering the use of force as the best way to defend the faith; of all the examples of complacency or of servility given by the clergy, despite a St. Gregory the Great or a Gregory VII, before the powerful of the earth, of all the examples too of the blind judgment of one's neighbor (Catholic neighbors and, especially, non-Catholic neighbors), of personal ambition, of clerical authoritarianism, of the lust for domination, of long-standing myopia in the face of the evidence and exigencies of reality, of the forgetfulness of the Gospels, and of unfaithfulness to what is most important and most necessary in the kingdom of God—in short, when we think of everything to which we can give the general name *compromises of Christianity* with the world and the spirit of this world and with the malice of the time; or, on the other hand, when we think of what might be generally called the *crises of Christianity*, though these crises are far from being strangers to the malice of the time and the troubled influences of the socio-cultural, nevertheless they affect the Church in its proper sphere here below—I am thinking of the development of the various schisms and heresies in which mistakes, blunders, and arrogance are intermingled inextricably from every direction: Well, all of this is in no way the work of the person of the Church; it is the work of its personnel. Still it must be added that, even though in all of this individual sins have not been wanting, in general many things which were of themselves, objectively speaking, very serious failings were perpetrated in all innocence of heart by the human subject simply because Churchmen like everyone else—and even the saints—are *of their time.*

And history also reveals to us an entirely different picture, this time luminous and worthy of the Church, where with our own eyes we can see daily examples of dedication to the truth and to the love of God and neighbor, of the constant giving of self for the salvation of souls, of care of the poor and the defense of the oppressed, of lives offered entirely to Jesus and to his cross, and of an invincible fidelity to the Gospel which can be seen also in the personnel of the Church, not just when it speaks and acts as the instrumental agent of the person of the Church, but also when it speaks and acts as proper cause; in this case I mean proper cause as docile to the demands of the vocation received and the assistance of the Spirit of God.

The fact remains that the spectacle of the failures and miseries of human free will is also there and that it too has its part in that experiential acquaintance with everything that have befallen the Church on this earth and which, given the time in which they were writing, were inevitably lacking to the Doctors of the first centuries.

Let us repeat that in the first tableau we looked at there was question of the personnel of the Church, not of its person. And the level on which we find ourselves is a completely empirical, human, and visible level which has nothing whatever to do with the proper life and the proper mystery of the person of the Church, with its living relationship of love with its Spouse, and with its progress in this love. And yet, with regard to this secret and invisible, this metaphysical and theological order, toward which the Canticle carries us and which is concerned with the sublimities of grace, does not the history of these miserable failures of human free will in the personnel of the Church have, for the mind that jumps from one level to the other, some relation or other that it is almost impossible for us to get a hand on, which nevertheless invites us to ask ourselves certain questions? This brings up the first of two difficult problems that I will have to face up to shortly, and which will force me—in self-defense—at least for an instant to look into the field of reflexivity.

9. It seems to me that a digression ahead of time here would not be inopportune—one about the notion of progress in general, and then one about the notion of progress in charity in particular.

There is a law of history, which I have often invoked, that in the things of this world and of human nature, wounded as it is, there is simultaneously progress in the line of good and in the line of evil. We have to accept this, and we have to think too, given the fact that the goodness with which God and the angels watch over human beings is greater than the propensity of human beings to become corrupted, that progress in the line of good is, after everything has been taken into consideration, greater and more profound, despite appearances and despite our groans, than progress in the line of evil. Primitive peoples were happier than we. But who would want to return to their condition? We know better than they just what the human being is made of, and we are more truly human than they were. A sparrow is less to be pitied than a human being, but we are worth much more than sparrows, "*multis passeribus pluris estis vos.*"[22]

In God's affairs the law of double simultaneous progress no longer plays a role. Here progress is made only in the line of good—evil, when we give in to it, being then no more than a parasite from which, in any event, Providence can realize a profit.

And in this passing from one good to a much greater good which is what progress in charity means, the evil which is in us has only an accidental role to play, I mean to say that by virtue of an accident which is the failure of our freedom, that has proved unfaithful to the loving attentions of grace, it may very well happen, and this is not rare, that repentance is the price of progress in love, and that to advance in grace and charity for us is to quit evil, to pass from evil to good. But what is *essential* to progress in grace and charity is to

---

22   Luke xii, 7.

pass from a certain degree of a priceless good to a higher degree of a priceless good.

Here language is equivocal and dangerous, for the word *imperfection* is often considered (wrongly) the equivalent of the word *evil*, even if it is an involuntary and pardonable evil. The fact is that an imperfection in itself is never an evil, however slight it may be. Charity that is still imperfect is in no way an evil; it is charity at a certain level, and one would have to be mad to consider charity at a certain level as evil, however low that degree of charity may be.[23] One of the worst stupidities we can commit is to confuse the passage from one good to a greater good with the passage from an evil to a good.

In what I call the here-below of his soul,[24] Jesus progressed in grace and charity until that great cry from the cross: *Father, into thy hands I commend my spirit*, which has resounded down through the centuries.

The immaculate Virgin progressed in grace and charity until she died of love, and in her body, which was immediately reclaimed and spiritualized by her blessed soul, she was borne up to be next to her Son.

And both of them, during the entire course of their progress in grace and charity, were without the slightest speck of evil.

And the Church too, in the whole course of its progress in grace and charity, is without the slightest speck of evil, without the slightest trace, in its person, of error, of lukewarmness, or of infidelity. Without any doubt she is "completely involved in sin," but in her members, not in her person:[25] in her person she is perfectly pure. Pure in her heart! And pure in her tears as well: torn as she is "between her Spouse who is God, and her children who are no more than poor human beings, and often enough no more than miserable wretches."[26] The Church's members and her personnel may make her weep; they can never tarnish her; all their failings are theirs, not Hers.

The love of the Bride for her Spouse increases in perfection here on earth, passes from a less perfect state to a more perfect state—this is the source of the trials and vicissitudes spoken of in the Canticle. While in the Canticle according to meaning no. 1 we have to do with Israel that has *returned to grace*, the entire historical background of failings and infidelities that were committed being forgotten, the Spouse of Christ, for her part, never returned to grace, she is and always has been *in grace*. And in contemplating her, her Beloved does not have to forget a single fault she may have committed. For in this case the

---

23   It is true that a soul whose fault is lukewarmness may have *too little* charity to accomplish some act that it ought to do at a given moment. In this case the evil is not the insufficient amount of charity, it is rather the lukewarmness which kept the soul from reaching the degree of charity to which it is called and which it should have attained.

24   Cf. my book *On the Grace and Humanity of Jesus*.

25   Cf. my book *On the Church of Christ*.

26   Thomas Dehau, *Le Contemplatif et la Croix* (Paris: Editions du Cerf, 1947), p. 148.

background is not a historical background, it is the entire background of human frailty, against which the person of the Church is secured. How is this so? By an invincible strengthening of grace which, each time she acts, makes her triumph over this fragility—as contrasted with us, in whom the baptism of water, while freeing us from original sin, leaves behind traces of that sin, wounds in our nature, and involuntary inclinations to some intellectual or moral failure.

10. Here we find ourselves face to face with a complication for which I apologize but which we are saddled with by the realities under consideration. When we say that the Church receives from God a supernatural personality because of the image she bears within her of the Christ Who has come, suffering, dying, risen, and evermore seated at the right hand of the Father,[27] there is question of the Church taken *in her fullness (her integrality)*, for she is one single unique person under two different states, the state of glory and the state of her earthly pilgrimage; and the image of Christ is in the multitude of the blessed in heaven as it is in the multitude of its pilgrims on earth. But when we say that the Church, each time she acts, triumphs over human frailty in virtue of an invincible strengthening of grace, there is question only of the Church *in her peregrinal state*, that is, the person of the Church here on earth; for the Church in heaven, in her beatitude and consummated charity, has no need for such a strengthening of grace. And then, from the perspective of the Canticle, is there no question of the Bride in her state of earthly pilgrimage, in which, through the various phases of her living relationship of love with her Spouse everything contributes to her growth in charity, which is not the case for the Church of heaven.

The baptism of water, which washes away original sin and every other sin, is received by the members of the Church—they were born sinners—and is a new birth for each of them. And from the nuptial bath of this baptism which makes them born again, the Church, as the community of the *re-born*, is herself born immaculate, absolutely pure and free of original sin or any other sin. It is *in order that she remain immaculate like this throughout the entire course of ages* and grow constantly in charity that she has need of a special strengthening of grace received at the very instant she is born without stain, and which, in each of her acts, will make her triumph over human frailty. (For anyone at all, either because he does not possess a divine privilege like Jesus and Mary, or because a special grace does not strengthen him in all his acts, remains prey to this frailty and risks falling victim to it some time or other. It is clear that the Church, *indefectibiliter sancta*, could not run such a risk.)

---

27   If the just of the Old Law, and those of preceding ages, waited in Limbo for the Resurrection and the Ascension to enjoy the beatific vision, is this not a sign that the ontological personality of the Church (it is into her person in heaven that they were received) was given (formally given) to her as the Church of Christ Who has come?

Let us say then that at the very instant when the Church both in heaven and on earth formally receives a supernatural ontological personality, and when the Church on earth—having become a social body visible to the eyes of men and acting among them, perfectly distinct from any temporal order—emerges absolutely pure and immaculate from the waters of baptism received by its members,[28] she herself receives as a person constituted from above a special strengthening of grace, another "baptism," the baptism *of fire and of the Spirit*,[29] which her Spouse gives to her from the instant that she rises in person before Him. Christ gives this baptism to the Church in the world in order to make it victorious over human frailty in all that she herself says and does. He gives it in order to purify, to enflame, and to keep ever pure.

And so it is at the same unique instant[30] that the Church on earth and in heaven receives its supernatural ontological personality, is born immaculate on earth by the baptism of water which gives its members a new birth, becomes a social body visible to the eyes of men and acting among them, and receives here below in her person the baptism of fire and of the Spirit, that baptism which enkindles for all time a conflagration of love.

11. Let me pursue my train of thought to its end. I believe that the mystery toward which I am trying to raise my eyes a bit took place on that day when, in the midst of men and of our sensible world, the apostolic college received the tongues of Pentecostal fire, while at the same time, in the Upper Room,

---

28 The Church in her *person* constituted from above keeps intact throughout the ages (by the strengthening of grace I mentioned) that immaculate purity which she has from the baptism of the "re-born" who are her members. But though these members are sanctified by baptism, nevertheless, exposed as they are every day to failure, they all, even the most saintly (except for the Virgin while she was living here below—she had no need to be baptized!) remain "sinners" to some degree or other, as is declared by the priest and the faithful in the formula of confession at the beginning of the Mass.

    So the Church on earth is destined by her mission to have *in her members* (by what in them *is not* hers) a very close contact with the weaknesses of the flesh and of the spirit and a most profound experiential knowledge of these weaknesses.

29 Welling up, like the baptism of water, from the virtue and the infinite merits of the baptism which Christ was so eager to receive (*"Baptismo autem habeo baptizari: et quomodo coarctor usquedum perficiatur?"* Luke xii, 50), and which Mary received with him at the foot of the cross, the baptism of blood, from the Blood of the Son of God poured out to the last drop. Jesus does not receive this baptism of fire and of the Spirit, but He gives it, and He alone can give it: *"Ipse vos baptizabit in Spiritu sancto et igni,"* Matt. iii, 11; cf. Luke iii, 16.—*"Super quem videbitis Spiritum descendentem, et manentem super eum, hic est, qui baptizat in Spiritu sancto."* John i, 33.—*"Joannes quidem baptizavit aqua, vos autem baptizabimini Spiritu sancto,"* Acts xi, 16.

30 A unique instant, composed of a plurality of "moments of nature."

and for all centuries to come, it was made the *very voice and the sovereignly vital instrument* of the Church henceforth constituted in the being of her personhood as the Church of heaven and earth, and, as the Church on earth, was made victorious, *in her person*, over the characteristic frailty of her members, as well as over the possibilities of evil and error which in them are the result of the first sin.[31]

The apostles for their part remained sinful men but became the unshakable pillars of the faith and the light of the world; they were made the dwelling-places of the Holy Spirit Who enflames their souls, enlightens their minds, guides and fortifies them in their immense mission. And through them on the day of Pentecost, the person of the Church cried out: It is done. Behold I am present here, I, the Spouse of Christ, in heaven and on earth, *Ecce adsum*.

And if, as it is recounted in the *Acts of the Apostles*,[32] they were "baptized that day in the Holy Spirit," it was also as sovereignly vital instruments of the person of the Church on earth, and as made participants in this way, to a certain degree, of that same baptism of fire and the Spirit first received by the Church, but received by her in such plenitude that it freed her in all her actions from our human frailty. What took place in the Upper Room was the sign and the manifestation among us of that unheard-of Event, a corollary of the Incarnation, in which all three Persons of the Holy Trinity took part. Through this Event—after millennia in which the Church of Christ Who was to come, in the diverse states through which it passed, tended more or less distantly toward a personality properly so called (at the time of the last stage it tended toward it quite closely)—the Church of Christ Who has come was supernaturally constituted, in heaven and on earth, a *person* in the first, full, and ontological sense of the word, while, at that very instant, this same person, on earth, was invincibly strengthened by the baptism of fire and the Spirit against human frailty.

This is so because, at the same time that the Church in heaven and on earth received its supernatural personality from the Father, the Church on earth

---

31   On the very day of the Resurrection, Jesus, having said to His disciples: *As the Father has sent me I also send you*, "breathed on them and said: Receive the Holy Spirit. If you forgive men's sins, they are forgiven them; if you hold them bound, they are held bound" (John xx, 21–23). This is sometimes called "the Johannine Pentecost," which is one with the Pascal mystery.

But it is after His Ascension and seated at the right had of the Father that Christ sends the Pentecostal fire to His apostles and makes them speak in tongues, as a manifest sign that, of His own royal authority, He established His Church on that day as the organized City of God, visible and universal, constantly aided by His Spirit. This is why I believe that, on this same day of Pentecost, the Church of heaven and earth received its supernatural personality from God and the Church on earth received from Christ the baptism of fire and the Spirit.

32   Acts i, 5: Ἰωάννης μέν ἐβάπτισεν ὕδυτι, ὑμεῖς δὲ ἐν πνεύματι βαπτισθήσεσθε ἁγίῳ οὐ μετὰ πολλὰς ταύτας ἡμέρας.–Cf. above, p. 461, n. 27.

received from the Incarnate Son the baptism of fire and of the Spirit in its
perfect and limitless plenitude. It is so because God made of this Church on
earth—this created collective person (in the full sense of the word) whose soul
is grace and charity—the Body of Christ and the fullness of Christ, to the most
intimate depths of which the Virgin, blest among all women, and her incomparable holiness are immanent, this Church God made to be the instrument
which the hand of the Father made use of to confer on the Church on earth, its
personality of grace, in indivisible unity with the Church in heaven.[33] And this
Church on earth, triumphing in all her actions over our human frailty, will
remain to the end of ages the immaculate one, the indefectibly holy one drawn
from poor humanity—the Beloved of Christ, the blessed Bride progressing
toward equality of love with the Bridegroom.

12. Now let us take up our two problems, keeping in mind that while it is
important in allegorical exegesis for the commentators of the Canticle in sense
no. 1 to follow in detail the history of Israel in order to keep certain guideposts
constantly in view, when, on the contrary, the Canticle is read in sense no. 2,
the course of events in the empirical world undoubtedly furnishes signs that
can be used anagogically but is good for nothing more than that. To stick too
closely to the course of history would be entirely useless in sense no. 2.

Our first problem has to do with the faults and errors which the personnel
of the Church happen to commit when acting as proper cause. For example,
let us think of the medieval Inquisition and of the primacy given to force and
fear in the defense of the faith. Could someone not ask: Since the Person of the
Church can make *instrumental* use of her personnel to makes its voice heard
by means of it, why did she not, instead of permitting the Inquisition and the
methods engendered by it to be set up, intervene herself by an act of the
extraordinary magisterium to prevent such things from taking place?

Just to ask such a question, which soars into the highest regions of the purely
abstract and the purely timeless, would be proof of a regrettable lack of
common sense. It would be to forget that out of love for her Spouse, the Church
has for its first duty to bring to us men, in each moment of our sad history and
according to all the expansion that it permits, the faith which saves and the
means to salvation, and to keep men in that faith for eternal life, those men for
whom He died and whom He has confided to her care. She is the *keeper of the
vines*, says the Canticle, the guardian of Jesus' vineyard. She feeds his flock in
any given historical age. And when that age is still afflicted with the infirmities
of childhood, these infirmities must certainly be tolerated as a lesser evil. Force
and violence were a part of the climate in which civilization developed during
the Middle Ages, and another climate was neither conceivable nor viable for
people at that time. What was essential and of the greatest urgency for the
Church was to announce divine truth—and to establish Christianity using the

33   Cf. my book *On the Church of Christ*, Chap. XI, pp. 137–138.

men of those particular times: if it was stained with blood and blackened by the smoke of burnings at the stake, too bad; that must be put to the account of those losses that our human nature will not let us avoid.

The Person of the Church surely did not like the Inquisition. She certainly did not approve of it and knew that it would draw down the wrath of God, that it caused Him to shed tears. There was no failing by omission on her part in letting her personnel establish it in those days—only sadness and wisdom. That personnel, like everyone else at the time, was incapable of seeing certain things that were evident in themselves. It would have been simply absurd to wish to keep them from considering as good, even as a holy duty, things which of themselves were not so. It was necessary that time bring a certain maturity. What Vatican II did in the twentieth century could not have been done in the eleventh century.

In our empirical world, this was undoubtedly useful in helping us to discern, in the relationship of love between the Bride and the Bridegroom, a level of perfection that was not very high and an expansion that was lacking in fullness, and to realize that much time would be required to pass beyond that level. But a "mad" boundless love for the Bridegroom was ever at work in the Bride who had to permit her personnel to do what she did not approve of. What we are shown here is the *patience* of the Person of the Church, that sorrowing patience to which she felt herself obliged with regard to the infirmities of the flock committed to her care by her Spouse.

13. Our second problem is of an entirely different order. Here we are not concerned with the patience of the Bridegroom with regard to the infirmities of His flock; here we are concerned with the Bridegroom's impatience to bring about at any price the growth of His Beloved in charity. The mystery then toward which we should raise our eyes is the mystery of the periods when His Beloved, the Person of the Church on earth, falls asleep, and of the periods of darkness She has to live through. Between sleep and the night there are surely certain affinities. And if one looks closely, one is surprised to see with what subtlety and in what a variety of distinctive modes those periods of sleep and the passive nights to which the Bride is subjected are presented in the Canticle. In formulating my most cherished hypotheses on this subject, I am not forgetting that in the predilections of this old collector, the sympathy that he feels for the frailty of their object naturally has had a certain influence (this is, after all, legitimate, at least as far as he is concerned).

First let me point out that the sleep of the Bride is mentioned four times in the Canticle: first in ii, 7; then in iii, 5; then in v, 2; and finally in viii, 4.

The first sleep is neither preceded nor followed by any night at all. After saying: *I am faint with love* (ii, 5), she falls asleep in the arms of her Bridegroom. She falls asleep, yes, but in the sense that the activities of the day have ceased for her. In reality, it is into the highest and most hidden activity, the one that is the most important in the life of the Church and in her living relationship of love with Christ, that He has introduced His Bride. I mean the silent ardor of holy contemplation, with eyes closed to everything else.[34] He wants her to be given over completely to love in contemplation by Love. Daughters of Jerusalem,[35] do not awaken, do not rouse love to all those things it ought to do in its actions among men. Let her remain alone with God as long as she wishes. This is a primary requirement for her progress in charity.

What signs of such a phase in the Dialogue of love between Christ and His Church can we find in the visible and the tangible and in the unfolding of what takes place among us? Here we can think of the Fathers of the Desert and of eastern monasticism, of St. Benedict (sixth century), of St. Bruno and of Citeaux (11th and twelfth centuries) . . .

The second sleep of the Bride (iii, 5) takes place *after* she has passed through the first night (iii, 1–4): this is *the night of the senses*, the tying up of the powers which are meant to help us seek out our good and direct our steps in the midst of life's vicissitudes. *I looked for him but could not find him.* She finally does find him, lays hold on him, and brings him to her mother's house. And there she falls asleep in the sleep of contemplation.

But he says to her (ii, 10): *Go toward yourself.* In its living relationship of love with Christ the Person of the Church must enter more deeply, not only into the mystery of God and His holy ways, but also into the mystery of nothingness which lies in the depths of her very self, into the abyss of impotence which by definition lies concealed in the creature as such. This is why she must first pass through the night, before being led into the silence and peace of a contemplation that is this time more profound and more abandoned than that of the first sleep, so that in this manner she may grow in charity: as if the Church on earth were well taught by the Church of heaven.

What signs of such a phase in the great Dialogue of love can be found in the spectacle that our empirical world presents to us? With regard to the passive night undergone by the Person of the Church, let us think back to all the missteps, on both sides, made by the personnel of the Church at the time (the 9th to the eleventh century) when the schism between Rome and Byzantium had its beginning,[36] and back to the kind of paralysis of the practical discern-

---

34   St. Thomas (or at least the author of the second commentary on the Canticle which has been attributed to him) also considers the sleep of the Bride as the *sleep of contemplation*: "Ne suscitetis *a somno contemplationis,* nec evigilare faciatis *a quiete dulcedinis,* dilectam Ecclesiam, donec velit" (*Opera omnia,* XVIII [Paris: Vivès, 1876], p. 631). This is how Gregory of Nyssa already understood the words "*ego dormio, et cor meum vigilat*" (hom. XI *in Cant.*, P.G., XIV, col. 994).

35   As I see it the daughters of Jerusalem are the blessed souls and the pure spirits of the Church in heaven.
         In the eyes of the cabbalists they were the souls of the just (cf. Chouraqui, *Le Cantique des Cantiques, suivi des Psaumes,* p. 9).

36   Under the title "Note sur l'unité de l'Eglise catholique et orthodoxe," Father M.-Vincent Leroy published a study in the *Revue Thomiste,* in which, making use

of, and criticizing when it was called for, the very important pages consecrated to the same subject by Father Louis Bouyer in his book *L'Eglise de Dieu, corps du Christ et temple de l'Esprit*, he sheds precious light and invites us to some very necessary meditation on this subject.

In my book *On the Church of Christ* (pp. 22–23 and 118, relative to the Person of the Church), I have myself spoken of the Orthodox Church in terms which, after reading this study, now seem to me only half true, and which I now consider far too cutting. This is the reason for this long note in which I would like to explain myself further and correct what I wrote, and in which, without trespassing on the domain of theology, I will express myself as a simple philosopher and have recourse to a simplistic image that is within my reach.

What I think it is absolutely essential to take note of is that, despite all the historical misfortunes, the mutual violence, and the mutual excommunications, a certain unity, lived out obscurely down deep, has actually continued to exist in spite of the schism. One might say that instinctively under the guidance of the Holy Spirit the Popes, even those who expressed themselves in the harshest of terms, always took care, in actual fact, not to push this rupture to the limit: whether they *accepted* in practice, avoiding any formal interdict, many things which make up the very life of the Orthodox Church (such as the validity of its episcopal and priestly ordinations and in general all of its sacraments), or whether in certain cases (as in the matter of spiritual jurisdiction) they themselves accorded *a free delegation*.

Here is the image that comes to my mind. I am thinking of a city composed of a central town and a peripheral town. In the central town everything that has an essential value presupposes an explicit and visibly marked communion with the Supreme Servant of the city as a whole. God crowns this central town with a sun which, in my metaphor, is the symbol of the personality supernaturally conferred upon the Church. But this sun, once the gift has been made to the central town, is a generous sun, which does not wish to be egotistically appropriated, nor constricted in its effects. The sun shines brightly and its rays spill over onto the peripheral town; in such a way that this part of the city, as far as it may be from recognizing the primacy of the Supreme Servant of the city, remains nevertheless in a kind of imperfect communion with him (a communion that is not openly professed, but implicitly, perhaps subconsciously, lived out, and never absolutely denied), and so participates, but by extension, in the privileges of the nuptial crown received from above by the central town.

A singular case, intermediary between the case of Israel and that of the Catholic Church inasmuch as it is directly and fully clothed with a supernatural created personality. The house of Israel remained a "moral person," the object of a divine choice, whose cohesion was so exceptionally strong that she could be called the spouse of Yahweh; and the Orthodox Church is much more than this. But since she participates, as I have just suggested, in the image I have chosen, in the supernatural created personality that was directly and fully received by the Catholic Church, she is an "ontological person," and therefore a Spouse of Christ to a less perfect degree than the Catholic Church.

There are not two Spouses; this is what Father Bouyer saw very clearly. And because of this I thought at first (remembering Pius IX and his letter *Etsi multa luctuosa*) that the Catholic Church alone can be called the Spouse of the Canticle. Today I think this is a much more complicated and nuanced question. I said earlier in this foreword that the Person of the Church can be considered under

ment that is required to conduct oneself properly, into which it fell at that time. Concerning that contemplation by which the Person of the Church enters, after this night, into the house of her mother where she has brought her Beloved, let us think of St. Gertrude the Great (second half of the thirteenth century), of St. Catherine of Sienna (fifteenth century), or of the great St. Teresa and St. John of the Cross (second half of the sixteenth century), and of the other great contemplatives who came after them.

The third sleep of the Bridegroom is mentioned in only one single line (the first line of verse 2 in chapter V) which lifts the curtain on the worst agonies to which the Bride will be subjected. "I am sleeping," she says. When we meditate on this *I am sleeping*, uttered at such a moment, we feel that it weighs very heavily. It is no longer a sleep into which, as in the two preceding ones, she lets herself slip gently. It is a leaden sleep which falls over her. Yet in it, at the very depths of her being, she is anxiously attentive to the slightest indication of her Lover's approach. *I am asleep, but my heart is watching*. As I see it, this is how this unique line where a third sleep is mentioned must be understood: it is still a sleep of contemplation, in which, however, no light remains and none of the sweetness of contemplation; nothing is left but the bitterness and the annihilation which contemplation implies as well, of being completely

---

two different aspects: the aspect of the work she has the mission to accomplish among men, and the aspect of the living relationship of love that she has with her Spouse. It is under this second aspect, and by the treasures of love in which she is so rich, that the Orthodox Church seems to me to manifest, and in what a magnificent manner, her participation in the ontological personality supernaturally conferred on the Church. But under the first aspect, in which there is question of bringing about progress in the explanations of the faith, and in theological truth as well, and of announcing the Gospel throughout all the earth, and of introducing action into the order of socio-temporal realities themselves— it seems to me that in the Orthodox Church participation in the supernatural personality of the Church is far less manifest. (Along with Father Bouyer, Father Leroy points out that the Eastern liturgy "will always be tempted to become a world in itself, a dream world closed in on itself, wanting to substitute itself for the real world, and, not being able to do so, limiting itself to making occult a reality that in great part has remained pagan.")

Let us say then that the Catholic Church and the Orthodox Church *together* are the Spouse of the Canticle, but in a unity that is *very imperfect*, minimal, which it is sovereignly important to change little by little into a unity of perfect act: when (after profound indispensable changes on both sides, and which have only just begun) the Eastern Churches that are now separated, but then reunited, would participate in the election of the Pope and would recognize in an explicit and visibly marked way the universal primacy of the successor of St. Peter, as a necessity for existing and acting in communion with him.

I hope Father Leroy will permit me here to render him a particularly fervent homage for his admirable pages on "the dialogue of charity" that is required today, and to join with all my heart in "the ardent hope" that he shares with us in the conclusion of his precious article.

engulfed in the abyss nothing, nothing, nothing. A sleep which this time precedes and acts as an immediate preface to that great night in which the highest and most precious powers of the soul will be bound and in which the soul will be besieged by temptations to go astray, under the crushing weight, felt in the heart, of having been abandoned by God.

It is in this *dark night of the soul* that the Canticle shows us the Bridegroom (v, 2–4). The Lover knocks at the door, she opens too late, and He has disappeared. *I looked for him and did not find him. I called him and he did not answer.* The guards beat and wound her. Now it is she who beseeches the daughters of Jerusalem, begging them to tell her Beloved if they find him that she is more than ever faint with love. She, the Bride herself, can no longer tell him this, for he hides from her and she does not know where he is. All she can do is sing of the beauty of her Absent Lover: a magnificent hymn of glorification, welling up from the most burning pain, and in which, without knowing it, she will perhaps find him once again to a certain degree at the center of her distress and her desperate desire.

What signs corresponding to what has taken place in this way in the Dialogue of love between Christ and His Church can we find in the visible and the tangible and in the historic events that have taken place among us? Regarding both the third sleep of the Person of the Church and the night of the spirit to which it is a preface, the personnel of the Church, in what it has made visible to us here below, has not been very careful about its contribution of significant edifying examples. All we have to do is think for example of the crises which the rise of Protestantism made so manifest, a crisis in the first years of which there reigned such a vast confusion of minds, and so many ministers of the Church turned to heresy. Or we have but to think of the present crisis as well, in which there is just as much confusion of mind.

All this must be charged to the account of those losses which our human nature will not permit us to avoid. But then God is rich enough in His mercy to let us hope for the salvation of many clerics and of laymen (the clerics are much more numerous in this regard, and far more zealous) who have no idea of what they are saying (this is why they do so much talking).

Then too we might very well ask, in order to be finally done with certain forms of sclerosis (in particular with a certain clericalism fixed fast by history in the mentality that is habitual to many of them, whether they are actually "out of touch with the times" or think they are part of the "avant-garde"), if twenty or thirty years of aberrations that are bent on destroying everything does not have its usefulness, and we might ask too if, on the whole, men being what they are, it would not be good for them, when their ancient wisdom has become so worm-eaten, to spend some time in an insane asylum before entering on a period of renewed wisdom which despite all the waste will probably be an improvement, freer and more open, and will save what is essential in the wisdom of the past.

In any case, what is certain is that, however serious it is, the damage caused within the personnel of the Church and by that personnel are far less important in the eyes of the Bridegroom than progress in charity in the Person of the Church, in its living relationship of love with Him. This is what He wants above all else and at any price: to have His Beloved grow in love. And we know that the sole end of these passive purifications is to bring her to a higher level of love, a level that cannot be attained except by that very price.[37]

The Holy Spirit helps those souls He has chosen for Himself to understand that if they wish to measure up a bit themselves to this great theological mystery, what is required of them is the unshakable gift of their entire self to Truth and to the Faith, a life of mental prayer and union with God that is open to all the misery of the world, a heroic devotion to contemplation along the way (*in via*) to that holy contemplation which will always remain the highest value in the Church,[38] and without which no lasting good can be accomplished. For without it those services demanded by the common good, however necessary they are and however fervent they may be, will in the end turn out badly.

The fact that the personnel of the Church did not understand this at the time of the Counter-Reformation, and that in the present post-Conciliar years it does all it can with even greater ardor not to understand, that is their affair. Nothing can be done about it.

14. Toward the end of the Canticle (viii, 4) there is again question of the sleep of the Bride, but this time for an entirely different purpose. For in this case the love between the Bridegroom and His Bride reaches its consummation.[39]

---

37 "Passive purifications are not meant principally to lead us to more or less elevated states of prayer, but to perfect us in faith, hope, and charity. . . . All the saints are unanimous on this point." It is impossible to escape this "great and terrible rule of St. John of the Cross: *You too must practice faith, hope and charity, and you cannot practice them in their full perfection except by undergoing very severe purifications.*" Thomas Dehau, *Le Contemplatif et la Croix* 2nd edition (Paris: Editions du Cerf, 1956), pp. 156–157.

38 In his book *Joie et Tristesse* (Paris, Editions du Cerf, 1945), Father Thomas Dehau reminds us that the contemplatives "are, as the great Cajetan says, *partes principaliores Ecclesiae*" (p. 51). They must be there and guarantee that service which the Church needs above everything else—even if in fact their number is not great—due to the "predominance, among most men, of the senses over reason, *plures manent in sensu*" (p. 66). "And yet it must be maintained against all the excuses of our cowardice, that the entire people has always been called to the living waters of mental prayer. . . . *Venite ad me omnes*, the source itself cries out. Some bit of desire is all that is needed: *omnes sitientes, venite ad aquas*. Not just many are called; all are called. Divine wisdom preaches this from the housetops, proclaims it in public squares, just as she whispers it in the ear and in the depths of the heart, *quod in aure auditis*. Her human instruments ought to do the same as she does, without hesitation or fear: *clamat in plateis. Praedicate super tecta*" (p. 65).

15. *Nigra sum, sed formosa.*

We know that during the patristic age the commentators of the Canticle were not at all embarrassed, when they could not involve the Church in their discussion, to switch over to a consideration—one entirely foreign to the poem itself—of the human soul or the Christian soul in general, and to make declarations on this subject which, however true they were in themselves, had nothing at all to do with the Canticle itself. Gregory of Nyssa, for example, wrote: "Though I was black with sin, and though my works made me one with darkness, he has made me beautiful by his love, wiping out by his purity my shame and the stains of my sins, and making me a sharer in his beauty. . . . As sinful and black as we were, God made us luminous and lovable by the splendor of his grace."[40]

(The Canticle says just the opposite that the blackness of the bride in absolutely no way alters her beauty.)

Let us discard immediately all this kind of parenetic commentary which, with the help of the worst facilities of language, sees in the dark complexion a symbol of the darkness and ugliness of the soul and which have no interest for anyone who is looking for a proper understanding of the Canticle.

"I, black and beautiful" (i, 5, Chouraqui's translation). If she is black it is not her fault. It is the sun that has darkened her skin, as she wore herself out looking after the vineyard. She was responsible as well (a simple change of image) for the Bridegroom's flock, while she stayed, beneath her veil, near the flocks of the companions of the Bridegroom.

> i, 6. *Take no notice of my swarthiness:*
> *It is the sun that has burnt me.*
> *My mother's sons turned against me in anger,*
> *They set me to caring for their vines.*
> *My own vine I did not care for.*[41]
> *[They took it away from her]*
>
> i, 7. *Tell me then, you who are the love of my heart:*
> *Where will you take your flock,*
> *Where will you let it rest during the noonday hour?*
> *Why am I here then under my veil*
> *Near the flocks of your companions?*[42]

What must be said of these two verses when the Canticle is read according to meaning no. 1? Must we think with Feuillet[43] that in the first chapter the

---

39   See further on, pp. 477–478.

40   Hom. II *in Cant.*, P.G. XIV, col. 790C and 791 A.

41   Translation of the Jerusalem Bible.

42   Translation of the Jerusalem Bible. (I changed the last two lines after consulting the Vulgate, Dhorme, and Chouraqui.)

43   Cf. A. Feuillet, *Le Cantique des Cantiques*, p. 93.

Bride, that is, the nation of Israel, is still captive to the Chaldeans, the sons of her mother[44] who turned against her in anger? Or must we think that she remembered only her captivity in Babylon, as verse 4 seems to indicate: *The King brought me into his private chambers?*[45] In any case the allusion to the sufferings of the exile is evident.

Concerning the vines that the Bride was to watch over, I believe personally that it is, above all and essentially, the vineyard of the Bridegroom—in other words the revelation entrusted to Israel. But as long as Yahweh does not yet reign over all the earth—and as long as Israel itself is exiled or dispersed among the nations—this refers also to the vines of the Gentiles and the nations among whom the chosen people lives and suffers, even if the wine they produce is a murky wine. Likewise, it is Yahweh's flock that she must essentially and above all else take care of. But, under her veil, she remains as well, in her exile, near the flocks of the companions of the Bridegroom, to the extent that in their baggage there may still remain some salutary truth. For Yahweh has His companions. He is infinitely transcendent; "but as shepherd of Israel, Yahweh can have companions, they are the foreign kings, whom the Bible on several occasions calls shepherds (Is. xliv, 28; Jer. vi, 3; xii, 10; xlix, 19 = Lam. 44; cf. Nah. iii, 18). Epigraphy tells us precisely that they frequently gave themselves this title. . . . We might note that in Psalm 45, the messianic king . . . is, according to verse 8, chosen and consecrated in preference to his companions."[46]

I said a moment ago that in the two verses cited above an allusion to the sufferings of the exile is evident. But there is not a single word in them to remind Yahweh of the faults and infidelities which preceded these sufferings. This does not prevent our exegetes, however, from falling headlong into that omission whose gravity I already pointed out:[47] they have kept in mind, and were perfectly right to do so, the faults committed by the chosen people. But they have not seen that *in this inspired poem* the Bride is the house of Israel restored to grace and that in the poem all these faults are entirely *forgotten*—the divine Bridegroom having wiped them out so completely that he himself no longer even remembers them. Apropos of the line "it is the sun that has burnt me" (which exonerates the Bride completely), A. Robert writes for example: "She *means* that her misfortunes, *as deserved as they may be*, do not turn from her the eyes of her Spouse."[48] And apropos of that vineyard of her own which she did not look after (the Bride's vineyard is Palestine, as he correctly points out, and as the Jerusalem Bible does as well; but what the Bridegroom says is simply that she was *dispossessed* of Palestine and that an

---

44   Cf. A. Robert, *Le Cantique des Cantiques*, p. 73.

45   Translation of the Jerusalem Bible.

46   A. Robert, *Le Cantique des Cantiques*, p. 79.

47   See above, p. 455 f.

48   A. Robert, *Le Cantique des Cantiques*, p. 72.

oppressor forced her into exile), Robert writes: "When she declares that she has not looked after her vineyard *she is alluding to her faults, which obliged God to banish her.*"[49] It is generous indeed on the part of the commentator to attribute to his author something that the latter never had in mind at all, but which he should have had in mind if he had exercised his judgment according to the norms of science—and this is what should always be done, is it not?

16. Now reading the Canticle according to meaning no. 2, let us try to get a glimpse in the two verses cited above of the ultimate truth and their prophetic meaning.[50]

It is the Bride of Christ, the Person of the Church who is speaking (the one same person under two different states but which the Canticle considers only under its pilgrim and terrestrial state, in which it grows in charity). And it is the Person of the Church *in statu viae*, it is the Church on earth which says: *I am black and I am beautiful.*

Let us not imagine that she is black because of the faults of her members and of her personnel. She suffers from these faults, she does penance for them, but they are completely foreign to her personality. If she is black, if she has a dark complexion; it is the sun of history that has burnt her.

Because she is in the world but not of the world, and because the world has an aversion for what is not its own, she is in exile as a stranger on this earth. Those who hold her in exile are the sons of her mother Eve. She is there to announce to them all that Truth which is Christ Himself; she does it as best she can. But what is so astonishing is the fact that, if her word has conquered many countries, and if on all the continents of the world there are baptized souls, she remains nevertheless (considering the mass of those who are visibly part of her) a flock quite limited in numbers—"*nolite timere, pusillus grex, quia complacuit patri vestro dare vobis regnum*"[51]—in comparison to the other great spiritual families which share the earth? It is only at the end of time, and when the cross of survival which is Israel's and the cross of redemption which is Jesus' cross will be but one single cross, that she will win the ultimate persecution together with the ultimate victory.

What her heart desires is to contemplate her Spouse in a faith so ardent and so illumined by the gifts of the Spirit that it will give her a foretaste of the

---

49   A. Robert and R. Tournay, *Le Cantique des Cantiques*, p. 75.

50   Let us take note of the fact that the ardent wish which the Bride expressed in the Canticle according to the original sense:

> *Oh, why are you not a brother*
> *nourished at my mother's breast!* (viii, 1)

has now been granted. Christ is God, but God incarnate, He is our brother; in His humanity he is brother to the Bride.

51   Luke xii, 32.

vision; that is, to remain enclosed in the arms of her Spouse, ecstatic in His love. But she is obliged by the heirs of the first sin to watch over the vines, and this is a difficult task. She is the guardian of the vineyard of her Spouse; she has to strengthen and constantly preserve in this vineyard the faith in the truth of divine revelation, to establish Christianities in all the regions of the world, to advance theological wisdom, even canon law, to watch over Christian morality, to defend this precious vine from the young foxes which ceaselessly threaten it on all sides.

Mary, the vineyard's queen, is a compassionate queen who never ceases to make supplication and who, with a love that is perpetually in action and at pains for her ungrateful children on earth, mingles with her glory and sovereign beatitude the mysterious equivalent of that sorrow which St. Theresa of Lisieux hoped to find again in heaven. Guided and urged on by her, the Bride, instead of remaining curled up in the arms of her Beloved, must battle without respite against the Enemy of men, the great conquered one, from whom we ask the Father each day to deliver us by His grace, but who will struggle till the end to maintain his title of Prince of this World and that power which led St. John[52] to exclaim: *"Totus in maligno positus est mundus."* Yes, the harsh sun and all the inclemencies of the weather will continue to darken the complexion of the All Beautiful Bride as long as history goes on.

And there are other vineyards of which, in the proper sense of the term, she is not the keeper, but which, in a certain sense, she does watch over because they too, but under an imperfect mode, belong to the Bridegroom (everything belongs to Him). She surrounds all these vines with her prayers and her co-redemptive sufferings; she is attentive to everything that happens in them; she wins grace and transmits it to them; she encourages her servants to study with indefatigable care the soil, the nature, and the history of these vineyards; she asks them to bring her word to these vineyards and even to suffer martyrdom; she asks her servants to become friends of the men who cultivate these vines, hoping that, by the simple fact of the interest and admiration that Christians show in wine stocks which in those vineyards produce a wine of wisdom and holiness, they will come to appreciate all the more those wine stocks on which the highest grace has been bestowed.

But what about the Bride's very own vineyard? *My very own vineyard I have not cared for.* What is most sacred and most uniquely hers in her very roots and in the secret of her being—all that she is and all that she has—she has given all of this to her Spouse, without keeping anything for herself.

> i, 7. *Tell me, then, you, the love of my heart:*
> *Where will you take your flock to graze,*
> *Where will you have them rest at noon?*[53]

---

52   I John v, 19.

53   Cant. i, 7, translation of the Jerusalem Bible.

The Spouse feeds Christ's flock. She would like to know a bit more about the last days of human history and also, like James and John, about what will happen in glory at the time of beatitude. But the Spouse leaves her ignorant of these things; besides, there are things which only the Father knows.

Then let her be content with what is given to her in the mystery of the highest knowledge possible this side of the beatific vision.

> *If you do not know this,*
> *You, the most beautiful of women,*[54]

follow the tracks of your kids, they will lead you where the instinct of the Holy Spirit takes them, toward the shepherds' tents, where these shepherds enjoy the delightful knowledge and the peace of loving contemplation. But she knows this much better than her kids and all the shepherds.

Finally there are other pastures which do not belong to the great tents of the Beloved—yet He has come for all men. The Church then must stay near these pastures as well. And in such spiritual families there are many men who by the grace of Christ, without knowing it, belong invisibly to the visible Church. And the Church itself is virtually and invisibly present in the life of every man, by that desire which dwells within him to save his being.[55]

This is why, when the Canticle is read according to meaning no. 2, it is preferable to think, not of the "flocks of the companions of Yahweh" (i, 7), but rather of those unfamiliar pastures where the secret friends of the Bridegroom are found. The Bride complains that her face is hidden by her veil when she is near these pastures. She would prefer to be there with her face uncovered, but this is impossible, since the very people in these pastures, who make up—invisibly-a part of the Bridegroom's flock and belong—invisibly—to the Bride do not know what and who the Bride and Bridegroom are.

But if she complains about the veil that covers her face, it is for another and more profound reason. She herself aspires to *see*, to pass, when the blessed hour of noon arrives, beyond the knowledge of Faith and enter totally into the Vision of the divine essence.

Toward the end of the Canticle an allusion is made to the fulfillment of this desire. The heavenly nuptials of the Lover and His Beloved are foreseen in iv, 11–12, are very near in vii, 11–14,[56] and are considered as accomplished in viii, 5–7.[57]

vi, 11–12. The Bridegroom goes down to look at the new shoots sprouting

---

54   Cant. i, 8.

55   "Man himself is the most fundamental and most universal 'Element of the Church,' in whatever region of the earth he happens to be, and whatever complementary help he may be able to receive form a religious family—Christian-dissident or non-Christian—in which he may have been born and may have been reared." On the Church of Christ, p. 131.

56   Cf. A. Robert and R. Tournay, *Le Cantique des Cantiques*, p. 291.

57   This is why, in my translation, I could speak as I did of the "little sister" (viii, 9).

from the earth—"he no longer knows"; it is not the new shoots that he sees; it is eternal glory which "fixes his soul," and appears before him, along with the triumphant chariots the immense people of whom He is the King.

vii, 12–14. Leave, O my love, says the Bride; there I shall give you the gift of my love, we will celebrate our nuptials. *The best of fruits are on our doorsteps, new kinds as well as old*, put aside for him by her in the freshness of that instant which will not pass away.

viii, 5–7. The Bride comes up from the desert, leaning on her Beloved. He has awakened her (for all time) under the apple tree, where her mother conceived her. May he set her as a seal on his heart, as a seal on his arm. For love is stronger than death, its burning is a conflagration of fire, *the flame of Yahweh!* The great waters can never extinguish that love, nor the rivers drown it.

*   *   *   *   *   *   *   *   *   *

18. A few words now about the subject of this present work.

In composing this unauthorized translation for private use, I proposed simply to read the Canticle *in the way that pleases me most*. With regard to what it may bring to the mind, I wanted its prophetically Christian meaning to be apparent to me in a way that was explicit and definite enough to bring me satisfaction in my mental prayer. With regard to what it brings to the ear, I hoped that, put in the form of a French poem sprung from a single continuous burst of inspiration, its incomparable beauty would become apparent in such a way as would satisfy my need for poetry, something that literal translations generally do not do (the more literal a translation of the Canticle is, the less fitting it seems to me to satisfy this need).

So nothing is further from a scientific study than what I proposed to try. I am the first to recognize that in the eyes of a man of science, a philosopher, an exegete, or a theologian, such an undertaking, carried out with the sole purpose of reading the Canticle according to my own taste and for my pleasure, must be judged as completely foreign to the domain of reason and might very well, from every point of view, be qualified as rather "nutty."

The problem is that I rather like what is a bit "crazy" and that, in spite of all the numerous philosophic works which put this off-limits for me, and in which I hope I have given proof of sufficient attachment to rational rigor, I have never considered myself a *doctor scientificus*. For a long time I have indulged in daydreams about a little study in which folly would be the servant of the rational and the rational in the service of folly. The occasion presented itself one day, without my looking for it, when, on rereading the Canticle in the excellent (and completely literal) translation of André Chouraqui, the idea mentioned above of a possible new version came to mind. Working on an unauthorized version of the Canticle for my own private use and just for my enjoyment propelled me definitely into the realm of folly. But for such a work to be carried out properly, a rational reflection as thorough as possible on the divers readings of the poem was necessary. I tried my hand at this in the present foreword. In this way then folly found itself in the service of the rational. On the other hand, the conceptual analysis which seemed to me required for a critical examination of the different readings of the Canticle themselves remained dependent on the folly of this undertaking so that in this way the rational found itself in the service of folly. Giving oneself up to the continual and painful racking of one's brains in such serious labors certainly involves some risk. But there are a number of people, in particular a few great theologians who call the old philosopher who wrote these lines their friend, who for such a naïve manner of existence experience what the Japanese call a good *kimochi* (an untranslatable word for which I propose as a rather imperfect equivalent "an instinctively favorable disposition of mind"). And it is for these few persons that I published as a booklet in a limited private edition this little work on the Canticle which I had first written out for myself alone.

19. Knowing no Syriac or Hebrew, I had no other recourse, to achieve my objective, than to compare and collate the different French translations that I had at hand,[58] so that I could at any time make my choice among the words used in them or modify them a bit if I chose. I am especially grateful to André Chouraqui for those passages where his translation, which follows the Hebrew text very closely, differed from the accepted classical translations. I found these passages particularly enlightening, especially i, 17; ii, 10; and viii, 4.

i, 17. Instead of saying: "The beams of our house are of cedar, the wainscoting is of cypress," according to Chouraqui we must say: *The cedars form the beams of our houses, the cypresses our wainscoting*. The Bride and the Bridegroom have not taken beams of cedar and wainscoting to build themselves a house. The cedars and the cypresses which grow freely in nature, the forests, all the verdure and vegetation of the earth, these are their dwelling places; they are at home everywhere. And if their house is the sacred House—the Temple—it is the Temple of the entire divine creation, sanctified by the presence of these two.

ii, 10. Instead of saying: "My Beloved raises his voice and says to me: Come now, my beloved, my beautiful one, come," we should say: "My Lover answered and said to me: Get up, my love, my beautiful one, and go toward yourself" (Similarly for ii, 13). "The translators who interpret the line "Come now, my beloved, come,' betray, it seems to me," wrote Chouraqui in his commentary (p. 50), "the most profound and significant movement of the Canticle—there is no possible doubt about the text: *Lekhi lakh*, which means

---

58   I am referring to the translations of André Robert (the one that appeared in the Jerusalem Bible, and the one which appeared after the death of the author in the book of Robert and Tournay), of Dhorme (Bible de la Pléiade), of André Chouraqui, and of the Bible ("En ce temps-là") published under the direction of André Frossard and André-M Gérard.

Set out toward yourself. The lover here finds once again the initial invitation of the vocation of Abraham: 'Lekh lekka' (Gen. xii, 1). . . . He does not tell her to *come toward him,* but to *set out toward herself."* In my version I have kept *Go toward yourself,* but interpreting it as I see fit.

viii, 4. Instead of saying, as the Jerusalem Bible does for example: "I beseech you, O daughters of Jerusalem, do not awaken, do not arouse my love, before the time that pleases her," we must say, according to Chouraqui: *I adjure you, O daughters of Jerusalem, how will you awaken, how will you arouse love, until she wishes it.* And in his commentary he writes (p. 76): "The cry of adjuration twice repeated to the daughters of Jerusalem (ii, 7; iii, 5) is heard a third time. But this time it is different in nature. The deer and the hinds are no longer taken to task. In its perfection the couple is sufficient to itself. And the expression *Im* ('if')[59] is replaced by *Ma* ('how?'). At the journey's end love must be awakened in a way that is total . . ." The word *how* completely changes the meaning of the verse. At this stage, as we saw above (cf. p. 475), the heavenly nuptials have been accomplished and love fully consummated in perfect joy. Why would the Bride want to close her eyes again to contemplate her Spouse? In viii, 4, she says to the daughters of Jerusalem, repeating, with a smile of tender and triumphant irony, the words which her Spouse used about her: "How could you ever awaken me again? I have done with sleep forever." This is what I tried to show in my version.

> *Je vous adjure, filles de Jérusalem,*
> *Comment feriez-vous désormais pour éveiller,*
> *Pour réveiller l'amour maintenant qu'en l'amante*
> *Il exulte à jamais au-delà du sommeil?*

> I beseech you, O daughters of Jerusalem,
> Why would you ever again want to awaken,
> To arouse love now that in this lover
> It exults forever beyond all sleep?

20. To compose an unauthorized version whose reading—a first completely open reading—brought me the satisfaction of mind I was looking for, it seemed to me that in order to better indicate the meaning of some particular verse, and sometimes to better insure the proper connection between ideas, it would not be entirely useless to have recourse to the addition of a few words, and on rare occasions of a line or two, and then to insert such glosses into the text with the same free and easy casualness that characterized the scribes and copyists of old. To distinguish these kinds of glosses from the actual text, I began by putting them in brackets where I inserted them into my version. But I quickly realized that what was more important was that nothing, in the typography itself, should hinder or interrupt the lines that the reader sees before him, when

---

59   In ii, 7, and iii, 5, the Bridegroom declares to the daughters of Jerusalem that they would betray His will if they roused His Beloved.

there is question, as there is here, of a poem that should be read or recited in a single uninterrupted flow. So following the example of the old copyists, I decided against using such distinguishing signs, telling myself that after all anyone who wants to go back to the actual text of the Canticle without such additions need only look in his Bible. But since I have been trained in modern intellectual disciplines, I have been careful, in order to spare myself too excruciating attacks of remorse, to draw up a list of the verses in which these interpolations are found and add it on at the end of the poem.

I just alluded to the free and easy casualness with which the copyists of old introduced their glosses into the text which it was their responsibility to transmit. Conscious of this fact, certain of our modern exegetes have peeled the Canticle in the same offhand way, supposing in their fantasy that it contained a mass of interpolations that it was their duty to throw out. To tell the truth, I think we should force the text of the Canticle to undergo no more than two operations of this kind—in chapter VIII.

The last three lines of verse 7 are, as the Jerusalem Bible points out, a late addition.[60] And as the Jerusalem Bible also points out,[61] the same must be said for verse 14, the last verse of the Canticle. This final addition,[62] I think is clearly due to some zealous teacher, who did not want the poem, at least in its final verse, to seem to deviate from the spurious orthodoxy of the high-priests and the Pharisees and to run the risk of letting their conception of the absolute transcendence of the God of Israel be forgotten. This addition in which the Bride asks her Spouse to fly far from her, onto the balmy mountains where he will be alone in his divinity, destroys the meaning of the Canticle and its very movement, which advances toward perfect *union* in the love of the *other*, loved in his very being. So I did not hesitate to eliminate it, just like the platitude added by a sage in verse 7 of the same chapter. And after eliminating verse 14, it seemed proper to me to substitute in its place, in order to end the Canticle as understood in the Christian sense, other words which were themselves pronounced in Israel by the Bridegroom Himself.[63]

Finally, let me point out that the traditional division (one that is undoubtedly quite arbitrary) of the Canticle into eight chapters runs the risk of making its unity unrecognizable. Some, like André Robert in the Jerusalem Bible,[64]

---

60   "He who would offer all the riches of his house to buy love would be justly disdained."—This, the Jerusalem Bible tells us, is the *aphorism of a sage.*

61   Cf. A. Robert and R. Tournay, *Le Cantique des Cantiques*, pp. 328 and 329. (They think that verse 13 was also added later, but in this case the reasons they offer as a basis for this opinion seem to me very questionable.

62   *Fly away, my Beloved,*
        Fly like a gazelle,
        Like the fawn of a deer,
        Up onto the balmy mountains.

63   John x, 7, 9, 14, 15, 16.

prefer to divide it into five poems and a denouement, but the risk remains the same. "The Canticle of Canticles is not a collection of songs, but one single poem with 117 stanzas."[65]

THE SONG OF SONGS[66]

I

1. The Song of Songs
From the treasures of Solomon.

She
2. Let him kiss me with the kisses of his mouth!
Caresses of his hands are better
Than the rapture of wild wine.

3. The ointment you pour out makes me drunk with sweetness
Your name drips with perfumes,
This is why all the maidens love you.

4. Take me with you, let us run away!
When the king has brought me
Into his private chambers
We shall exult with gladness,
All our joy will be in you,
We shall praise your caresses
More ardently than with any wine of this world
Everything that is right lives by your love.

5. I am black, and I am beautiful,
O daughters of Jerusalem,
Like the tents of Kedar,
The pavilions of Solomon.
6. Be not surprised that I am dark,
It is the sun that has burned me.
The sons of my mother have exiled me.

---

64   Cf. A. Robert and R. Tournay, *Le Cantique des Cantiques*, pp. 56–57.

65   André Chouraqui, *Le Cantique des Cantiques, suivi des Psaumes*, p. 11.

66   Translator's note: I am not a poet, at least not by profession. Except for a turn of phrase here and there I have not attempted to replicate in English whatever poetic elements there are in Jacques Maritain's version of the Song of Songs. So this is meant to be no more than a rather literal translation.

Like a stranger on the earth,
Here I am, the keeper of the vineyards
Of your vineyards.
My own vineyard I have not kept,
I have given my all to you.

7. Tell me then, you, the love of my heart,
Where will you take your flocks to graze,
Where will you have them rest at noon?
While near the flocks who stray
Where your secret friends are,
I am the one who watches over those who have your mark on
their brow.
Tell me! And from my face
Let the veil finally fall away,
That I may see!

Chorus
8. If you do not know this,
O most beautiful among women,
Then go out on your own along the tracks of the flock,
And go with your little goats
To let them graze near the shepherds' tent,
There where love knows.

He
9. To my thoroughbred mare
Out in front of the Pharaoh's prize horses
I compare you, O my love.

10. Your cheeks among all those curls hold me spellbound
As does your neck under those flowing necklaces.

11. We will make you pendants of gold
Inlaid with touches of silver.

She
12. As I wait for my king
To arrive with his retinue
My spikenard pours out its fragrance.

13. My lover is a sachet of myrrh
At rest between my breasts.

14. O Beloved, a cluster of cypresses
Among the vines of En-Gaddi!

He

15. How beautiful you are, my love.
How beautiful you are here before me.
Your eyes are doves!

She

16. You are here too, my love,
How handsome you are, full of grace and truth,
Your whole being is sweetness.
And our only bower is the verdure
Of an eternal springtime which grows up around us.
Alone with each other! The two of us in a single breath of love.

17. The cedars form the beams of our houses,
The cypresses are our wainscoting.

II

She

1. I am the lily of Sharon,
The rose of the low places.

He

2. Like a rose amid the brambles
Is my love among all other women.

She

3. Like an apple tree in the forest
Is my lover among the other men.
I longed for his shade,
And there I sat down.
His fruit is sweet to my palate.

4. He led me to the wine house,
With his banner spread above me: Love.
5. Surround me with live coals,
Revive me with apples,
For I am faint with love.
6. His left hand is under my head,

And his right arm embraces me.

He

7. I entreat you, O daughters of Jerusalem,
By the gazelles and hinds of the plains,
Do not arouse, do not stir up love,
As long as she gives herself up to sleep.

She

8. Voice of my beloved: Behold him, he is coming,
Leaping from mountain to mountain, bounding over the hills,
Like the gazelle, like the fawn of the hinds, behold him,
Standing behind our wall,
Looking in at each window,
Peering through the lattice.

10. He speaks. To me he has spoken! He said to me:
"Rise, my love, my all-beautiful one,
Go toward yourself.
Be strong, go toward yourself,
Know yourself!

11. For see, the winter is past,
The rains are over and gone.

12. The flowers have appeared on the land,
The season of song is here,
The cooing of the turtledove
Is heard throughout the land.

13. The fig tree already has its sweet-smelling buds.
The blossoming vines have spread their fragrance.
Well, the time for it is here.
O sweetness of all the world and sweetness all my own.
Arise my love, my all-beautiful one, go,
Enter into the desert of yourself."

He

14. My dove in the clefts of the rock,
In the secret of the painful ascent,
Show me your face.
Let me hear your voice,
That voice which fills me with freshness,
Your face which enraptures my heart,
Even if you feel yourself forsaken.

15. Catch the foxes for us,
The little foxes that spoil the vines.
Our vines are full of blossoms.

She

16. My beloved is all mine,
And I am all his alone,
This shepherd among the roses.

17. I think I understand what he told me.
Till the breath of day comes
And till the shadows flee,
My love, go hide yourself for me in your glory.
Abandoning me until the morning.
You are the one no name can name,
O my deer, my fawn of the hinds,
On the eternal hills
Where being comes apart.

III

She

1. In my bed, through the long dark nights,
I sought my soul's true love.
I sought him but did not find him.

2. I will arise then
And go about the city,
In its narrow lanes and markets
I will seek my soul's true love.
I sought him but did not find him.

3. The watchmen came upon me
As they made their rounds of the city:
"Have you seen my soul's true love?"
4. Scarcely had I passed them by,
When I found him, found my soul's true love.
I took hold of him, I did not let him go
Until I brought him
Into the house of my mother,
Into the alcove of her who conceived me.

He
5. I entreat you, O daughters of Jerusalem,
By the gazelles, by the hinds of the prairie,
Do not awaken, do not rouse love,
As long as she gives herself up to sleep.
Far, far from here I shall enrapture her
In the house of my father.

Chorus
6. What is this, rising from the desert
Like columns of smoke,
Clouds of myrrh and incense
All the perfumes of the universe?

7. It is the bed on which Solomon is borne,
Surrounded by sixty heroes,
All of them heroes of Israel.

8. Each one carries his sword,
Each is skilled in combat:
Each has a sword at this side
Against ambushes in the night.

9. The palanquin of King Solomon
Was made for him of wood from Lebanon.

10. Its columns are of gold
Its baldaquin of silver
And the seat is all in purple.
Everything in it is radiant with the love
Of the daughters of Jerusalem.

11. Go outside, O daughters of Sion,
Go see Solomon the king,
With the glory of the crown
With which his mother crowned him
On his wedding day,
The day of his heart's true joy.

IV

He
1. You are here, my love, you are here,

You are beautiful, O how beautiful you are!
Your eyes are doves beneath your veil!
You hair, a flock of goats
Frisking down the slopes of Gilead.

2. Your teeth, a flock of new-shorn lambs
Coming back from the watering-hole,
Each one along with its twin.

3. Your lips, a ribbon of scarlet,
From which your words spring sovereignly pure.
Under your veil your temple
Is like a slice of pomegranate.

4. Your neck is the tower of David
Built for trophies
And hung with a thousand shields,
With the quivers of all our heroes.

5. Your two breasts, the twin fawns of a hind
That graze among the lilies.

6. Until the breath of day arrives
And the shadows flit away,
I will go and give thanks
On the mountain of myrrh,
On the hill of incense.

7. You are all beautiful, my beloved,
In you there is not a single blemish.

8. You will come with me from Lebanon, my love, my betrothed.
With me from Lebanon you will come,
From the uplands of the North,
From the peaks of Amanna
From the summits of Senir and of Hermon,
From the lion dens,
From the leopard lairs,
You will contemplate our horizons.

9. You have seized my heart,
My betrothed, my sister,
You have captured it whole and intact

By one single glance of your eyes,
By one little curl on the nape of your neck.

10. How very lovely are your caresses,
My betrothed, my sister,
How good are these caresses of yours,
More exalting than wine!
And the perfume of your ointment
Is better than all spices together.

11. Your lips, my tender bride to be,
Distill sweet nectar.
Under your tongue is the milk and honey
Of the Promised Land.
Like the odor of incense
Is the smell of your garments.

12. You are an enclosed garden,
O my betrothed, my sister,
A walled-in spring of fresh water
A fountain guarded with a seal.

13. Your very being is eternal sweetness.
It is a paradise of pomegranates
Filled with exquisite perfumes,
With hedges of privet and nard.

14. Nard and saffron,
Calamus, cinnamon,
Myrrh, aloes,
The first fruits of all the balm-trees.

15. A pure spring in the gardens,
A deep well of coolness and delight,
Living waters flowing down from Lebanon!

She
16. O wind of the north, arise, come quickly, wind of the south,
Waft through my garden,
So that it may give forth its perfumes!
May my lover enter into his garden,
May he eat the fruit I offer him,
All of my soul is in his hand.

V

He

1. I have come into my garden,
My sister, my betrothed,
I have picked my myrrh and my balm,
I have eaten of my honeycomb,
I have drunk my wine and my milk,
Eat, my friends, drink yourselves drunk with love.

She

2. I am asleep, but my heart is awake.
His voice! He comes, he knocks at the door:
Open up, my sister, my love,
My dove, my immaculate one.
My head is wet with the dew,
My locks are drenched with the dewdrops of night.

3. But when I had scarcely awakened
why was I troubled for an instant?
I am naked, I have taken off my tunic,
How can I dress quickly again?
My feet are washed, am I to dirty them
By running in the dust?

4. My lover stretches his hand through the opening,
My heart for him is all atremble.

5. I rose from my bed
To open the door to my beloved.
Myrrh dripping from my hands,
And from my fingers virgin myrrh
Trickled down on the door-bolt's handle.
6. I myself opened the door to my beloved.
But he was gone, he had disappeared.
My soul almost left my body,
I could do no more than cry after him.
I looked for him but did not find him.
I called to him, he did not answer.

7. The watchmen came across me
As they made their rounds about the city.
They beat me, they wounded me,

They tore off my cloak,
These guardians of the city walls.

8. I entreat you, O daughters of Jerusalem,
If you find my beloved,
What should you tell him?
Tell him that I am faint with love.

Chorus
9. What is this lover of yours compared to other lovers,
O most beautiful of women,
What is this lover of yours compared to other lovers
That you should entreat us so.

She
10. My beloved is both pale and ruddy.
He is like a standard raised high
Above the multitude.

11. His head is gold, of the purest gold,
His locks flow black like the crow.

12. His eyes, like doves on the waters of a lake,
And washed in milk,
Find rest in plenitude.

13. His cheeks are flower-beds of aromatic spices,
Towers of perfume.
His lips, which are roses,
Diffuse their myrrh and their purity.

14. His hands are golden baskets
Set with jewels of chrysolite,
His flanks are of pure ivory
Adorned with many sapphires.

15. His legs are columns of alabaster
Set on pedestals of gold.
He is sought after and prized
Like the cedars of Lebanon.

16. His mouth is sweetness itself,
He is nothing but delight

Such is my love, my beloved,
O daughters of Jerusalem.

VI

Chorus
1. Where then has your lover gone,
O most beautiful of women,
Which way did he go?
We will help you find him.

She
2. He has gone down to his garden,
To the flower-beds of the spice bushes,
To lead his flock to pasture
And gather roses there.

I belong to my beloved,
And he belongs to me,
This shepherd among the roses.

He
4. You are beautiful, my love, like Tirzah.
Splendid like Jerusalem,
Terrible, irresistible,
Like standards drawn up in battle array.

5. Turn your eyes from me.
They are taking me by storm.
Your hair, a flock of goats
Frisking down the slopes of Gilead.
6. Your teeth, a flock of new-shorn lambs
Coming back from the watering-hole,
Each one along with its twin.

7. Under your veil your temple
Is like a slice of pomegranate.

8. There are sixty queens,
And eighty concubines,
And numberless women throughout the world.
9. But she is unique, different from all the rest.
My dove, my perfect one,

The only daughter of her mother,
The immaculate daughter of the one who bore her.
All the other daughters saw her and proclaimed her blessed.
The queens and the concubines celebrated her.

10. Who is she who in her freshness
Rises like the dawn,
As beautiful as the moon,
More brilliant than the sun,
Terrible as the standards
Of an army charging to the attack?

11. I went down to the walnut orchard
To see the little plants pushing up through the earth
In the dried up stream-bed,
To see the flowering vines
And the blossoms on the balm-trees.

12. And lo, I am dazzled
By the ineffable accomplishment
Of the purposes for which I was sent.
O conquering love! O glory,
O chariots, O holy people whose king I am,
And you too, my queen, carried off with me.

VII

Chorus
1. Come back, come back, O Shulamite,
You who bring us the gift of Peace,
Come back, come back, that our eyes may look upon you.

She
What will you see in the Shulamite?
A dance from two camps:
Friends of the Bridegroom, from among his companions,
Friends of the Bridegroom, from among his foreigners.

He
2. I see you in your glory.
And your feet, how very beautiful they are
In their sandals, O princely daughter!

Your thighs are gracefully curved
Like a pure chalice, the work of a master's hand.

3. Your bosom is an exquisite vase, in form
More delicate than a crescent of the moon,
Full of the fire of life.
Your belly, a heap of wheat
Encircled with roses.

4. Your two breasts, the twin fawns of a hind.

5. Your neck, a tower of ivory,
Your eyes, the lakes of Heshbon
At the gate Bat-Rabbim;
Your nose like a tower of Lebanon
On guard before Damascus.

6. Your head stands erect like Carmel,
Its braids shine brilliant as purple
A king is held captive in its curls.
7. How very beautiful you are, fresh and sweet as a lily,
O my love, my queen of delights!

8. Your waist seems like a palm tree,
And your breasts like grape-arbors.

9. I said: I will climb that palm tree,
I will gather its clusters of dates.
Let your breasts be my grape-arbor,
Your breath like the golden scent of apples.
10. Your palate, like good generous wine
Restoring the noble heart with a courage
That can set the lips of death itself atremble.

She

11. I belong to my beloved,
Totally sustained by his desire.

12. Let us run off together, let us go out to the open fields,
Find lodging in the hamlets.

13. At daybreak we will go to the vineyards,
To see if there are blossoms on the vine,

If its flowers are forming their fruit,
If the pomegranate trees are budding.
There you will cover me with your caresses.

14. The mandrakes have exhaled their perfume,
Above our doors masses of glorious fruit hang drying,
Fruits old and new
Which I have put by for you, my love.

VIII

She

1. Let me dream in your arms,
Ah! Why are you not my brother
Nursed at my own mother's breasts!
Then I would kiss you without fear in public.
A dream? No, this is holy reality,
Yes, our embraces are fraternal.
Brother of men, O blessed God,
And for all eternity you are my Bridegroom and my brother!

2. I will take you, I will lead you
Into the house of my mother.
There you will teach me my first lessons and I will slake your thirst
With spiced wine
And the juice of my pomegranates!

3. His left hand holds up my head,
And his right arm embraces me.

4. I beg you, O daughters of Jerusalem
Why would you ever again want to awaken,
To stir up love now that in me
It exults forever beyond all sleep?

He

5. Who is this making her way up from the desert,
Leaning on her beloved?
I have awakened you forever, under the apple tree,
In the place where your mother conceived you,
At the very spot where she who bore you brought you forth.
6. Set me as a seal on your heart,

As a seal on your arm,
For love is as strong as death.
Its jealousy as hard as Hell.
Like violent conflagrations
Are the blazing fires of love,
Flame of Yahweh, of the Uncreated!

7. The waters of the seas cannot
Extinguish this love.
No river will ever drown it.

She

8. We have a little sister,
Whose breasts are not yet formed.
What shall we do with our little sister,
The day when people begin to talk about her?

9. If she is a high wall,
We will crown it with silver crenelations,
If she is a door, we will reinforce it
With beams of cedar.
Little sister, are you not
Myself walking along on earth in days gone by
Whom I now see from heaven above?

10. I who speak, I am the Bride
In the glory of my Spouse.
I am a wall, and my breasts are its towers.
Before his eyes, this is how
The Shulamite stands,
As a true bearer of Peace.

He

11. Solomon had a vineyard
At Baal-hamon.
He entrusted it to care-takers,
Each of them paying him a thousand silver shekels
As a price for the grapes he harvested.

12. Here before me is my very own vineyard,
The only one I have, I alone will care for it.
Take your thousand shekels, Solomon
Use them well,

And two hundred more for the care-takers!

Chorus

You who dwell in the gardens,
There happy friends listen to you.
O Blessed one, let me hear your voice!

He, when He Himself spoke to us here on earth

14. I am the door for the sheep.
Whoever enters through me will be saved.
I am the good shepherd,
I give my life for my sheep.
And I have other sheep,
That are not of this fold.
Them also I must bring,
And they will hear my voice.
And there will be only one flock
And one shepherd.

INTERPOLATIONS

A list of the verses in which a few words, and on occasion a few lines, have been added or changed:

I, vs. 1; 2; 4; 6; 8; 16.
II, vs. 10; 13; 14; 17.
III, vs. 5.
IV, vs. 6; 8; 11; 13; 15; 16.
V, vs. 3; 6.
VI, vs. 4; 9; 12.
VII, vs. 1; 2.
VIII, vs. 1; 4; 5; 9; 10; 12; vs. 14 in its entirety.